WOMEN'S REALITIES, WOMEN'S CHOICES

WOMEN'S REALITIES, WOMEN'S CHOICES ♀

An Introduction to Women's Studies

THIRD EDITION

Hunter College Women's Studies Collective

Ülkü Ü. Bates
Florence L. Denmark
Virginia Held
Dorothy O. Helly
Shirley Hune
Susan H. Lees
Frances E. Mascia-Lees
Sarah B. Pomeroy
Carolyn M. Somerville

New York   Oxford
OXFORD UNIVERSITY PRESS
2005

Oxford University Press

Oxford   New York
Auckland   Bangkok   Buenos Aires   Cape Town   Chennai
Dar es Salaam   Delhi   Hong Kong   Istanbul   Karachi   Kolkata
Kuala Lumpur   Madrid   Melbourne   Mexico City   Mumbai
Nairobi   São Paulo   Shanghai   Taipei   Tokyo   Toronto

Published by Oxford University Press, Inc.
198 Madison Avenue, New York, New York 10016
www.oup.com

Oxford is a registered trademark of Oxford University Press

Library of Congress Cataloging-in-Publication Data

Women's realities, women's choices : an introduction to women's studies / Hunter College
   Women's Studies Collective.—3rd ed.
     p. cm.
   Includes bibliographical references and index.
   ISBN 13: 978-0-19-515035-3(pbk. : alk. paper)

     1. Women's studies—United States. I. Hunter College. Women's Studies Collective.

HQ1181.U5W653 2005
305.4'0973—dc22

                                                          2004056091

Printing number: 9 8 7 6 5

Printed in the United States of America
on acid-free paper

Sue Rosenberg Zalk, 1945–2001

We dedicate this book to our late colleague in recognition of the important role she played in this project from its inception, as both a feminist and a friend. We miss her presence but remember the joy she brought into our lives. She was both courageous and wise.

CONTENTS

BOXES AND TABLES

Tables

FOREWORD TO THE THIRD EDITION

If the first edition of this book deserved fireworks and the second edition an acknowledgment of the sophistication that had developed in women's studies a decade later, this third edition by the Hunter College Women's Studies Collective must be celebrated for the compelling presentation of what has become, over two decades later, a complex, increasingly specialized, and still profoundly pertinent examination of women's lives.

There is a reason that women's studies as a discipline has grown from strength to strength since the early 1970s: it reveals the basic structures of society and the way gender in all its contexts (race, class, ethnicity, nationality, religion, age, and culture) has been and continues to be critical for understanding how those structures function and how they can be transformed.

This book was launched when I was president of Hunter College. It took on new stature while I was U.S. Secretary for Health and Human Services. Now, presiding once more over an academic institution, it is clear to me that the authors must be hailed again for their success in bringing these truths home to a new generation of university students.

I am also happy to see the book dedicated to the late Sue Rosenberg Zalk, an original author and an important founding figure in this field.

February 2, 2004   Donna E. Shalala, President
University of Miami

PREFACE

In the two decades since the first publication of this introductory textbook in women's studies, there has been a revolution in scholarship. Consideration of gender as a factor of analysis is now recognized as necessary by scholars in every field, and the issues raised by the modern women's movement have transformed much of public discourse.

Unlike single-authored books by a scholar trained in one discipline and anthologies by many authors each tackling one subject, *Women's Realities, Women's Choices* has been written by nine authors from as many disciplines. The authors have shared with each other and share with the reader the multiple perspectives they bring to this examination of women's lives and experiences, treating women as subjects rather than objects, looking at the world through women's eyes.

Rethinking the world through women's eyes has affected the very basis of knowledge in our universities. Until this revolution in scholarship, only men's experiences, and especially those of privileged men, were seriously studied, with the assumption that to understand them was to understand all that was worth knowing. Nearly 40 years of research focused on women has not only added new information about their lives historically and cross-culturally but also changed our understanding of history and culture.

The writing of this book continues to be a collaborative effort, each author contributing to all chapters. The organization of the book, dealing with women as individuals, as family members, and as members of society, reflects the experiences and perspectives of most readers. In every chapter, we point out the contradictions between social or cultural "givens" that generally have been structured by men in their own interests and what we perceive to be women's realities. At each point, we consider what changes would be required to open better choices for women. The title of the book acknowledges our awareness of the gap between women's realities and women's choices, and the book sets out to analyze that gap and to find ways of bridging it.

The history of this book goes back to 1978–9, when a year-long interdisciplinary seminar for faculty members at Hunter College met weekly and taped their discussions. The purpose was to design an introductory course for the women's studies program instituted in 1976. As the outline for such a course emerged, so did a core group of faculty willing to carry the project forward into published form. With a grant from the National Endowment for the Humanities, eight authors proceeded to turn these materials into a text and were able to test it out in various campus situations before completion of the manuscript. Oxford University Press published it in 1983. The second edition, published in 1995, saw the loss of one original author but benefited from the addition of two more, for a total of nine. Soon after we signed the contract for a third edition, our beloved colleague Sue Rosenberg Zalk, to whom we dedicate this edition, died suddenly. In consequence, we asked Frances Mascia-Lees, an anthropologist with a specialty in cultural studies, to join us. As we wrote, we found it critical to ask another colleague who teaches at Hunter College to act as a consultant for the chapter updating women's health and the health system. Kathryn Rolland, who has taught courses on women's health and on AIDS, agreed, and we are grateful to her for undertaking this task so successfully at relatively short notice.

From its inception in the 1970s, a great many people have been generous to us with their time and expertise. Early reviewers of the first manuscript, to whom we still owe a debt of gratitude, included Nancy Hartsock, Joyce Ladner, and Catherine Stimpson. For the third edition, we are grateful to Georgia Tsouvala, Nicholas Jumara, and Holly Troy for their efforts to keep our paper (and electronic) work in order. We also wish to thank the Public Relations office of the Graduate School of the City University of New York for supplying the photograph of Sue Rosenberg Zalk for our dedication page. We continue to be grateful to the willingness of our first acquiring editor, Spencer Carr, to take on what was then so experimental a project. Other editors at Oxford University Press who have aided us include Valerie Aubrey, David Roll, Gioia Stevens, Susan Hannan, and, more recently, Jeffrey Broesche, Sean Mahoney, Peter Labella, Shiwani Srivastava, and Christine D'Antonio. We are also delighted to be published by a press whose president is now a woman, Laura Brown. Finally, we are grateful to Donna Shalala, president of Hunter College when we first published this book, later U.S. Secretary for Health and Human Services, and now president of Miami University, for agreeing for a third time to write a foreword.

THE AUTHORS

Ülkü Ü. Bates is Professor of Art History at Hunter College, where she teaches Islamic art. Born in Romania and raised in Turkey, she studied in Istanbul, Freiburg (Germany), and the University of Michigan, where she received her Ph.D. She is the recipient of several fellowships, a Fulbright among them. She is on the editorial board of the journal *Muqarnas* (Harvard–MIT) and a director on the board of the American–Turkish Cultural Society.

Professor Bates has published on Turkish–Ottoman art, particularly the architecture, and on the patronage of Muslim women in the arts. Her current research is on the political and intellectual colonization of the Islamic countries in the eighteenth and nineteenth centuries and the reaction of Muslim artists and patrons in a multicultural world. She has one son.

Florence L. Denmark is the Robert Scott Pace Distinguished Research Professor at Pace University in New York, where she has served as chair of the Psychology Department for 13 years. She previously taught at Hunter College for 26 years. A social psychologist, who received her doctorate from the University of Pennsylvania, she has published extensively on the psychology of women and gender. She is a fellow of the American Psychological Association (APA) and served as its eighty-eighth president in 1980. In addition, she was president of the International Council of Psychologists, the Eastern Psychological Association, the New York State Psychological Association, and Psi Chi. She was vice president of the New York Academy of Sciences. She has four honorary doctorates and is the recipient of many awards including APA's Distinguished Contributions to Education and Training, Public Interest, and the Advancement of International Psychology. Professor Denmark is currently an APA nongovernmental organization representative to the United Nations and continues to teach graduate courses at Pace University. She has two surviving children, three stepchildren, and four grandchildren.

Virginia Held is Distinguished Professor of Philosophy at the City University of New York Graduate Center and Professor Emerita at Hunter College. Among her books are *The Public Interest and Individual Interests* (1970); *Rights and Goods: Justifying Social Action* (1984); *Feminist Morality: Transforming Culture, Society, and Politics* (1993); the edited collections *Property, Profits, and Economic Justice* (1980) and *Justice and Care: Essential Readings in Feminist Ethics* (1995); and the coedited collections *Philosophy and Political Action* (1972) and *Philosophy, Morality, and International Affairs* (1974). In 2001–2, she was president of the eastern division of the American Philosophical Association. She has been a fellow at the Center for Advanced Study in the Behavioral Sciences and has had Fulbright and Rockefeller fellowships. She has been on the editorial boards of many journals in the areas of philosophy and political theory. She has also taught at Yale; Dartmouth; the University of California, Los Angeles; and Hamilton. She is currently working on a book on the ethics of care and its implications. She has a daughter and a son and five grandchildren.

Dorothy O. Helly is Professor Emerita of History and Women's Studies at Hunter College and the City University of New York Graduate Center. A graduate of Harvard University, she has served as an associate dean at Hunter College and coordinator of its women's studies program. She was also a Senior Associate Member of St. Antony's College, Oxford University, and a scholar-in-residence at the Rockefeller Study Center at Bellagio, Italy. For a decade she cofacilitated a university faculty seminar on transforming the curriculum, which won an American Association of University Women award in 1997.

Professor Helly cochaired the program committees for the Seventh Berkshire Conference on the History of Women and the Fourth International Interdisciplinary Congress on Women. She currently serves on the board of directors of the Feminist Press and the editorial board of *Women's Studies Quarterly*. She coedited *Gendered Domains: Rethinking Public and Private in Women's History* (1992) and is at work on a biography of Flora Shaw, Lady Lugard (1852–1927), the first woman journalist to serve on the permanent staff of *The Times* (London) (1893–1900). With the late Helen Callaway as coauthor, she has published three articles on Shaw's exploits and has written the entry for Shaw for the *New Dictionary of National Biography*. She has a daughter.

Shirley Hune serves as Associate Dean for Graduate Programs, Graduate Division, at the University of California, Los Angeles (UCLA); she is also Professor of Urban Planning and Asian American Studies and a faculty affiliate of the Center for the Study of Women. Before joining UCLA in 1992, she was professor of educational foundations and associate provost at Hunter College. She holds a Ph.D. in American civilization and has published in the areas of U.S. immigration policy, nonaligned countries, human rights and migrant workers, and Asian American studies. She has a decade of research experience at the United Nations on migrant workers' rights and the global agenda of developing states. She is a past president of the Association for Asian American Studies. Her recent publications include *Asian/Pacific Islander American Women: A Historical Anthology* (2003), *Asian Pacific American Women in Higher Education* (1998), and *Teaching Asian American Women's History* (1997). Her family includes two adult stepchildren, four grandchildren, and a dog.

Susan H. Lees is Professor of Anthropology at Hunter College and a member of the Ph.D. programs in anthropology and earth sciences at the City University of New York Graduate Center. She has carried out field research in Latin America, Israel, and more recently the United States, primarily in rural communities, and has published extensively on human ecology and rural economies. While continuing to work on issues of rural life in coastal Maine, she has also been researching, publishing, and teaching about religion and human rights. She coedited the interdisciplinary journal *Human Ecology* from 1977 to 1996 and since 2001 is co-editor-in-chief, with Frances Mascia-Lees, of the *American Anthropologist*, the journal of the American Anthropological Association. She has two sons and one stepdaughter.

Frances E. Mascia-Lees is Professor of Anthropology and Chair of the Department of Anthropology at Rutgers University. She is also currently co-editor-in-chief of the *American Anthropologist*, the flagship journal of the American Anthropological Association. She has taught at Sarah Lawrence College, Hunter College, State University of New York at Albany, and Simon's Rock College of Bard, where she also directed the women's studies program from 1986 through 1996.

She has written widely on feminist and anthropological theory, the female body and subjectivity, and the "race"/gender politics of cross-cultural representation. She has conducted fieldwork in the Caribbean, Mexico, and multiple sites in the U.S. Her books include *Taking a Stand in a Postfeminist World: Toward an Engaged Cultural Criticism* (2000), *Gender and Anthropology* (2000), *Tattoo, Torture, Mutilation, and Adornment: The Denaturalization of the Body in Culture and Text* (1992), and *Toward a Model of Women's Status* (1984). In 1998 she was awarded the American Anthropological Association's Mayfield Award for Excellence in the Teaching of Anthropology. She is currently at work on the book *Gender and Difference in a Global World*. She has two sons.

Sarah B. Pomeroy is Distinguished Professor of Classics and History, Emerita, at Hunter College and the City University of New York Graduate Center. She was the first chair of the Women's Classical Caucus, the first coordinator of the women's studies program at Hunter College, and the first coordinator of the certificate program in women's studies at the City University of New York Graduate Center. When she taught at the University of Texas in Austin, she flew her own plane and now is interested in astronomy. Professor Pomeroy is the author of many publications about women in antiquity, including *Goddesses, Whores, Wives, and Slaves: Women in Classical Antiquity* (1975, 1994), *Women in Hellenistic Egypt from Alexander to Cleopatra* (1984, 1990), *Families in Classical and Hellenistic Greece: Representations and Realities* (1997), and *Spartan Women* (2002). She is currently working on *Regilla, Wife of Herodes Atticus: My Quest for Women in Antiquity*. Professor Pomeroy has two daughters and a son and four grandchildren.

Carolyn M. Somerville is Associate Professor of Political Science at Hunter College and at the City University of New York Graduate Center. She has also served as director of the women's studies program at Hunter College. Her research and writing interests include political and economic liberalization in western and southern Africa. She has published in *Sex Roles: A Journal of Research*, *PS: Political Science and Politics*, the *Oxford Companion to Politics of the World*, and *Globalization and Survival in the Black Diaspora*.

Besides teaching and research, Professor Somerville has also done community work with young women in after-school programs. She has a daughter and a son.

WOMEN'S REALITIES, WOMEN'S CHOICES

Introduction

- Today, more women than ever serve as members of their country's legislative bodies at the local, regional, and state levels. In Namibia (southern Africa), women account for 44% of local government officials. In Denmark, Norway, and Sweden, women make up more than 36% of the legislators at the national level, and they are making a difference in creating public policy beneficial to women.
- Today, in the United States, almost 50% of all women of working age work in the labor force, and career opportunities have expanded for women.
- Today, rape during times of war is treated as a crime against humanity, punishable by the International Criminal Court, an international court created by the United Nations and launched in 1998.

Why Women's Studies

Forty years ago, few women dared to run for political office, and women in political office were viewed as unnatural by both women and men. Forty years ago, only 32% of working-age women in the United States worked in the labor force. Forty years ago, the rape of women during armed conflict was viewed as just an unfortunate but all too common event.

In the past 40 years, the feminist revolution has expanded women's opportunities and women have made many impressive gains and achievements. Women are active politically, economically, and socially in ways that were unimaginable decades ago. Political and economic rights acquired by women allow them to live their lives quite differently from their foremothers. Reproductive rights allow women the freedom to choose when to have or not have a child.

With these tremendous gains achieved by women, why would anyone want to study feminism and women's studies in the twenty-first century? Many opportunities for girls and women are wide open, there to be seized; and some wonder why women would want to dwell on their "victimhood" or the "past" instead of just steaming ahead toward their goals. Young women today, they say, are confident they can do as they please with respect to how they look, with whom they have sex, how they identify themselves, and what they do with their time. They have never known a time before "girls can do anything boys can" (Baumgardner and Richards, 2000; Findlen, 1995). Others associate women's studies with feminism and feminism with something that may have been needed in the past but is now passé.

To a considerable extent, opportunities are much more open to many women today than they were in the 1970s, when efforts by students, faculty, and others began to bring women's studies courses to campuses around the United States and to make women's studies a legitimate discipline. However, this is largely because the changed consciousness and political activism brought about by the women's movements of the last quarter of the twentieth century made this possible. Women's studies is intimately linked to that changed consciousness that came of the women's liberation movement of the 1970s, providing understanding and ideas for personal and political action.

Progress comparable for its time was made in the 1920s and 1930s in the United States and then lost in the 1950s. For most girls in the 1950s and 1960s, career choices were extremely limited. By 1930, one in seven Ph.D.'s was earned by a woman; but by 1960, the figure had dropped to about one in ten (Howe, 2000). Sexual double standards were rampant, and mothers were expected to care for their children full-time until they were grown if they could afford it. To prevent such reversals of women's gains from happening again, the consciousness brought about in the 1970s and later needs to be kept alive; and women's studies is a way of doing this.

Some of us (the authors) can remember that when we were young women, the "suffragettes" who demonstrated and won the vote for women early in the twentieth century were no models of who we wanted to be. We did not want to lose the vote, but our image of the suffragists was of women who were dowdy, frumpy, and definitely not sexy. We wanted to be attractive, contemporary, and focused on our own lives. We thought we were interested in the same things as men. Only later did we appreciate the achievements of the suffragists and begin to see how far we

still needed to go to achieve the equality for which gaining the vote was only a beginning.

The culture of the early twenty-first century has brought about a view of feminists that is somewhat like our own early view of the suffragists: feminists are often seen by young women today as unattractive, shrill, hostile toward men, and definitely not fun or sexy. Many young women avoid identifying themselves as feminists: some see no point in feminism anymore, and others fear that the young men in whom they are interested will be put off. However they do not want to give up the gains in equality that have been achieved. With more experience and more knowledge, they often come to see that women still have a long way to go before feminism is obsolete.

Young women since the 1990s who do consider themselves feminist may think that the feminism of the 1970s and 1980s, which they call "second-wave" as distinct from their own "third-wave" feminism, does not speak to their media-savvy, culture-driven generation (Baumgardner and Richards, 2000; Dow, 1996). They celebrate what they call "girlie culture," in which young women in tight clothes and streaky hair make zines and music and web sites and flaunt their sexuality, confidence, and self-worth. "Girlie culture is a rebellion against the false impression that since women don't want to be sexually exploited, they don't want to be sexual," some say (Baumgardner and Richards, 2000:xviii, 137–8). These observers recognize, however, that Girlie culture is mistaken when it also suggests that politics is a second-wave activity no longer needed, instead of understanding that politics is inherent to feminism. (Baumgardner and Richards, 2000: xviii, 137–8.)

As threats of losing reproductive rights and other gains become more imminent, young women often appreciate the need for political organization along with their self-confident lifestyles and want to learn from earlier generations of feminists.

Feminism seeks to overcome the subordination of women in all its forms. Most women share this goal, though they may interpret it differently. Women's studies is the study of women's conditions and achievements, of how and why women's subordination takes place, and of how it can be overcome. It remains central to maintaining women's gains and achieving further progress.

Women's Studies in the Twenty-First Century

Consider some reasons for a continuing focus on women.

- Events in Afghanistan in 2001–2 brought to the attention of the whole world the plight of women there. Women were prevented by the religious fundamentalists who ruled the country from going to school and from working outside the home. Although the Taliban government was overthrown, the attitudes toward women that characterized it still prevail in many parts of the region. However, one may ask, is this not an isolated problem?
- Nearly two-thirds of the world's hundreds of millions of illiterates are women. In southern Asia and sub-Saharan Africa, where populations are rising fast and many girls still do not go to school, the numbers of illiterate women are still growing in the twenty-first century (United Nations, 2000:87). Mortality rates for girls are significantly higher than for boys in the enormously populous countries of China and India, due to discrimination in providing nutrition and health care (United Nations, 2000:56).
- In large parts of the world, violence against women is still pervasive and under-reported. In some studies, over half of all women report having been subjected to physical violence by an intimate partner (United Nations, 2000:153). Being free from domestic assault and from gender discrimination are just beginning to be recognized as rights to which all women are entitled as women's rights come to be seen as human rights (United Nations, 2000).

- Are these problems only for women elsewhere than the reader's own society? In 2003, dozens of women cadets at the U.S. Air Force Academy complained that they had been raped at the academy and that when they reported the incidents they were subjected to retribution. They described a pervasive attitude at the academy characterized by demeaning women and resenting their presence there (Janofsky, 2003; Janofsky and Schemo, 2003).
- Figures for 2002 showed that although women's pay rates compared to men's had improved very slightly compared to a decade earlier, full-time female workers still made only 77.5% of what their male counterparts did (Leonhardt, 2003), and the accumulated earnings of women lag much further. For the years 1983–98, women earned only 38% of what men earned. To care for family members, women more often give up their jobs or work part time, and the tendency is self-reinforcing: because women earn less, they are more apt than men to interrupt their careers (Madrick, 2004).

One may think, perhaps, that such problems as these are just the results of pockets of resistance and that they are being corrected. Most people probably disapprove of such realities, but it takes time for behavior to catch up with new thinking about women. Some activism may still be called for, but is not the work of studying and theorizing about women already done? Do we really still need women's studies?

Consider whether the changed thinking brought about by women's movements, feminism, and women's studies has achieved its goals and whether all that is left is implementation. In many fields of study, taking women's experience seriously has already deeply changed the basic assumptions made, concepts used, and issues examined, transforming what had been considered to be knowledge in them. For example, taking women's experiences seriously has made a profound impact on disciplines such as history, anthropology, political science, the classics, literature, philosophy, and biology. Further transformation of these fields continues; the work is nowhere near done. An example is economics. A collection of essays called *Beyond Economic Man* (Ferber and Nelson, 1993) describes itself as the first book to provide a feminist critique of the foundations of economics. Economics is built on the assumptions that behavior is based on rational self-interest and interactions between individuals occur only when each believes it to be in his or her own interest. These assumptions are often generalized from market behavior to all behavior (Radin, 1996). From the perspective of women's experience in the family and with friendship, these are highly dubious and misleading assumptions and making them has consequences, such as undermining cooperation, that are often harmful. Questioning such assumptions requires entirely new ways of thinking about economic activity and how it should be organized.

Another field transformed in the light of feminist critique is international relations. Traditionally, the field of international relations has refused to acknowledge the roles played by women in war, peace, and diplomacy (Enloe, 1989). Also, the basic assumption of this field of study, that individual states pursue their own interests in ways analogous to how individual persons are thought to pursue theirs, aiming to contract with their equals for the restraints of justice on how they do so, is dubious (Tickner, 2001). States are grossly unequal, and relations between them are often characterized more by force and fraud than by voluntary contracts. Improving such relations will require thinking beyond the dominant male views of contracts between equals based on self-interest. In just these examples, we can see how the rethinking needed in our pursuit of knowledge continues and how women's studies often leads the way.

What Is Women's Studies?

Women's studies is not simply the study of women. It is the study of women that places power at the center of the process. It examines the world and the human beings in it with questions, analyses, and theories built directly on women's experiences. Because not all women's lived experiences are the same, women's studies is also about differences—in race, ethnicity, nationality, sexual identity, generation, class, religion, physical ability, and other identity markers. While many might characterize the field as concerned with victimhood, we disagree. We believe the ultimate aim of women's studies is to show women in a role of agency: analyzing the social construction of gender and power, challenging old knowledge about women, creating new knowledge about gender, and becoming active in the transformation of society through the creation of alternatives to the present constructions of power and inequality in order to help women and men to fulfill their human potential.

Knowledge about ourselves and our world has usually been divided, for the purpose of study, into distinct disciplines and has largely been constructed from the point of view of men, not women. Some fields have a long past, as in the case of history or philosophy. Various other fields, such as sociology and psychology, have developed only in the past century. However long these areas of study have been in existence, each involves a relatively distinctive approach to knowledge. Each also involves an explicit set of observations concerning what is "true" and rests on an implicit set of assumptions and ethical views. These observations and assumptions provide us with guidelines for human action. Yet, if these observations and assumptions reflect a predominantly masculine perspective on reality, the interpretations they elicit may not be as true for women as for men. They often do not reflect women's experiences of reality, and they are often poor guides for women. They represent men's studies without awareness of their limitations, in contrast with the new field of men's studies now developing which calls attention to issues of gender and questions traditional assumptions about women's and men's roles. Women's studies focuses on women's experiences and points of view. It seeks to provide observations and to develop concepts and theories that can help us understand women's realities and enable women to better choose their goals.

Women's studies is both a complement and correction to established disciplines and a relatively new academic field of its own. It requires other fields to reexamine and revise the basic assumptions and methods on which they rest. As a more recent discipline, women's studies crosses the boundaries between established fields, providing fresh views of their subject matter and creating coherent new ways of seeing the world. Women's studies contributes to change of a fundamental kind as a result of its search for knowledge.

Women's Studies and Feminism

Feminism has been defined in various ways, but it is widely agreed that it is committed to overcoming the devaluation of women and those who are oppressed. Feminism insists that women and men be valued for the attributes they choose to value, not for those imposed on them by others for their own purposes. Feminism rejects cultural images that denigrate women, social structures that treat women as subordinate, and behavior that fails to accord women equality. Feminists strive to contribute to the cooperative efforts of women to shape their own destinies.

Supporting feminism means rejecting the assignment of social roles with their corresponding norms according to whether a person is female or male. Feminists reject evaluations that esteem presumably "masculine" qualities, such as being aggressive and autonomous, when found in men while deploring these qualities in women; and they affirm the moral importance, for men as well as for women, of various presumably "feminine" qualities, such as being caring and compassionate. Any quality may appear in any human being and should be evaluated on its own merits, not in terms of the gender of the person in whom it appears. Understanding that cultural attitudes and beliefs about women have often been based on false premises and faulty observations, feminists are working to replace ignorance and fantasy with views that have greater validity. Realizing that discriminatory laws and practices have oppressed women, that this oppression is disgraceful and harmful to all human beings, and that people can through their persistent and collective efforts bring about change for the better, feminists seek such change. Many men are also feminists because they recognize the validity of feminism's positions.

However, just as the failure to understand women's experiences and lives impoverished traditional disciplines, so too must women's studies move beyond just the categories, issues, concepts, and theories of concern to middle-class women in industrialized countries. Minority feminists in industrialized countries and feminists in developing countries have criticized the perspectives of feminist scholars and activists in the industrialized countries. The 1980s and 1990s witnessed the emergence of new feminist scholarship in the form of minority, postmodern, and postcolonial women's studies that criticized the weaknesses of research coming out of the West (Spivak, 1999; Abu-Lughod, 1998; Nicholson, 1990). Much recent work among feminists has been devoted to better understanding the oppressions of race, class, sexual orientation, and ethnic identity and the ways they are related to the oppression of women. For all women to be liberated, concerted efforts are needed to overcome many different kinds of discrimination and oppression. Finally, younger feminists, called "third-wave" feminists, are speaking and writing about their differences with the previous generation of feminism (Walker, 1995).

History of Women's Studies

The development of an academic manifestation of feminism has been a relatively recent addition to the history of feminism. Although there were scattered courses in areas such as women's history or women in literature, women's studies was not taught under that name on U.S. college campuses until 1970. In the late 1960s, concurrent with the civil rights, students' rights, and anti-war movements and the creation of black studies, courses sprang up around the country exploring the status of women, discrimination experienced in public roles and private lives, and gender bias in general in society, literature, and learning. Dozens of courses, some official and some unofficial, were launched in a variety of contexts by instructors with many different academic backgrounds but most often in the liberal arts: humanities, sociology, psychology, and history. During the next six years, such courses proliferated on American campuses. Instructors exchanged syllabi and

ideas about how to teach in the feminist mode.

From 1970 to 1976, women's studies began to be articulated as a distinctive, increasingly integrated field. Journals in women's studies were established, including, in the United States alone, *Feminist Studies, Quest, Sex Roles, Signs, Women's Studies,* and *Women's Studies Quarterly.* Anthologies of writing and books in women's studies were published. These began to establish it as a discipline. The National Women's Studies Association was founded in 1977 to facilitate the sharing of information among individuals involved in women's studies and other feminist pursuits.

The roots of the discipline are in feminist critiques of existing scholarship and higher education. Other academic fields had virtually overlooked women's experiences and points of view, the contributions of women scholars and writers had gone unrecognized, and women were grossly underrepresented among academics (Chamberlain, 1988). By now, there has been a virtual explosion of scholarly books and articles on women, and feminist perspectives have transformed much of the work in fields as varied as literature and poetry, health and medicine, history, psychology, philosophy, law, political science, economic development, communications, and management. Profound questions are being raised about what has been taken to be knowledge and about the ways human beings should organize the societies in which they live.

A distinctive characteristic of women's studies, inherited from its earliest days, has been the development of collective modes of production. Although women who are scholars, professionals, artists, and the like often work alone, they also often pool their resources of skills and energy for collective work that does not emphasize individual achievement but rather the shared product

> ### Box I.1   STUDYING WOMEN
>
> In 1970, when scholar-activists established the first program at San Diego State University, no one could have predicted just how successful women's studies would be. Just three decades later . . . there are approximately 615 programs in the United States, and women's studies enrolls the largest number of students of any interdisciplinary field.
>
> ---
>
> Source: *The Politics of Women's Studies. Testimonies from 30 Founding Mothers*, edited by Florence Howe. New York: Feminist Press at the City University of New York, 2000:xv.

made possible only by cooperative group effort. This book is one example.

Missing Information About Humans

One focus of women's studies is the search for "missing information" about women. For example, for many years archeologists of prehistory refined theories about human origins based on increasing knowledge about tools and behavior associated with what is generally considered a man's activity: hunting. They concluded that hunted animals provided the entire food supply for these ancient populations; but when feminist anthropologist Sally Slocum (1975) asked what women were doing, it was realized that little or nothing was known of women's activities in preagricultural communities. This led to the discovery that among some "hunting" societies up to 80% of the diet consisted of vegetable foods gathered by women (Haraway, 1989; Tanner, 1981). Our ancestors are now referred to as "hunter–gatherers."

Historians may have imagined that they knew a great deal about the Renaissance until feminist historian Joan Kelly asked whether *women* had a Renaissance. What were women doing during that period in Europe? It was discovered that developments that were gains for men of the upper classes were losses for women and that if women were taken as the basis for conceptualizing periods of history,

the periods would have to be divided very differently (Kelly, 1987; Ferguson et al., 1986).

One reason women have been "invisible" has to do with the way their "silence" has been sustained. Women have generally been excluded from recorded public discourse and confined to the domestic sphere of home and family and to less valued "woman's work." Because women were only rarely taught to write, there is relatively little direct documentary material about most of our foremothers' lives. Compared to the numbers of male artists, few women were engaged in creating the painting, sculpture, and architecture that historians traditionally study; and work of lasting value done by women was often forgotten through neglect. Many creative women tended to use such forms as music, dance, weaving, tapestry making, quilting, and gardening—forms that were fragile, ephemeral, and anonymous. Women are still poorly represented in the arts establishment among those who decide which paintings will be hung in museums and which books published.

Not only have women had fewer opportunities to express themselves to others, but scholars and critics, usually men, in the past have not selected as interesting the things that women recorded or did. They have felt that the restricted set of activities open to women was simply not very important: what was important was what men did—governing, fighting, producing "great" works of art, etc. The work of women was often ignored because it was done by women. That is why some women chose to write under male pen names, such as nineteenth-century novelists George Eliot (Marian Evans) and George Sand (Amandine Aurore Lucie Dupin Dudevant).

It is a distortion of history to think that the course of social events has been directed by men's activities alone. Men's wars could not have been fought and male-controlled industrialization could not have taken place without the integral support of women's work and activities. Economic and social changes in men's lives could not have taken place in the same way without the concurrent—if different—changes in women's lives, but these have been largely overlooked.

Today, economic planners are beginning to ask what the impact of technological development is on women around the world. Educators are looking at the effects of particular pedagogical methods on girls' learning of mathematical concepts. In this way, they are gaining a new view of phenomena they once thought they understood—from explanations of the origins of culture to the events of a historical period to the processes of social development to the impact of primary school teaching to the development and use of ideologies like that of public and private spheres (Helly and Reverby, 1992). The raising of our consciousness is opening our eyes to the realities that have shaped the lives of women and men and constrained their interactions.

Changed Views of Women and Men

The discovery that a great deal of information is missing about humans has contributed to another discovery: some very serious misconceptions about humans, particularly about women, are widely believed. Feminist research has uncovered a large number of mistaken views about women's bodies, mental capacities, activities, and achievements. This book addresses many of these misconceptions and their implications for a better and broader understanding of human nature and society.

The discipline of women's studies searches to understand how these misconceptions in other disciplines came about, how they affect these disciplines today, and how we might improve the processes of inquiry to develop more reliable knowledge. The historian who wishes to understand why we know so little about women's activities during a particular period might observe that only a limited set of written documents was used to study that time and place, primarily those relating to "public" events or leaders. This historian might then look for other kinds of sources, such as those dealing with local and family records. These records add new kinds of information and yield new insights into the previously used materials. The researcher who asks how women contributed to development in postcolonial African nations might observe that calculations of gross national product were based on men's wage labor and ignored unpaid agricultural production largely done by women. To find out what that production was, the researcher might have to develop new means of collecting data and new types of analysis. It might be necessary to reexamine such basic concepts as "work" and "production" and to rethink the whole notion of how an economy functions.

Women's studies may begin with questions about women, but it leads to many other questions about men and societies and about the methods used to study them. When questions such as these are pursued, they can radically alter the way whole areas of knowledge can be conceptualized (Zalk and Gordon-Kelter, 1992). For instance, most moral theory can be seen to be gender-biased; it has given priority to the norms of "public" life where men have predominated and has discounted as of little moral significance the "personal" interactions largely conducted by women; it has given priority to the rules and rationality traditionally associated with men and denigrated the sensitivity and caring traditionally associated with women (Held, 1993). The ethics of care developed by feminists disputes this priority.

Women's studies raises questions about all that we have been taught and all that we have learned. It has become increasingly clear that if women are not well understood, neither are men. Just as social systems based on beliefs about "natural" gender roles perpetuate stereotypic female roles, pressuring women to conform to a "feminine" ideal, so do they perpetuate stereotypic male roles, pressuring men to conform to a "masculine" ideal. Women's liberation will also contribute to the liberation of men.

Issues and Goals

Race, Class, and Other Oppressions

Like any academic discipline, women's studies has multiple goals and confronts many issues, although it may be more explicit than most about what it hopes to accomplish. High among its concerns is integrating considerations of race, class, ethnicity, sexual orientation, and other differences into its understanding of women.

Members of oppressed groups may find it particularly difficult to see what they have in common with those women and men they have come to classify as members of privileged, dominant groups. To attain their own self-esteem, they emphasize and positively express their differences from the dominant group. They do not want to be "assimilated" according to the values of others but insist on being accepted on their own terms. Freedom from racial, class, ethnic, or homophobic oppression may rank highest among their priorities; and to focus on divisions between women and men within their groups may seem diversionary. Thus, African American women may rightfully argue that their lives and relations with men are shaped by racism and that they have more in common with African American men than with white women. Women who are lesbians may feel closer to gay men who understand homophobic hatred and discrimination than to straight women.

Still, the various kinds of discrimination people experience arise from some similar sources. All forms of discrimination rely on stereotypes that provide rationalizations for exploitation or disdain. To fight against one kind of discrimination is to aid the fight against other kinds. Women of all groups are learning the value of alliances between groups devoted to social justice as they learn to resist also the sexism or racism or homophobia within such groups.

Women from relatively more silenced groups increasingly are gaining a hearing for the expression of their concerns, experiences, and points of view (Collins, 2000; Smith, 2000; Chideya, 1999; Spivak, 1999; Abu-Lughod, 1998; Williams, 1991; Anzaldúa, 1990; hooks, 1990). As they do so, women who lack awareness of these experiences learn from them and incorporate these different points of view into their own thinking. The more such a diversity of perspectives is considered, the more it can contribute to formulating feminist goals, understanding how to reach them, and addressing the concerns of all women everywhere.

Women's Studies as an Academic Discipline

Focusing on women from a particular disciplinary perspective is not the same as drawing from many disciplines to answer question that focus on women. Different disciplines ask different kinds of question and often use discipline-based methods to find the answers. For this reason, many people now believe that women's studies should be its own discipline and not simply a focus on women integrated into existing fields.

As women's studies grows, universities have begun to offer advanced work in women's studies as well as undergraduate concentrations. Master's level and even doctoral programs exist, although they are growing slowly. To date, there are over 700 women's studies undergraduate programs and 100 graduate-level programs in the United States. Other women's studies programs and research centers can be found throughout the world in Asia (the Philippines, India, Japan, and Korea), the Caribbean (West Indies), Latin America (Brazil), Europe (Hungary, the Czech Republic, and the Netherlands), Africa (South Africa), Australia, and New Zealand. As in other disciplines, individuals in women's studies are very likely to specialize in some particular area of the study of women as the field is too broad for anyone to be an "expert" in all its aspects.

Women's studies allows scholars to draw from all the other academic fields and to select whatever perspectives, information, and approaches are most useful to a particular question. Doing so has allowed women's studies scholars to develop their own conceptual frameworks and to build new theories while engaging in research that will test, revise, and expand them.

The study of women provides a basis for critical examination both of existing disciplines and of the social practices they study. Women's studies sharpens people's awareness of the connections between ideas and behavior, placing women's studies scholars in the forefront of efforts to transform knowledge and society.

Women's Studies as a Source of Strength

One of the most important achievements of women's studies as an academic discipline has been to recover the successes of women in the past and to sustain the work women are now doing. Many isolated women in the past accomplished extraordinary things that were then buried through lack of interest by those controlling cultural life. Previous feminist ferment produced significant social change and outstanding academic and intellectual efforts that were then submerged by waves of reaction. Examples of losses that have been

---

Box I.2   The War Against Women

Running for the White House in the fall of 2000, George W. Bush did not talk about ending the right to abortion . . . . Yet two years into the Bush presidency, it is apparent that reversing or otherwise eviscerating the Supreme Court's momentous 1973 ruling that recognized a woman's fundamental right to make her own childbearing decisions is indeed Mr. Bush's mission. The lengthening string of anti-choice executive orders, regulations, legal briefs, legislative maneuvers and key appointments emanating from his administration suggests that undermining the reproductive freedom essential to women's health, privacy, and equality is a major preoccupation of his administration—second only, perhaps, to the war on terrorism . . .

Source: New York Times, Editorial, Jan. 12, 2003. Copyright © 2003 by the New York Times Co. Reprinted with permission.

recovered are Christine de Pizan's *Book of the City of Ladies* (1405, 1982) and Elizabeth Cady Stanton's *Woman's Bible* (1895–8, 1972). Also, today's exchanges of books between the United States, Europe, Asia, and Africa—works of imagination and scholarship—create a new global women's community that looks for knowledge and literature from multiple sources that reflect many different realities. Women need to ensure that today's women's movements remain strong and are not submerged again.

An institutional base for women's studies at as many universities and colleges as possible will help make visible the work women have done and are now doing, even when such work is unwelcome in the wider society. Independent centers for research on women, community-based women's organizations, lobbying in governmental circles, and organizing for political and cultural influence can all gain from women's studies. Women's studies can in turn gain knowledge from what is found in women's practical endeavors and experiences, especially from women's work for women, such as in battered women's shelters, in rape crisis centers, in the work to keep abortion clinics safe and available to all women, and in women's development efforts around the globe.

Whatever their major fields of interest in school, most people will use their education in the nonacademic world. What they learn from women's studies will help them to make better decisions about how to live and work and vote, how to express themselves, and how to strive for their ideals.

How This Book Presents Women's Studies

The field of women's studies is still so new that it has no traditional subgroupings, no standard ways of presenting materials, not even a general agreement about its definition. In this book, we present the discipline as we see it, in the continuing process of defining itself. As far as possible, we avoid disciplinary boundaries in order to focus on our subject: women as human beings.

We begin with a focus on women as individual persons; we then move to women in the family, and lastly, to women in society. The order could easily be reversed; indeed, many might prefer to view things that way. We have visualized the subject matter as three concentric circles. Moving from the self outward, we suggest that what occurs in each circle has profound reverberations throughout the others.

Women are not one group of people with common backgrounds, experiences, and perspectives. When we wrote the first edition of this book in the early 1980s, there was much more information on white, middle-class women and women in the majority classes of more industrialized countries than on other women, including women from industrially developing parts of the world and in earlier periods of history. As women's studies has grown and as more women with diverse backgrounds are contributing to it, literature and scholarly work continue to be developed by and about women who had previously not received enough attention. This third edition of the book incorporates many rich insights, new points of view, and added information provided by such material. Clearly, understanding women and women's experiences historically, across cultures, races, classes, generations, and sexual orientations—indeed, across all the barriers that potentially divide women—requires a heightened awareness of both their differences and their similarities.

In keeping with the new insights and points of view on women, the third edition has removed references to women as an undifferentiated whole. In the previous editions, the term "we" was often used to describe all women, minimizing differences across categories of women. In this latest edition, we avoid claiming a universal woman. Another term we struggled over was that for countries referred to as the "Third World." Historically, the "First World" referred to the industrialized Western countries; the "Second World" included the Soviet Union and its allies in Eastern Europe and Central Asia; and the "Third World" included Africa, Asia, and Latin America. With the collapse of the "Second World" as a distinctive grouping, the term "Third World" has fallen out of favor. After much discussion and in recognition of the new political realities and current thinking on Africa, Asia, and Latin America, we have substituted "developing" for "Third World."

Women's studies is devoted to the study of all women. For this, one needs to understand the consequences of being assigned membership in a human group socially labeled "women" and the enormous differences among women. Women's studies seeks to understand the possibilities of what one can make of one's life as a human being.

References

Abu-Lughod, Lila. *Remaking Women: Feminism and Modernity in the Middle East*. Princeton: Princeton University Press, 1998.

Anzaldúa, Gloria, editor. *Making Face, Making Soul. Haciendo Caras: Creative and Critical Perspectives by Feminists of Color*. San Francisco: Aunt Lute Books, 1990.

Baumgardner, Jennifer, and Amy Richards. *ManifestA: Young Women, Feminism, and the Future*. New York: Farrar, Straus and Giroux, 2000.

Chamberlain, Mariam K., editor. *Women in Academe: Progress and Problems*. New York: Russell Sage, 1988.

Chideya, Farai. *The Color of Our Future*. New York: William Morrow, 1999.

Collins, Patricia Hill. *Black Feminist Thought: Knowledge, Consciousness, and the Politics of Empowerment*. New York: Routledge, 2000.

de Pizan, Christine. *The Book of the City of Ladies* (1405), translated by Earl Jeffrey Richards. New York: Persea, 1982.

Dow, Bonnie J. *Prime-Time Feminism: Television, Media Culture, and the Women's Movement Since 1970*. Philadelphia: University of Pennsylvania Press, 1996.

Enloe, Cynthia. *Bananas, Beaches, and Bases: Making Feminist Sense of International Politics*. Berkeley: University of California Press, 1989.

Ferber, Marianne A., and Julie A. Nelson, editors. *Beyond Economic Man: Feminist Theory and Economics*. Chicago: University of Chicago Press, 1993.

Ferguson, Margaret W., Maureen Quilligan, and Nancy J. Vickers, editors. *Rewriting the Renaissance: The Discourse of Sexual Difference in Early Modern Europe*. Chicago: University of Chicago Press, 1986.

Findlen, Barbara, editor. *Listen Up: Voices from the Next Generation*. Seattle: Seal Press, 1995.

Haraway, Donna. *Primate Visions: Gender, Race, and Nature in the World of Modern Science*. New York: Routledge, 1989.

Held, Virginia. *Feminist Morality: Transforming Culture, Society, and Politics*. Chicago: University of Chicago Press, 1993.

Helly, Dorothy O., and Susan M. Reverby, editors. *Gendered Domains: Rethinking Public and Private in Women's History* (*Essays from the Seventh Berkshire Conference on the History of Women*). Ithaca: Cornell University Press, 1992.

hooks, bell. *Yearning: Race, Gender, and Cultural Politics*. Boston: South End Press, 1990.

Howe, Florence, editor. *The Politics of Women's Studies. Testimony from 30 Founding Mothers*. New York: Feminist Press of the City University of NewYork, 2000.

Janofsky, Michael. Air Force begins an inquiry of ex-cadets' rape charges. *New York Times*, Feb. 20, 2003, A18.

Janofsky, Michael, and Diana Jean Schemo. Women recount life as cadets: Forced sex, fear and silent rage. *New York Times*, Mar. 16, 2003, A1.

Kelly, Joan. Did women have a Renaissance? In *Becoming Visible: Women in European History*,

2nd ed., edited by Renate Bridenthal, Claudia Koonz, and Susan Stuard. Boston: Houghton Mifflin, 1987.

Leonhardt, David. Gap between pay of men and women smallest on record. *New York Times*, Feb. 17, 2003, A1, 15.

Madrick, Jeff. The earning power of women has really increased, right? Take a closer look. *New York Times*, June 10, 2004. Economic Scene.

Nicholson, Linda J., editor. *Feminism/Postmodernism*. New York: Routledge, 1990.

Radin, Margaret Jane. *Contested Commodities: The Trouble with Trade in Sex, Children, Body Parts, and Other Things*. Cambridge, MA: Harvard University Press, 1996.

Slocum, Sally. Woman the gatherer: Male bias in anthropology. In *Toward an Anthropology of Women*, edited by Rayna R. Reiter. New York: Monthly Review Press, 1975.

Smith, Bonnie G. *Global Feminisms Since 1945*. London: Routledge, 2000.

Spivak, Gayatri Chakravorty. *A Critique of Postcolonial Reason*. Cambridge, MA: Harvard University Press, 1999.

Stanton, Elizabeth Cady. *The Woman's Bible* (1895–8), reprint. New York: Arno Press, 1972.

Tanner, Nancy M. *On Becoming Human*. New York: Cambridge University Press, 1981.

Tickner, J. Ann. *Gendering World Politics: Issues and Approaches in the Post-Cold War Era*. New York: Columbia University Press, 2001.

United Nations. *The World's Women 2000: Trends and Statistics*. New York: United Nations, 2000.

Walker, Rebecca, editor. *To Be Real: Telling the Truth and Changing the Face of Feminism*. New York: Anchor, 1995.

Williams, Patricia J. *The Alchemy of Race and Rights*. Cambridge, MA: Harvard University Press, 1991.

Zalk, Sue Rosenberg, and Janice Gordon-Kelter, editors. *Revolutions in Knowledge: Feminism in the Social Sciences*. Boulder, CO: Westview Press, 1992.

Part *I*

Defining Women

To study women, we need a conception of what we are studying. What is it about women that leads us to group them together and to refer to women's studies as a discipline?

As women's studies has developed over the years, it has reformulated its basic assumptions concerning this question. During the 1970s, it was often simply taken for granted that women had similar experiences, if not because of common biological traits (e.g., all women menstruate), at least because they share a social position as "the second sex," always seen, or treated, as inferior to men. Since then, however, feminist scholars have found it increasingly difficult to locate shared features among women and have discovered instead that women's diversity is the more appropriate focus for the discipline. Women's studies today is committed to understanding the social, political, economic, and cultural factors that give rise to different conceptualizations, and the differential treatment, of women both across cultures and within the same society. Feminist scholars understand that whether a woman lives in a poor or rich nation will have a significant impact on her life. They are concerned with how being part of an ethnic minority or a lesbian or how coming from a poor class or caste within a country will differentially affect a woman's opportunities and choices. Thus, the very cat-

egory "woman" has been problematized within women's studies. Why, then, have a field devoted to the study of women if there is not one simple "object of study"?

One important answer to this question lies in how women have traditionally been treated in scholarship: women's own ideas and experiences have been overlooked and omitted within academic disciplines. Privileged men, with the power and authority to control ideas and their dissemination, have been the main producers of knowledge about the world and about women's and men's place in it. One important consequence of this control of knowledge has been that the male has been viewed as the "ideal" and, thus, "male" characteristics have been more highly valued than "female" characteristics.

In contrast, women have traditionally been thought of primarily as those who are "not men"; they have been constructed as the "other." Their characteristics have been devalued because they have been viewed as defective or incomplete males, inherently less than "ideal," and even less than human. In Western thinking, for example, women have been seen as less rational, more frivolous, closer to nature, more nurturing, and less aggressive than men and, because of these traits, inferior or defective. The conceptualization of women as "other" has led to an emphasis in much thinking and research on the differences between women and men, rather than the similarities shared by all humans. Since the most obvious differences between women and men are anatomical, it has not been unusual for women to be defined in terms of their reproductive systems and for their biological differences to be taken as the explanation and rationalization for their differential treatment.

Thus, women have been understood and studied as the "other" for centuries; only recently, with the advent of the modern women's movement and women's studies, has there been a sustained effort to understand women from the perspective of women themselves, to put the elements of women's daily lives at the center of analysis, to value women's contributions to ideas, to acknowledge their creativity, and to document the central role women play in the maintenance, reproduction, and development of their society, wherever they may live. Although it has been a slow process, and there is much more progress to be made, recently more and more women from racial and ethnic minorities within their own countries or from less-privileged classes have entered the academy. Many feminist scholars, especially in the humanities and social sciences, have analyzed and critiqued not only traditional views of

"woman as other" but also newer views, some produced by other women. They have shown that just as gender has traditionally differentially privileged men over women, so too have such factors as "race," class, ethnicity, ability, age, and sexual preference differentially privileged some women over others and even some women over some men. This insight has led to the development of a dual focus in women's studies. Feminist scholars study and analyze how ideas about "woman" maintain and reproduce gendered power relations and how ideas about "race," ethnicity, and other forms of difference intersect with ideas about gender to reproduce other forms of social stratification.

Women, from whatever social group, need not read the scholarly literature on women to know how they have been seen and understood. Definitions of women and assumptions about "race," ethnicity, sexual preference, and differential ability are communicated in multiple ways in all nations. They are communicated through images, language, and nonlinguistic symbols in myths, rituals, folklore, and the media. In the course of socialization and education, whether in a household, a classroom, or a movie theater, girls and women are told how they should act, what they should desire, who they should strive to be, and how they should value themselves.

The implications and consequences of such definitions of women affect their daily lives, molding their identity and sense of self from childhood to old age. Such definitions impose on women the expectations of society and provide a framework within which to censor women who do not, or will not, conform to those expectations.

The chapters in Part I investigate how the question "What is a 'woman'?" has tradition- ally been answered, primarily, although not exclusively, in Western thinking. They focus on how the idea of "woman" has been con- structed through images and ideas about women's "nature," their bodies, personalites, and "proper" social roles. They assess how these images and ideas vary cross-culturally and how they differentially affect the lives and choices of women within a society.

chapter 1

Imagery and Symbolism in the Definition of Women

The Meaning of Imagery and Symbolism

Experience, Perception, and the Symbolic Construction of Reality

Classification and Perception. If we were suddenly transported to another world, where none of the objects, smells, sounds, colors, or other sensations was anything like what it is on earth, we would feel greatly confused. Our senses might be open to everything, but we would have difficulty knowing what we were experiencing. Until we learned to classify what we sensed, we would have no clear perception of this strange world. What we perceive is dependent on the way we order our experience. We select certain characteristics and say that they typify an object; other characteristics are dismissed as unimportant and erased from our consciousness. The ordering that we do in our minds structures our experience for us and renders it intelligible. Without some order, there is no meaning.

The capacity to organize our perceptions is innate, but we must learn the categories we will use to classify them. In our first years of life, we learn from people around us distinctions that have meaning within our own cultural settings. We learn to distinguish colors such as green from yellow, objects that are food from those that are "not to eat," and things that are for girls from things that are for boys. Soon we take the meanings of our classificatory system so much for granted that we cease to question them. We believe that we are perceiving "reality," even though, to a large extent, we are seeing only our culture's interpretation of it.

When we need to teach a child or a stranger the distinctions meaningful to us, we see how capricious they are. A little boy needs to be taught that he cannot wear a pink ruffled tutu. Such outfits are arbitrarily classified as "feminine," although there is nothing intrinsically feminine about them. Through distinctions such as these, children quickly learn to identify gender by clothing. A modern North American child—despite unisex jeans and jumpsuits—might easily be confused by the dress of a Scottish bagpiper or a traditional Arab sheikh.

In organizing our experience, we make use of symbols to give meaning to our perceptions. A symbol, such as a word, a color, or an object, is used arbitrarily to represent something else. Paper money is a cultural or public symbol, a representation widely understood and agreed upon by members of society. There can be private symbols as well, representations that individuals make to themselves in their own dreams and fantasies.

Our perceptions of women and men are shaped by our symbolic constructs of "femininity" and "masculinity." We select very particular features of personality and physical shape on which to focus while we ignore others. We reinterpret what we see according to these preconceptions about what is important. The symbols we allow to represent "feminine" and "masculine" are often arbitrary. For example, round hips may be designated as a feminine characteristic, but both sexes can (and do) have round hips. In any culture, the social construct of "femininity," dependent as it is on symbols, is artificial.

An image is an idea or picture formed in the mind. It may be composed of symbols, or it may serve as a symbol itself. The Statue of Liberty is an image formed out of symbols representing womanhood, light, and strength; as a symbol itself, it represents liberty, welcome, security—also the United States, particularly New York City. Imagery is a medium of expression that depends on the symbolic associations of the creator and the perceiver.

Shaping of Reality. Not only do we construct and interpret the reality of the external world through the application of names and symbols but the same names and symbols *gradually construct us.* Consider our appearance. In places where most people have an image of women as persons who wear makeup and skirts, women who are eager to be perceived as "feminine" do indeed wear makeup and skirts. Social constructs also influence more profound matters of conduct, personality, and intellect. To conform to a cultural representation of femininity, women may think of themselves as being—and act as though they are—physically weak, incapable of understanding electronics, and preoccupied with getting married and having babies. Furthermore, such constructs govern the behavior of others toward the individual in such a way as to reinforce the actuality of the image. If women are assumed to be incapable of learning mathematics, they will not be taught mathematics.

As children, we learn to view ourselves and to behave according to others' perceptions and expectations of us. Cultures vary widely in their attribution of characteristics to femininity and masculinity. In some cultures, women are thought to be naturally strong and hardy, while in others they are thought to be delicate and in need of remaining indoors and being protected. In the United States, it has been common to associate pale skin with femininity and darker skin with robustness and masculinity. African American women have experienced the politics of skin color and hair, of having an appearance that does not replicate the dominant image of white feminine beauty.

Imagery and Symbolism in the Definition of Women

We live in a world doubly shaped by mental constructions. We learn to classify objects and to combine symbols into imagery in subtle, inexplicit ways so that we are not even aware of how we learned what we have learned. Understandings about the meanings of symbols are conveyed through language, art and literature, folklore and popular media. This chapter is about these symbolic media, the images they convey about women, and the significance of their representations for women's behavior and ideas about women.

It is important to remember that to the extent that symbolic expression, through whatever medium, is dominated by one segment of society, the imagery conveyed is that group's imagery. If men, not women, are the artists, then the images of women depicted in painting and sculpture will be men's; women's images of themselves will not be conveyed either to men or to women. If women have access to the products of this creativity only as "consumers"—if, for example, they listen and read but do not speak or write—then the perceptions of women who listen and read will be shaped by a one-sided view of reality. In the

---

Box 1.1   MEDIA IMAGES

The moment the women's movement emerged in 1970, feminism once again became a dirty word, with considerable help from the mainstream news media. News reports and opinion columnists created a new stereotype, of fanatics, "braless bubbleheads," Amazons, "the angries," and "a band of wild lesbians." The result is that we all know what feminists are. They are shrill, overly aggressive, man-hating, ball-busting, selfish, hairy, extremist, deliberately unattractive women with absolutely no sense of humor who see sexism at every turn. . . .

Yet in a culture saturated by representations of happy brides and contented moms, and then by representations of feminists as deranged, karate-chopping, man-repelling witches, a women's movement did burst on the scene and continues, against great odds, to flourish. . . . The mass media helped make us the cultural schizophrenics we are today, women who rebel against yet submit to prevailing images about what a desirable, worthwhile woman should be. . . .

The media, of course, urged us to be pliant, cute, sexually available, thin, blonde, poreless, wrinkle-free, and deferential to men. But . . . the media also suggested we could be rebellious, tough, enterprising, and shrewd. And much of what we watched was porous, allowing us to accept *and* rebel against what we saw and how it was presented. The jigsaw pieces of our inner selves have moved around in relation to the jigsaw imagery of the media, and it is the ongoing rearrangement of these shards on the public screens of America, and the private screens of our minds, that is the . . . story of American culture over the past thirty-five years.

Source: Susan J. Douglas, *Where the Girls Are: Growing Up Female with the Mass Media.* New York: Times Books, 1994: 7–9.

---

history of the world's best-documented civilizations, men have indeed predominated as the creators of symbolic expressions. This results in an imbalance, a lack of reciprocity: men have been the providers of images and women and men have been the recipients.

The Construction of Images and Symbols

The images built out of our symbol-controlled perceptions are usually grouped into categories and classified in different ways depending on our immediate purposes. Different purposes will result in classification of the same objects in different ways. We may have three articles of clothing: a pink sweater with a ruffle, a bikini, and swimming trunks. We may classify the two bathing suits together if we are interested in function, but we may classify the sweater and the bikini together if we are interested in the gender of the wearer.

How does this apply to the classification of people? For some purposes, the ancient Greek philosopher Aristotle (384–322 B.C.E.), in his book *Politics* (350 B.C.E.), classified women and children together. Since he believed that neither had fully developed rationality, he concluded that the male should rule both females and children and be responsible for them. This attitude, pervasive in Aristotle's time and culture, was reflected in a social system in which women and children were excluded from public life. In the contemporary world, we still find some similar attitudes.

How is this type of classification represented symbolically? A "feminine" woman

Box 1.2   WOMEN, WRITING, AND LANGUAGE

I shall speak about women's writing: about *what it will do*. Woman must write her self: must write about women and bring women to writing, from which they have been driven away as violently as from their bodies—for the same reasons, by the same law, with the same fatal goal. Woman must put herself into the text—as into the world and into history—by her own movement.

Every woman has known the torment of getting up to speak. Her heart racing, at times entirely lost for words, ground and language slipping away—that's how daring a feat, how great a transgression it is for a woman to speak—even just open her mouth—in public. A double distress, for even if she transgresses, her words fall almost always upon the deaf male ear, which hears in language only that which speaks in the masculine.

It is by writing, from and toward women, and by taking up the challenge of speech which has been governed by the phallus, that women will confirm women in a place other than that which is reserved in and by the symbolic, that is, in a place other than silence. Women should break out of the snare of silence. They shouldn't be conned into accepting a domain which is the margin or the harem.

Source: Excerpted from Helene Cixous, The Laugh of the Medusa, *Signs* 1, 875–93, 1976, Chicago: University of Chicago Press. Reprinted in Cixous, 1981:245; 251.

may affect childish mannerisms and cultivate an appearance of ignorance and helplessness. Womanhood may be idealized as essentially childlike and associated with innocence, unworldliness, and vulnerability; the ideal woman portrayed in a novel or play may be vested with these characteristics. Thus, the cultural classification of women and children together, in opposition to men, is represented in a variety of symbolic images, some contributed by men but some contributed by women as they mold themselves to fit the classificatory system that exists. It is obvious that in a classificatory system that views

Box 1.3   TELEVISION IN INDIA: PROGRAMS AND COMMERCIALS

The affirmed aspects of womanhood are situated and contained within the home, the most private of social spaces. The denied aspects of womanhood are largely located in public spaces which . . . are the domain of the male . . . the active, energetic male goes to the passive, waiting, and accepting woman. . . .

[The role of the media] is the maintenance of the integrity of the public and private realms. . . . Through gender identification, women see themselves as sexual beings that exist for men.

Source: Originally published in Prabha Krishnan and Anita Dighe. *Affirmation and Denial: Construction of Feminity on Indian Television.* Copyright © UNICEF, 1990. All rights reserved. Reproduced with the permission of the copyright holder and the publishers, Sage Publications India Pvt. Ltd., New Delhi, India. Reprinted in Brunsdon et al., 1997:50–2.

women as the polar opposite of men but erotically connected only with men, lesbians will have no place.

Heterosexism involves the negative representation or treatment of gays and lesbians. Realistic images of homosexual behavior have rarely existed in literature and art, though recent decades have seen an increase in scholarship that aims to reclaim gay and lesbian history. In recent years, the media have also offered some sympathetic portrayals of gay and lesbian characters.

Negative images have been challenged in the fictional and nonfictional works of lesbian and gay writers of color. *The Gilda Stories* (Gomez, 1991), *Compañeras: Latina Lesbians* (Ramos, 1987), and *The Very Inside: An Anthology of Writing by Asian and Pacific Islander Lesbian and Bisexual Women* (Lim-Hing, 1994) are all works that fill this void.

The Use of Symbols and Their Influence

A woman does not need to be told explicitly that women are separate from and considered unequal to men. Women learn this in many different ways, through various symbolic media, including language, myths, fantasies, and cultural imagery.

Language. Language is inherently a symbolic system. The language that women use for thought and speech contains the message of inequality in many forms. Through language we learn that *man* means "people" and that *he* is the standard singular pronoun. One *masters* material; one does not *mistress* it. *Patrons* support the arts; *matrons* serve as custodians in prisons. *Patrimony* describes an inheritance from one's ancestors, including women, while *matrimony* refers to marriage.

These verbal matters are not frivolous and insignificant. Such use of language teaches the young girl that men are the doers and owners and that women are valued mainly as caretakers and supportive partners. When there are only postmen and firemen and spokesmen, the young girl may assume that only men "man" these posts. *Effeminate* is always a "bad" word, meaning weak, flaccid, irresolute. *Feminine* is a "nice" word as applied to women, but applied to anything else it is likely to be uncomplimentary. Language has always expressed cultural biases, whatever they are; sexism is only one of them. In other ways, for example, our language is phallocentric. Consider how metaphors reflect a male-centered view of the world in the way that they reflect the close linkage implied between the male sex and machines. Wanting to provide "input," a male "plugs into" a conversation to get its "thrust" and "penetrate" the problem. Or consider how ideas are referred to as "seminal," not "germinal." It is no longer news that much of our daily language, spoken and written, is sexist. Such use of language tends to reinforce sexist behavior and organization in our society, to promote stereotyping by gender, and to perpetuate inequality. Feminists have urged those involved in the public media to change their use of language and other imagery in favor of nonsexist usage.

An entirely new language is not necessary to present equal treatment of the sexes. Very conservative change, using common, traditional language but with balance, can be effective. Many publishers now have explicit editorial policies about nonsexist usage. Guidelines concerning language usage suggest that the terms *man* and *mankind*, when used to denote humanity at large, should be replaced by *human being, person, humanity,* or *people*. The term *man-made* can be replaced by *artificial, synthetic, constructed,* and so forth. To avoid repetition of the pronouns *she, he, her,* and *his,* authors can use plural terms or words like *personal* and *individual*. Instead of "The student can buy his or her books at the campus bookstore," we can write "Students can buy their books . . ." or "The student can buy books for personal use at the campus bookstore." When a single student is being discussed, the gender of the pronoun can be alternated in different cases: "If . . . she graduates with honors," or "He must fulfill the requirements." Use of "men and women" can signal an author's sensitivity to the issue of sexism in language. Substitution of *Ms.* for *Mrs.* or *Miss*, *representative* for *congressman*, *firefighter* for *fireman*, *flight attendant* for *stewardess*, and so on is a battle that feminists have fought and won. There is nothing difficult or jarring about these changes for either the writer or the reader. They are minor, easily achievable reforms of language usage. Some writers have attempted more radical changes, but the extent to which they can affect usage is not yet clear.

Myths, Fantasies, and Imagery. More insidious perhaps than the spoken word, because their messages are subliminal, are myths and fantasies. In one version of the story of Adam and Eve, an origin myth for Christians and Jews, man is created by God "in his own image." Here, we learn that man came first and that God is like man (because man is like God). Eve was made as a companion to Adam and constructed from his rib. This tells women that they are subordinate to men in that they are made from men (but not the reverse) and that they exist to serve men's needs. The next event in this creation myth is that Eve, defying God, eats the apple and leads Adam into sin. From this, women learn that they are morally weak, that they cannot resist temptation, and that their weakness leads men into trouble. In this case, the trouble is great: Adam and Eve are expelled from paradise and cursed. The curse itself is interesting: Adam's curse is that he shall have to work for a living, and Eve's is that she shall bear children in pain. This suggests that it is men, not women, who engage in produc-

tive labor and that women deserve the pain of childbirth (see Chapter 8).

The Koran, the holy book of Muslims, does not indicate the order in which the first couple was created. However, in Islamic traditionalist literature inscribed in the period following the Muslim conquests, Eve is once again referred to as created from a rib. This is an example among others of how Islam conformed to religions which were already established in adjoining regions and in which segregation of the sexes and use of the veil were already common practices (Ahmed, 1992).

Cultural imagery, largely originating in men's minds, expresses ideas about women and their roles. The messages conveyed are complex; there may be contradictions and multiple aspects and many levels of communication. The symbolic devices themselves constitute the creative content of culture: sculpture, painting, literature, dance, drama, ritual, clothing, gesture, words (spoken and written), and other ways that humans use their imaginations to express ideas.

Some Predominant Imagery

Various art forms in different cultures and different historical periods have expressed certain basic ideas of women in similar ways. We will now take a look at some of the ways that women have been represented through symbolic constructs. Symbolic constructs of woman appear in a number of different societies. Five themes that commonly appear in many cultures around the world are the following: frightening females, venerated madonnas, sex objects, earth mothers, and invisible women. These themes may not be universal, but they are also not confined to any type of society or geographical region. Also, although the messages conveyed are not necessarily consistent, contradiction itself makes a statement about the arbitrary nature of symbols.

Frightening Females

Men's fear of women is expressed in a vast number of symbolic modes. Rituals and beliefs suggesting that women's anatomical parts or physiological processes are polluting have been found to be extremely widespread. Women in many cultures are secluded during menstruation and during and after childbirth, after which they must undergo a purification ritual lest they contaminate men. In some cultures, men are prohibited from sexual intercourse with women prior to engaging in warfare or religious rituals. Many religions prohibit the participation of women in the most sacred ceremonies and even their witnessing them.

Folk tales present a more direct image of women as fearsome objects. Witches, sorcerers, and other semi-supernatural figures able to transform men by spells are frequently females. Sometimes these threatening figures are deceptively beautiful, but often they are old and ugly. In the Western heritage of fairy tales, the wicked stepmother has no male counterpart; she is the embodiment of evil—selfish, powerful, and dangerous to men and children alike.

Female deities and mythical women are also often portrayed as evil, dangerous, and powerful. The Hindu goddess Kali is the very powerful, supernatural agent of destruction. In Greek mythology, numerous female monsters threaten men: Scylla squeezes men's bones together and eats them, while Charybdis, the whirlpool, draws men into her watery depths. These cultural expressions of men's fear of women have inspired numerous explanatory treatises. Psychohistorical arguments rest on Freudian analysis, which begins with early-childhood conflicts that become projected in fantasies. Sociologist Philip Slater (1968) argues that the close, stifling relationship of mothers and sons in ancient Greece accounts for the terrifying females of Greek mythology. He claims that mothers, confined to the women's quarters, vented their baffled energies on their small and defenseless sons, whose understandable fears were the basis for the bloodthirsty female figures of myth they grew up to write about.

Some nineteenth-century social thinkers, such as Johann Jacob Bachofen, author of *Mother Right* (1861), as well as a few contemporary feminists have argued that myths representing female figures as powerful and dominant over men have a historical explanation. They believe that at an earlier stage of human history, women ruled. This form of social organization, called *matriarchy*, was later overthrown by men. Awesome, uncivilized female figures are interpreted, in this argument, as representative of a more ancient order, a mirror image of and a threat to patriarchy, the more recent rule of men. Some anthropologists who have sought the explanation for men's fear of women in social conditions conclude ironically that fear of women is greatest where women are most oppressed (Ember, 1978). Fear of women may or may not be universal; as we shall see below, it is certainly variable in its manifestation.

Venerated Madonnas

While women are perhaps most widely portrayed as objects of fear, they are also idealized as objects of love and veneration. The wicked witch has a counterpart in the fairy godmother; the destructive goddess has a counterpart in the heavenly madonna. Woman in this guise is self-sacrificing, pure, and content. Her job is to make men (and children) feel happy and successful. This message is conveyed in sex manuals and child-rearing manuals alike. The madonna construct is fascinatingly unbiological; she has no blemishes and no body functions. One imagines that she does not menstruate, urinate, defecate, or

The Hindu goddess Kali portrays woman as monster. This goddess is assigned the attributes of death and destruction and usually depicted with four arms, red palms and eyes, and bloodstained tongue, face, and breasts; her hair is matted with blood, her eyes are crossed, and she has fang teeth. She sometimes wears strings of skulls around her neck, while her earrings resemble corpses. Sometimes her waist is depicted as girdled by snakes.

even perspire. Incorporated in the image of the Virgin Mary, the madonna has existed in Western culture for centuries: she is the young, beautiful, and pure woman who is at once mother and virgin, source of comfort and support, fulfilled in giving, submerged in the male figures who make use of her (God and Jesus). She is symbolically represented as the new Eve, whose obedience and humility redeemed "mankind" from the curse the first Eve brought upon "him." Through her perpetual virginity, she serves as a symbol of the "good" woman. Through her maternal nature, she nourishes and comforts her offspring in this vale of tears.

How do we account for this image, the converse of the frightening witch? The warm and nurturing relationships small children can enjoy with their mothers may provide the basis for the mythical madonna figures. However, madonna-like images do not predominate where women are more equal to men; rather, they sometimes seem to accompany the fearsome images as foil or counterpart in situations of inequality (Cornelisen, 1976; Wolf, 1969). They may be understood not only as idealizations but also as wish fulfillments: women defanged and declawed, women now sanctified for their compliance with men's wishes. The "good" woman, stripped of her dangerous elements, desires nothing, demands nothing. Sometimes she receives worship, not equality. Sometimes she seems to worship the man she is with. Contemporary advertisements often present images of women as passive and unthreatening.

Sex Objects

Images of women as witches or madonnas leave out an inescapable fact. The first image suggests that sexual relations with women are dangerous to men; the second suggests that sexual relations are unnecessary. However, sexual relations with women obviously occur,

and without them men cannot have children. The idea of woman as sex object focuses on male sexual gratification. Images of women as sex objects are affected by other notions about women. If they are perceived as dangerous, then before they can be sexually attractive, their dangers must be overcome. If "good" women are pure and asexual, then the objects of sexual desire and release must be invented as "bad," impure.

Most heterosexual pornography attempts to reduce female human beings to sexual objects. While the nonerotic witch-woman may consume men (the vagina is sometimes imagined to have teeth), the erotic sex object offers herself to be "eaten." She is displayed as merchandise and popularly called "sugar," "honey," or "peach." She may be reduced to a bodily part and called "cunt" or "pussy." If she is perceived as threatening, she may be rendered more harmless by being portrayed as childlike. If she is perceived as being too pure to be accessible, her breasts and buttocks may be exaggerated. The adult female may be depicted as bound and helpless or as an irresistible seductress. "Hard" pornography does not confine itself to binding women but displays scenes of mutilation; breasts are sliced off, throats bleed, and genitals are penetrated with broken glass. Sometimes women are portrayed as being dismembered and killed. Vulnerable women, debased, in chains, and totally available to male penetration, constitute the fantasy of hard pornography.

Antipornography feminists speak out against pornography because it is degrading to women, encourages violence, and perpetuates sexist images of women in general (Russell, 1993). Feminist responses to the problem vary greatly. Some antipornography feminists (notably Catharine MacKinnon, 1993, and Andrea Dworkin, 1979) promote legislation against images deemed to be degrading to women. Others (Vance, 1990; Ellis et al., 1986; Burstyn, 1985), who fear that such legislation can lead to an erosion of crucial First Amendment rights in the United States, favor social policies that promote non-sexist education and the protection of women from sexual violence or its effects (by establishing rape crisis centers, battered women's shelters, and abortion services).

Critics of feminism charge that feminists are anti-sex, opposed to the pleasures of sexuality. Feminists respond that this is simply untrue: it is not women's sexuality or nudity to which they object, but how images of women are manufactured to reinforce the social, political, and economic subjugation of women (Lewallen, 1989) and how pornography contributes to violence against women (Cornell, 2000). Many advocate reducing the consumption of pornography through changing attitudes toward it, rendering it less socially acceptable, if not illegal.

Earth Mothers

If the depiction of women as sex objects depends largely on cultural artifice, the counterpart, the earth mother, is seen as embodying what is "natural." In her early work, anthropologist Sherry Ortner (1974) claimed that women are universally devalued and that this is tied to the symbolic association of women and "nature." Her argument runs as follows. Every culture controls and transforms nature by means of symbols and artifacts. "Culture" is equated with human consciousness and its products (thought and technology), which humans use to control a threatening "nature." Culture is superior to nature, for it can transform nature according to its needs or wishes. Women have been associated with "nature" and men with "culture"; hence, women are seen as inferior to men and easily controlled by them.

Women are not identified solely with nature but have long been considered closer to it than men. There are three reasons for this

position. *(1)* Because women also participate in culture, they are considered intermediate between culture and nature. What is distinctive about women's physiology is connected with their reproductive role, and their bodily involvement with reproduction is greater than men's. Thus, women are seen as more a part of nature than men. *(2)* Because women nurture infants and children, they are associated with children, who have not yet acquired culture (and are therefore closer to nature). Again, however, women are intermediate between culture and nature because their role is to socialize children, that is, to transform "natural" humans into "cultural" ones. Women who care for children are kept closer to domestic cycles, hence to the "natural" family, than men, who circulate in the more artificial "cultural" settings of society beyond the family. *(3)* Woman's psyche is thought to be closer to nature. Women deal more with what is concrete, while men deal more with what is abstract. This results from the difference between the ways females and males are socialized by their mothers (Ortner, 1974).

Women, seen as being closer to nature than men, have long been accordingly consigned to lower status. Images of women as earth mothers take many forms. Men, who have historically been the image-makers, have culturally manipulated their ideas about women to clarify their own position with regard to controlling nature. The representations of women in cultural imagery—ritual, mythology, art forms, and so forth—are affected by the relations between men, culture, and nature.

Woman as Invisible

The subsuming of women under the category "man" that has taken place in the conceptions prevalent in much theorizing has often led to the virtual disappearance of women from conscious thought. When Aristotle proclaimed man a "political" (i.e., civilized) animal, he certainly did not mean to include women. The "brotherhood of man" is not a sisterhood. When anthropologists refer to "man the hunter" or literary scholars refer to "man the hero," it is hard to believe they mean to include women. In many respects, this systematic exclusion of women results from the image of woman as part of nature, and perhaps not fully human. This final image more emphatically denies women a place in culture because in it women are neither threats, saints, sex objects, nor earth mothers; they simply are not there.

The Effect of the Images on Women

It would be a mistake to assume that any one image of the female is predominant in a society or at a particular time; in fact, the apparently contradictory images are different expressions of the same idea: woman as "other," the anomalous being who is both like and unlike man. A myth cannot be understood in isolation from the full repertoire of the mythology of a society.

The message that the imagery of women conveys lies not only in its content (woman is dangerous, woman is natural) but also in its form, the opposition of extreme elements: good versus evil, natural versus artificial. All these images serve to set women apart as "other," to make them more creatures of the imagination than real people. They are conceptualized only in their parts, not as whole human beings. This kind of conceptualization, according to sociologist Nancy Chodorow (1978), reflects a male way of thinking, a tendency to deal with categories rather than people, which results from the socialization process applied to boys (see Chapter 5). That it predominates in a culture attests to male control over symbolic construction itself—language, religion and ritual, and the arts. Although the imagery we have

discussed may well originate in the male mind, women certainly subscribe to and use it. They often socialize their children to live in a male-dominated world. They teach their daughters to be feminine and their sons to be masculine (however those terms may be construed).

Do women conform to male images simply to survive, knowing that they must placate men? Do they adopt male fantasies because they have none of their own? No. It is more likely that women's own imagery has been hidden as a result of male control of symbolic communication. Since women have for the most part been confined to the domestic world, their thoughts rarely emerge in public. Often, they communicate orally exclusively to other women. Denied opportunities to speak or write or paint or engage in ritual, it is difficult for them to communicate their imagery in any lasting way to one another or to men. Men may, in any case, ignore what women produce because they devalue it. If, in other cultures or other times, historians or anthropologists had the opportunity to observe women's imagery, they paid little or no attention to it. In the past, most historians and anthropologists have been men, trained by men. They have communicated with men about what interests men (Ardener, 1975).

Social imagery provides a rationalization for the real social order. The social distancing established by the notion of women as "other" provides an excuse for the actual devaluation of women, for the treatment of women as less than human, for exploitation and abuse, and for the denial of their rights to self-determination. The same ideological devices are used against various ethnic groups and social classes exploited by the elite of a stratified and unequal social order. As a result, women in these communities face the consequences of a double burden of devaluation. This makes the challenge to change it even more formidable (Wallace, 1990).

Changing Reality by Changing Images

If our sense of ourselves and of the ways we feel and act is shaped by predominant social images of gender, then presumably our perceptions, feelings, and behavior can be changed in part by a change in imagery.

It is often argued that "the production of meaning is inseparable from the production of power" (Chadwick, 1990). Feminists now contest images perceived to represent women negatively, often by creating diverse alternatives in academia, art, literature, and the media (Rakow, 1992). In the 1970s, scholarship on women set out to disprove that the unequal status of women around the world is biologically determined, a notion that suggests that women's social inferiority is natural. Feminists saw this as an essential first step in combating images of women that suggested that women were inferior to men for it affirmed that women's social inferiority is brought about by culture, not determined by nature. For example, most contributors to *Women, Culture and Society* (Rosaldo and Lamphere, 1974) located women's subordination, which in this work was deemed to be universal, within women's culturally prescribed role as mothers and nurturers because it associated them with nature.

Another anthology took a different approach: *Toward an Anthropology of Women* (Reiter, 1975) suggested that the nature/culture dichotomy and models of child socialization have been most useful in describing Western, middle-class cultures and cannot be used to generalize about women from non-Western cultures. Moreover, this volume questioned the universality of the nature/culture dichotomy on historical grounds. Reiter's volume thus shifted analytical focus from a search for universals to a deeper understanding of how the experiences of women around the world may differ (Morgen, 1989).

There has been a move away from the search for universal symbols of women's experience to the recognition that diverse groups of women may interpret the same cultural images differently. Perhaps most important, it is also understood that different women can and must produce their own symbols to represent their own experiences. Perhaps the most important contributions to the understanding of the diversity of women's experience in the United States have come from women of color, such as Cherríe Moraga, Gloria Anzaldúa, bell hooks, Angela Davis, and Barbara Smith, among many others. Two of these important contributions are *This Bridge Called My Back* (Moraga and Anzaldúa, 1983) and *Making Face, Making Soul—Haciendo Caras* (Anzaldúa, 1990). They include statements from women of diverse national, ethnic, and racial backgrounds. As Angela Davis (1989) points out, it is essential that mainstream feminism not overlook the experiences and contributions of women of color. Such an omission can never be benign. Patricia Hill Collins notes that suppressing the knowledge produced by any oppressed group makes it easier for dominant groups to rule because the seeming absence of an independent consciousness in the oppressed can be taken to mean that subordinate groups willingly collaborate in their own victimization. Maintaining the invisibility of black women and their ideas is critical in structuring patterned relations of race, gender, and class inequality that pervade the entire social structure (Collins, 2000:5).

Women's oppression is at least three-tiered: economic, political, and ideological. The last, the subject of this chapter, is represented by "controlling images" of women (Collins, 2000). According to bell hooks, African Americans have made less progress in the realm of representation than in the economic and political spheres. Whereas improvements have been made in education and employment, images of African Americans in the media continue to be often stereotypical and negative. Whites may see African Americans through the lens of such negative images, and African Americans may see themselves the same way (hooks, 1992). Negative stereotypes are so dominant that they can affect women's esteem for one another. For example, hooks (1990) points out that African American feminists and other feminists of color must be careful not to dissociate themselves from one another while competing for places within the white feminist hierarchy.

The Beauty Myth (Wolf, 1991) and *Backlash* (Faludi, 1991) are two books that view the glamorous female image promoted by the commercial fashion and cosmetics industries as dangerous to women. Many women suffer a lack of self-esteem aggravated by the proliferation of images of female "perfection." The shopping mall serves as a forum and a bazaar where women cultivate and shape their body images by visiting the beautician, the plastic surgeon, or Weight Watchers and, of course, by shopping for clothes (Mascia-Lees and Sharpe, 2000). Susan Douglas (1994) notes that despite all the advances in the last thirty years, women are still haunted, and diminished, by unrealizable longings to be as beautiful as the images by which they are surrounded. This trend seems to be expanding around the world instead of receding.

Participating in Imagery Construction

An important function of the creative arts— literature, drama, poetry, painting, sculpture, and music—is the creation of imagery with which we can see, express, and order the world. Women artists have a very significant role to play in orienting women to their own female identities.

Television is the most powerful and influential medium of communication in the world, cutting across national and class barriers. In recent years, the number of women who work

as news anchors and correspondents on major channels has risen to more than one-third of the total and includes some of the best-paid, most successful people in the business (Marlane, 1999:246). Christiane Amanpour and other women have been reporting from the front lines of wars and upheavals, showing how women are no longer confined to "soft" topics. Also, it certainly has made a difference to millions of viewers to watch and hear women in positions of authority discussing the latest events that used to be labeled as "masculine," including business, international politics, and men's sports.

Women Define Themselves

The courageous motto written by the nineteenth-century mathematician Sonya Kovalevsky (1850–91) on a prize-winning essay was "Say what you know, do what you must, come what may" (Osen, 1974). This is splendid advice for those who know that they do know something and have a strong sense of what they must do, but self-definition is problematic for many women. In many parts of the world, the majority of women have not been taught to use their critical faculties and have little self-esteem and few ways to develop it apart from society's narrowly approved means. The deepest problems may revolve around their internalization of society's views and their lack of realization that they have a "self" to fulfill or even that they have any wishes beyond those of pleasing their families or others around them. In what follows, we will look at ways in which women have searched for self through art and literature.

Women's Search for Self Through Art

Historical Perspective. A few examples from the history of women as painters illustrate the

---

Box 1.4   NETWORKING IN TELEVISION

Connie Chung on ageism:

I think that's the one area that women have made some very healthy progress—thanks to Barbara Walters, who will be on the air until she's 202 because she looks terrific and she is the hardest worker and the most successful person . . . in television news. . . . And because she has created her niche in the television news industry . . . all of us will be able to stay on the air longer. We're in the next generation. All of us are in our fifties now and we are lasting very nicely. . . .

We're very supportive of one another. . . . Barbara Walters moms all of us. . . . And she will drop us a note if she thinks we did a particularly good interview. . . . When I left *CBS News*, Lesley Stahl gave me a great lunch. . . . The camaraderie that I felt and the sisterhood was beyond my comprehension.

Source: Marlane, 1999:34, 133–4.

---

problem of gaining self-definition. As Ann Sutherland Harris and Linda Nochlin (1977:41) say, "Most women artists before the nineteenth century were the daughters of artists. Those who married often married artists as well. Most women artists before 1800 were trained by their fathers, or by their husbands or some other male relative."

Men were more or less free to choose such a field of endeavor, but women could not think of taking up painting without the approval, chaperonage, support, and teaching of a male relative. To be taught to write or to paint by imitating a style is not unusual; but to be an accomplished artist, one must learn independence of mind and judgment, qualities not stressed in the training of women. Writing of another era, Harris and Nochlin (1977:57) acknowledge the high price women paid:

The result of . . . discriminatory attitudes—whether veiled or overt—was often achievement at a level of competent mediocrity by those women artists tenacious enough to pursue professional careers. . . . Simply being persistent enough to devote a lifetime of effort to being a serious artist was a considerable

accomplishment for a nineteenth-century woman, when marriage and its concomitant domestic duties so often meant the end of even the most promising careers.

Some women artists did follow a personal vision. Like many successful women artists of the Renaissance, Artemisia Gentileschi, who was born in 1593 in Rome, was the daughter of a painter (Harris and Nochlin, 1977; Borzello, 2000). Working in a "man's world," she was raped in 1611 by the painter Agostino Tassi, whom her father had engaged to teach her. In a celebrated trial which tarnished Gentileschi's reputation, her father sued Tassi for the theft of both his daughter's virginity and some paintings. Although Tassi was imprisoned for eight months, he eventually was acquitted. The following year, Gentileschi married the painter Pietro Stiattesi, with whom she had four children, including at least one daughter she taught to paint. She separated from her husband after about 14 years of marriage and then lived as a single mother until her death in 1652–3. Women artists like Gentileschi had to rely on the assistance of family members: her brother served as her business manager. Although men painted both female and male nudes, women were limited to female models. Nevertheless, Gentileschi was a highly successful artist. Confident in her own talent, she portrayed herself as the personification of the allegorical figures of Painting and Fame, in the latter perhaps asserting that her reputation was beyond reproach, indeed exemplary. In a letter she wrote to one of her noble patrons, she declared "This will show your Lordship what a woman can do" (Harris and Nochlin, 1977:119). Women artists of the Renaissance often portrayed biblical and mythological heroines. The beheading of the Holofernes, general of Nebuchadnezzar, was a popular theme. The heroine Judith, a beautiful widow, is usually shown assisted by a loyal maidservant.

In the past, the designation of much of women's work as mere "craft" rather than "high art" has caused their creations to be devalued. Some contemporary women are reviving such skills as weaving and quilting and (like the authors of this textbook) finding a special pleasure in the collaborative nature of much of their creative work.

Since the first edition of this textbook was published over twenty years ago, art historians, including Nochlin and Harris, have brought women's work into the mainstream of art history. Knowledge about artists such as Gentileschi makes it no longer possible for critics to ask "Why were there no great women artists?" Though much frustration remains, some contemporary women artists have seen their works installed in prestigious museums like the Museum of Modern Art in New York. The National Museum of Women in the Arts in Washington, D.C., which was founded in 1981, displays works exclusively by women artists from the Renaissance to the present. Not only painters but silversmiths, textile makers, potters, and others are given due attention (Heller et al., 1980:158–9). Included in the collection is a jar by one of the most prominent Native American artists

of the twentieth century, Maria Martinez (1887–1980). Like Gentileschi, Martinez was born into a family of artists and taught to make pottery by her grandmother and aunt, who made pots for practical and ritual use. Martinez did not even sign her pots until collectors began to recognize them as works of art. Pottery making is often a collaborative effort. Martinez's fame brought prosperity to her family and pueblo in New Mexico.

Contemporary Feminist Imagery. Feminism has created a new context within which women artists may work, with feminist and mainstream critics commenting on their work. Feminist artists are beginning to flourish. The multiplicity of their work demonstrates that there is no single form of expression that must be labeled "feminist."

Some contemporary feminists, like women artists of the past, record and interpret women's lives and fantasies about such experiences as birth, motherhood, food preparation, and being in the presence of other women. In 1971, Judy Chicago and Miriam Shapiro, two feminist artists, along with their students, created a "*womanhouse.*" This environment "included a dollhouse room, a menstruation bathroom, a nude womannequin emerging from a (linen) closet, a bridal staircase, a pink kitchen with fried egg–breast decor, and an elaborate bedroom in which a seated woman perpetually made herself up and brushed her hair" (Lippard, 1976). Like other feminist artists, Chicago availed herself of the freedom of the twentieth century to express herself through explicitly female sexual imagery. Working for six years with hundreds of other women and a few men, Chicago created *The Dinner Party*, a work that celebrates women's heritage and employs arts traditionally cultivated by women, including needlework, lacemaking, and china painting. On an equilateral triangular table that measures forty-eight feet on each side, thirty-nine places are set for

Judith and Maidservant with the Head of Holofernes, Artemisia Gentileschi (c. 1625). In this Baroque painting, the artist casts herself as the heroine Judith.

Blackware jar by Maria Montoya Martinez. Abstract designs painted by Martinez's husband, Julian Martinez. A self-made artist, Martinez worked in collaboration with her husband and brought fame and prosperity to herself, her family, and the pueblo. On the right side is a photograph of Martinez, teaching a pottery class.

goddesses and women, from prehistoric earth goddesses to the contemporary American artist Georgia O'Keeffe (1887–1986). The table rests on a floor of triangular tiles on which the names of 999 women are written. The triangular shape is based on the configuration of the female pubic mound. For the plates, Chicago adapted the imagery of flowers and butterflies to represent the female genitalia. This imagery derives from the work of O'Keeffe, who developed the painting of flowers into a serious subject but herself denied that being a woman influenced her painting. *The Dinner Party* is controversial even among feminists. Some question its artistic merit; others express concern that the one plate of an African American—Sojourner Truth—does not use the imagery of all the

others (Pois, 1979, 1981; Kuby, 1981). *The Dinner Party* is now installed permanently in New York at the Brooklyn Museum.

Feminist artists are also critical of the art establishment. Artists such as Karen Finley protest the commercialization of art by creating public art and performance art that cannot be stored in a gallery to acquire value through time. Others, such as Jenny Holzer, Cindy Sherman, Barbara Kruger, Silvia Kolbowski, Marie Yates, and Mary Kelly, have criticized dominant media constructions of women through their own art (Chadwick, 1990).

The work of other feminist artists does not explicitly express a feminist identity. For example, when architect Maya Lin was starting in her profession, her work was not judged to be that of a woman.

A striking image created by a woman. One of the most frequently visited and celebrated national images is the Vietnam Memorial in Washington DC on the Mall. The memorial is a gift to the nation from the creative mind of Maya Lin (left, b. 1960). In its understated and pure form comprising two walls that create an open triangle, the memorial represents abstract concepts of remembrance, sadness, loss, and love, among other feelings that we link with the war in Vietnam. The visual impact of this image of the Vietnam War is stunning and serene. Maya Lin was in her early twenties and a student in the School of Architecture at Yale University when she won the design competition for the Vietnam Memorial in 1981. In 1989, another of Maya Lin's creations, The Civil Rights Memorial, was placed in Montgomery, Alabama.

The Dinner Party (1979) by Judy Chicago, now in the permanent collection of the Brooklyn Museum of Art, New York, celebrates women of myth and history. A central motif for the decoration of the plates is the vaginal shape, which traditionally has signified women's hidden sexual identity, with implications of shame, weakness, and inferiority. The transformation of such an image into a celebration of women's greatness and achievements represents the work of feminist artists bent on self-definition.

Women's Search for Self Through Literature

The earliest woman writer in Western literature whose works are extant is Sappho, who lived on the Greek island of Lesbos in the sixth century B.C.E. She wrote poetry for and about a group of younger women who spent time with her before they departed for marriage. The emotions expressed by Sappho run the gamut from love to jealousy to hate, and they were all inspired by women. Although she lived in a male-dominated culture, Sappho asserted women's values. She would not trade her daughter for limitless treasure, she appreciated the beauty of other women, and she preferred love to war. Despite her

Box 1.5   APHRA BEHN: TO ALEXIS IN ANSWER TO HIS POEM AGAINST FRUITION

Man! our great business and our aim,
For whom we spread our fruitless snares,
No sooner kindles the designing flame,
But to the next bright object bears
The Trophies of his conquest and our shame:
Inconstancy's the good supreme
The rest is airy Notion, empty dream!

Then, heedless Nymph, be rul'd by me
If e're your Swain the bliss desire;
Think like Alexis he may be
Whose wisht Possession damps his fire;
The roving youth in every shade
Has left some sighing and abandon'd Maid,
For tis a fatal lesson he has learn'd,
After fruition ne'er to be concern'd.

Source: From Louise Bernikow, *The World Split Open: Four Centuries of Women Poets in England and America*, Vintage 1974:71–2.

preoccupation with women's culture, Sappho was admitted into the mainstream of classical literature because of her technical versatility. Male poets could adopt her erotic imagery for homosexual or heterosexual purposes.

Sappho's poetry is an artistic rearrangement and interpretation of reality, though it appears to be frank and personal. In fact, most women's literature is personal to such a degree that the confessional style of writing has been labeled "feminine" even when men employ it. Owing to the circumstances of their lives, women writers have often turned inward to explore the private sphere.

Discovering Models in Women's Culture. Virginia Woolf once said "Anonymous was a woman." In the past, it was often difficult for women writers (like painters and sculptors) to maintain respectability if they made their work public. As in the case of painting, many works of literature whose creators are now unknown may have been produced by women.

Instead of working anonymously or as an amateur, Aphra Behn (1640–89) became the first woman author in England to support herself through writing. Restoration literature is tolerant of talk of sex, but Aphra Behn showed courage and originality in speaking of the game of love from a woman's viewpoint. "The Disappointment" is about premature ejaculation. In "A Thousand Martyrs I Have Made," she writes about sexual pleasures; but in another poem, "To Alexis in Answer to His Poem Against Fruition," she recounts a common experience that women faced after satisfying a lover's pleas (Box 1.5). Like Gentileschi who became notorious because she was a victim of rape, Behn was labeled a prostitute for her outspokenness (Bernikow, 1974).

The Heroine. The word *heroine* is ambiguous. It has been applied both to the female protagonist in a literary work and to females whose actions are admirable. By what criteria are we to judge those heroines of Greek tragedy who, motivated by personal concerns, threatened the masculine fabric of the state? Queen Clytemnestra slew her husband Agamemnon upon his triumphant return from Troy in order to avenge his sacrifice of their daughter Iphigenia. Antigone dared to disobey the edict of her uncle, King Creon, by giving her brother, a traitor, a proper burial. Clytemnestra was murdered by her son, and Antigone, condemned to death, committed suicide. Are these women heroines or villains? Our answer depends on who we are and the period of history in which we live. Doubtless, some members of the Athenian audience in the fifth century B.C.E. sympathized with Clytemnestra and Antigone for the wrongs they suffered but condemned their actions. Women's experimental theater groups nowadays reenact the old myths so as to leave no doubt that, in our assertion of female values, Clytemnestra and Antigone are heroines in every sense of the word.

In *The Woman Warrior* (1976), Maxine Hong Kingston conjures up a myth derived from stories told by women in her family. A Chinese American girl raised in a hardworking family that earned a living by operating a laundry envisions herself as a warrior woman in China fighting barbarians, bandits, and even the emperor. She takes vengeance on behalf of the people of her village, whose grievances were inscribed on her back with knives, thus avenging her family for grievances experienced in the United States, such as being called "chink" and "gook." Heroines are women who do not accept their fate passively. They think, choose, and act.

The search for self—even for a brief duration—is a luxury that has been enjoyed by few of the world's women, but that does not mean the theme should be rejected as unimportant (Jelinek, 1980). The written text need not reveal—directly or distortedly—the experience of the majority. We are looking forward to a world where more options will be available to greater numbers of women. Literature serves as a testing ground for new models. In *Drinking the Rain* (1995), feminist Alix Kates Shulman describes her own regeneration at the age of fifty after a divorce. Shulman abandoned a busy life in New York City and lived in seclusion in a cabin on an island in

---

Box 1.6   WHEN WOMEN WRITE

While I was writing he spit up orange juice on the tablet that I was writing on, and I distinctly remember writing around it, because I thought I had this really perfect sentence that might not come back if I stopped and wiped up his puke.

My work requires me to think about how free I can be as an African-American woman writer in my genderized, sexualized, wholly racialized world. My project rises from delight, not disappointment. It rises from what I know about the ways writers transform aspects of their social grounding into aspects of language.

Source: Quotations from Toni Morrison. First from website for Oprah's Book Club, Writers on Writing, accessed June 20, 2001, http://www.oprah.com/obc/writers/obc_writers_mother.jhtml. Second reprinted by permission of the publisher from *Playing in the Dark: Whiteness and the Literary Imagination* by Toni Morrison, p. 4, Cambridge, MA, Harvard University Press. Copyright © 1992 by Toni Morrison

Maine without electricity, running water, neighbors, or shops. Learning to appreciate her environment, living off the land and sea, Shulman renewed herself as an independent creative woman.

The paucity of books relating to the experiences of women of color, which critique negative stereotypes of women of color as well as provide alternative images, has been partially rectified in the 1980s and 1990s. Important nonfiction works by women of color include *Homegirls* (Smith, 1983), *Borderlands/La Frontera* (Anzaldúa, 1987), *Black Popular Culture* (Wallace, 1992), *Women of Color in U.S. Society* (Baca Zinn and Thornton Dill, 1994), *A Patchwork Shawl* (Das Gupta, 1998), and *Asian/Pacific Islander American Women* (Hune and Nomura, 2003). Novels such as *The Color Purple* (Walker, 1982) and *Beloved* (Morrison, 1987) have been widely read and acclaimed. Toni Morrison was awarded the Nobel Prize for literature in 1993. While pregnant, Sethe, the protagonist in *Beloved*, escapes from a cruel master with her children. When her master finds her, she kills her baby Beloved rather than see her grow up as a slave. Later, during Reconstruction, when Sethe is free, she cannot escape the memories of slavery and her daughter Beloved returns to haunt her.

Women's Words. Language itself shapes social realities, for words are our primary system of communication. Some people claim that changes in language are an important step in developing awareness of reality and that such changes are essential for reforming society. Like the visual arts, however, language is controlled by those in power and enables them to structure women's individual and collective unconscious, though this power can sometimes be subverted. Some women argue that the goal of women authors should be to employ the standard language and to write of common human experience, rather than to examine the truths particular to female life. On the other hand, if men have labeled and catalogued everything and have thus forged our system of thought, then to do this women must think and write in a dialect and mode that is foreign to them (Spender, 1980). Feminist scholars are now attempting to determine whether there is a distinct language, a distinct quality of the imagination, and a separate literary style that are appropriate for women (Cixous, 1981; Todd, 1980).

According to Robin Lakoff's (1975) analysis, women's language has been shaped by socialization. Their vocabulary is expected to be ladylike, and their phraseology and intonation are shaped by their role as language teachers to young children.

WOMEN'S LANGUAGE: Oh dear, you've put the peanut butter in the refrigerator again, haven't you?

MEN'S LANGUAGE: Shit, you've put the damn peanut butter in the refrigerator again.

Such differences may be decreasing as women enter the workforce and the locker room and as men take on a larger share in childrearing; but differences may remain (Tannen, 1990), and women writers may still seek voices distinctive to women.

Women's Identity in Utopia. Science fiction is a kind of laboratory for testing suppositions and presenting new paradigms. Women's utopian science fiction attempts to create better worlds for everyone but pays particular attention to what is beneficial for women. Feminist writers disagree about whether to emphasize the differences between the sexes in such a world and to honor women's distinctive characteristics, such as the ability to bear children and perhaps to excel in caring activities. Some think the goal, instead, should be *androgyny* (blending of female and male), with the separate identities of the sexes reduced to a minimum. Some feminists prefer a separate women's culture, and others prefer freedom from gender (Ketchum, 1980).

Marge Piercy's *Woman on the Edge of Time* (1976) uses the science fiction genre to suggest two opposing possible futures. To include all women, Piercy makes her work multiethnic and multiracial. Her vision of two different possible futures, one sexist and one nonsexist, are conveyed in part through terms that underscore social inequality and equality. In the nightmarish sexist future, women are designated "*fems*." If they are not "richies" (members of the upper class), they try to survive as "contracties" (women who arrange to get a contract for sexual service to men). The contracts range for periods of a night or a month to several years; only a "bulgie" (a shapely woman) can get a long-term contract. Reproduction is limited mainly to women who are professional babymakers, "moms." Women are generally considered useful only for sexual entertainment. If they fail to get a "prospect" (client), they might end up in a "knock-shop" (house of prostitution); by forty, they are useless and, hence, likely to be "ashed" (cremated). If they misbehave, they might be sent to an "organbank" so their organs can be used for someone else. The nonsexist utopian future has sex and sexuality but not gender. The pronouns *him* and *her* are replaced by *per*, for "person." People select their own names at adolescence; these names have no particular gender reference but reflect the personalities and preferences of their owners. The term *mother* applies to all parents regardless of sex or genetic tie to the child; each child has three co-mothers. Persons who are closest friends form a core, but there are no marriages. Piercy challenges us to see the sexism implicit in the institutional arrangements that stan-

dard terms for social relationships represent. She suggests that in a society not governed by sexual stereotyping, a whole new set of concepts, and therefore new language, would be necessary.

Some feminists have written of utopias or *dystopias* (negative utopias) as a way of criticizing contemporary society. In *The Handmaid's Tale* (1986), Margaret Atwood describes a feminist dystopia called Gilead in which a totalitarian regime imposes roles on women that are extensions of what some people have always believed women should be. Some young women are categorized as "handmaids," while older, sterile women are called "wives." The obligation of the handmaids is to produce babies for the sterile upper-class couples to whom they are assigned. All women are safe from the random rape and violence of men other than those to whom they have been allocated, but they are forced to have sexual relations with the men, called "commanders," for whom they are to produce babies. Often, due to the terrifying environmental conditions in Gilead, the men are sterile or the baby is "an Unbaby, with a pinhead or a snout like a dog's, or two bodies, or a hole in its heart or no arms, or webbed hands and feet." Abortion and reproductive technology that might have predicted such conditions are outlawed (Atwood, 1986:112). Nevertheless, the handmaids are blamed if they do not produce normal babies or any baby at all and are assigned the job of cleaning up nuclear waste. Because of the "brainwashing" and constant surveillance inherent in any totalitarian system, many women support the regime.

The Propagation of Feminist Imagery of Women

Is there a female aesthetic? If so, what are the artistic principles by which we may evaluate works created by women about women's experience for a female audience? The problem of self-definition through art extends to criticisms of women's work by a cultural establishment dominated by men. Consider needlepoint, quilt making, and painting on porcelain. These have been termed *crafts* or *arts*, as in "arts and crafts," rather than art. Such terms demonstrate that political power dictates the assignment of labels and categories. Contemporary strategies are developing to aid women's self-definition. One strategy has long been known to women in small communities: using the support of other women. Just as the larger society has found that people with a common concern gain strength from meeting together, so women have learned to use their common experiences to illuminate and support themselves, to show that they are not alone in their experience as women.

Networking is another variation of this strategy. Having observed the way "old boys' networks" operate, women are developing their own networks, through increasing numbers of regional, national, and even international conferences. Women are learning that in helping each other they constitute a force of considerable magnitude in the world (see Chapter 12).

Groups have formed in which women band together to gain and sustain employment and to enjoy and participate in women's culture. Collectives have formed in this country and elsewhere to display the work of women. Music groups are flourishing, as are graphics collectives and galleries to exhibit women's art.

Conclusions: Being Whole

The efforts of many feminists in a wide variety of professions, including writing, law, health, and art, have been directed toward establishing an idea of woman as a whole human being. Women should not be reduced to the subordinate member of a relationship (wife of *x*, mother of *y*, secretary of *z*) or a body part (breasts, uterus, legs). This complex process implies, to many, a radical rethinking of what human beings are and what their society has made of them.

Most feminists today reject self-definitions that deny any one of their parts as much as they reject a self-definition in terms of one or more of these characteristics. They do not, that is, deny the fact that they have families, children, lovers, friends, or dependents; on the contrary, such relations are appreciated. Their obligations to and pleasures with others are emphatically a part of their lives. They seek to incorporate these parts into their perceptions, into their work, and into their activities. This may mean working for certain practical changes, such as accommodations for children in the workplace or in other public places (movie theaters, restaurants, and so forth). It may especially call for public support of caring activities and such changes in the workplace as flexible hours and appropriate paid leaves.

Being whole also means accepting and taking pride in one's physical self, not feeling ashamed or awkward or limited because of bodily parts and processes, sexual preferences, or a less than "perfect" appearance. This acceptance entails adopting different attitudes toward menstruation, childbirth, menopause, and sexuality as well as toward breasts, vaginas, legs, and faces. Women see their bodies in terms of what they mean for them, not simply in terms of what they may mean for others. From this perspective, older images of women (witch, polluter, saint, savior) make no sense whatsoever.

Should women's new images of themselves actually become established, through the arts, the media, medicine, and law, many women and men would be obliged to reexamine their identities and self-definitions. Men, in particular, would have to seek new self-images. If men have defined themselves as "not-woman," characterizing manliness in terms of male superiority toward, conquest of, or disdain for women, the concept of manhood would have to be rethought. Once *woman* along with *man* means "human," we can begin reconceptualizing everything in which difference or contrast has been an organizing principle.

Nor are there secrets, mysteries, or privileges of sex. Women would give this up in exchange for the ability to express themselves. Menstruation and menopause are neither dirty secrets nor sacred mysteries. No longer hidden and no longer threatening, they cannot be used to manipulate others. Having insisted that they are not simply nurturers, consolers, and sources of pleasure for men and for children, women must admit to their human shortcomings and admit the competence of others, including men, to be nurturers, consolers, and sources of pleasure.

It should not be surprising that the effort to create an image of oneself, true to one's own experience and knowledge, is difficult. Any difficult endeavor depends considerably on the extent of cooperation and support people receive from one another. Women who have sought to change their self-images have shifted away from seeking male approval and have depended importantly on other women. The literature of feminism is filled with references to support groups and networks of women who share ideas, motivations, time, and effort. In this, women have cooperated as they have in the past, whether just to survive in the face of pressure, work, and resistance or to bring about change.

Summary

The ideas that women and men have had about who they are, how they relate to one another, and their potential are the products of their cultures. An important part of any culture is its system of symbolic representations of reality—the attribution of meaning to perception. We (or our cultures) shape our perception of what is "out there" on the basis of the ways we have learned to interpret reality. These perceptions, or images, are social creations whose shape and origin need to be explained rather than accepted at face value.

Notions of what women are have been shaped by social imagery. Society conveys imagery through ordinary language, social behavior, and creative works. The images themselves have served to set women aside from humanity by reducing them to one or a few aspects of their personalities, physiologies, or behavior. Thus, the image of woman as either witch, madonna, sex object, earth mother, or invisible reduces all women to something less than whole, individual human beings. This symbolic reduction of women then becomes a rationale for their unequal treatment and self-devaluation. Women often shape themselves according to this demeaning imagery simply to survive in a world dominated by men. This imagery is damaging. Why is it so widespread and how can it be changed?

One important factor in explaining the biased imagery depicting women is the predominance of men in producing and disseminating it: men have dominated the fields of public discourse and professional activity in the past. Few women have had the opportunity to present their views of themselves, although feminist scholars are now discovering many self-defining women hidden by men's history. Now, many more women are self-consciously producing images of women, drawing from their own life experiences and perceptions guided by a feminist appreciation for women's worth.

We have examined some of the past obstacles and current strategies that enhance this development. Imagery and symbolism are of great importance in shaping not only works of art but all perceptions of reality, including those to be discussed in the next chapters. The ways that scientists and scholars have perceived women have been no less influenced by the subtle constructions of culture than have been the perceptions of artists.

Discussion Questions

1. Describe a woman and a man as portrayed in a popular song, television show, or film. Note the difference in language and imagery both the writer and you have used to describe each.
2. Remember a fairy tale or folk tale or the words of a song that a woman told you when you were young. Which of the stereotypes that we have discussed in this chapter appear in this tale? What message is being conveyed to the listener?
3. Examine a women's fashion magazine. Discuss the images of women with which the fashion and cosmetics industries surround us. What "feminine" qualities are emphasized? What qualities are ignored? What sorts of women are not shown in the photos? If you were designing clothing, what would you create?
4. Does heterosexual pornography harm women? How? If it does, what should be done to prevent such harm?

Recommended Readings

Douglas, Susan J. *Where the Girls Are: Growing Up Female with the Mass Media*. New York: Times Books, 1994. A readable account of the love–hate relationship women have with the media and of how girls can learn to talk back to its messages.

Kaplan, E. Ann. *Women & Film: Both Sides of the Camera*. New York: Methuen, 1983. The development of feminist film criticism beginning in the early 1970s focused in particular on the question of the male gaze, seen as having a "controlling power over female discourse and female desire" (p. 2). Kaplan explores this concept of image making through a number of specific films. She includes in her introduction a useful glossary to the language of feminist film criticism.

Modleski, Tania. *Loving with a Vengeance: Mass-produced Fantasies for Women*, orig. pub. 1982. New York: Routledge, 1988. A study of three forms of popular culture designed for a female audience: Harlequin romances, gothic novels, and television soap operas. Modleski examines the way each type of narrative contains elements of resistance to the subservient role women are expected to play, yet shows women ultimately endorsing the patriarchal myths and institutions which subordinate them.

Ringer, R. Jeffrey, editor. *Queer Words, Queer Images: Communication and the Construction of Homosexuality*. New York: New York University Press, 1994. Among the proliferation of books on lesbian theory and queer theory, this volume has a section on the portrayals of lesbians and gay men in the media. Issues include the way television has portrayed homosexuality and AIDS, heterosexism, and lesbian and gay characters.

References

Ahmed, Leila. *Women and Gender in Islam: Historical Roots of a Modern Debate*. New Haven: Yale University Press, 1992.

Anzaldúa, Gloria. *Borderlands/La Frontera: The New Mestiza*. San Francisco: Aunt Lute Books, 1987.

———, editor. *Making Face, Making Soul—Haciendo Caras: Creative and Critical Perspectives by Feminists of Color*. San Francisco: Aunt Lute Books, 1990.

Ardener, Edwin. Belief and the problem of women. In *Perceiving Women*, edited by Shirley Ardener. London: Dent, 1975.

Atwood, Margaret. *The Handmaid's Tale*. Boston: Houghton Mifflin, 1986.

Baca Zinn, Maxine, and Bonnie Thornton Dill, editors. *Women of Color in U.S. Society*. Philadelphia: Temple University Press, 1994.

Bachofen, Johann Jakob. *Myth, Religion and Mother Right. Selected Writings of J. J. Bachofen* (1861), reprint, translated by Ralph Manheim. Princeton: Princeton University Press, 1967.

Bernikow, Louise. *The World Split Open: Four Centuries of Women Poets in England and America, 1552–1950*. New York: Vintage, 1974.

Borzello, Frances. *A World of Our Own. Women as Artists Since the Renaissance*. New York: Watson-Guptill, 2000.

Brunsdon, Charlotte, Julie D'Acci, and Lynn Spigel, editors. *Feminist Television Criticism: A Reader*. Oxford: Oxford University Press, 1997.

Burstyn, Varda, editor. *Women Against Censorship*. Vancouver: Douglas and McIntyre, 1985.

Chadwick, Whitney. *Women, Art, and Society*. London: Thames and Hudson, 1990.

Chodorow, Nancy. *The Reproduction of Mothering: Psychoanalysis and the Sociology of Gender*. Berkeley: University of California Press, 1978.

Cixous, Hélène. The laugh of the Medusa. In *New French Feminisms*, edited by Elaine Marks and Isabelle de Courtivron. New York: Schocken, 1981. (Originally published as Le rire de la meduse, *Signs* 1:875–93, 1976.)

Collins, Patricia Hill. *Black Feminist Thought: Knowledge, Consciousness, and the Politics of Empowerment*, 2nd ed. New York: Routledge, 2000.

Cornelisen, Ann. *Women of the Shadows: The Wives and Mothers of Southern Italy*. Boston: Little, Brown, 1976.

Cornell, Drucilla, editor. *Feminism and Pornography*. New York: Oxford University Press, 2000.

Das Gupta, Shamita, editor. *A Patchwork Shawl: Chronicles of South Asian Women in America*. New Brunswick, NJ: Rutgers University Press, 1998.

Davis, Angela. *Women, Culture, Politics*. New York: Random House, 1989.

Douglas, Susan J. *Where the Girls Are: Growing Up Female with the Mass Media*. New York: Times Books, 1994.

Dworkin, Andrea. *Pornography: Men Possessing Women*. New York: G. P. Putnam, 1979.

Ellis, Kate, Nan D. Hunter, Beth Jaker, Barbara O'Dair, and Abby Tallmeret, editors. *Caught Looking: Feminism, Pornography and Censorship*. New York: Caught Looking, Inc., 1986.

Ember, Carol. Men's fear of sex with women: A cross-cultural study. *Sex Roles*, 4, 657–78, 1978.

Faludi, Susan. *Backlash: The Undeclared War Against American Women*. New York: Crown, 1991.

Gomez, Jewelle. *The Gilda Stories*. Ithaca, NY: Firebrand Books, 1991.

Harris, Ann Sutherland, and Linda Nochlin. *Women Artists 1550–1950*. New York: Knopf, 1977.

Heller, Nancy G., Susan Fisher Sterling, Jordana Pomeroy, Britta Konau, and Krystyna Wasserman. *Women Artists. Works from the National Museum of Women in the Arts*. Washington, DC: National Museum of Women in the Arts, 1980.

hooks, bell. *Yearning: Race, Gender and Cultural Politics*. Boston: South End Press, 1990.

———. *Black Looks: Race and Representation*. Boston: South End Press, 1992.

Hune, Shirley, and Gail M. Nomura, editors. *Asian/Pacific Islander American Women: A Historical Anthology*. New York: New York University Press, 2003.

Jelinek, Estelle C., editor. *Women's Autobiography: Essays in Criticism*. Bloomington: Indiana University Press, 1980.

Ketchum, Sara Ann. Female culture, woman-culture and conceptual change: Toward a philosophy of women's studies. *Social Theory and Practice*, 6, 151–62, 1980.

Kingston, Maxine Hong. *The Woman Warrior*. New York: Knopf, 1976.

Krishnan, Prabha, and Anita Dighe. *Affirmation and denial: Construction of femininity on Indian television*. New Delhi: Sage Publications India (for UNICEF), 1990.

———. Affirmation and denial: Construction of femininity on Indian television. In *Feminist Television Criticism: A Reader*, edited by Charlotte Brunsdon, Julie D'Acci, and Lynn Spigel. Oxford: Oxford University Press, 1997.

Kuby, Lolette. The hoodwinking of the women's movement. *Frontiers*, 6, 127–9, 1981.

Lakoff, Robin. *Language and Woman's Place*. New York: Harper & Row, 1975.

Lewallen, Alice. Lace: Pornography for women? In *The Female Gaze: Women as Viewers of Popular Culture*, edited by Lorraine Gamman and Margaret Marshment. Seattle: Real Comet Press, 1989.

Lim-Hing, Sharon, editor. *The Very Inside: An Anthology of Writing by Asian and Pacific Islander Lesbian and Bisexual Women*. Toronto: Sister Vision Press, 1994.

Lippard, Lucy R. *From the Center. Feminist Essays on Women's Art*. New York: Dutton, 1976.

MacKinnon, Catharine A. *Only Words*. Cambridge, MA: Harvard University Press, 1993.

Marlane, Judith. *Women in Television News Revisited. Into the Twenty-First Century*. Austin: University of Texas Press, 1999.

Mascia-Lees, Frances E., and Patricia Sharpe. *Taking a Stand in a Postfeminist World: Toward an Engaged Cultural Criticism*. Albany: SUNY Press, 2000.

Moraga, Cherríe, and Gloria, Anzaldúa, editors. *This Bridge Called My Back: Writings by Radical Women of Color*. Latham, NY: Kitchen Table/Women of Color Press, 1983.

Morgen, Sandra, editor. *Gender and Anthropology: Critical Reviews for Research and Teaching*. Washington, DC: American Anthropological Association, 1989.

Morrison, Toni. *Beloved*. New York: Knopf, 1987.
———. *Playing in the Dark: Whiteness and the Literary Imagination*. Cambridge, MA: Harvard University Press, 1992.

Ortner, Sherry. Is female to male as nature is to culture? In *Woman, Culture and Society*, edited by Michelle Z. Rosaldo and Louise Lamphere. Stanford: Stanford University Press, 1974.

Osen, Lynn M. *Women in Mathematics*. Cambridge, MA: MIT Press, 1974.

Piercy, Marge. *Woman on the Edge of Time*. New York: Knopf, 1976.

Pois, Anne Marie. The Dinner Party. *Frontiers*, 4, 72–4, 1979.
———. A reply to Kuby's review. *Frontiers*, 6, 129–30, 1981.

Rakow, Lana F., editor. *Women Making Meaning: New Feminist Directions in Communication*. New York: Routledge, 1992.

Ramos, Juanita. *Compañeras Latina Lesbians*. New York: Latina Lesbian History Project, 1987.

Reiter, Rayna Rapp. *Toward an Anthropology of Women*. New York: Monthly Review Press, 1975.

Rosaldo, Michelle Zimbalist, and Louise Lamphere, editors. *Woman, Culture and Society*. Stanford: Stanford University Press, 1974.

Shulman, Alix Kates. *Drinking the Rain*. New York: Farrar, Straus, Giroux, 1995.

Slater, Philip. *The Glory of Hera*. Boston: Beacon, 1968.

Smith, Barbara, editor. *Homegirls: A Black Feminist Anthology*. Latham, NY: Kitchen Table/Women of Color Press, 1983.

Spender, Dale. *Man Made Language*. Boston: Routledge & Kegan Paul, 1980.

Tannen, Deborah. *You Just Don't Understand: Women and Men in Conversation*. New York: Morrow, 1990.

Todd, Janet, editor. *Gender and Literary Voice*. New York: Holmes & Meier, 1980.

Vance, Carol S. Negotiating sex and gender in the attorney general's commission on pornography. In *Uncertain Terms: Negotiating Gender in American Culture*, edited by Faye Ginsburg and Anna Lowenhaupt Tsing. Boston: Beacon, 1990.

Walker, Alice. *The Color Purple*. New York: Washington Square Press, 1982.

Wallace, Michele. *Black Popular Culture*. Seattle: Bay Press, 1992.
———, editor. *Invisibility Blues: From Pop to Theory*. New York: Verso, 1990.

Wolf, Eric R. Society and symbols in Latin Europe and in the Islamic near east: Some comparisons. *Anthropological Quarterly*, 42, 287–301, 1969.

Wolf, Naomi. *The Beauty Myth: How Images of Beauty Are Used Against Women*. New York: William Morrow, 1991.

chapter **2**

Ideas and Theories About Women

Do women have a "nature"? Is it "natural" for women to care for children, and are social roles for women inevitable or "prescribed by nature"? Many have thought so, but when we look at what we mean by "nature," it should be clear that nature cannot prescribe anything. This conclusion leads to such questions as whether women should be thought of as equal to men and what we mean by "equality." What values are especially important for and to women, and what should social arrangements be like to reflect them? Though philosophers have dealt with such questions but inadequately, now philosophers and thinkers who are feminists are changing traditional views about women (Kourany, 1998).

Definitions and Theories

When people want to know the meaning of a word, they look in a dictionary; but dictionaries are written by people (traditionally male) and can be rewritten. For the most part, they merely record usage at a given time: usage can change, and the ideas that people have can cause usage to change. For instance, *fathering* used to mean begetting a child by impregnating a woman; lately, it is often taken to mean something comparable to *mothering*, involving the actual care of a child.

Definitions are starting points or building blocks. They give us the terms with which we can make assertions about what is in fact the case or about what is normatively valid. Then, we can consider whether these assertions are true or false, depending on the evidence and arguments. For instance, once we have defined *nurse* without assuming that by definition a nurse must be female, we can gather evidence on what percentage of nurses are male. Once we find that, in fact, most doctors are men and most nurses are women, we can decide if this work is distributed properly or whether it should be changed.

We also need definitions to construct theories, both theories about what is and theories about what ought to be. Human beings need theories to deal with life and experience—to understand the world and to act in it. For example, it is a theory that lets us expect that the sun will rise tomorrow because it has risen every previous day. (Of course, we now have a different theory to explain this from the one people had before Copernicus showed that the earth revolves around the sun.) It is a theory about what it is to be a "person" that allows us to think we are the same persons as when we were children. A theory also lets us decide that government ought to be based on the consent of the governed rather than imposed upon people.

A definition may reflect an assumed theory. For instance, we are assuming one theory if we define *earth* as "the center of the universe" and another if we define *earth* as "a planet in the solar system." Definitions of *woman* have often reflected faulty theories that people have had about the "nature" of women, and the very language in which women have been considered and talked about has contained hidden, implicit sexism (Vetterling-Braggin, 1981). Definitions of women have often been the result of fear or ignorance and have almost always been affected by the distorted perspective of one part of humanity seeing another part as "other" than itself and drawing unjustified inferences from this partial perspective.

The definitions and theories in this chapter, evolving from the sciences and social sciences, on the one hand, and conceptions of justice and equality, on the other, are largely Western notions, in contrast with the images, myths, traditions, and religious views discussed in Chapters 1 and 9.

Women as "Other"

The philosopher Simone de Beauvoir's extraordinarily rich and perceptive book *The Second Sex* appeared in 1949, at a time when there was no women's liberation movement to sustain the views she presented. Better than anyone, she explored the implications of defining women as "other." The dominant view, she writes, is that it is men who are agents in the world: they act, they make history, they are conscious, they think and work and rule. She shows that whenever concepts of the "self" or of the self as "agent" had been developed, they had male exemplars. From the perspective of the male agent, women are "other," "different." Men look upon women as other than themselves: man, the agent, acts and thinks; woman, the "other," exists.

Man is active; woman is passive. According to this view, woman is a part of nature or of the external world on which and with which man, who is human and conscious, acts. Yet, woman is sufficiently conscious to be able to recognize man's humanity and achievement. By being a conscious "other," woman is able to affirm him in his manhood in a way in which inert matter (or nature) cannot. By possessing this passive yet conscious "other," man both asserts himself and reassures himself about his selfhood and his humanity.

To understand himself as a human being, man, the subject, needs other human beings rather than merely nature. Other men do not serve this purpose, however. They only present him with an interminable conflict. Each man, de Beauvoir writes, "aspires to set himself up alone as sovereign subject. Each tries to fulfill himself by reducing the other" (de Beauvoir, 1953:130). Since all men are trying to triumph over all other men, conflict is constant.

Woman presents man with neither "the hostile silence of nature" nor the opposing will that leads other men to strive to be master: "woman is defined exclusively in her relation to man." Such definitions, de Beauvoir continues, are truly man-made: "Representation of the world, like the world itself, [is] the work of men; they describe it from their own point of view, which they confuse with absolute truth" (de Beauvoir, 1953:133).

We might want to question de Beauvoir's assumption that the archetype of the "free agent" is the ideal of human life, but as an existentialist, she saw that ideal as what all human beings should consciously become. Since men have held the positions of power and privilege that have enabled them to label and to define from their own perspective, it is not surprising that their view of women as "other" has led to many unjustifiable theories and false assertions. Secure in their own experience of the world, men have felt little need to question their views (Hartsock, 1998). The more women understand themselves and interpret experience in their own terms, the less

Simone de Beauvoir (1908–86), photographed here in 1964, 15 years after publication of *The Second Sex*. She had been all her life an activist in political causes and a member of French intellectual circles. Her essential contribution to modern feminism was to point out that most of what had ever been written and considered important had been written by men, and in consequence women were always portrayed as acted upon, as the eternal "other," in relation to the male agent.

likely they are to accept the misconceptions that have prevailed throughout history as valid ideas about "woman" and women's "nature." They will recognize these views as claims, frequently false, about what women are like and recommendations, frequently invalid, about how women should behave.

Women can begin with ostensive definitions, definitions which point to the entities designated. In this case, the entities are real.

Box 2.1   DE BEAUVOIR LOOKS BACK

This book was first conceived . . . almost by chance. Wanting to talk about myself, I became aware that to do so I should first have to describe the condition of woman in general; first I considered the myths that men have forged about her. . . . in every case, man put himself forward as the Subject and considered the woman as an object, as the Other.

. . . I began to look at women with new eyes and found surprise after surprise lying in wait for me. It is both strange and stimulating to discover suddenly, after forty, an aspect of the world that has been staring you in the face all the time which somehow you have never noticed. One of the misunderstandings created by my book is that people thought I was denying there was any difference between men and women. On the contrary, writing this book made me even more aware of those things that separate them; what I contended was that these dissimilarities are of a cultural and not of a natural order.

Source: de Beauvoir, 1964:185–7.

They are women. Any definition of women that does not refer to women as they know themselves to be is faulty. Of course, there is a catch in "know themselves to be" because in the past they have too often known themselves only through the eyes and words and theories of men. As they increasingly see for themselves their own reality and express it in their own words and ways, they can reject the definitions of women that belie that reality. Let us now look at some of the distorted philosophical definitions that have prevailed in the past.

Women's "Nature"

In writing about women, male philosophers have by and large shared in the distorted views characteristic of their times and places, however original or antitraditional their views may have been on other issues (Mahowald, 1994). There have been a few notable exceptions, such as Plato (c. 427–347 B.C.E.), the Marquis de Condorcet (1743–94), and John Stuart Mill (1806–73), but the list is distressingly short. The implication is not that the philosophical mode of inquiry is suspect but

that feminist philosophers must make sure that philosophy is enriched by women's views and women's realities. Contemporary feminist philosophers are striving to do this (Kourany, 1998; Tong, 1998; Alcoff and Potter, 1993; *Hypatia*, 1983–present).

A so-called definition of *woman* which has had an enormous and pervasive influence on vast segments of human thought, however ludicrous we recognize it to be, holds that "a woman is a defective man." This view was suggested by Aristotle in the fourth century B.C.E. Aristotle was one of the most influential philosophers of ancient Greece. His work was rediscovered by Christian theologians in medieval Europe, who referred to him as "the philosopher" and adapted many of his views.

Aristotle's view of women was based partly on a theory that among animal species females have less vital heat than males. He reasoned that woman, lacking this heat, was unable to impart shape to what flowed away as menstrual blood. Woman's part in conception was merely to supply the container, the "flower pot" one might say, in which the distinctive seed, implanted by a man, grows:

The most important principles of generation are the male and the female; the male since it possesses the principle of movement and of generation, the female since it possesses that of matter. . . . By "male" we mean that which has the power to generate in another, while by "female" we mean that which can generate in itself. That is why in discussing the nature of the world too, they speak of the nature of the earth as something female and name it "mother," while they address the heaven and the sun and anything else of that kind as "generator," and "father." (Aristotle, 1943:716a)

Contemporary Efforts to Define Woman

In most classical theories, even though they did not play a central role in the system as a whole, claims about women's nature were explicit. In the dominant theories of more recent times, in contrast, women have usually not been discussed. This very silence, however, is significant. It suggests either that standard moral or political theories, such as natural rights theory, Kantian moral theory, or utilitarianism apply to women without need for revision, or that they simply do not apply to women. "In other words, from contemporary philosophers' silence about women one might infer either that there are no differences between women and men that are relevant to political philosophy or that women are not part of the subject matter of political philosophy at all" (Jaggar, 1983:21).

Feminists make clear that there is a problem here. Their critique shows that every aspect of social life is affected by gender and that "all of social life is structured by rules that establish different types of behavior as appropriate to women and men" (Jaggar, 1983:21). Feminists criticize social structures oppressive to women and insist that theory must recognize the role of gender and change accordingly.

Let us begin by examining Aristotle's view that woman is both a "monstrosity" and an "accidental necessity of the species." In this view, the norm of the human species is male and women are lesser, "defective" men or inferior to men (Lange, 1983:12). In terms of biology, of course, the "facts" imagined by Aristotle and others are false. Furthermore, his definition of women in terms of reproductive capacity obviously excludes prepubertal and postmenopausal females. Nevertheless, though we can now dismiss Aristotle's "biological theory" of woman's nature as mistaken, we have to appreciate its long-lasting significance. We need only look to modern theories of women as "defective men," such as the influential views of Sigmund Freud (1856–1939), to understand the point. Freud thought of females as anatomically defective because they lack penises and, hence, as psychologically defective (see Chapter 4).

The view of women as inferior was thought to be confirmed by the attributes assigned to being "feminine" in the Western tradition. The concept of "feminine" was always shaped by the concept of what constituted "masculine." The belief that "reason" characterized "masculinity" was pervasive. If "male" meant being rational, "female" meant being irrational, emotional, and intuitive. The task of rationality was to dominate nature, the body, the emotions, and the inferior parts of the soul, each of which came thus to be identified with the "feminine" or with "woman's nature" (Lloyd, 1984). Western philosophers since Aristotle have assigned women subordinate roles in the creation of knowledge, that is, in the life of the mind and the use of "reason." We shall investigate these ideas again in many other contexts (see, for example, Chapters 4 and 10).

A discussion of facts, however, is not the end of the matter. The more significant question is why anyone would suppose that from such "facts" about a biological process or reality, conclusions of an evaluative kind could be drawn. To suppose that a woman is a defective man, less important as a human being, or of lesser worth or that she ought to be ruled by men or passive does not follow from any facts of biology or psychology.

The contemporary version of such arguments is that women have some biologically based trait, such as being less aggressive, which is properly reflected in society, as in having men dominate women in major activities. No such conclusion, however, can follow from any statement of biological fact. Even if

it were true that men are innately more aggressive, society might be organized so as to restrain and discourage, far more than it now does, the aggressiveness of men, rather than to reinforce and reward it. We use medicine to counter the "natural progression" of disease and can adopt social policies to counter "natural tendencies" harmful to women, if they exist.

Because women give birth to babies, it has often been supposed that this is their primary

---

Box 2.2   "AIN'T I A WOMAN?"

Sojourner Truth was born as a slave in New York State about 1797 and was freed in 1827. She challenged conventional ideas about women and slaves.

She delivered her famous "Ain't I a Woman?" speech, as it was later called, at the Women's Rights Convention in Akron, Ohio, in 1851. Several ministers had come to the convention and spoke of differences between women and men, highlighting men's superior intellect. Years later, Frances Dana Gage, the president of the convention, recounted Sojourner Truth's speech: "Nobody eber helps me into carriages, or ober mud-puddles, or give me any best place"; and, raising herself to her full height . . . "And ar'n't I a woman? Look at me! Look at my arm. . . . I have

Sojourner Truth (1797–1883).

plowed, I have planted and I have gathered into barns, and no man could head me. And ar'n't I a woman? . . . I could work as much, and eat as much as man (when I could get it) and bear de lash as well! And ar'n't I a woman? I have borne thirteen chillen, and seen 'em mos' all sold off into slavery, and when I cried out with a mother's grief, none but Jesus heard me. And ar'n't I a woman?" The women in the audience began to cheer wildly. She pointed to a minister. "He talks about this thing in the head. What's that they call it?" "Intellect," whispered a woman nearby. According to the Salem, Ohio, *Anti-Slavery Bugle* of 1851, which quoted Sojourner Truth's words somewhat differently from Gage, then she said: "As for intellect, all I can say is if woman have a pint and man a quart, why can't she have her little pint full? You need not be afraid to give us our rights for fear we will take too much—for we won't take more than our pint'll hold."

Source: Mabee and Newhouse, 1993:76, 81

function and that it is somehow fitting that women be confined to the role of mother, nurturer, or homemaker. Again, no such conclusion follows from the biological facts, but innumerable thinkers, from ancient times to the present, have made such gross mistakes of reasoning when the subject was women.

Aristotle, again, gives us a good example. He assumed that we could understand what a thing is by understanding what it does, as when we see that a knife is a thing whose function is to cut. The prime function of woman, he thought, is to bear children, whereas the prime function of man is rational activity. He did not argue that the function of man was to beget children. He also argued that since the function of woman is not the same as the function of man, virtue for women is different from virtue for men. A woman's virtue could be found only in serving men. A "good woman" is one who produces children and confines herself to this function.

Aristotle's view of human society was hierarchical. He thought it right and proper for free, adult males to rule over women, children, and slaves, for he believed that only some adult males are capable of being fully rational. Aristotle held that slaves, both female and male, lack the ability to deliberate, that children have this ability only in an underdeveloped form, and that in all women the ability is only partial or defective. We now recognize such theories of intelligence, or reasoning ability, to be false. Nevertheless, even if there were a difference of intelligence, this would not entitle us to conclude that those with greater intelligence ought to be in a privileged position in society. Society can be based on equal rights even if persons are "naturally" different in intelligence, strength, or psychological tendencies (see discussion in Chapter 13).

Arguments drawn from psychology or evolutionary biology that claim to justify social advantages for men take many forms. We need to be on guard against the many current misuses of such arguments to the disadvantage of women.

Rethinking "Knowledge"

Feminist theorists have explored questions of whether there are distinct approaches to knowledge characteristic of women's experience. Many theorists suggest that even the physical sciences and certainly biology and the social sciences will have to be understood very differently if they are to reflect the perspectives of women as fully as they reflect those of men (Fausto-Sterling, 2000; Alcoff and Potter, 1993; Zalk and Gordon-Kelter, 1990; Harding, 1987).

In one field after another, radical reconceptualizations are seen to be required to overcome the bias that has been built into what has been taken to be "knowledge." Not only have topics of interest to women and of less interest to men, such as rape, the sexual abuse of children, employment patterns among women, or the histories of women's lives, been left out of traditional disciplines, but the very concepts and assumptions with which inquiry has proceeded have often reflected a male rather than a universal point of view. Feminists of color have shown how the perspectives of race, gender, and global position overlap and interact, requiring radical rethinking of what has been thought of as impartial and objective knowledge (Collins, 2000; Narayan, 1997; Williams, 1991).

For example, to suppose that the objects of study in psychology are individuals and their states (as when an individual is in a state of fear or a state of sexual arousal) rather than relationships between individuals may reflect a masculine "way of seeing" (Harding and Hintikka, 1983); or to conceptualize social and political and economic life as characterized by contracts between rationally self-interested "men" may again be the result of

Box 2.3   CHICANA VIEWPOINTS

Chicana feminist Sonia Saldívar-Hull (2000) points out that it is essential not to lose sight of specific ethnic distinctions in feminist theory.

I use *Third World feminism* to indicate how our histories as Chicana/Latina feminists force us to examine geopolitics as well as gender politics. As our alignment with women of the Third World indicates, our subject position exists in the interstices of national borders. More to the point, we are aligned as women whose specific needs have largely been ignored by most of our own male theorists as well as by many Euro-American feminists. . . . We Chicanas, along with other previously unlistened-to subaltern women, now insist on our agency to speak for ourselves. The question remains—who will listen and how well equipped with relevant information is that audience?

Source: Sonia Saldívar-Hull, *Feminism on the Border: From Gender Politics to Geopolitics*, p. 55. Berkley: University of California Press, 2000. Copyright © 2000 The Regents of the University of California.

male bias rather than the reflection of a gender-neutral view (Folbre, 2001; Held, 1993; DiStefano, 1991).

Examining such issues as these makes clear that "knowledge" is seldom the impartial, objective, unbiased enterprise it has often been claimed to be. Feminists are increasingly concerned with the ways knowledge ought to contribute to human liberation, rather than, as much of it has, to human oppression. They are asking how to proceed, in constructing theory, in ways that will listen to those excluded from dominant discourses not only by gender but also by race, class, sexual orientation, and history (Card, 1995; Anzaldúa, 1990; Spelman, 1988).

Feminist Diversity

Among the insights to which women come as they examine their experiences is that they are not merely women; they are white or black or Latina or Asian, they are heterosexual or lesbian, privileged or poor, Western or among the previously colonized, and so on (Collins, 2000; Narayan, 1997; Williams, 1991; Spelman, 1988). Issues of race and class

are often just as important to human identities and our hopes for better lives as are issues of gender, and we need to consider how to improve the lives of women in a global context, not just within our own societies (Eschle, 2001; Nussbaum and Glover, 1995). As we examine the ways diverse women see themselves and their problems, better ideas and theories about women can be formulated. A good example is how African American feminist theory in the United States has improved the ideas of middle-class white feminists, who tended at first to generalize from their own experience as housewives or aspiring professionals, disregarding the way many women have always worked outside their homes, often as domestics. Furthermore, non-Western feminists have corrected what they see as the individualistic bias of many liberal feminists, emphasizing the more communitarian approaches with which they are familiar.

Ideas About Freedom and Equality

The first major repudiation of the hierarchical traditions that characterized much of Western thought from the time of Aristotle occurred in the seventeenth and eighteenth centuries. Enlightenment philosophers deliberately rejected notions of original sin and of the innate inferiority of some men compared with others. They emphasized instead the essential equality of men and the importance of liberty. This liberating movement formed the background of the new American nation in the late eighteenth century, and its ideas have helped to shape the society of the United States to a significant extent ever since. The familiar words of the American Declaration of Independence express the dominant ideas of the liberal tradition:

> We hold these truths to be self-evident, that all men are created equal; that they are endowed by their Creator with certain inalienable rights; that among these are life, liberty, and the pursuit of happiness. That, to secure these rights, governments are instituted among men, deriving their just powers from the consent of the governed.

The ideas of the Enlightenment that inspired the Declaration of Independence formed a liberal tradition that encouraged the further development of political democracy. As it has been developed in the West, political liberalism requires such aspects of political democracy as periodic free elections, an independent judiciary, laws that respect the rights of citizens to be treated fairly, and a government that is responsive to the will of its citizens as expressed through the political process.

In the expansive economic developments of the nineteenth century, traditional liberalism fostered the acceptance of *laissez-faire*, the view that government should not interfere with the economic activity of its citizens. This political policy allowed the relatively unrestrained growth of capitalist forms of economic production and corporate ownership. Liberalism did not require economic institutions to be democratic, for that would have

been seen as interfering with the free exercise of what were thought to be rights to private property. Though government may, and later did, enact laws that businesses must obey, the liberal view regards economic activity as part of the "private sphere." The term *private enterprise* specifically indicates that economic activity is considered to be outside the sphere of democratic political control and decision, that it is to be free to develop (its critics would say free to exploit) without governmental interference.

Criticism of exploitative capitalism also developed in the nineteenth century, and there were calls for political restraints on "free enterprise" along with more radical demands for the overthrow of capitalism. Critics of capitalism pointed out that being free from governmental interference is worth little to workers who cannot find jobs; to be free one must have the resources to live. Many contemporary social critics point out that the modern corporation is an extraordinarily undemocratic institution and that the vast disparities of wealth and inherited position in an economic system such as that of the United States are incompatible with the spirit and principles of democracy. They suggest that it is misleading to think of a giant multinational corporation as "private"; such corporations have far more power than many national governments.

In the tradition of political liberalism, however, democracy applies to the political sphere of activity, not to the economic. This view of democracy continues to dominate opinion in the United States and, to a lesser extent, Western Europe. Many socialists also advocate democracy, but democratic socialism argues that economic activity ought to be organized to serve the needs of the whole society rather than allowing individuals to own the means of production and to profit from this private ownership. The liberal tradition and the alternative democratic socialist tradition differ in their views of the sort of economic

---

Box 2.4   WHAT IS FEMINISM?

In the most basic sense, feminism is exactly what the dictionary says it is: the movement for social, political, and economic equality of men and women. Public-opinion polls confirm that
when women are given this definition, 71 percent say they agree with feminism, along with
61 percent of men. We prefer to add to that seemingly uncontroversial statement the following: Feminism means that women have the right to enough information to make informed
choices about their lives. And because *women* is an all-encompassing term that includes
middle-class white women, rich black lesbians, and working-class straight Asian women, an or-
ganic intertwining with movements for racial and economic equality, as well as gay rights, is
inherent to the feminist mandate. Some sort of allegiance between women and men is also an
important component of equality. After all, equality is a balance between the male and female
with the intention of liberating the individual.

Breaking down that one very basic definition, feminism has three components. It is a *movement*, meaning a group working to accomplish specific goals. Those goals are *social* and *political change*—implying that one must be engaged with the government and law, as well as social
practices and beliefs. And implicit to these goals is *access* to sufficient information to enable
women to make responsible choices.

The goals of feminism are carried out by everyday women themselves, a point that is often
lost on the media.

Source: Jennifer Baumgardner and Amy Richards, *ManifestA: Young Women, Feminism, and the Future,*
New York: Farrar, Straus, and Giroux, 2000:56; italics in original. Reprinted with permission.

---

system we ought to have, but both claim to be democratic.

The liberal tradition has made the concepts of freedom and equality central to our ways of thinking. Most of us characteristically begin our discussions of what society ought to be like with commitments to democracy, to free-dom, to equality, and to the rights of individuals; but liberalism has not yet applied these principles in a satisfactory way to women.

Liberalism and Feminism

Feminists often take for granted the princi-ples that liberalism first espoused, such as that people have the right to be free and to be treated as equals and that social arrangements ought to be based on consent and not simply imposed by the strong on the weak. These ideas were developed in Europe and America in the seventeenth and eighteenth centuries but, until very recently, had not been applied to women, even in the political domain. Women were only given the vote, the ab-solute minimum of political equality, in England in 1918 and 1928, in the United States in 1920, in France in 1945, and in Switzerland in 1971; and they do not vote or participate in decision making in all coun-tries (see Chapter 13). Nevertheless, liberal ideas are the foundations on which feminists have often built, and many continue to do so. They offer conceptions of freedom and equality, although they acknowledge the need to reconceptualize and expand these con-cepts. For instance, women cannot live freely if they are sexually dominated in the "private" sphere, and they are not free if they have no means to feed and care for themselves and their children.

The citizens for whom liberal government as developed in the eighteenth century was thought legitimate turned out to be male heads of households. The interests of women were thought to be covered by taking account of the interests of these men. As James Mill (1773–1836) expressed it as late as 1820 with respect to who should be permitted to vote:

> One thing is pretty clear, that all those individuals whose interests are indisputably included in those of other individuals, may be struck off without inconvenience. In this light may be viewed all children up to a certain age, whose interests are involved in those of their parents. In this light also, women may be regarded, the interest of almost all of whom is involved either in that of their fathers or in that of their husbands. (James Mill [1821] 1992)

Most liberal thinkers were not explicit on the subject of women. They took the family as given, and they saw women as confined to the family. They neither included women in the political realm as free and equal citizens nor considered the possibility of relations within the family becoming egalitarian and consensual. As Susan Moller Okin (1979:202) writes, "Whereas the liberal tradition appears to be talking about individuals, as components of political systems, it is in fact talking about male-headed families. . . . Women disappear from the subject of politics."

Not all of the fathers of democracy and liberalism were silent about women. Jean-Jacques Rousseau (1712–78), one of the most important figures of the Enlightenment, argued that liberal principles could not be applied to women or government would be impossible. He exemplified the contradiction between an egalitarian view of men in society and an inegalitarian view of women in relation to men. In his book *Émile* (1762), he maintained that women must learn to submit to men's will and to find happiness in doing so.

Along with many others, Rousseau invoked nature to keep women subordinate. The so-called philosopher of freedom declared the following:

> Nature herself has decreed that woman, both for herself and her children, should be at the mercy of man's judgment. . . . When the Greek women married, they disappeared from public life; within the four walls of their home they devoted themselves to the care of their household and family. This is the mode of life prescribed for women alike by nature and reason. (Rousseau [1762] 1966:328–30)

Since the essence of being human, for Rousseau, is freedom, women in his conception are less than fully human. Rousseau argued that within the family there must be a dominant authority (which must be the father); without the rule of the man within the family, society would fall apart. Rousseau was unwilling either to apply the principles of freedom and equality to relations between women and men in the family or to apply to the wider society his conception of the necessity for clear lines of authority in the family. If Rousseau was right that not even two persons with ties of affection and common concerns can reach decisions on the basis of mutuality rather than domination and submission, it would suggest that there is little hope for the democratic, consensual organization of any larger society that he so passionately advocated. On the other hand, if the liberal and democratic view of government is correct—that is, if government should be based not on tradition or force but on consent between free and equal individuals, as most of us now believe—it is remarkable that its adherents have been and often still are so unwilling to extend such ideas to the family, often a bastion of tradition and coercion (Okin, 1989).

Wollstonecraft

Mary Wollstonecraft (1759–97) is one of the first woman philosophers to make a place for herself in history, although few histories of philosophy mention her. Writing in England in the late eighteenth century, she shared fully in the Enlightenment's rejection of all authority based on arbitrary power and reliance on human reason alone to assure endless human progress. She was a journalist and author, struggling to live on her own earnings and concerned that other middle-class women were unable to find ways of sustaining economic independence. Aware of society's maxims about "woman's nature"—women's idleness and weakness—and the barriers society placed around women's ability to gain their own economic livelihood, she argued forcefully against Rousseau's views that women are inferior in reasoning and that virtue in a woman is thus different from virtue in a man (Eisenstein, 1981):

> Men, indeed, appear to me to act in a very unphilosophical manner when they try to secure the good conduct of women by attempting to keep them always in a state of childhood.... It is a farce to call any being virtuous whose virtues do not result from the exercise of its own reason. This was Rousseau's opinion respecting men: I extend it to women. (Wollstonecraft [1792] 1967:50, 52)

Wollstonecraft said that women had been taught to be creatures of emotion rather than of reason. Instead, women should have educations comparable to those that enable at least men not corrupted by too much wealth to become rational and responsible beings. She was not discouraged by the magnitude of the changes needed in human behavior; along with many other Enlightenment thinkers, she celebrated the distance already traveled by men.

To Wollstonecraft, the principles of the Enlightenment were correct and ought to apply fully to women as well as to men (see also Chapter 10). Unfortunately, Rousseau's ideas, rather than Wollstonecraft's, appealed to those who have made history and the history of ideas in their own image. Whatever gains women made in the political turmoil of the eighteenth century were soon lost, even in theory.

Various rationalist philosophers on the European continent continued to maintain that women are defective in rationality, however admirable in other respects, such as beauty or sensitivity. In Germany, the influential philosopher Immanuel Kant (1724–1804) developed a morality based on reason alone, seeing the fundamental principles of morality as required by rationality. Since women in his view are emotional rather than rational beings, they are not capable of fully moral action. Kant's identification of pure reason with traits defined as "masculine," fitting into the preceding views of male philosophers about "woman's nature," were powerful precursors of later psychological theories and theories of development, which also measured human nature in masculine terms. Kant's own vision of morality was deeply marked by his assumptions about sexual difference (Lloyd, 1984). Thus, the great moral principles enunciated so forcefully by Kant, which added to the liberal tradition of respect for individual rights the concept of respect for persons as persons, were thought to be not applicable to women.

Mill and Taylor

Almost all the giants of the liberal tradition excluded women from the political world in one way or another, but there were a few exceptions. John Stuart Mill, the son of James Mill, argued for an end to the subjection of women (J. S. Mill, [1869] 1970). Mill's lifelong companion and eventual wife, Harriet Taylor Mill (1807–58), helped him develop his feminist positions. In his treatise *On the*

Harriet Taylor Mill (1807–58) left us only a small legacy of her writing, but her views about women and the issues of women's emancipation were essential to the analysis made of this subject by the nineteenth-century philosopher John Stuart Mill.

Subjection of Women, Mill argued that the liberal requirements of equal rights and equal opportunities should be extended to women and that women ought to be able to own property, to vote, to receive education, and to enter into any profession for which they were qualified. These views were the height of rad-icalism in mid-nineteenth-century England, but discussions of Mill as late as the 1960s usually failed to include his ideas on women among his important writings.

Mill's arguments ran counter to those of the French philosopher Auguste Comte (1798–1857), often considered the "father of sociology." Comte asserted that women are biologically inferior to men and will always be so. Biology, he claimed, was already "able to establish the hierarchy of the sexes, by demonstrating both anatomically and physiologically that, in almost the entire animal kingdom, and especially in our species, the female sex is formed for a state of essential childhood" (Okin, 1979:220).

Mill rejected the view that observable deficiencies found among women are due to innate inferiority. He argued that since women have never been given a chance to gain the same education and intellectual development as men, their capacities cannot be known. It may well be, he thought, that the social environment, rather than any innate incapacity, has caused women to achieve less than men so far.

Mill believed that society would benefit if women were given all the educational opportunities given men. Nevertheless, even he thought that, although women should be free to choose a career, marriage was itself a career. Despite Harriet Taylor's objections, he continued to think that while men could enjoy both parenthood and an occupation, women could choose only one or the other. It was not until a century later that the women's movement gathered widespread support for the view that this limitation is highly unfair.

Harriet Taylor's own writings on women were even more forceful than Mill's in demanding equality for women. She derided the faulty arguments through which men tried to support their refusal to accord women equality:

> The world were once persuaded that the supreme virtue of subjects was loyalty to kings, and are still persuaded that the paramount virtue of womanhood is loyalty to men. . . . Self-will and self-assertion form the type of what are designated as manly virtues, while abnegation of self, patience, resignation,

and submission to power . . . have been stamped by general consent as preeminently the duties and graces required of women. The meaning being merely that power makes itself the center of moral obligation, and that a man likes to have his own will, but does not like that his domestic companion should have a will different from his. (Harriet Taylor Mill, 1970:97)

Contemporary Liberal Feminism

Liberal feminists today, like those of the past, view biological difference as irrelevant to the question of women's rights. They pursue efforts to show that women share most capacities with men and emphasize the need for fair educational and occupational opportunities (Jaggar, 1983; Littleton, 1987). They fight discrimination against women, particularly in areas such as education, employment, constitutional rights, and rights to reproductive freedom, and emphasize how far women are from having such rights implemented in much of the world (Nussbaum, 1999; Smith, 1993; Rhode, 1989). It was the desire to end all sex-biased laws that led to the attempt to pass the Equal Rights Amendment in the 1970s (see Chapter 13). These efforts continue, as do efforts to assure the rights of lesbians and battles against sexual double standards, rape, domestic violence, sexual harassment, and gender stereotypes.

Liberal feminists continue the task begun by Mary Wollstonecraft, Harriet Taylor Mill, and John Stuart Mill: to extend liberal principles to women not only when they enter the public realm but also within the family. Equality, it is argued, can never be realized for most women if they are forced by social convention or law to choose between parenthood and a career. The marriage contract can never be a free and voluntary agreement as long as women are forced by economic necessity to marry or stay married and as long as the terms of the contract are so clearly unjust within what used to be the standard marriage. It is unfair that the primary responsibility for household tasks, child care, and care of aged parents falls on the mother, while the opportunities for economic independence and advancement are much greater for the father (Okin, 1989).

Since those who do housework and especially care for children or the elderly perform hard work, often for very long hours, the economic value of this work should be recognized (Folbre, 2001). Some feminists favor wages for housework, although pay for housework (as distinct from support payments to provide for children) may do little to change the unjustifiable division of labor within most households that assigns tasks on the basis of gender. A more plausible liberal solution is the equal sharing of housework, child care, and the responsibility to support the family economically (Bem and Bem, 1993).

Liberal feminists also call for the equalization of women and men in the realms of political life and economic activity, where liberals have always professed commitment to equality of opportunity (though not to "economic democracy"). The liberal tradition should be seen to imply that women have an equal right to as much education as men, to develop an occupation that is as fulfilling, to hold public office, to choose to have or not have children, and to be a parent with adequate resources and some leisure for further self-development.

To make equality of opportunity a reality, special efforts of "affirmative action" to open up opportunities for qualified women in nontraditional employment, such as police and fire departments, have been made. The rationale behind affirmative action is to give qualified women and the men of subordinated racial and ethnic groups who have consistently experienced a pattern of discrimination in the past a right to be considered, sometimes even ahead of similarly qualified white

men, until discrimination is overcome. Providing women and subordinated men such openings has been met with a backlash among those who were previously given preference for such positions. Despite some advances made in opening up opportunities previously closed, much remains to be done. Other efforts, such as to achieve equal pay for equal work or for work of "comparable worth" (see Chapter 12), also continue.

Feminists have also contributed a fundamental critique of the traditional division between the public and the private. Public laws and practices have often supported women's subordination as they have allowed men to rule to their advantage in the "private" realm of the family or the corporation and even to engage in domestic violence without public interference (Landes, 1998).

The resistance of many men and of society to the changes that their own traditions indicate should be made tells us something about the extent to which self-interest rather than a commitment to principles of equality often motivates the behavior of the fortunate (see Chapter 13). During many of the great periods of "progressive" change in history, such as classical Athenian civilization, the Renaissance, and the French Revolution, women not only failed to share in the progress but actually suffered a relative loss of status (Kelly, 1984). The fact remains that among the strongest arguments feminists can make is that the traditions of liberalism and democracy inherently require many of the changes they seek (Eisenstein, 1981).

At the same time, as we shall discuss below, many feminists have become aware of the deficiencies of the individualism at the core of liberalism.

Conservative Sentiments and Feminism

Conservatives have often claimed to be concerned about many aspects of life important to women: the family, the voluntary association, and the moral standards of society. In the nineteenth century, conservatives upheld ties of family and friendship against the more calculated and competitive relations advocated by traditional liberalism. Conservatives understood the emotional value of traditions and ethnic ties as well as the role of habits of discipline or responsibility. Liberals then, and still today, sometimes appear willing to decide everything in the marketplace; to a conservative then, though rarely today, there are things that should not be bought and sold, such as a person's honor.

Feminists, too, understand the importance of family relations, although they have different notions of what constitutes a family. They consider lesbian couples a valid family and do not give precedence to the rights of the unborn fetus over the right of a woman to control her own body. Conservatives have so far shown no inclination to transform their views on such subjects in a way that would be compatible with mainstream feminism. The traditional values conservatives try to uphold include that of the place of woman in the home, as wife and mother, giving emotional support to a husband who supports her economically and to whom she is subordinate. Furthermore, contemporary conservatives continue to uphold economic and social privileges and are often the greatest enthusiasts of the market.

Conservatives (even more so than traditional liberals) favor less governmental regulation of the activities of business corporations. Yet, conservatives (unlike liberals) favor more governmental regulation of the sexual behavior of individuals. The idea that the activities of a large corporation, which affect the lives of millions, are "private" while what consenting adults do in bed is "not private" does not stand up well to critical reflection, nor does the claim that conservatives respect women if at the same time they expect women to "stay in their place."

Alternative Contemporary Feminist Views

There are a wide range of goals that women who call themselves "feminists" choose to emphasize. Liberal feminism remains an important strand of feminism, but many feminists find other approaches more promising. Some call themselves variously "eco-feminists," "global feminists," "prolife feminists," etc. We will look next at some of the more popular views.

Socialist Feminism

Many feminists have looked to the socialist tradition for the most satisfactory source of ideas for a women's movement that will improve society (Jaggar, 1983). They reject as corporate propaganda promoted by a media dominated by corporate interests the idea that socialism is dead because of the disintegration of the Soviet Union. The latter was not a socialist society as democratic socialists envision it. Socialist feminists see conservatism as conserving a sexist status quo and fear that liberalism will merely promote an expanded market and an even more generalized pursuit of self-interest than already exists. They see deep connections between male domination and capitalism. In Eastern Europe, for instance, as capitalism has replaced communism, patriarchal policies and attitudes have often regained ascendancy and women have paid a heavy price in lost jobs, freedoms, and social supports (Funk and Mueller, 1993). Capitalist globalization has often been particularly damaging to women.

Socialist feminists fear that too many of the few women in a liberal capitalist system who will taste success will learn to scramble for self-advancement in the corporate hierarchy, striving for profits regardless of the good of society, just as men do, and that too many other women will simply be left out, especially poor women, Third World women, and women whose racial and ethnic heritage differs from that of those who control society. Some feminists claim that liberalism has never paid enough attention to economic power because of its individualism and its tradition of laissez-faire. Women could gain many individual legal rights and still be left in a condition of economic dependence and disadvantage damaging to their self-respect and their efforts to win liberation. Liberalism combats individual discrimination but fails to see the oppressive structure of a society dominated by corporate power.

The unfortunate effect of the economic dependence of women was recognized by Karl Marx (1818–83) and Friedrich Engels (1820–95). In *The Origin of the Family, Private Property, and the State*, Engels ([1884] 1972) argued that the institutional and cultural manifestations of a given historical period, including the monogamous family, result from economic causes. According to this nineteenth-century view of historical evolution, it was at the stage of human development when property began to be accumulated by men (though it is not clear why it was men who did the accumulating) that men became the first ruling class.

In the middle-class family of Western capitalism, as seen by Marx and Engels, the wife had sold herself sexually for economic support. In the eyes of many other writers as well, the wife and mother in the successful bourgeois family of Victorian times was "elevated" to a position of powerlessness: cared for by hired servants, flattered but sexually imprisoned, denied any chance for self-development or personal freedom. Women of the lower classes, meanwhile, were economically exploited in factories and needle trades and as domestic servants even more brutally than were men. Economic and social "progress" by late in the century had moved many married women from the factory into the home. They aspired to the status and promised security

of the middle-class wife, not realizing how few could achieve it or how unsatisfactory this goal could turn out to be. The point was well made by Charlotte Perkins Gilman (1860–1935), the author of *The Yellow Wall-Paper* ([1899] 1973) and of *Women and Economics* ([1898] 1966):

> When the woman, left alone with no man to "support" her, tries to meet her own economic necessities, the difficulties which confront her prove conclusively what the general economic status of women is. . . . We see the human mother worked far harder than a mare, laboring her life long in the service, not of her children only, but of men; husbands, brothers, fathers, whatever male relative she has. . . . The human female, the world over, works at extramaternal duties for hours enough to provide her with an independent living, and then is denied independence on the ground that motherhood prevents her working! (Gilman, [1898] 1966:10, 19–20)

The Marxist view held that the working class must gain control of the means of production and thus end the exploitation of workers by capitalists. In this view, if women enter the labor force in large numbers, their problems will be soluble along with the problems of the working class. Feminists, however, recognize that this picture needs revision: there are some problems that affect women as women, rather than as members of the working class (see Chapter 12).

Dissatisfaction with corporate capitalism and the lack of awareness among traditional Marxists of the views and problems of women have led to the development of a socialist feminism that is influential among Western feminists (Hartsock 1998; Jaggar, 1983). Thus, Sheila Rowbotham (1973) and Juliet Mitchell (1973) argue that many transformations of the economy called for by socialists are necessary before women—confined primarily to the lowest-paying and least secure jobs—can begin to gain real economic independence.

For society to begin to provide what women need, many specific demands made by socialists will have to be accepted. All feminists can enthusiastically join in demanding publicly funded child care, medical care, care of the elderly, decent housing for all, and non-exploitative jobs for all who can work (Harrington, 1999). They can join in working for the changes that will be necessary to make these possible. Socialist feminists also recognize that traditional socialism has failed to understand the specific ways in which women are oppressed (Jaggar, 1983; Sargent, 1981). The traditional gender division of labor within the family, for instance, as well as outside it will have to disappear, as will the many forms of violence against women.

Radical Feminism

Radical feminists often start thinking about women's oppression by looking at the way sexuality is socially constructed. In Catharine MacKinnon's view, men sexualize hierarchy; the male sexual role "centers on aggressive intrusion on those with less power. Such acts of dominance are experienced as sexually arousing, as sex itself" (MacKinnon, 1989:316).

Radical feminism sees the basic hierarchy with regard to sexuality as extended to all aspects of social life. Consequently, two cultures are created: the visible world of male culture, which is divided into national boundaries, and the invisible world of women's culture, which exists universally "within every culture" (Jaggar, 1983:249). According to radical feminists, dominant male culture portrays a picture of social reality in which men are, and should be, positive, aggressive, dominant, objective, strong, and intellectual, while women are, and are in most cases even valued for being, passive, emotional, intuitive, mysterious, childish, dependent, evil, and submissive. Liberal feminists and socialist feminists often seem to accept this picture as an accurate depiction of reality but see it as socially constructed. Liberal feminists believe women have as much potential for autonomy and rationality as men, and socialist feminists see the contrast in terms of women's oppression and alienation (Bartky, 1990; Jaggar, 1983).

Radical feminists claim that the picture of reality presented by male culture conceals the destructive values that underlie this culture and "obscures the positive contributions of the female culture" (Jaggar, 1983:251). For instance, male culture seems to focus on death and on dying for gods or countries, while relegating human birth and childrearing to mere "natural" events (Held, 1993; Hartsock, 1983). Radical feminists think liberal and socialist feminists have internalized the values of male culture and that their efforts for change are a striving to make women more like men by men's standards. Radical feminists revalue the attributes assigned to women in men's culture and reclaim them with new meanings for "womanculture." Radical feminists coined the slogan "the personal is political" (Jaggar, 1983:255).

Radical feminists have viewed patriarchy as a system of pervasive domination by males, most clearly expressed in efforts to control women's bodies. They see failures to provide adequate contraception and abortion as aspects of compulsory motherhood and motherhood as it is institutionalized under patriarchy as one of the bases for women's subordination. Pervasive sexual harassment, rape, prostitution, and pornography are other ways by which men dominate women through sexuality (MacKinnon, 1987). Radical feminists' focus on women's oppression in intimate relations is a contribution to feminist thought, just as liberal feminists contribute an analysis of barriers to legal equality and socialist feminists an analysis of what women need for full participation in the economic and political worlds.

It follows from the radical feminist view of women's oppression that heterosexual relationships are always in danger of being reduced to male control of female bodies, whether expressed in marriage, motherhood, prostitution, or any sort of intimate relation. From that perspective, separatism may be an answer, and separatism may take the form of sexual celibacy or lesbianism, which may or may not take a sexual form. Charlotte Bunch writes the following:

> Being a Lesbian means ending identification with, allegiance to, dependence on, and support of heterosexuality. It means ending your personal stake in the male world so that you join women, individually and collectively, in the struggle to end your oppression. Lesbianism is the key to liberation and only women who cut their ties to male privilege can be trusted to remain serious in the struggle against male dominance. (Bunch, 1975:36)

For some radical feminists, the very fact that lesbianism is sexual makes it political. As Adrienne Rich (1980:648) expresses it: "Lesbianism is a threat to the ideological, political, personal, and economic basis of male supremacy. The Lesbian threatens the ideology of male supremacy by destroying the lie about female inferiority, weakness, passivity, and by denying women's 'innate need for men.'"

Some feminists consider themselves radical because they see the overthrow of gender domination as the most fundamental and radical change possible in human history and society. Many think this change can occur within as well as by rejecting close relationships with men and sometimes with men as allies, and some believe that racial and class oppression are in important ways dependent on gender domination.

Other Western Feminisms

Among theorists who call themselves "poststructuralists" or "postmodernists," usually working in a continental European rather than an Anglo-American tradition, language is often seen as reflective of struggles for power. It is clear that the meanings attached to "women's nature" or biological difference have changed over time, reshaped with the emergence of the medical profession in the nineteenth century, for example, or the rise of psychiatry in the twentieth (Foucault, 1978, 1986). In poststructuralist or postmodernist terms, the different processes by which meanings are shaped are called "discourses." Language is seen as the site of battles within a discourse over meanings. For example, assumptions, as in the discourse called evolutionary psychology, that motherhood and childrearing are natural for women carry many political, social, and economic messages with regard to women who do not choose to become mothers as well as to those who do. "Natural femininity and masculinity," as depicted in much sociobiological discourse, are claimed to "necessarily fit women and men for different types of jobs and social and familial tasks" (Weedon, 1987:130). Differences between "woman's nature" and "man's nature" are presented as fixed and, by virtue of the tasks assigned, hierarchical; and men have greater access to the power that determines the nature of society. Yet, sociobiologists characteristically assume that as scientists they are independent of particular social and moral values and interests and that the language they use is merely a tool for expressing facts, rather than the material out of which conflicting versions of the facts are constructed. If, however, meanings are contested and our very subjectivity is constantly being constructed in the context of the battle going on over those meanings, how can gender differences be understood?

Postmodernist insights have helped many feminists "deconstruct" the ideas they were taught about the impartiality and universality of much that has been presented authoritatively

---

Box 2.5   WOMEN AND CARE

[W]omen not only define themselves in a context of human relationship but also judge themselves in terms of their ability to care. Women's place in man's life cycle has been that of nurturer, caretaker, and helpmate, the weaver of those networks of relationships on which she in turn relies. But while women have thus taken care of men, men have, in their theories of psychological development, as in their economic arrangements, tended to assume or devalue that care. When the focus on individuation and individual achievement extends into adulthood and maturity is equated with personal autonomy, concern with relationships appears as a weakness of women rather than as a human strength.

Source: Reprinted by permission of the publisher from *In a Different Voice. Psychological Theory and Women's Development* by Carol Gilligan, p. 17, Cambridge, MA: Harvard University Press. Copyright © 1982, 1983 by Carol Gilligan.

---

as "scientific knowledge" and as required by "rationality," and some even contest the category "woman." Some feminists are concerned, however, that contemporary efforts to undermine previous, biased claims to "truth" and "objectivity" are now being used, in turn, to undermine the insights of feminists. If all discourses and theories are relative and without foundation, feminist criticisms and reconstructions of them are as dismissible as those they replace (Hartsock, 1998). Postmodernists respond that even though there is no absolute objective truth, some partial views are better than others (Benhabib, 1992; Young, 1990).

The Ethics of Care

An approach that has had wide influence among contemporary feminists, especially radical ones, concerns morality: the ethics of care. It involves reevaluating activities and practices long associated with women and coming to appreciate both their enormous importance in society and the neglected moral values they incorporate. Then, with a new understanding of the importance and value of caring relations in society, theorists

have been exploring how this new ethic should be applied to areas other than those with which women have been associated: for instance, to medical practice, public and political life, even international relations (Tong, 2001; Kittay, 1999; Robinson, 1999; Held, 1993; Tronto, 1993; Sherwin, 1992).

Early in the development of feminist theory in the 1970s, feminists began to consider the implications of thinking about the traditional ideals of rationality and objectivity as "male" rather than as universal (Lloyd, 1984). Interest in the issue was intensified by the studies of moral development made by Carol Gilligan (1982) and others. Gilligan showed that the most widely accepted theory of moral development, that of Lawrence Kohlberg, is, like Freud's theories, male-biased. Proposed as a universal theory but based on an interpretation of the cognitive development of 84 boys, Kohlberg's scale of moral development was constructed to represent progress in moral reasoning. On Kohlberg's scale, the highest level of achievement is seen as the internalization of formal, abstract principles or rules of justice.

Gilligan set out to study women to determine why they seemed to become stalled

---

Box 2.6 STANDARD MORAL THEORIES

In examining contemporary moral theories and their modern antecedents feminists find kindred preoccupations, assumptions, and points of view. These theories idealize relations of nonintimate, mutually independent peers seeking to preserve autonomy or enhance self-interest. . . . They mirror spheres of activity, social roles, and character ideals associated with socially advantaged men. . . . The canonical form of moral judgment in dominant theories tracks gendered social positions and prerogatives. . . . In this "theoretical-juridical" picture "the" moral agent in action resembles a judge, manager, bureaucrat, or gamesman. . . . The normative subject thus conjured up is not (typically) a woman; but he or she is also not a child, a person of disadvantaged economic, educational, or professional position, or someone of despised racial, caste, ethnic, sexual, or religious identity.

Source: Copyright © 1998. From *Moral Understandings: A Feminist Study in Ethics*, pp. 20–1, by Margaret Urban Walker. Reproduced by permission of Routledge/Taylor & Francis Books, Inc.

---

at the middle stage of Kohlberg's scale, a situation that implied that women are deficient in the development of moral judgment. Gilligan found that many women follow a different path to moral development than most men and that there exists a morally "different voice" from the one that Kohlberg identified as definitive of mature judgment (Kittay and Meyers, 1987). Studying a group of women making real-life decisions regarding abortion, Gilligan discovered that instead of applying abstract rules of justice, her subjects were concerned with preserving actual human relationships and expressing care for those for whom they felt responsible. This "ethic of care" was a different way of interpreting moral problems from that enunciated by the "ethic of justice" of Kohlberg's scale. As Gilligan (1982:19) put it: "This conception of morality as concerned with the activity of care centers moral development around the understanding of responsibility and relationships, just as the conception of morality as fairness ties moral development to the understanding of rights and rules."

Although Gilligan's analysis suggests how women and men act and think about themselves, it does not explain why they develop

differently or whether an "ethic of care" is equivalent, inferior, or superior to an "ethic of justice." One danger, according to some of Gilligan's critics, is that the idea of a morally "different voice" lends itself to biological typecasting such as has been used through the centuries to keep women in their "place," confined to a "separate sphere," and assigned to do the world's dirty work by praising their capacities for selfless devotion to others. Some feminists suggest that women's different moral expression may result from their historically subordinate social position.

Joan Tronto draws on studies showing that African Americans tend to construct morality in terms that resemble an ethic of care; she notes that people of color, as well as women, do a disproportionate amount of the work of caring for the ill and elderly—for instance, as poorly paid hospital attendants. Thus, tendencies to use an ethic of care may depend less on gender than on lacking power and privilege (Tronto, 1993). However, once people recognize the value of caring, they can advocate its wider practice and the need for social recognition and support for the activities it involves (Folbre, 2001). Tronto and others see a lack of caregiving experiences by

---

Box 2.7 PERSONHOOD

[T]he prevailing conception of moral personhood in contemporary social contract theory assumes that individuals are neither dependent on others for care nor encumbered by responsibilities to care for dependents. Yet, viewing such independence as a universal norm becomes suspect once one takes women into account. . . . Women's traditional role reminds us not only that many adults do not fit the regnant model of personhood but also that all of us spend a lengthy childhood dependent on others and that many of us will return to a condition of dependency in old age. Insofar as a culture's rules of moral salience occlude dependency, many women's moral concerns will be denigrated, and the needs of dependents will be marginalized.

Source: Meyers, 1997:200.

---

privileged males as leaving them morally deprived, misleading them into thinking that moral beliefs can be expressed in abstract, universal terms as if they were purely cognitive questions, like mathematical ones.

Empirical studies of how people tend to approach moral problems are suggestive of how standards should be questioned. Nevertheless, for understanding what moral approaches ought to be favored, a normative rather than empirical inquiry is required. Feminist moral philosophers have been doing this work, exploring the kinds of morality that might adequately reflect what has significant value in the experience of women (Walker, 1998; Held, 1993; Tong, 1993; Card, 1991). The activity of caring for children and the aged and ill is not something that just takes place; it has enormous value, and moral judgment is needed to guide it so that it will be the best care possible. However, caring may not be enough to deal with such issues as fairness and justice: parents may care for a daughter but still provide her with fewer opportunities than her brother.

Perhaps an "ethic of care" should be combined with an "ethic of justice," or perhaps the context of caring relationships between actual persons and of concern for the next generation should be the primary context for the development of moral thinking (Clement, 1996; Held, 1995; Ruddick, 1989; Noddings, 1984). Feminists have been developing ideas and theories about care. They examine those aspects of the practice of care that should be changed because they reflect how women and the less powerful have been compelled into performing this unpaid or ill-paid and devalued activity. They also show why this activity should be highly valued and done in the best possible ways and how the moral theory that adequately appreciates caring is suitable not just for the household but also for the wider society.

Feminists have also come to a different view of persons from that of the person as abstract liberal individual. The ethic of care understands persons as relational, embedded in human relationships and in an actual historical context, as well as embodied (Mackenzie and Stoljar, 2000; Meyers, 1997; Clement, 1996).

A Feminist Agenda

After several early years of exploring an ideal of "androgyny," which sought to overcome discrimination by minimizing differences between the sexes, feminists began to celebrate difference and to build theories recognizing women's unique experiences and contributions to culture. Some feminists then became concerned that the "woman" at the core of such theories, in their emphasis on the uniqueness of women's experience, "maternal thinking," "voices," and "ways of knowing," is too close at heart to an essentialist view of "women's nature."

Essentialism is the view that there is an essential, innate human nature based on biological reality. In the past, biological thinking about women has upheld a doctrine of "separate spheres," tying women as a group to their "natural" domestic place, supposedly "for their own good." Essentialist thinking was often couched in universals, forcing all women into a single grouping because the paramount characteristic of "woman" was seen as her difference from "man." Critics of essentialism have emphasized that "women's nature" has been socially and culturally constructed and is subject to significant change over time and place. Increasingly, there have been explorations and celebrations of differences among women and appreciation of the complexities of subjective identities. The question of defining "women" must now be broached in terms of a multitude of racial, ethnic, religious, class, and sexual identities and histories.

Still, without falling into essentialism, women can affirm their distinct contributions. Feminist philosopher Linda Alcoff suggests they take a "positional perspective":

> The concept of positionality allows for a determinate though fluid identity of woman . . . woman is a position from which a feminist politics can emerge rather than a set of attributes that are "objectively identifiable." Seen in this way, being a "woman" is to take up a position within a moving historical context. (Alcoff, 1988:435)

Principles in Action

Feminists understand how caring about and for people requires that their needs be met, and they advocate societies that take responsibility for doing so (Folbre, 2001). They support efforts to meet people's needs for child care, health care, employment, and care of the elderly. They do not accept the currently popular ideology of social Darwinism: every man for himself and may the fittest become super-rich.

In regard to economic issues, feminists sometimes start with the workplace, advocating units of economic activity in which a concern for the environment and for providing satisfying work are more important than bulging profits or high salaries. Many seek work arrangements that encourage cooperative and egalitarian, rather than hierarchical and coercive, interaction among members.

Just as in the household, the following question must be asked outside the home: what work needs to be done? Obviously, much of the work that is done in both business and bureaucratic societies does not need to be done. People are persuaded to buy things they do not need, and children are enticed to seek entertainment that undermines education so that corporations can increase their sales and dividends. Officials try to multiply the occasions on which they can exercise their authority over citizens, regardless of whether this serves a useful purpose. On the other hand, important work often is not done: children go uncared for and inexpensive housing goes unbuilt because those with the capital to invest do not believe there is adequate profit to be made in these areas.

Feminists deciding what work needs to be done begin with the meeting of real human needs. The next questions may concern how to divide the work so that each person does her or his fair share and how to structure the work so it is done cooperatively, with a

> **Box 2.8   GLORIA STEINEM ON FEMINIST LABELS**
>
> In the label department . . . I would prefer to be called simply "a feminist." After all, the belief in the full humanity of women leads to the necessity of totally changing all male-supremacist structures, thus removing the model and continuing support for other systems of birth-determined privilege. That should be radical enough. However, because there are feminists who believe that women can integrate or imitate existing structures (or conversely; that class or race structures must be transformed first, as a precondition to eliminating sexual caste), I feel I should identify myself as a "radical feminist." "Radical" means "going to the root," and I think that sexism is the root, whether or not it developed as the chronologically first dominance model in prehistory. . . . The tolerance of a habit as pervasive as male-dominance not only creates an intimate model for oppression as "natural," but builds a callousness to other dominations—whether based on race, age, class, sexuality, or anything else.
>
> *Source:* Steinem, 1978:92–3.

minimum of hierarchy. Then, attention may be turned to making work as joyful and creative an activity as possible.

A feminist business that produces a product or performs a service genuinely useful to women and uses its earnings to train other women and to help them increase their economic independence will not be a "capitalist enterprise" in the usual sense (Folbre, 2001; Hartsock, 1998). It may respond voluntarily to community, regional, or even national planning. It should certainly take responsibility for maintaining the health of its workers or neighbors and preserving the environment for future children, and it may be expected to do so without government intervention. Though it may well seek to expand, its goal will not simply be to maximize profits and increase its control over others but to perform useful work in ever more humanly satisfying ways.

How should the changes needed in society be brought about? Those with power in corporations and those with power in bureaucracies, whatever the form of the economic system, are predominantly male. Women must usually work from the bottom up: they must organize, persuade, and build their strength gradually and steadily. Feminists emphasize that women do not want to be liberated in order to be increasingly like men. A basic aspect of feminist thought will continue to resist such absorption into male structures of domination and oppression. Feminists often start by attempting to make communities more humane and cooperative places to live and work. They may go on to develop ways of governing ever wider communities that will enhance, rather than pollute and destroy, our environments. They may change the culture from one that induces greed and egotism to one that fosters mutuality and respect and in which disputes are settled without violence or war (Ruddick, 1989) or imperialistic ventures (Robinson, 1999). Women are finally choosing for themselves the conceptions of women with which they wish to live.

Summary

Definitions of *woman* have often reflected faulty theories about the "nature" of women.

Distorted definitions result from men seeing women as something "other" than themselves and drawing unjustified inferences from this perspective. Men tend to view themselves as active subjects and women as passive objects.

Aristotle's definition of woman as "defective man" has had enormous influence on human thought. Biological "facts" about women, regardless of their validity, should not be misused to draw evaluative conclusions about women's rights. What has been thought to be impartial and objective "knowledge" has often represented the point of view of men only. Changes are essential in the very definition of knowledge, even in the sciences.

Some contemporary feminists emphasize the way language and our most basic concepts result from one group having imposed its conceptual schemes. Meanings, for instance, of *equality* and *democracy* more adequate than those common in patriarchal culture must be devised.

Philosophers of the Enlightenment rejected hierarchical traditions of Western political thought—but not for women. The liberal principles of equality and freedom that helped to shape democracy applied to men and to male heads of households. Many liberal thinkers were silent on the subject of women. Jean-Jacques Rousseau, however, was outspoken in his opinion that the existence of society required woman's subordination to man. Many philosophers believed that women were deficient in rationality.

The Enlightenment philosopher Mary Wollstonecraft argued that women had not yet been taught to favor reason rather than emotion and that women should have an education comparable to men's. John Stuart Mill also believed women's capacities would increase with more education. Harriet Taylor Mill argued even more forcefully for women's equality.

Contemporary liberal feminists favor equality in the home as well as in the public realm, advocating that wives and husbands should share equally in child care and household tasks. Affirmative action programs may be needed to provide women and minorities with equal job opportunities.

Some conservative views coincide with feminist concerns for the family and moral values. Conservatives, however, are usually opposed to feminism, maintaining that woman's place is only, or primarily, in the home.

Some feminists have been influenced by the socialist tradition. Since traditional Marxism did not understand many of the problems of women, socialist feminism has developed its own positions. It focuses on the oppression of women as women, not merely as workers, but pays special attention to the economic structures around the world that oppress the disadvantaged.

Radical feminism moves beyond the ideas familiar in any existing social theories. It emphasizes aspects of sexuality and reproduction as the sources of women's oppression and appreciates the values and strengths of women's culture.

The ethics of care has developed as an influential feminist approach to moral issues and to questions about how society should be organized. It especially values caring relations between persons and emphasizes these in both personal and social contexts.

Although feminists frequently disagree, all share one goal: to overcome the oppression of women. They are interested in work that meets human needs, with the work fairly divided and cooperatively organized, and believe society should be governed with a minimum of domination and subordination.

Women no longer have to accept the conceptions that others have had about them and about society. They can choose for themselves what ideas to accept and what their goals should be.

Discussion Questions

1. Do women have a "choice"? Discuss the ways in which women can or cannot choose to *(1)* "accept" subordinate roles, *(2)* believe in the "natural" inferiority of women, *(3)* act as free and responsible persons, and *(4)* do what they would like rather than what others would like them to do.

2. In what ways can you see a male rather than a universal point of view as predominant in *(1)* traditional moral or political theory and *(2)* a social science with which you are familiar?

3. What would be needed for women to have *(1)* legal equality, *(2)* equal opportunities, *(3)* equality within the family, and *(4)* full equality?

4. What sorts of governmental policy might be recommended by an ethic of care?

5. Discuss the importance of feminist theory in your own experience. Has it helped you to understand, to choose, to act? If so, how? What are the major areas in which you think feminist theory needs to be improved?

6. What does feminism mean for the vast majority of women in the world?

Recommended Readings

de Beauvoir, Simone. *The Second Sex*, 1949, translated by H. M. Parshley. New York: Knopf, 1953. A classic book on how women have been thought about and how they can begin to think for themselves about themselves.

Hypatia. A Journal of Feminist Philosophy (Bloomington: Indiana University Press), with continuing new theorizing about women's issues.

Kourany, Janet, editor. *Philosophy in a Feminist Voice: Critiques and Reconstructions*. Princeton, NJ: Princeton University Press, 1998. A sample of feminist reconceptualizations of the various fields of philosophy such as epistemology, ethics, history of philosophy, and philosophy of science.

Lloyd, Genevieve. *The Man of Reason: "Male" and "Female" in Western Philosophy*. Minneapolis: University of Minnesota Press, 1984. Lloyd demonstrates that Western philosophers have celebrated the ideal of "reason" in ways that, upon close investigation, required the rejection of whatever, at various stages of history, was associated with the female.

Tong, Rosemarie Putnam. *Feminist Thought*, 2nd ed. Boulder, CO: Westview Press, 1998. A comprehensive introduction to varieties of feminist thinking, such as liberal feminism, socialist feminism, radical feminism, psychoanalytic feminism, existentialist feminism, and postmodern feminism.

References

Alcoff, Linda. Cultural feminism versus post-structuralism: The identity crisis in feminist theory. *Signs* 13:3, 405–36, 1988.

Alcoff, Linda, and Elizabeth Potter, editors. *Feminist Epistemologies*. New York: Routledge, 1993.

Anzaldúa, Gloria, editor. *Making Face, Making Soul—Haciendo Caras: Creative and Critical Perspectives by Women of Color*. San Francisco: Aunt Lute Books, 1990.

Aristotle, *The Generation of Animals*, vols. 1 and 4. Translated by A. L. Peck. Cambridge, MA: Harvard University Press, 1943.

Bartky, Sandra. *Femininity and Domination. Studies in the Phenomenology of Oppression*. New York: Routledge, 1990.

Baumgardner, Jennifer, and Amy Richards. *ManifestA: Young Women, Feminism, and the Future*. New York. Farrar, Straus & Giroux, 2000.

Bem, Sandra, and Daryl Bem. Homogenizing the American woman. In *Feminist Frameworks*, 3rd ed., edited by Alison M. Jaggar and

Paula S. Rothenberg. New York: McGraw-Hill, 1993.

Benhabib, Seyla. *Situating the Self: Gender, Community and Postmodernism in Contemporary Ethics*. New York: Routledge, 1992.

Bunch, Charlotte. Lesbians in revolt. In *Lesbianism and the Women's Movement*, edited by Nancy Myron and Charlotte Bunch. Baltimore: Diana Press, 1975.

Card, Claudia. *Lesbian Choices*. New York: Columbia University Press, 1995.

———, editor. *Feminist Ethics*. Lawrence: University Press of Kansas, 1991.

Clement, Grace. *Care, Autonomy, and Justice*. Boulder, CO: Westview Press, 1996.

Collins, Patricia Hill. *Black Feminist Thought: Knowledge, Consciousness, and the Politics of Empowerment*, 2nd ed. New York: Routledge, 2000.

de Beauvoir, Simone. *The Second Sex*, translated by H. M. Parshley. New York: Knopf, 1953.

———. *Force of Circumstance*. Translated by Richard Howard. New York: Putnam, 1964.

DiStefano, Christine. *Configurations of Masculinity: A Feminist Perspective on Modern Political Theory*. New York: Cornell University Press, 1991.

Eisenstein, Zillah. *The Radical Future of Liberal Feminism*. New York: Longman, 1981.

Engels, Friedrich. *The Origin of the Family, Private Property, and the State* (1884), translated by Alec West, edited by Eleanor Burke Leacock. New York: International Publishers, 1972.

Eschle, Catherine. *Global Democracy, Social Movements, and Feminism*. Boulder, CO: Westview Press, 2001.

Fausto-Sterling, Anne. *Sexing the Body: Gender Politics and the Construction of Sexuality*. New York: Basic Books, 2000.

Folbre, Nancy. *The Invisible Heart: Economics and Family Values*. New York: New Press, 2001.

Foucault, Michel. *The History of Sexuality. An Introduction*, vol. 1, translated by Robert Hurley. New York: Pantheon, 1978.

———. *The History of Sexuality. The Use of Pleasure*, vol. 2, translated by Robert Hurley. New York: Pantheon, 1986.

Funk, Nanette, and Magda Mueller, editors. *Gender Politics and Post-Communism: Reflections from Eastern Europe and the Former Soviet Union*. New York: Routledge, 1993.

Gilligan, Carol. *In a Different Voice. Psychological Theory and Women's Development*. Cambridge, MA: Harvard University Press, 1982.

Gilman, Charlotte Perkins. *Women and Economics* (1898), reprint, edited by Carl Degler. New York: Harper Torchbooks, 1966.

———. *The Yellow Wall-Paper* (1899), reprint, afterword by Elaine R. Hedges. New York: Feminist Press at CUNY, 1973.

Harding, Sandra, editor. *Feminism and Methodology: Social Science Issues*. Bloomington: Indiana University Press, 1987.

Harding, Sandra, and Merrill B. Hintikka, editors. *Discovering Reality: Feminist Perspectives on Epistemology, Metaphysics, Methodology, and Philosophy of Science*. Dordrecht: D. Reidel, 1983.

Harrington, Mona. *Care and Equality: Inventing a New Family Politics*. New York: Knopf, 1999.

Hartsock, Nancy C. M. *Money, Sex, and Power*. New York: Longman, 1983.

———. *The Feminist Standpoint Revisited and Other Essays*. Boulder, CO: Westview Press, 1998.

Held, Virginia. *Feminist Morality: Transforming Culture, Society, and Politics*. Chicago: University of Chicago Press, 1993.

———, editor. *Justice and Care: Essential Readings in Feminist Ethics*. Boulder, CO: Westview Press, 1995.

Hypatia. A Journal of Feminist Philosophy. Bloomington: Indiana University Press, 1983–present.

Jaggar, Alison. *Feminist Politics and Human Nature*. Totowa, NJ: Rowman and Allanheld, 1983.

Kelly, Joan. *Women, History, and Theory: The Essays of Joan Kelly*. Chicago: University of Chicago Press, 1984.

Kittay, Eva Feder. *Love's Labor: Essays on Women, Equality, and Dependency*. New York: Routledge, 1999.

Kittay, Eva Feder, and Diana T. Meyers, editors. *Women and Moral Theory*. Totowa, NJ: Rowman and Allanheld, 1987.

Kourany, Janet, editor. *Philosophy in a Feminist Voice: Critiques and Reconstructions.* Princeton, NJ: Princeton University Press, 1998.

Landes, Joan B., editor. *Feminism: The Public and the Private.* New York: Oxford University Press, 1998.

Lange, Lynda. Woman is not a rational animal. In *Discovering Reality*, edited by Sandra Harding and Merrill Hintikka. Dordrecht: D. Reidel, 1983.

Littleton, Christine. Reconstructing sexual equality. *California Law Review* 25:1279–1337, 1987.

Lloyd, Genevieve. *The Man of Reason: "Male" and "Female" in Western Philosophy.* Minneapolis: University of Minnesota Press, 1984.

Mabee, Carleton, and Susan Mabee Newhouse. *Sojourner Truth: Slave, Prophet, Legend.* New York: New York University Press, 1993.

MacKenzie, Catriona, and Natalie Stoljar, editors. *Relational Autonomy: Feminist Perspectives on Autonomy, Agency, and the Social Self.* New York: Oxford University Press, 2000.

MacKinnon, Catharine. *Feminism Unmodified. Discourses on Life and Law.* Cambridge, MA: Harvard University Press, 1987.

———. Sexuality, pornography, and method: "Pleasure under patriarchy." *Ethics,* 99:2, 314–46, 1989.

Mahowald, Mary Briody, editor. *Philosophy of Woman: An Anthology of Classic to Current Concepts,* 3rd ed. Indianapolis: Hackett, 1994.

Meyers, Diana T., editor. *Feminists Rethink the Self.* Boulder, CO: Westview Press, 1997.

Mill, Harriet Taylor. The enfranchisement of women (1851). In *John Stuart Mill and Harriet Taylor Mill, Essays on Sex Equality,* edited by Alice S. Rossi. Chicago: University of Chicago Press, 1970.

Mill, James. Government. (1820). *Political Writings of James Mill.* Cambridge Texts in the History of Political Thought, edited by Terence Ball. Cambridge: Cambridge University Press, 1992.

Mill, John Stuart. On the subjection of women (1869). *In John Stuart Mill and Harriet Taylor Mill, Essays on Sex Equality,* edited by Alice S. Rossi. Chicago: University of Chicago Press, 1970.

Mitchell, Juliet. *Woman's Estate.* New York: Vintage, 1973.

Narayan, Uma. *Dis-locating Cultures: Identities, Traditions, and Third-World Feminism.* New York: Routledge, 1997.

Noddings, Nel. *Caring: A Feminine Approach to Ethics and Moral Education.* Berkeley: University of California Press, 1984.

Nussbaum, Martha. *Sex and Social Justice.* New York: Oxford University Press, 1999.

Nussbaum, Martha, and Jonathan Glover, editors. *Women, Culture, and Development.* Oxford: Clarendon Press, 1995.

Okin, Susan Moller. *Women in Western Political Thought.* Princeton, NJ: Princeton University Press, 1979.

———. *Justice, Gender, and the Family.* New York: Basic Books, 1989.

Rhode, Deborah L. *Justice and Gender: Sex Discrimination and the Law.* Cambridge, MA: Harvard University Press, 1989.

Rich, Adrienne. Compulsory heterosexuality and lesbian existence. *Signs,* 5:4, 631–60, 1980.

Robinson, Fiona. *Globalizing Care: Ethics, Feminist Morality, and International Relations.* Boulder, CO: Westview Press, 1999.

Rousseau, Jean Jacques. *Émile* (1762), translated by Barbara Foxley. New York: Dutton, 1966.

Rowbotham, Sheila. *Woman's Consciousness, Man's World.* Baltimore: Pelican, 1973.

Ruddick, Sara. *Maternal Thinking: Toward a Politics of Peace.* Boston: Beacon Press, 1989.

Saldívar-Hull, Sonia. *Feminism on the Border. Chicana Gender Politics and Literature.* Berkeley: University of California Press, 2000.

Sargent, Lydia, editor. *Women and Revolution: A Discussion of the Unhappy Marriage of Marxism and Feminism.* Boston: South End Press, 1981.

Sherwin, Susan. *No Longer Patient: Feminist Ethics and Health Care.* Philadelphia: Temple University Press, 1992.

Smith, Patricia, editor. *Feminist Jurisprudence*. New York: Oxford University Press, 1993.

Spelman, Elizabeth V. *Inessential Woman: Problems of Exclusion in Feminist Thought*. Boston: Beacon Press, 1988.

Steinem, Gloria. From the opposite shore, or how to survive though a feminist. *Ms*, 7, 65–7, 90–4, 105, 1978.

Tong, Rosemarie. *Feminine and Feminist Ethics*. Belmont, CA: Wadsworth, 1993.

———, editor. *Globalizing Feminist Bioethics*. Boulder, CO: Westview Press, 2001.

Tronto, Joan C. *Moral Boundaries: A Political Argument for an Ethics of Care*. New York: Routledge, 1993.

Vetterling-Braggin, Mary. *Sexist Language*. Totowa, NJ: Littlefield, Adams, 1981.

Walker, Margaret Urban. *Moral Understandings: A Feminist Study in Ethics*. New York: Routledge, 1998.

Weedon, Chris. *Feminist Practice and Poststructuralist Theory*. Oxford: Blackwell, 1987.

Williams, Patricia J. *The Alchemy of Race and Rights*. Cambridge, MA: Harvard University Press, 1991.

Wollstonecraft, Mary. *A Vindication of the Rights of Woman* (1792). New York: Norton, 1967.

Young, Iris Marion. *Justice and the Politics of Difference*. Princeton, NJ: Princeton University Press, 1990.

Zalk, Sue Rosenberg, and Janice Gordon-Kelter, editors. *Revolutions in Knowledge: Feminism in the Social Sciences*. Boulder, CO: Westview Press, 1990.

Women's Bodies

The Body as Cultural Construct

The human body is not merely flesh and bones; it is also a cultural construct. This means that the body, despite its apparent "naturalness," is not a purely biological entity: its meaning and significance are shaped by differing cultural ideas. The North Mekeo people of New Guinea, for example, do not think that things can be done to the body because, in their culture, the body is not understood as an object (Strathern, 1981:61). By contrast, in many societies throughout the world, the body has been considered an object that can be manipulated and controlled, a conceptualization that has had profound

The corset.

consequences for women. As Susan Bordo (1993:143) points out, "female bodies have historically been significantly more vulnerable than male bodies to extremes in both forms of cultural manipulation and control." Women's bodies, at one time or another, have been stretched, scarred, corseted, crippled, pierced, contorted, and deformed in the name of everything from religion to fashion. In China, for example, the feet of high-status women were once painfully broken and tightly wrapped to produce tiny, erotically charged "lotus-feet" so small that many of these women were unable to walk. Today's high-heeled shoes are similarly considered fashionable and erotic by many (as their ubiquity in pornography suggests), and they too can deform women's feet, sometimes severely enough to require surgery (see Box 3.1). In countless societies around the world, assaults

---

Box 3.1   DEFORMED FEET: BUNIONS AND CORNS

Bunions are a common problem experienced mostly by women. The deformity can develop from an abnormality in foot function, or arthritis, but is more commonly caused by wearing improper fitting footwear. Tight, narrow dress shoes with a constrictive toe box (toe area) can cause the foot to begin to take the shape of the shoe, leading to the formation of a bunion. [Bunions] can worsen to the point where surgery is necessary.

Corns . . . develop from an accumulation of dead skin cells on the foot, forming thick, hardened areas. They contain a cone-shaped core with a point that can press on a nerve below, causing pain. Some of the common causes of corn development are tight fitting footwear, high heeled footwear. . . . Complications that can arise from corns include bursitis and the development of an ulcer.

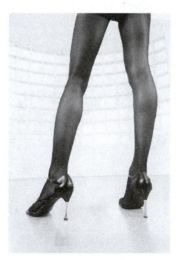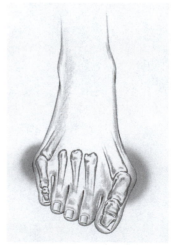

High-heeled shoes and foot deformities.

Source: www.foot.com

on women's bodies serve to constrain their movements, acting as a powerful form of social control. Such strategies of control use women's bodies to maintain power relations.

Differing conceptualizations of the body affect how individuals in different times and places experience their own bodies. In Egypt today, for example, a woman who dresses in a traditional chador and covers her face with a veil might experience her "lived body" with modesty, understanding it as a site for demonstrating piety and devotion to Allah (Mahmood, 2001), similar to a Catholic nun in her traditional habit. By contrast, some U.S. teenagers experience the body as a prison and try to escape its confinement and limitations through self-starvation.

The meaning of the body can also vary within a society according to such factors as age, ability, class, sexual orientation, and race. For example, lesbian feminist Carolyn Martin Shaw describes how racist ideas affected her understanding and experience of her own body and sexuality as a young African American woman growing up in the United States in the 1950s. She was caught between contradictory messages from a popular culture littered with images of sexy women, on the one hand, and religion and racial discourse, on the other: "While I wanted to be sexy and alluring," Shaw (2001:110) writes, "I was constrained by my need for social approval in the black community and by my fear and mistreatment at the hands of whites who would see me as a workhorse or a whore." Poet and essayist Nancy Mairs (1997:301) has written eloquently about how, as a woman with multiple sclerosis, she experienced her body as doubly shameful: first, because she had a body at all and, second, because her body had become "weakened and misshapen by disease." She echoes the experience of many disabled women when she recounts how those around her rendered her invisible and erased her sexuality because her body did not conform to standard notions of beauty and health. In many Western cultures, the aging female body is similarly viewed as unattractive due to its departure from the idealized body of youth. Older women are bombarded with advertisements for products to remove their wrinkles and erase their gray hair, convincing them that their physical appearance and the aging process itself is undesirable. As these examples suggest, the experience of the body is mediated by cultural assumptions, constructs, and images.

Not only the meaning of the body but also its physiological processes are affected by cultural expectations and practices. A Jul'hoansi woman from the Kalahari Desert, for example, might have only a few menstrual periods during her lifetime due to a combination of a strenuous workload and long periods of breast-feeding, both of which can stop monthly ovulation. Due to its rarity, the experience of menstruation may have minimal significance for her life. Most premenopausal U.S. women, by contrast, have fairly regular monthly cycles throughout their lifetimes, interrupted only periodically by pregnancy. Perhaps not surprisingly, Jul'hoansi women report no relationship between menstruation and mood changes (Shostak, 1983), while some U.S. women describe themselves as the victims of premenstrual hormones that can radically affect their dispositions and behaviors.

Feminism and the Body

Since the first organized women's movement in the United States during the late nineteenth and early twentieth centuries (see Chapter 13), feminists have recognized the body as a site of political domination. They have protested cultural constraints placed on women's bodies and argued for women's rightful control of their own bodies. Women at the First Feminist Mass Meeting in the

United States in 1914, for example, argued that the right "to ignore fashion" was a political one. U.S. feminists in 1968 echoed their call; they threw their bras into "a freedom trash can" during a demonstration of the Miss America Pageant to symbolically protest how women's bodies are controlled, whether through codes of fashion, ideal notions of femininity and beauty, forced sterilization, abuse, or rape (Bordo, 1993:15–23). In the United States today, maintaining a woman's reproductive freedom remains a centerpiece of feminist political struggle (see Chapter 13).

The body is a complex construction: it is a material entity whose movements can be forcefully and subtly controlled and manipulated; a site on which gender differences seem materially inscribed; and a symbolic construct to which notions of selfhood, identity, and self-worth are intimately tied and through which they can be contested and resisted (Conboy et al., 1997:7–8). Understanding how the body is variously constructed and the impact of such constructions on women's lives, experiences, and choices has been essential to feminist scholarship since its inception. Today, research on the body continues to play a central role in feminist studies and is, according to some, "the topic generating the most exciting new research and the most interdisciplinary theoretical inquiry" (Conboy et al., 1997:7–8). Much of this research understands the body as a site of contestation on which battles for competing ideologies are waged, acknowledging how the body can also be a locus of resistance to standard assumptions about gender and femininity, like those discussed in the next two sections (Conboy et al., 1997:7–8).

Women's bodies are constructed through discourses, practices, and representations. Each of these can give rise to different ideologies of the body and its relationship to the self, often producing intersecting, overlapping, contradictory, and confusing conceptualizations. Feminists are divided over whether these complex, contradictory constructions are detrimental for women or offer women agency, the ability to protest conventional understandings of the female body and to act on their own behalf. Susan Bordo, for example, suggests that they can be problematic: she shows that anorexia nervosa is some young women's response to the contradictory messages arising, on the one hand, from feminism, which recognizes women's autonomous selfhood, and, on the other, the conservative backlash against feminism that reinscribes woman as mother, body, and object (Bordo, 1993:171–4). Feminist cultural critic Janice Radway (1986), however, sees the liberating potential of contradictions: she argues that when different practices and discourses intersect, their point of connection is characterized by a seam that exposes a weakness in dominant ideology. Like a seam of clothing, it can be ripped open and altered, refashioned into a new ideological construction by women on their own behalf. The discussion below focuses on both the constraints placed on women by various constructions of the body and how women have creatively resisted such conceptualizations and altered their bodies in protest against them.

Whether concerned with women's subjugation or their agency, whether focused on the sexed, commodified, reproductive, cyborg, or performative body, feminists have repeatedly exposed the tenacity of "body politics." They have made clear just how very personal the political can be when the body is the site of struggle. They have also offered exciting alternative visions of what the body is and what it can become, both in theory and in practice.

Mind/Body Dualism

In Western thought, at least since Plato, the body has been juxtaposed with the mind and seen as inferior to it. This distinction between mind and body is an aspect of what is often referred to as "Cartesian dualism," named for the Western philosopher René Descartes. Descartes' famous dictum "I think, therefore, I am" vividly encapsulates the widespread association in Western culture of the mind and its reasoning processes with the self. The body places limitations on the self, according to this view, and must, therefore, be transcended. Everyday language encodes this understanding of the body as an entity distinct from the self: a person is likely to say "I have a body," not "I am a body" (Mairs, 1997:298). Cartesian dualism is so taken for granted that it can be understood as an unwritten, official doctrine of Western societies.

This mind/body dualism is also part of the Christian tradition that has influenced Western thinking: the body is seen in opposition not only to the mind and the self but also to the "soul" and the "spirit." The body, in this view, represents the animal side of human existence, possessing unruly appetites and desires that must be willfully controlled and suppressed for salvation.

What is most significant for women about this conceptualization is that "woman" has been associated with the body, while "man" has been linked with the mind. "Woman" equated with the body is, therefore, not mind and not self. She is not subject but object, not spirit but flesh. She is aligned against reason (a woman is more emotional, intuitive, and irrational than a man, we still hear today) and against spiritual salvation (woman, it is still widely believed, is naturally a temptress and seductress, as we saw in Chapter 1). She is in need of control.

This set of associations has had profound significance for how women have been valued, treated, and constrained in their opportunities and choices. As Simone de Beauvoir argued in *The Second Sex*, the entrapment of women in their bodies means that women have been made "the second sex," defined by a lack of masculine qualities and traits that men assume stem from a natural defectiveness (Conboy et al., 1997). More recently, Bordo has remarked as follows:

> The cost for such projections to women is obvious. For if, whatever the historical content of the duality, the body is the negative term, and if woman is the body, then women are that negativity, whatever it may be: distraction from knowledge, seduction away from God, capitulation to sexual desire . . . failure of will, even death. (Bordo, 1993:5)

The Body as Natural

The association of women with the body also allies them with the negative term in another set of associations: nature/culture. The body has been seen as natural and the mind, the source of human cultural control over nature's destructive forces. Although in the contemporary United States, the environmental and New Age movements might suggest otherwise, the predominant view in Western thinking is that nature acts against human interests and, therefore, needs to be tamed and subdued. The association of women with nature arises from the function of woman's body in giving birth and nurturing children (see Chapter 1), but de Beauvoir's (1953) insights are again instructive: she argues that if women's bodies have constrained them, it is not because this is natural or inevitable but because women have been interpreted through the lens of culture, thought of as "natural" by men who have created the very category of "nature" to serve their own aims. Evidence from around the world indicates that women have combined motherhood with almost every task imaginable. This suggests the cultural, rather than the natural, character of such limitations in Western culture where "woman" has been defined by her body and seen as trapped in nature because of it. This has not only rendered her as object not as subject, as other not as self, but has also served as a rationalization for her domination and subordination. In contemporary society, science plays a particularly important role in this subordination because scientific theory and practice are concerned with knowledge of, and mastery over, nature (Jardanova, 1993). In nineteenth-century science, nature was often even conceptualized as a woman "to be unveiled, unclothed, and penetrated by masculine science" (Jardanova, 1993:376).

The construction of the female as natural has had particular consequences for non-Western women and women of color, who have been seen as doubly natural and "other" due to both gender and race. In Western racial discourse, the "naturalness" of black and brown bodies has been equated with animality, in particular with an animal-like sexuality. This belief was perhaps nowhere clearer than in Victorian England, where, under the guise of scientific interest, the African woman Sartje Bartman,

known as the "Hottentot Venus," was displayed nude in a public pornographic exhibition disguised as science (Collins, 1990). She was probed at by anatomists and stared at by a repulsed, but fascinated public audience. Her distinctive bodily traits—enlarged vaginal lips and protruding buttocks—were taken as signs of a rampant and animalistic sexuality (Gilman, 1985). This conclusion reinforced the notion at the time that African women were savages, devoid of the sexual modesty necessary for achieving "true" femininity. More recently, this equation of the black female body with nature and a "primitive" sexuality can be found in contemporary advertisements to entice consumers to buy everything from vacations in the Caribbean (Cohen and Mascia-Lees, 1993) and perfumes (Bordo, 1993) to unwanted hair remover (Williamson, 1986). During the late nineteenth and early twentieth centuries, not only "racial" bodies were displayed for public consumption but so too were those of

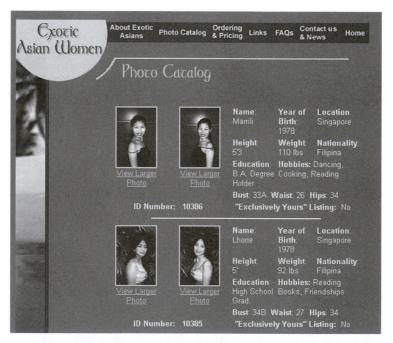

Sample page from on-line catalog for "exotic Asian women" mail-order brides.

"disabled" people. Thought of as "freaks," extraordinary bodies were viewed as exotic spectacles in U.S. and European circuses, fairs, and zoos (Thomson, 1996).

The bodies of Asian women have also been represented as particularly erotic and exotic, but unlike the bodies of black women, they have not been associated with savagery and rampant desire but with smallness, timidity, and subservience, traits that have made them desirable to many men in Western societies. This perception has even led to the development of a highly profitable mail-order business in which Asian women are sold to Western male consumers as brides.

In Western thought, the body has also been understood as the physical ground of gender differences. Because the body has conventionally been understood as a natural, relatively unchangeable entity and gender differences are thought to arise from the body, they too have been seen as natural and, thus, inevitable. The differences between the bodies of women and men have therefore been taken as the justification for treating women and men differently.

Feminist scholarship on the body in the last 30 years, however, reveals that the body is far from being a stable ground of sex differences. As we will see below, whether focused on brain structure and function, hormones, or chromosomes, we know of no biological difference that distinguishes all women from all men, making any current biological definition of the sexes inadequate. Indeed, the very instability of the body as a ground for gender difference allows women to use their bodies to resist constraining definitions of femininity.

The Nature of Sex Differences

As indicated in Chapter 2, Western philosophical definitions of "woman" have been based on faulty theories and biased cultural assumptions. This is also true of biological definitions of the sexes focused on the body, but while today it may be easy to see that Aristotle's view of women as "imperfect men" was an ideological construct which served political ends, it is more difficult to conclude the same for definitions of the sexes grounded in scientific research. Is science not, after all, the unbiased, objective pursuit of truth? Are scientific definitions of the sexes not based on biological facts that can be observed and measured with precise and accurate instruments?

Historians of science have documented repeatedly how the gender, race, and class assumptions of scientists influence their supposedly objective, scientific experiments and the conclusions drawn from them (for example, Fausto-Sterling, 2000; Haraway, 1989; Keller, 1985; Longino and Doell, 1987; Martin, 1987, 1994). Thus, although science is framed in a language of rationality and objectivity, the apparent neutrality with which it speaks and through which it gains authority conceals its cultural assumptions (Jackson et al., 1993:363). Because science has so often been used in the service of women's subordination, revealing its cultural biases has been an important feminist project.

Cultural factors affect the very questions scientists deem important enough to ask and which studies are deemed important enough to fund. That researchers in many Western countries choose to focus on identifying the differences between women and men, rather than the similarities, is itself a product of the history, as well as the social and political agendas, of these nations. This interest in difference is so deeply embedded in U.S. society, for example, that suggesting that the study of gender differences might be misguided and that research on gender similarities might be productive tends to strike most people as absurd. Why? Today, most scientists believe it is wrong-headed to look for biological explanations of many other kinds of difference. Yet, it was not that long ago that learned cultural differences between Jews and non-Jews were attributed to biological causes, an assumption that found its most hideous expression in the notion in Nazi Germany that Jews were so different from non-Jews that they were actually "life unworthy of life" and therefore in need of extermination. Today, most scientists find claims that vast biological differences exist between groups of people to be unwarranted, and the idea that biological factors best explain ethnic and cultural differences between people rightfully strikes many people as ludicrous. Might this not be true for gender as well?

The Gendered Brain

Cultural assumptions have been shown to affect scientific investigations not only at the level of the question asked but at every stage of the research process as well. The history of brain research into gender and racial differences clearly indicates this. The claim that women and men have differing brains, and therefore necessarily think differently, has been a longstanding one in Western society. Such supposed natural "brain differences" have been used historically to rationalize and further systems of oppression and to determine social policy. For example, toward the end of the nineteenth century, it was erroneously concluded that white men were naturally superior to women in intelligence because of the larger size of their brains. This assumption was used to justify women's exclusion from higher education. Measurements were also taken of African Americans and Native Americans, two other groups assumed to have intelligence levels inferior to those of white men, and a similar conclusion was reached: their smaller brain size was taken as evidence of lower intelligence. We know now, however, that the size differential noted by these scientists was based on measurement techniques affected by pre-existing cultural assumptions about the supposed inferior intelligence of white women and of women and men of color. Craniometrists consistently un-derestimated the cranial capacity of these groups, which biased their results. Even if such measurements had been correct, they would hold no significance today since it has been repeatedly shown that variation in human brain size is not related to intelligence.

Today, it is not brain size but differences in brain structure and in the way women and men use their brains that supposedly explain gender differences, and questions of measurement are still an issue. Women and men have been repeatedly studied to discern whether they use the left or right hemisphere of the brain for certain functions. The focus of such studies has been on differences in the *corpus callosum*, the band of white matter connecting the left and right hemispheres of the brain, which supposedly produce gendered styles of thinking. In the wake of one study conducted in 1982, which reported a difference in size in one area of this structure in nine men and five women, a virtual industry of brain lateralization research has arisen. However, as molecular biologist Anne Fausto-Sterling has detailed in her book *Sexing the Body* (2000), this research is not as straightforward as we might suppose. The corpus callosum is so complex and irregularly shaped that it is impossible to define it with certainty: "The corpus callosum is a structure that is difficult to separate from the rest of the brain, and so complex in its irregular three dimensions as to be unmeasurable" (Fausto-Sterling, 2000:120–1). This has not stopped scientists from trying, although the results of this research indicate the intractability of the corpus callosum as an object of study: Fausto-Sterling's review of 34 scientific papers written between 1982 and 1997 found that there is no consensus on sex differences in the corpus callosum (2000:130–5).

Given the highly inconclusive results of corpus callosum research, conclusions about how and why women and men think differently may be as faulty today as those of the craniologists who measured people's skulls to determine intelligence 100 years ago. Nonetheless, scientists and popular culture alike have made broad claims for the significance of brain function differences in males and females. In 1992 alone, *Newsweek*, *Time*, *Elle*, the *Boston Globe*, and the *New York Times* each featured stories about gender differences in the brain, claiming that they were responsible for everything from women's intuition and difficulties with physics to women's stronger verbal skills and more holistic way of thinking, differences that have not been clearly substantiated (Fausto-Sterling, 2000:116–17). Also, the search for brain differences today has not concentrated on questions of gender alone. Just as nineteenth- and early twentieth-century craniometrists sought explanations for "racial" differences in varying brain size, so contemporary thinkers have searched for them in brain functioning (Fausto-Sterling, 2000:119).

What physiological characteristics, then, should we look for in distinguishing females from males? Surely, differences in genital anatomy, hormones, or chromosomes allow us to define women and men as biologically distinct. At first glance, this might seem the case, but a closer look at the range of variation among females and males in basic bodily traits suggests otherwise.

Sex(ing) Hormones

Some scientists differentiate women and men on the basis of hormones. The view that differences in women's and men's behavior are explicable in terms of the presence of differing "sex hormones" in their bodies is also a popularly accepted one, often difficult to dislodge. It has, for example, become commonplace to blame complex human behaviors, such as male aggression, on the supposed "male" hormone testosterone or women's discontent on fluctuating levels of the supposed "female" hormone estrogen, although studies of these hormonal effects have produced contradictory and equivocal results. Some critics of women's participation in politics have even argued that female hormonal fluctuations might cause erratic behavior, which would preclude responsible decision making. During the Cold War, it was not unusual to hear that women could never be entrusted with the presidency of the United States since such biologically based erratic thinking might lead to nuclear disaster. How hormones are invoked to explain behavior is also gendered:

> although male hormones are used to account for general masculine proclivities (such as aggression) only rarely is any individual man's behaviour explained in these terms. When a man loses his temper we seldom hear anyone say "It's just an excess of androgen," yet how often women's anger is explained in terms of the "time of the month," (Jackson et al., 1993:364)

Such ideas reinforce the image of woman as more trapped in her body than man.

Do hormones provide the key to the differences between women and men? Anne Fausto-Sterling (2000), in documenting the history of hormone research, has shown that it has been no less burdened with unproven assumptions and misinterpretations than the history of brain research, which she has also studied. She painstakingly shows how the choices endocrinologists have made about what to name a particular hormone, how to measure it, and how to interpret its effects have been so greatly influenced by cultural ideas about gender as to render the assumption that "sex hormones" exist questionable.

The primary role of hormones in the bodies of both women and men is not to control behavior but to work at the cellular level to govern cell growth, cell differentiation, cell physiology, and cell death. Hormones may be present in different quantities in males and females and might affect the same tissues differently, but all hormones operate throughout the bodies of both women and men. There is, in other words, no hormone specific to either men or women. Despite this, scientists have labeled some of these chemical secretions "male" hormones (*androgen*, meaning "to create a man") and others "female" hormones (*estrogen*, meaning "to create estrus," which itself means "crazy," "wild," or "insane" and which also refers in animals to the period when females are "in heat"), thus gendering them and infusing them with cultural assumptions about women and men. The results of research on the activities of these substances in the bodies of women and men have been similarly affected by preexisting gendered assumptions, leading Fausto-Sterling and other biologists to call for abandoning the organizing metaphor of the sex hormone in endocrinology studies altogether.

Does this problematic history of endocrinology mean that there are no hormonal differences between women and men? Not necessarily, but it does suggest that any claims presently made for such differences have been so clouded by faulty research assumptions that they are premature at best, dangerous at worst.

Genital Anatomy

The difference between genital organs might seem an obvious way to distinguish a woman from a man, but a number of people throughout the world have "ambiguous" genitals, which look neither distinctly male nor female. Such features include a larger-than-typical clitoris, an absent vagina, a smaller-than-typical penis, and irregularly shaped scrota and labia (Kessler, 1998). Reproductive anatomy is also insufficient as a clear basis for assigning gender: although most women have the machinery for gestation (pregnancy) and men do not, not every woman can have a child. This does not make her "not a woman." Some individuals, such as "true hermaphrodites," are born with both ovaries and testes, making any clear designation of their sex on the basis of anatomical characteristics alone impossible.

Chromosomes

The modern biological definition of a man and a woman is a genetic one: an individual with two X chromosomes is designated a female and an individual with one X and one Y chromosome, a male. Yet, there are a number of chromosomal anomalies that make even this definition problematic. For example, some "genetic males" with an XY chromosomal complement have a rare mutation of the Y chromosome that results in a lack of male genitalia. These individuals look typically female, including having fully developed breasts at puberty. Other people have such chromosomal combinations as XO, XXY, XXX, and XYY, making their clear assignment into the category "male" or "female" difficult. Usually such "intersexed" individuals are assigned to one sex or another by physicians and parents based on cultural assumptions about gender. They may even undergo "clarifying" surgery to bring their external appearance in line with social expectations about masculinity and femininity. Recently, in the United States, an "intersex movement" has emerged, composed of individuals who protest such surgery, claiming that it is a form of genital mutilation that ruins future sexual pleasure (Lorber, 2001:228). It has been estimated that approximately 1.7% of all births in the United States today are intersexed, a rate that would result in a city of 300,000 having 5,100 intersexed individuals in its population (Fausto-Sterling, 2000:53–4).

The Politics of "Nature"

These examples suggest that defining males and female biologically, that is, determining their "sex," is a complicated business. In practice, in most Western societies, a female is simply defined as someone whose anatomy and physiology will allow her to menstruate, lactate, and become pregnant. However, as we have seen, not all people labeled "female" possess these characteristics.

No one definition, whether based on anatomical, physiological, or genetic differences, has yet been able to clearly and unambiguously distinguish all men from all women. Yet, the desire to make such distinctions is strong: millions of dollars are spent annually on such research. This is because "our debates about the body's biology are always simultaneously moral, ethical, and political debates about social and political equality and the possibilities for change" (Fausto-Sterling, 2000:255). The stakes are high in such debates: if women and men can be shown to be different, then it is an easy next step to conclude that such differences, and the benefits and drawbacks associated with them, are natural. In a world in which what is natural is often associated with what is "inevitable," demonstrating a clear biological basis for sex differences provides a powerful ideological rationalization for treating women and men differently.

Discourse/Knowledge/Power

In the last few decades, feminist scholarship has focused on how the female body is created through discourses, practices, representations, commodification, reproduction, and technology. The role of language in the body's construction has been a particularly fruitful area of feminist inquiry.

Language is a system through which we construct and order reality, interact and live in the world, and transform social existence. It is also a system tied to how power is distributed both socially and materially in any given society. Language is tied to power through *discourses*, systems of knowledge supported by institutions and practices that create a picture for people of what is true and what is not. Historically, various institutions, such as the medical, psychological, and religious establishments, have produced images of women as frail, helpless, dependent, passive, submissive, childlike, and emotional creatures, defining these traits as inevitable, natural, and normal. This "discourse of femininity" not only circumscribes women's lives and choices but also brings them into "the norm," in line with the standard ideas and behaviors desired by adherents with the power to construct and disseminate discourses. In contemporary Western societies, science is a privileged discourse, one that is widely believed to "speak the truth" about sex differences and women's bodies. Individuals who diverge from what science claims is natural, normal, or healthy are labeled "deviant," "abnormal," or "sick" and often feel themselves to be just that.

The Medicalization of Women's Bodies

Scientific discourse has been central in defining women's bodies. This has occurred primarily through the medicalization of the body. In the nineteenth century, the female body became a site of medical knowledge and practice as the field of medicine became professionally organized. Prior to that time, women had been healers, midwives, even physicians and surgeons. However, as medicine became an increasingly commercial activity—rather than a part of caretaking centered in the home that had traditionally been part of women's domestic duties—women were increasingly excluded, and often forcefully so, from the business of medicine. Medicine became a male-dominated profession charged with gaining "knowledge" of the body. As in many other spheres of Western thought, the male was taken as the norm and the Female was found deficient by comparison. In medical discourse, these deficiencies were pathologized; women's bodies were thus viewed as inherently diseased. Bodily functions such as menstruation and menopause were understood as pathologies.

In her analysis of contemporary medical discourse *The Woman in the Body* (1987), Emily

Martin reveals that these views are still wide-spread today. She shows how the language used to describe physiological processes in medical textbooks is far from objective and neutral. Frequently, the metaphors used to explain female bodily processes like menstruation and menopause have been drawn not from science but from aspects of Western economic systems. Menstruation, for example, has been likened to the failure of a factory system: the female body fails to create a useful embryo, instead producing a worthless product, menstrual blood. Menstruation is therefore a productive system gone awry (Martin, 1987:46). Production metaphors drawn from the world of the factory are also used to describe childbirth. Women are seen as passive laborers in a process in which doctors bring about a desirable "product" in the form of a healthy child. Women's "productive capacities" are also described in such language. A young woman recently reported being told by her physician that her difficulty in becoming pregnant was due to her "incompetent cervix."

Menopause is described in language derived from the communication industry, with its focus on "information-transmitting systems with a hierarchical structure" (Martin, 1987:41). Martin describes the depiction of menopause in college text thus: in menopause, the ovaries become "unresponsive" to stimulation

> from the gonadotropins, to which they used to respond. As a result, the ovaries "regress." On the other end of the cycle, the hypothalamus has gotten estrogen "addiction" from all those years of menstruating. As a result of the withdrawal of estrogen at menopause, the hypothalamus begins to give "inappropriate orders."... what is being described is the breakdown of the system of authority.... At every point in the system, functions "fail" and falter. (Martin, 1987:42)

This portrayal of menopause as a failure of the authority structure of the body contributes

to our society's negative view of it. As one textbook says, with the onset of menopause "a woman must readjust her life from one that has been physiologically stimulated by estrogen and progesterone production to one devoid of these hormones" (Guyton quoted in Martin, 1987:51). This statement implies that women cannot continue a vigorous life after menopause (they are no longer "stimulated") and must think of themselves as lacking something that invigorated them previously (they are now "devoid" of hormones). Recently, a number of women authors have worked to dispel such negative notions about menopause (for example, Sheehy, 1998).

U.S. society is not the only one that has constructed negative notions of female bodily processes. In many societies, for example, menstruating women are viewed as polluting and dangerous, as capable of defiling anyone or anything that comes in contact with them. In some societies, this belief has given rise to taboos that require women's seclusion during their menstrual period. Such taboos, however, may not always have negative implications. Among some Native Americans, for instance, the menstrual blood of sequestered women is seen as a source of power.

Women are not affected equally by the language and practices of medical discourses of the body. Martin found, for example, that white middle-class women are more likely to hold a worldview consistent with a "scientific" one and thus are more apt to accept the views of their bodies offered by contemporary medical discourse. In contrast, women from working-class backgrounds are more likely to resist such views. Martin (1987:190–1) proposes that these different responses arise because the people most oppressed by a system are more likely to be critical of it and to call for fundamental changes in it.

Rayna Rapp's study of *amniocentesis*, a technique used to reveal fetal anomalies such as Down syndrome, has produced similar results regarding a variety of responses from women to the claims of medical discourse. She has shown how a woman's race, class, and ethnicity can affect her decision to abort a child who in medical discourse is seen as "defective." White middle-class women in her sample tended to be more ambivalent about the idea of raising a disabled child than were Latina women. According to Rapp (1990:36), Latina women often recall friends and family members with sickly children and see the care given to these children by their mothers as consistent with a self-sacrificing view of motherhood that is valued by them. A number of other studies have substantiated Martin's and Rapp's conclusions that responses to the medicalization of women's bodies through discourse vary by ethnicity and class (for example, Ginsburg and Rapp, 1991).

Since the beginning of second-wave feminism, women have wrested some control of their bodies back from the male-dominated medical profession. The groundbreaking book *Our Bodies/Ourselves* was a crucial tool for raising women's consciousness about the benefits of self-knowledge about their bodies. More recently, *Ourselves, Growing Older* (Doress and Siegal, 1987) has similarly empowered older women. Although women in the United States today are more likely to confront their physicians armed with knowledge and questions, the nation has become an increasing medicalized society, with medicine, and its discourses and practices, penetrating into women's bodies and psyches in ever more far-reaching ways than before. Our organs can now be transplanted, our DNA removed and tested, and every inch of our bodies—from head to toe, from inside to outside—imaged and surveyed, at least for those who can afford such "benefits." Health and fitness have become increasingly dominant values as they have become increasingly big business, paradoxically even as obesity has become a significant health problem for many people throughout the world.

Discourses of Sexuality

Since the nineteenth century, the discourses of science and medicine have increasingly gained hold over women's sexuality. This process has had significant consequences for how women experience their bodies and their selves. Susan Bordo describes how, during this time period, the incessant probing of the body and the mind of the patient for knowledge about sexual practices paradoxically forced sexuality inward, interiorizing it. What may have been sexual acts before being subjected to science's scrutinizing eye became perversions as a range of sexual behaviors were pathologized:

> the medicalization of sexuality in the nineteenth century . . . recast sex as a family matter into a private, dark, bodily secret that was appropriately investigated by such specialists as doctors, psychiatrists, and school educators. The constant probing and interrogation . . . ferreted out, eroticized and solidified all sorts of sexual types and perversions, which people then experienced (although they had not done so originally) as defining their bodily possibilities and pleasures. The practice of the medical confessional, in other words, in its constant foraging for sexual secrets and hidden stories, actually created new sexual secrets. (Bordo 1993:142–3)

Medical and psychiatric researchers produced "knowledge" of women's bodies and sexual behaviors and declared that certain of those behaviors were natural and others were aberrant, based on standard assumptions of ideal femininity. In general, those women with little or no sexual desire but who complied to satisfy their husbands' sexual needs and to have children were deemed "good" women. The sexual woman was viewed as sick, dangerous, and whorelike. Sigmund Freud, perhaps the most significant sex researcher of the day, deviated from this view. He saw women as sexual beings and identified repression of their sexual desires as the cause of neurosis. He, nonetheless, had his own notions of what constituted normal female sexuality: he believed, for example, that women's sexual fulfillment could come about only in the form of vaginal orgasm (as distinct from clitoral orgasm, which Freud considered "masculine" and childish) and the subsequent bearing and nurturing of children. Lesbian sexuality, according to Freud, was a neurosis based on lesbian women's inability to give over their early masculine identification with the clitoris, the "inferior penis," to the vagina, thereby rejecting their true feminine role as passive receptacles in heterosexual vaginal intercourse.

Through such "normalizing discourses," women's sexual appetites and behaviors were tamed and new identities created. Nowhere was this more evident than in the creation of "homosexuality." As people's sexuality became an important focus of study, medical and psychiatric researchers and practitioners sought and gained information about same-sex sexual behaviors, organizing it into a "discourse of homosexuality," deeming heterosexuality normal and homosexuality abnormal. This created the very idea of "the homosexual." Before this time, homosexual acts occurred but the social identity "homosexual" did not exist (Foucault, 1980). Medicine and psychiatry created this category of identity through organizing information about same-sex sexual relations under the heading "homosexuality."

What is particularly significant about this and other discourses is that people have great difficulty constructing identities outside of them. Indeed, just the opposite occurs: people find meaning and identity in them. Discourses create categories of identity to sustain power relations and patterns of domination by speaking the supposed truth about an individual's normality. The norms produced through such discourses are inculcated by individuals; their power then works from within. If people think of themselves in the way such normalizing discourses do, for example, they will recognize themselves in talk about normality and abnormality. If their behavior diverges from the norm, they will most likely feel aberrant or deviant, and may even secretly believe something is wrong with them, rather than seeing talk about normality as a form of social control. Lesbian sexuality, for example, still widely understood within standard cultural constructions of femininity and masculinity, continues to be labeled unnatural and deviant.

Psychoanalytical theories like Freud's dominated Western beliefs about sexuality for many decades and represented a set of assumptions about "normal" sexual behavior and roles for women. In the 1940s and 1950s, Alfred Kinsey conducted an extensive survey of the sexual behavior of women and men. His findings, based on interviews, astonished his contemporaries. He found that many people engaged in a range of sexual behaviors considered to be atypical by standards of that time. Masturbation, same-sex sex, and oral–genital sex were found to be practiced by a significant proportion of the population.

Beginning in the 1960s, sex researchers Masters and Johnson continued to produce unexpected results. Their research was an influential corrective to long-held heterosexist and androcentric beliefs about female sexuality. For example, their findings that orgasms result from clitoral stimulation and that the phases of female sexual response are the same regardless of the source of stimulation reject the notion that a woman's full sexual satisfaction requires sexual intercourse with a man. Their studies indicated that women generally reach orgasm more quickly and with greater intensity from manual stimulation of the clitoris, especially when they stimulate themselves. This finding suggests that delays in achieving or failure to achieve orgasm during intercourse may be a result of techniques that are not compatible with women's physiological responsiveness.

Box 3.2   USES OF THE EROTIC: THE EROTIC AS POWER

There are many kinds of power, used and unused, acknowledged or otherwise. The erotic is a resource within each of us that lies in a deeply female and spiritual plane, firmly rooted in the power of our unexpressed or unrecognized feeling. In order to perpetuate itself, every oppression must corrupt or distort those various sources of power within the culture of the oppressed that can provide energy for change. For women, this has meant a suppression of the erotic as a considered source of power and information within our lives.

We have been taught to suspect this resource, vilified, abused and devalued within Western society. On the one hand, the superficially erotic has been encouraged as a sign of female inferiority; on the other hand, women have been made to suffer and to feel contemptible and suspect by virtue of its existence.

It is a short step from there to the false belief that only by the suppression of the erotic within our lives and consciousness can women truly be strong. But the strength is illusory, for it is fashioned within the context of male models of power.

But the erotic offers a well of replenishing and provocative force to the woman who does not fear its revelation, nor succumb to the belief that sensation is enough.

Source: Reprinted with permission from *Sister Outsider* by Audre Lorde, 53–4. Copyright © 1984 by Audre Lorde, The Crossing Press, a division of Ten Speed Press, Berkeley, CA. 94707, www.tenspeed.com.

While laboratory studies of sexuality and physiological sexual responses have discredited many old assumptions and raised new possibilities, they are limited in addressing the varied and changing experience and meaning of sexuality for diverse individuals. Sexuality is a complex social construction; many feminists have pointed out that privileging biology in our attempts to study and understand it is problematic: sexuality cannot be reduced to objective measures or divorced from its social and personal contexts. African American feminist poet Audre Lorde has made the significance of understanding sexuality as more than a biological process abundantly clear. She identifies "the erotic"—women's deepest sexual feelings—as a creative resource and basis of power for women (see Box 3.2).

Body as Text

Like Lorde, other feminist scholars have looked to the body as a possible source of female creativity. The conceptualization of woman as body has meant that women have traditionally been consigned to the role of object of male artistic representation and not as a subject capable of acting creatively in the world. The female body has been seen as the instigator of male desire, spurring male creativity: woman is a muse but cannot be an active creator of art herself.

Feminist literary critic Susan Gubar has shown how the Western literary tradition repeatedly excludes "woman" from literary creation through such ideas. Woman, she writes, has been conceptualized not as a writer but, instead, as a "blank page" in need of inscription by the male pen, which itself has been conceptualized as a metaphorical penis. She provides a persuasive chronicle of examples in Western literature of the "textualization" of the female body, from Ezra Pound's statement to the poet H.D. "You are a poem, though your poem's naught" (Gubar, 1982:75) to Ishmael Reed's description of sex: "He got good into her Book tongued her every passage thumbing her leaf and rubbing his hands all over her binding" (Gubar, 1982:76). Gubar (1982:78) asserts that in this tradition, where the female body and women's sexuality are identified with textuality, "many women experience their own bodies as the only available medium for their art." She hypothesizes that this may help to account for women's historical preference for media like dance and acting, which directly use the body (1982:82).

Although many feminists have protested the construction of woman as "blank page" incapable of artistic creation and have reclaimed her as mind, others have appropriated the equation of the female body with text and turned it to feminist ends. In one of her performances, contemporary feminist artist Carolee Schneemann, for example, read from a long scroll she removed from her vagina, thereby symbolically equating the female body with text but also suggesting it as a creative wellspring not just of babies but of words as well.

French feminists, such as Hélène Cixous and Luce Irigaray have theorized that because women's difference from men is located in the body, it is the female body and female sexuality to which women must turn for a source of female creativity that is authentic and disruptive. Cixous has referred to this as *l'écriture feminine*, "writing in the feminine." In her article "The Laugh of the Medussa," she exhorts women to "write yourself. Your body must be heard. Only then will the immense resources of unconscious spring forth" (Cixous, 1981:250). Cixous turns to a mythical maternal body for the source of this creative inscription.

In contemporary U.S. culture, many women have begun to take this exhortation literally: through tattooing and piercing, they inscribe their own bodies and use them to "write their own stories." Women often explain their body modifications in terms of exerting control over meaning, as a means of replacing the cultural inscription of the body with their own marks of signification. As Margo DeMello (2000:173) writes, for women, the tattoo is often "an important step in reclaiming their bodies, and the narrative in which they describe this process is equally important." Frances Mascia-Lees and Patricia Sharpe (1994) have found that women speak of piercing and tattooing as enabling them to control pain which they could not do in situations where they felt victimized, to dictate some of their own terms in the sexualization and eroticization of their bodies, to accept the body as desirable, and to resist inscription from without, using the body as a canvas for their own self expression. As one woman writes on a website:

> Tattoos are an important part of who I am. They let me take control of my own body and appearance. They make me feel better about myself, and they improve my self-image. They let me express who I am and what I believe, and they will always be a part of me. (http://www.wiccan-refuge.com/tattoorant.html, 28 Sept. 2004)

Some feminists have protested the turn toward the body by women scholars, particularly by the French feminists. They claim that this focus merely reproduces and underscores Western culture's objectification of women and re-essentializes the difference between women and men. Any attempt to define woman by the body, they claim, is dangerous. Others, as we have seen, see it as liberating: they are envisioning alternatives, suggesting that if we do not have new ways to imagine the body, there can be no vantage point from which to transform culture (Bordo, 1993:41).

The Commodified Body

Today, both in the United States and throughout the globalized world, the marketplace has become increasingly central to the

Tattoos.

construction of women's bodily needs and desires. Consumption has become so fundamental to many women's lives that their diverse bodily wants are mediated by mass-produced images in commercial ads found in magazines, on TV, and on the web. Through such images, women are offered more than simply products; they are promised a more beautiful body, a more gratifying life, and a more gratified self (Rosenblatt, 1999:8). Everyday life, these images suggest, can be transformed through the style on view or on sale. Yearning for these better ways of looking, living, and being drives consumption.

Since the late nineteenth century, with the rise of industrial society and consumer society in Europe and the United States, women have been seen as the ideal consumer. With the development of the department store, such as the Bon Marché in Paris, elite women were titillated by commodities that offered fantasies of a more desirable self. With the increasing "democratization of consumption" throughout the twentieth century, women from the working classes were offered compensation and respite from the bodily drudgery of their daily lives through purchasing products. Although women were enticed to buy newer and better commodities to improve the home, their "proper" domain, a woman's primary act of consumption was aimed at making herself into an object of desire.

Today, women's consumption continues to be critical to the success of a capitalist economy: in the United States, for example, women account for 85% of all purchases (Maine, 2000:7). Much of this expenditure is directed at the body and, in particular, at the pursuit of beauty. Today, U.S. women spend over $20 billion each year on beauty products, yet they feel more negatively about their bodies than women in most other cultures (Faludi, 1991). Standards of beauty vary across cultures and within societies due to differences based on such factors as sexual orientation, age, race, and ethnicity. However, media images of ideal beauty are so widespread and ubiquitous in the world today that they exert a powerful normalizing and homogenizing effect. The ultraslim, toned body of the tall white model continues to be the dominant image in advertising. Toni Morrison's provocative novel *The Bluest Eye* portrays the devastating consequences for black women of this idealized notion of the beautiful, desirable woman as "white." The significance of this ideal of beauty affects not only U.S. women: a prevalent form of cosmetic surgery in Asian countries, for example, is one that alters the shape of the eyelid to mimic the appearance of the "Western eye," and a rise in the incidence of anorexia nervosa and bulimia among recent immigrants to the United States has been reported for Korean, Latina, African, Middle Eastern, and Asian women. In Western countries in particular, older women are increasingly undergoing expensive and often dangerous cosmetic surgery, including face-lifts, liposuction, and Botox injections, as a means of retaining the youthful sense of beauty prescribed by the larger culture, while younger women risk their health by electing to have cosmetic surgery, such as breast enlargement, at increasingly younger ages.

Pursuit of the "body beautiful" requires not only exorbitant spending but also an inordinate amount of time. Despite feminist gains since second-wave feminism, women today spend more time and money on their appearance than ever before. The requirements for obtaining a beautiful body and appearance have become more stringent as fashion magazines promote new ideas, new images, and new products (Maine, 2000:65). New discourses of health overlay these images of beauty: the ideal female body today is also a healthy one that is toned and firmed by hours in the gym. Some women spend nearly as much time trying to look good as they do working. As Naomi Wolf (1991) puts it, women today work three shifts: one at their job, one taking care of their home and family, and one trying to meet the beauty demands of our culture.

Women's bodies are constructed as much through bodily practices of deportment and the automatic and habitual activities of their daily regimens as through internalized images and cultural inscription. The time-consuming regimen many women undertake daily in the pursuit of a feminine ideal of beauty acts to discipline women's bodies:

> Through the pursuit of an ever-changing, homogenizing elusive ideal of femininity—female bodies become docile bodies—bodies whose forces and energies are disciplined and habituated to external regulation, subjection, transformation, "improvement." Through the exacting and normalizing disciplines of diet, make-up and dress—central organizing principles of time and space in the day of many women—we are rendered less socially oriented and more centripetally focused on self-modification. Through these disciplines, we continue to memorize on our bodies the feel and conviction of lack, of insufficiency, of never being good enough. (Bordo, 1993:166)

Must the demands of the cult of beauty be understood as nothing more than expressions of women's subjection in capitalist society? Do fashion and cosmetics merely fix women visibly in their oppression? In *Adorned in Dreams*, Elizabeth Wilson warns against simply seeing fashion as a "moral feminist problem." If we do, she suggests that we will miss the richness of its cultural–political meanings (Wilson, 1985:13). Fashion can be used as a form of self-expression or self-enhancement and to signal one's affiliation with a subcultural group, often with a strong political orientation. The punk fashion of the 1970s, with its torn and slashed clothing, vinyl, bondage gear, and outrageously dyed, spiked, and sculpted hair, for example, presented a mockery of traditional style. Punk style and other "antifashion aesthetics," such as the slacker styles of the 1980s and the cyberpunk styles of the 1990s, were attempts to resist standard encodings of beauty, femininity, female sexuality, and class.

Feminist literary critic Mary Russo has taken such ideas a step further and theorized

The antifashion aesthetic of punk style.

an "anti-aesthetic of the body." She notes that in Western culture the ideal body is the classical body of the male, which is monumental, static, and closed (1986). By contrast, the woman's body, with its oozing fluids of menstruation and lactation, disrupts the boundaries of the enclosed body and challenges respectability and social order; it is the open, protruding, extended, secreting body of the "grotesque." It is a body conceived by society as impure, threatening, and dangerous, as anthropologist Mary Douglas has theorized. Russo suggests that the grotesque body need not be despised and contained as has traditionally been the case; instead, she argues that women co-opt this unruly body and its "aesthetic of the ugly," recognizing that the grotesque presents us with a body "of becoming, of process" (1997:325). It provides an image of transgression and change that can be used toward political ends.

These processes of self-creation, resistance, and transgression through the body and fashion exist within capitalist formations and gendered power relations and, thus, will necessarily be influenced, mediated, and constrained by them. However, women are active creators and, as such, can use the resources offered by these formations, if not to escape or transcend them then to negotiate, protest, and resist them. To understand shopping and fashion only as frivolous, empty-headed feminine activities reproduces the denigration of the body with which women have so long been associated. It devalues a traditional sphere of women's activities and concerns, and it does not allow for the diverse ways in which women can use these activities to improve their lives. Some women might starve themselves to death in the pursuit of impossible images of beauty and perfection, but others will playfully adorn themselves and seek pleasure in their own bodies (Mascia-Lees et al., 1990). Some will subject themselves to potentially dangerous cosmetic surgery, but others will find empowerment in the strong and sculpted body they build at the gym. In addition, a strong body is an important element of self-defense, which can serve as a valuable tool in providing women comfort and security. The manipulation of the body and its adornment can also result in the tangible accumulation of both symbolic and economic capital (Brydon and Niessen, 1998). Yet, it is also important to recognize that practices of fashioning the body are deeply embedded in worldwide relations of inequality: they depend on the hard physical labor of the bodies of women in poor countries, their tired backs, exhausted limbs, and failing eyesight.

The Visibility Politics of the Body

Hollywood movies, perhaps today's most powerful cultural medium, are a primary site of commodification of the female body.

Feminists have turned to an analysis of film to understand "the visibility politics of the female body" in a commodified culture (Conboy et al., 1997:9). Although roles for women in film have expanded somewhat in recent years, many films continue to objectify the (young) female body, offering it as an object of pleasure for the male viewer. Women, of course, are also consumers of films and their images and stories; but feminist film theorists have pointed out how female viewing and male viewing may be different due to the way the film camera structures "looking" to endorse dominant ideas of sexual difference.

The camera has traditionally provided "shots" of the female body as though through the eyes of the male on-looker, positioning the male as spectator and the woman as object of the "cinematic gaze." In perhaps the best-known article in feminist film theory, "Visual Pleasure and Narrative Cinema," Laura Mulvey (1975), drawing on psychoanalytical theory, argued that viewing and contemplating the female body inevitably arouse castration anxiety in men; cinematic images of women, thus, threaten to undermine the very pleasure they are supposed to provide for the male viewer. This anxiety is managed through voyeurism, which, according to psychoanalytical theory, is pleasurable; the voyeur takes other people as objects and controls them through looking. Women are denigrated through this voyeuristic control, thereby enabling the male spectator to take sadistic pleasure in contemplating their bodies. Women have no choice but to view a film from the perspective the camera presents, and that perspective, according to Mulvey's theory, is male. Pleasure for women in film thus comes, in the terminology of psychoanalytical theory, only from masochistic identification with their own objectification or from narcissism, becoming the object of their own desire.

The theory of the gaze provided feminists with a powerful tool for understanding how commodification of the female body in film reproduces powered gendered relations and how women are positioned in Western culture to participate in their own objectification. Over the last few decades, however, feminists have both expanded and critiqued Mulvey's formulation. The most trenchant critique of the theory of the gaze points out that individuals walk into a movie theater already positioned as social (not merely psychological) spectators: they actively and variably respond to filmic images on the basis of such prior experiences as gender, race, sexual orientation, and class. This approach focuses not on a hypothetical spectator but on the actual audience that attends particular films at particular historical moments. This restores to film theory the social world in which films are produced and received, the world outside and prior to the movie theater. Proponents of this approach contest Mulvey's totalization of the spectator as male and the spectacle as female, arguing that the spectator position is not singular and inflexible. They have suggested that women can "read against the grain," finding alternative positions from which to enter into a film's narrative and images and to resist the encoding of the female as object. Lesbian spectators, in particular, offer a challenge to any theory, such as that of the gaze, grounded in assumptions of heterosexual desire.

African American feminist cultural critic bell hooks indicates how historically oppressed people can come to resist identification with a film's discourse and images. Blacks, in particular, have traditionally done this as they were confronted with racist and dehumanizing images of themselves in Hollywood cinema. They learned the power of a resistant gaze under the historical situation of black subjugation, hooks argues, and brought it to bear on filmic interpretation. During slavery, black slaves could be brutally punished for appearing to observe the whites they were serving. They learned experientially that there is a critical, oppositional gaze (hooks, 1992:116–17). Black female spectators have had to develop a particular "resistant gaze," hooks says, because they

> have had to develop looking relations within a cinematic context that constructs our presence as absence, that denies the body of the black female so as to perpetuate white supremacy and with it a phallocentric spectatorship where the woman to be looked at and desired is "white." (hooks, 1992:118)

Little attention has been paid to the differential viewing position older women might take. Research into this area could provide valuable information about whether the exclusion of the older woman's body as object of the cinematic gaze similarly produces a "resistant gaze."

Today, it is necessary to combine multiple approaches in our attempts to understand the role film plays in reproducing traditional power relations through the commodification of images and the objectification of bodies, as well as to seek sources of resistance to them. We must inquire into the actual uses made of cultural forms by particular receivers of filmic images based on their historical and social circumstances. We also need to understand how a film itself constructs and constrains possible interpretations and viewing positions since no text is open to any and every interpretation.

The Reproductive Politics of the Body

Biological reproduction is at the center of social life in societies across the globe. Like gender, it is highly culturally mediated. Because of procreation's centrality to the reproduction of social life, it has been a significant focus of power and control. Feminists have, thus, made understanding the cultural role of reproduction central to their analyses of women's lives. Women's realities and choices have been con-structed and constrained through political and religious ideologies regulating their procreative functions, whether through state policies restricting Chinese women to one child, forced sterilization of Jewish women in Germany and of mentally disabled and poor women in the United States, denial of abortion rights to women in Portugal and Poland and to young women in the United States without parental consent, or the threat to deny women the right to abortion altogether.

As we have seen, because of their role in procreation, women have been associated with the natural. This construction has been used to deny them full participation in society and equal access to prestige, status, and resources. However, it has become harder and harder to sustain the fiction of reproduction as a natural process in our world of highly technologized reproduction. Indeed, the body has now crossed into the realm of the cyborg, a part human/part machine organism, as such technological prostheses as pacemakers, artificial hearts, and ceramic hip joints become increasingly prevalent.

From conception to birth, technology plays a role like never before in a woman's procreative life. Her fertility can be enhanced with drugs, her eggs removed from her body and implanted in another's, the DNA of her fetus removed and tested for "birth defects," and, increasingly throughout the world, her child's birth monitored and assisted in a hospital. New technologies have so changed the face of procreation that a new reproductive politics is only still emerging. Reproductive practices and policies unfold on a transnational landscape of inequalities, where poor women's bodies are, for example, the testing ground for new birth control options for women in industrialized nations and the devaluation of currencies in the global marketplace can make fertility drugs too expensive for importation to poor countries (Ginsburg and Rapp, 1995:1–7).

Biomedical practices affecting women's reproduction have been both welcomed and opposed by women around the world. Some have appreciated the chance to give birth in a hospital under sterile conditions, for example, while others, such as Inuit women of Canada, have resisted attempts to take birth out of the hands of local women (O'Neil and Kaufert, 1995). Feminists have organized locally, as well as on an international scale, to voice their concerns about new reproductive practices and to exert pressure on policy makers. For example, women in India, fearing the differential abortion of female fetuses, successfully waged a campaign against the use of amniocentesis— the extraction of genetic material from the amniotic fluid surrounding a fetus for genetic testing—to determine the sex of an unborn child. Despite the 1994 ban on such tests, however, their use has become commonplace, and female fetuses are routinely aborted. This practice of sex selection through abortion continues a trend that became marked in India in the 1980s: in 1981, the number of girls per 1,000 boys was 962; in 2001, that number dropped to 927 (Dugger, 2001:12).

Debates over new reproductive policies also pit groups of women against each other, just as in the fight over abortion in the United States. U.S. women, for example, are divided in their stance on genetic testing of fetuses for genetic diseases. Amniocentesis is now routinely used to test a fetus for a range of genetic abnormalities and diseases, and women are counseled to seek abortions if tests indicate their presence. Many women consider their right to know such information part of their reproductive freedom. Other women, particularly disability rights activists, argue that aborting a fetus is a new form of eugenics, selective breeding against undesirable traits. They argue that such practices narrowly define what is normal and desirable and perpetuate discrimination against those living with disabilities (Rapp, 2000). Many women wonder what will happen when genetic technologies are used not only to screen for potential diseases and disabilities but also to create "designer" children with "desirable" traits. Regardless of where they stand on such issues, feminists have for too long understood the impact on women of narrow definitions of acceptability and the consequences of them for women's sense of body and of self to leave such issues solely in the hands of bureaucratic policy makers.

Summary

The human body is a cultural construct; its meaning and significance are shaped by differing cultural ideas. Women's bodies are subject to cultural practices that use the body to exert political control over them. Feminists have recognized the body as a site of political domination and protested cultural constraints placed on women's bodies, arguing for women's rightful control of their own bodies.

Historically, women have been associated with the body and nature and men with "self," "soul," and culture, profoundly affecting how women have been valued, treated, and constrained in their opportunities and choices. The body has also been understood as the physical ground of gender differences, which science has been charged with uncovering. However, today, no clear biological sex difference has been unquestionably, scientifically demonstrated.

The female body is created through discourses, practices, representations, commodification, reproduction, and technology. Medical discourse, in particular, has constructed negative notions of the female body and sexuality. Literary discourse has conceptualized the female body as a "blank page," rendering her an object to be "written upon," not an artist herself.

Bodily needs and desires today are constructed in the marketplace. Through mass-media images, women are promised a more beautiful body through buying products and maintaining time-consuming daily beauty regimens. Women have found places in consumer culture to use their bodies and fashion for self-expression and self-enhancement and to signal political commitments. Hollywood movies also construct the female body as a commodified object, but women can resist this encoding.

Today, women's reproductive functions are greatly mediated by technology. Reproductive practices and policies unfold on a transnational landscape of inequalities. Feminists have been centrally involved in debating new reproductive technologies and practices and exerting pressure on policy makers.

Discussion Questions

1. The body can be experienced as a site of control, contestation, and empowerment. Compare and contrast times when you felt cultural pressures controlling your body, when you felt yourself challenging and resisting cultural definitions of your body, and when your body acted as a source of empowerment. What does this analysis reveal about the relationship of the body to culture?

2. Analyze a scientific article that claims that women and men are biologically different for any cultural assumption about masculinity and femininity that may affect its "objectivity." How, for example, do such assumptions influence the question asked, research methodology employed, or conclusions reached?

3. Analyze a description of one of women's biological or physiological processes in a popular magazine. How does the language affect the interpretation of that process?

4. Interview women from diverse backgrounds about the clothes they wear. What is the relationship of their clothing to their experiences of their bodies? How do popular images of women in the media affect these experiences?

5. Choose a Hollywood film and pay close attention to how it constructs a viewing position for you as spectator, especially in relationship to the women's bodies on the screen. Interview spectators for their reactions to the film, paying particular attention to how factors such as race, class, sexual orientation, and ethnicity affect them. Compare your analyses of the film based on these two approaches for their strengths and weaknesses regarding the "visibility politics of the female body."

Recommended Readings

Bordo, Susan. *Unbearable Weight: Feminism, Western Culture, and the Body*. Berkeley: University of California Press, 1993. A cultural analysis of the contemporary female body and the myths, ideologies, and practices that construct, manipulate, and constrain it. It focuses on the commodification of the female body, analyzing how consumption "normalizes" women's bodies and leads some to discipline their bodies so rigorously that it produces dangerous extremes in behavior that might harm or even kill them.

Conboy, Katie, Nadia Median, and Sarah Stanbury, editors. *Writing on the Body: Female Embodiment and Feminist Theory*. New York: Columbia University Press, 1997. A collection of essays by leading feminist theorists. It uses the metaphor of "writing on the body" to investigate how the body can and has been "read," how bodies are produced, how they speak women's experience, and how they are performed.

Fausto-Sterling, Anne. *Sexing the Body: Gender Politics and the Construction of Sexuality*. New York: Basic Books, 2000. An in-depth analysis of the role of science in constructing "truths" about sexuality, sex differences, and sexual identity. It focuses specifically on past and current research on intersexed individuals, sex-based brain differences, and "sex hormones," showing how the gender politics have been, and continue to be, at work in each of these areas.

Staiger, Janet. *Interpreting Film: Studies in the Historical Reception of American Culture.* Princeton, NJ: Princeton University Press, 1992. A historical analysis of the impact of social, political, and economic conditions on spectators' responses to films. It pays particular attention to how gender, race, class, sexual preference, and ethnicity enter into film viewers' interpretations.

Thomas, Rosmarie Garland. *Freakery: Cultural Spectacles of the Extraordinary Body.* New York: New York University Press, 1996. An interdisciplinary collection of essays focused on how non-Western, racialized, and disabled bodies have historically been commodified and turned into spectacles for viewing, whether in circuses, museums, and fairs or, more recently, on TV.

References

Bordo, Susan. *Unbearable Weight: Feminism, Western Culture, and the Body.* Berkeley: University of California Press, 1993.

Brydon, Anne, and Sandra Niessen. *Consuming Fashion: Adorning the Transnational Body.* Oxford: Berg, 1998.

Cixous, Hélène. Laugh of the Medussa. In *New French Feminisms,* edited by Elaine Marks and Isabelle de Courtivron. New York: Schocken Books, 1981.

Cohen, Colleen, and Frances E. Mascia-Lees. The British Virgin Islands as nation and destination: Representing and siting identity in a post-colonial caribbean. *Social Analysis,* 33, 130–51, 1993.

Collins, Patricia Hill. *Black Feminist Thought.* London: Unwin Hyman, 1990.

Conboy, Katie, Nadia Median, and Sarah Stanbury, editors. *Writing on the Body.* New York: Columbia University Press, 1997.

de Beauvoir, Simone. *The Second Sex,* translated by H. M. Parshley. New York: Knopf, 1953.

DeMello, Margo. *Bodies of Inscription: A Cultural History of the Tattoo.* Durham, NC: Duke University Press, 2000.

Doress, Paula Brown, and Diana Laskin Siegal. *Ourselves, Growing Older: Women Aging with Knowledge and Power.* New York: Simon and Schuster, 1987.

Douglas, Mary. *Natural Symbols: Explorations in Cosmology.* New York: Vintage Books, 1973.

Dugger, Celia. Abortion in India spurred by sex test skew the ratio against girls. *New York Times,* Apr. 22, 2001, 12.

Faludi, Susan. *Backlash: The Undeclared War Against American Women.* New York: Doubleday, 1991.

Fausto-Sterling, Anne. *Sexing the Body: Gender Politics and the Construction of Sexuality.* New York: Basic Books, 2000.

Foucault, Michel. *The History of Sexuality.* New York: Vintage Books, 1980.

Gilman, Sander. *Difference and Pathology: Stereotypes of Sexuality, Race, and Madness.* Ithaca: Cornell University Press, 1985.

Ginsburg, Faye, and Rayna Rapp, editors. *Conceiving the New World Order.* Berkeley: University of California Press, 1995.

Gubar, Susan. "The blank page" and the issue of female creativity. In *Writing and Sexual Difference,* edited by Elizabeth Abel. Chicago: University of Chicago Press, 1982.

Haraway, Donna. *Primate Visions: Gender, Race, and Nature in the World of Modern Science.* New York: Routledge, 1989.

hooks, bell. *Black Looks: Race and Representation.* Boston: South End Press, 1992.

Jackson, Stevi, Jane Prince, and Pauline Young. Introduction to science, medicine and reproductive technology. In *Women's Studies: Essential Readings,* edited by Stevi Jackson. New York: New York University Press, 1993.

Jardanova, Ludmilla. Natural facts: An historical perspective on science and sexuality. In *Women's Studies: Essential Readings,* edited by Stevi Jackson. New York: New York University Press, 1993.

Keller, Evelyn Fox. *Reflections on Gender and Science.* New Haven: Yale University Press, 1985.

Kessler, Suzanne. *Lessons from the Intersexed. Piscataway,* NJ: Rutgers University Press, 1998.

Kinsey, Alfred C., et al. *Sexual Behavior in the Human Male.* Philadelphia: W. B. Saunders;

Bloomington, IN: Indiana University Press, 1948.

———. *Sexual Behavior in the Human Female.* Philadelphia: W. B. Saunders; Bloomington, IN: Indiana University Press, 1953.

Longino, Helen, and R. Doell. Body, bias and behavior: A comparative analysis of reasoning in two areas of biological science. In *Sex and Scientific Inquiry*, edited by S. Harding and J. F. O'Barr. Chicago: University of Chicago Press, 1987.

Lorber, Judith. *Gender Inequality: Feminist Theories and Politics*, 2nd ed. Los Angeles: Roxbury Publishing, 2001.

Lorde, Audre. Uses of the erotic: The erotic as power. In *Sister Outsider: Essays and Speeches.* Freedom, CA: Crossing Press, 1984.

Mahmood, Saba. Feminist theory, embodiment, and the docile agent: Some reflections on the Egyptian Islamic revival. *Cultural Anthropology*, 16, 202–36, 2001.

Maine, Margo. *Body Wars.* Carlsbad, CA: Gürze Books, 2000.

Mairs, Nancy. Carnal acts. In *Writing on the Body*, edited by Katie Conboy, Nadia Median, and Sarah Stanbury. New York: Columbia University Press, 1997.

Martin, Emily. *The Woman in the Body: A Cultural Analysis of Reproduction.* Boston: Beacon Press, 1987.

———. *Flexible Bodies: Tracking Immunity in American Culture from the Days of Polio to the Age of AIDS.* Boston: Beacon Press, 1994.

Mascia-Lees, Frances E. and Patricia Sharpe. The anthropological unconscious. *American Anthropologist*, 96, 649–60, 1994.

Mascia-Lees, Frances E., Patricia Sharpe, and Colleen B. Cohen. The female body in postmodern consumer culture: A study of subjection and agency. *Phoebe: An Interdisciplinary Journal of Feminist Scholarship, Theory and Aesthetics*, 2, 29–50, 1990.

Masters, William H., and Virginia E. Johnson. *Human Sexual Response.* Boston: Little, Brown, 1966.

Mulvey, Laura. Visual pleasure and narrative cinema. *Screen*, 16, 6–18, 1975.

O'Neil, John, and Patricia Kaufert. Irniktakpunga! Sex determination and the Inuit struggle for birthing rights in northern Canada. In *Conceiving the New World Order*, edited by Faye Ginsburg and Rayna Rapp. Berkeley: University of California Press, 1995.

Radway, Janice. Identifying ideological seams: Culture, analytic method, and political practice. *Communication*, 9, 93–123, 1986.

Rapp, Rayna. Constructing amniocentesis: Maternal and medical discourses. In *Uncertain Terms: Negotiating Gender in American Culture*, edited by Faye Ginsburg and Anna Lowenhaupt Tsing. Boston: Beacon Press, 1990.

———. *Testing Women, Testing the Fetus.* New York: Routledge, 2000.

Rosenblatt, Roger, editor. *Consuming Desires: Consumption, Culture, and the Pursuit of Happiness.* Washington, DC: Shearwater, 1999.

Russo, Mary. Female grotesques: Carnival and theory. In *Feminist Studies: Critical Studies*, edited by Teresa de Lauretis. Bloomington: Indiana University Press, 1986.

Shaw, Carolyn Martin. Disciplining the black female body: Learning feminism in Africa and the United States. In *Black Feminist Anthropology*, edited by Irma McClaurin. Piscataway, NJ: Rutgers University Press, 2001.

Sheehy, Gail. *The Silent Passage: Menopause.* New York: Pocket Books, 1998.

Shostak, Marjorie. *Nisa: The Life and Words of a !Kung Woman.* New York: Vintage, 1983.

Strathern, Marilyn. Between a melanesianist and a deconstructive feminist. *Australian Feminist Studies*, 10, 49–69, 1981.

Thomson, Rosmarie Garland. *Freakery: Cultural Spectacles of the Extraordinary Body.* New York: New York University Press, 1996.

Williamson, Judith. Woman is an island: Femininity and colonization. In *Studies in Entertainment*, edited by Tania Modleski. Bloomington: Indiana University Press, 1986.

Wilson, Elizabeth. *Adorned in Dreams: Fashion and Modernity.* Berkeley: University of California Press, 1985.

Wolf, Naomi. *The Beauty Myth: How Images of Beauty Are Used Against Women.* New York: William Morrow, 1991.

chapter **4**

Women's Personalities

The nature of the psychological characteristics distinguishing females from males has been a focus of speculation for a wide array of theorists over the centuries. Whether philosopher, theologian, or scientist, writers have contemplated and theorized about women's mental capabilities and psychological makeup, have frequently pronounced them deficient in comparison to men's, and have prescribed a wide range of remedies for addressing women's supposed shortcomings. These theorists have asked whether women's psychic structures and abilities differ fundamentally from men's, whether there is a specifically "female" way of thinking and making decisions (see Chapter 2), and if women as a group possess certain behavioral characteristics, linked to a specific psychological makeup, that distinguish them from men. Table 4.1 presents a sample of the psychological and behavioral traits commonly assumed in U.S. society today to differentiate females from males and the values placed on them.

In the last chapter, we saw how women's identities are constructed through discourses of the body and how cultural practices, such as the consumption of products and images, are implicated in the construction of women's subjectivity and sense of self. In this chapter, we are particularly concerned with *personality*, a term that refers to a complex of motivations, traits, and behaviors produced in the process of psychological development. Because theorists have assumed that women and men differ in terms of this complex of traits, they have often investigated personality in relationship to the development and acquisition of gender-identity. Our emphasis in this chapter is on theories of personality that focus on gender-identity development to explain women's supposedly unique psychological constitution.

Explanations for Differences Between Women and Men

Nature Versus Nurture

Some theories attribute gender identity and gender-related personality traits to "nature," that is, biology (our bodies). Others explain it as a result of "nurture," that is, socialization—how individuals learn to behave as a result of being raised female or male. Attempts to attribute behavioral and personality differences to biological causes have focused on the influence of prenatal hormones on the system, brain lateralization, different characteristics associated with the sex chromosomes (XX, XY), the reproductive hormones estrogen and the androgens (see Chapter 3), and the development of gender-differentiated behaviors that supposedly helped our species survive over the course of its evolution. However, since females and males differ not only

TABLE 4.1 Typical and Desirable Characteristics: Differences in Ratings of Male Versus Female Targets

Typical Man > Woman	*Typical Woman > Man*
Independent	Emotional
Aggressive*	Grateful
Not excitable in	Home-oriented
minor crises*	Strong conscience
Skilled in business	Kind*
Mechanical aptitude*	Cries easily
Outspoken	Creative
Acts as leader*	Understanding
Self-confident	Considerate
Takes a stand	Devotes self to others
Ambitious	Needs approval
Not easily influenced	Gentle*
Dominant*	Aware of others' feelings
Active	Excitable in a major crisis
Knows ways of world	Expresses tender feelings*
Loud	Enjoys art and music
Interested in sex	Does not hide emotions
Makes decisions easily	Tactful
Does not give up easily	Feelings hurt
Stands up under	Helpful to others
pressure	Neat*
Not timid	Religious
Good at sports*	Likes children
Likes math and science	Warm to others
Competitive*	Need for security
Adventurous	
Sees self running show	
Outgoing	
Intellectual	
Feels superior	
Forward	

*Gender differences were considered desirable as well as typical.
Source: Adapted from T. L. Ruble. Sex stereotypes: Issues of change in the 1970s. *Sex Roles*, 9, 397–402, 1983. With the kind permission of the author and Kluwer Academic Publishers.

physiologically in some ways but also experientially, it is virtually impossible to separate the effects of "nature" versus "nurture" to determine the role of biology in behavior and emotions. To uncover the biological basis of gender behaviors, much research has depended on studies using laboratory animals. Extrapolating these results to humans, however, is a notoriously fraught endeavor. Other studies have focused on people born with gender-atypical genitals due to prenatal hormonal exposure, but even with this group, it is difficult to disentangle biological from environmental influences since results may indicate as much about these individuals' atypical social status as their physiology.

Feminists have tended to be particularly skeptical of theories positing innate causes for supposed differences between women and men because of the historical uses to which such arguments have been put. However, it is not for this reason alone that most feminists remain wary of biological explanations of gender difference. In actuality, there is no clear substantiating evidence of universal and innate differences between women and men despite easy and widespread claims to the contrary both in the scientific literature and in U.S. culture more broadly. Instead, research suggests that the gender differences found in individual studies are amenable to change and often vary depending on the circumstances of the research situation. Differences that do appear are never consistently found, which undermines the validity of claims for universal, biologically based differences between women and men. Even where differences do exist, they refer to group averages; and the overlap between groups is considerable, indicating that women and men share many behavioral characteristics often associated with only one or the other gender. Table 4.2 presents a summary of research findings about supposed gender differences.

The one area of personality difference between women and men in which hormonal differences have been strongly implicated is the greater propensity of men for aggression. Most of this support, however, is based on laboratory animal studies, which suggest a relationship between testosterone and aggression. Interestingly, there is also evidence that providing male monkeys with an opportunity

TABLE 4.2 Summary of Research Findings About Hypothetical Gender Differences

COGNITIVE

Intellectual aptitude: No difference.

Memory: No difference.

Verbal skills: Essentially no difference, although girls show a slight edge on some tasks.

Quantitative skills: No difference before high school; males show an edge in problem-solving tasks and in the incidence of math genius.

Visual-spatial abilities: Males perform somewhat better, especially if tasks involve rapid mental rotation of images.

Cognitive styles: No difference in analytic or computer abilities. Possible difference in style preferences, with males preferring an autonomous and females a connected style.

Creativity: Unclear. Females sometimes have an edge.

PERSONALITY AND TEMPERAMENT

Personality: Girls describe themselves as more people-oriented, males as more instrumental and power-oriented.

Temperament: Unclear. Females may be more timid.

COMMUNICATION PATTERNS

Verbal: Males dominate conversations; females listen, qualify, and self-disclose more. Situational and sex-typing factors are important.

Nonverbal: Males dominate after childhood; females are more expressive and more sensitive to nonverbal cues. Situational, cultural, and sex-typing factors are important.

PROSOCIAL BEHAVIORS

Affiliation: Females show greater interest by adolescence.

Empathy: Unclear. Females express more interest in others' feelings. Situational and sex-typing factors important.

Nurturance: Unclear. Females more likely to be in nurturant roles.

Altruism: Unclear. Females express more concern, but males are more likely to help strangers. Situational factors important.

Morality: Unclear. Females may be more concerned about the feelings of others.

POWER-RELATED BEHAVIORS

Aggressiveness: Males tend to be more physically aggressive.

Assertiveness: Unclear. Situational and sex-typing factors important.

Dominance: Dominance appears more important to males. Definitional, sex-typing, and situational factors important.

Competitiveness: Males tend to be more competitive. Situational and sex-typing factors important.

Achievement: No difference in motivation. Definitional, sex-typing, and situational factors important.

Noncompliance–nonconformity: Males tend to be less compliant and conforming. Situational factors important.

Source: From *Gender: Stereotypes and Roles*, 3rd ed., p. 101, by Susan A. Basow © 1992. Reprinted with permission of Wadsworth, a division of Thomson Learning. www.thomsonrights.com Fax: 800-730-2215.

to dominate increases their testosterone levels (Rose et al., 1972). This suggests that environmental situations also affect biology. While human males are more likely to behave aggressively than females, such differences are not consistently found (Eagly and Steffen, 1986), and recent research suggests that males and females may differ more in terms of the style of aggression than in aggressive behavior per se. Males tend to be more physically

---

Box 4.1   THE POWER OF INTERPRETATION

Take the case of hormonal differences between men and women. Women's apparently greater hormonal variability has been sued to buttress charges of emotional instability. Of course, men are also affected by hormones, and one former President of the American Psychological Association suggested that antitestosterone pills be taken by male leaders to reduce war. . . . If men were more hormonally variable rather than women, however, it would probably be argued that because they were more flexible and more in touch with themselves and their social environment, they were thus better suited by "nature" to fill important leadership positions.

Source: From: Phyllis A. Katz et al., *Psychology of Women*, edited by F. L. Denmark and M. A. Paludi, p. 261. Copyright © 1993 Greenwood Press. Reproduced with permission of Greenwood Publishing Group, Inc., Westport, CT.

---

aggressive than females, while females tend to use their interpersonal relationships to hurt others (see, for example, Simmons, 2002; Wiseman, 2002), although evidence for this type of female aggression has been questioned (see Meadow, 2002). In considering studies of aggression and of other supposed differences between males and females, it is important to remember that, as Katz et al. (1993:261) point out, "it is not only the accuracy of a documented difference but also the interpretation and the power of the interpreter that can be potentially damaging" (see Box 4.1).

Biases in Research Studies

Feminists have also shown that the results of many research studies of gender differences in personality are biased, rendering them highly questionable. Most systematic observations in Western countries of hypothetical differences between females and males, for example, involve white, middle-class people, both as observers and as subjects. The labels the researchers use to classify behavior may reflect their own biases, as when they label nurturance or passivity "feminine." Furthermore, the context of observation influences the results. Women might, for example, behave one way at home, another way at school or work,

and still another way in a laboratory situation; and the effects of these environments may differ for women and men. The observer may influence the subject's behavior without even being aware of it. If the person administering a psychological test behaves one way toward female subjects and another way toward males—say, by smiling more often at women or speaking more abruptly to men—then the results may reflect the differential treatment of the subjects. Finally, research reporting gender differences is more likely to be published than research failing to find differences, and there is a strong tendency to magnify gender differences even when the evidence is questionable. As a result, there is considerable potential for confusion about the results of empirical research on personality and behavioral differences between women and men.

Another source of bias in gender research studies is the neglect of variation among women and among men. Women and men differ considerably among themselves in terms of many of the traits analyzed in research studies of personality, motivation, and behavior. Life experience, social context, class, ethnicity, and age are important dimensions of variability. Unfortunately, such variables have been neglected in most studies of gender differences in personality, even though they most directly challenge previous assumptions about women and explanations grounded in earlier male-dominated theory.

Is Anatomy Destiny?

Evolutionary Theories

Recently, evolutionary psychology, a new form of sociobiology, has gained popularity as an approach to understanding gender differences in personality. Sociobiology was first formulated by E. O. Wilson (1975), who argued that psychological traits are selected in a population because they are adaptive and help maintain that population. Evolutionary psychologists, following Wilson, are particularly concerned with the different behaviors and psychological characteristics men and women have developed over the course of evolution to increase the likelihood that their genes will be passed on to later generations. They argue that these differences pit men and women against each other in an evolutionary "battle of the sexes," are inherent, and are, thus, natural.

As sociobiologist Richard Dawkins explains, male and female gender behavior is motivated by "selfish genes." That is, males and females can be thought of as trying to exploit the other, trying to force the individual of the other sex to invest more in their offspring in order to optimize the chances that their own genes will be passed down to future generations (Dawkins 1976:150). To increase this "genetic fitness," males need to impregnate as many females as possible. Males are thus genetically programmed for behaviors and psychological traits that will ensure this, according to evolutionary psychologists, such as hypersexuality and philandering. These traits propel them to have frequent sex with multiple partners.

Females, however, according to this hypothetical scenario, must be chaste to increase the chances of passing on their genes. Once pregnant, more frequent sexual relations will not increase a female's chances of successfully passing on her genes since she can be pregnant only once at a time. Once her child is born, a female increases the chances of her initial investment paying off by investing even more time and energy in the rearing of her child. To relieve some of this burden, a woman encourages a man to help her care for her dependent child. Women, thus, have developed personality and behavioral traits that help them keep a man around so that he does not leave her in order to spread more of his own genes. One such trait is "coyness." By being coy and playing "hard to get" in the mating/dating game, evolutionary psychologists hypothesize, a woman is more likely to attract a male willing to wait. It is in the female's interest to find such a man since he might also be more willing to remain after the birth of a child and help her with child-care responsibilities than a man who wants sex without commitment.

It is important to note that sociobiology and evolutionary psychology attempt to explain conditions only after the fact. These theories provide only a possible explanation for events that occurred in the past, about which we can never be certain since such explanations are not amenable to testing. In addition, these theories overlook data that do not support the evolutionary framework and fail to consider the cross-cultural evidence that contradicts their characterization of women as naturally chaste and coy and men as more highly sexual. It is not surprising then that the characteristics associated with males and females in the "selfish gene" model are strikingly similar to those found in the dating behavior of many Western men and women, although the model is more reflective of dating mores in the 1950s than in the twenty-first century. This Western focus is also evident in the capitalist economic language used in evolutionary psychological models: men and women are locked in a fierce "competition" in which they must protect their "investments."

Evolutionary psychologists discount cross-cultural variation in personality traits and behaviors even though evidence for this variation has been available for decades. For example, Margaret Mead (1901–78), an anthropologist and pioneer in research on the cultural and social context of personality development, studied men and women in a number of non-Western societies in the early part of the twentieth century. She began with the following question: Do universals of personality development exist? She empirically tested propositions about universals by comparing people in different cultural settings. Comparing men and women in several South Pacific societies with those in her own society, the United States, Mead discovered that what many people think of as feminine and masculine are culturally produced traits, not inherent biological differences (Mead, 1949) (see Box 4.2).

Box 4.2   SEX AND TEMPERAMENT

We have now considered in detail the approved personalities of each sex among three primitive peoples. We found the Arapesh—both men and women—displaying a personality that, out of our historically limited preoccupation, we would call maternal in its parental aspects, and feminine in its sexual aspects. We found men, as well as women, trained to be cooperative, unaggressive, responsive to the needs and demands of others. We found no idea that sex was a powerful driving force either for men or for women. In marked contrast to these attitudes, we found among the Mundugumor that both men and women developed as ruthless, aggressive, positively sexed individuals, with the maternal cherishing aspects of personality at a minimum. Both men and women approximated to a personality type that we in our culture would find only in an undisciplined and very violent male. Neither the Arapesh nor the Mundugumor profit by a contrast between the sexes. . . . In the third tribe, the Tchambuli, we found a genuine reversal of the sex-attitudes of our own culture with the woman the dominant, impersonal, managing partner, the man the less responsible and the emotionally dependent person. These three situations suggest, then, a very definite conclusion. If those temperamental attitudes which we have traditionally regarded as feminine—such as passivity, responsiveness, and a willingness to cherish children—can so easily be set up as the masculine pattern in one tribe, and in another be outlawed for the majority of women as well as for the majority of men, we no longer have any bias for regarding such aspects of behavior as sex-linked. And this conclusion becomes even stronger when we consider the actual reversal in Tchambuli of the position of dominance of the two sexes. . . .

. . . Only to the impact of the whole of the integrated culture upon the growing child can we lay the formation of the contrasting types. There is no other explanation. . . . We are forced to conclude that human nature is almost unbelievably malleable, responding accurately and contrastingly to contrasting cultural conditions. The differences between individuals who are members of different cultures, like the differences between individuals within a culture, are almost entirely to be laid to differences in conditioning, especially during early childhood, and the form of this conditioning is culturally determined. Standardized personality differences between the sexes are of this order, cultural creations to which each generation, male and female, is trained to conform.

Source: Excerpt from *Sex and Temperament in Three Primitive Societies,* pp. 279–80, by Margaret Mead. Copyright © 1935, 1950, 1963 by Margaret Mead. Reprinted by permission of HarperCollins Publishers, Inc. William Morrow.

Margaret Mead (1901–78) was one of the most influential and widely read anthropologists of her time. Her fieldwork among different societies in the South Pacific illustrated the great diversity one can find in the cultural definition and shaping of gender roles and personalities. This very diversity, in her view, indicated that what is thought to be "feminine" and "masculine" is culturally, not biologically, determined.

Traditional Psychoanalytical Theory

Traditional psychodynamic theory, or psycho-analytical theory, was founded by Viennese neurologist Sigmund Freud (1856–1939). Freud became intrigued by the number of patients he saw whose symptoms appeared to be the result of sexual conflicts and repressions. Based on case studies of these patients, he developed a theory of personality development called "psychosexual development," which explained what Freud saw as fundamental characteristics of the female personality: dependence, passivity, masochism, and an inferior sense of justice. For Freud, sexual drives underlie all personality development and arise from a fundamental difference in anatomy that differentiates males from females: the presence or absence of a penis. Thus, for Freud, "anatomy is destiny" (see Freud, 1925).

Freudian theory stipulates that the significant turning point in the formation of gender identity occurs at about age 3. Before this time, sensual pleasure is centered first on oral, then on anal, gratification. During the subsequent *phallic stage*, the sexual organs become the source of pleasure. It is then that girls notice that boys and men have penises. According to Freud, this recognition leads girls to develop a sense of inferiority and the desire for a penis, a wish he labeled *penis envy*. Women's supposed tendency to be masochistic was thought to arise from their self-loathing due to this lack. At the same time, boys notice that girls and women do not have penises, and this leads boys to suspect that girls' penises were somehow denied or taken away. Freud concluded that this produces anxiety in boys that they will also lose their principal source of pleasure, the penis. Freud called this anxiety the *castration complex*. He argued that girls blame their "inferior anatomy" on the mother. Girls then turn affections toward the father, hoping to get the desired object (a penis) or a substitute (a baby) from him. Girls later learn that the father cannot provide either and must replace him with another man to provide gratification. Since a girl's penis envy is mollified only by "gaining" a penis through marrying a man and having children, women, according to Freud, are naturally dependent on men and passive. Boys, on the other hand, possess a desire to have sex with their mothers and replace their fathers but fear that their fathers will retaliate for this desire by castrating them. A resolution of this *Oedipal conflict* is generally achieved by relinquishing the mother as love object while identifying with the father. This identification with the father removes a boy from the realm of competitor, thus reducing castration fears. As a result of this identification with the father, the boy develops a male identity and internalizes parental moral standards. Girls identify with the mother. According to Freud, girls do so reluctantly because this identification does not help obtain the wished-for penis. Girls' own moral standards are weaker and less developed than those of boys because they do not evolve in response to castration fears but, rather, to counteract the shame of having been castrated. Because internalization of moral standards is essential to maturity, girls are seen as having more difficulty maturing than boys. Thus, according to Freudian theory, gender identity and the foundation for all later personality development is established in the first 6 years of life and indirectly derived from anatomy.

Alternative Feminist Psychodynamic Theories

Some psychoanalysts have pointed out the lack of empirical evidence for Freud's theo-

ries, noting that findings from both direct-observational studies of children and clinical reports lend little support to Freud's formulation of female psychosexual development. Fliegel (1980), for example, rebukes those analysts who rigidly adhere to this dynamic in the face of contradictory information and notes that a belief in penis envy has "almost become a test of doctrinaire loyalty." However, this has not caused feminists to reject Freud entirely. Indeed, Dorothy Dinnerstein suggests this would be a mistake:

> I am disturbed . . . by the sexual bigotry that is built into the Freudian perspective. But I am disinclined to let the presence of the bigotry deflect my attention from the key to a way out of our gender predicament that Freud, in a sense absent-mindedly, provides. Feminists' preoccupation with Freud's patriarchal bias, with his failure to jump with alacrity right out of his male Victorian skin, seems to me wildly ungrateful. The conceptual tool that he has put into our hands is a revolutionary one. (Dinnerstein, 1976, xi)

A number of feminists have drawn on some aspects of Freudian theory while questioning others. The "dissidents" discussed in the next two sections, for example, reject the androcentric Freudian premise that "anatomy is destiny" but share with traditional psychoanalytical models the belief that individuals form a core gender identity based on early childhood experiences. They argue that psychological development must be understood within the cultural context within which girls and boys develop. Although these theories are based primarily on Western families, their focus on the cultural context of psychological development allows them to better accommodate cultural diversity than Freud's theory.

The Importance of Culture

Karen Horney (1885–1952) and Clara Thompson (1893–1958) were among the first women psychoanalysts to diverge from the classical Freudian theory of female psychology and to elaborate on the cultural constraints that contribute to the formation of the feminine personality. Horney suggested that psychological traits, such as women's dependence on men and female masochism, could be explained without reference to anatomical determinants. For example, Horney attributed women's dependence on, and "overvaluation" of, love, which she observed in normal as well as neurotic women of her time, to their economic and social dependence, which limits direct access to security and prestige (Horney, 1939). Horney argued that the vicarious aspect of women's status and accomplishments can explain why they may seem to be more afraid of losing love than men. According to Horney, it is not necessary to attribute this to the symbolic desire for a penis. Similarly, she saw masochism as an attempt on the part of women to achieve personal safety and satisfaction by appearing inconspicuous and dependent, not as a reaction to the recognition of the lack of a penis.

Thus, Horney's explanation of "feminine psychology" suggests that social change might be able to remedy traits deemed undesirable. If socialization practices were changed so as to permit the development of women's sexuality and independence, the female personality would be different. This view is in stark contrast to that of those who attribute femininity to penis envy and biological makeup. Horney also pointed out that women have anatomical features and capacities that men lack and may even envy. The wish for a penis may be no more significant than the frequently observed

Karen Horney (1885–1952) published a major feminist critique of Freudian psychoanalysis and women in her 1926 paper "The Flight from Womanhood." She pointed out that the masculinist mode of thought represented by the psychoanalysts of her day was not surprising given the male domination of all institutions. Thus, both social reality and theoretical constructs were based on male views of the inferiority of women. She attributed this male perspective to a deep envy of the primacy of women in reproduction.

wish of boys for breasts and the ability to give birth to a child. Horney ([1922] 1973) suggests that this envy of women is at the root of misogyny and male oppression of females; in fact, research suggests that males in many societies experience feelings of breast and womb envy (Zalk, 1980, 1987; Mead, 1949).

Thompson challenged the classic assumption that discovery of the penis invariably causes psychic trauma for a girl. However, she agreed that this might be true if the lack of a penis is associated with lower status and fewer privileges within the family, which has historically been the case in many Western societies (Thompson, 1942, 1943). Rather than attribute the adolescent female's renunciation of the "active" role in life to the resolution of penis envy, Thompson attributed it to external social pressures. Insofar as the requirements of a culture are unchangeable or unchanging, it may be a more positive adaptation for the female to find pleasure in pain and self-sacrifice than to reject the life of a woman altogether and refuse to marry and bear children. In *Psychoanalysis and Feminism* (1974), Juliet Mitchell, like Thompson and Horney, viewed Freudian theory in a cultural context, taking the position that psychoanalytical theory is an analysis of a patriarchal society, not a recommendation for one.

The Importance of Relatedness

Attempts by feminists to understand female psychological development within a psychoanalytical or psychodynamic framework have led many theorists to explore the mother–daughter relationship and the differential impact on girls and boys of being raised by a female caretaker. These writers focus not on genitals but on the impact on early identity formation of having a same-sex or an other-sex caretaker. The fact that the female child is cared for and raised primarily by a parent or a parent-surrogate of the same sex may engender feelings and conflicts that differ from those elicited in the mother–son relationship (Denmark, 1977).

Chodorow (1978) discusses the effect that predominantly female parenting has on the establishment of the boy's gender identity. In order for him to develop his appropriate gender role, the boy must break away from the female-dominated world from which he emerges. The devaluation of femininity and female activities may represent the male's attempt to differentiate himself from that feminine world. According to Chodorow, males have an easier time establishing autonomy than do females but a less stable gender identity and less access to feelings of empathy, nurturance, and dependence, which are a reminder of their early identification with their mothers. Indeed, some research has shown that males do demonstrate a greater concern with maintaining gender-role distinctions than do females (Silvern and Katz, 1986). Because females initially identify with a same-sex caretaker, Chodorow hypothesizes that they have less trouble establishing a positive gender identity but more difficulty developing feelings of autonomy than do males. This is seen to disadvantage women because, in traditional psychodynamic theory, establishing an independent, autonomous identity is taken as the hallmark of mental health and is seen as necessary for obtaining mature, intimate, and trusting relationships (Erikson, 1963).

Other psychodynamic theorists have challenged this claim. Jean Baker Miller (1984) and her colleagues at The Stone Center at Wellesley College, for example, argue that relatedness is the central goal of development and that it is only within the context of relatedness that autonomy can develop. Miller's self-in-relation theory proposes that it is the give-and-take relationship between the caretaker and the child that forms the core "self" and that this reciprocal relationship is the precursor of empathy, nurturance, and connection with others. Miller notes that females are more likely to be encouraged in these experiences than are males; that, as a result, they possess a greater capacity for emotional connectedness, empathy, and intimacy; and that this relational self is a core self structure for them.

Feminism and the Lacanian Turn

Recently, a number of psychoanalytical feminists have turned to Freud to understand those aspects of the female psyche often overlooked in mainstream psychological theory and studies: women's pleasures, desires, and fantasies. Juliet Mitchell and Jacqueline Rose (1982), for example, see in Freud's theory of the unconscious a potent tool for analyzing how women's desires are channeled in a patriarchal society to reproduce their own subjugation.

These theorists have tended to draw on the work of French psychoanalyst Jacques Lacan (1901–81), who has reinterpreted aspects of Freud's theory, focusing specifically on how a child comes to be either one sex or the other. Lacan's conceptualization of this process centers on how a child becomes a "subject," or an "I" like the subject of a sentence. In other words, Lacan asks how children come to have a conscious understanding of themselves as distinct from the mother, as possessing their own identity, and suggests that it is through entry into the symbolic realm of culture, through the acquisition of language. This entry, based on the recognition of oneself as distinct, however, splits the child from its mother, producing a sense of loss and a constant desire for this unattainable lost object (see Wright, 2000). To disavow this lack and to make up for the lost object, the male projects fantasies onto the female: she becomes the desired *object*. However, this has different consequences for women because of their differing relationship to language.

Unlike Freud, who saw male and female genital anatomy as the basis of sexual identity and sex difference, Lacan sees no predetermined nature to sex difference; instead, sex difference is a "construction in culture." For him, it is not the penis (the biological organ or lack of one) which is associated with one's actual father that is significant in the development of gender identity but the "phallus," the cultural sign or symbol of the father, a metaphor for society's rules and laws and their imposition. The symbolic order, according to Lacan, is organized around the phallus, meaning that in language the male is taken as the norm (e.g., the word *man* subsumes both men and women) and the female is defined as "lack of maleness." Since coming into language produces subjectivity, but there is no subject position in language for the female, the female subject is constituted as an exclusion. Constituted by lack and defined by men as an object onto which their fantasies are projected, "woman" does not exist. In other words, the phallic order of language and society excludes woman and assigns her to the position of fantasy. What is significant about this formulation is that it places emphasis not on women's psychological inadequacies, as Freud did, but on society's.

The Lacanian idea that woman is constructed in language as an absence has been combined with a similar insight developed by the distinguished psychoanalyst Joan Riviere (1883–1962), who wrote in the 1920s and 1930s. According to Riviere, feminine identity is a masquerade, not an essence but a role played; gender, in other words, is a performance (Riviere [1929], 1986). Riviere studied assertive and intellectual heterosexual women who, in their anxiety that their behavior was overly male, adopted a compensatory exaggerated femininity. These women, thus, understood themselves as both male and female, allowing them to identify across, as well as by, gender. One significant implication of Riviere's theory is its questioning of the distinction between genuine "femininity" and pretence (Wright, 2000:54). Through an understanding of femininity as masquerade, women have a means to negotiate their subjectivity within the constraints of a phallocentric social order. Although some feminists have seen liberatory potential in this conceptualization of female identity, not all concur.

In the formulation of feminine identity as a performance, "femininity" is like "drag." Judith Butler argues that drag is not necessarily subversive and can even reproduce essential notions about gender and sexuality. Although drag might seem to call attention to gender as something "put-on" and "made-up," rather than essential, she argues that it also can reinforce heterosexual norms. As Elizabeth Wright (2000:38) summarizes, "in drag, there is an exaggerated miming of the opposite sex . . . a form of gender melancholia, an unconscious grief for the loss of the same-sex person, a renunciation of the possibility of homosexuality."

Neo-Freudian theory, especially that derived from Lacan, has also been put to use by feminists to understand such topics as women's reading preferences, their consumer practices, and, as we saw in Chapter 3's discussion of theories of the "gaze," the role cinema can play in the reinscription of woman as object. Tania Modleski (1982:30), for example, has argued that feminists need to mine the liberatory potential of Freudianism, which lies in its encouragement of people to explore the sources of their repression and discover in their dreams and fantasies the long-hidden wishes which might ultimately lead to a critique of a repressive culture. Modleski explores such potential in her analysis of the appeal of "mass-produced fantasies"

for women: Harlequin romances, Gothic novels, and television soap operas. She shows that it is inadequate to understand these popular forms only as forces that oppress women through imposing false needs or a false consciousness on them. Instead, she suggests that these forms also address women's desires in a culture in which there are inadequate ways for women's longings to be fulfilled. She argues that each of these forms satisfies a particular psychological need of women. Readers of romance novels, for example, derive some of their pleasure from the elements of a revenge fantasy embedded in these stories; the female protagonist often is able to bring the man in the story "to his knees" (Modleski, 1982:45). The desire on the part of the female character in these stories to be taken by force can be understood, Modleski argues, as concealed anxiety about rape and longings for power and revenge.

Cognitive-Developmental Theory

Other schools of psychological thought offer alternative explanations for the development of female and male gender identities and roles, dismissing the basic assumptions that underlie Freudian theory because the events are largely unconscious developments that cannot be observed directly. Cognitive psychologists focus on the individual's internal need to fulfill a learned gender identity (Kohlberg and Ullian, 1974; Kohlberg, 1966). Cognitive psychologists are interested in how people organize and understand their perceptions of physical and social reality and how these perceptions change at different developmental stages. They have suggested that at age 2 girls and boys begin to learn gender categories based on experiences with representatives of each gender, although they are not initially aware of anatomical distinctions and do not conceive them to be unchangeable characteristics. Once children have classified themselves as female or male and recognize that their gender does not change (at about age 5), they are motivated to approximate to the best of their ability the social definitions of this identity. In the case of female children, the motivation to fulfill their gender identity presses them toward the ideal of femininity (as socially defined), independent of externally mediated rewards or punishments for attaining such a goal. This explanation for gender-role acquisition may account for the fact that often girls and boys will conform to stereotypic gender roles even when their parents or other socializing agents do not differentially reinforce feminine and masculine behavior in them (Kohlberg and Zigler, 1967).

Socialization Theories

All societies teach their young culturally prescribed gender roles. This gender socialization often begins at the moment of birth. Socialization theories focus attention on the social context of this learning of gender roles that gives rise to characteristically female and male personality traits and behaviors. They are particularly interested in the messages a child receives from others in the social environment and how these messages are conveyed. Parents and peers are powerful socializing agents, but gender expectations are communicated in many different ways. Television, school, books, clothing, toys, and even fairy tales operate as socializing agents.

Social Learning Theory

Like cognitive–developmental theory, social learning theories stress the acquisition of personality traits within a social context and not as inherent in the individual. However, while cognitive theory of gender-role development focuses on the internal motivations of females and males to excel at the roles in which

they find they have been classified, social learning theorists emphasize the role of external pressures imposed on the developing girl and boy.

Social learning theory associates gender-role conformity with the external reinforcements (rewards and punishments) that people receive from behaving in particular ways. This theory holds that individuals learn "female" and "male" behavior by observing others. However, the behavior actually performed is a function of whether it is rewarded or punished. Social learning theorist and experimental psychologist Albert Bandura (1965) suggests that the introduction of rewards for cross-sex behavior will enable girls and boys to expand their behavioral repertoires with little difficulty.

Gender Schema Theory

Sandra Bem (1981, 1983, 1985) proposes a gender schema theory, which incorporates cognitive, child-rearing, and cultural factors to explain the development of gender identity and personality triats. All people have mental categories that are a network of associations. In order to understand or make sense of information, individuals try to place it into these categories, which form a sort of blueprint in the mind. These *schema* are descriptive and consist of associations and assumptions. For example, schemas for "teacher" and "student" include the descriptors "one who teaches" and "one who learns," respectively, as well as myriad associations about authority, judgment, power, expertise, interdependence, and more.

One of the most culturally salient categories in which people are grouped is gender, with the development of gender schema beginning early in childhood. Children learn quickly to categorize people by gender and develop a gender schema that incorporates cultural gender roles, norms, attributes, and definitions of *feminine* and *masculine*. Bem proposes that gender schemas become part of an individual's self-concept:

> As children learn the contents of the society's gender schema, they learn which attributes are to be linked with their own sex and, hence, with themselves. This does not simply entail learning where each sex is supposed to stand on each dimension or attribute—that boys are to be strong and girls weak, for example—but involves the deeper lesson that the dimensions themselves are differentially applicable to the two sexes. (Bem, 1981, 355)

According to Bem, people fall on a continuum from having more to having less developed gender schema. There is some evidence to support Bem's suggestion that the more developed our gender schema, the more gender-typed our self-concept and behavior and, alternatively, that people who are less gender-typed have less developed gender schema (for example, Bigler and Liben, 1990; Bem, 1985). Bem does not consider gender typing as inevitable; she suggests that raising children in gender-aschematic homes and school environments, in which *sex* refers only to anatomy, results in fewer gender-typed behaviors, traits, and expectations.

Social Interactions and Gender Roles

The above theories attempt to explain how individuals develop gender identities and personality traits and the relationship between gender identity and gender roles. Other theories place greater emphasis on social roles; rather than view gender-typed traits and behaviors as primarily a function of internalized gender identities, they understand them as an outcome of gender-differentiated role assignments and expectations and the unequal distribution of power between females and males. These theories hold that gender-typed personality traits or behaviors are, at least in part, behavioral displays that are shaped by, or result from, social demands, interactions, or oppression, rather than necessarily representing internal or stable characteristics.

Alice Eagly (1987), for example, explains gender-typed traits as compliance to gender-role expectations. Her social/role theory suggests that women and men demonstrate different personality characteristics because the family and occupational roles to which they are assigned require them. Thus, women are communal because of their roles in the family as caretakers and nurturers and men, more agentic because of their roles in the workplace. Although roles may be changing in much of the world, even in the United States women and men continue to assume different family and workplace responsibilities and roles (for example, Ruble, 1988). Women are more likely to assume the child-care and domestic work in the home, and half of employed women are in service-related jobs (Neft and Levine, 1997).

Candace West and Don Zimmerman (1987) present a thoughtful argument for conceiving of gender as a verb rather than a noun. In other words, they view gender as something people *do*, not as something they *are* (see Box 4.3). Other researchers have presented a model that explains the display of gender-typed traits and behavior rather than their acquisition. They propose that the enactment of gender takes place within the context of social interactions, is highly flexible, and is context-dependent (Deaux and Major, 1987). In other words, gender-related traits and behaviors are an outcome of the individual's self-perception, emitted expectation of another, and the context of ongoing social interactions.

That such behaviors are related to the characteristics of social interactions rather than to those of particular individuals is borne out by research on low-status individuals, both male and female. Henley (1977), for example, found that when females relate to males and

Box 4.3   DOING GENDER

When we view gender as an accomplishment, an achieved property of situated conduct, our attention shifts from matters internal to the individual and focuses on interactional and, ultimately, institutional arenas. In one sense, of course, it is individuals who "do" gender. But it is a situated doing, carried out in the virtual or real presence of others who are presumed to be oriented to its production. Rather than as a property of individuals, we conceive of gender as an emergent feature of social situations: both as an outcome of and a rationale for various social arrangements and as a means of legitimating one of the most fundamental divisions of society. . . .

    To elaborate our proposal, we suggest at the outset that important but often overlooked distinctions be observed among sex, sex category, and gender. Sex is a determination made through the application of socially agreed upon biological criteria for classifying persons as females or males. . . . Placement in a sex category is achieved through application of the sex criteria, but in everyday life, categorization is established and sustained by the socially required identificatory displays that proclaim one's membership in one or the other category. In this sense, one's sex category presumes one's sex and stands as proxy for it in many situations, but sex and sex category can vary independently; that is, it is possible to claim membership in a sex category even when the sex criteria are lacking. Gender, in contrast, is the activity of managing situated in conduct in light of normative conceptions of attitudes and activities appropriate for one's sex category. Gender activities emerge from and bolster claims to membership in a sex category.

    . . . Doing gender also renders the social arrangements based on sex category accountable as normal and natural, that is, legitimate ways of organizing social life. Differences between men and women that are created by this process can then be portrayed as fundamental and enduring dispositions. . . . Thus if, in doing gender, men are also doing dominance and women are doing deference, . . . the resultant social order, which supposedly reflects "natural differences," is a powerful reinforcer and legitimator of hierarchical arrangements.

Source: Candace West and Don H. Zimmerman, Doing gender, *Gender and Society* 1, 126–7, 146, 1987.

subordinate males relate to more dominant males, they touch less, smile more, make less frequent eye contact, and are more tentative. The effect of male dominance on women may be a direct and powerful influence on gender-related traits and behaviors in other ways as well. MacKinnon (1987), for example, suggests that women behave differently from men because they grow up and live under the constant threat of physical violence and sexual exploitation. It is understandable that women may behave in ways that minimize a challenge to male dominance and the possibility of being victimized (Zalk, 1987).

Research on Gender Socialization

Although how gender is learned may not differ significantly among groups of people, research clearly indicates that the experience of growing up male or female in different cultures is quite varied. Theorists have had a great deal to say about the development of gender identity stage by stage, but traditionally, these models have been developed based on observations of twentieth-century Western society and often limited to the white middle class. The following section focuses on the results of such studies. It is followed by sections concerned with studies of gender expectations and gender-role socialization among African Americans, Asian Americans, and Latinos in the United States, although there are significantly fewer of these studies than of those focused on white children. It is important to remember that when researchers conduct studies of women of color, the broad ethnic designations they use—African American, Hispanic/Latino, Asian American, or Native American, for example—often obscure important ethnic and cultural variations among individuals. Moreover, like much gender research, that on U.S. females of color has been plagued with biases and unfounded assumptions. Consequently, generalizations about the experiences that shape the personalities of women of color, as well as the personalities themselves, are apt to be inaccurate for many individuals. Although this research suggests variation in traits, motivations, and behavior among groups of women, what many women do have in common is the experience of discrimination. What many women of color share is the pressure to reconcile family expectations and values with those imposed on them by the larger culture of which they are a part.

Chicanas, for example, have roots in a Mexican Indian heritage. Historically, Mexican Indian women had a responsible role in the social, religious, and economic life of the community (Nieto-Gomez, 1976). With the arrival of a colonizing Spanish culture and the Catholic Church, the opposing concepts of good woman–bad woman began to predominate. The Spanish "lady," representing a different set of traditional roles, became the new ideal, and the place of Mexican Indian women was diminished and denigrated within that culture.

The divergent pulls of personal heritage and dominant cultural expectations impose additional stresses and conflicts on women of color in the United States, who often struggle to maintain cultural roots that are different from those of the dominant culture while establishing an individual identity. In doing this, women confront not only the inherent sexism of both cultures but the racism as well. The importance of this struggle cannot be underestimated (see Box 4.4). As Cherrie Moraga (1981:34) writes in *This Bridge Called My Back*, "I think: what is my responsibility to my roots—both white and brown, Spanish speaking and English? I am a

---

Box 4.4   THE SOCIALIZATION OF LAS CHICANAS

Marianisma is the veneration of the Virgin Mary. . . . Through the Virgin Mary, the Chicana begins to experience a vicarious martyrdom in order to accept and prepare herself for her own oppressive reality. . . . To be a slave, a servant, woman cannot be assertive, independent and self-defining. . . . She is conditioned to believe it is natural to be in a dependent psychological condition as well as dependent economically. The absolute role for women is not to do for themselves but to yield to the wishes of others. . . . Her needs and desires are in the charge of others—the patron, her family, her father, her boyfriend, her husband, her God. She is told to act for others and to wait for others to act for her . . .

The basis for La Mujer Buena, the good, respectable woman in La Casa Grande, was the upper class Spanish woman whose role was to stay home. . . . The concept of Marianisma reinforced this Spanish role as a positive ideal for everyone to follow . . .

. . . Marianisma convinced the woman to endure the injustices against her.

Source: Nieto-Gomez, 1976:228–33.

woman with a foot in both worlds; and I refuse the split" (see Box 4.5).

The Gender Socialization of White Girls

Studies of early parent–child interaction among white middle-class participants reveal that within the first 24 hours after birth parents attribute gender-stereotypic traits to their infants, viewing boys as firmer and stronger and girls as softer and finer (Rubin et al., 1974). From the earliest age, mothers also look at and talk to female infants more than male infants. Differences have been observed in the ways in which mothers hold sons and daughters and in patterns of physical contact and proximity (Lips, 2001).

Research by Money and Ehrhardt (1972) on changes in gender assignments of infants born with ambiguous genitals dramatically illustrates the impact of such gender labeling on parental behavior; even small children altered their behavior toward siblings whose gender label was changed. Another study (Seavey et al., 1975) shows how one can demonstrate the effects of gender labeling on the treatment of infants on an experimental basis. Adults who were told that a 3-month-old baby was a girl were more likely to engage in one sort of treatment (such as playing with a doll) than they were when told that this same baby was a boy.

Table 4.3 summarizes the results of studies demonstrating the different expectations U.S. middle-class white parents have for their daughters and sons and the different ways mothers and fathers treat their daughters and sons.

The structure of schools, teachers' behavior, and peer group pressure are also powerful

---

TABLE 4.3 Some Differential Expectations and Treatment of Boys and Girls by U.S. Parents

- Boys are expected to be more independent than girls and less fragile, resulting in their being less restricted than girls and allowed more freedom to explore the environment (Aberle and Naegele, 1952). By the age of 13 months, boys spend longer periods of time away from their mothers and explore further distances; girls spend more time talking with and looking at their mothers than do boys.
- By age 2, girls are socialized into nurturing activities through doll play, while boys are encouraged in play with toy vehicles, which develops motor activity (Liss, 1983; O'Brien and Huston, 1985b).
- Parents respond differently to girls' and boys' moods, displays of anger, and aggressive behaviors (Fivush, 1989; Tronick and Cohn, 1989).
- Parents talk to sons and daughters differently. In addition, mothers talk more and use more supportive and negative speech than fathers (Leaper et al., 1998).
- Caretakers attend more to assertive behaviors in boys and to verbal behavior in girls in children as young as age 1 (Fagot et al., 1985).
- Activities assigned at home follow gender-role expectations such that girls are more likely to be assigned domestic chores (such as cooking) and boys, maintenance chores (such as mowing the lawn) (Burns and Homel, 1989; Goodnow, 1988). This pattern is more exaggerated among people in lower economic classes and increases from childhood to adolescence.
- Parents discourage children from engaging in other-gender activities and toy play and reinforce gender-appropriate activities. This is more pronounced with sons than with daughters (Antill, 1987; Lytton and Romney, 1991). Fathers are more concerned with their children's conformity to gender-appropriate behavior than are mothers. They view their children in more gender-stereotypic ways and are more likely to interact with their daughters and sons in ways that encourage gender-appropriate behaviors and toy playing than are mothers. This is particularly true with sons.

Source: Adapted from Jacklin et al., 1984:413–25.

Box 4.5   THE BRIDGE POEM

I've had enough
I'm sick of seeing and touching
Both sides of things
Sick of being the damn bridge for everybody

Nobody
Can talk *to* anybody
Without me
Right?

I explain my mother to my father my father to my little sister
My little sister to my brother my brother to the white feminists
The white feminists to the Black church folks the Black church folks
To the ex-hippies the ex-hippies to the Black separatists the
Black separatists to the artists the artists to my friends' parents . . .

Then
I've got to explain myself
To everybody

I do more translating
Than the Gawdamn U.N.

Forget it
I'm sick of it

I'm sick of filling in your gaps

Sick of being your insurance against
The isolation of your self-imposed limitations
Sick of being the crazy at your holiday dinners
Sick of being the odd one at your Sunday Brunches
Sick of being the sole Black friend to 34 individual white people

Find another connection to the rest of the world
Find something else to make you legitimate
Find some other way to be political and hip

gender-socializing agents; and this is true from the preschool years through post-secondary education. Both peers and teachers have been shown to reward gender-appropriate behavior and punish gender-inappropriate behavior. Peer pressure to conform to gender-typed be-havior is strong from preschool through ado-lescence, and children who engage in more traditional gender-role activities are more socially acceptable to peers than those who do not (Martin, 1989). The terms *sissy* and *tomboy* serve to pressure peers toward gender-role

I will not be the bridge to your womanhood
Your manhood
Your human-ness

I'm sick of reminding you not to
Close off too tight for too long
I'm sick of mediating with your worst self
On behalf of your better selves

I am sick
Of having to remind you
To breathe
Before you suffocate
Your own fool self

Forget it
Stretch or drown
Evolve or die

The bridge I must be
Is the bridge to my own power
I must translate
My own fears
Mediate
My own weaknesses

I must be the bridge to nowhere
But my true self
And then
I will be useful.

Source: From *This Bridge Called My Back: Writings by Radical Women of Color,* xxi–xxii, edited by Cherríe Moraga and Gloria Anzaldua. © 1981 Donna Kate Rushin. Reprinted by permission

conformity. Not surprisingly, given the greater status of males in U.S. society, a sissy is viewed considerably more negatively than a tomboy (Martin, 1990). Even the instructional materials used in schools depict females and males differently. From elementary school through college, males dominate the curricula and the textbooks (Ferree and Hall, 1990; Schau and Scott, 1984). The material presented continues to depict sexist attitudes and beliefs, thus disseminating stereotypes.

Gender segregation, that is, girls grouping with girls and boys grouping with boys, begins in the preschool years and increases through adolescence. Same-gender grouping seems to be an outcome of the differential status of females and males in societies, and males are particularly intent on dissociating themselves from females in societies where the higher status and better treatment of men is most blatant (Whiting and Edwards, 1988). It appears that the give-and-take between girls and boys favors boys in group interactions. For example, girls offer help to both girls and boys, while boys rarely offer help to girls (Lockheed, 1985). As a result of this sex segregation, girls and boys grow up in different subcultures and the subcultures support the process of gender socialization. The role of peer groups in gender socialization intensifies in the adolescent years (Donelson, 1999).

The Gender Socialization of African American Girls

Studies suggest that the socialization of African American children is less likely to reinforce gender stereotypes as prescribed by the larger society than that of white children. Both African American females and males are encouraged toward independence, employment, and child care (Bardwell et al., 1986; Hale-Benson, 1986). Large discrepancies in power and status between girls and boys are more infrequent among African American children than white children due to the combined influence of the upbringing of African American girls, which promotes competence and decisiveness, and the relative absence of gender stereotyping (Chisholm, 2000). In a study of African American preschoolers, the elimination of conventional roles in childrearing was found to be related to higher achievement (Carr and Mednick, 1988).

The "ideal" woman described by black women and black men is more independent than the "ideal" woman described by white women and white men (Crovitz and Steinmann, 1980). More African American women than white women are heads of households. The socialization of African American girls is a preparation for these realities of adult life. This is particularly true among those living in poverty. Joyce Ladner's (1971) study of African American girlhood suggests that, unlike white middle-class girls, black girls in urban ghetto environments develop emotional stability, strength, and self-reliance early in life in order to cope with harsh conditions. Ladner also points out that poor African American girls are given a great deal of responsibility and independence at a young age and are more likely to spend time in peer groups without adult supervision at a younger age than are their white counterparts. Hill (2001) found that black families embrace African and American practices simultaneously and teach honesty, academic success, and family responsibility to their children.

In reviews of the research on the work patterns and gender roles of African American women, Janice Porter Gump (1975) notes that African American girls grow up with the expectation of working; it is an integral and accepted part of African American identity. Although many African American women's attitudes about marriage, children, and gender roles are traditional, work and motherhood are not seen as incompatible. According to Gump, intelligent, competent African American women are more attractive and less threatening to African American men than are similar white women to white men. African American women express greater feelings of competence and self-confidence than do white women. This is consistent with the evidence suggesting that African Americans hold less polarized gender-role stereotypes and have more equalitarian childrearing practices (Lewis, 1975).

The Gender Socialization of Asian American Girls

In contrast to African Americans, among Asian Americans, the split between the "ideal" woman and man has traditionally been quite extreme and girls are often taught from birth to be subservient to men. While Asian culture encourages affiliation, altruism, adaptability, and timidity for women and men, women are particularly discouraged from acquiring such traits as activism, independence, and competitiveness (Chow, 1987). Fujitomi and Wong point out the consequences of these expectations:

> Since the image of the passive, demure Asian woman is pervasive the struggle for a positive self-identity is difficult. Within the Asian community, the family supports the development of the male's personality and aspirations, while the sister is discouraged from forming any sense of high self-esteem and individuality. (Fujitomi and Wong, 1976:236).

Although attitudes about family and gender roles are much less traditional among Asian American women today than in the past, the Asian American male is far more reluctant to make such changes than the Asian Amerian female (Chisholm, 2000).

The Gender Socialization of Latina Girls in the United States

Latino culture, too, relies on strict gender roles that serve as deterrents to women who want to venture outside of traditional gender boundaries and to the development of characteristics such as assertiveness and independence (see Mednick and Thomas, 1993, for a review of the literature on the psychology of achievement). The larger Hispanic community often perceives college-educated, career-oriented women as elitist and threatening to their male counterparts, a factor that has been shown to discourage Chicanas from breaching traditional gender roles by participating in the workforce (Gonzales, 1988). Recent research indicates that Latinas also face economic hardship because of dual minority status; however, they suffer from even more unyielding gender-role guidelines and limitations than do white or African American women. Consequently, they are subjected to barriers on all fronts: pay discrimination along with criticism from family members.

The Impact of Gender Socialization

Do differences in the treatment of girl and boy infants by their parents have any clear impact on the children's behavior or on their later lives? While we can only speculate on the long-term effects of the differential treatment of children, research strongly suggests that it influences gender behavior in children and adolescents. Many studies have found, for example, that children demonstrate gender-stereotyped behaviors and toy preferences by 18–24 months (for example, Huston, 1985; O'Brien and Huston, 1985a; Perry et al., 1984; Caldera et al., 1989). This is not surprising given the propensity of parents to encourage gender-appropriate activities in their children. The gender-role attitudes and expectations of parents do seem to have a direct link to children's gender-role conformity and self-esteem. For example, mothers who believe that boys have greater aptitude for math tend to have daughters who have lower confidence in their math abilities even when they obtain good grades in their math courses (Eccles, 1989; Eccles and Jacobs, 1986). Parents with nontraditional gender attitudes encourage less stereotypic behavior in their children, and sons tend to hold less traditional gender attitudes if their fathers do (Antill, 1987; Weisner and Wilson-Mitchell, 1990). Women are more likely to perceive women's roles as involving satisfaction and freedom of choice if their mothers are employed than if they are not (Baruch and Barnett, 1986). Lesbian mothers hold more egalitarian views about daughters and sons than do heterosexual mothers and are more likely to encourage daughters in nontraditional role expectations (Hill, 1988).

Is There a Lesbian Psychology?

Is there such a thing as a "lesbian personality"? Stereotypes about lesbians and gay men are numerous and almost always negative. Lesbians are thought to be less attractive and extroverted than heterosexual women (Dew, 1985). Lesbians are often thought to be "man-haters," inadequate women, suffering from a traumatic sexual experience, or socially and psychologically maladjusted. However, research does not indicate greater pathology among lesbians than among heterosexual women. It also does not suggest greater adjustment problems among their children (see Garnets and Kimmel, 1991; Patterson, 1994). Also, there is remarkable similarity between lesbian, gay, and heterosexual couples in the processes that regulate relationship satisfaction (Kurdek, 1994).

Terms like *butch* and *dyke* are crude and hostile labels, implying that lesbians are more like men than women or that lesbians want to be men. These are stereotypes and assumptions with no research backing. Sexual orientation is independent of gender identity or roles. The sexual politics of such references and beliefs are evident by the fact that these labels are often applied to women who fail to conform to traditional gender roles, without regard to their actual sexual orientation. This reflects the fear aroused when confronting women who do not conform to societal gender-role dictates and serves as a mechanism to maintain the status quo. As Garnets and Kimmel (1991:149) point out, "lesbians may be perceived as having greater power than heterosexual women because they live independently of men, and do not depend on men for sexual, emotional, or financial support."

A question continually posed is "Why are some people lesbian or gay?" One might as well ask "Why are some people heterosexual?" While the psychological theories cited above offer different theoretical answers to these questions, little is known about the origins of sexual orientation. One of the problems blocking greater understanding of sexual orientation is the assumption that it is bipolar: that people are either homosexual or heterosexual. Bisexuals are frequently grouped with homosexuals in research studies, contributing to the idea that sexual orientation is dichotomous (Garnets and Kimmel, 1991). Additionally, the almost exclusive focus on sexual acts in analyses of sexual orientation blocks more complex understanding: it ignores the distinctions among such things as lifestyle, attraction, fantasies, and identification. An individual may be "heterosexual" in one of these areas and "homosexual" in another. Garnets and Kimmel prefer the terms *homophilia* and *heterophilia* because they emphasize love (*philia*) and suggest that these are two parallel continuums and that an individual may be high in one and low in the other, high in both, or low in both.

> A complex set of factors interact, varying from individual to individual, to produce lesbian and gay adults. Likewise, the gay male and lesbian community is diverse and multiethnic and differs by gender [and] socioeconomic status, and few generalizations apply across cultural borders. (Garnets and Kimmel 1991:174)

Additionally, sexual orientation is not always stable and may change over the life span, although lesbian and gay sexual orientation is generally established during adolescence (see Table 4.3). Multiple factors, including cultural, historical, and psychosocial ones, influence one's sexuality.

Nonetheless, lesbians (and gay men) do have different experiences than heterosexual women (and men). Many of these result from the hostile treatment they encounter in a homophobic society: lesbians and gay men may be subject to hate crimes, victimization, and verbal abuse, all factors which have negative consequences for mental health (Herek, 1991). Even heterosexuals who are not overtly hostile often bring stereotyped attitudes and treat lesbians differently, for example, avoiding contact or judging them negatively (see Kite, 1994). As a result, lesbians may choose to "pass" as heterosexuals (see Greene, 1994). Lesbians may avoid acknowledging sexual orientation to family members and friends for fear of evoking disappointment, rejection, misunderstanding, and loss of support and to coworkers and neighbors for fear of job and housing discrimination, respectively.

While passing as heterosexual may be practical in that there is overt and subtle discrimination against lesbians and gays, it has its problems (Greene, 1994a). Passing can put up a barrier to intimacy and closeness between lesbians and others, causing feelings of isolation and making it more difficult to identify a community of other lesbians for support and emotional relationships. Pretending to be something one is not can create personal identity conflicts. *Coming out*, that is, accepting one's lesbian or gay identity and revealing it to other people, is related to psychological adjustment. Lesbians and gays with a positive homosexual identity have fewer depressive, neurotic, and anxious symptoms and higher self-esteem than do those with a less positive identity (Savin-Williams, 1989).

While white lesbians confront both sexism and heterosexism in their daily lives, lesbians of color face what Beverly Greene calls "*triple jeopardy*"—sexism, racism, and homophobia. "Just as the experience of sexism is 'colored' by the lens of race and ethnicity for women of color, so is the experience of heterosexism similarly filtered for lesbian women of color" (Greene, 1994b). The particular meaning and value of family, gender roles, and community held by a cultural and ethnic group is imposed upon one's attitudes and responses to lesbianism. For racially oppressed groups, lesbianism may seem like a betrayal of the ethnic community. Among African Americans and Native Americans, for example, reproductive sexuality may be viewed as contributing to the survival of a group subject to racist genocidal attempts (Kanuha, 1990).

Immigrant lesbians may be more dependent on their families and local ethnic communities because of separation from their homeland, family members, and friends. They may have difficulty identifying lesbian communities as well as lesbians within their ethnic groups. In some ethnic minority groups, such as Asian American and Latino, lesbians may be "invisible" because of the rigidly held traditional gender-role beliefs (Donelson, 1999).

In spite of the negative attitudes held by the dominant culture, lesbians and gay men have adopted strategies to cope with oppression and to manage their lives and differences from the mainstream. Lesbian communities provide support and encourage a positive group and individual identity, enabling individuals to form a positive sense of self and self-esteem. As a result of the feminist movement, which has challenged traditional ideas about sexuality and gender, lesbianism became more visible and, increasingly, is viewed not as abnormal but as "*normatively different*" (Brown, 1989).

Lesbians are a diverse group. While lesbians may be grouped into a category based on some limited criteria of sexuality, homosexual women are as different from one another as are heterosexual women. However, lesbians have more in common with heterosexual women than they do with gay men. Some lesbians adhere to rather traditional roles and beliefs, while others explore nontraditional options. Nonetheless, the rejection of a heterosexual lifestyle allows many lesbians to experiment with more androgynous gender-role behaviors and to develop relationships in which the two partners are more equal in power, decision making, and role responsibilities.

Women and Aging

Why do so many women seem much more concerned with signs of aging than do men? With the loss of women's reproductive and active parenting roles, Western cultures devalue their worth. Indeed, in the United States and elsewhere, elderly women are devalued considerably more than elderly men, who gain status from experience and, perhaps, even power as they age. For women, however, the value of youth and physical attractiveness, as well as the emphasis on reproductive functioning, diminishes the respect and value granted them as they get older, which may have consequences for women's attitudes, motivations, and feelings of self-esteem. The devaluation of older women is not universal however. In other cultures, older women are often respected, viewed as wise, consulted on community and family decisions, and allowed to participate in events barred for younger women.

Despite the general devaluation of older women in U.S. society, there is a great deal of variation in how women react to aging: personal responses to the process are usually the result of a complex set of circumstances—physical health, social realities, and a sense of psychological well-being. In each case, the messages an older woman receives from her culture and those with whom she interacts can make a significant difference in how smoothly she ages. It is a matter of whether aging comes to mean the shutting down of possibilities or new and different opportunities for self-expression. Many older women experience the benefits of increased self-confidence tied to the emotional and economic independence that comes with paid employment. Life for many women continues to be exciting and fulfilling after the age of 40, 50, 60, and 70 years. These women often undertake new interests and endeavors and may be involved more intensely in social interactions or in a number of community interests (see Lott, 1987). Middle-aged and older women, provided that they are economically stable and in good health, report looking forward to satisfying experiences provided by work, sociability, travel, and study.

Two age-related events that have generally been thought to negatively affect women's personalities, moods, and behaviors and to cause depression are menopause and the occurrence of the "empty nest," when a woman's children grow up and leave home. Some women do suffer emotional distress during menopause (see Chapter 11), but studies of menopausal and postmenopausal women indicate that most women do not view menopause as a stressful or even a very important event in their lives (for example, Black and Hill, 1984). "Contrary to assumptions . . . menopause is rarely a crisis to women. There is more dread in the anticipation than difficulty in the experience; and, far from being upset at the loss of an important biological function, most women feel relief to have it behind them" (Rossi, 1980:285). In a cross-cultural study of women's behavioral changes at menopause, Joyce Griffen (1979) notes that in some cultures there are no associated behavioral changes; in others, postmenopausal women are granted special privileges and status; and in still others, there are negative attitudes toward menopause and associated emotional conflicts. After reviewing the literature on these cultures, she suggests that "the magnitude of symptoms associated with menopause is positively correlated with the paucity of roles (or of availability of demeaning roles only) available to the postmenopausal woman" (Griffen, 1979:493).

Research also provides little support for the idea that the "empty nest" causes distress in most women. Indeed, studies suggest that once children have left the home marital happiness increases and women experience less depression than those whose children remain at home (Donelson, 1999). Again, however, there is variation: in her research on depression in older hospitalized women, Pauline Bart (1971) found that women who embrace the traditional feminine role and norms are more prone to depressive reactions when their children leave. This might also explain her finding that black women were less likely to have depressive reactions in middle age than white women. It is not surprising that women who have developed few extrafamilial activities and interests and whose lives have been extremely child-centered are more likely to experience distress at the departure of children (Lehr, 1984).

Widowhood is another stress women are likely to experience in the later years. Loneliness is one of the greatest difficulties widows confront. However, this is less problematic for women who have social and familial support (McGloshen and O'Bryant, 1988). Research suggests that men have more difficulty dealing with the loss of a spouse than do women (Stroebe and Stroebe, 1983). This may be because women are more effective at maintaining social networks. Women's acclimation to spousal loss is noteworthy in light of the fact that widowhood most often carries with it the additional burden of economic distress, which is less the case for men.

Women and men do change later in life, often becoming more alike. Research indicates that both women and men become more androgynous, demonstrating both "feminine" and "masculine" psychological characteristics. Women in the United States and other societies display more independence and assertive behaviors and men demonstrate more nurtu-rance and feelings of affiliation as they get older.

Psychology and Culture: Implications for Feminism

In the last decade or so, one particular model of psychology has come to dominate explanations of men's and women's behavior in U.S. popular culture: self-help discourse. This has led to a virtual therapeutization of U.S. society in which self-help explanations have infiltrated into many areas of public life, displacing other models through which human behavior has been understood. For example, the success of the Clinton–Gore ticket in the presidential election of 1992 was explained by Naomi Wolf in these terms: Clinton's threat to fathers who failed to pay child support and Gore's story of his political conversion in the face of his son's near-death accident allied these candidates with a "kind of therapeutic family democracy both at home and nationwide" (Wolf, 1992:24). Richard Weissbourd (1992) suggested a similar basis for Clinton's appeal to voters, noting that Clinton's biographical film, featured at the Democratic convention, was what helped him win the election. It aligned Clinton not with the abandoning father but with the abused child and suggested that, because of this experience, Clinton himself would be the kind of father/president who would not abdicate his responsibilities to his children/ constituents. Court dramas in the 1990s, like that of the Menendez brothers, who murdered their parents, or Lorena Bobbitt, who cut off her husband's penis, also showed the infusion of therapeutic models into new arenas: in these cases, what once may have been primarily understood as criminal behavior in need of punishment or rehabilitation, now came to be widely seen as a pathology in need of a cure (see Mascia-Lees and Sharpe, 2000).

Many feminists have been wary of self-help discourse because it depoliticizes women's circumstances (see especially Kaminer, 1992). It draws focus away from political and structural inequalities and instead instructs the individual to find a "cure" for her or his ills through giving up control by submitting to a higher power, whether God explicitly or an ideal of authority manifest in a self-help group and its program for "recovery." Self-help's prescription for changing the "dysfunctional" U.S. society is to encourage people to change themselves, not to take action in the world.

Feminists have also pointed to the dangers inherent in the way self-help discourse allows individuals to deny responsibility for their own problematic behavior. For example, in the conceptual framework of self-help, abusers are encouraged to envision themselves as a wounded inner child encased in an unfeeling false persona. It is this exterior identity that is thought to be prey to addiction and guilty of abuse, whether of substances or people, while the "true" self is seen as innocent and pure. All abusive behavior is interpreted as itself a product of some sort of victimization of the perpetrator long in the past when he or she was a defenseless child. The victimizer is invited to identify with the powerlessness of those he or she has wronged and to see himself or herself as a victim. In such a model, distinguishing victims from perpetrators becomes merely a matter of perspective (Kaminer, 1992:153). It denies the degrees of injustice experienced not only by women in comparison to men but also by people of color in comparison to whites.

Summary

The nature of the female mind and women's mental capabilities and psychological makeup have been the focus of speculation for a wide array of theorists over the centuries. Explanations for women's supposed psychological differences from men are usually explained in terms of either biology (nature) or the effect of the social environment in which children are reared (nurture). Much of the research into female and male differences is affected by the biases of the researchers. Nonetheless, there is little research substantiation for most presumed differences. When differences are found, they vary among women and within the same woman at different times and in different contexts.

Biological differences, psychodynamic theories, and socialization practices have all been used to explain why women and men differ. Strictly biological explanations refer to genetically derived factors, such as hormones, which may influence behavior and emotions. Evolutionary psychology assumes that there are differences in male and female behaviors and psychological traits and then offer scenarios for how these may have been selected in the course of human evolution. Such theories are fundamentally untestable and often based on cultural assumptions, rather than on scientific data, about men's and women's behaviors.

According to psychodynamic theories, females and males develop different personality structures as a result of early childhood experiences with their caretakers and identification with the same-sex parent. Traditional psychodynamic theory, psychoanalytical theory, founded by Sigmund Freud, proposes that sexual drives start playing a key role in gender personality development at age 3. Freud attributed many developmental consequences, including a sense of inferioritiy, to girls's "penis envy." Males, in contrast, were said to struggle with "castration anxiety."

Freud's theories have been criticized both within and outside of psychodynamic schools of thought. Psychoanalysts Karen Horney and Clara Thompson stressed the role of social–cultural factors, such as economic and social dependence on men, in the development of a female personality and suggested that men's envy of women may account for misogyny and the oppression of women. Feminist psychodynamic explanations, such as Nancy Chodorow's analysis of the impact of female caretakers on gender-role development or Jean Baker Miller's self-in-relation theory, offer alternative perspectives on female development. Other psychoanalytical feminists draw on the reformulation of Freud's theories by Lacan, who focused on the role language plays in the development of subjectivity.

Cognitive–developmental theory holds that girls and boys feel internal needs as well as external pressures to conform to a gender-appropriate identity and role. Social learning theory gives greater weight to external factors, such as the reward of gender-appropriate behavior and the punishment of cross-gender behavior.

Sandra Bem proposes a gender schema theory, which incorporates cognitive, child-rearing, and cultural factors to explain the development of gender identity and roles. Other theories place greater emphasis on social roles and explain gender-typed behaviors as primarily a function of gender-differentiated role assignments and expectations and the unequal distribution of power between females and males.

All societies teach their young culturally prescribed gender roles. Parents and peers are powerful socializing agents, but gender expectations are communicated in many different ways. Television, school, books, clothing, toys, even fairy tales operate as socializing agents. Parents, particularly fathers, encourage different behaviors in girls and boys. Teachers have different expectations and responses to female and male students from the preschool through the postsecondary levels.

Evidence indicates that the experience of growing up in different cultures is quite varied. Even within the United States, the socialization experiences differ among ethnic and cultural groups. Women of color in the United States confront a "double jeopardy"—racism and sexism—and these experiences contribute to their socialization.

Lesbians are subject to a range of hostile and unsubstantiated stereotypes. They are exposed to homophobic and heterosexist beliefs and discrimination and struggle with the consequences of openly acknowledging their sexual orientation. The lesbian and gay rights movements, the women's movement, and the visibility of lesbian social communities have facilitated the development of a positive lesbian identity, which is related to more positive mental health. Lesbians, freed from expectations of emotional and social dependence on men, are freer to explore nontraditional roles. Lesbian couples are more likely to have role equality in their relationships.

In Western cultures, older women are devalued because of the emphasis placed on women's reproductive roles and physical attractiveness. There are many negative stereotypes about older women, such as asexuality, hypochondria, and menopausal depression. Experience of the older years of life is a result of many factors, including health, financial status, and support systems. For many older women, the later years are a time of increased self-confidence and new interests and activities. Both women and men tend to become more autonomous in the later years. In many cultures, older women are respected, viewed as wise, and consulted on community and family decisions.

In the last decade or so in U.S. popular culture, self-help discourse has come to dominate explanations of men's and women's behavior. Feminists have been wary of self-help discourse because it depoliticizes women's circumstances.

Discussion Questions

1. List three differences between girls/women and boys/men that have been reported in research. These can be differences in personality, skills, or conduct. What kinds of contrasting explanation can you give for them? Which do you find most convincing and why?

2. Most psychological theory tends to focus attention on the formation of personality in the younger years. What questions should be explored with regard to mature women?

3. Theories of personality development offer different explanations for gender identity and gender roles. What experiences did you have as a child that shaped your gender-role behaviors and attitudes? Explain these from two or three different theoretical positions. Are they consistent with the research on gender-role socialization, or do they contradict it?

4. Review some popular children's fairy tales or stories, such as *Cinderella, Jack in the Bean Stalk*, or *Sleeping Beauty*, and discuss how girls and boys are portrayed. How might these operate to socialize girls' and boys' attitudes and behaviors? Similarly, analyze the depiction of females and males in popular television programs. Give particular attention to the gender, ethnicity, class, and age of the characters. Are heterosexist assumptions apparent in the show?

Recommended Readings

Chesler, Phyllis. *Women and Madness*. New York: Four Walls Eight Windows, 1997. Chesler explores mental illness in women as a cultural phenomenon reflecting sexist standards and pressures on women.

Chodorow, Nancy. *The Reproduction of Mothering: Psychoanalysis and the Sociology of Gender*. Berkeley: University of California Press, 1978. Employing psychoanalytical principles, Chodorow develops an original thesis showing how the traditional family structure, in which women have the primary responsibility for child care and nurturing, shapes female (and male) development and results in the generational reproduction of gender roles.

Denmark, Florence L., Vita Rabinowitz, and Jeri Sechzer. *Engendering Psychology: Bringing Women into Focus*. Boston: Allyn and Bacon, 2000. This comprehensive text applies a feminist theoretical framework to the psychology of women and gender. It is attentive to issues of diversity and thorough in its exploration of the issues, research, and perspectives in the field.

Mead, Margaret. *Coming of Age in Samoa*. New York: Morrow, 1928.

———. *Sex and Temperament in Three Primitive Societies*. New York: Dell, 1935.

———. *Male and Female: A Study of the Sexes in a Changing World*. New York: Dell, 1949. These three books by anthropologist Margaret Mead are pioneer works in the cultural relativity of gender roles and the way in which social structures shape female and male personalities according to the demands of society.

Modleski, Tania. *Loving with a Vengeance: Mass-Produced Fantasies for Women*. New York: Routledge, 1982. An insightful exploration of the appeal of "mass-produced fantasies" for women: Harlequin romances, Gothic novels, and television soap operas.

Rose, Hilary, and Steven Rose. *Alas, Poor Darwin: Arguments Against Evolutionary Psychology*. New York: Harmony Books, 2000. This collection of essays by leading biologists, psychologists, and philosophers presents an engaging and accessible critique of evolutionary psychology's basic ideas and an alternative view of humankind and gender difference.

Simmons, Rachel. *Odd Girl Out: The Hidden Culture of Aggression in Girls*. New York:

Harcourt Brace, 2002. This book questions the stereotype of girls as the kinder, gentler gender and provides evidence that because girls are raised not to express anger overtly, they instead develop "a hidden culture of silent and indirect aggression" that can be devastating for its targets.

References

Aberle, David F., and Kasper D. Naegele. Middle-class father's occupational role and attitudes toward children. *American Journal of Orthopsychiatry*, 22, 366–78, 1952.

Antill, John K. Parents' beliefs and values about sex roles, sex differences, and sexuality: Their sources and implications. In *Sex and Gender*, edited by P. Shaver and C. Hendrick. Newbury Park, CA: Sage, 1987.

Bandura, Albert. Influence of models' reinforcement contingencies on the acquisition of imitative responses. *Journal of Personality and Social Psychology*, 1, 589–95, 1965.

Bardwell, Jill R., Samuel W. Cochran, and Sharon Walker. Relationship of parental education, race, and gender to sex role stereotyping in five-year-old kindergarteners. *Sex Roles*, 15, 275–81, 1986.

Bart, Pauline B. Depression in middle-aged women. In *Women in Sexist Society: Studies in Power and Powerlessness*, edited by Vivian Gornick and Barbara Moran. New York: Basic Books, 1971.

Baruch, Grace K., and Rosalind C. Barnett. Fathers' participation in family work and children's sex-role attitudes. *Child Development*, 57, 1210–23, 1986.

Basow, Susan A. *Gender Stereotypes and Roles*, 3rd ed. Pacific Grove, CA: Brooks/Cole, 1992.

Bem, Sandra L. Gender schema theory: a cognitive account of sex typing. *Psychological Review*, 88, 354–64, 1981.

———. Gender schema theory and its implications for child development: Raising gender-aschematic children in a gender-schematic society. *Signs*, 8, 598–616, 1983.

———. Androgyny and gender schema theory: A conceptual and empirical integration. In *Nebraska Symposium on Motivation, 1984: Psychology and Gender*, edited by T. B. Sonderegger. Lincoln: University of Nebraska Press, 1985.

Bigler, R. S., and Lynn S. Liben. The role of attitudes and interventions in gender-schematic processing. *Child Development*, 61, 1440–52, 1990.

Black, S. M., and Hill, C. E. The psychological well-being of women in their middle years. *Psychology of Women Quarterly*, 8, 282–92, 1984.

Brown, Laura S. New voices, new visions: Toward a lesbian/gay paradigm for psychology. *Psychology of Women*, 13, 445–58, 1989.

Burns, A., and R. Homel. Gender division of tasks by parents and their children. *Psychology of Women Quarterly*, 13, 113–25, 1989.

Caldera, Yvonne M., Aletha C. Huston, and Marion O'Brien. Social interactions and play patterns of parents and toddlers with feminine, masculine, and neutral toys. *Child Development*, 60, 70–6, 1989.

Carr, Peggy G., and Martha T. Mednick. Sex role socialization and the development of achievement motivation in black preschool children. *Sex Roles*, 18, 169–80, 1988.

Chisholm, June F. Culture, ethnicity, race and class. In *Engendering Psychology: Bringing Women into Focus*, edited by Florence L. Denmark, Vita Rabinowitz, and Jeri Sechzer. Needham Heights, MA: Allyn and Bacon, 2000.

Chodorow, Nancy. *The Reproduction of Mothering: Psychoanalysis and the Sociology of Gender*. Berkeley: University of California Press, 1978.

Chow, Esther N. The influence of role identity and occupational attainment on the psychological well-being of Asian-American women. *Psychology of Women Quarterly*, 11, 69–81, 1987.

Crovitz, Elaine, and Anne Steinmann. A decade later: black–white attitudes toward women's familial roles. *Psychology of Women*, 5, 170–6, 1980.

Dawkins, Richard. *The Selfish Gene*. New York: Oxford University Press, 1976.

Deaux, Kay, and Brenda Major. Putting gender into context: An interactive model of gender-related behavior. *Psychological Review*, 94, 369–89, 1987.

Denmark, Florence L. What sigmund freud didn't know about women. Convocation address, St. Olaf's College, Northfield, MN, January 1977.

Denmark, Florence L., and Michele A. Paludi, editors. *Psychology of Women: A Handbook of Issues and Theories.* Westport, CT: Greenwood Press, 1993.

Dew, M. A. The effects of attitudes on inferences on homosexuality and perceived physical attractiveness in women. *Sex Roles,* 12, 143–55, 1985.

Dinnerstein, Dorothy. *The Mermaid and the Minotaur.* New York: Harper & Row, 1976.

Donelson, F. E. *Women's Experiences: A Psychological Perspective.* Mountain View, CA: Mayfield, 1999.

Eagly, Alice H. *Sex Differences in Social Behavior: A Social-Role Interpretation.* Hillsdale, NJ: Erlbaum, 1987.

Eagly, Alice H., and V. J. Steffen. Gender and aggressive behavior: A meta-analytic review of the social psychological literature. *Psychological Bulletin,* 100, 309–330, 1986.

Eccles, Jacqueline S. Bringing young women to math and science. In *Gender and Thought: Psychological Perspectives,* edited by M. Crawford and M. Gentry. New York: Springer-Verlag, 1989.

Eccles, Jacqueline S., and J. E. Jacobs. Social forces shape math attitudes and performance. *Signs,* 11:21, 367–80, 1986.

Erikson, Erik. *Childhood and Society.* New York: Norton, 1963.

Fagot, Beverly I., R. Hagan, M. D. Leinback, and S. Kronsberg. Differential reactions to assertive and communicative acts of toddler boys and girls. *Child Development,* 56, 1499–1505, 1985.

Ferree, M. M., and E. J. Hall. Visual images of american society: Gender and race in introductory sociology textbooks. *Gender and Society,* 4, 500–33, 1990.

Fivush, R. Exploring sex differences in the emotional content of mother-child conversations about the past. *Sex Roles,* 20, 675–91, 1989.

Fliegel, Zenia. Half a century later: Current status of freud's controversial views of women.

Paper presented at the American Psychological Association Conference, Montreal, Canada, 1980.

Freud, Sigmund. Some psychological consequences of the anatomical distinction between the sexes. *International Journal of Psychoanalysis,* 8, 133–43, 1925.

Fujitomi, Irene, and Diane Wong. The new Asian-American woman. In *Female Psychology: The Emerging Self,* edited by Sue Cox. Chicago: Science Research Associates, 1976.

Garnets, Linda, and Douglas Kimmel. Lesbian and gay male dimensions in the psychological study of human diversity. In *Psychological Perspectives on Human Diversity in America,* edited by J. Goodchilds. Washington, DC: American Psychological Association, 1991.

Gonzales, J. T. Dilemmas of the high-achieving chicano: The double-blind factor in male-female relationships. *Sex Roles,* 18, 367–80, 1988.

Goodnow, J. J. Children's household work: Its nature and functions. *Psychological Bulletin,* 103, 5–26, 1988.

Greene, Beverly L. Lesbian and gay sexual orientations: Implications for clinical training, practice, and research. In *Lesbian and Gay Psychology: Theory, Research, and Clinical Applications,* edited by B. Greene and G. M. Herek. Thousand Oaks, CA: Sage, 1994a.

———. Lesbian women of color: Triple jeopardy. In *Women of Color and Mental Health,* edited by L. Comas-Diaz and B. Greene. New York: Guilford Press, 1994b.

Griffen, Joyce. A cross-cultural investigation of behavioral changes at menopause. In *Psychology of Women,* edited by Juanita Williams. New York: Norton, 1979.

Gump, Janice Porter. A comparative analysis of black and white women's sex role attitudes. *Journal of Consulting and Clinical Psychology,* 43, 858–63, 1975.

Hale-Benson, Janice E. *Black children: Their roots, culture, and learning styles,* revised ed. Provo, UT: Brigham Young University Press, 1986.

Henley, Nancy M. *Body Politics: Power, Sex, and Nonverbal Communication.* Englewood Cliffs, NJ: Prentice-Hall, 1977.

Herek, Gregory M. Stigma, prejudice, and violence against lesbians and gay men. In *Homosexuality: Research Findings for Public Policy*, edited by J. C. Gonriorek and J. D. Weinrich. Newbury Park, CA: Sage, 1991.

Hill, Marjorie. Child rearing attitudes of black lesbian mothers. In *Lesbian Psychologies: Explorations and Challenges*, edited by Boston Lesbian Psychologies Collective. Urbana: University of Illinois Press, 1988.

Hill, Shirley. Class, race, and gender dimensions of child rearing in African American families. *Journal of Black Studies*, 31:4, 494–508, 2001.

Horney, Karen. Flight from womanhood: The masculinity complex in women. *International Journal of Psychoanalysis*, 7, 324–39, 1926.

———. *New Ways in Psychoanalysis*. New York: Norton, 1939.

———. On the genesis of castration complex in women (1922). In *Psychoanalysis and Women* edited by Jean Baker Miller. New York: Brunner/Mazei, 1973.

Huston, Athea C. The development of sex-typing: Themes from recent research. *Developmental Reviews*, 5, 1–17, 1985.

Jacklin, Carol N., J. A. DiPietro, and Eleanor E. Maccoby. Sex-typing behavior and sex-typing pressure in child/parent interaction. *Archives of Sexual Behavior*, 13:5, 413–25, 1984.

Kaminer, Wendy. *I'm Dysfunctional, You're Dysfunctional: The Recovery Movement and Other Self-Help Fashions*. Reading, MA: Addison-Wesley, 1992.

Kanuha, Valli. Compounding the triple jeopardy: Battering in lesbian of color relationships. *Women and Therapy*, 9, 169–83, 1990.

Katz, Phyllis A., Ann Boggiano, and Louise Silvern. Theories of female personality. In *Psychology of Women: A Handbook of Issues and Theories*, edited by F. L. Denmark and M. A. Paludi. Westport, CT: Greenwood Press, 1993.

Kite, Mary E. When perceptions meet reality: Individual differences in reactions to lesbian and gay men. In *Lesbian and Gay Psychology: Theory, Research, and Clinical Applications*, edited by B. Greene and G. M. Herek. Thousand Oaks, CA: Sage, 1994.

Kohlberg, Lawrence. A cognitive-developmental analysis of children's sex-role concepts and attitudes. In *The Development of Sex Differences*, edited by E. E. Maccoby. Stanford, CA: Stanford University Press, 1966.

Kohlberg, Lawrence, and Dora Z. Ullian. Stages in the development of psychosexual concepts and attitudes. In *Sex Differences in Behavior*, edited by R. C. Friedman, R. M. Richard, and R. L. Vande Wiele. New York: Wiley, 1974.

Kohlberg, Lawrence, and Edward Zigler. The impact of cognitive maturity on the development of sex-role attitudes in the years 4–8. *Genetic Psychology Monographs*, 75, 89–165, 1967.

Kurdek, Lawrence A. The nature and correlates of relationship quality in gay, lesbian, and heterosexual cohabiting couples: A test of the individual difference, interdependence, and discrepancy models. In *Lesbian and Gay Psychology: Theory, Research, and Clinical Applications*, edited by B. Greene and G. M. Herek. Thousand Oaks, CA: Sage, 1994.

Ladner, Joyce. *Tomorrow's Tomorrow: The Black Woman*. New York: Doubleday, 1971.

Leaper, Campbell, Kristin Anderson, and Paul Sanders. Moderators of gender effects on parents' talk to their children: A meta-analysis. *Developmental Psychology*, 34, 3–27, 1998.

Lehr, Ursula. The role of women in the family generation context. In *Intergenerational Relationships*, edited by V. Garms-Homolova, E. M. Hoerning, and D. Schaeffer. Lewiston, NY: C. J. Hogrefe, 1984.

Lewis, Diane K. The black family: Socialization and sex roles. *Phylon*, 36, 221–27, 1975.

Lips, Hilary. *Sex and Gender: An Introduction*. Mountain View, CA: Mayfield, 2001.

Liss, Martha B. *Social and Cognitive Skills: Sex Roles and Children's Play*. New York: Academic Press, 1983.

Lockheed, Marlaine E. Sex and social influence: A meta-analysis guided by theory. In *Status, Relations, and Rewards*, edited by J. Berger and M. Zeldich. San Francisco: Jossey-Bass, 1985.

Lott, Bernice L. *Women's Lives: Themes and Variations in Gender Learning.* Monterey, CA: Brooks/Cole, 1987.

Lytton, Hugh, and David M. Romney. Parents' differential socialization of boys and girls: A meta-analysis. *Psychological Bulletin*, 109, 267–96, 1991.

MacKinnon, Catharine A. *Feminism Unmodified: Discourses on Life and Law.* Cambridge, MA: Harvard University Press, 1987.

Martin, Carol L. Children's use of gender-related information in making social judgments. *Developmental Psychology*, 25, 80–8, 1989.

———. Attitudes and expectations about children with nontraditional and traditional gender roles. *Sex Roles*, 22, 151–65, 1990.

Mascia-Lees, Frances E., and Patricia Sharpe. Self-help Hollywood-style: Masculinity, masochism, and identification with the child within. In *Taking a Stand in a Postfeminist World: Toward an Engaged Cultural Criticism.* New York: SUNY Press, 2000.

McGloshen, Thomas H., and Shirley L. O'Bryant. The psychological well-being of older, recent widows. *Psychology of Women Quarterly*, 12, 99–116, 1988.

Mead, Margaret. *Sex and Temperament in Three Primitive Societies.* New York: Morrow, 1935.

———. *Male and Female: A Study of the Sexes in a Changing World.* New York: Dell, 1949.

Meadow, Susannah. Meet the gamma girls. *Newsweek*, June 3, 2002, 44–50.

Mednick, Martha T., and Veronica G. Thomas. Women and the psychology of achievement: A view from the eighties. In *Psychology of Women: A Handbook of Issues and Theories*, edited by F. L. Denmark and M. A. Paludi. Westport, CT: Greenwood Press, 1993.

Miller, Jean Baker. The development of women's sense of self. In *Work in Progress, Stone Center Working Paper Series 12*, Wellesley, MA: Stone Center, 1984.

Mitchell, Juliet. *Psychoanalysis and Feminism.* New York: Random House, 1974.

Mitchell, Juliet, and Jacqueline Rose. *Jacques Lacan and the École Freudienne: Feminine Sexuality*, translated by Jacqueline Rose. London: Macmillan, 1982.

Modleski, Tania. *Loving with a Vengeance: Mass-Produced Fantasies for Women.* New York: Routledge, 1982.

Money, John, and Anke Ehrhardt. *A Man and Woman, Boy and Girl.* Baltimore: Johns Hopkins University Press, 1972.

Moraga, Cherrie. La guera. In *This Bridge Called My Back*, edited by C. Moraga and G. Anzaldua. Watertown, MA: Persephone Press, 1981.

Nieto-Gomez, Anna. Heritage of la hembra. In *Female Psychology: The Emerging Self*, edited by Sue Cox. Chicago: Science Research Associates, 1976.

O'Brien, Marion, and Aletha C. Huston. Development of sex-typed play in toddlers. *Developmental Psychology*, 21, 866–71, 1985a.

———. Activity level and sex stereotyped toy choice in toddler boys and girls. *Journal of Genetic Psychology*, 146, 527–34, 1985b.

Patterson, Charlotte J. Children of the lesbian baby boom: Behavioral adjustment, self-concepts, and sex role identity. In *Lesbian and Gay Psychology: Theory, Research, and Clinical Applications*, edited by B. Greene and G. M. Herek. Thousand Oaks, CA: Sage, 1994.

Perry, David G., Adam J. White, and Louise C. Perry. Does early sex-typing result from children's attempts to match their behavior to sex role stereotypes? *Child Development*, 55, 2114–21, 1984.

Riviere, Joan. Womanliness as masquerade. In *Formations of Fantasy*, edited by V. Burgin, J. Donald and C. Kaplan. New York: Methuen, 1986.

Rose, Robert M., Thomas P. Gordon, and Irwin S. Bernstein. Plasma testosterone levels in the male rhesus: Influences of sexual and social stimuli. *Science*, 178, 643–45, 1972.

Rossi, Alice S. Aging and parenthood in the middle years. In *Life-Span Development and Behavior*, vol. 3, edited by P. B. Baltes and O. G. Brim, Jr. New York: Academic Press, 1980.

Rubin, Jeffrey, Frank J. Provenzano, and Zella Luria. The eye of the beholder: Parents' views on sex of newborns. *American Journal of Orthopsychiatry*, 4, 353–63, 1974.

Ruble, Thomas L. Sex stereotypes: Issues of change in the 1970s. *Sex Roles*, 9, 397–402, 1983.

Rushin, Donna K. The bridge poem. In *This Bridge Called My Back*, edited by C. Moraga and G. Anzaldua. Watertown, MA: Persephone Press, 1981.

Savin-Williams, Rich. Coming out to parents and self-esteem among gay and lesbian youth. *Journal of Homosexuality*, 18, 1–35, 1989.

Schau, Candace G., and Kathryn P. Scott. Impact of gender characteristics of instructional materials: An integration of the research literature. *Journal of Educational Psychology*, 76, 183–193, 1984.

Seavey, Carol A., Phyllis A. Katz, and Sue Rosenberg Zalk. Baby X: The effect of gender labels on adult responses to infants. *Sex Roles*, 1, 103–9, 1975.

Silvern, Louise, and Phyllis A. Katz. Gender roles and adjustment in elementary-school children: A multidimensional approach. *Sex Roles*, 14, 181–202, 1986.

Simmons, Rachel. *Odd Girl Out: The Hidden Culture of Aggression in Girls*. New York: Harcourt Brace, 2002.

Stroebe, Margaret S., and Wolfgang Stroebe. Who suffers more: Sex differences in health risks of the widowed. *Psychological Bulletin*, 93, 279–301, 1983.

Thompson, Clara. Cultural pressures in the psychology of women. *Psychiatry*, 5, 331–9, 1942.

———. Penis envy in women. *Psychiatry*, 6, 123–5, 1943.

Tronick, Edward Z., and Jeffrey F. Cohn. Infant–mother face-to-face interaction: Age and gender differences in ordination and the occurrence of miscoordination. *Child Development*, 60, 85–92, 1989.

Weisner, Thomas S., and Jane E. Wilson-Mitchell. Nonconventional family life-styles and sex typing in 6-year-olds. *Child Development*, 61, 1915–33, 1990.

Weissbourd, Richard. Trust fund. *New Republic*, November 9, 1992, 24–5.

West, Candace, and Don H. Zimmerman. Doing gender. *Gender and Society*, 1, 125–51, 1987.

Whiting, Beatrice B., and Carolyn P. Edwards. *Children of Different Worlds: The Formation of Social Behavior*. Cambridge, MA: Harvard University Press, 1988.

Wilson, E. O. *On Human Nature*. Cambridge, MA: Harvard University Press, 1975.

Wiseman, Rosalind. *Queen Bees & Wannabes*. New York: Crown, 2002.

Wolf, Naomi. Father figures. *New Republic*, October 5, 1992, 22, 24–5.

Wright, Elizabeth. *Lacan and Postfeminism*. Cambridge, UK: Icon Books, 2000.

Zalk, Sue Rosenberg. The re-emergence of psychosexual conflicts in expectant fathers In *Pregnancy, Birthing and Bonding*, edited by Barbara Blum. New York: Human Science Press, 1980.

———. Women's dilemma: Both envied and subjugated. Paper presented at the Third International Interdisciplinary Congress on Women, Trinity College, Dublin, Ireland, June, 1987.

chapter 5

Diversity Among Women: Gender, Race, and Class

Social Roles and the Individual

Every community assigns social roles to those within it, and the way we interact with each other ordinarily takes place within the terms of those roles. Social roles are not the same in different cultures, and they change over time. Our sense of self is affected by these social roles; it is a process negotiated throughout our lives. Pressures from family, school, community, religion, and the media continually remind us of what our culture considers gender-appropriate behavior. Gender affects what social roles we are assigned, as do age, race, ethnicity, class, sexuality, nationality, religion, and physical ability; and we take our identity from the particular configuration that describes us. Growing up a "girl" or a "boy," our experiences differ with these many different combinations and the range of our "choices" in life is shaped by them. The ways that human beings interact are shaped by the roles that they play in relation to one another. Each role consists of a set of rules or guidelines which establish what an individual is expected or required to do—and what is not expected or forbidden. All socially prescribed conduct is organized in terms of these roles. Roles may be familial (wife, mother, daughter) or occupational (teacher, salesclerk, doctor) or relate to some other social context (hostess, citizen, religious figure).

The Determinants of Role Assignment

Gender. The meaning of gender in human identity is always affected by class, race, ethnicity, religion, age, and physical ability, as well as the particular situation in which a person acts. Theoretically, however, we can think about gender as a single factor to examine how it functions in the assignment of social roles. Individuals are assigned specific roles by their societies, not on the basis of their own choice but because of the supposed attributes they possess by virtue of membership in some social category, such as gender. For example, by virtue of being identified at birth as "female," girls are assigned the roles of "daughter" and "wife," as these roles are interpreted in their society. Girls are generally taught these roles as part of their upbringing. For most of human history, women, wherever born, have rarely been given the option of rejecting these roles or of opting for a change in how they are defined. (For ways women have at times succeeded at opting out of marriage and motherhood, see below and Chapters 7 and 8.)

Societies assign most roles on the basis of gender. This classification, together with other social restrictions based on class and race, for example, in the past made it less likely that a woman would play such roles as "judge" or "ruler" or "chief executive officer"

At an early age, girls work longer and have less leisure than boys. Here, a girl in Colombia, South America, carries firewood.

of a corporation. Since the women's movement in the late 1960s, there has been erosion in the United States and elsewhere of some of these barriers, but these gains may mask underlying continuities in gender relationships. One person may be asked to play a multiplicity of roles over a lifetime, with changes occurring with age or social mobility. Within families, a woman will be a daughter at the outset of her life and always remain one, but she will then add on such roles as sister, wife, mother, or grandmother. Each role entails another script, sometimes with requirements or restrictions on behavior that will involve conflicts. The role of a daughter may sometimes conflict with that of a wife, in terms of loyalties and duties to parents and husband. Many other roles will be piled on to these: a sister, wife, or mother may also be an office manager, a community organizer, and a church

volunteer. She may also act as a hostess, a plaintiff in a court case, a volunteer health-care worker, and a lover. Some roles seem at times to be mutually exclusive. Dependent upon the script of class, race, ethnicity, or religion, for example, being a wife and mother has been deemed to be in conflict with working outside the home for wages or taking any public role. The role of gender is clear in differentially affecting how women and men experience their roles, for being a husband and father has never been deemed to conflict with such roles.

The roles to which people are assigned on the basis of attributes like gender and age are also associated with social status. Social status is an expression of a person's rights and entitlements or power and influence over others. We play certain roles because of the social status—high or low—to which we are assigned, and we are often assigned to a particular status because of the value which society places on our roles. Our status is reflected in the privileges bestowed on us or of which we are deprived by society. For example, being a chief executive officer of a large corporation is a high-status occupation in economically developed countries; it entitles the person who plays it to a high salary, which in turn makes it likely that the person will be able to own a large and comfortable residence, take luxurious vacations, and employ workers to perform a variety of domestic tasks. Being a domestic worker, by contrast, is a low-status occupation, which entitles the person playing it to a low salary and denies the opportunity to own a large and comfortable home, take luxurious vacations, or employ anyone at all. Because of other role assignments and their statuses, it is more likely that the chief executive officer will be a man than a woman and that the domestic worker will be a woman than a man.

Women scholars who do research in sex-segregated societies, like anthropologist Lila Abu-Lughod, who lived with the Bedouin in the Egyptian Western Desert in the late 1970s, note that, as women, they have more access to the society than do male researchers. She notes that "the structure of information flow between the men's and women's worlds was not symmetrical" (Abu-Lughod, 1988:151). Alien women have access to what men do and say among themselves since in a patriarchal society they are written off as invisible, while they have full access to what women are doing and saying because they are women. In addition. Abu-Lughod found that men of lower status often supplied information about men's affairs to their mothers, aunts, grandmothers, and wives, while "a conspiracy of silence excludes men from the women's world" (Abu-Lughod, 1988:151).

Race and Class. Gender and age are not the sole determinants of who becomes a chief and who becomes a servant. Other social categories intersect with gender and age to determine which roles are open to and expected of individuals and which are denied them. Most common among these restrictive categories are class, race, ethnicity, sexual orientation, physical handicap, and religious affiliation; and these often intersect.

Taking race and class as our examples, we see that these categories are hierarchically arranged and membership in a particular group will in itself entitle an individual or disenfranchise her or him from the roles that belong to a particular social status—that is, these social categories are often in themselves the basis of discrimination. Membership in a dominant group in any society tends to entitle individuals to assume certain privileged roles which are denied to members of a subordinate group while freeing them from undesirable roles assigned to members of the subordinate group. In the United States, the person holding the position of chief executive officer of a corporation is most likely not only male but also white; his domestic employee, on the other hand, is just as likely to be a woman of color.

However, and this is a very important point, if the chief executive officer is a white male, his wife will probably also be white; and even though she is female, she will experience the privileges of his high status (ownership of a large and comfortable home, luxurious vacations, domestic employees) by virtue of being his wife, despite the fact that her femaleness and role as wife make it unlikely that she herself will be a chief executive officer in his corporation. Her membership in the category of "white people" makes it more likely that she will play the role of the wife of a chief executive officer than will a woman of color. (Of course, statistically, only a very few white women play this role while, conversely, some women of color play it as well, so we are speaking here only of probabilities.)

If we translate this into a Middle Eastern society, we find many examples of this phenomenon. Not surprisingly, we learn that a woman from a landed upper-class family has more power, authority, and status than a male "sharecropper." This class position is underpinned by the fact that in this region the family continues to be a significant political and economic unit. A woman's access to power in this situation comes through her male kin, who hold the primary positions of control, and the degree of her power is closer to that of her male kin than to both men and women of other classes (Aswad, 1978:473–4).

Postmodern Perspectives. Such differences resulting from the assignment of roles and status to members of society on the basis of attributes other than gender, like race and class, add major complexities to our understanding of the social meaning of gender itself. Is it possible to generalize about gender attributes and experiences across class, ethnic, racial, religious, and other social categories? How can generalizations capture the differences in gender roles that depend on such specific differences? What are the implications of our differences for our understanding of women's circumstances now and through history? As feminist scholars have pursued the study of women since the 1960s, these questions have become increasingly central to the methods employed to understand women's lives, now and in the past.

Almost from the beginning of the second wave, as the women's movement that arose in the late 1960s has been called, the issue of "difference" was raised, particularly by African American feminists who objected to descriptions of women's lives that did not acknowledge such differences as race and sexuality (Lorde, 1984; Dill, 1983; Frye, 1983; hooks, 1982; Lugones and Spelman, 1983;

Davis, 1981; Joseph and Lewis, 1981; Eisenstein and Jardine, 1980). Nancy Hartsock, for example, raised the need to look at both "difference" and "dominance," suggesting what is called "standpoint theory" to emphasize that how each of us understands the world depends on where, literally and figuratively, we stand (Hartsock, 1983:285–91). In *The Feminist Standpoint Revisited and Other Essays* (1998), Hartsock revisits that theory and emphasizes that, in her view, the historical conditions of the material life of a woman structure how she experiences it.

Postmodernist perspectives in feminist theory have also drawn our attention to the importance of difference (Tong, 1998:193–211; see also Chapter 2). Proponents of a postmodern feminist view, such as British writer Denise Riley (1988) or French writer Julia Kristeva (1997), have argued convincingly that there is no "essential woman" but, rather, a multiplicity of experiences which reflect the great diversity of lives women have led as a result of attributes other than gender. To be a British literary critic or a French lesbian feminist in Paris in the year 2005 remains quite a different experience from that of a farmer's wife in Chile or a rural Egyptian mother of six. To make a generalization which would comprehend these views solely on the basis of being women would be fairly meaningless.

Feminist scholars have deplored the misrepresentation of women found in standard literary and scholarly works, resulting from the fact that the majority of writing about women in the past has been done by men who generally assumed that their own experiences gave them sufficient information to portray accurately women's lives and views. Postmodernist scholars, in a similar way, point out that theories about women written in more recent years by women, who are themselves more likely to be urban intellectuals than landless rural mothers, are just as likely not to include in any adequate way the realities of the latter

(Alcoff, 1995). As a result, the argument goes, the lens through which women are seen and portrayed in feminist theory will continue to be distorted unless and until the significance of that difference of experience is recognized in describing the lives of women (Mohanty, 1991, 2002).

The most extreme version of this argument would claim that we can see the world only through our own experience and cannot, and should not (because it is presumptuous), generalize about the experience of all women (or men). If the problem so far lies with the tendency to "universalize" to all people on the basis of a specific life experience, the problem with a swing in the opposite position would, logically, suggest that we can understand and write about ourselves only as individuals. This would undermine efforts to reduce the oppression to which women, regardless of their differences, are subject throughout the world. A practical compromise lies in the view that we can attempt to understand others but need to learn from them as far as possible how they understand themselves. We continue to try to understand past lives and experiences of people who have left no written records of themselves. Scholars who study the past, particularly the ancient world and prehistory, grapple with the issue all the time.

Here, as we explore the different roles women have been assigned by virtue of being women, we can be aware as well of how these roles have varied because of other social attributes, such as membership in specific racial, ethnic, class, and other social categories. In examining these social roles, wherever possible, we need to pay close attention to the descriptions of the experience of being placed in these categories that have been made by members of these groups. In recent years, feminist scholars have devoted a great deal of attention to discovering ways of describing how these several social categories come into play to influence the way women identify

themselves, develop self-images and self-esteem, or become linked into systems of discrimination and inequality (for example, Lorber, 2001; Boris and Janssens, 1999; Brewer, 1991; Haraway, 1989; Spelman, 1988; Minh-ha, 1987; Cole, 1986; Hammonds, 1986).

Social Roles and Social Stereotypes

One of the problems of generalizing too broadly is that it leads to stereotyping, and that prevents us from seeing people as individuals. Social stereotypes encourage us to react to people on the basis of our expectations of the characteristics that they, as a group, have been assigned by our culture. Negative stereotypes are usually *caricatures*, broad characterizations that emphasize a negative valuation of the categories of gender, race, class, age, and sexuality. Such caricatures are based on negative assumptions that create labels like "dumb blonde," "lazy black," "scheming Jew," "terrorist Muslim," "aggressive dyke," or "nagging mother-in-law." These expectations, based on repeated generalizations, become stereotypes and are too often reflected in day-to-day interactions. For example, both U.S. Supreme Court Justices Sandra Day O'Connor and Ruth Bader Ginsburg have reminisced that when each first got her law degree and went job hunting, the personnel offices of the legal firms they approached all assumed that, because each was a woman, she was seeking a job in the secretarial pool, not as a lawyer (Maveety, 1996, Schneir, 1994:483).

The Social Construction of Gender

Even though many women never marry, bear children, or nurse them, women are socially defined by the capacity to do so and by the social expectation that this capacity is a basic characteristic of a woman's existence. What

Storekeepers in Egypt. Women from poorer economic classes have always worked at home and outside all over the world. These three women have installed and maintain a small grocery store.

this means, of course, varies from context to context. Social definitions of women include many physical, psychological, and behavioral characteristics, the sum of which, for any society, represents the gender label "woman" for that group. Since every society makes a gender assignment at birth, an infant is immediately heir to all these social expectations. Essential to the construction of gender is the notion of polarity, that there are only two genders (which is so with some cultural exceptions) and each is the "opposite" of the other (which is so only by cultural definition). By this reasoning, girls and boys (and women and men) are each partially defined in terms of what the other is not.

Socialization of children consists of introducing them to the rules or norms of behavior, the social expectations by which they can make sense of how others act toward them and how they should in turn behave. The extent to which women and men conform, even

Woman spinning and weaving. From this early fourteenth-century book illustration, we have a sense of the age-old assignment to women in the Western world of such domestic needs as the clothing of the family. Other cultures, as in many countries of North Africa, may assign to men the tasks of sewing, tailoring, and clothes making.

partially, to the stereotypes of gender-appropriate behavior depends in part upon their successful socialization, the degree to which they have internalized the cultural pressures to conform (see Chapter 4). Some societies have specific rites of passage in which girls and boys are explicitly taught to be women and men. These rites and other forms of deliberate education suggest that a person *becomes* a woman or a man, rather than that a person is biologically designed to be one or the other at birth.

The social structure, which defines gender-appropriate behavior, is composed of a pattern of values, beliefs, and customs embedded in a specific material way of life. As these variables change over time, the norms within societies also change; but they do not do so all at once. The social roles and behavior of women in any society represent some measure of change over past time, but there is usually a lag between changes of behavior and changes of values or expectations. While change occurs for some women, it does not for others, who are affected instead by reinforced traditional values and expectations that resist change. For example, some decades ago, when women's rate of work outside the home had increased strikingly, public schools in the affluent neighborhood of Shaker Heights, Ohio, continued to send all children home in the middle of the day for lunch, with the assumption that their mothers would be there to feed them. Only public demonstrations by concerned parents changed the situation. Employers, following cultural norms, also change their policies slowly; and their company policies often have not recognized the parental responsibilities of their workers until those workers have raised the problem. Parental leave, common in Europe, is still a relatively recent and far from universal phenomenon in the United States (see Chapter 12). Rarer still is any ready accommodation by employers for the long period after infancy when parents are expected to be available to take children to pediatricians and dentists and to attend parent–teacher conferences. The lower the status the job has and the lower the pay, the more difficult it may be for mothers to make such arrangements.

Whether or not they are wives or mothers, women who pursue jobs in male-dominated fields experience daily conflict between the male-defined norms of that activity and the social roles expected of them as women. Being a "woman" in a work world hitherto dominated by men, where the patterns of the workday reflect men's lives, is to experience boundaries on the range of behavior that is socially acceptable. The situation automatically creates tension for those who seek to combine different sets of roles traditionally divided along gender lines. Despite the fact that more women than ever before have become lawyers, for example, they find that the law office expects a 50–60 hour work week and that they need to honor it if they wish to rise in the firm to the level of partner. Such hours present problems for family and personal life for both men and women, but the expectations regarding the social roles of women outside work, not just as mothers but increasingly in the care of elderly family members, present continuing barriers to career success (Williams, 2000; Drachman, 1998).

Despite the feminist gains since the 1960s, therefore, even women in the United States continue to experience social challenges in relation to education, choice of work, mobility, forms of cultural expression, and political participation. They also face discriminatory treatment in terms of their health care (see Chapter 11) and even whether they may—or must—have children. These social controls limit women's choices from the moment of birth and affect their range of individual autonomy and self-expression; they govern women's social realities as "women." Women's decisions to accept or resist particular social assignments or to give priority to one or another of them at different times depend on their circumstances, political needs, or strategies for making change. The many social expectations attached to the gender label "woman" from birth expose women to the positive and negative assumptions, and stereotypes, with which they will have to deal as they grow up and form an image of themselves—for themselves and for others.

Race

"Race," like sex and gender, is a social construct, one whose meaning has differed over historical time and place. The term at various times has been used to designate what might otherwise be called "ethnic," "religious," or "national" (for example, "the Irish race" or "the Jewish race" or "the French race"), categories which clearly include people with a broad range of physical characteristics. "Race" has also been used for presumed biological groups (Asians, Pacific Islanders, or African Americans) whose genetic roots are extremely diverse, often combining presumably separate groups. The assignment of a racial label to a group of people, in other words, is in the biological sense fairly arbitrary and has its origins in the meanings assigned by society rather than in any specific biological reality. In the United States, this arbitrariness becomes particularly clear when we attempt to define, for official purposes like the government census, what it means to be "white," "Native American," "African American," "Asian American," or "Hispanic

There is great diversity among Muslim women regarding the use of veils, headscarves, and burkas. Some Muslim women wear none of these. The practice is governed by national law, ideological purpose, and custom. Here, a burka enshrouds a woman in Afghanistan. Elsewhere, especially among Muslim women living in Western countries, choice and ideology play an important role in the use of headscarves.

American." We must ask how many of our ancestors we should use, and in what proportions and how far back in time, to determine into which category we may, or must, place ourselves.

Until recently, "race" in the United States has meant being "not white." Now, increasingly aware of the socially constructed nature of race, scholars have begun to examine the social meanings of "whiteness" and how those meanings have changed over time (Clark and O'Donnell, 1999; Frankenberg, 1993, 1996; Sacks, 1994; Ware, 1992). For example, one study has demonstrated the way the U.S. Supreme Court, asked repeatedly to define *whiteness* for legal purposes, has shifted its position over time; tracing this process has revealed how historically situated and arbitrary these definitions have been (Haney Lopez, 1996). For Native Americans, to establish legal membership in a particular tribe or nation necessitates documentation that at least a single grandparent was a member of that group; however, Native Americans often have so mixed a heritage that this requirement can be quite problematic (Gould, 1992). Until recently, having a single African American great-grandparent was sufficient in some states to place a descendant in the category "African American." For many Latinas and Latinos, having a Spanish surname was both necessary and sufficient to place one in the category still officially called "Hispanic" by the U.S. census. Like members of the other "official" racial categories, people carrying this label may have light or dark hair, round or

---

Box 5.1   THE COMPLEXITIES OF LABELING

Not all Third World women are "women of color"—if by this concept we mean exclusively "non-white." I am only one example. And not all women of color are really Third World—if this term is only used in reference to underdeveloped or developing societies (especially those not allied with any superpower). Clearly then it would be difficult to justify referring to Japanese women, who are women of color, as Third World women. Yet, if we extend the concept of Third World to include internally "colonized" racial and ethnic minority groups in this country, so many different kinds of groups could be conceivably included, that the crucial issue of social and institutional racism and its historic tie to slavery in the U.S. could get diluted, lost in the shuffle. . . .

I don't know what to think anymore. Things begin to get even more complicated when I begin to consider that many of us who identify as "Third World" or "women of color," have grown up as or are fast becoming "middle-class" and highly educated, and therefore more privileged than many of our white, poor and working-class sisters.

Source: Quintanales, 1983:151.

---

almond-shaped eyes, and dark or light skin color.

Race (now that we have established its arbitrariness as a term, we will drop the quotation marks) is socially constructed to serve a range of political and social purposes. The particular context of time and place in which race is experienced—and it differs over the globe—remains critical to how and how much an individual is conscious of it (see Box 5.1).

The condition of slavery, for example, which circumscribed the experience of African Americans for over a century, has taken its toll on the lives of some four generations and shaped indelibly the consciousness of those who are descended from them. Toni Morrison's Pulitzer Prize–winning novel *Beloved* (1987) makes this point eloquently, as does *Playing in the Dark*, her examination of "whiteness" in the American literary imagination (1992). The conditions of social and economic life experienced by freed slaves after 1865; the hierarchies of a rural, sharecropping world; and the harsh conditions of employment that confronted those who migrated to

urban areas of the South and North created the circumstances which continue to shape race consciousness among both African Americans and those with whom they interact.

To be an African American woman, or a woman of color (a term that assumes "white" is colorless), in a northeastern city in the United States today means confronting a specific set of cultural prejudices. Yet, a woman of color in this context who is a recent immigrant from the Caribbean has a different set of historical and personal roots to bring to her identification with race than those whose forebears migrated north two or three generations ago (Jones, 1985:152–95). The writer Audre Lorde has explored the realities of growing up West Indian in New York in *Zami: A New Spelling of My Name* (1982) and novelist Paule Marshall, who wrote about growing up in Brooklyn in *Brown Girl, Brown Stones* (1981), again explores the lives of West Indian women in Brooklyn in *The Fisher King* (2000). A white woman growing up in the south (Pratt, 1984) is likely to have a very different consciousness of race from one who grows up in Maine or California, although modern mass media has increasingly tended to obscure these differences. She will certainly have a different consciousness of being white from an Italian woman who "discovers" this identity only when she comes to live in the United States (de Lauretis, 1986:8–9). An Asian American woman, depending upon her country of origin and circumstances of her parents' or grandparents' migration to the United States, similarly has varying personal understandings of race. Consciousness of difference as a part of coming of age in the United States has been explored by several Chinese American authors, such as Amy Tan in *The Joy Luck Club* (1989) and, most recently, in *The Bonesetter's Daughter* (2000). Another Chinese American writer, Gish Jen, in her novel *Mona in the Promised Land* (1996), examines the second-generation experiences of assimilating cultures in American suburbia through the eyes of a teenage Chinese American girl who decides to convert to Judaism because her best friend is Jewish.

Ethnicity

Just as race proves to be a fairly arbitrary classificatory system, the difference between race and ethnicity is equally subjective. The distinctions of ethnicity are in some ways subtler, for ethnic identity generally refers to inherited cultural traits that have often in the past been identified with nationality. Ethnically aware groups themselves have a history and change over time (Mullings, 1978). There is also a great variety of ethnicities that are claimed among African Americans, Native Americans, Asian Americans, Latinas/Latinos as well as groups today identified as "white."

In fact, most people designated on official forms as "white" in the United States actually think of themselves as "Irish," "Armenian," "Norwegian," "Greek," "Jewish," a mixture of two or more ethnicities, depending on the ethnic origins of their parents. Major U.S. cities have neighborhoods designated not as "white" but in ethnic terms, like "Polish" or "Italian." "White" becomes a racial–ethnic category only in dualistic opposition to "people of color." It is a category which often obscures what is felt by its members to be their own identity. "White," in other words, covers at least as diverse an ethnic conglomeration as "Latinas/Latinos," a label now used for a heterogeneous group in the United States that includes Puerto Ricans, Chicanas/Chicanos, Cubans, Colombians, and Dominicans, among many others. It is as difficult to generalize about the experiences and identity of "Latinas," therefore, as it is for women designated as "white," "Asian American," or "African American" (Latina Feminist Group, 2001; Moraga and Anzuldúa, 1983). Some novels which have graphically explored these nuances for women from the Dominican Republic, Antigua, and Cuba are *How the García Girls Lost Their Accents* (1991) by Julia Alvarez, *Lucy* (1990) by Jamaica Kincaid, and *Dreaming in Cuban* (1991) by Christina García.

Understanding Contextual Difference

In the earlier years of second-wave feminism, "women" and "men" were treated as single, meaningful categories; this has now given way to an understanding of the complexities of these terms and a greater appreciation of how these complexities are compounded by diversities. In part, this new analysis arises from intellectual critiques that include "deconstructionist" theories, which demand that we reexamine our use of the concept "woman" (see above and Chapter 2). In part, this shift in understanding is also inspired by political forces within the women's movement and throughout the world itself. Nevertheless, current feminist thought acknowledges that, as in the past, the dominant discourse of any society sends out powerful messages about the ideals of "femininity" and "womanhood." Such ideologies have set up archetypes of beauty and behavior that not only do not conform to the historical experience of many within the dominant group but also exclude absolutely the realities of women within subordinate groups subject to the power and norms of the dominant group. Slavery in the United States was accompanied by very different ideologies about womanliness. White women were defined as weak, homebound, nurturing mothers, creatures always in need of male protection; black women were considered primarily as strong workers to be used for the hardest labor, mothers whose children could be sold away from them, and creatures who could be treated with the severest physical punishments.

Histories of slavery and lynching for African Americans, genocide for Native Americans, and military conquest for Mexican Americans and Puerto Ricans, for example, serve as contexts for understanding how these groups developed a sense of distinctive identity. Understanding the overall experience of a group, however, does not specifically tell us of the nature and history of women's experiences within that group, "the physical abuse, social discrimination, and cultural denigration suffered by women" (King, 1988:45). We need to seek in the histories of racial and ethnic groups the gendered meaning of their experiences in order to determine what these circumstances mean for the social roles of women.

After slavery, for example, African American women assumed powerful leadership roles within their communities, founding schools and churches, organizing unions, and establishing commercial enterprises. African American women have also played leading roles in the ongoing struggle for racial justice, such as Harriet Tubman, who organized the Underground Railway for runaway slaves before the Civil War; Ida B. Wells-Barnett, who led an antilynching crusade in the early twentieth century; Rosa Parks, who precipitated the antisegregation Montgomery bus boycott in 1955; and Fannie Lou Hamer and Ella Baker, who played pivotal roles in the 1960s civil rights movement (Hine et al., 1993; Sterling, 1984). Nineteenth-century educators and writers like Anna Julia Cooper and Frances Watkins Harper and twentieth-century writers and activists such as Pauli Murray, Audre Lorde, and Angela Davis all sought to define broad educational and political roles for African American womanhood. An understanding of the roles these particular women have played in American history requires an understanding of the specific contexts in which they have acted, spoken, and written (Collins, 2000).

Women's roles in society depend not only on the traits attributed to them but also on the way they claim an identity, and that in turn depends on the social, economic, political, and historical circumstances of their lives. Since racial and ethnic groups have histories, the extent to which women are aware of them determines how much they claim from them in asserting their identities. When we try to understand how diverse women claim their own histories, we have to learn about those histories and the experiences of the women who lived them. A virtual explosion of literature by women from the 1970s onward—novels, autobiographical accounts, analyses of their heritages—has made this possible. Rediscovery and republication of earlier literature by women has supplied the diverse voices and experiences we need to understand some of these women. To recover such voices has been the object of The Feminist Press at the City University of New York, for example, which has republished many of those lost voices for over three decades and has now instituted a "memoir" series to capture contemporary women's voices and experiences that span the globe from Turkey, India, and Malaysia in works entitled *Lion Woman's Legacy* (Avakian, 1992), *Fault Lines* (Alexander, 2003), and *Among the White Moon Faces* (Lim, 1996), respectively.

One very striking example of the emergence of a substantial literature illustrating differences among women is by and about Native American women. The peoples represented in this literature are enormously diverse, from the Arctic north to the southern woodlands, from the deserts of the southwest to the urban concentrations of both coasts. The quality of life described varies immensely in its texture, reflecting not only local environments but also significant historical differences of custom, belief, and aesthetic. Even so, there are common themes derived from certain shared experiences of oppression, specifically those related to conquest, decimation, dislocation, adjustment, and resistance (Allen, 1989). One such theme is the problem of remembering and holding onto the traditions—knowledge, belief, ritual—of the past in the face of the loss of hundreds of thousands of people to war and disease with the coming of European conquerors and colonists. Stories are told of how Native American women have secretly sustained traditions and lovingly passed them on, one generation to the next. A second related theme is the abduction of children, forced to live in boarding schools to learn "American" or white men's versions of religion and cultural values, humiliated out of speaking their own languages and observing their own religious practices. Separation, loss of parents and children, and the loneliness of isolation from one's kin are central themes of this literature. Yet another important theme is resistance, not only through insistent memory of customs but also through recounting the actual history of struggle by those who fought back. Finally, it is important to understand the continuity and the ties between pre-Conquest, post-

Conquest, and present times. Paula Gunn Allen's anthology *Spider Woman's Granddaughters* (1989) illustrates all of these themes. Her more recent book of personal reflections, *Off the Reservation* (1998), continues her deconstruction of Western values and assumptions in comparison with Native American life and literature. Leslie Marmon Silko also uses the pivotal events of the Native American experience of the late nineteenth century to write about the lives of three generations of women in the southwest in *Gardens in the Dunes* (1999).

Like the experiences of Native American women, those of Asian American women are extremely diverse: their histories, homelands, and experiences in the United States are very far from uniform. *Asian/Pacific Islander American Women* (2003), edited by Shirley Hune and Gail M. Nomura, suggests that diversity in selections about Cambodian, Chamoru, Chinese, Filipino, Hmong, Indian, Japanese, Korean, Native Hawaiian, and Vietnamese American women. Its chapters consider the wide range of these women's experiences as immigrants, U.S.-born children of immigrants, military brides, refugees, lesbians, organizers, low-income workers, professionals, entertainers, beauty contestants, mothers, daughters, and grassroots activists. In viewing women in this fashion, as active participants in history, negotiating hierarchies of power that include gender, race, class, sexuality, generation, language, religion, and status, we can become aware of the complexities of Asian/Pacific Islander American women's roles and lived realities in households and communities in the United States as well as under globalization. In Asian/Pacific Islander American literature, mother–daughter relationships are a common theme, as is the struggle of an American-born daughter of immigrants to find herself between the demands of two cultures, as Amy Tan (1989, 2000) and Gish Jen (1996) show so well in their novels.

Class, Race, Ethnicity, and Gender: Discrimination

A *social class* is a group sharing the same social or economic status. Generally speaking, in complex, stratified societies, racial, ethnic, and class divisions reinforce one another. That is, ethnicity and race, depending on the historical and regional context, often become stereotyped signs of class position. In the United States, this means that being "black" has been identified with being poor and the poor have been identified as being often associated with criminal activities. Both assumptions are the result of generalizations, and belief in such generalization leads to the problem of treating people in advance as if such assumptions were true. Such generalizations can become the basis for official policies that discriminate against individuals on the basis of their group identity; one result has been *racial profiling*, a practice by which police officers stop more drivers of color than white drivers because the color of their skin signals "wrongdoer" to the police, with no other evidence needed. Such racial discrimination operates on a system opposite from the U.S. legal system, which holds that an individual is innocent unless proven guilty. The assumption has become a stereotype and is so strong that stereotypes of class, such as expensive clothing, an educated voice, a high-priced car, which ordinarily mark those who bear them as law-abiding citizens, are ignored. Stereotypes of gender, like those of race, led women professionally trained in medicine in an earlier era, when job hunting, to descriptions of positions that included "Doctor wanted, Women need not apply."

The same problem has faced other groups in the United States, like Jews, where discrimination on the grounds of religion has weighed more than class markers of higher socioeconomic status to make it difficult to buy homes in particular locations, join private clubs, or gain entrance into Ivy League universities and medical schools. Quotas, to keep the number of persons in one group to a minimum in any social setting, were also used for admitting women to most medical schools before the practice was declared illegal in the early 1970s. Such instances go against the pattern of privilege, which more often has assured individuals with relatively more wealth at their disposal of the enjoyment of social privileges not available to those with less wealth and class status.

Rationalization and Resistance

Subordinate groups learn to rationalize their position in terms promulgated by dominant groups, emphasizing the "natural" condition of subordination and dominance. It is possible to understand the characteristics and actions of members of dominant and subordinate groups by means of this rationalization and of instances of resistance to it. Group members come to define themselves in terms of the attributes of superiority or inferiority ascribed to them by others; alternately, they resist such attribution in various ways. This process applies to many of the characteristics which combine to describe the social person in a complex society: age, gender, race, religion, abilities, and sexual orientation. Negative stereotypes which develop to rationalize power relations usually persist despite the way they obviously contradict reality, as in the case of Sojourner Truth and the ideology of the "weaker sex" (see Chapter 2). Women who make other women the center of their emotional lives face the consequences of negative stereotypes if they want to adopt children or even if they wish to visit a dying partner in a hospital (see below, The "Heterosexual Prescription").

What social function does this stereotyping serve? For one thing, it is easier to exploit people if you think they are inferior and easier still if they think they are inferior. Stereotypes distance people and position them hierarchically in relation to each other. As Charlotte Bunch has written:

> We learn in childhood that such things as sex and race bring differences in power and privilege, and that these are acceptable. This idea that difference justifies domination is deeply embedded in society and defended as natural . . . as women who have challenged the so-called naturalness of male supremacy, feminists must also question it in other areas of domination. (Bunch, 1987:150)

Fear and distrust contribute to the maintenance of the privileges of the powerful. Negative stereotypes lower the self-esteem of their targets. Even "positive" stereotypes, such as the belief that Asian Americans are especially gifted in mathematics and the sciences, may serve to lower the self-esteem of those individuals who cannot live up to the group stereotype.

Internalization of these images helps to perpetuate the social order which promotes them. Resistance, in the form of alternative interpretations and reverse stereotyping, undermines the power structure by encouraging opposite ways of acting or thinking. The Black Power movement of the 1960s was such an effort at resistance. Its slogan, "Black is Beautiful," affected African Americans' self-image and, therefore, their power to resist negative stereotypes. Finding a voice, a new sense of identity, is always complicated; in addition, resistance to social control and oppression of one kind often leads to reactions of other kinds, as Claudette Williams explains in Box 5.2.

Resistance often takes the form of interrogating the dominant attitudes toward a social group and finding ways of giving voice to a new assertion of a social identity. Latinas in contemporary Puerto Rico are keenly aware of the gendered messages of popular music like salsa on popular culture and women's lives. Feminist scholar Frances Aparicio notes the way contemporary Puerto Rican writers

---

Box 5.2   BLACK CONSCIOUSNESS AS RESISTANCE FOR WOMEN

The arrival of the Black Panther movement and the Black consciousness era offered me the necessary knowledge and confidence to survive. . . . Black power taught me to value myself and others like me in a way I had not experienced before. "Black is Beautiful," "Be Proud To Be Black" carried their unique message to my heart.

I was presented with a history, people and struggle of which I was a part; and I found out that there was much beauty and pride in being a Black woman. I was able to recognize the significance of pressing my hair, and bleaching my skin. While consciously I did not want to be white, everything I had learned and was surrounded by told me that to be white was "good," but here for the first time in my life were other Black people addressing "me" and my personal doubts and inadequacies. I was being told not to be ashamed or afraid of what, and who I am.

. . . Black consciousness enabled me to make the connection between class and racism. . . . However, with political enlightenment came contradictions that became very antagonistic with women's demands for autonomous groups.

The "brothers" took it hard. They saw autonomy as a threat to male leadership and male egos. Gender oppression was reduced to sexuality, and lesbianism became a weapon to deter women from organizing independently.

Source: Williams, 1988:152, 155–6.

Box 5.3   EXAMINING POPULAR MUSIC AS A FORM OF RESISTANCE

For all of us in every culture, but particularly in the Caribbean, music has been a strong influence in our formative years, and both song lyrics and the social practice of dancing have had a tremendous impact on the formation of our sexuality. . . . Sexual politics also come into play, as popular music reproduces the struggles between men and women in a contemporary urban world where gender identities and sexual roles are being drastically transformed.

. . . Despite isolated attempts to raise the issue of women's representation in Caribbean popular music and in salsa . . . salsa lyrics have remained virtually uncontested by women musicians, authors, listeners, and critics. However, two contemporary Puerto Rican women authors, Ana Lydia Vega and Carmen Lugo Filippi, have dismantled constructions of women in salsa in a short story entitled "Cuatro selecciones por una peseta" ("Four selections for a quarter"). . . . Two characters who, while listening to Latin popular music, utter (as authors) their own diatribes against women. The underlying irony is the narrator's voice and the parodic inscription of musical and phallocentric discourses allow this text to participate in the questioning of patriarchal models of being and of social constructs of the feminine. Thus as authors and narrators Vega and Filippi deploy a feminist politics of listening to salsa; they listen woman and then listen as women, undoing and rewriting patriarchal salsa lyrics from a female-centered perspective.

Source: Aparicio, 1997:259, 261.

Ana Lydia Vega and Carmen Lugo Filippi began to explore this subject as a form of cultural resistance in Box 5.3.

Like other stereotypes, those that apply to gender generally promote subordination. Some women may be in multiple jeopardy, being oppressed not only on the basis of gender but also on account of race, ethnicity, class, age, and sexual orientation. As a result of being discriminated against for any and all these attributes, a woman may all too readily come to accept society's attribution of inferiority because of her gender. Yet, women do continue to find ways of resisting a social identity that denigrates them, as Williams and Aparicio demonstrate.

Constraints on Choice

Women learn to conform to society's dominant images of them as they learn to accept the constraints that limit their choices, becoming educated into the social roles deemed appropriate to them. Such education includes understanding how limited is their access to the resources they need to shape their lives. Individuals and groups in subordinated positions are oppressed by the power of the dominant culture to curb their ambitions, and in the end, the process may sharply limit attempts at self-realization. When women work to fulfill their potential by struggling against these dominant forces, they increase their understanding of the real effects of subordination and oppression upon them (Hurtado, 1989:834).

Ironically, those who seek to enforce subordination on others also experience the negative effects of oppression themselves. In a project carried out in the Netherlands, small groups of women met over a period of 5 months, each organized around issues such as racism, anti-Semitism, and homophobia. The women in these groups found that oppression and domination are experienced "as a mutually re-inforcing web of insecurities and rigidities . . . [and] the psychological consequences . . . surprisingly alike . . . the fear of violence one feels as a victim of oppression reinforces the fear of revenge she feels as an agent of oppression" (Pheterson, 1990:45).

Resistance

One source of support for those experiencing discrimination at the hands of the dominant group is to form groups whose members can aid each other to resist the recurring pattern of low achievement and low self-esteem. Consciousness-raising groups beginning in the 1960s have provided women of all kinds with the strength to resist the dominant stereotypes that denigrated them and have helped them mobilize for making change. This is as true today as it was then. Women caught within patterns of poverty have learned how to work together successfully to aid themselves, their children, and their neighborhoods (Omolade, 1994:67–78). African American women built on existing traditions of community and church activism. Patricia Hill Collins (2000) reminds us of the rich African American oral tradition among women as storytellers which, as mothers, teachers, musicians, and preachers, has created a continuing source of ideas and strategies for resistance to the daily disparagements that set up barriers to social achievement (see also Riley, 2000; Gilkes, 1992).

A New Consciousness of Choice

The successes of what is now called the second wave of the U.S. women's movement are evident in many areas of life in the United States, but the daughters of that generation, the third wave, critique what they see as its failures so far as their lives are concerned. Second-wave feminists had to resist the pres-sures of the traditions into which they were born and to chart new ways of shaping freer, more autonomous lives for themselves and their generation. To the extent that they succeeded, their resistance to social constraints on them as women created a greater consciousness of the choices that were possible. Christina Looper Baker and Christina Baker Kline, a mother and daughter who themselves represent second- and third-wave feminism, explored the generational issues involved. They interviewed mothers and daughters who have been involved in feminist activities in *The Conversation Begins: Mothers and Daughters Talk About Living Feminism* (1996). Their examples of mothers and daughters range widely in age as well as in racial and ethnic identities. They found that mothers understand that the consciousness-raising process they went through to resist the constraints on their lives also affected their daughters' lives. Daughters admire their mothers' activism or professional ambitions but remember feeling deprived of that endless, selfless love and attention that society taught them to expect from mothers. As adults, some of these daughters have come to understand more directly the conflicts of work and parenting faced by their mothers. They appreciate the ways their mothers have helped transform the world in which they now make choices, while remembering in some cases the distress that meant for them as children (Baker and Kline, 1996) (see Chapter 6).

Commonalities of Experience

Johnnetta Cole has remarked cogently that "Among the things which bind women together are the assumptions about the way women think and behave, the myths—indeed the stereotypes—about what is common to all women" (Cole, 1986:2). The myths about women as madonnas or temptresses (see Chapter 1), assumptions about women's

Chief Wilma P. Mankiller, the first woman to lead the Cherokee nation, was acclaimed for her authority and guidance. She was only 38 years old when appointed chief in 1985. She was elected in 1987 and reelected in 1991; she retired in 1995. In her own words, "you don't have to have a title or a position to be effective" (*New York Times*, 4/6/94).

irrationality and otherness (see Chapter 2), claims and warnings about women's bodies (see Chapter 3), and assertions about women's personalities (see Chapter 4) all form part of a system of stereotypes about women which relates to social expectations of their subordinate and supporting roles in society. Women are also bound by their common assumptions about those to whom they are subordinate or for whom they are supportive, men as a group. We can identify the supportive and supporting roles women are commonly assigned and regularly play in relationship to men, but we must allow for the diversity women experience, what women do not have in common due to culture, class, ethnicity, and race (Spelman, 1988:111–13). We also need to acknowledge the diversity among men.

For example, many wives perform hostess duties on behalf of their husbands and their husbands' careers or social positions. How much and how this is done, however, greatly differ from class to class, from country to country, from culture to culture. As Susan Ostrander (1984:146) notes, "When women arrange men's social lives and relationships, men of every class are spared investing the time and energy required to meet their social needs." Women also tend to family relationships on behalf of husbands, the forms varying widely depending upon the social group. As more women have entered the impersonal workplace in the United States, they have usually undertaken to oil the social wheels as well with celebrations of birthdays and seasonal holidays, thereby indirectly aiding their—primarily male—employers to maintain social harmony within the work organization (Di Leonardo, 1987).

Family Roles

Commonalities among women most often have to do with their family roles as daughters, sisters, wives, and mothers. Whatever

the particular arrangements are, due to race, ethnicity, culture, religion, or historical period, daughters experience their roles in connection with parental figures to whom they owe duties of obedience and loyalty and for whom they may indeed experience tenderness and love. Daughters may also feel bonds of love and bonds of jealousy toward siblings, depending upon circumstances, and bonds of responsibility depending upon the age relationship. Whether women marry or not, stay at home or not, their obligations often grow over the years in relation to their families, for daughters more than sons may find themselves directly responsible for providing care for elderly parents.

If women marry, whoever they are, they undertake a new set of obligations that sometimes involves a husband alone but may also extend to the new kin group, including parents-in-law. In societies where polygamy occurs, women are co-wives and have obligations to these other wives as well. In terms of commonalities, marriage around the world generally means household responsibilities, social obligations, and a new status derived from the husband's social position. In the Muslim world, with the exception of Turkey, family law is closely linked to religious doctrine and increasingly has become a political symbol of Islam as a culture. The treatment of women in family law symbolizes that linkage. On the one hand, when areas like northern Nigeria adopted Islamic family law in recent years, they proclaimed a fundamentalist Muslim identity. On the other hand, Islamic family law has been undergoing reform throughout the twentieth century.

Commonalities also occur when women become mothers. Motherhood may have many different meanings in different cultural contexts, but in general it brings responsibility for the continued nurture and health of a new life and must be undertaken in addition to any and all other obligations and responsibilities of

---

Box 5.4   THE FAMILY'S LESSONS IN INEQUALITY

A patriarchal society expects mothers to be totally giving and available, downplaying their own needs, ambitions, and desires, as well as fears and guilts.

Revolutionizing the family, not just mothers and daughters, is necessary if we are to have any chance at women's liberation. After all, the home is still the most powerful and primal seat of patriarchy, housing and teaching the most basic inequalities between the sexes.

For masses of Second Wave households, the rhetoric of women's rights was part of the dinner-table discussion. But the conversations didn't necessarily reflect what was going on inside the house—Dad never doing the laundry and Mom saying "Ask your father" when it came to finances. If it wasn't a feminist-informed household, it was likely to be more repressive inside the home in response to advances women were making in public.

Source: Jennifer Baumgardner and Amy Richards, *ManifestA: Young Women, Feminism, and the Future,* New York: Farrar, Straus, and Giroux, 2000:211, 213.

---

living and working. Women's arrangements to cope with this unceasing obligation yield a world full of common experiences.

In their book *ManifestA: Young Women, Feminism, and the Future,* third-wave feminists Jennifer Baumgardner and Amy Richards examine these common social roles of mothers in U.S. families over the past three decades and the lessons in inequality daughters have learned from them (Box 5.4).

Alternative Roles. Wherever choice has been possible, some women have always chosen not to marry. Single women have become nuns in the Christian and Buddhist worlds; single women have devoted themselves to caring for others outside the family, to traveling through the world, to living alone or together with other women in groups, or to living as couples in loving relationships. For those who prefer these choices, different kinds of commonality exist. Yet another alternative choice is made by women who do not want to have children. A different position from that of women who find themselves unable to bear children, this decision is often made with both fear and guilt bred by the social pressures of family and kin, who might brand such a decision as, at best, "selfish." The conscious choice not to marry— yet not to become a nun or devote life to the service of others, traditional choices for alternatives—is also subject to social pressures, as Sandra Cisneros's poem "Old Maids" suggests (Box 5.5).

Society and Social Control

The "Heterosexual Prescription"

The social assumption that all women will marry and become mothers is taught girls from babyhood, and teaching women to believe this assumption has been an important method of social control. As noted above, a percentage of women has always chosen not to marry and have children, but the social script remains unchanged. Some 10%–20% of women through time in the Western world have remained single, despite the fact that single women have usually been looked down upon and pitied as leading a "lesser" life. Those who choose to live with other women because they love one another have always existed, but only since the late nineteenth

Box 5.5   OLD MAIDS

My cousin and I,
we don't marry.
We're too old
by Mexican standards.

And the relatives
have long suspected
we can't anymore
in white.

Who won't
dress children,
and never
saints—
though
we undress them.

The aunts,
they've given up on us.
No longer nudge—You're next.

Instead—
What happened in your childhood?
What left you all mean teens?
Who hurt you, honey?

But we've studied
marriages too long—

Aunt Ariadne,
Tia Vashti,
Comrade Penelope,
querida Malintzin,
Señora Pumpkin Shell—
lessons that served us well.

century has the label "lesbian" been attached to loving women. The term was adopted from the name of the island of Lesbos, where the Greek poet Sappho lived in the sixth century B.C.E. and wrote poetry revealing an erotic and emotional life centered on women (Pomeroy, 1975).

The lesbian poet Adrienne Rich, trying to understand the hostility and homophobia lesbians have often faced, made what has become the classic analysis of the "heterosex-ual prescription." Basing her analysis on an-thropological literature about women across time and cultures, she notes how the various kinds of power men have traditionally exer-cised over women has been used to enforce heterosexuality on them. Some of these accu-sations against male use of power include seeking to convince women, by force if nec-essary, that marriage and a sexual orientation toward men are both "natural" and "in-evitable." Not to turn to men for the expres-sion of their sexuality, therefore, is defined by men as "unnatural." Men have historically used methods ranging from arranged mar-riages, harems, pornography, and rape to force male sexuality upon women; they have controlled contraception and abortion to en-force motherhood upon them; they have claimed legal rights over wife and children and confined women to their homes by pur-dah, foot binding, and sexual harassment on the streets; they have used women to facilitate deals between men; they have exploited them as artists's models; and they have kept them from acquiring the knowledge that would make them independent of men's control (Rich, 1980:638–40).

Even women who seek heterosexual fulfill-ment understand that this relationship has been marked by brutality and coercion over the centuries. The message of Hollywood movies in the 1930s was that a woman slapped around by her boyfriend understood that this behavior meant he "really liked" her. What-ever their sexuality, therefore, women have in common a past of many kinds of sexual subor-dination that only a future of sexual equality can undo.

The Social Construction of Human Beings

A vast array of changes in social practice and thought is required to overcome the perpetu-ation of sex and gender oppression. Consider the reactions of people to a young adult dressed and groomed in such a way that it is not possible to tell whether the person is fe-male or male. Responses may vary from dis-comfort (confusion/curiosity) to anxiety to anger or even disgust. The key issue raised by this scenario is why people feel compelled to place human beings immediately into the so-cial category "woman" or "man." Since we have all learned from childhood to respond to people in terms of gender, such reactions are not surprising. We have no experience in treating people as genderless. By means of gender, we learn to place people in society and to react to them accordingly.

Unfortunately, placing people also implies patterns of dominance and subordination, which then govern our reactions. The unease or outright distress that people may feel when facing an indefinitely gendered person makes clear they have been well socialized to treat others first and foremost in specific gen-der terms. Sadly, this early learning of social roles makes it impossible for them to respond to a person simply as another human being. In fact, it makes possible—encourages—group hatreds based on stereotypes (see Box 5.6).

Some feminists have argued that if gender assignment to nurturing roles were less rigid, if all children grew up expecting to take care of others, especially the next generation and the elderly, some of the "difference" that di-vides the two genders and the roles assigned them would disappear. Other feminists be-lieve that even to consider this kind of future is to engage in hopeless utopian thinking. In-stead, they urge us to solve the problem of un-equal access created by sexism in practical and legal ways. Human rights activists take this view of countering human oppression by such means wherever it is found (Dimauro, 1996; Young, 1990).

Box 5.6   SOCIAL IDENTITIES BEYOND NEGATIVE STEREOTYPES

MINNIE BRUCE PRATT: If I have come to the point of consciousness where I have begun to understand that I am entrapped as a woman, not just by the sexual fear of the men of my group, but also by their racial and religious terrors; if I have begun to understand that when they condemn me as a lesbian and a free woman for being "dirty," "unholy," "perverted," "immoral," it is a judgment that has been called down on people of color and Jews throughout history by the men of my culture, as they have shifted their justification for hatred according to their desires of the moment; if I have begun to understand something of the deep connection between my oppression and that of other folks, what is it that keeps me from acting, sometimes even from speaking out, against anti-Semitism and racism? . . .

    As I try to strip away the layers of deceit that I have been taught, it is not hard to be afraid that these are like wrappings of a shroud and that what I will ultimately come to in myself is a disintegrating, rotting nothing: that the values that I have at my core, from my culture, will only be those of negativity, exclusion, fear, death. And my feeling is based in the reality that the group identity of my culture has been defined, often, not by positive qualities, but by negative characteristics: by the absence of: "no dogs, Negroes, or Jews"; we have gotten our jobs, bought our houses, borne and educated our children by the negatives: no niggers, no kikes, no wops, no dagos, no spics, no A-rabs, no gooks, no queers. . . .

BARBARA SMITH: Relationships between Black and Jewish women are the very opposite of simple. Our attempts to make personal/political connections virtually guarantee our being thrust between "the rock" of our own people's suspicion and disapproval and "the hard place" of the other group's antagonism and distrust. It is a lot easier to categorize people, to push them into little nastily-labelled boxes, than time and again to deal with them directly, to make distinctions between the stereotype and the substance of who and what they are. It's little wonder that so often both Black and Jewish women first label and then dismiss each other. All of us resort to this tactic when the impact of our different histories, cultures, classes, and skins backs us up against the wall and we do not have the courage or the desire to examine what, if anything, of value lies between us. . . . We are certainly damaged people. The question is, finally, do we use that damage, that first-hand knowledge of oppression, to recognize each other, to do what work we can together? Or do we use it to destroy?

Source: Pratt, 1984:38–9, 85.

Summary

From the earliest ages, children try out social roles according to the gendered social rules they observe concerning what is required and what is forbidden. Roles may relate to family, work, or some other social context. Women are generally assigned wife and mother roles, and gender can determine which social roles people will play or be forbidden to play. The roles people are assigned on the basis of gender and age are associated with social status. In complex societies, class, race, caste, ethnicity, and religious affiliation often intersect with these social categories to establish hierarchies of groups, membership in which affects the likelihood of various roles individuals play.

    Postmodern perspectives in feminist theory draw our attention to the importance of differences among women, making generalizations about women difficult. This chapter explores the different roles women have been assigned and how these roles have varied with other social attributes, such as racial, ethnic, class, and other social categories. When we stereotype people, we react to them on the basis of our expectations rather than our knowledge of them as individuals. Negative stereotypes are usually caricatures, emphasizing a negative valuation of gender, race, class, and other labels.

At birth, the label "biological woman" is commonly based on anatomy; the social construction of "woman" as a gender is then based on social expectations, and societies may and do differ. Essential to the construct, however, is the notion that there are only two genders and that each gender is what the other is not. Socialization introduces children to the rules or norms of behavior of a particular society and what becomes gender-appropriate behavior. Social norms are embedded in specific material ways of life, which change over time, sometimes creating a gap between norms and needs, as in the case of working mothers and the social expectations of motherhood roles based on nonworking mothers. We all take our identities from a variety of culturally imposed and individually claimed social constructions: gender, race, ethnicity, religion, class, age, sexual orientation, and physical abilities.

Race is a social construct, too. The term assumes biological characteristics, but the genetic roots of groups so identified are both diverse and often mixed with those of other groups. The term *Hispanic*, as used by the U.S. census, for example, merely refers to a Hispanic surname and covers a wide range of physical appearance. What is important is that the context of the use of the label is critical to the individual's consciousness of its meaning and that both contexts and meanings have changed through time. Ethnicity similarly refers to a social construct that devel-

oped over time and sometimes to what in the past was called "nationality." African Americans, Native Americans, Asian Americans, Latinas/Latinos, and whites all are divided by ethnicities.

We can begin to understand "difference" only when we examine the specific context in which it operates over time, place, and circumstances. Our roles in society depend not only on what is attributed to us but also on what we lay claim to as our identity. Native American women, though representing diverse groups and diverse experiences, find identity in common themes of oppression related to conquest, decimation, dislocation, adjustment, and resistance. Similarly, for example, the many groups who make up "Asian American," and differ from each other in striking ways, still have common themes as daughters of immigrants balancing between two cultures.

Ethnicity and race often become stereotyped signs of class position. Social class can divide groups or provide a unifying factor. Subordinate groups learn to rationalize their position in terms of negative stereotypes that suggest that subordination to another, dominant, group is "natural." This hierarchical thinking maintains the privileges of the powerful and lowers the self-esteem of their targets, perpetuating the social order that promotes that relationship. Resistance, like the Black Power movement of the 1960s, fought against the negative stereotypes.

Conforming to dominant images of women constrains their choices. Internalized oppression fosters the negative self-images that reinforce negative stereotypes. Poverty comes from having limited access to the material resources of society, and negative self-images abet the process of keeping women of oppressed groups out of educational channels that would increase their social mobility, career choice, and self-realization. However, even within poor groups of women, there have been successful attempts to provide mutual self-help, to resist society's negative stereotypes, and to create a positive self-identity.

Women have experiences in common that cross many of the lines that divide them. These commonalities have to do with family roles. Some women have always chosen alternatives, however, despite the assumption learned from childhood that all women must become wives and mothers and care for husbands, homes, and children. Women who love other women have always existed, though the term *lesbian* dates only to a century ago. Lesbians have had to face work and legal discrimination, public disparagement, and sometimes outright violence. To overcome gender oppression, society needs to be transformed to give everyone the chance to develop whatever potential he or she has without negative stereotypes, without patterns of hierarchical dominance, without all the problems of unequal access created by sexism; but only by being aware of these issues, and they are human rights issues, can we begin.

Discussion Questions

1. How does the social construction of women relate to the biological factors introduced in Chapter 3 and the philosophical issues about "women's nature" raised in Chapter 2?
2. Read one of the books mentioned in this chapter that deals with the experiences of women of a cultural group other than your own. Either write an essay or make an oral presentation indicating the differences and commonalities of that experience compared to your own.
3. Make a list of all the negative stereotypes of women of which you are aware. Who is served by these negative images? What barriers to choice do they create for the women at whom they are aimed?

4. Considering the real differences that exist and have existed between women of various groups, and indeed among women of the same group, discuss the possible commonalities they face.
5. Look around for the projects organized by women on your campus or in your community. What are their objectives and what women have formed an alliance to carry them out?

Recommended Readings

Allen, Paula Gunn. *Off the Reservation: Reflections on Boundary-Busting, Border-Crossing Loose Canons*. Boston: Beacon Press, 1998. Standing herself in the ethnic crosssroads of three heritages, Laguna Indian, Lebanese, and Scots, Allen explores these and other boundary issues in a series of personal essays on late twentieth-century Native American literature and the contrast between Native American culture and the dominant white culture.

Hune, Shirley, and Gail M. Nomura, editors. *Asian/Pacific Islander American Women: A Historical Anthology*. New York: New York University Press, 2003. Through women's eyes and voices and using oral history, ethnic publications, and archival research, the complex and nuanced lives of Cambodian, Chamoru, Chinese, Filipino, Hmong, Indian, Japanese, Korean, Native Hawaiian, and Vietnamese women are recovered as sites of oppression and resistance. The book explores their experiences as picture brides, military wives, refugees, beauty contestants, girls' club members, lesbians, health-care workers, and union organizers.

Latina Feminist Group. *Telling to Live: Latina Feminist Testimonios*. Durham, NC: Duke University Press, 2001. Differing in generational, class, religious, ethnic, racial, linguistic, and sexual ways, while writing as particular

Puerto Rican, Chicana, Native American, Mexican, Cuban, Dominican, Sephardic, and Central American women, a group of Latina feminists look for common ground, using the Latin American form of *testimonio* to tell their stories.

Nafisi, Azar. *Reading Lolita in Tehran: A Memoir in Books.* New York: Random House, 2003. An Iranian professor of English and American literature, educated in the United States, living and teaching in Tehran, writes of her experiences with university students, young women and men, who study with her. She recounts her and their experiences when the Islamic revolution turns their lives upside down, ordering all women to cover themselves in public or face dire penalties. Nafisi describes how it feels to live under these restrictions, for herself and her women students, and their reactions to the books she teaches.

References

Abu-Lughod, Lila. Fieldwork of a dutiful daughter. In *Arab Women in the Field: Studying Your Own Society*, edited by Soraya Altorki and Camillia Fawzi El-Solh. Syracuse: Syracuse University Press, 1988.

Alcoff, Linda Martin. The problem of speaking for others. In *Who Can Speak? Authority and Critical Identity*, edited by Judith Roof and Robyn Wiegman. Urbana: University of Illinois Press, 1995.

Alexander, Meena. *Fault lines*, 2nd ed. New York: Feminist Press at the City University of New York, 2003.

Allen, Paula Gunn. Deep purple. In *Spider Woman's Granddaughters: Traditional Tales and Contemporary Writing by Native American Women*, edited by Paula Gunn Allen. Boston: Beacon Press, 1989.

———. *Off the Reservation: Reflections on Boundary-Busting, Border-Crossing Loose Canons.* Boston: Beacon Press, 1998.

Alvarez, Julia. *How the García Girls Lost Their Accents.* Chapel Hill: Algonquin Books, 1991.

Aparicio, Frances. '*Así Son*': Salsa music, female narratives, and gender (de)construction in Puerto Rico. In *Daughters of Caliban: Caribbean Women in the Twentieth Century*, edited by Consuelo López Springfield. Bloomington: Indiana University Press, 1997.

Aswad, Barbara C. Women, class, and power: Examples from the Hatay, Turkey. In *Women in the Muslim World*, edited by Lois Beck and Nikki Keddie. Cambridge, MA: Harvard University Press, 1978.

Avakian, Arlene Voski. *Lion Woman's Legacy: An Armenian American Memoir.* New York: Feminist Press at the City University of New York, 1992.

Baker, Christina Looper, and Christina Baker Kline. *The Conversation Begins: Mothers and Daughters Talk About Living Feminism.* New York: Bantam Books, 1996.

Baumgardner, Jennifer, and Amy Richards. *ManifestA: Young Women, Feminism, and the Future.* New York: Farrar, Straus and Giroux, 2000.

Boris, Eileen, and Angélique Janssens. Complicating categories: An introduction. *International Review of Social History*, 44, (Suppl.), 1–13, 1999.

Brewer, Rose M. Gender, class and the woman's movement: The role of black feminist intellectuals. In *The Third Wave: Feminist Perspectives on Racism*, edited by Norma Alcaron, Lisa Albrecht, Jacqui Alexander, Sharon Day, and Mab Segrest. New York: Kitchen Table/Women of Color Press, 1991.

Bunch, Charlotte. *Passionate Politics: Feminist Theory in Action.* New York: St. Martin's Press, 1987.

Cisneros, Sandra. *Loose Woman: Poems.* New York: Vintage Books, 1995.

Clark, Christine, and James O'Donnell, editors. *Becoming and Unbecoming White: Owning and Disowning a Racial Identity.* Westport, CT: Bergin & Garvey, 1999.

Cole, Johnnetta B. Commonalities and differences. In *All American Women: Lines that Divide, Ties that Bind*, edited by Johnnetta B. Cole. New York: Free Press, 1986.

Collins, Patricia Hill. *Black Feminist Thought*, 2nd ed. New York: Routledge, 2000.

Davis, Angela. *Women, Race and Class*. New York: Vintage Books, 1981.

de Lauretis, Teresa. Feminist studies/critical studies: Issues, terms, and contexts. In *Feminist Studies/Critical Studies*, edited by Teresa de Lauretis. Bloomington: Indiana University Press, 1986.

Di Leonardo, Micaela. The female world of cards and holidays: Women, families, and the work of kinship. *Signs: Journal of Women and Culture*, 12:3, 440–53, 1987.

Dill, Bonnie Thornton. Race, class, and gender: Prospects for an all-inclusive sisterhood. *Feminist Studies*, 9:1, 131–48, 1983.

Dimauro, Julie. Toward a more effective guarantee of women's human rights: A multi-cultural dialogue in international law. *Women's Rights Law Reporter*, 17:3, 333–44, 1996.

Drachman, Virginia G. *Sisters in Law: Women Lawyers in Modern American History*. Cambridge, MA: Harvard University Press, 1998.

Eisenstein, Hester, and Alice Jardine, editors. *The Future of Difference*. New Brunswick, NJ: Rutgers University Press, 1980.

Enloe, Cynthia. *Beaches, Bananas, and Bases: Making Feminist Sense of International Politics*. Berkeley: University of California Press, 1988.

Estrich, Susan. *Sex and Power*. New York: Riverhead Books, 2000.

Femenia, Nora Amalia. Argentina's mothers of Plaza de Mayo: The mourning process from junta to democracy. *Feminist Studies*, 13:1, 9–18, 1987.

Frankenberg, Ruth. *White Women, Race Matters: The Social Construction of Whiteness*. Minneapolis: University of Minnesota Press, 1993.

———. When we are capable of stopping we begin to see: Being white, seeing whiteness. In *Names We Call Home: Autobiography on Racial Identity*, edited by Becky Thompson and Sangeeta Tyagi. New York: Routledge, 1996.

Frye, Marilyn. *The Politics of Reality*. Trumansburg, NY: Crossing Press, 1983.

García, Christina. *Dreaming in Cuban*. New York: Knopf, 1991.

Gilkes, Cheryl Townsend. A case study: Race–ethnicity, class, and African American women: Exploring the community connec-

tion. In *Revolutions in Knowledge: Feminism in the Social Sciences*, edited by Sue Rosenberg Zalk and Janice Gordon-Kelter. Boulder, CO: Westview Press, 1992.

Gould, Janice. The problem of being "Indian": One mixed-blood's dilemma. In *De/colonizing the subject: The politics of gender in women's autobiography*, edited by Sidonie Smith and Julia Watson. Minneapolis: University of Minnesota Press, 1992.

Hammonds, Evelynn. Race, sex, AIDS: The construction of the "other." *Radical America*, 20:6, 28–36, 1986.

Haney Lopez, Ian F. *White by Law: The Legal Construction of Race*. New York: New York University Press, 1996.

Haraway, Donna. *Primate Visions: Gender, Race and Nature in the World of Modern Science*. New York: Routledge, 1989.

Hartsock, Nancy C. M. The feminist standpoint. In *Discovering Reality*, edited by Sandra Harding and Merrill Hintikka. Dordrecht, Holland: Reidel, 1983.

———. *The Feminist Standpoint Revisited and Other Essays*. Boulder, CO: Westview Press, 1998.

Hine, Darlene Clark, Elsa Barkley Brown, and Rosalyn Terborg-Penn, editors. *Black Women in America: An Historical Encyclopedia*, 2 vols. Brooklyn, NY: Carlson Publishers, 1993.

hooks, bell. *Ain't I a Woman? Black Women and Feminism*. Boston: South End Press, 1982.

Hune, Shirley, and Gail M. Nomura, editors. *Asian/Pacific Islander American Women: A Historical Anthology*. New York: New York University Press, 2003.

Hurtado, Aida. Relating to privilege: Seduction and rejection in the subordination of white women and women of color. *Signs: Journal of Women in Culture and Society*, 11:4, 833–55, 1989.

Jen, Gish. *Mona in the Promised Land*. New York: Knopf, 1996.

Jones, Jacqueline. *Labor of Love, Labor of Sorrow: Black Women, Work and the Family, From Slavery to the Present*. New York: Basic Books, 1985.

Joseph, Gloria, and Jill Lewis. *Common Differences: Conflicts in Black and White Perspectives*. Garden City, NY: Anchor, 1981.

Kincaid, Jamaica. *Lucy*. New York: Farrar, Straus and Giroux, 1990.

King, Deborah K. Multiple jeopardy, multiple consciousness: The context of a black feminist ideology. *Signs: Journal of Women in Culture and Society*, 14:1, 42–72, 1988.

Kristeva, Julia. *The Portable Kristeva*, edited by Kelly Oliver. New York: Columbia University Press, 1997.

Latina Feminist Group. *Telling to Live: Latina Feminist* Testimonios. Durham, NC: Duke University Press, 2001.

Lim, Shirley Geok-Lin. *Among the White Moon Faces: An Asian-American Memoir of Homelands*. New York: Feminist Press at the City University of New York, 1996.

Lorber, Judith. *Gender Inequality: Feminist Theories and Politics*, 2nd ed. Los Angeles: Roxbury Publishing, 2001.

Lorde, Audre. *Zami: A New Spelling of My Name*. Freedom, CA: Crossing Press, 1982.

———. *Sister Outsider*. Trumansburg, NY: Crossing Press, 1984.

Lugones, Maria C., and Elizabeth Spelman. Have we got a theory for you! Feminist theory, cultural imperialism and the demand for "the woman's voice." *Women's Studies International Forum*, 6:6, 573–81, 1983.

Marshall, Paule. *Brown Girl, Brown Stones*. New York: Feminist Press at the City University of New York, 1981.

———. *The Fisher King*. New York: Scribner, 2000.

Maveety, Nancy. *Justice Sandra Day O'Connor: Strategist on the Supreme Court*. Lanham, MD: Rowman & Littlefield, 1996.

McGlen, Nancy E., Karen O'Connor, Laura van Assendelft, and Wendy Gunther-Canada. *Women, Politics, and American Society*, 3rd ed. Boston: Allyn & Bacon/Longman, 2000.

Minh-ha, Trinh. Difference: A special third world women issue. *Feminist Review*, 25, 5–22, 1987.

Mohanty, Chandra Talpade. Under Western eyes: Feminist scholarship and colonial discourses. In *Third World Women and the Politics of Feminism*, edited by Chandra Talpade Mohanty, Ann Russo, and Lourdes Torres. Bloomington: Indiana University Press, 1991.

———. "Under Western eyes" revisited: Feminist solidarity through anticapitalist struggles. *Signs*, 28:2, 499–536, 2002.

Moraga, Cherríe, and Gloria Anzaldúa, editors. *This Bridge Called My Back: Writings by Radical Women of Color*. New York: Kitchen Table/Women of Color Press, 1983.

Morgen, Sandra, and Ann Bookman. Introductory essay. In *Women and the Politics of Empowerment*, edited by Ann Bookman and Sandra Morgen. Philadelphia: Temple University Press, 1986.

Morrison, Toni. *Beloved*. New York: Knopf, 1987.

———. *Playing in the Dark: Whiteness and the Literary Imagination*. Cambridge, MA: Harvard University Press, 1992.

Mullings, Leith. Ethnicity and stratification in the urban United States. In *Papers in Anthropology and Linguistics*, edited by May Ebihara and Rosamund Gianutsos. New York: New York Academy of Sciences, 1978.

Nafisi, Azar. *Reading Lolita in Tehran: A Memoir in Books*. New York: Random House, 2003.

National Council for Research on Women. The world's women: A demographic and statistical overview. Prepared for Citigroup's Women's Summit, September 2000.

Omolade, Barbara. *The Rising Song of African American Women*. New York: Routledge, 1994.

Ostrander, Susan. *Women of the Upper Class*. Philadelphia: Temple University Press, 1984.

Palmer, Phyllis Marynick. White women/black women: The dualism of female identity and experiences in the United States. *Feminist Studies*, 9:1, 151–70, 1983.

Pheterson, Gail. Alliances between women: Overcoming internalized oppression and internalized domination. In *Bridges of Power: Women's Multicultural Alliances*, edited by Lisa Albrecht and Rose M. Brewer. Philadelphia: New Society Publishers, 1990.

Pomeroy, Sarah B. *Goddesses, Whores, Wives, and Slaves: Women in Classical Antiquity*. New York: Schocken, 1975.

Pratt, Minnie Bruce. Identity: Skin blood heart. In *Yours in Struggle: Three Feminist Perspectives on Anti-Semitism and Racism*, edited by Elly Bulkin, Minnie Bruce Pratt, and Barbara Smith. New York: Kitchen Table/Women of Color Press, 1984.

Quintanales, Martha. I paid very hard for my immigrant ignorance. In *This Bridge Called My Back: Writings by Radical Women of Color*, edited by Cherríe Moraga and Gloria Anzaldúa. New York: Kitchen Table/Women of Color Press, 1983.

Rich, Adrienne. Compulsory heterosexuality and lesbian experience, *Signs* 5, 631–60, 1980.

Riley, Denise. *Am I that Name? Feminism and the Category of "Women" in History*. Minneapolis: University of Minnesota Press, 1988.

———. *The Words of Selves*. Stanford, CA: Stanford University Press, 2000.

Rubin, Gayle. The traffic in women: Notes on the political economy of sex. In *Toward an Anthropology of Women*, edited by Rayna Rapp Reiter. New York: Monthly Review Press, 1975.

Sacks, Karen Brodin. How did Jews become white folks? In *Race*, edited by Steven Gregory and Roger Sanjek. New Brunswick, NJ: Rutgers University Press, 1994.

Schneir, Miriam, editor. *Feminism in Our Time*. New York: Vintage, 1994.

Silko, Leslie Marmon. *Gardens in the Dunes*. New York: Simon & Schuster, 1999.

Spelman, Elizabeth V. *Inessential Woman: Problems of Exclusion in Feminist Thought*. Boston: Beacon Press, 1988.

Sterling, Dorothy, editor. *We Are Your Sisters: Black Women in the Nineteenth Century*. New York: Norton, 1984.

Tan, Amy. *The Joy Luck Club*. New York: Ivy Books, 1989.

———. *The Bonesetter's Daughter*. New York: G. P. Putnam's Sons, 2000.

Tong, Rosemarie. *Feminist Thought: A Comprehensive Introduction*, 2nd ed. Boulder, CO: Westview Press, 1998.

Ware, Vron. *Beyond the Pale: White Women, Racism, and History*. London: Verso, 1992.

Washington, Mary Helen. Introduction: "The Darkened Eye Restored." Notes toward a literary history of black women. In *Invented Lives: Narratives of Black Women 1860–1960*. New York: Anchor Press, 1987.

Williams, Claudette. Gall . . . you come from foreign. In *Charting the Journey: Writings by Black and Third World Women*, edited by Shabnam Grewal, Jackie Kay, Liliane Landor, Gail Lewis, and Pratibha Parmar. London: Sheba Feminist Publishers, 1988.

Williams, Joan. *Unbending Gender: Why Family and Work Conflict and What to Do About It*. New York: Oxford University Press, 2000.

Young, Iris Marion. *Justice and the Politics of Difference*. Princeton: Princeton University Press, 1990.

Part II

Families

Images of families in the popular media—television, films, magazines—inform us about family forms considered acceptable and unacceptable and ways to play roles within them. In the United States, traditional nuclear families were a staple of prime-time television. Since the 1980s, television viewers have seen depictions of families—related genetically or by legal acts such as adoption and marriage—headed by single mothers or single fathers and families composed of combinations of relatives incorporating grandparents, aunts and uncles, siblings, nieces and nephews, in-laws, or cousins or blended households with stepparents and their children, even if these representations were idealized. Viewers also have been made more aware of cultural differences in family organization and roles through the portrayals of ethnic households, as in *The Sopranos*, a television drama of an extended Italian family. It is noteworthy that among the most watched television programs of the past decade are those about the unique relationships among friends and housemates, some of whom are gay: *Will and Grace* is an example.

The popular representation of the woman's traditional role in the U.S. family as a married stay-at-home mother engaged in full-time domestic work is being replaced by other images. She may be portrayed as a married mother with a career, trying to balance work outside the home and family responsibilities, or as a single working parent seeking to have a personal life as well. Even if never married or divorced, the adult woman is often depicted as a dutiful daughter who worries about her parents and other family members and may even move back to her childhood home to live with them. She might also choose to be a mother without marrying. Only 12% of the nation's households are headed by two parents. Reflecting these norms, in 2002, Rachel Green, a character on the television show *Friends*, gave birth in a much-watched episode to a baby she chose to have with one of her male friends outside of marriage.

Daughterhood, sisterhood, wifehood, and motherhood are socially defined roles women play in a family context. Our understanding of these roles is shaped from the earliest childhood experience. It can be argued that all our roles in society are governed by family-role expectations. Families, however structured and realized, are significant organizing units for all known societies, from the preindustrial hunter–gatherers and cultivators to the highly urban industrial (and, some say, postindustrial) nations. In all these societies, families tend to be assigned the organization of childrearing, marriage, and various aspects of domestic life. In many societies, past and present, women have been defined largely in terms of domestic concerns and family-role assignments, while men, though also tied to families, have been defined in other ways as well.

Historical studies and cross-cultural comparisons inform us that the sentiments and activities ascribed to women's family roles are variable; they are not "natural" but are socially shaped. Society may tell us that daughters are "naturally" obedient, sisters competitive, mothers loving of their children, or wives dependent on their husbands; and women may indeed conform to these social expectations because they have been taught to do so. Nevertheless, an examination of contemporary family interactions in U.S. society as well as in other times and places reveals that there are many diverse ways to fulfill family expectations.

To understand family roles and how they have shaped women, we need to understand both social expectations and the scope for variation in women's choices in how they fulfill prescribed roles. We must also take into account the conflicts that may arise between women's different family roles and between those roles and others that may be assigned to them or to which they may aspire.

Women have sometimes seen the family as too constricting and limiting for the fulfillment of their aspirations. At times, they have had the option of developing alternative ways of organizing themselves at the household or domestic level, of fulfilling their assigned roles, or even of replacing households and families with other social forms. This section will examine the ways that women have been defined by their family roles and the ways they have sought to redefine families.

The family circle can be seen as a warm, enfolding, supportive center to women's lives, or it can be viewed as a small, confining cage that they long to escape. Many women have experienced both kinds of feeling toward families at different times in their lives and at the same time.

chapter 6

Daughters and Sisters

Traditional studies of family history and comparative kinship structures have tended to emphasize the role change females experience as they grow from daughter to wife and mother and to draw attention away from their permanent attachments to parents and siblings. Nevertheless, the ties between daughters and mothers and between sisters in their natal families last beyond their girlhood even though most women eventually leave home. These relationships constitute the formative experience of women's lives, and they continue in some manner until their deaths. Thus, investigating how daughterhood and sisterhood are constituted is essential for understanding women's lives and choices.

Daughter in the Family

The conception and birth of a child is usually a welcome event in the history of a family. Sometimes, however, it is inconvenient or even disastrous to a household's economic survival. The physical survival of the mother and older children, especially an unweaned child, may be threatened by the arrival of another child. Where contraceptive and abortive methods are unknown, unavailable, or undependable, the only "choice" may be infanticide. Even in societies with forms of birth control available, infanticide has been practiced.

Those readers who believe that there is a "maternal instinct" that naturally causes mothers to protect their children must wonder what could prompt women to kill them instead. Inability to care for a child, particularly if it is "illegitimate" or if the other parent or other members of the society are not available for assistance, may be a motive. In some situations, a mother may suffer from postpartum depression or a debilitating physical or mental illness. Where infanticide is a socially recognized option, it may be the father alone who makes the decision and it may be the midwife or another party who carries it out. Historians and anthropologists have not documented the emotions of mothers in the face of such directives. Reflecting the inequality that women face worldwide, the death rate of infant girls far exceeds that of infant boys, an outcome of parental and societal discrimination, family resource allocations, and government policy (Croll, 2000).

Female Infanticide

In 1 B.C.E., a husband in Alexandria wrote to his wife in the Egyptian countryside: "I beg you and urge you . . . if by chance you bear a child—if it is a boy, let it be; if it is a girl, cast it out" (Hunt and Edgar, 1932). Such abandonment was usually tantamount to infanticide.

Until recent times, female infanticide has been the only method of population control that enables the responsible parties to make decisions on the basis of sex. The Greeks abandoned many more girls to die than boys, and the Romans had a law requiring fathers to raise all healthy sons but only one daughter (Pomeroy, 1975). In medieval Christian society, where church law strictly forbade infanticide, there is evidence that it was still carried out extensively. Girls were the most common victims of "accidents" where women claim to have "overlaid" (smothered) children at night. When foundling homes were established, as in Florence in the fourteenth century, the records provide incontrovertible evidence that parents discarded many more females than males (Trexler, 1973).

Where infanticide has not been practiced, it might be expected that the genetic advantages of girls would result in women making up slightly more than half of the adult population. Often, this is not the case. Today, it is possible to perform tests in early pregnancy to discover the sex of the fetus. In many countries in East and South Asia, for example, families have used such technologies to abort fetuses identified as female, to both limit family size and select the sex of their children. Although one daughter may be viewed as ideal for help in the home, a second may be seen as a burden. Recent studies note the excessive female mortality and widening male–female sex ratio in East and South Asia and have called attention to the "missing girls" in their societies (Croll, 2000).

Why in many societies outside the United States do more girls than boys die in infancy and early childhood? Are there "natural" causes, or can this phenomenon be better explained by social practices? One answer seems to be that male children get better treatment. If one child is systematically allotted less food, neglected during illnesses, and overworked or abused physically, that child is more likely to die. In many families, when protein has been scarce, women have customarily stinted themselves and their daughters in favor of the husband and sons. This has prejudiced the daughters' chances of survival and helped to socialize those who survived to play the same role later in their own households. The neglect of daughters is masked almost everywhere by the assertion that girls do not require as much food as boys. This belief might account for more discrepancy in the size and physical strength of girls and boys than is generally acknowledged. In other cases, when a daughter is unwanted, girls are simply abandoned, put up for adoption, or even sold (Croll, 2000; Dickemann, 1979).

Worldwide, more couples still prefer to have a son than a daughter, particularly if it is the first child, and many couples tend to continue having children until they have a son. There is virtually no society that positively prefers girl babies to boys.

The Value of Daughters

The selective destruction of female babies by individual families throughout history would not have been possible unless society as a whole condoned it. Why the murder or abandonment of female children should be a method of population control, why effective and safe contraceptives took so long to develop and become widely accepted and used, and why so many people display a preference for sons over daughters are questions for both women and men. Many of the answers lie in the social patterns that define women's place and their value to the society at large.

One theory suggests that female infanticide can be understood in terms of the high valuation given males in societies engaged in chronic warfare. If men are the warriors, sons must be raised and "masculine" qualities stressed. Because investment in daughters detracts from investment in sons, daughters are sacrificed.

The evidence supporting this argument shows systematic correlation between female infanticide, chronic warfare, and male supremacist cultural values (Divale and Harris, 1978).

Another theory rests on speculations concerning the marital strategies of individual families, which are political and economic decisions, and if properly utilized can enhance family wealth and power. This theory suggests that where the potential marital pool is known and limited, parents may sacrifice daughters for whom there are no possibilities of a profitable future marriage settlement (Coleman, 1976). In many societies, brides must be accompanied by wealth when leaving their fathers' houses. In others, daughters represent potential wealth that will be paid their parents in exchange for them (see Chapter 7). Clearly, these economic and political prospects play an important role in a family's decision making about the value of girls.

Still another theory emphasizes gender ideologies that devalue daughters because they are viewed as temporary members of a family, while sons generally and historically have inherited property, carried on the family line, fulfilled cultural rituals, and had responsibilities for parents and female members of the household. Thus, son preference is reinforced (Croll, 2000).

Recent studies by economists document how girl devaluation in the U.S. is embedded in family practices, oftentimes through very subtle choices, and how these decisions contribute to the differential well-being of girls and boys. For example, since the 1940s, couples with girls have been more likely to get divorced than those with boys. As children from divorced households demonstrate higher rates of dropping out of high school and becoming parents while teenagers and being jobless as young adults, female children carry a greater share of the costs of divorce. Another study found that parents invested more of their resources into improving their housing when

they had a son. Other investigators found that fathers who read to their children and put them to bed also fed, changed, and played with boy babies more often than with girl babies. Thus, while boy preference is less widespread today, girls in the United States are still treated as less worthy of resources and attention from their parents (Leonhardt, 2003).

Decisions that favor women seem to exist only in the realm of fantasy. Ancient Greek myths about Amazons tell of women warriors who preferred girl babies to boys. According to this legend, sons were maimed, killed, or immediately sent to their fathers. Feminists have adopted this myth about strong women but have modified its ugly features. In *The Female Man* (1975), for example, Joanna Russ created a fictional utopia where women live without men and have only girls. Reproduction is accomplished by the merging of ova, and children are raised communally.

Naming the Daughter

Women's names given at birth are sometimes the most powerful indicators of their value and place in the family and social scheme. Because the process of naming is profoundly political, we can learn much about the status of women in different societies by understanding naming patterns.

A name generally designates the sex of a child. The more emphasis a society places on the difference between girls and boys, the more carefully it distinguishes their names. Medieval Europeans usually got through life with a single name, which often repeated the father's name or embroidered on it, such as *Charles*, *Charlotte*, or *Charlene*. When named for fathers, daughters were given a close feminine form of his name: *John/Joan; Robert/Roberta*. Custom may reserve the privilege of naming sons for fathers and give mothers the right to select names for daughters. Boys are almost never given names identified with girls, but the reverse can occur, perhaps reflecting the greater worth attached to male associations. Sons are frequently named for their fathers. Daughters are far more rarely named for their mothers. Some mothers seek to express pleasure in having daughters or to transfer desirable qualities through a name like *Joy* or *Linda* ("beautiful" in Spanish). They may name daughters for admired objects such as flowers or jewels or for a character in a movie or novel. Today, some daughters in the United States are given gender-neutral names, such as *Blair*, *Taylor*, or *Jordan*, which suggests perhaps the desire of contemporary parents to reduce gender stereotyping in naming.

The importance of children for the continuity of a lineage is reflected in the use of *patronymics* (fathers' names). For example, the ancient Romans did not give their daughters individual names: they were automatically called by the feminine form of the father's name. Thus, all the daughters of a Claudius were called Claudia and referred to informally in numerical order: *Claudia prima*, *Claudia secunda*, *Claudia tertulla*.

In some areas, patronymics continued into modern times. The Russian heroine of Tolstoy's novel (first published in 1875–77) was named *Anna Arkadyevna* ("daughter of Arkady") Karenina ("wife of Karenin"). African American slaves in the American South named sons for their fathers in an effort to retain family ties despite the breakup of the conjugal unit through sale (Gutman, 1977). The use of patronymics in modern Europe and the United States has commonly rigidified into a permanent family name (such as *Jackson* or *Richardson*). Names associated with a parent, a profession, or a geographical location also have hardened into "family" names, bestowed alike on daughters and sons at birth, and reflect the perpetuation of a male lineage since they are derived from the father's name, profession, or place of birth.

Traditionally in Korea, Confucian custom deemed female status too low even for married women to be permitted to use the family name of their husbands. In contrast, Burma (now Myanmar), with its Buddhist tradition and a matrilineal past, did not have a family name system. Both females and males were registered using their own individual names, and historically women did not change their names after marriage (Matsui, 1987:109–10). In Spanish-speaking societies, women often retain their father's name by adding it (with *y*) to the husband's name. Among noble families, it is often possible to trace a whole genealogical history by a recitation of the full name of an individual. In other societies, children will often perpetuate the name of their mother's family as a middle name or even as a first name.

In the modern Western world, a daughter's surname generally changes at the time of marriage as she takes on that of her husband. Women have reported feelings of a loss of identity when they suddenly stop using their own names and become, instead, Mrs. _____. A woman's married name designates a position rather than a person, and a first Mrs._____ may be replaced by a second or third with the same surname. Many U.S. couples today experiment with combining both names as a family name; women may keep their family name when they marry, as they are legally entitled to do, and some do so for their professional lives. It is still most common for U.S. children to have the surnames of their fathers, but it is perfectly possible to register them under other names, alternating the names of mother and father with each child, for example, according to the sex of the child. Some women reject the surnames of both fathers and husbands and choose their own, as did artist Judy Chicago (see Chapter 1).

Daughters' Work

Although not all societies value females in and of themselves, girls can occupy an important position within their natal families on the basis of the work they perform. Certain tasks must be done for a household's survival. In most households, including those in the contemporary Western world, daughters are expected to care for younger siblings and assist in food preparation and other domestic chores. In developing societies, where child labor is common, girls fetch water and firewood, feed chickens, go to the market, wash clothes, help with the dairying, do agricultural work, and undertake income-producing tasks like garment work.

Daughters also have a certain intrinsic value because if there is to be a future generation, women must be raised to produce it. The universal taboos against the mating of members of the immediate family make it necessary to procure a daughter-in-law for the production of grandchildren. In traditional cultures, the most common way in which a family gets a daughter-in-law is in exchange for a daughter. Some societies operate on a rigid one-to-one basis: the even exchange of cousins, for example, is seen as the right and normal way of pairing off young people. Thus, daughters are valuable directly or indirectly as chips in the bargains that make up the composition of society.

In many parts of the world, daughters are thought to be critical for parents' old-age security. They are generally expected to provide their parents with a home, personal care when needed, affection, and other emotional supports. Although sons are liable for the same responsibilities, all too often they limit their contributions to cash, have their wives (the daughters-in-law) undertake much of their obligations, or manage to escape altogether. It is an old saying among the Turks that only a daughter can be relied upon on a dark day. The son will defect to his wife's family when he is most needed. There is also the following saying in the Western world: "A son's a son till he gets him a wife. A daughter's a daughter the whole of her life."

In the United States today, the value of daughters' (unpaid) work to families and societies is most evident in a 1988 U.S. House of Representatives report, which points out that the average woman in the United States is likely to spend 18 years looking after elderly parents and in-laws in addition to 17 years of childrearing. Regardless of their racial, ethnic, and class background, many women willingly assume dependent-adult caring responsibilities. Brothers and husbands, however, often do not share this work. Hence, while some women may not choose the "mother track," they retain for the most part the "daughter track." The strains of elder care can affect the health of daughters, complicate their personal and professional responsibilities, and often require them to make major alterations in their everyday life (Beck, 1990). Feminists, however, argue that equality for women calls for elder care to be recognized as a societal responsibility (Harrington, 1999) and not one left to individual women.

Young women, then, start their lives on the basis of a series of considerations about their future worth to the family. They enter into a political system in which parents, sisters, and brothers all figure in a series of shifting alliances and antagonisms. They struggle for identity and material advantage within a pattern imposed by chance and social convention.

Parental Relationships

From the moment a girl is born and named, she is started on a track that will take her through her whole life. Social conventions tend to prescribe parental behavior. A girl is handled, dressed, and trained to fulfill a role in the family as a daughter.

Daughters and Mothers

Western feminist studies have identified three major phases in a daughter's relationship with her mother (Applebaum, 2001). First, there is the attachment in early infancy and the power

Box 6.1   MOTHERS AND DAUGHTERS

They perpetuate themselves
one comes out of the other
like a set of Russian dolls.

Each is programmed to pass on
her methods to the daughter
who in turn becomes a mother.

They learn to cry and get
their way and finally to say
"I did it all for you."

When they are old and can't
be mended they're either burnt
or laid in boxes in the dark.

Sometimes their sons are sad.
Their daughters go away and weep
real tears for themselves.

Russian dolls.

Source: Feaver, 1980, reprinted by permission.

of same-sex bonding. According to the psychological theory developed by Nancy Chodorow and other theorists, children experience the mother as the first "other" and a daughter's sense of self must be forged out of that opposition. Since the mothering person, however, is nearly always a woman, daughters tend to experience stronger feelings of identity with the mother than do sons and may have more difficulty than their brothers in separating psychologically from their mothers and becoming their own persons (Chodorow, 1978). The developmental task is made harder if mothers see daughters as a reflection of themselves as children. In traditional cultures, where girls grow into women looking forward to a predictable life and women's and men's roles are distinctly defined, this is probably not a matter for distress and does not seem to create a great deal of tension between generations. Mothers act easily as role models and guides for young women. In societies that reward a highly developed sense of individu-

alism, daughters may suffer much confusion in separating from their mothers, as is suggested by the title of Nancy Friday's *My Mother/My Self: The Daughter's Search for Identity* (1977).

The second phase identified by this particular theory of Western psychological development centers on the years of adolescence and early adulthood, which are often difficult as daughters seek to distance themselves from their mothers and differentiate themselves as individuals while also maintaining the closeness of a mother's love. Mothers may inhibit the development of a separate sense of identity by expecting daughters to remain at home or closer to home more often than they expect sons to stay. This may reflect a traditional pattern in which boys are sent out into the world at a relatively early age to be shaped for their predicted adult role. Girls, in contrast, are generally expected to help with "women's work" around the home. A daughter is often shaped into a "little mother" and taught nurturing skills. Mothers may mold daughters in their own images, or they may consciously set out to create daughters who will not repeat their experiences.

Jane Flax (1997) argues that even after separation from their mothers daughters continue to experience their mothers as an ever-present framework through which they evaluate their own developing selves. She notes that the relationship between a daughter and her mother can be both rich and laden with conflict. Many young women report separation from their mothers as being accompanied by feelings of regret and longing. Lynn Glasman (2002) finds that women struggle with the idea of being similar to or different from their mothers. Some daughters react with rage to their mother's dependence. Others react against their mother's independence. Whatever confusion and tension may have occurred between daughters and mothers, their relationships may shift and enter a third phase, one of increased mutual interdependence. As daughters become adults and marry, work, and become mothers themselves they often draw closer to their mothers, seeking their support and advice. Finally, their roles may reverse when mothers become elderly and frail and daughters often mother their mothers (Beck, 1990; Fischer, 1986).

The ability of daughters to define and redefine themselves can be evidence of assertiveness and strength; it can also betray the absence of a sense of a fixed inner core. A common motif in the work of women artists is the mirror in which women search for themselves and beautify their bodies. In her painting of a daughter and mother, Mary Cassatt portrays a mother who is helping her daughter find the image of herself in a mirror. Women's art is commonly haunted by the fear that a woman will look into the glass and see nothing; it is "an allegory of nonidentity . . . fear of desertion, of dependence upon an insufficiently integrated self" (Peterson and Wilson, 1976:4). The double female image is another common theme, for women often view themselves as part of a daughter–mother dyad.

Although the daughter–mother relationship generally takes place within a patriarchy, mothers may also be the strongest allies in helping daughters to realize their dreams. Examples include the French author Colette ([1930] 1953), who wrote of the encouragement she received as a child in her mother's house. The leader of the militant British suffrage movement, Emmeline Pankhurst (1858–1928), raised her daughters to live independent and creative lives. Sylvia Pankhurst (1882–1960) first chose an artistic career and then became the socialist leader of working-class women. Christabel Pankhurst (1880–1958) also became a leader in the fight for women's rights. Adela Pankhurst (1885–1961) immigrated to Australia and became a social reformer there. Less known are the hopes and struggles of working-class women and the role of their mothers and other womenfolk in helping them make difficult life choices. One Mexican American migrant worker's daughter, for example, Elizabeth Loza Newby, left home to attend college with a scholarship and her mother's support and insistence in the face of her traditional father's disownment at her decision (Newby, 1981).

U.S. daughters of many racial and ethnic backgrounds whose mothers were second-wave feminists have also expressed their gratitude for the new opportunities made available to them by their mothers. The doors that their mothers forced open have given them personal and social rewards through new occupational and professional experiences. Their mothers have also provided them with alternative ways of being and with a sense of social commitment and political activism. Hence, these daughters do not view marriage as their only option in life (Glickman, 1993). Some daughters, however, have expressed ambivalence about those feminist mothers who

Dame Christabel (1880–1958), Sylvia (1882–1960), and Adela (1885–1961) Pankhurst, daughters of Richard and Emmeline Pankhurst, followed their parents' commitment to working for radical social and political reform in England. Christabel, with her mother, established the radical Women's Social and Political Union in 1906 to gain women's suffrage. Sylvia established a women's suffrage movement specifically among the working class in London's East End. Adela emigrated to Australia, where she was active in socialist politics.

seem to devalue motherhood. In one study, conversations between 23 contemporary feminists and their daughters reveal both connection and conflict (Baker and Kline, 1996).

The psychological development model discussed above is not universal, however. Women of color in the United States have challenged the (white) feminist and Eurocentric notion of motherhood, with its identification with domestic activities and its emphasis on daughter–mother relationships, as constantly fraught with conflict. Such a depiction, they have argued, is an incomplete and unbalanced portrayal of their experiences as daughters and mothers. For example, Patricia Hill Collins (2000) and Gloria Joseph (1981, 1991) call attention to the importance of other female figures in mothering, such as grandmothers, siblings, aunts, cousins, and women who are not biologically related, as well as men who "mother" African American children. Joseph also writes of the respect and affection of daughters for their mothers and mother surrogates in recognition of the obstacles the women (and occasionally men) confront in holding households together under conditions of racism and economic constraints, in addition to gender discrimination, that often require them to work long hours outside the home. She also points out that, contrary to the views expressed by Chodorow (see above), black lesbian mothers do not believe that a father figure is essential for a daughter's development. Many African American mothers have purposely raised girls to be independent and able to enhance their capacity to survive for themselves and their households. The literary critic Mary Helen Washington acknowledges the persistent image of the strong black mother and dedicates her anthology *Black-Eyed Susans: Classic Stories by and About Black Women* (1975) "to the fine black women who brought me up." Sometimes to provide for children mothers need to send them away to be raised by grandmothers

or other relatives or leave them behind while the mothers emigrate to obtain work. In extreme cases, daughter–mother relationships are conducted thousands of miles apart, as occurs under globalization today (see Chapter 12). For example, some Filipinas mother from afar as part of a transnational household while they work in the United States as domestic workers caring for the elderly. Daughters, in particular, and other female relatives acknowledging the mother's sacrifice assume major household responsibilities in the Philippines and stay connected by a stream of regular phone calls and packages from their mothers that can continue for years (Tung, 2003).

Consequently, the struggle to sustain ethnic communities in the dominant Anglo-American culture that has treated racial groups as inferior has strengthened daughter–mother relationships as well as contributed to tensions. Chinese garment workers' daughters who have become professionals and community activists often speak with pride about their hardworking mothers and view them as role models (Bao, 2003). In assessing Chicana poetry, Marta Sanchez (1985) discusses the "double ambivalence" borne by Mexican American women in their struggles against racism in the United States and sexism from within and without the community and the lives of their mothers, grandmothers, and mother surrogates as inspiration. The theme of daughter–mother interdependence underlies much of American ethnic literature (see Box 6.2).

Young women frequently find that their struggles to break away from the pattern of their mothers' lives entangle them more deeply in a mesh of invisible threads. This can be heightened, for example, in the case of U.S.-born or U.S.-raised daughters of immigrant mothers, who often negotiate different notions of daughterhood and womanhood offered by their peers and their parents' culture.

Box 6.2   THE BONESETTER'S DAUGHTER

In her novel The Bonesetter's Daughter *(2001), Amy Tan shows how the power of a woman's memories of her own girlhood and of family secrets concerning her mother, a daughter of a Chinese bonesetter, can affect her relationship with her daughter.*

She pulled out a clipped stack of paper from the bottom of the drawer, guessing she could toss out whatever had lain there the longest by neglect.

They were pages written in Chinese, her mother's writing. LuLing had given them to her five or six years before. "Just some old things about my family," she had said, with the kind of awkward nonchalance that meant the pages were important. "My story, begin little-girl time. I write for myself, but maybe you read, then you see how I grow up, come to this country." Ruth had heard bits of her mother's life over the years, but she was touched by her shyness in asking Ruth to read what she had obviously labored over. The pages contained precise vertical rows, without cross-outs, leaving Ruth to surmise that her mother had copied over her earlier attempts.

Ruth had tried to decipher the pages. Her mother had once drilled Chinese calligraphy into her reluctant brain, and she still recognized some of the characters: "thing," "I," "truth." But unraveling the rest required her to match LuLing's squiggly radicals to uniform ones in a Chinese–English dictionary. "These are the things I know are true," the first sentence read. That had taken Ruth an hour to translate. She set a goal to decipher a sentence a day. And in keeping with her plan, she translated another sentence the next evening: "My name is LuLing Liu Young." That was easy, a mere five minutes. Then came the names of LuLing's husbands, one of whom was Ruth's father. Husbands? Ruth was startled to read that there had been another. And what did her mother mean by "our secrets gone with them"? Ruth wanted to know right away, but she could not ask her mother. She knew from experience what happened whenever she asked her mother to render Chinese characters into English. First LuLing scolded her for not studying Chinese hard enough when she was little. And then, to untangle each character, her mother took side routes to her past, going into excruciating detail over the infinite meanings of Chinese words: "Secret not just mean cannot say. Can be hurt-you kinda secret, or curse-you kind, maybe do you damage forever, never can change after that. . . ."

Source: From *The Bonesetter's Daughter* by Amy Tan, pp. 12–3. Copyright © 2001 by Amy Tan. Used by permission of G. P. Putnam's Sons, a division of Penguin Group (USA), Inc.

Some daughters who have grown up, married, and become mothers may still be haunted by their mothers' "nagging" voices telling them how to do everything, setting standards of perfection that they can never reach. This is an irritating experience if the voices come to them daily over the telephone or in person. It is even more maddening if the maternal voice has been internalized in the daughters' sense of permanent inadequacy. Other daughters recognize their mother's voice as they themselves speak and smile as they find themselves becoming more like their mothers. As the daughter of the newspaper advice columnist Ann Landers (Esther "Eppie" Lederer), Margo Howard, who herself now writes an advice column, poignantly noted after her mother's death, "I miss telling her what's going on. . . . But a girl's mother is always alive in her head" (Witchel, 2003).

Daughters and Fathers

Historically, fathers have had social, economic, and political power over their daughters as well as certain obligations, such as arranging for a proper marriage. Under conditions such as slavery, feudalism, and colonialism, many fathers were limited in serving as the head of the household and able neither to provide adequately for their daughters nor to protect them. Daughters, on the other hand, have usually deferred to their fathers. Immigrant daughters in the United States often brought home all their earnings to their fathers. As the historical and legal conditions of a father's power over his children have changed, so has a daughter's relationship with her father (Devlin, 2001). Nowadays, in the United States, for example, it is possible to find feminist fathers who shoulder a fair share of parenting and treat daughters and sons in a reasonably equal way.

The same psychological theory discussed above in terms of a girl's relationship to her mother suggests that a daughter's relationship with her father can sometimes be fraught with tension and instability. Daughters often find themselves in league with their mothers against the "foreign" male element represented by their fathers. On other occasions, hunger for a father's approval makes them vulnerable to the subtle training males give young women on how to become attractive and socially desirable women in maturity.

Fathers who want to bring up their daughters as "little women" will actively discourage their efforts to break out of the conventional restrictions of their feminine role and will compliment girls on pretty clothing and beguiling ways. They will frown if girls are messy or "tomboyish." They will also let daughters know that straightforward competition will not earn paternal respect. When early feminist Elizabeth Cady Stanton (1815–1902) won a first-place Latin award in school to compensate her father for the son he had lost, her father sighed heavily, "You should have been a boy" (Stanton, 1971:23). Only after years of marriage and motherhood, conforming to the roles so clearly marked out for her, did Stanton return to the ambitions of her youth, pursuing a career as a writer and feminist agitator.

An extreme form of a father's domination of a daughter is incest, a social taboo in almost all societies and a cruel exercise of power. Freud came to believe that when his female patients talked of incest with their fathers, they were revealing wishes rather than reporting facts. Other male family members—uncles, stepfathers, brothers, cousins, and grandfathers—also perpetrate sexual abuse of females. Yet, father–daughter incest is the most commonly reported type of incest in the United States, and its effects are many. Research indicates it often leaves deep and lasting trauma. It may drive girls away from home as runaways, into a premature and unwanted marriage or pregnancy, or to drug addiction and prostitution. Even if abused girls remain at home and the relationship runs its course, they may be haunted by anxiety attacks, adult sexual dysfunction, and difficulties in social relationships (Russell, 1986).

To prevent such violations becoming public knowledge, a daughter and mother may engage in a conspiracy of silence lest the offending father be imprisoned and his wages lost to the family. They may also fear the removal of the daughter to a hostile or unfamiliar environment. If a daughter seeks help, she may be held responsible for the family's dissolution, punished for "misbehavior," and loaded down with a misplaced burden of guilt that may emotionally cripple her. If a daughter becomes a mother of her father's child, the damage to all concerned may be extraordinary.

Fathers can also be very supportive. Many prominent women have noted with gratitude their fathers' role in helping them establish a career beyond the domestic sphere. Historically, in many cases, however valuable the emotional support of mothers to aspiring daughters, the sheer material support that the father commands can make the difference in determining their fates. Maria Mitchell (1818–89), the astronomer from Nantucket who became the first woman elected to the American Philosophical Society in 1869, began by spending many hours with her father gazing at stars through his telescope. In 1847, she discovered the comet that is named for her. Marie Skiodowska (1867–1934) began her scientific career under the instruction of her father, a professor of physics in Warsaw. Without his assistance, it is doubtful that she would have been sent to study in Paris, married Pierre Curie, and used his laboratory facilities in her discovery of radium, which contributed to her becoming the first person ever to receive two Nobel prizes. Indira Gandhi (1917–84), prime minister of India during 1966–77 and 1980–4 and the first woman elected to lead a democratic state, credited her father, Jawaharlal Nehru, with preparing her for a world of politics. He purposely educated her by sending her letters about world history while he was imprisoned for opposing British colonialism and took her along to meetings in his role as India's first prime minister after the country gained its independence in 1947 (Bhatia, 1974).

Research into the lives and careers of a group of women who were among the few to hold top management positions in U.S. business and industry in the early 1970s revealed a distinct pattern. The women were generally the firstborn of girls or only children, and all had a close daughter–father relationship in which the daughter was given strong support to pursue her interests (Hennig and Jardin, 1976).

The relationship of women with their father has not received much attention in recent feminist literature. Domineering fathers may provoke reactions in their daughters that release their feminist impulses and creative potential. Yet, it is also true that the fathers of many feminists and women artists, women scientists, and other creative women were sympathetic and actively involved in the rearing of their daughters. The full participation of both parents, where possible, provides children with more opportunities of finding helpful role models and with the support necessary to cultivate their talents and ultimately to form their own characters (see Box 6.3).

Girlhood

Until the 1990s, feminists had given little attention to girlhood. In their investigations, they have found that although girls generally hold a subordinate position in their families and societies compared to their male counterparts, the experiences of girlhood, past and present, can vary widely across the globe and within societies given differences in backgrounds, cultures, and family dynamics in specific historical eras. In the United States today, for example, girlhood as a daughter of migrant farm workers differs significantly from girlhood as a daughter of professional parents in a predominantly white middle-class suburb (Forman-Brunell, 2001). Moreover, girls throughout the world are experiencing changing and oftentimes competing notions of what it means to be female not only within their own societies but also more generally from the influence of the globalization of Western culture through its advertisements, media, and products (Inness, 1998).

In the early 1990s, feminist studies of girlhood (more precisely, Euro-American middle-class girlhood) in the United States emphasized girls' vulnerability, including problems of body

Box 6.3   ANNE FRANK ON HERSELF

Anne Frank and her family lived for 2 years in the Netherlands in hiding from the Nazis, who were rounding up the Jews for extermination. Her diary records the atrocities of the Holocaust as well as the thoughts of an adolescent girl living in close confinement with her parents, sister, and a few other people. On July 15, 1944, at the age of 15, 1 month before she was led to her death, she wrote the following:

I have one outstanding trait in my character, which must strike anyone who knows me for any length of time, and that is my knowledge of myself. I can watch myself and my actions, just like an outsider. The Anne of every day I can face entirely without prejudice, without making excuses for her, and watch what's good and what's bad about her. This "self-consciousness" haunts me, and every time I open my mouth I know as soon as I've spoken whether "that ought to have been different" or "that was right as it was." There are so many things about myself that I condemn; I couldn't begin to name them all. I understand more and more how true Daddy's words were when he said: "All children must look after their own upbringing." Parents can only give good advice or put them on the right paths, but the final forming of a person's character lies in their own hands. In addition to this, I have lots of courage, I always feel so strong and as if I can bear a great deal, I feel so free and so young! I was glad when I first realized it, because I don't think I shall easily bow down before the blows that inevitably come to everyone.

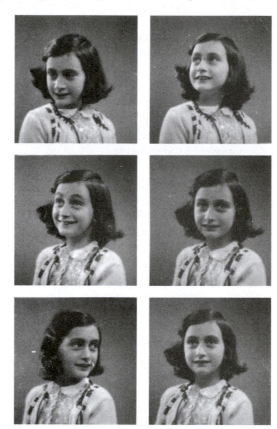

Strip of six photographs of Anne Frank. Her notes on these photos included "pity about the ugly teeth," "obviously a flop," "nice," and "I stuck the same photograph in before." Frank was able to look at herself through the eyes of a creative young woman and analyze the facets of her own personality.

Source: From *The Diary of Anne Frank, The Critical Edition* by Anne Frank, copyright © 1986 by Anne Frank-Fonds, Basle/Switzerland, for all texts of Anne Frank. Translation by Arnold J. Pomerans, pp. 689–90. Copyright © 1989 by Doubleday, a Division of Random House, Inc., and by Penguin Books, Ltd. Used by permission of Doubleday, a division of Random House, Inc.

image and eating disorders, lack of self-esteem, neglect by schools (see Chapter 10), and the need to be protected from the pressures of consumer culture with its Barbie and Ken dolls and sexualized representations of girls. Lyn Mikel Brown and Carol Gilligan's (1992) study of the psychological development of girls found that girls tended to lose their confidence (and hence their authentic voice) and were hesitant to express their thoughts and feelings as they made the transition into adolescence. Their study also pointed out that as the dominant "male-voiced" culture began to play a larger role in children's lives as they grew up, girls as well as boys began to distance themselves from relationships with women, such as their mothers, who are viewed as having less authority than males.

Other feminists who examine girls' realities find that girls are not necessarily sweet, passive, and "good." Sharon Lamb (2001), for example, concludes that "good" girls can be "bad," in their verbal and physical abuse of other girls but suggests that such acting out is also a form of resistance that must be recognized and channeled. That girls could be "mean" to other girls, bullies, and cliquish (Simmons, 2002; Wiseman, 2002) has contributed to concerns among protective parents about their daughters' welfare but has also broadened our understanding of girlhood. These studies on girls' aggression have been balanced by others that give attention to girls who are emotionally and socially confident, do well in school, are active in sports, have close relationships with their parents and girlfriends, and feel no need to be popular (Meadows, 2002).

Investigators are beginning to shift the focus of girlhood from an emphasis on the multiple ways in which girls are disadvantaged compared to their brothers to one that also promotes strategies and programs to support and enhance girls' empowerment. Feminist efforts to advance girls' empowerment have contributed to and been supported by policy changes to address gender inequality between girls and boys. These include Title IX in the United States, which opposes sex discrimination, and a number of global treaties and conferences, such as the United Nations Convention on the Rights of the Child ratified in 1990, the United Nations Fourth World Congress on Women in Beijing in 1995 that gave attention to discrimination and violence against the girl child, and the World Congress against Commercial Sexual Exploitation of Children in Stockholm in 1996, all of which seek to strengthen the human rights of girls as well as women. As non-governmental organizations have addressed the issues facing girls globally, especially those who need to work to support themselves and their families, who are young mothers, or who are exploited sexually, they have devised model programs to promote the education, health, and human rights of girls (Barker et al., 2000). Girlhood, then, is a more complex period than formerly understood and warrants more attention by scholars.

Sibling Relationships

Girlhood is defined by sibling relationships as well as relationships with parents and other adults. Siblings also shape a girl's personality by assigning her an individual role among them. The most common means of discriminating among siblings aside from gender is age ranking. In some ways, age ranking is an inescapable result of the facts of social interaction. The firstborn child will tend to be given more responsibility for the care of younger children and assigned leadership in the organization of family chores. The older child will generally go to school first and break the path in obtaining privileges, such as an extended bedtime, from the parents. In addition, many societies reserve specific privileges for older children. For example, the upper ranks of English society as well as feudal Japan long held a tradition of passing the family wealth and property to the oldest male offspring. Parents also discouraged younger daughters from marrying until an older sister was settled. Folklore and fairy tales are replete with stories like Cinderella, Cupid and Psyche, and Hansel and Gretel that tell of the plight of younger children obliged to make their way in a hostile world controlled by their elders.

Personality characteristics may derive from a child's place in the family, as noted in studies of U.S. households. An older child will often emerge as the more aggressive, achievement-oriented, responsible member of the family. A younger child is likely to feel cheated, being outfitted with hand-me-down clothes and toys and treated as an inferior in the games and conversations of older siblings. Nevertheless, younger children may also emerge as more insouciant, carefree personalities, the darlings of parents and older siblings; and the middle child often feels neglected by parents and lost between other siblings (Leman, 1985; Sutton-Smith and Rosenberg, 1970).

A fictional illustration of the interaction of age-ranked siblings that conforms to the findings of some modern psychological studies can be found in *Little Women* by Louisa May Alcott (1832–88), which was published in 1873. In the book, four sisters struggle to help their mother make ends meet while their father is away at war. Their life experiences shape their parts in the family scenario. Meg, the oldest, is the "little mother," the somewhat straitlaced, responsible leader of the flock. Her seriousness and occupation of the adult role leave the next sister, Jo, free to occupy the part of tomboy, mischief-maker, and eventually liberated woman. The third sister, Beth, is the family saint, whose peacemaking role continues even after her pathetic death. Amy is the family beauty, whose childish vanity and self-centeredness is a cause of concern

for her censorious older sisters. The Bennet girls in the 1813 novel of English sisterhood *Pride and Prejudice* by Jane Austen (1775–1817) reveal a similar assortment of role assignments.

The sibling dynamics established in childhood may last throughout life. The labeling imposed by parents, rivalry between siblings, and reactions against family roles sometimes influence young adults into certain career paths and life goals. Even late into life, jealousy of one another and rivalry for the attention of parents who may long since have died can mark the relationship.

Siblings can be sources of strength as well as conflict. In a period of widespread divorce, many individuals find relationships with sisters and brothers a core of stability in lives that are otherwise gravely troubled. Continuing and successful sibling relationships appear to have positive effects in heightening women's sense of security and in improving their social skills in the wider community.

Sisters as Opposites and Companions

Sisters often view themselves and are viewed by others as alike and not alike. The Bible provides two examples of sisters who reflect and complement one another: Leah and Rachel in the Old Testament and Martha and Mary in the New Testament. Leah was the older, maternal sister and Rachel, the younger and long childless sister; both were the wives of Jacob. Martha was the careful, domestic sister engaged in making Jesus and his companions comfortable in her house; Mary was the intellectual, visionary sister who cast aside her domestic responsibilities in order to listen to Jesus' teaching.

In the contemporary United States, despite their occasional rivalries and jealousies, even tantrums, sisters have affectionate and long-lasting bonds as well. Swapping of clothes,

---

Box 6.4   WHEN WE WERE SISTERS

Alice Sebold had told the story of her own rape as a student in Syracuse in her first book (Lucky). *In her best-selling novel* The Lovely Bones, *the oldest daughter is raped and murdered. She continues to live in her sister's memory:*

Two sisters dressed identically in velvet or plaid or Easter yellows. We held baskets of bunnies and eggs we had sunk in dye. Patent leather shoes with straps and hard buckles. Smiling hard as our mother tried to focus her camera. The photos always fuzzy, our eyes bright red spots. None of them, these artifacts left to my sister, would hold for posterity the moments before and the moments after when we two girls played in the house or fought over toys. When we were sisters.

Source: From *The Lovely Bones* by Alice Sebold, Boston: Little Brown and Company © 2003:179–80.

---

boyfriends, advice, and support often overshadow hostility, playing against one another in lifelong dialogue. This relationship was dramatically expressed by Jessamyn West in her memoir *The Woman Said Yes* (1976), a record of her sister's bout with cancer in which the author assisted her first with home care and finally with a peaceful death. In the course of the long ordeal, the sisters spent the nights reliving their youth together, comparing and reconciling the differences in their experiences. The Delany sisters, Sadie (1889–1999) and Bessie (1891–1995), both of whom lived to over 100 years of age, also documented their lives together over the span of the twentieth century in a best-selling memoir, *Having Our Say* (1993). The book portrays the loving and bantering closeness of the two sisters who never married and the political and social changes that their distinguished African American family experienced from emancipated slavery through Jim Crow segregation in the South. It also highlights their struggles to overcome racism and sexism and to support one another as part of the first generation of black professionals in New York City (see Box 6.5).

Older sisters provide models and assistance to younger ones. In many cultures, past and present, one of the roles of married sisters is to chaperone younger sisters at social gatherings and to use their husbands' contacts to look for husbands for their sisters. They may also provide a home for younger sisters or brothers. Thus, older sisters who emigrate to another country, relocate to a different city, marry, or become established in jobs often provide a base for younger siblings who come looking for similar opportunities. In old age, the original bonds may reassert themselves. Divorced, widowed, and maiden sisters often come at last to share households.

Sister–Brother Relations

Age ranking is too often nullified by sex ranking. The privileges and importance that a girl might expect as the oldest child can be brutally canceled by the appearance of a brother. Many U.S. feminists received the first jolt of awareness of "woman's place" when they realized that the leadership role was destined for a new baby by right of his gender alone (Shaarawi, 1987). Throughout the early

Box 6.5 THE DELANY SISTERS

In the following excerpts from their memoir, the Delany sisters talk about how they complement one another yet remain distinct.

SADIE: Bessie is my little sister, only she's not so little. She is 101 years old, and I am 103. . . . Neither of us ever married and we've lived together most of our lives. . . . After so long, we are in some ways like one person. She is my right arm. . . . Bessie and I still keep house by ourselves. We still do our shopping and banking. We were in helping professions—Bessie was a dentist and I was a high school teacher—so we're not rich, but we get by . . .

Bessie was what we used to call a "feeling" child; she was sensitive and emotional. . . . I always did what I was told. I was calm and agreeable. The way I see it, there's room in the world for both me and Bessie. We kind of balance each other out.

The Delany sisters.

BESSIE: If Sadie is molasses, then I am vinegar! Sadie is sugar, and I'm the spice. You know, Sadie doesn't approve of me sometimes. She frowns at me in her big-sister-sort-of-way and says it's a wonder I wasn't lynched. . . . Most of the things that make me mad happened to me because I am colored. As a woman dentist, I faced sexual harassment—that's what they call it today—but to me, racism was always a bigger problem. . . .

Now, Sadie doesn't get all agitated like this. She just shrugs it off. It's been a little harder for me, partly because I am darker than she . . . and because I have a different personality than Sadie.

. . . I'm alive out of sheer determination, honey! Sometimes I think it's my *meanness* that keeps me going.

Source: From *Having Our Say: The Delany Sisters' First 100 Years* by Sarah Delany and A. Elizabeth Delany, with Amy Hill Hearth, pp. 5–11. New York: Kodansha International, 1993. Reprinted by permission of Kodansha America, Inc.

years, girls and boys are almost always routed along different tracks. This is often formalized by the practice of special initiation ceremonies for boys alone. According to a common story, a young girl attending a *brith* (a Jewish circumcision ceremony) was told not to be dis-tressed at the baby's discomfort, "for," said her aunt, "it is a small price to pay for being a man." In some societies, boys are "breeched" or otherwise endowed with the garb of a man at an early age, while girls do not change their mode of dress to signify womanhood.

In all too many families, the achievements and talents of sisters may be subordinated to the ambitions of brothers. In the nineteenth century, for example, poet Dorothy Wordsworth devoted her life to the care of her poet brother, William. The talents of Charlotte, Anne, and Emily Brontë far overshadowed those of their brother, Branwell; but they were able to gain recognition only by publishing their novels under male pseudonyms. Before the current generation of Kennedys—a preeminent U.S. political family—it was the brothers and their male offspring, rather than the Kennedy women, who garnered the most family support in the pursuit of their aspirations.

Some sisters conditioned to the inequities faced by women may accept their second-class status. Others may resent the preference that their families (often backed by the laws of the state) have shown to their brothers and the freedom, education, friends, and favored treatment boys receive at home. Resentments of this kind may open deep gulfs between sisters and brothers and may be reflected in their relationships with their spouses and their own children. In horticultural communities in Kenya, for example, girls aged 5–7 may spend half their time doing chores, while boys of the same age spend only 15% of their time at work and never do women's work unless there is no sister available to help the mother (Ember, 1973). Among the Hopi, men teach boys to weave cloth and women teach girls to weave baskets. In the United States, even though it is the law that both girls and boys must go to school, girls tend to be steered into different and less educationally valued subjects and different extracurricular activities, on the basis of gender (see Chapter 10). Age ranking still plays a role in establishing the relationship between sister and brother. Older sisters may be forced to give precedence to their brothers in the family's strategies, but they may also be cast in the role of "mothers" to them, establishing a burden that may last throughout life. On the other side, older brothers tend to play the masculine role toward their sisters, being protective in some cases and, in more extreme cases, assuming a bullying tone. The males become stronger and more confident as they grow older, while the females may find themselves restricted by limitations and a suffocating protection that deprives them of the confidence that can come only from the experience of success. Often, societies impose this role on young men whether they like it or not. "A man's honor lies between his sister's legs" is a common saying throughout the Mediterranean world. Young men are thus encouraged to police the behavior of their sisters and personally to avenge any infringement of the customary male code of honor by both the sisters and their chosen lovers. Among some Native American tribes, for example, the brothers take an active role in arranging their sisters' marriages, even if the fathers are still alive, on the understanding that it is they who will have to live longest with the proposed brothers-in-law.

Inheritance

As women carry with them the emotional legacies of sibling and parental interaction through their mature lives, they also contend with a formal legacy defined through custom, law, and social institutions. The family, however defined, is the recognized unit that bestows status, class, property rights, privilege, or position upon its members, whether biological or adopted. The determination of legitimacy is the first social characteristic that girls derive from their families. If the sexual relationships of one's parents have followed a prescribed pattern of propriety or if they have fulfilled a socially approved set of rituals governing formal adoption, daughters will usually be legitimately established—or confined—in that social place.

The inheritance of social status may include legacies from both parents. Women may derive their citizenship in a modern state from either mother or father or from both, depending on the laws set by the state. Jews, for example, inherit Jewish affiliation through the mother's line and, therefore, the right to claim Israeli citizenship. In the United States, illegitimate children of a woman citizen inherit the mother's position. Often, lower status or dependent status (slavery, serfdom, or noncitizenship) comes through the mother. Thus, in the American South in the era of slavery, the children of slave women were born slaves, even if fathered by a freeman, slaveholder, or man who became the president of the United States (in the case of Thomas Jefferson).

Sex affects inheritance among sisters and brothers. Patrilineal societies pass authority, property, and descent directly through the male line from father to son. Matrilineal societies sometimes pass authority and property through males, but descent passes through females; property, like tools for producing clothing and food, often passes from mothers to daughters. Although matrilineal societies, such as the Native American Navajo and Iroquois and the African Bemba, tend to confer greater authority upon women than do patrilineal societies; observers have noted that these societies have a less rigid system of authority in general. Where extensive trade or manufacturing exists, matrilineal systems appear to vanish and even patrilineal systems are modified in favor of a bilateral system, allowing a child to inherit from both parents.

Historically, a household head in Japan without children would often adopt a boy to be raised as the successor to manage the family's economic matters, inherit property, and worship the ancestors. If he had only daughters, the household head would adopt a son-in-law as his successor, who would also assume the head's surname (Yanagisako, 1985). Even in the simplest societies, where personal property is restricted to a few effects

that are buried with their possessor, the inheritance of parental skills or privileges will generally be apportioned according to a child's sex. In capitalist societies, patterns of inheritance of property and position favor sons over daughters. In socialist societies, which typically aim at reducing disparities of private property, it remains possible to inherit status or position informally. There, too, it is fairly clear that discrimination favors the male.

Commonly, a system that allows the passage of property to and through women is accompanied by the development of class and caste hierarchies with strict rules for controlling individual heirs, particularly females. Generally, women are admitted to the inheritance of their fathers and/or brothers only when strong measures exist to control their marriages and sex lives in general. These societies are careful to enforce adultery laws against women, to link "honor" with virginity before marriage and fidelity after, and to endow fathers and brothers with strong coercive powers over the female members of their families (Goody, 1977).

Many societies have had laws that restricted the leaving of property. These laws may recognize *primogeniture* (passage of the patrimony to the firstborn son), *entail* (strict line of succession to property, which then cannot be sold off, usually through the oldest related male), and *coverture* (husband's complete control over his wife's property). The more wealthy and productive a society has been, the more likely that a social hierarchy of class has formed that has caused women to lose status in a variety of ways. Where it has been possible for women to write wills, they have generally left their personal property to daughters and other women in the family.

The Sisterhood of Women

Women's identities are informed by the ideals of womanhood that the family accepts from the larger community as well as by relationships with parents and siblings in the natal family. In this way, women receive two levels of self-consciousness from their childhood: their sense of womanliness and their sense of individuality. Their ability to accept their own identities with self-confidence in mature life is largely dependent on the feelings that women have developed about other women.

As discussed earlier, Western psychological theory suggests that the relationship between daughter and mother is complex and emotionally charged. Mothers often become the standard against which daughters measure their own relationships. Although identity development is commonly viewed as a process that takes place during adolescence, contemporary young women are faced with far greater opportunities and a different timetable of establishing relationships from what their mothers experienced at the same age (Glasman, 2002). Thus, identity consolidation may now be occurring well into one's twenties, in part due to the current societal norms in which women are marrying later and remaining financially dependent on their parents for longer periods of time.

Sibling relationships also contribute to a woman's development. Siblings of both sexes experience rivalry and competition with one another, which can be particularly intense between same-sex siblings. In the context of societies that award privileges to males, sisters rival one another as well as their mothers for the love and attention of their fathers. Brothers are able to diffuse this rivalry in adult life by choosing from a wide range of competitive possibilities in the public sphere, but these possibilities have generally been more restricted among women. Women's memoirs and literary writings, as expressed in the title of the anthology *Forever Sisters* (O'Keefe, 1999), for example, identify the special bonds shared by sisters and underscore the importance of female sibling relationships in building a broader sisterhood. More attention also needs to be given to the role that sharing between sisters and their encouragement of one another plays in a girl's development to womanhood and beyond and in her relationships with other women.

Box 6.6   SISTERHOOD: POLITICAL SOLIDARITY AMONG WOMEN

Male supremacist ideology encourages women to believe we are valueless and obtain value only by relating to or bonding with men. We are taught that our relationships with one another diminish rather than enrich our experience. We are taught that women are "natural" enemies, that solidarity will never exist between us because we cannot, should not, and do not bond with one another. We have learned these lessons well. We must unlearn them if we are to build a sustained feminist movement. We must learn to live and work in solidarity. We must learn the true meaning and value of Sisterhood . . .

. . . Some feminists now seem to feel that unity among women is impossible given our differences. . . . Solidarity strengthens resistance struggle. There can be no mass-based feminist movement to end sexist oppression without a united front—women must take the initiative and demonstrate the power of solidarity. Unless we can show that barriers separating women can be eliminated, that solidarity can exist, we cannot hope to change and transform society as a whole.

Source: From *Feminist Theory: From Margin to Center* by bell hooks, pp. 43–4. Cambridge, MA: South End Press, 2000.

In 1986, Susan Hellauer, Ruth Cunningham, Marsha Genensky, and Johanna Rose joined together to create the vocal ensemble Anonymous 4. Their focus is on medieval chant and polyphony, which was until then almost exclusively performed by men. Anonymous 4 is known for its purity of voice, language, and historical style. Despite avant-garde trends in music, the group plays what its members enjoy, and audiences delight in Anonymous 4 performances worldwide. After seventeen releases, Anonymous 4 continues to create "early music" that is vital to our times and enjoyable to modern ears. The four women are an example of a "professional sisterhood."

One of the challenges that women's studies must meet in redefining women from the center of their own experiences is to expose the power relationships that threaten to oppress them and then to reconstruct womanhood as a positive experience. Many feminists believe that the struggles that now mark the relationships between daughters and mothers and between sisters are a consequence of inflexible family, sex, and gender roles and of the oppression of women, including the notion of heterosexuality as the norm. A woman's identity based on the rejection of mothers and sisters contributes to self-denigration and dependence. The early slogan of women's liberation, "Sisterhood is powerful," sought to establish the bonds between women that male-oriented kinship and political structures have so often obscured. Collaborations among women, like the vocal ensemble Anonymous 4, have been efforts to use the concept of "Sisterhood" for mutual support and creativity. Through the agency of consciousness raising, many women began painfully to reexamine the real histories of their lives to see how they had been damaged in their individual integrity and alienated from their sister women by false myths and oppositions. Most difficult of all, perhaps, is the effort to reach past the long and painful barriers of age and experience and see their mothers, in particular, and their sisters as full members in the sisterhood of women. It is a task that all women must undertake to reach full appreciation of their own selves.

Women must also reach out across the differences of culture, race, class, and nationality without ignoring them. Every woman is the daughter of another woman. Every mother is a daughter. All women are potential sisters.

Summary

Virtually no society expresses a preference for girl babies over boy babies. In some societies, the first decision to be made on the birth of daughters is whether they are to live at all. Female infanticide is a way of controlling the population on the basis of sex. In general, girl babies receive less careful treatment than boy babies, thus reducing girls' chances for survival. The devaluation of daughters has its roots in the low value placed on women in society at large. Warriors, for example, tend to be more highly valued than mothers; but daughters do provide valuable services to the family. They can be relied on more than sons to take care of aging parents. They help to carry out the household tasks. Daughters also have intrinsic value in that they represent the reproducers of the next generation.

The names given to daughters indicate their place in the social scheme. Most societies are careful to distinguish the sex of the child by the name. Most surnames perpetuate the male lineage, reflecting a name, profession, or place of birth. In general, women have changed their surnames on marriage, but many today keep their own names.

Daughters tend to identify with their mothers. Gender identity is thereby made easy, but the task of developing one's own individuality becomes complicated. Mothers may inhibit this development by expecting daughters to be at home more than sons and to help with "women's work." In this way, daughters are socialized into accepting an established role model of dependence. As noted by many Western feminist studies, daughter-mother relationships may be marked by conflict, especially in the case of daughters who want to break away from the patterns of their mothers' lives or who resent maternal dependence. Women of color in the United States identify strong bonds between daughters and mothers as well as ambivalence and tensions as mothers have helped prepare their daughters to survive and thrive in unsupportive racial environments.

A close and supportive daughter-father relationship can enhance a daughter's self-worth and educational and occupational achievements. Sometimes daughters' relationships with fathers are tense and unstable. Girls often desire paternal approval, which makes them vulnerable to the training fathers give daughters to become socially desirable women. Father-daughter incest is the most commonly reported type of incest and may cause lasting trauma.

Girlhood in the United States is complex. Some studies emphasize the vulnerability of girls in the face of societal pressures. Others note that girls can be aggressive and mean, and still others find girls to be well balanced and confident. Societies globally are seeking to promote policies, strategies, and programs to support daughters' empowerment.

Families commonly discriminate among siblings on the basis of age ranking. The first-born child enjoys certain responsibilities and privileges denied to later-born children. Certain personality characteristics, which have consequences in later life, also go with one's birth order.

Sisters are both opposites and companions. They may be rivals for their parents' affection but also have close bonds with one another. Older sisters often provide role models and assistance for younger sisters as well as younger brothers.

Sex ranking may nullify age ranking. The rights and privileges of the oldest child may be canceled if that child is a girl and a brother is born. Household division of labor further differentiates sisters and brothers. A daughter's talents and ambitions are often subordinated to those of her brother.

Age ranking helps establish the type of relationship a sister and brother have. Older sisters are often cast in the role of "mother" to younger brothers, and older brothers frequently play the role of protector of younger sisters.

Women inherit legitimacy and social status from their parents. Sex often determines legal inheritance rights. Most societies favor sons over daughters in the inheritance of property and position. Even where rights may descend from either parent to any of the children, custom or law often curtails inheritance for women.

Women who develop an autonomous self-image by transferring identity from the mother to the father often suffer a conflict about their identity as women. This is complicated by sibling rivalry. The emphasis on women's alienation from one another detracts from the ways in which mothers, daughters, and sisters support one another. Women need to examine their life histories for sources of support in building a sisterhood of women within their own households and with women everywhere.

Discussion Questions

1. Draw a chart illustrating naming patterns of all the members of your extended family. What conclusions can you draw?
2. What changes occurred in your own relationships with your mother, father, and other parenting figures as you were growing up? Does your experience fit the patterns sketched by Chodorow and Flax or that of Collins and Joseph?
3. Describe your changing relationships with your sisters and brothers as you grew older. If you could, how would you change them now?

4. Write a brief essay on one of the following slogans, defending or refuting the premise: "Sisterhood is powerful," "sisterhood is global," or "sisterhood is forever."

Recommended Readings

Baker, Christina Looper, and Christina Baker Kline. *The Conversation Begins: Mothers and Daughters Talk About Living Feminism*. New York: Bantam Books, 1996. An exploration of the mother–daughter relationship between second- and third-wave feminists, this book reveals the tensions and satisfactions experienced by 23 pioneer feminists of the modern U.S. women's movement as they have tried to live by new rules in bringing up their daughters. It also reveals through conversations with both daughters and mothers that the experiment has not been easy. These mothers assess their feminist discoveries in the context of family life, while their daughters define new agendas for themselves in light of the legacies they have inherited. Their conversations are both painful and rewarding.

Bell-Scott, Patricia, Beverly Guy-Sheftall, Jacqueline Jones Royster, Janet Sims-Wood, Miriam DeCosta-Willis, and Lucie Fultz, editors. *Double Stitch: Black Women Write About Mothers and Daughters*. Boston: Beacon Press, 1991. With a foreword by Maya Angelou, 47 African American feminists write about black daughters and mothers, drawing attention to the specific dynamics of the black family, lesbian families, and black women's relationships with men. This book includes stories, poems, and essays by such writers as bell hooks, June Jordan, Audre Lorde, Sonia Sanchez, and Alice Walker.

Davidson, Cathy N., and Esther M. Broner, editors. *The Lost Tradition: Mothers and Daughters in Literature*. New York: Frederick Ungar, 1980. An exploration of the theme of mothers and daughters in literature, including the myths of ancient Greece, nineteenth- and twentieth-century literature, and the works of women of color. Despite its age, the book includes an excellent bibliography.

Forman-Brunell, Miriam. *Girlhood in America: An Encyclopedia*. Santa Barbara: ABC-CLIO, 2001. This encyclopedia on girlhood in the United States synthesizes scholarly work on the everyday lives of girls from different ethnic, racial, and class backgrounds and considers their many activities under nearly 120 topics from acquaintance rape to zines.

Morgan, Robin. *Sisterhood Is Forever*. New York: Washington Square Press, 2003. After the landmark anthologies, *Sisterhood Is Powerful* (1970) and *Sisterhood Is Global* (1984), Morgan has compiled a "women's anthology for the new millennium." Sixty authors address a range of topics and female experiences in the United States and consider where women have been, where they are, and where they are going.

Woolf, Virginia. *The Three Guineas* (1938). New York: Harcourt Brace, 1966. As an "educated gentleman's" daughter, Woolf presents a critique of the educated fathers and brothers who monopolize the ruling structures of the state, its government, educational establishments, and professions to the exclusion of daughters and sisters. Her footnotes present a feminist history of the English women of her class from the nineteenth century to her own day.

References

Alcott, Louisa M. *Little Women* (1873). New York: Western, 1977.

Applebaum, Susan. Daughters and mothers. In *Girlhood in America: An Encyclopedia*, vol. 1, edited by Miriam Forman-Brunnell. Santa Barbara: ABC-CLIO, 2001.

Austen, Jane. *Pride and Prejudice* (1813). New York: Dell, 1959.

Baker, Christine Looper, and Christine Baker Kline. *The Conversation Begins: Mothers and Daughters Talk About Living Feminism*. New York: Bantam Books, 1996.

Bao, Xiaolan. Politicizing motherhood: The Chinese garment workers' campaign for daycare centers in New York City, 1977–1982. In *Asian/Pacific Islander American Women: A Historical Anthology*, edited by Shirley Hune and Gail M. Nomura. New York: New York University Press, 2003.

Barker, Gary, and Felicia Knaul, with Neide Cassaniga and Anita Schrader. *Urban Girls: Empowerment in Especially Difficult Circumstances*. London: Intermediate Technology Publications, 2000.

Beck, M. Trading places. *Newsweek*, July 16, 1990.

Bhatia, Krishan. *Indira: A Biography of Prime Minister Gandhi*. New York: Praeger, 1974.

Brown, Lyn Mikel, and Carol Gilligan. *Meeting at the Crossroads: Women's Psychology and Girls' Development*. Cambridge, MA: Harvard University Press, 1992.

Chodorow, Nancy. *The Reproduction of Mothering: Psychoanalysis and the Sociology of Gender*. Berkeley: University of California Press, 1978.

Coleman, Emily. Infanticide in the early Middle Ages. In *Women in Medieval Society*, edited by Susan Mosher Stuard. Philadelphia: University of Pennsylvania Press, 1976.

Colette, Sidonie-Gabrielle. *My Mother's House and Sido* (1930), translated by Una Vincenzo and Enid McLead. New York: Farrar, Straus and Giroux, 1953.

Collins, Patricia Hill. The meaning of motherhood in black culture and black mother–daughter relationships. In *Double Stitch: Black Women Write About Mothers and Daughters*, edited by Patricia Bell-Scott, Beverly Guy-Sheftall, Jacqueline Jones Royster, Janet Sims-Wood, Miriam DeCosta-Willis, and Lucie Fultz. Boston: Beacon Press, 2000.

Croll, Elizabeth. *Endangered Daughters: Discrimination and Development in Asia*. London: Routledge, 2000.

Delany, Sarah, and A. Elizabeth Delany, with Amy Hill Hearth. *Having Our Say: The Delany*

Sisters' First 100 Years. New York: Kodansha International, 1993.

Devlin, Rachel. Daughters and fathers. In *Girlhood in America: An Encyclopedia*, vol. 1, edited by Miriam Forman-Brunell, Santa Barbara: ABC-CLIO, 2001.

Dickemann, M. Female infanticide, reproductive strategies, and social stratification: A preliminary model. In *Evolutionary Biology and Social Behavior: An Anthropological Perspective*, edited by Napoleon Chagnon and William Irons. Duxbury, ME: Duxbury, 1979.

Divale, William, and Marvin Harris. Population, warfare, and the male supremacist complex. *American Anthropologist*, 78, 521–38, 1978.

Ember, Carol. Feminine task assignment and social behavior of boys. *Ethos*, 2, 424–39, 1973.

Feaver, Vicki. Mothers and daughters. *Times Literary Supplement*, February 29, 1980.

Fischer, Lucy Rose. *Linked Lives: Adult Daughters and Their Mothers*. New York: Harper & Row, 1986.

Flax, Jane. Forgotten forms of close combat: Mothers and daughters revisited. In *Toward a New Psychology of Gender*, edited by Mary M. Gergen and Sara N. Davis. New York: Routledge, 1997.

Forman-Brunell, Miriam. *Girlhood in America: An Encyclopedia*. Santa Barbara: ABC-CLIO, 2001.

Frank, Anne. *The Diary of Anne Frank: The Critical Edition*, edited by David Barnouw and Gerrold Van Der Stroom. New York: Doubleday, 1989.

Friday, Nancy. *My Mother/My Self: The Daughter's Search for Identity*. New York: Dell, 1977.

Glasman, Lynn. Mother "there for" me: Female-identity development in the context of the mother–daughter relationship. A qualitative study. *Dissertation Abstracts International. Section B: The Sciences and Engineering*, 62 (7-B), 3377, 2002.

Glickman, Rose L. *Daughters of Feminists*. New York: St. Martin's Press, 1993.

Goody, Jack. *Production and Reproduction*. Cambridge: Cambridge University Press, 1977.

Gutman, Herbert. *The Black Family in Slavery and Freedom, 1750–1925*. New York: Vintage, 1977.

Harrington, Mona. *Care and Equality: Inventing a New Family Politics*. New York: Knopf, 1999.

Hennig, Margaret, and Anne Jardin. *The Managerial Woman*. New York: Pocket Books, 1976.

Hooks, bell. *Feminist Theory: From Margin to Center*, 2nd ed. Cambridge, MA: South End Press, 2000.

Hunt, A. S., and C. C. Edgar. *Select Papyri I: Non-Literary Papyri, Private Affairs*, no. 105. Cambridge, MA: Harvard University Press, 1932.

Inness, Sherria A. Introduction. In *Millennium Girls: Today's Girls Around the World*, edited by Sherrie A. Inness. Lanham, MD: Rowman & Littlefield, 1998.

Joseph, Gloria. Black mothers and daughters: Their roles and functions in American society. In *Common Differences: Conflicts in Black/White Feminist Perspectives*, edited by Gloria Joseph and Jill Lewis. Garden City, NY: Doubleday, 1981.

———. Black mothers and daughters: Traditional and new perspectives. In *Double Stitch: Black Women Write About Mothers and Daughters*, edited by Patricia Bell-Scott, Beverly Guy-Sheftall, Jacqueline Jones Royster, Janet Sims-Wood, Miriam DeCosta-Willis, and Lucie Fultz. Boston: Beacon Press, 1991.

Lamb, Sharon. *The Secret Lives of Girls*. New York: Free Press, 2001.

Leman, Kevin. *The Birth Order Book*. Old Tappan, NJ: Fleming H. Revell Co., 1985.

Leonhardt, David. It's a girl! (will the economy suffer?) *New York Times*, Oct. 26, 2003, sect. 3, 1 and 11.

Matsui, Yayori. *Women's Asia*. London: Zed Books, 1987.

Meadows, Susannah, with Mary Carmichael. Meet the GAMMA girls. *Newsweek*, June 3, 2002.

Newby, Elizabeth Loza. *A Migrant with Hope*. Kansas City, MO: Beacon Hill Press, 1981.

O'Keefe, Claudia, editor. *Forever Sisters*. New York: Pocket Books, 1999.

Peterson, Karen, and J. J. Wilson. *Women Artists: Recognition and Reappraisal from the Early Middle Ages to the Twentieth Century*. New York: Harper Colophon, 1976.

Pomeroy, Sarah B. *Goddesses, Whores, Wives, and Slaves: Women in Classical Antiquity*. New York: Schocken, 1975.

Russ, Joanna. *The Female Man*. New York: Bantam, 1975.

Russell, Diana E. *The Secret Trauma: Incest in the Lives of Girls and Women*. New York: Basic Books, 1986.

Sanchez, Marta Ester. *Contemporary Chicana Poetry*. Berkeley: University of California Press, 1985.

Sebold, Alice. *Lucky*. New York: Back Bay Books, 1999.

———. *The Lovely Bones*. New York: Back Bay Books, 2002.

Shaarawi, Huda. *Harem Years: The Memoirs of an Egyptian Feminist (1879–1924)*, translated, edited, and introduced by Margot Badran. New York: Feminist Press at the City University of New York, 1987.

Simmons, Rachel. *Odd Girl Out: The Hidden Culture of Aggression in Girls*. New York: Harcourt, 2002.

Stanton, Elizabeth Cady. *Eighty Years and More* (1898). New York: Schocken, 1971.

Sutton-Smith, Brian, and Benjamin G. Rosenberg. *The Sibling*. New York: Holt, Rinehart, & Winston, 1970.

Tan, Amy. *The Bonesetter's Daughter*. New York: Putnam, 2001.

Trexler, Richard. The foundlings of Florence, 1395–1455. *History of Childhood Quarterly: The Journal of Psychohistory*, I, 259–84, 1973.

Tung, Charlene. Caring across borders: Motherhood, marriage, and Filipina domestic workers in California. In *Asian/Pacific Islander American Women: A Historical Anthology*, edited by Shirley Hune and Gail M. Nomura. New York: New York University Press, 2003.

Washington, Mary Helen, editor. *Black-Eyed Susans: Classic Stories by and About Black Women*. Garden City, NY: Doubleday, 1975.

West, Jessamyn. *The Woman Said Yes*. New York: Harcourt, Brace, 1976.

Wiseman, Rosalind. *Queen Bees and Wannabes: A Parent's Guide to Helping Your Daughter Survive Cliques, Gossip, Boyfriends, and Other Realities of Adolescence*. New York: Crown Publishers, 2002.

Witchel, Alex. "Dear Margo," the voice still says. *New York Times*, Oct. 23, 2003, D1, D11.

Yanagisako, Sylvia Junko. *Transforming the Past: Tradition and Kinship Among Japanese Americans*. Stanford: Stanford University Press, 1985.

chapter 7

Family Configurations: Wives, Partners, Alternatives

As far as we know, the most ancient and most universal unit of social organization is what we call the "family," comprised of people who consider themselves to be related to one another by marriage or "blood." In the simplest, smallest-scale societies, virtually all social life takes place within or between families: food production, exchange of goods, religion and ritual, struggles for power, and the making of war and peace. A woman's place within the family as wife and mother is essentially all there is to define her role in many societies, in all these spheres of life.

In modern society, although there are other arenas for women to work and participate in social life, politics, and religion, families continue to be of great importance to most women. For adult women in most societies in the world today, the roles of wife and mother continue to occupy huge segments of their daily routine and family obligations remain primary in their decisions about what else they might do with their lives. Girls and young women the world over are educated in anticipation of their assuming the roles of wife and mother, regardless of what else they might do. Women who do not (or have not yet) become wives and then mothers are, more often than not, socially condemned or pitied (unless they assume other socially esteemed roles such as nun) and more likely than not to feel a sense of inadequacy or deprivation. Consequently, most families strive to ensure that their daughters become married, and most adult women do marry. Through time, there have always been women who did not marry, but it has been only in the past few decades that any significant number of women in the world have had the option to not be married and to not be mothers as a matter of personal choice.

In this chapter, we examine some of the family configurations produced by different sorts of marriage. We look at the situation of women who become unmarried because of divorce or the death of their husbands and at alternatives to conventional marriage for women.

Conventional Marriage

Why Marry?

We take marriage so much for granted that it rarely occurs to us to question the institution and ask "why marry?" One important reason is that marriage forms the basis for what has usually been thought of as the smallest building block of society, the *nuclear family*, comprised of a wife and husband and their offspring. In many societies, of course, this smallest building block is part of a larger family, sometimes called the *extended family*, comprised of one or more nuclear families and other relatives.

For most of human history, marriage was regarded as necessary for women and men because the division of labor was such that a man needed the products of women's work and a woman needed the products of men's work. For the most part, this division of labor could be seen as somewhat arbitrary (though men usually are assigned the roles of large game hunter and military fighter and women are assigned roles closely related to the care of infants and young children). A man without a wife might have nobody, for example, to prepare his food or clothing, to care for his children, perhaps to build or repair his house. A woman without a husband might have no protector, no source of meat or hides, no means to obtain trade goods from distant places. To establish themselves as adult participants in society, each would need a spouse. Thus, a common explanation for why people marry is economic: women need men and men need women for practical, subsistence purposes. To a certain extent, this obtains even in modern industrial societies, especially where women and men continue to engage in traditional divisions of labor. However, some people can purchase services in the household traditionally performed by one gender or another (a woman can hire a plumber, a car mechanic, or a carpenter to do what husbands used to be expected to do; a man can hire a housecleaner, a cook, or a child caretaker to do what wives used to be expected to do), and of course they can learn to perform these tasks themselves. However, in most families, it can be a struggle for a woman to manage without a husband and a man to manage without a wife (see Chapter 12).

There is another reason why people marry, much less evident in large, mobile, industrialized societies than in smaller ones: to regulate sexuality. In every known society, there is a prohibition against incest, generally defined as sexual relations among close kin: parents and children, siblings, and other family members. In order to have sexual relations and bear children, people must seek a mate outside the family circle. In earlier times and in small-scale societies, this often meant looking beyond the local community, where people were likely to be closely related, to "marry out." Commonly, it was the daughters of the household who were sent away to their husband's home (in a postmarital pattern known as *virilocal* or *patrilocal* residence) so that the local community would be comprised of men who were closely related and their unrelated wives and offspring. Typically, then, a young bride would begin her married life in the home of her husband's mother. Sometimes, however, it was the men who left home (*uxorilocal* or *matrilocal residence*). A man, then, would live in the home of his mother-in-law. One can imagine how the dynamics of these households would differ.

In such situations, it was families who planned their children's marriages. They would decide where to send their sons or daughters based not only on the expected compatibility between their children and those of the other family but also on what was anticipated in an alliance between the two families brought together by their children's marriage. Often, this alliance had implications for mutual defense in warfare, for trade and other economic relationships, and perhaps for diplomacy and other mutual assistance. In these cases, the bride and groom had rather little to say about the match and could only hope that a match could be found for them and that it would be tolerable. In cases where marriages were arranged (and this was probably true of most marriages in most societies for most of human history), marriage was generally accompanied by an exchange of gifts between the families of the bride and the groom. Sometimes, the much larger gift would be given by the family of the groom,

The Arnolfini Wedding (1434) in Flanders, oil painting by Jan Van Eyck. Marriage vows, called "hand-giving," were performed in private homes or church vestibules, not inside churches, in the fifteenth century in Europe. Here, a wealthy merchant has commissioned a painting to commemorate the occasion. The bride gathers up her skirt to her waist, giving the appearance of pregnancy and alluding to the promise of future motherhood.

especially when the bride was leaving her family of birth to join the household of his parents. The gift (sometimes known as *bride-price* or *bridewealth*) was in compensation for the loss of her economic contribution to her natal family and would be used to help her brothers to acquire wives. However, it was also a kind of marriage insurance for the husband's family: the bride's own family, having accepted a substantial gift, would be reluctant to return it so would discourage her from leaving her husband if she felt inclined to do so. In some societies, notably in historical Europe among elite families but also in contemporary India, it is the bride's family that is expected to give the groom, or the groom's family, a gift, known as *dowry*. Families without sufficient funds to provide a dowry despair of finding a good marital match for their daughters; and in modern times, young women in Sri Lanka are strongly motivated to find work in factories (manufacturing underwear for Victoria's Secret, for example) in order to make money to contribute toward their dowries so that they can marry.

Whether in arranged marriages or not, couples who marry usually anticipate having children—in most cases, most people think this is the purpose of marriage. Marriage gen-

erally legalizes a man's claim to his children, a woman's claim to support for her children by a man, and the children's claim to some part of their father's income or property. Childlessness is often seen as tragic for both men and women and frequently regarded as justification for divorce. It can be heartbreaking for a woman in a society which sees a woman's role as wife to be primarily to provide her husband with heirs. While husbands in many societies may discard wives who fail to bear them children, there are also traditions of tenderness by husbands toward barren wives, as in the biblical story traditionally recited on the first day of the Jewish New Year of a man, Elkanah, and his two wives, Peninnah and Hannah (see Box 7.1).

Although having children is seen as a principal goal of marriage, sexual intimacy is itself a goal and marriage is commonly seen as the only legitimate realm for this activity. Not all societies confine sex to marriage, and in practice, even in societies where sex outside of marriage is strictly forbidden, it is clear that extramarital sex occurs. However, adultery is generally prohibited, particularly for women (who might bear another man's child), and is often a cause of strife. In some societies, the punishment for women's adultery is severe,

---

Box 7.1   CHILDLESSNESS

Whenever Elkanah offered sacrifices, he would give portions to his wife Peninnah, and to all her sons and daughters; but he would give a double portion to Hannah, for he loved her, though the Lord had made her childless. Her rival would taunt her severely because she was childless. This went on year after year. Whenever she went up to the house of the Lord, Peninnah would so distress her that she wept and would not eat. Elkanah her husband would ask her: "Hannah, why do you weep, and why do you not eat, and why is your heart so sad? Am I not better to you than ten sons?" [As the story goes on, Hannah prays and is granted a son, whom she dedicates, in gratitude, to God's service.]

Source: Samuel, 1:1–2:10. Greenberg and Levine, 2001:213.

ranging from gang rape to death by stoning; and sometimes a woman accused of adultery will prefer death by suicide to social ostracism and the other sanctions which will result from this accusation. It is nearly always the case that society is more lenient to male adulterers.

In sum, then, in the past at least, people were expected to marry, for mutual economic support, to have children, to allow families to make alliances, and to engage in socially approved sexual intimacy. Family-based households were the basis of society, and marriages were their foundation. These social functions of marriage have been superseded in industrial, urban society by many other social, political, and economic institutions. Consequently, many of the earlier motivations for marriage have been undermined. When technology and economic organization provide alternatives to divisions of labor by gender, women and men in industrial societies are less motivated to marry just to be provided with services that the other gender is socially assigned to perform, though this motivation does not entirely disappear. Further, even in industrial societies, since men still make more money than women do, on the whole (see Chapter 12), and because it is hard for a woman with young children to support herself alone, many women still feel a strong motivation to marry for financial reasons. Arranged marriages for family alliances are uncommon in the Western world; but in Asia, the Middle East, Africa, and elsewhere, these persist, as they do to a certain extent among immigrant communities from these regions in the Western world. Among some sectors in the West and elsewhere, sexual relations and having children without being married are becoming acceptable; but in most regions, the sanction of marriage is preferred for both sexual unions and parenthood. Just because unmarried sex and parenthood are more common in some societies does not mean that there is no longer pressure to marry.

Whom to Marry

As we have seen, in most societies in most of the world, a woman has not had to "find a husband" nor a man a wife: this was the task of their families, particularly of their parents. In some societies, the parents turn to professional matchmakers to pair up their children with an appropriate mate and to smooth the path of betrothal up to the wedding itself. In some cases, children are betrothed in infancy or childhood; in others, the prospective couple is allowed to meet before betrothal, although this is not always the case.

When marriage is a matter for whole families, the suitability of the individuals to be married as a couple is considered of less importance than the appropriateness of the tie between the families. Families are chosen for their wealth, stability, and social standing. Often, a family has an obligation to marry their daughter to an appropriate kinsman— say, the father's sister's son—if such a kinsman is available (*cross-cousin marriage*). Sometimes, a family has the right or obligation to provide a close kinsman as a husband to a widow of one of their members (*levirate marriage*). Thus, in traditional societies, individual choice is simply not an issue. It is hoped that the bride and groom will get along, perhaps develop a fondness for one another over time, so that the marriage will be stable and even happy.

In more complex societies, individual preference has become a primary factor in the choice of a spouse, but even so, people marry largely within certain socially acceptable boundaries. That is, they are likely to choose somebody within a similar social class, race, caste, religion, and ethnicity, as well as other social commonalities. They are likely to choose somebody within their own age group, educational background, and even geographic origin. Women are more likely to marry somebody older (sometimes much older) than

The Wedding of Humay and Humayun. This Persian miniature (1396) depicts women attendants displaying the "bloody sheet" to signal the virginity of the Chinese princess upon her marriage to an Iranian prince. He, meanwhile, is showered with gold coins by their friends, who celebrate the couple's new status with music making and dancing. As this painting demonstrates, marriages throughout the world have shared similar customs.

are men and more likely to marry someone wealthier than are men. However, great disparities of age and wealth are likely to raise eyebrows even in the United States, which has a very liberal and permissive society.

In the West, and increasingly elsewhere, marriage is coming to be understood as a romantic commitment rather than a pragmatic arrangement. Thus, the ideal choices of a husband involve good looks, sex appeal, and romantic attraction at least as much as money-making potential and social standing. Much is made of the romance of falling in love, getting engaged, preparing for a wedding, having the wedding itself. Couples often find themselves disappointed afterward, when the romance has faded. Divorce has become very frequent in societies where it is permitted, partly because of this disappointment and partly because individuals now more frequently are able to live independently of a spouse. However, the practical consequences of divorce for women are complex and something we will discuss in detail below.

The Marital Household

Although a marital household is based on a married couple and their children, what this means in a practical sense is quite variable from society to society and situation to situation. In many societies, as mentioned above, either the bride moves into the household of her mother-in-law or the groom moves into the household of his mother-in-law (though there are many variants of each of these practices). The household might be comprised of several generations of couples and their children and various unmarried adult sisters and brothers of different ages. The experience for a young married woman, and the way this experience evolves as she matures, depends on the configuration of her household. If she is alone with her husband when she starts out, life might be quite difficult because she might have a great deal to learn about managing her household and might have little or no help. However, if she is in a large household, while she will have teachers and helpers, she might suffer the criticism of older women, particularly her mother-in-law. Alternatively, her life as a wife alone might be yet more difficult when she has children, unless she is wealthy and can afford a great deal of hired help; but in a larger household, she will have help at hand and her status will rise with motherhood.

Some societies allow *polygamy*, the practice in which an individual may have more than one spouse. For example, Muslim religious law permits a man to marry up to four wives. However, the ideal of *polygyny* (marriage to more than one wife) is achieved only by the minority of men who can afford to support multiple wives. The converse, *polyandry*, in which a woman marries more than one man, is truly rare—a well-known example comes from the Himalayas, where in land-scarce areas several brothers might share one wife rather than splitting up their land holdings to provide for several families (Levine and Silk, 1997). Polygyny, however, is found on every continent, including in the modern United States, where although now outlawed, it continues to be practiced among some Mormons in Utah. Some women have argued that there are advantages in having co-wives in a large household, particularly in the pooling of wealth and labor to raise children. In other parts of the world, such as East Africa, it is often the case that one wife, or even two, is not enough to produce the wealth to provide a comfortable standard of living for all. It takes teamwork among a number of wives to cultivate land, care for livestock, and take care of children. However, it is also often the case that polygyny is not a happy state for women. There is often jealousy and bitterness among the wives, a subject of poetry and literature from the Hebrew Bible to contemporary novels and essays. A good example is Mariama Ba's *So Long a Letter* (1981), which recounts a modern West African woman's unhappiness upon learning that her husband has decided to take a new, younger wife. Further, even when husbands are limited by law to only one wife, in many parts of the world it is common for them to make second and even third families; and such practices are not limited to the wealthy and powerful. While the husband might keep his mistresses and their children secret from his legal wife, often the wife knows of them and the children know of one another.

This complex situation reflects the traditional subordination of wives to husbands. Although marriage presumably guarantees a wife certain rights and entitlements, it has generally been the case, in most parts of the world, that these have been secondary to those of her husband. In marriages in which the bride has left her home at marriage to live either in a new home or in the home of her mother-in-law, her standing is below that of her husband and her role is to serve and support him. She becomes his dependent, often owning very little or no property of her own, lacking in inheritance rights or control over finances except those of immediate household management. In such cases, a wife may have virtually no identity of her own. It is her job to provide her husband with sexual satisfaction when he wishes it, physical comfort in his home, and food as well as to provide these for their children and, for that matter, his family and guests. She is judged by him, his family, and her own family, as well as the neighbors and society at large, according to how well she performs as a homemaker and mother, for these are the primary roles of a wife. Her upbringing will be geared to preparing her for a life as a good servant to her husband.

This asymmetry in traditional marriage is reflected in myriad ways, from the frequent practice of changing a woman's name to that of her husband upon marriage in Western societies to the unequal household maintenance tasks allocated wives and husbands in most societies today. Wives continue to put in much more time on a daily basis than husbands in such domestic activities as cooking and cleaning, even when both have full-time jobs outside of the home (see Chapter 12).

The Incorporated Wife. Many careers and occupations involve not one person but two, a wife and husband, and sometimes the whole family. In many traditional societies, past and present, this has been the norm: whatever a man does for a living, his wife is to be his supportive junior partner. Her "job" is to help him do his job. Thus, if a man is a farmer, his wife is a "farmer's wife": that is her occupation. In complex societies, where most people are employees, the incorporation of a wife (more often than a husband) into a spouse's job is less explicit. Often, there is no job title and the spouse does not appear on the payroll or receive benefits in her own right; but she is expected to contribute, and sometimes her contributions to both her husband's career and the company's objectives are recognized (though not remunerated). Wives are expected to support their husbands' activities, especially by taking care of all their domestic needs but also by taking an active interest in company functions. They are expected to entertain (depending on the husband's rank in the company) and to appear with their husbands at all social functions run by the company. If the job involves travel overseas for long periods of time, the wife is expected to go with her husband and perform those domestic and social functions in the overseas posting.

For example, the wife of a diplomat or an oil company worker who is posted overseas is often expected to subordinate her interests to her husband's work, going with him wherever he is sent and associating with other diplomats' or oil company workers' wives. Until recently, the wives of professors, doctors, and clergymen had important roles to play in the conduct of their husbands' work—both assisting with the work itself and making a social life for the husband's work community. The work of a politician's wife is very apparent in today's world, especially at the higher levels. This poses something of a dilemma for professional women married to politicians. The various debates about Hillary Rodham Clinton during her husband's presidency of the United States (1992–2000), for example, brought home to many Americans not only the importance of the role of "first lady" but also its limitations.

Although the first lady position is recognized as a kind of job, in the sense that the person holding it is assigned a staff to carry out her duties, most incorporated wives are not so recognized or provided with such support. Although performance of their roles contributes to the well-being of the company, in the end her only claim is to the benefits of her husband and his career. This surfaces when she might sue for divorce, claiming a share of his earnings because of the role she has played in his earning capacity (Callan and Ardener, 1984). In recent years, in recognition of the fact that many wives also have careers, some companies posting their employees to different cities and states or recruiting new personnel will assist in finding a new job for the wife or, if the employee is a wife herself and her rank is high enough, for the husband.

Children in the Family

While having children is one of the expected consequences of a marriage, in the United States the rise in the number of children born to single mothers indicates a profound change. This change, which reflects the trend in many developed countries, has been politi-
cized and narrowed down to a debate on the acceptable form of "family." (We shall examine various alternate forms or configurations of families later in this chapter.) "For the sake of the children," the presence of both parents in the marriage is said to be preferable not only by political conservatives but by many social scientists as well. For example, sociologists Linda Waite and Maggie Gallagher defend even bad marriages, which they believe, with enough determination and work from both spouses, are capable of improving and becoming quite satisfactory. Marriage, they argue, benefits a woman and her children financially. Waite and Gallagher see divorce as a punishment for the wife as well as for her children and counsels women to work out a marital partnership (see Waite and Gallagher, 2000). Others, however, would argue that a bad marriage does not benefit either wife or children and, if the husband is physically abusive, preserving the marriage can endanger all of them. The view that long-term damage is inflicted on children by divorce has been argued (Wallerstein et al., 2000), but some scholars have a more positive prediction for the children of divorce (Hetherington and Kelly, 2002). A U.N. study found that 75%–80% of children whose parents divorced adapted to the change and within 6 years were as well-adjusted and happy as children from intact families (United Nations, 2000).

According to the most recent statistics, attitudes toward sexual and reproductive rights have changed considerably over the past three decades (United Nations, 2000). Today, in many countries, women and men can choose when and whom to marry and whether to have children. The number of children desired (as expressed by women) has declined significantly in developing countries, according to surveys taken in the 1980s and 1990s. The largest absolute decline is in sub-Saharan Africa, where women want, on average, two fewer children than did women in the 1980s. However, women in some developing countries still want a large number of children—for example, in Cameroon, seven, and in Senegal, six. In all regions of the world—and in all countries—fertility rates are declining. Between 1990 and 2000, fertility rates decreased by at least 10% in all regions of Asia (except South Asia, where the decline is relatively less), North Africa, Eastern Europe, and Central America. In East Asia (except Mongolia) and in all Western European countries, fertility is now below replacement level (i.e., the number of children born to a woman is less than 2.1). The decrease in fertility in the People's Republic of China is a reflection of the government's one-child policy, with penalties for parents who have more than one child. In most countries, the reasons for smaller numbers of children derive from women's increased participation in economic activities, often made possible by private and public investments in educational and career opportunities for young women. Women who take advantage of such opportunities tend to delay marriage and childbirth.

Throughout the world, women bear most of the responsibility for rearing children, and an increasing number of mothers are also in the labor force. Attitudes toward employed mothers have changed profoundly during recent decades. Often, when women lack adequate child care, they must take their children to work with them. In 10 of the 12 countries surveyed in sub-Saharan Africa and in Pakistan and Peru, over 40% of women have their small children with them when they work away from home. Maternity leave with pay before and after childbirth, institutions that provide quality child care, and the possibility of free or inexpensive health care and medicine for mothers and their children would benefit working mothers. In the United States, a developed and highly industrialized country, such benefits lag far behind those in many developed, even several developing, countries.

Western Marriage in Historical Perspective

In precolonial and revolutionary America, as well as later, the status of the wife was determined by the husband's occupation and place in society. In a 1792 critique of this inequity, Mary Wollstonecraft called for *A Vindication of the Rights of Woman*, advocating education for young women so they would not be subject to the "slavery of marriage" (see Wollstonecraft, [1792], 1975, and Chapters 2 and 10). Between 1776 and 1830 in Western

---

Box 7.2   MONOGAMOUS MARRIAGE AS ECONOMIC EXPLOITATION

The first class opposition that appears in history coincides with the development of the antagonism between man and woman in monogamous marriage, and the first class oppression with that of the female sex by the male. Monogamy was a great historical step forward; nevertheless, together with slavery and private wealth, it opens the period that has lasted until today in which every step forward is also relatively a step backward, in which prosperity and development for some is won through the misery and frustration of others. It is the cellular form of civilized society in which the nature of the oppositions and contradictions fully active in that society can already be studied.

Source: Engels [1884], 1972:129.

Europe and the United States, although property, family, and social status remained important criteria for selecting a mate, love in marriage came to be considered desirable, prefiguring the notion that has come to dominate the ideal for love today (Farrell, 1999). The ideal was nurtured in the United States during the eighteenth and early nineteenth centuries by the fact that there were more men than women, allowing women to choose among them. Down to the twentieth century in the United States, poor women were more likely to have unformalized or "common law" marriages with the men with whom they lived, and they continued to work both at home and outside it, caring for their men and children and marrying only when and if there were enough leisure time and extra money for a ceremony. The ideal for middle- and upper-class white women was to stay home in the privacy of their own domain. In these classes, the husband was expected to be the sole provider, and his world was deemed outside the home, in the public arena. In the nineteenth century, magazines and other kinds of literature were published to aid wives to care for their homes and families. Such advice manuals and women's journals have continued into the twenty-first century, directing women how to make their houses and gardens more beautiful and how to take care of their children.

In the United States, by the late nineteenth century, women were making some gains toward equality. In 1848, feminist reformers, including Elizabeth Cady Stanton (1815–1902), who would be a wife for almost 50 years (and a mother of seven) and Quaker Lucretia Coffin Mott (1793–1880), met at Seneca Falls, New York, and proclaimed a *Declaration of Sentiments* which demanded redress for many inequalities in the legal code. In their view, "the only acceptable marriage was based on love, sympathy, and equality between the sexes" (see Hartog, 2000; Stanton, 1971; and

Chapter 13). Reforms in the United States concerning equality, however, were slow to come. By the 1890s, some new rights for wives had been established in a law: a wife could keep her property and earnings in her own name when married, and if separated or divorced, she could claim custody over her children. So long as she was legally a "wife," however, the state expected her husband to provide for her. These advances were of particular aid to white women in the northern states. Under the federal system in the United States, civil law codes vary according to the state or territory. In the western states/ territories, where women were in short supply through the nineteenth century, women were granted rights earlier than in other areas, perhaps to attract more of them to these rough regions. In Wyoming, for example, women were allowed to vote in 1864, and three more western states legalized women's suffrage by 1896.

Marriage for women in the southern states was quite a different story. Until after the Civil War (1860–5), only free black women could legally marry; their slave sisters, as the property of their owners, could not. After the Civil War, interracial marriage was forbidden by state laws in the South, these laws remaining in place until very recently (in Alabama, for example, until 2000).

White women of the propertied class in the South were supposed to be treated like "rare flowers." They were taught not to "unsex" themselves by acquiring too much learning and developing aspirations that did not suit their place in society. These southern women generally accepted their dependence upon their menfolk, until the Civil War changed their situation drastically. The loss of more than half a million men in the Confederacy compelled a number of southern women, married or not, to consider some form of work outside their homes, as so many of their northern and western sisters did. Southern women faced the situation that had held true for New England women earlier in the century, a shortage of available men (Yalom, 2001:204–8).

The turning point for American women came late in the nineteenth century, when the Civil War and its aftermath had effected changes in social conventions and constructs. In 1874, the reformist Abba Goold Woolson gave voice to the changes: "I exist . . . not as a wife, not as a mother, not as a teacher, but first of all, as woman, with a right to existence for my own sake" (Yalom, 2001:280). Hers was the voice of a changing self-definition of women in the United States. Women went to work, although in many cases they had to choose between marriage and a career. Rooming houses and dormitories that were set up in cities or mill towns where women worked in ever larger numbers provided women with an opportunity to separate themselves from families, at least until they entered a marital arrangement. It was at about this time that lesbian partnerships, as long as they appeared to be devoid of physical intimacy, came to be somewhat tolerated by the larger society; such unions were called "Boston marriages" (Yalom, 2001; Rothblum and Brehony, 1993). The choice that women were forced to make between working and marrying/having children in the late nineteenth century has not completely disappeared in the early twenty-first century.

The introduction of large numbers of married women into the workforce began when the United States entered World War I (1916–8) and was necessitated again by World War II (1941–5). With adult men in military service, women filled in the ranks at factories, offices, and shops. When the servicemen returned and demanded their old jobs, women were forced out of them and married women were told to return home, a message, justified by a "new" image of the wife. As depicted in the popular media, the young middle-class wife was now idealized as one who cleans and polishes her house, shops and cooks, puts her children to bed, and pretties herself, waiting for her (corporately employed) husband to return from work to drink the cocktail she has prepared for him. A good wife lived vicariously through the accomplishments of her husband and the achievements of her children. Her job as "wife" entailed the sacrifices and devotion to her family that would make this rosy picture possible. That description of a "wife" prevailed in the United States in the 1950s. This image cloaked the reality that many women continued to work at sex-segregated and lower-paid jobs (see Chapter 12) and many were unhappy and dissatisfied with their lot. Those with higher education wanted to use it to get work and pursue careers. The divorce rate began to rise sharply in the 1960s, with one out of two marriages ending in divorce. Despite the prevailing ideology of domesticity, many wives were not satisfied with being relegated to care of households and children. Mirra Komarovsky's 1962 study *Blue-Collar Marriage* depicted the struggles of working-class women who had to work both at low-paying jobs and at home with little acknowledgment or appreciation by their husbands, describing how children added to the strains of marriage. Betty Friedan published *The Feminine Mystique* in 1963, in which she laid bare what she saw as the monotony, drudgery, and isolation of the suburban wife. The book struck a chord in the lives of discontented wives, and many of them began to rethink their situations as a new women's liberation movement gained momentum by the late 1960s.

One of the significant outcomes of the new women's movement came in 1973: the U.S. Supreme Court's decision *Roe* v. *Wade*. This invalidated state laws prohibiting abortion and left the decision largely to the woman and her doctor. This legal decision, along with the recent development of a contraceptive pill, provided a degree of sexual liberation for women. Because pregnancy and childbearing were no longer the inevitable outcome of sexual intercourse, a woman had more options available, including having sex without necessarily getting married. Another outcome was that women, particularly wives, actively began to confront domestic physical and verbal abuse, rape, and inequalities they experienced at home and outside it, in part motivated by a "raised consciousness" that was produced by the social activism of the new women's movement (see Chapter 13). What followed from this growing resistance to past subordination was an increase in divorce, trends toward choosing later motherhood and single parenting, far more women participating in the workforce, and an emerging ideal of a far more egalitarian form of marriage than had been envisioned before. These changes in traditional marital unions did not occur without heated debates and vociferous protests, often in the name of "family values." Not surprisingly, therefore, these changes have continued to be at the forefront in the agendas of our national political parties.

Infidelity

Between marriage partners, sexual relations may not be a microcosm of unequal gender relationships in a society. For some couples, sex may offer a respite from daily battles to survive and to achieve, the only private time wife and husband have in a day to share thoughts and intimacies. Lovemaking for such a couple may be an expression of these mutual feelings and may provide a moment when both can respond to physical needs that transcend social roles.

In a marital partnership, both women and men continuously make compromises to accommodate one another, the society in which they are living, and their offspring. Yet, marriages often do not go smoothly, even those which are amicable and affectionate. As the spouses go through physical and psychological changes, as their economic and geographical terrains change, as children grow up and leave, and particularly if children present some problems which appear unsolvable, the marriage often strains, shows cracks, and may not persist even with considerable effort on both sides. One partner in the marriage may "stray off" to find relief, consolation, comfort, or merely distraction in an affair with someone else. The "affair" distracts the involved spouse, but once it is discovered by the other, the marriage often moves onto rocky ground. In modern times, when love has become the basis for a marital union, an extramarital affair which develops into a love affair leaves little hope for the marriage to endure. "Love" becomes a force that can make or unmake unions between two people.

Whether love is there before marriage or grows between spouses later, many wives and husbands have sought romance and love outside of marriage ever since marriage began as an institution. In medieval Europe, for example, among the elite love was not assumed to exist between married couples but was thought to be found outside of marriage, or so it was suggested in many of the songs that the thirteenth-century French troubadours sang (Amt, 1993). After the 1450s, the attitude in Europe toward marriage in the upper classes began to change; a wife was seen to uphold the family honor by being chaste, attentive to decorum, and absolutely faithful to her husband and by producing heirs to bear the family name. If wedlock was primarily expected to produce legitimate offspring, love hardly had anything to do with it. Even much later, a wife, especially a mother, was not meant to stray away from the nuptial bed; and many cautionary novels, such as Gustave Flaubert's *Madame Bovary* (1854) and Leo Tolstoy's *Anna Karenina* (1875–7), continue to remind their readers of the terrible end that awaits married women who search for fulfillment and self-definition through adultery.

Divorce

Not all societies treat divorce the same way. In one anthropologist's sample, women and men had approximately equal rights to initiate divorce in 75% of societies, while men enjoyed superior rights in only 15%. In 10%, women had superior rights. In a matrilocal society, such as that of the Iroquois, wives could divorce husbands by dumping their belongings outside the door (Murdock, 1950). The majority of societies disapprove of divorce, and Western society is no exception—as testified to by the many legal obstacles to divorce in the laws of both church and state. Although laws, rules, customs, and attitudes toward divorce have changed in the Western world over the centuries, it is undeniable that there is social stigma assigned to a divorced woman to this day. Even though divorce has become commonplace, the experience of marital failure is hard to take, and its emotional impact may be felt for years after the event.

In ethnically complex societies, such as those where new nations comprise disparate groups with different customs and different languages or where older nations incorporate large numbers of immigrants or workers from abroad, family law (which is generally where divorce is placed) becomes complex. Some nations assign responsibility for legal decisions about marriage and divorce to special courts from each ethnic or religious group, with no civil law on these matters, while others struggle to devise ways to accommodate religious/ethnic diversity, with varying degrees of success. In the United States, polygamy is not officially recognized, and no matter what the religious convictions of the parties, neither men nor women can be legally married to more than one spouse at a time.

Divorce is a primary contributor to an increase in the number of impoverished women and children. Most of the families in the United States that are living in poverty are female-headed households, and the 1998 census data indicate that the single-parent family has increased 190% since 1970. In part, this impoverishment has to do with gender roles in marriage. While women are married, they contribute domestic labor. By the mid-1980s, if they worked outside the home, their income contribution came to, on the average, only 22% of the total family income (Arendell, 1987) (see Table 7.1). When a woman is divorced, she generally loses access to the financial resources that were available through a husband and, as a consequence and because the children usually stay with her, her

TABLE 7.1 Which U.S. Wives Work?

	Married Couples with One or More Children Under Age 6 Where the Husband Works Full-Time		
	Wife Works Full-Time	*Wife Works Part-Time*	*Wife Does Not Work*
Number of families	3,540,000	3,629,000	3,130,000
Median income	$69,008	$56,975	$44,942
Family income			
Under $50,000	24.9%	40.4%	55.3%
$50,000–$100,000	52.7%	49.8%	22.1%
Over $100,000	22.4%	9.8%	22.6%

Source: Bureau of the Census, Money Income in the United States, 1999.

standard of living declines. Because women continue to be discriminated against in the job market (see Chapter 12) and continue to bear major responsibility for the care of children (see Chapter 8), divorce can have a devastating impact on their economic situations, just at the moment when they and their children may be emotionally vulnerable.

Since the divorce rate in the United States is fairly high, many, perhaps most, women's economic futures depend more on their own job situations than on those of their husbands. The wife (who is still often assumed to be a stay-at-home wife) is expected to provide the wifely services, which include caring for children, cooking, cleaning, and so on, but with no monetary or guaranteed compensation such as a retirement plan or unemployment benefits. A wife is not judged as an equal partner in the financial arena. While the law requires former husbands to pay child support in most cases, fewer than half of divorced fathers pay anything at all and only a small proportion pay what the court has ordered them to pay. In those states which require an equitable split in the marital assets between wife and husband, divorce may involve a bitter struggle over the division of property and money, resulting in high legal fees and unhappy feelings all around.

It is relatively easy to marry in the United States, while it is difficult, although not as difficult as in the past, to get divorced. To marry, a couple of legal age need do no more than register with the local government, have a blood test (in most states), exchange brief vows in the presence of an official and a witness, and pay a very small fee. Waiting time is usually about 3 days, often less. No parental consent is needed, nor any promise of family support. To get divorced, on the other hand, couples usually require lawyers, legal documents, one or more court hearings, and often a considerable amount of time, even when both parties are in agreement over the desire

to divorce and the terms of separation. If the couple disagrees about the terms of divorce, as is likely when the marriage has dissolved in discord and there are children and property rights in dispute, the legal cost of settlement can be high, while the costs in time and personal agony may be incalculable. The issue of the burdens borne by children in divorce is usually of profound concern to parents as well as to the courts and other involved parties.

The process of divorce can exacerbate the pain of marital failure. Divorce laws in some states require evidence of misbehavior or inadequacy, even when both parties agree that neither was "at fault." Reasons for divorce vary and often are not mutual for the couple in question. In addition to personal incompatibility, infidelity (in some states), mistreatment, and abuse, common causes for seeking divorce are abandonment, premarital misrepresentations, and economic or sexual problems.

Widowhood

Women in most countries of the world have a greater life expectancy than men; consequently, a larger number of women than men are widowed. With the exception of Japan, in most industrially developed countries, the elderly are likely to live alone. In some societies, it is not uncommon for a widow to be permanently ensconced in the house of her in-laws, who possess and control her dowry and the chances of her remarriage. An extreme example of this treatment is the case of young Indian widows, who may be barred from remarriage and treated as pariahs and who may be believed (according to the laws of karma) to have caused the death of the husband by some evil committed in a previous life, if not in this one (see Box 7.3).

Nonetheless, a husband's death does not end a woman's life. Tomioka Taeko (b. 1935), a Japanese poet and fiction writer, captures

Box 7.3   WIDOWHOOD IN CONTEMPORARY INDIA

About 10 percent of women in India are widows, compared to only three percent of men, according to the 1991 census. Fifty-four percent of women aged 60 and over are widows, as are 12 percent of women aged 35–59. Remarriage is the exception rather than the rule; only about 10 percent of widows marry again.

According to a study based on qualitative information, widowers do not suffer the social stigma, restrictions and taboos associated with widows. They retain their economic resources and are much more likely to remarry. In contrast, the approximately 33 million Indian widows are expected to lead chaste, austere, ascetic lives. Meeting those expectations is possible only for women who come from households prosperous enough to care for a dependent widow. Reports describe brothers-in-law who usurp the widow's share of property and do not offer her a harvest share or daily maintenance; sons who live separately and do not support the widowed mother; and brothers who do not support the widowed sister although they inherited her share of the father's property.

Widows have a basic repertoire of strategies. They may try to exert their claims on male kin (if any). If not, widows may adopt a son or negotiate a daughter's marriage to a son-in-law willing to support them. Widows who own land are more likely than landless widows to be able to negotiate such arrangements. Widows may remarry or enter partnerships with men who offer support. They may continue to work in small-scale farming, trading or producing goods for sale, or they may enter the wage labour force. Others adopt a religious way of life, living from begging, chanting prayers or singing devotional songs. Still others become prostitutes or concubines to earn enough money to support themselves.

The sensational circumstances of small numbers of widows receive more attention than the less visible and quiet deprivations of millions. These deprivations do not show up in economic and social statistics, so the standard household-level analyses tell very little about widows and their well-being. Female-headed households are not reported by marital status, so widow-headed households cannot be compared with other households.

Source: From United Nations, *The World's Women 2000*, based on Martha Alter Chen, *Perpetual Mourning: Widowhood in Rural India*, Oxford University Press © 2000.

the state of widowhood in her story "Family in Hell" in these words: "After all what is it they say? When a man's left a widower the maggots start to crawl, but when a woman's left a widow flowers come out in bloom!" (Tanaka and Hanson, 1982:176).

Marriage as an Institution at the Beginning of the Twenty-First Century

As the twenty-first century starts, it is helpful to take a look at the institution of marriage in the United States, where some of the data of the 2000 census have been analyzed and published. The following information is based on newspaper reports that appeared on after the U.S. census of 2000 (Schmitt, 2001). Fewer than one-quarter of U.S. households consisted of married couples with children, firstly because women and men are delaying marriage and having children and secondly because the number of single-parent families is growing much faster than the number of married couples. For the first time, the number of

Americans living alone, 26% of all households, surpassed the number of married-couple households with children.

People are marrying later or not at all and are more often choosing to remain single after divorce or widowhood. The median age at the first marriage has increased for women from 20 in 1960 to 25 in 2000 and for men from 22 in 1960 to 27 in 2000. Although it has not increased significantly since the 1960s, divorce is one of the reasons for the large numbers of single adult women (numbers of single older men are smaller). Better health care, retirement and nursing homes, and institutions that provide assisted living contribute to longer and improved quality of lives for both women and men. The increasing economic independence of women is yet another reason for them to delay marriage or to stay single.

Perhaps it is not surprising that cohabitation of an unrelated woman and man has grown to 5.5 million couples in 2000 from 3.2 million in 1990. The number of nonfamily households makes up about one-third of all households. They grew at twice the rate of family households in the 1990s. Related to this change in the constitution of households is the decline in childbirth, including out-of-wedlock births. The percentage of married-couple households with children younger than 18 has declined to 23.5% of all households in 2000 from 25.6% in 1990 (see Table 7.2). That married couples choose to postpone having children seems to be widespread among the developed nations. For example, the birth of a daughter to the relatively older Japanese Crown Princess Masako (just a few days before her thirty-eighth birthday) has effected a change in the social acceptability of delayed childbirth in that country. She had already blazed a trail when she married the prince because she was a Harvard-educated former diplomat, around age 30, and a commoner. Japanese women who have been customarily delegated the role of "stay-at-home wife and mother" are at a crossroad where more

TABLE 7.2 U.S. Domestic Demographics: 1970 and 1998

	1970	1998	Change
Total population	203,302,000	269,067,000	+32.3%
Annual births	3,731,000	3,942,000	+5.7%
Marital births	3,332,000	2,693,000	−19.2%
Nonmarital births	339,000	1,249,000	+223.6%
Women aged 40–44 who have not married	5.4%	9.9%	+83.3%
All married couples	44,278,000	54,317,000	+21.4%
Married with children	25,541,000	25,269,000	−1.1%
Single-parent families	3,271,000	9,491,000	+190.2%
Children living with unmarried couples	196,000	1,491,000	+665.5%
Single mothers who have never married	9.1%	42.2%	+363.7%
Distribution of births			
White	78.1%	59.9%	−23.3%
Black	13.7%	15.0%	+9.5%
Latino	6.8%	18.6%	+173.5%
Asian and other	1.4%	6.5%	+364.3%

Source: Bureau of the Census and National Center for Health Statistics, 1999.

TABLE 7.3 Percentage of Young Adults Currently Married, 1993–8

	Age 20–24		Age 25–29	
	Women	*Men*	*Women*	*Men*
WESTERN EUROPE				
Belgium	23	9	60	43
Denmark	9	3	32	19
Finland	10	4	34	23
France	10	3	39	26
Germany	14	5	39	23
Iceland	8	3	34	22
Ireland	7	3	41	27
Netherlands	13	4	42	25
Norway	8	3	32	18
Sweden	7	2	28	16
Switzerland	17	7	48	31
OTHER DEVELOPED REGIONS				
Australia	16	7	50	35
Japan	13	7	50	32
New Zealand	12	5	48	39
United States	27	16	55	44

Source: United Nations, *The World's Women* 2000.

professional women, if they choose to marry, can do so at an advanced age and keep their professions. The postponement of marriage and childbearing is one way of fulfilling a woman's wish to be professionally successful and economically independent in Japan and elsewhere. In most developed countries, marriage has become increasingly rare for young adults, particularly young men (see Table 7.3).

A trend in changing mores in the United States regarding marriage was already on its way in the twentieth century when divorce became commonplace and out-of-wedlock children no longer were branded "illegitimate." The swelling prosperity of the 1990s allowed some women to make adequate income to bear or adopt children without a husband, and better-quality child-care facilities and child care takers were available to the working mother who would not be necessarily dependent on a partner. The relaxation of the traditional family composition of the mid-1950s, which consisted of a father and a mother and their children, brought the existence of alternative family configurations into the open. Although not all alternative families are acceptable to all segments of the population of the United States or of many developed countries, let alone universally, some of these configurations are currently viable and gradually becoming established institutions.

Alternatives to Conventional Marriage

Many societies have had alternatives to conventional marriage, but often these have been hidden because of social stigma and because researchers have paid more attention to the dominant forms. More equal relationships between husbands and wives have coexisted with the more common patriarchal family, for example. The old ideal of *"companionate marriage"* has been reformulated under such new labels as "egalitarian marriage," "equal partnership," and "marital equality," although in most cases "his" marriage continues to be better than "hers," as when marriage ends in divorce and the woman suffers from loss of earnings and insufficient (if any) child support. A historical precedent to an egalitarian marriage was set in 1855 when Lucy Stone married Henry Blackwell after a long and determined resistance to his suit. In pursuit of women's rights, the pair signed a contract which was a manifesto criticizing and abjuring the legal authority of husbands, their conjugal rights to sex on demand, the female duty of constant childbearing, and the obliteration of the wife's personality (Rossi, 1964).

A partnership means that both spouses contribute to the economic and physical maintenance of the home and both have the opportunity and the responsibility to pursue other interests. Each may take turns at completing educational programs or starting new jobs or caring for young children, but in terms of contribution and responsibility, there must be true parity (Okin, 1989; Held, 1979).

The alternative configurations to conventional family roles and lives are diverse. Some have been devised without women's input or consent, and some have evolved as a "last resort" because women have not had the option to marry and have children. Here, however, we review mainly the options that women have shaped for themselves, the ways of living that they have chosen, designed, or dreamed. We begin with considerations of different types of community for women—religious, educative, work-oriented, and supportive. At times, women who were able to have joined ideological communities based on religious or political convictions rather than be in a traditional marriage. We describe a few here. We then look at families that retain some features of conventional family life but whose members have reshaped their roles by choice. These include families of single parents, cohabitating or domestic partners, consensual or informal unions, visiting unions, and women only. Women also can choose not to mother while remaining in a union with partners. Finally, we consider the lives of women who choose to be on their own.

Religious Communities

Buddhist and Christian orders of nuns have enabled women to live outside the boundaries of the family circle for centuries. Christian

---

Box 7.4   "DELAYED TRANSFER MARRIAGE": AN ALTERNATIVE FORM OF MARRIAGE IN CHINA

Janice Stockard (1989) has recorded the existence of "delayed transfer marriage," a form of marriage almost undocumented in previous literature on Chinese society but widely established in the Canton Delta:

In striking contrast to the orthodox Confucian form of marriage, brides in delayed transfer marriages were required to separate from their husband shortly after marriage and return to live with their parents for at least three more years. During this customary period of separation, brides were expected to visit their husband on several festival occasions each year. Ideally, brides became pregnant about three years after marriage and then settled in the husband's home. . . .

Source: Janice Stockard, *Daughters of the Canton Delta: Marriage Patterns and Economic Strategies in South China, 1860–1930.* Copyright © 1989 by the Board of Trustees of the Leland Stanford Jr. University. Used with the permission of Stanford University Press, www.sup.org.

convents go back to the fourth and fifth centuries in the Mediterranean area and, like the churches to which they are attached, have had a complex and varied history (McNamara, 1996). Buddhism also has a long history of monasticism for women in Asia and a comparable complexity (Falk, 1980). In certain forms, both Buddhism and Christianity are turned intensely toward an otherworldly vision. This attitude provides the basis for monasticism. However, both Buddhism and Christianity are formally male-dominated institutions, and this fact is reflected in the regulation of the lives of nuns.

Christianity has valued chastity above marriage. Many women have had genuine longing for the celibate religious life, to take vows to remain a virgin, and "to keep herself for God to serve Him freely and for no man besides" (Amt, 1993:140–2). However, such fervent convictions were not always heeded. Medieval annals tell of women whose desires to dedicate themselves to God were frustrated because their and their families' poverty made impossible the payment of the "dowry" for their "marriage to God" and upkeep in the convent. Some women lamented the unwillingness of their families to relieve them from the duty to marry and bear children.

Despite these frustrations, convents provided an arena in which many women not only realized religious aspirations but also found scope for their economic, political, and intellectual talents. The convent provided women with opportunities to exercise their abilities in administration, handiwork, music, art and literature, and scholarly learning, as well as spiritual exploration. Renunciation of sex was not too high a price for the many women of every rank and condition who desired and were able to choose this alternative. During the religious crises of sixteenth- and seventeenth-century Europe, nuns were able to overcome the restrictions of cloistering and to expand teaching, charitable, and nurs-

ing activities. The nun of early modern times stood out as a public model for generations of European women seeking a respectable alternative to conventional duty to home and hearth.

With the wider availability of other alternatives and a decline in the authority of organized religion, many nuns today leave orders while relatively few women decide to join. The decline in the numbers of women and men who dedicate themselves to God may require the Catholic Church to make changes to allow women in religious life to move into positions of power and authority, but this has not yet happened. Today, convent life takes many different forms; women who are nuns vary widely in work, dress, and social relationships. What has not changed are a dedication to spiritual life (though this may take many forms), a decision not to marry or engage in any sexual relationships, and a commitment to a community of like-minded women organized in convents and orders. Noncontemplative orders are extremely variable in their patterns of life. Members of these orders may be committed to teaching, nursing, helping the poor, providing shelter for orphans or unwed mothers, working with drug addicts, or fighting for human rights. Indeed, some Christian nuns have been in the forefront of the struggle for social justice in the world— and in the Church.

Women who choose to walk the path of Buddha and become nuns must give up family and marriage, take vows of celibacy, abstain from most kinds of food, forsake the external world, and undergo a relentlessly demanding instructional period which includes prayer and study of scriptures. Women can be ordained as nuns in the countries dominated by the Mahayana school of Buddhism. (Female ordination is not practiced, however, in several Buddhist countries, including Japan and Cambodia.) Novices with shaved heads and white robes are little better than servants for the monks, cleaning and cooking in exchange for monastic shelter and food provided by the men. As in Christianity, the number of women attempting to become Buddhist nuns is on the decline.

Convents have traditionally housed schools for girls, and many modern women's institutions have been based on that model. The women's experiences of an all-girls school or college provide them with an opportunity to study, excel, and develop skills and goals without the pressures and restrictions inherent in settings dominated by men (see Chapter 10). School experiences often bear fruit in life-long relationships, such as those narrated by Mary McCarthy in *The Group* (1963). The range of leadership roles possible in single-sex education has created advocates for such experiences.

Laboring Communities

Many women, by necessity or choice, have attempted to become self-supporting outside a family circle. Social pressure in the form of low wages, abuse of unprotected women, and sometimes outright coercion have sometimes led working women to organize on a collective basis. In Europe, in the Low Countries, for example, unmarried women, including widows, formed quasi-religious communities based on the idea of collective housekeeping and economic enterprise. The famous Belgian tapestries and lace were produced in such workshops. The religious element in these *beguine* organizations ensured their social respectability and enabled members to claim the protection of local ecclesiastical authorities. Nevertheless, women met with hostility and even violence from the guildsmen, who would neither admit women to the craft "brotherhoods" nor allow them to compete by working for lower wages or longer hours (McDonnell, 1976).

Industrialization in the nineteenth century brought to Western Europe and the United States a major social shift away from the organization of production by the individual artisan to factories and machines owned by industrial capitalists. A feature of early factory communities was the careful supervision and control of unmarried girls and young women who had left home to work in the mills. The most famous experiment of a protected mill community was located in Lowell, Massachusetts, in the 1820s. Rural young women were recruited into the textile factories there; they lived in company boardinghouses, where morals as well as physical needs were carefully monitored. They enjoyed the benefits of urban life; lectures and other culturally enriching events were scheduled in the few leisure hours. Several young women produced a magazine, *The Lowell Offering*, and some were sufficiently inspired to go on to more rewarding careers (Eisler, 1977). The Lowell experiment, however, lasted fewer than two decades and was not to be repeated. In *North and South* (1855), mid-nineteenth century British novelist Mrs. Elizabeth Gaskell (1810–65) described the independence of the factory girls in Manchester, England. For most women, the experience of the factory system was not an idyll but a life of hard labor, tuberculosis, and sexual exploitation. However, for some women in Europe and the United States, industrialization made possible a new image as well as a new kind of role, an alternative to those of "wife" and "mother."

Utopian and Experimental Communities

Utopia was first used by philosopher Thomas More (1478–1535) as a name for an imaginary community whose design would eliminate social ills such as injustice and moral degeneracy. The elements of the design reveal the author's critique of society as it exists, as well as providing a proposal for how to correct society's flaws, however fanciful or unrealistic the construction might be. Many utopias focus on the conventional family and its assigned roles. They see this institution as the root of many social problems and propose radical alternatives. Some attack the institution of marriage itself, while others target the nuclear family. Both can limit human, particularly women's, potential.

The "solutions" envisioned are diverse and often radical: elimination of sexual intercourse, keeping sex but eliminating sexual exclusivity, communal childrearing, and, the most fanciful, eliminating men altogether and/or altering the body so that reproduction does not rely on coupling. While the last of these has not occurred so far, the others have been attempted experimentally as well as dreamed and described in writing. Some of these literary and real utopian (or "intentional") communities can be described as feminist, and some are explicitly so.

The most frequently cited utopian writer of antiquity is the Greek philosopher Plato. His *Republic*, written in the fourth century B.C.E., is perhaps the prototype of antifamily utopias. He imagined a state governed by an elite group, the "guardians," in which women and men would participate on equal terms. Reproduction would be carefully regulated. When children are born, they would be taken from the mother and put under the supervision of special caretakers, a group that included both women and men. Mothers would breast-feed at random and would be prevented from knowing which of the infants are theirs. Women would participate in the job of governing and develop concern and affection for all the society's children (Plato, 1998). Later male utopian writers tended to take a dim view of marriage and parental control over children; their ways of solving these problems were far less innovative than their suggestions for dealing with government or property. Plato's *Republic* has sometimes been seen as feminist because it challenges male su-

premacy and frees women from the constraints of child care.

We know of no utopian constructs written by women in antiquity, but a number of modern utopias have been conceived by women. "Ladyland" is such a place described by the Bengali author Rokeya Sakhawat Hossain in her story *Sultana's Dream* (1905; see Hossain, 1988). It is a land where the private and public roles of women and men have been reversed. Women are able to take control over Ladyland after men prove incapable of defending the country through conventional warfare. Men are relegated to seclusion, thus eliminating both crime and sin. Women take over all public and political functions, while men are assigned the job of child care. Women rule in Ladyland not through the traditional male manner of domination and oppression but through more cooperative means and working with nature for example, to extract the sun's energy. As a result of a less exploitative approach to nature, many disasters, such as drought, are eliminated.

Herland, written by Charlotte Perkins Gilman ([1915] 1979) a decade later, solves the problem of women's inequality through the simple device of eliminating men from society altogether. In her utopia, women find a way to conceive children by *parthenogenesis* (nonsexual reproduction) and motherhood is a venerated achievement. All of society is oriented toward nurturance, of human beings as well as of nature. This is a society of mothers and women who see themselves as potential mothers and yet do not ever have to be wives.

Utopias and *dystopias* (the repellant opposite of utopias) have been imagined by many modern feminist writers in the guise of fantasy and science fiction. Many utopian writers rely on radically modifying not only marriage and the family but also the process of reproduction. This suggests that while social inequality is the "problem," the root of inequality is the biology of reproduction (Lees,

1984). Change this and everything changes; without changing this, they suggest, we have little chance of changing anything else.

Celibacy seems to have been the central rule for many communities based on religious conviction. Celibacy, communitarians have argued, reorders the priorities of a community over those of the individual (Muncy, 1973). For the community of Shakers, celibacy was a theological issue; its founder, Ann Lee (1736–84) preached equality of women with men, deemed possible only by eliminating sexual relations, which would distract women and men from their religious duties, and motherhood, which would create inequality. There were communities which approved sex but not marriage. The most famous and longest-lasting community was known as the "Perfectionists" in Oneida, New York, who practiced "complex marriage," in which each member was married to every other person of the opposite sex; exclusive attachments between couples were forbidden. Young women who were chosen to bear children had to give them up to specialists to raise them. In this community as in many others, the rights of women were still limited, although equality among the members was advocated. Contrary to theory, friction arose between the mothers and the rest of the community of the control of the children.

Since the nineteenth century, there have indeed been experimental communities that attempted to create societies with very unconventional marriage and childrearing practices. Few have been led by feminists, and few have succeeded for very long. The early Israeli kibbutz was long viewed as a success in the tradition of communes based on socialist ideals of equality and shared effort. Everyone worked, and all economic conditions, profits and debts, were shared communally. In the first decades, children were raised in "children's houses," seeing their parents at the end of the workday but sleeping apart from them, with other children of their age group. Housework was eliminated for the most part because shopping, cooking, washing up, and laundry were done communally. The ideology of women's equality with men and the subordination of private interests to those of the collective were fundamental to the kibbutz movement. Yet, traditional gender distinctions have emerged. When they have children, most kibbutz women prefer to work closer to home, and that means doing "domestic" work in the kitchen and the laundry or in the children's houses. In recent years, moreover, most kibbutz communities have restored the nuclear family household, with its attendant extra housework (Safir, 1991; Palgi, 1991).

Other communal social arrangements have been more short-lived for a variety of reasons, but utopian communities are not the only alternative to conventional family life.

Alternative Families

Single Parents. *Single-parent*, or *lone-parent*, families, in which children are raised by only one parent, usually the mother, are becoming more common in many higher-income countries (United Nations, 2000). In Italy, for example, 90% of children whose parents divorced stayed with their mothers. In the United States in 1998, of all families with children, a third—almost 12 million—were single-parent families, up from 28% in 1990. Never-married women represent an increasing proportion of single mothers; in the United States in 1998, 42% of single mothers had never been married, while in Canada in 1996, the proportion of unmarried mothers was 24%. Everywhere in the developed regions single mothers tend to be poorer than mothers who live with a partner and even poorer in comparison to single fathers (United Nations, 2000). Children living with a divorced parent, however, generally fare better than those living with a never-married mother, who is more likely to have a low level of education and, as a result, fewer employment opportunities. In an economic system such as that of the United States, which provides fewer social services and less social support for human needs than almost any other advanced industrial country, single mothers and their children have long faced very difficult hurdles (Edelman, 1987).

While in most cases single mothers are not single by choice, this is increasingly an option actively chosen by many women at various levels of the economic scale. There is still controversy over the desirability of single parenthood as a choice, but in the United States, it is no longer a new or shocking subject as it was in 1992 when Vice President Dan Quayle publicly chastised a fictional television character, Murphy Brown, for having and raising her child as a single mother.

Domestic Partners, Cohabitation, Consensual Unions. Significant proportions of women and men do not marry in some regions of the world, particularly in Latin America and the Caribbean (in Caribbean countries, 22% of women and 19% of men). In Western Europe, the proportion is lower: 9% of both women and men do not ever marry. On the other hand, cohabitation or informal unions of women and men are generally high—for example, 28% of women aged 15–49 in Haiti and 36% in the Dominican Republic. In sub-Saharan African countries, the number of consensual unions is fairly high. In Mozambique, the proportion of women in consensual union reaches 55%. The increase may be due to the disappearance of sanctioned polygamy (men married fewer women) and to the shift from a rural to a cash economy, which leads to the migration of laborers to urban centers and, thus, a shortage of men in rural villages. The shortage of men in villages, for example, in South Africa and in Peru, has increased the number of women who seek partners other than their husbands

and enter informal unions or cohabitation. In most countries, it has proven quite difficult to gather information on nonmarital unions due to general disapproval, economic reasons (women threatened with the loss of a widow's pension or alimony), and the rather fluid formations of partnerships.

Informal unions, including cohabitation, have become more common in some countries in the developed regions. In northern European countries in 1996, more than half of women aged 20–24 were in cohabiting unions—in Sweden, more than three-quarters. Cohabitation generally becomes less common with age, suggesting marriage at a later age for both sexes. Yet, a significant proportion of women aged 30–34 (33% in Sweden, 18% in France, and more than 10% in other countries of Europe) remained in nonmarital unions. Elsewhere in the developed countries, with the exception of the United States, where both women and men tend to marry early, cohabitation is relatively high. In Canada, for example, 46% of women were in unions between the ages of 20 and 24, as were 16% of women aged 30–34. The proportion of women in informal unions in New Zealand reaches 67% for those aged 20–24 and 19% for those over age 30. The increase in consensual unions in various forms, including domestic partnerships or cohabitation without necessarily sexual relationship or children, points to the weakening of the institution of marriage, formalized by legal processes or religious ceremonies. The acceptance of children born out of wedlock by the society in most regions of the world is another contributing factor. It seems that informal union or cohabitation among consenting adults is still underreported, and members of alternative family configurations may show up as singles in a census.

Visiting Unions. Movement of large numbers of adults all over the world, from one region to the other, among countries, even continents, has never been so massive. Migrant workers move from rural areas to urban centers, from poorer regions to those where jobs may be available, or to countries which encourage "seasonal" laborers or seek workers to do jobs that local inhabitants may not want to do. Drastic conditions in home countries or villages, such as natural or economic disasters, political pressures (such as civil war or invasions), or social circumstances, may force many women and men to seek refuge elsewhere in order to survive. We can add to these groups of migrants and immigrants students who pursue higher education in cities or in other countries. Workers, refugees, immigrants, or students may enter informal unions while being in a marital union in the area of original residence. Some of the informal unions can be formalized with or without the knowledge and consent of one or more other partners, thus ending up as polygynous marriages. Men more than women are mobile (unhindered by pregnancy and small children) and more prone to form more than one union. Those who do not cut themselves off from any of the partnerships may pay regular or occasional visits to their various "families." Women in "visiting" unions may be disadvantaged relative to women in legal marriages with respect to financial commitments in case of separation. Since informal unions are more common among poor women, the social and financial consequences of the dissolution of such unions are even more severe for them.

Role Reversals. Crossing gender roles, though not widespread, has been accepted in some societies. A typical example is that of "women marriage" among the Igbo of southeast Nigeria, where women could marry other women by paying a bride price. This Igbo institution provided an opportunity for women who had skills and economic resources to operate as men did, within socially sanctioned

patterns (Uchendu, 1965). Role reversal may be available to men too, as in the case of the *berdaches* of the Cheyenne, a term for men who adopted the clothing and behavior of women and became "wives" (Hoebel, 1960).

The view in developed countries that men in general would not willingly take on "housewifely" roles and become fathers who take care of children has weakened considerably. Some men choose to be more involved with parenthood; others are led to be so through unemployment. The traditional low regard conferred on domestic jobs to which women have traditionally been relegated is hard to change, but associations between kinds of work or activity and gender are becoming less rigid (see Chapter 8).

Families of Women. Only with the emergence of lesbian consciousness in the context of the feminist movement has the concept of lesbian families gained clarity. Women insist that they should have the freedom to delimit themselves. The law usually defines a family in terms of blood relationships and heterosexual marriage, shared property, and the legitimization of children. This limited and conventional definition excludes same-sex unions, which are based on the commitment of emotion, property, and time for each other and the children. In Germany and the Netherlands, same-sex civil marriages are recognized as legal. In the United States, Vermont has accepted "civil unions" and a high court in Massachusetts has opened the prospect of gay marriage. Elsewhere, domestic partnerships may be legally registered. These are beginnings of the legalization of various forms of households. They often encounter societal resistance. For instance, permitting lesbian couples to have or keep their children from previously dissolved marriages is often opposed. Poet Adrienne Rich (1980) has exposed the stereotypical thinking that has caused even the most "enlightened" to

A lesbian wedding. Anna Bulkin, stepdaughter of coauthor Susan Lees, exchanges vows of commitment with Sherry McClintock in Massachusetts in October 2003. The ceremony was celebrated with joy by family members and friends.

imagine that the categories of "lesbian" and "mother" are mutually exclusive.

Women have discovered that "sexual liberation" has made them frank with themselves in acknowledging their sexual orientations. Until recently it was not so. Only a few courageous and economically independent women could publicly "come out" and live in lesbian relationships. Gertrude Stein (1874–1946) was one of them. Many of those who were not privileged were condemned to tragic lives. Radclyffe Hall (1880–1943) depicts that reality in her classic *The Well of Loneliness* ([1928], 1975).

Choosing Not to Mother, Childless Couples

The number of women who choose to remain unmarried and to not have children has increased in recent years (see Table 7.2).

Women and men living in domestic arrangements as partners is becoming acceptable and normal, without the stigma attached to it in the past. The bases of this alternative form of union include the frequent dissolution of legal marriages, the dissatisfaction of women with the traditional role of "wife," various economic and financial reasons, the nature of jobs that force women and men into long working days away from home or "traveling for business," or the ordinary choice to not marry and to not have children.

In some countries, and in the United States until recently, wives achieved "adult status" primarily by becoming mothers, as if women were created for the sole purpose of being vessels to carry babies. Some women cannot, or by choice do not, bear children. Others may seek careers, avocational interests, or commitments to political and social causes that they feel might hinder their dedication to motherhood or take them away for long periods of time when they would be needed by their children. The overpopulation of the world, the impoverished children here and abroad, diseases, worsening natural disasters, pollution, dire economic conditions, and discord among nations and human beings, which are increasingly threatening an acceptable life for all, force some women to question the fairness of having children for self-gratifying reasons (Ratner, 2000).

Women on Their Own

Today, young women are marrying at a later age than their mothers did, if at all. Economic, educational, and job opportunities have relieved many women from the dependent wifely role. Many married (and divorced) women who were "housewives" are returning to school or the workplace or are founding businesses that they can perform at home. Many women who are divorced or widowed prefer not to marry again. With improved financial standing, the need to marry or stay married for economic security has become less compelling to women. The first requirement for women's emancipation, and for a greater range of choices, is a source of income—for most, a job that pays enough to live independently.

Freedom to find love and emotional sustenance outside of conventional marriage and family and the opportunity to be self-supporting are prerequisites to choosing an alternate arrangement to the marital union. This choice is not available to vast numbers of women in the world in societies that do not readily condone the unmarried status of a woman and that continue to censure the independent and autonomous woman. Today, in the United States, the richest country in the world, the majority of poor people are women and children. The search for personal auton-

omy may be difficult and costly even for women with economic means. Pressures to marry and have children continue to be immense. It takes considerable psychic and emotional strength to resist such pressures, which in fact most women have internalized from childhood. Some 87% of women marry at one time or another; but even without such pressures, most women might still want to get married, have a wedding ceremony, stay in the marriage happily till death, and hope to become mothers.

Summary

In most societies, most people marry and form families based on marital households. Marriage is often explained as a way to organize the labor needed to produce food and shelter and to raise children; gender division of labor implies an interdependence between women and men, which is most often formalized in marriage. Marriage also regulates sexuality. After marriage, couples may reside with the wife's natal family, the husband's, in a new household of their own, or according to some other pattern. Every society has customary rules and expectations about the formation of households.

In traditional societies, past and present, parents and families usually select mates for their children, often according to traits desired by the family and according to the economic, social, and political interests of the family. In modern industrial societies, it is more often the case that individuals expect to make their own choices; in these cases, ideas about personal attraction and love play a greater role.

Marital households usually include a husband, wife, and children; but some societies allow and even encourage more than one spouse (*polygamy*). Having multiple husbands (*polyandry*) is extremely rare, but having multiple wives (*polygyny*) is a common ideal of men, though the cost of providing for such wives prohibits most men from achieving it. Whether single or multiple, wives in traditional marriages in most societies are deemed to be subordinate to husbands. This traditional subordination can also be expressed in modern industrial societies, as illustrated by the concept of the "incorporated wife," such as the wives of politicians (the "first lady").

The question of the role of marriage in the welfare of children is controversial. Most societies, like many social scientists, regard a two-parent household as ideal but are not necessarily in agreement about the effects of single-parent homes after divorce on children. Traditionally, it has been argued that women who are or expect to be mothers should marry and stay married for the sake of the children. Today, many women have the option of birth control, which reduces the necessity to marry or stay married. Nevertheless, social pressures on women to get married persist in the modern industrial world.

Divorce, for marriages that do not work out, is an option in many societies; in the United States, it tends to result in unfavorable economic consequences for women. Usually, the husband makes more money; while he may be legally obliged to provide child support, many divorced fathers fail to do so or provide only small contributions. Women who have stopped working to be stay-at-home mothers and wives may find it difficult to re-enter the workforce, much less to attain the level of pay and benefits available to their ex-husbands.

By the end of the twentieth century, many people were choosing not to marry, many couples were choosing cohabitation without marriage, and many couples were choosing to delay parenthood, to sharply limit the number of children they had or to not become parents. Increasing numbers of women choose to have children without marriage. Thus, the character of marriage and of household organization has been changing.

Alternatives to conventional marriage have existed in earlier times as well as in the present and in a variety of contexts. Some couples, for example, have rejected inegalitarian marriages, in which women are subordinates, for true parity. Larger nonmarital communities have existed as an option for women; a clear example is the religious community, or convent, in which Buddhist and Christian nuns have lived for centuries. These communities have provided some of their members with opportunities to develop their skills and talents and to serve their societies in ways that could never be realized had they lived as wives and mothers. Utopian communities constructed by male and female writers have critiqued the conventional family and imagined alternative roles for women and men, though often by means of celibacy and eliminating reproduction. Actual "utopian" communities have experimented with similar methods to produce ideal societies, though these have proven very difficult to sustain for any length of time.

Single parenthood, role reversals for women and men, the choice to remain childless, and the choice to live alone are all increasingly experienced as alternatives to conventional family life. However, choice is highly limited for most women in the world, and in fact, most women continue to wish for the ideal conventional marriage and family.

Discussion Questions

1. Make a score pad for the advantages and disadvantages of marriage and alternative forms of family configuration. Compare and discuss your findings concerning each form of union. How would you rate the future of each family configuration?

2. Make a review of current popular journal publications on married life, brides and weddings, housekeeping, home life, and babies/children. What is the image of the "*wife*" that emerges from the articles,

stories, advertisements, letters to the editor, and photographs? In your opinion, do these publications have an effect on the definition and formation of the *wifely roles* in the United States, in your own family, in your circles?

3. Housework causes frequent friction between couples in any type of union. Discuss the underlying reasons for the friction, and come up with possible solutions to ease the disagreements.

4. What, in your view, would be an ideal family configuration? What social conditions would be necessary for this kind of marriage to be possible?

5. If you could write your own script for your role in the family, what would it be? What would be the roles of others in your family? What are the risks of writing your own script?

Recommended Readings

Allende, Isabel. *The House of the Spirits*, translated by Magda Bogin. New York: Bantam, 1986. A novel that offers examples of women supporting women over several generations of Latin American extended families.

Ba, Mariama. *So Long a Letter*, translated by Modope Bode-Thomas. London: Heinemann, 1981. First published in French in 1980, this long "letter" from a recently widowed Senegalese schoolteacher to her girlhood friend is a story of marriage and polygamy in modern, urban Africa. It is a short, deeply moving narrative about the practice and meanings of polygamy.

Jarvis, Cheryl. *The Marriage Sabbatical: The Journey That Brings You Home*. New York: Perseus, 2001. Jarvis finds the contemporary conventional marriage in trouble. She conceives a novel paradigm to save the institution of marriage: that a woman loosens the rules that control a marriage by taking a sabbatical

leave. A wife can design for herself an escape without renouncing marriage; she may take time out for a while for an invigorating experience, focused on human fulfillment.

Mukherjee, Bharati. *Desirable Daughters*. New York: Thelia/Hyperion, 2002. A gripping novel about a Brahmin woman, Tara, whose marriage to an equally privileged young man was arranged in Calcutta when she was 19. After the couple moves to the United States, Tara tries to fight the constraints imposed by her traditional marriage and her Indian heritage and becomes a single mother caught between two cultures. This is a story of familial relationships, and the attempts of a woman to transform her identity, her history, her present and future.

Yalom, Marilyn. *A History of the Wife*. New York: Harper Collins, 2001. An easy-to-read but informative survey of the history of the "wife" in the Western world, from the ancient Greeks to the contemporary United States.

References

Alford-Cooper, Finnegan. *For Keeps: Marriages That Last a Lifetime*. Armonk, NY: M. E. Sharpe, 1998.

Amt, Emilie, editor. *Women's Lives in Medieval Europe: A Sourcebook*. London: Routledge, 1993.

Arendell, Terry. Women and the economics of divorce in the contemporary United States. *Signs*, 13:1, 121–35, 1987.

Callan, Hilary, and Shirley Ardener, editors. *The Incorporated Wife*. London: Croom Helm, 1984.

Chen, Martha Alter. *Perpetual Mourning: Widowhood in Rural India*. New York: Oxford University Press, 2000.

Edelman, Marian Wright. *Families in Peril: An Agenda for Social Change*. Cambridge, MA: Harvard University Press, 1987.

Eisler, Benita, editor. *The Lowell Offering: Writings by New England Mill Women*. New York: Harper & Row, 1977.

Engels, Friedrich. *The Origin of the Family, Private Property, and the State* (1884), translated by Alec West, edited by Eleanor Burke Leacock. New York: International Publishers, 1972.

Falk, Nancy Auer. *Unspoken Worlds: Women's Religious Lives in Non-Western Cultures.* New York: Harper Collins, 1980.

Farrell, G. Betty. *Family: The Making of an Idea, an Institution, and a Controversy in American Culture.* Boulder, CO: Westview Press, 1999.

Friedan, Betty. *The Feminine Mystique.* New York: Norton, 1963.

Gaskel, Elizabeth. *North and South,* edited by Dorothy Collin. Harmondsworth, UK: Penguin Books, 1970.

Gilman, Charlotte Perkins. *Herland* (1915). New York: Pantheon, 1979.

Greenberg, Rabbi Sidney, and Rabbi Jonathan D. Levine, editors. *The New Mahzor for Rosh Hashana and Yom Kippur.* Bridgeport, CT: Prayer Book Press, 2001.

Hall, Radclyffe. *The Well of Loneliness* (1928). New York: Pocket Books, 1975.

Hartog, Hendrik. *Man and Wife in America: A History.* Cambridge, MA: Harvard University Press, 2000.

Held, Virginia. The equal obligations of mothers and fathers. In *Having Children: Philosophical and Legal Reflections on Parenthood,* edited by Onora O'Neill and William Rudrick. New York: Oxford University Press, 1979.

Hetherington, E. Mavis, and John Kelly. *For Better or For Worse: Divorce Reconsidered.* New York: Norton, 2002.

Hoebel, E. Adamson. *The Cheyennes: Indians of the Great Plains.* New York: Holt, Rinehart, & Winston, 1960.

Hossain, Rokeya Sakhawat. *Sultana's Dream and Selections from the Secluded Ones,* edited and translated by Roushan Jahan. New York: Feminist Press at the City University of New York, 1988.

Komarovksy, Mirra. *Blue-Collar Marriage.* New Haven, CT: Vintage, 1962.

Lees, Susan. Motherhood in feminist utopias. In *Women in Search of Utopia,* edited by Elaine Baruch and Ruby Rorlich-Levy. New York: Shocken Books, 1984.

Levine, Nancy E., and Joan B. Silk. Why polyandry fails: Sources of instability in polyandrous marriages. *Current Anthropology,* 38, 375–98, 1997.

McCarthy, Mary. *The Group.* New York: New American Library, 1963.

McDonnell, Ernest. *Beguines and Beghards.* New York: Octagon, 1976.

McNamara, JoAnn Kay. *Sisters in Arms: Catholic Nuns Through Two Millennia.* Cambridge, MA: Harvard University Press, 1996.

Muncy, Raymond L. *Sex and Marriage in Utopian Communities in 19th Century America.* Bloomington: Indiana University Press, 1973.

Murdock, George P. Family stability in non-European cultures. *Annals of the American Academy of Political and Social Science,* 272, 175–201, 1950.

Okin, Susan Moller. *Justice, Gender, and the Family.* New York: Basic Books, 1989.

Palgi, Michal. Motherhood in the kibbutz. In *Calling the Equality Bluff,* edited by Barbara Swirski and Marilyn Safir. New York: Pergamon Press, 1991.

Plato. *The Republic,* translated by Robin Waterfield. Oxford: Oxford University Press, 1998.

Ratner, Michelle, editor. *Bearing Life: Women's Writings on Childlessness.* New York: Feminist Press at the City University of New York, 2000.

Rich, Adrienne. Compulsory heterosexuality and lesbian existence. *Signs,* 5, 631–60, 1980.

Rossi, Alice. Equality between the sexes: An important proposal. *Daedalus,* 93, 607–52, 1964.

Rothblum, Esther, and Kathleen Brehony. *Boston Marriages: Romantic but Asexual Relationships Among Contemporary Lesbians.* Amherst: University of Massachusetts Press, 1993.

Safir, Marilyn. Was the kibbutz an experiment in social and sex equality? In *Calling the Equality Bluff,* edited by Barbara Swirski and Marilyn Safir. New York: Pergamon Press, 1991.

Schmitt, Eric. For the first time, nuclear families drop below 25% of households. *New York Times,* May 15, 2001, A1.

Stanton, Elizabeth Cady. *Eighty Years and More: Reminiscences 1815–1897* (1898). New York: Schoken Books, 1971.

Stockard, Janice E. *Daughters of the Canton Delta: Marriage Patterns and Economic Strategies in South China, 1860–1930*. Stanford, CA: Stanford University Press, 1989.

Tanaka, Yukiko, and Elizabeth Hanson, translators and editors. *This Kind of Woman: Ten Stories by Japanese Women Writers, 1960–1976*. New York: Pedigree Books, 1982.

Uchendu, Victor. *The Igbo of South East Nigeria*. New York: Holt, Rinehart & Winston, 1965.

United Nations. *The World's Women 2000: Trends and Statistics*. New York: United Nations, 2000.

Waite, Linda, and Maggie Gallagher. *A Case for Marriage: Why Married People Are Happier, Healthier, and Better Off Financially*. New York: Doubleday, 2000.

Wallerstein, Judith, Julia Lewis, and Sandra Blakeslee, editors. *An Unexpected Legacy of Divorce*. Boulder, CO: Hyperion, 2000.

Wollstonecraft, Mary. *A Vindication of the Rights of Woman* (1792), edited by Miriam Krammick. Harmondsworth, UK: Penguin Books, 1975.

Yalom, Marilyn. *A History of the Wife*. New York: Harper Collins, 2001.

chapter **8**

Motherhood

And then I realized what the first word must have been: ma, the sound of a baby smacking its lips in search of her mother's breast. For a long time, that was the only word the baby needed. Ma, ma, ma. Then the mother decided that was her name and she began to speak, too. She taught the baby to be careful: sky, fire, tiger. A mother is always the beginning. She is how things begin.

(AMY TAN, *THE BONESETTER'S DAUGHTER*, 2001)

Among the social roles that a woman fills, motherhood is the most difficult to define; being a mother is a multifaceted and multidimensional predicament. It is the hardest role a woman may play, whether she is the biological (natural/birth) mother or assumes that persona as an adoptive or foster mother, mother-in-law, grandmother, stepmother, godmother, or unrelated surrogate mother. In real life and in fiction, the mother is loved and hated, loving and vengeful, nurturing and destructive, all-giving and completely withholding; but in every individual's life she is potentially the most dominant person. What makes a "mother" so significant and all-powerful in our lives? Although only a woman can bear a fetus, both nature and society have dictated the limitations on her capacity to become a mother: when and how, even where she can have a baby.

In this chapter, we examine why mothers are central to human emotions, their power as the sole promoters of the continued existence of the human species, and how that power affects the other roles that women assume. To ensure the continuity of the human species, which is generally considered of paramount importance, control of a woman's body has been strictly maintained, beginning with legal and theological dicta, which in turn affect social and cultural norms and the medical and other scientific tools that foster, enrich, and inhibit mothering. Since society agrees that the most important function of a woman's body is to bear a child, motherhood is subject to regulations in all its aspects, biological and social. In the twenty-first century, when we live in an overpopulated world with dwindling resources, to focus on women's bodies as reproductive machines may seem rather simplistic, but we cannot deny the reality that the biological aspect of the female body is intimately intertwined with political and economic realities.

The starting point for understanding motherhood is to investigate how it is constructed, that is, how in any society motherhood is defined by belief systems and visual images. This reveals how ideas about motherhood are reflected in and shaped by social processes. Attitudes toward the biological aspects of motherhood are also informative, such as ideas about a "maternal instinct" and the responses of a woman's body to pregnancy, childbirth, and lactation. These biological events are also shaped by society at large. Motherhood is such a critical role assignment that many people, particularly men, have been determined to design it according to their own convictions and the cultural mores of the day. The state of becoming and being a mother has fostered heated arguments and feelings from legislators in the U.S. Congress to theologians in the Vatican. In Muslim countries, girls are molded to become mothers in the privacy of their homes according to well-defined rules. Men in the public sphere, however, have most often controlled the choices made for motherhood: whether, when, and how often to become a mother.

Human babies are born helpless, often needing a well-placed slap on the back to get their lungs to breathe on their own, and remain dependent on their mothers or caretakers longer than do other primates. Their infancy stretches beyond months before babies can crawl, then stand, and finally walk. The dependence of the human child on its mother has often required mothers to seek help to care for herself and her baby. In the last section of this chapter, we shall turn to a consideration of support systems, whether offered by her mate, her neighbors (her "village"), or some other system of networks. The mother and her clinging infant have to be sustained by individualized or institutionalized help. Support for mothers has become both a private and a public concern—from grandmothers to commercial establishments—and the help to be extended to mothers and infants is highly politicized. We shall see how society is recruited to institute support systems to guide a mother through her early parenting period. Motherhood is here to stay so long as women are willing to become mothers, and mothering will continue to be political.

Images of Motherhood

Mother is a multilayered term, implying many concepts depending on the context. It may be a metaphor, as in "the mother of all evil," an adjective denoting the superlative. It appears as a prefix, as in *motherland*, meaning the country one identifies as one's own. Even when the term is limited to its most common and stereotypical usage, the woman who undertakes that role can evoke multiple images, such as a pretty woman embracing a child, a complaining mother-in-law, or an evil stepmother. Images of mothers, as depicted in mythology, religious texts, and the visual arts, as well as in written and oral literature and the performing arts, are usually of central importance. These images, on the one hand, instruct people about the currently acceptable role ascribed to mothers and, on the other hand, inform us about the notions of motherhood that prevail in a particular culture. Yet, there has been surprisingly little investigation of the representational forms of motherhood through the ages and in different cultures, as though the very concept has been deemed too sacred to be subjected to inquiry. We can survey briefly the existent literary and visual arts in the West to construe how this social role has been scripted for women.

Perspectives: Who Creates the Image?

Images project and convey the ideas of their creators, who in turn reflect certain notions of their culture. In the West, where mass media and representational arts are abundant, the imagery of mothers predominantly represents the idealized bond between mother and child. As the larger numbers of artists and writers have been men, these images are from their perspective, informed by their experience as sons or partners of women. Mothers have generally had little opportunity to reflect on their condition as mothers or to describe motherhood in formal ways. The time-consuming task of mothering has historically left little leisure for women to engage in creative arts. In the modern era, however, women have made rich contributions to the imagery of mothers. The poet Adrienne Rich, for example, has written "Once in a while someone used to ask me, 'Don't you ever write poems about your children?' The male poets of my generation did write poems about their children, especially their daughters. For me poetry was where I lived as no one's mother, where I existed as myself" (Rich, 1976).

Daughters' explorations of their relationships with their mothers are also a relatively new phenomenon in Western literature (see Box 8.1).

Sons' relations to their mothers, on the other hand, are more commonly found in both myth and literature. For example, two powerful myths that appeared in ancient Greece more than twenty-five hundred years ago express the extreme feelings of sons toward their mothers, one who loves his mother too much and another, too little. The "loving son," Oedipus, without knowing who his natural parents were, murdered his father, married that man's widow (his own mother), and had four children by her. Upon discovering that he had committed incest and patricide, tortured by guilt, he blinded himself. In another myth, Orestes murders his mother, who had killed his father. Orestes, like Oedipus, was tormented by a guilty conscience. The gods then invented the first court of law to try

---

Box 8.1   THE PATTERN

Little has come down to me of hers,
a sewing machine, a wedding band,
a clutch of photos, the sting of her hand
across my face in one of our wars
when we had grown bitter and apart.
Some say that's the fate of the eldest daughter.
I wish now she'd lasted till after
I'd grown up. We might have made a new start

as women without tags like *mother, wife,
sister, daughter,* taken our chances from there.
At forty-two she headed for god knows where . . .

Sometimes I'd have to kneel
An hour before her by the fire,
a skein around my outstretched hands,
while she rolled wool into balls.
If I swam like a kite too high
amongst the shadows on the ceiling
or flew like a fish in the pools
of pulsing light, she'd reel me firmly
home, she'd land me at her knees.

Tongues of flame in her dark eyes,
she'd say, "One of these days I must
teach you to follow a pattern."

Source: By kind permission of the author and The Gallery Press, Loughcrew, Old Castle, County Meath, Ireland. From *The Man Who Was Marked by Winter,* 1991, by Paula Meehan.

these two cases of murder. The gods declared that a father is more truly a parent than a mother, and Orestes was acquitted. These myths illustrate a more general theme: sons must dissociate themselves from their mothers and identify with their fathers or pay an enormous penalty (Baruch, 1991).

Male authors of the twentieth century, heavily influenced by Freudian theories, have written in a similar vein of the destructiveness of their mothers' seductive and engulfing love and of conflicts of interest between growing sons and overpowering mothers. This literature depicts mothers as emasculating, possessive, dangerous, and antithetical to adult maleness. Only by overpowering the mother can the son free himself of infantilism and go forth into the civilized world of adult men. The theme of men freeing themselves from the control of a once-powerful mother is similar to some of the myths discussed in Chapter 1.

"The Happy Mother": A Western Image as Political Ideology

Depictions of mothers, fathers, and children have a long history in the Western world, but the nonreligious image of a mother and her child(ren) are relatively rare before the sixteenth century in Europe. Most paintings depicting specific mothers were commissioned by the members of various courts as propaganda for a prince to show off his private riches, as the famous double portrait of Eleanora di Toledo and her son by Agnolo Bronzino around 1545 (now at the Uffizi Gallery in Florence), which portrays the

Cornelia, Mother of the Gracchi (c. 1785) by Angelica Kaufmann (1741–1807). In the second century B.C.E., when a woman showed off her jewelry to Cornelia, daughter, widow, and mother of Roman heroes, she pointed to her children and responded "These are my jewels." Like Artemisia Gentileschi, Kaufmann was the daughter of a male artist. Famous in her day, she painted primarily women and historical subjects and was one of the founders of the Royal Academy of Art in London.

The Mother by Pieter de Hooch (1658). Lacing her bodice beside a small cradle, this seventeenth-century Dutch mother faced numerous tasks in addition to feeding her infant. She was expected to keep her house spotless and her children clean and to provide both food and domestic tranquility for her family.

beautiful mother in her exquisite dress and jewels and the heir to the Medici of Florence. Representations of ordinary mothers and their children, both inside and outside of their homes, became popular in seventeenth-century Netherlands, where the Calvinist Dutch eschewed traditional depictions of the virgin and child. The interiors of houses were represented as places where all the human virtues were combined, and cleanliness was held as next to godliness. More often than fathers, it was mothers who figured in Dutch paintings and prints as the protectors of the pure household. Some of the most affecting family scenes in Dutch genre painting are of children submitting to their mother's inspection of their head for nits and lice.

Images portraying mothers in blissful ecstasy proliferated in Western Europe as wealth spread to the expanding middle class in the eighteenth century (Duncan, 1973). In Jean-Baptiste Greuze's painting *The Beloved Mother* (1765), for example, marriage and domestic life are depicted as a major source of happiness, not simply as a legal and economic structure. The new emphasis on domesticity and the elevation of maternity to an exalted state challenged earlier assumptions about marriage, families, and children. This type of genre painting in Europe accompanied a shift in attitudes that reflected intellectual, economic, and social changes beginning in seventeenth-century maritime and mercantile Holland and slightly later among the bourgeoisie of France. Heredity had less to do than before with one's success in life, and the environment of the home took on increasing importance in the education and formation of children for society. Though many mothers and children were subsequently forced to work for pitiful wages in horrendous conditions as the Western world industrialized, the image that was held up for aspiration was that of woman as joyful guardian of the peaceful home. The paintings of this idealized home life convey a clear moral message: a woman's place is in her clean home, a symbol of purity where she cares for her children. This early form of media representation continued to change along with social and cultural conditions, but the core remained unaltered. The image was increasingly popularized in the United States and elsewhere with the mass-media development of women's magazines, advertising, motion pictures, and television. This was the encouraging image that accompanied the burgeoning generation of "baby boomers," who were born during and after World War II and whose mothers were urged to devote themselves to raising them.

Representations of mothers and children are not common in the Muslim world or generally in Asian cultures. For the men of these societies, the privacy of home, with wife (or wives) and children, has traditionally been considered too sacrosanct to be subjected to the gaze and examination of any stranger or any man not related to them.

"Ethnic Mothers" and Social Mobility

The United States, a nation comprised largely and from its beginnings of immigrants, has displayed an enduring fascination with ethnicity. The literature of the last hundred years in particular is replete with ethnic and racial stereotypes. Among these, two female figures are particular U.S. phenomena: the Jewish mother and the black mother. Both have been treated as stereotypes in literature, movies, and television and subjected to scholarly study, as stereotypes in the public media, by sociologists and psychologists. Some authors of fiction have written eloquently, without stereotyping, about mothers, Jewish or

African American, inspired by their own experience. Scholarly books have exposed the way ethnic stereotypes have become internalized by many people in such a way that their racist and sexist overtones are not obvious and they have been accepted as "truths."

The stereotypic Jewish mother in literature has undergone dramatic changes that correspond to real changes in the Jewish family itself in U.S. society during the twentieth century. In the first part of the century, increasing numbers of Jews emigrated from Eastern Europe to North America. Some were highly educated, but most were poor. Without knowledge of English or marketable skills, Jewish men often continued to rely on their wives, the strong and practical mothers of their children, who had been the breadwinners in the "old country," while they prayed and studied. Their U.S. sons depicted their Jewish mothers in fiction as supporters of traditional values, respecting the father in the family, and above all as self-sacrificing protectors of their children. As these children, particularly sons, began to make their way in the New World by adopting new, materialistic values with their mothers' encouragement, their fathers began to fade in their consciousness, often seen as weak or as social outsiders. In contrast, they saw their mothers increasingly as the de facto head of the family, adjusting to necessary changes. These mothers became increasingly ambitious for their children, pushing them upward socially through education. The children measured their achievements by their mothers' yardstick. By the 1960s, the image of the pushy Jewish mother had become ubiquitous in U.S. ethnic literature and the popular media. She had at once become a comic figure and an object of alarm. Freudian theory suggested that the emotional problems of Jewish sons stemmed from their early erotic relationships with their mothers. The son saw his mother as the primary obstacle to his own maturity and freedom. Turning her into a

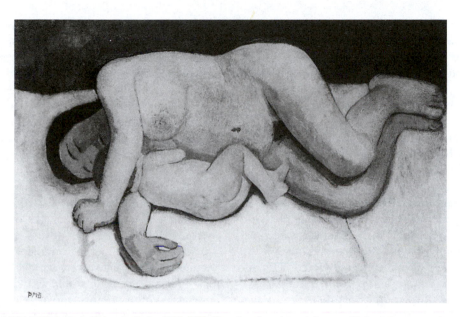

Mother and Child (1906) by Paula Modersohn-Becker (1876–1907). The painter has portrayed the sensual intimacy between mother and child of which some mothers speak.

comic figure was a way of reducing her imagined power (Bienstock, 1979).

In an era of rapid social change in the twentieth century, when people felt uneasy about undefined roles for women and men, the problem of the Jewish son and his mother held a message comprehensible to a broad range of U.S. citizens who could identify with the hostility and anxiety of the uprooted, upwardly mobile son. Although mothers were the immediate targets of the sons' rage, they represented much more. They stood for virtually every social inhibition, every anxiety-provoking element of the past. Recognition of the pain of the assimilation experience in the United States was often made tolerable through ridicule.

The experience of African Americans was very different from the Jewish one, yet there are elements of similarity. Like the Jewish mother, the African American mother has been stereotyped as the "black mammy" ser-vant familiar from U.S. movies and novels like *Gone with the Wind*. This stereotype had its roots in the slave experience, which, like the experience of immigration, evoked extreme strength and endurance from mothers to protect families.

After slavery ended, African American families were faced with economic survival. Racial prejudice virtually barred social mobility and denied job opportunities in nearly every sphere. Those jobs that were open to men paid very little and offered little security. To feed their children, women were obliged to work at low-paying menial tasks. While African American men often suffered low esteem and humiliation, women struggled to keep their families together morally and physically. African American mothers, like Jewish mothers, were seen as the moral backbone of their homes. Also like Jewish mothers, idealized African American mothers "pushed" their children, in this case usually their daughters, upward, emphasizing the role of education in the achievement of their ambitions for the future. The image of the strong, supportive, and protective African American mother grew alongside an image of a weak, ineffective father. Sociological literature refers frequently to the "matrifocal household" as if it were the product of slavery or the African heritage; in fact, where it exists, it is part of a survival strategy, an adjustment to contemporary conditions (Collins, 2000). This image of a strong mother and weak or absent father has been propagated in the popular media as well. As the family has become more involved with the mainstream of U.S. life, mothers have increasingly acted as mediators between past and present. They are depicted as the source of their children's strength.

Asian American women writers have been productive in writing about mothers, daughters, and families in general. Maxine Hong Kingston (*The Woman Warrior*, 1976) and Amy Tan (*The Bonesetter's Daughter*, 2001; *The Joy Luck Club*, 1989) write about the experiences of Chinese American mothers and daughters, while Anita Desai (*Fasting, Feasting*, 1999) and Bharati Mukherjee (*Desirable Daughters*, 2002) tell the stories of Indian and Bengali women caught between the old traditions of the "mother" country and their new lives in the West. In each case, these writers move beyond stereotypes to portray mothers as complex beings with complicated histories, motivations, and aspirations.

Motherhood and the Media

An ideology of motherhood is "sold" to us along with a variety of commercial products in the public media. Magazine advertising and television commercials are blatant in the image they convey of motherhood as "it ought to be." The most effectively designed mothers appear on television, a medium largely directed to family viewing. Although in the last thirty years or so the representation of the mother has undergone considerable change, stereotypes have persisted. One of the early images was in the series *I Remember Mama* (1950s), a sentimental reconstruction of immigrant Swedish family life in San Francisco based on memoirs written by a daughter. That "mama" was depicted as gentle and comforting, a moral force, and a hardworking housewife. Almost to the 1970s the depiction of the U.S. mother figure remained a weak woman who had few significant anxieties or nondomestic functions and was always neat, well dressed, calm, eminently middle class, and suburban. She rarely was shown having a job, making major decisions, and being sexually desirous. As the feminist movement became stronger, so did the image of the mother. Ethnic mothers began to appear in the media, including African American, Jewish, and Italian women; some were "liberated," others divorced or otherwise independent. These mothers voiced opinions, held jobs, and expressed anxieties. Yet, the majority of the TV mother characters continue to be idealizations, representing a perfection that average mothers cannot actually achieve. When idealized, mothers are in fact trivialized.

Magazines intended explicitly for parents also demonstrate what the image of motherhood means in the popular media. Motherhood is marketable; articles on the web and magazine stories, like the advertisements that support them, create "needs" by spelling out the requisites of mothering. The few men depicted are shown as "experts," primarily obstetricians and pediatricians. Mothers, on the other hand, are shown as dependent on these experts for constant advice on the most trivial matters and are warned to ignore the advice of their mothers or grandmothers. The articles purport to be reassuring; in fact they emphasize the mothers' helplessness. Although holding jobs outside the home for mothers is suggested, mothers most often are shown at home attending to their babies' comfort. Expensive "breast-feeding kits" with all sorts of equipment are marketed as obligatory for women, although women are fully equipped by nature to nurse babies. If they must be absent from their babies, however, women do need to collect their milk in bottles for others to feed to the baby.

In most cases, the advertisements and advice that saturate the media foster feelings of personal inadequacy and dependence in women. The media largely serve the interests of commercial enterprises, whose goal is to sell products and bolster the view of the professionals, such as obstetricians and pediatricians, who advise women on proper mothering and feeding. If the public image of motherhood reflects women's social position in general, we must conclude that, despite considerable changes in women's economic roles during the last thirty years, little has changed in their social roles. Parenting is not generally assumed to be the equal responsibility of both women and men. Depictions of men who occasionally take sole responsibility are usually played for comic relief.

Mothers Speak Out

The women's movement has encouraged awareness by mothers and self-expression about the contradictions and conflicts of their experience. Some of this self-expression has taken the form of autobiographical literature. Adrienne Rich's treatise on motherhood, *Of Woman Born* (1976), and Phyllis Chesler's diary of her first year of motherhood, *With Child* (1979), combine autobiography with analysis of being a mother, exposing it to scrutiny to disrupt ideological assumptions. Rachel Cusk's *A Life's Work: On Becoming a Mother* (2002) is part of a new wave of "backlash" literature that confesses that negative feelings are part of mothering. Rich, Chesler,

and other feminist theorists are exploring the implications of the central but neglected human experience of mothering (Held, 1993). Sara Ruddick (1980), for instance, examines the distinctive thinking involved in the practice of mothering. She sees it as characterized by the mother's interests in the child's preservation, growth, and acceptable development and notes that mothers are oriented toward the peaceful solution of conflict.

Parental Behavior: "Instinct" and Culture

The popular media is a window into the society, which produces and receives it; by investigating the constructions of motherhood and mothering in the media, we can learn about cultural attitudes toward parenting. The cultural shaping of mothering is intertwined with the biological bases of being a mother. Mothering is a central issue for humanity since each one of us is born to a mother; feelings about mothers run deep, and emotions cannot easily be separated from intellectual reasoning. Motherhood is such a sensitive issue that many, particularly men who wield power, wish to affect the design. Legislators and theologians want to be designers of motherhood as much as scientists and medical personnel. How, then, can we separate the ideology from the reality of motherhood? The task of extricating the cultural construction from the biological events is complex. One method is to weigh each stage of mothering, from pregnancy to birth to social and physical nurturing, against the physical and sociological realities.

All organisms come from other organisms. In this sense, all organisms have "parents." Although many plants have female and male reproductive functions, we do not speak of "mother" and "father" plants. Even when parents never see a child after birth, they are called its "mother" and "father" (biologically if not practically). For other animals, like birds or cats, we assume parenting activities are "instinctive"; that is, their nervous systems are so programmed by genetic inheritance that, as parents, they will automatically behave in certain ways. Feeding and protecting the offspring are two basic parental instincts. Among mammals, a classification named for the breast (in Latin called *mamma*) of its female members because they *lactate* (produce milk), there is considerable variability in parental roles.

When we consider more complex animals, particularly primates like ourselves, we begin to question the applicability of the notion of "instinct" (Hrdy, 1999). Studies show that for complex animals maternal behavior must be learned and that its expression by females or males depends on their experience and social conditions. Is there such a thing as "maternal instinct" in humans, and is it present only in women? The emotional and developmental need of children for mothering is most likely met by one of the child's progenitors assuming the role of "mother." However, humans who mother need not be female, even though only females can breast-feed a baby. Of course, humans do have some relatively simple instincts, or reflexes. For example, women who breast-feed experience the *let-down reflex* (involuntary ejection of milk) in response to the sensation of the infant's sucking. However, the maternal instinct is not this simple reflex. Mothering, even the desire to mother, does not exist in all women who give birth and often does exist in women who do not.

Humans have innate predispositions for complex and varied sorts of behavior; however, genetic inheritance provides the general pattern, not the details, of such conduct. Of all primate species, humans are the most utterly helpless at birth and remain dependent on their caretakers for the longest time. When advanced apes, such as the chimpanzee, reach the age at which they can have their own babies, human infants are only beginning to venture away from their parents'

arms. The dependent period of the human child lengthens in industrialized countries, where there is less urgency for the child to separate itself from the family in search of other means of support, be it a job or a spouse. This phenomenon of dependence on the part of the child causes a symbiotic relationship between it and its caretakers/parents in which the child demands and the parent gives. Because of the necessity even today in most societies for a woman to provide her child with breast milk, it is not uncommon for a woman to form emotional bonds with her baby from the moment of birth. Emotions and biological needs intermingle, and traditions in almost every society work to strengthen mother–child togetherness, to ensure the survival of the child, and to maintain the continuity of the human species.

The "selfless" mother, who is expected to attend to the child, can often be consumed by its seemingly endless dependence. The baby demands to be nursed at least every few hours, and if the babies come frequently, the mother can be continuously pregnant and breast-feeding. As babies turn into toddlers, mothers have to be vigilant, protecting them from dangers that lurk everywhere—from modern electric sockets to bathtubs—and feeding and clothing them, along with other chores that may seem endless. Thus, what nature starts, society soon takes over: biology dictates women's capacity for motherhood, but society enlarges the task of mothering, assigning a multitude of nurturing tasks to women. It is possible that other people, women and men, can care for a child and, in doing so, form an intimate bond. A willing and nurturing person of either sex can carry out the "mothering" of the child.

Motherhood: Ideology and Reality

The stereotypical view that motherhood comes naturally to women may have no biological basis in fact, but the acceptance of this view by society does have an influence on women's feelings and attitudes. Many cultures regard motherhood as a major source of fulfillment and satisfaction for women and disapprove of negative behavior toward childbearing and childrearing. Despite these cultural biases and the general denial that a woman may not want to mother ("it is unnatural"), some women have begun to express feelings of ambiguity, dissatisfaction, fear, resentment, inadequacy, and anger about the experience of mothering (Ratner, 2000; see also Box 8.2 and Box 1.6). Expectations and standards of mothering are set so high that women often develop feelings of inadequacy (often turning to columns in women's magazines and child-care manuals for help) and even resentment. In the mid-twentieth century, the suburban middle class in the United States seemed to carry this to an extreme (Friedan, 1963). Often isolated at home with children and with no help from spouses or public services, middle-class suburban women in particular had virtually no socially acceptable outlet other than mothering, whether in the form of employment outside the home, intellectual activity, or social purpose. Raising children was their "job" in life; falling short of managing this job was seen as a shortcoming. Yet, this job offered no pay, no pension plan, and no paid or unpaid vacation. The mother, conscious of unfulfilled yearnings, could feel like a domestic slave.

The contradictions written into the job of mothering are puzzling: if being a mother is a responsible position subject to high standards and demands, why is it not appreciated as "real work"? If we take a mother who is only doing her "natural" assignment for granted, why is she considered so important that society has been intensely occupied with the definition of and qualifications for the job? Women may be told, for example, depending on the society in which they live, how many children they can have or if they can have any at all without a husband. They may even be denied any choice in having a baby or terminating an unwanted pregnancy. Society may determine if they can raise a child by themselves, whether they should nurse their children, how often they may do so, where they may do so, and so on.

Because mothering as a job is assigned to women, fathers have traditionally been excluded (or may exclude themselves) from an active role in childrearing (though some younger fathers in recent years have been affected by the messages of the women's movement and the positions taken on the subject by their wives). Why have fathers generally not shared or even helped mothers in the care of their young children? Besides what we saw in Chapter 5, that socialization and ideology have traditionally combined to teach boys that "men do not do a woman's job" and a home and children are a "woman's territory," men are more likely to feel detached from babies (after all, no one gave them baby dolls to play with while growing up) and tend not to spend time with them. The emotional differences between human females and males toward their offspring have also been detected among other species. The nine-month-long investment in carrying her young, the pains of birthing, and the early bonding with the child may prepare a woman to accept the job of mothering. This seems to be true for most women all over the world. The father/partner may also feel neglected while the new mother spends so much of her time caring for the baby; he may feel jealous because he does not have the claim and access to her that he did before the child was born. Some men, like some other primates, may roam and look for other mates; but most men who presume they are the biological father are willing to provide for their child (Hrdy, 1999:226–34). The monogamous pairing of women and men is the most prevalent type of marriage arrangement in non-Islamic countries. In exchange for the provision that a husband makes, the woman accepts the job of mothering, sheltered within a monogamous marriage. (For other forms, see Chapter 7.)

The dependence of the mother and child on the husband/father may often contribute to the superior attitude men take toward women. Women who are or intend to be full-time mothers may find that their identities become submerged in the identities of their husbands and children. Many popular novels written by women in the second half of the twentieth century, such as Marilyn French's *The Women's Room* (1977) and Sue Miller's *The Good Mother* (1986), explore the problems of the full-time mother who is seeking and finding independence and sexual fulfillment. Maya Angelou, in her autobiographical novel *I Know Why the Caged Bird Sings* (1969), writes about the relationship of a young girl with her glamorous but elusive mother in contrast to her bonds with the grandmother who cares for her through most of her childhood.

Are oppressive conditions the inevitable consequence of motherhood? Numerous feminist writers have seen the roots of women's oppression in their reproductive function (Firestone, 1970). Because only women can bear children, men, who are excluded from this creativity, try to create everything else and deny women access to their world (de Beauvoir, 1953). Other feminist writers argue that it is not motherhood itself but the way that society has institutionalized it that oppresses women, children, and men (Rich, 1976). Charlotte Perkins Gilman's fantasy novel *Herland* ([1915] 1979) depicts a world in which motherhood is gratifying, not oppressive, and does not preclude other forms of creativity and achievement. *Herland*, however, has no men. Other feminists see motherhood as the possible source of the most fundamental pride and empowerment in women; they ask that society be reshaped from the point of view of mothers so that it respects first of all the well-being of children and, thus, of those who care for them (Treblicot, 1984).

In the United States today, as in other countries, diverse forms of family configuration have emerged (see Chapter 7). Families in which men engage equally in the activities of mothering are not uncommon. Families formed as alternatives to traditional monogamous marriages have radically challenged conventional ideas of motherhood. Even within the once standard Western "family," mothers' roles have shown considerable change. Increasingly, with the rise in divorce and remarriage, many women are called upon to mother not just their own children but also the children of their new partners. Adjustment, redefinition, and changing descriptions of mothering and motherhood are being made and remade. Second-wave feminism, for over thirty years, has subjected these issues to new thought and new behavior, as has the increased role of women in the workplace (see Chapter 12).

The Assignment of Motherhood: Whose Interest Does It Serve?

A woman's biological contributions to reproduction, though costly in time, energy, and risk, are of relatively short duration compared to the social role of motherhood, which lasts decades. Rearing children is very hard work, and usually it is mothers who have borne the primary responsibility for this indispensable contribution to human society.

Why does a woman want to be a mother? Societal norms everywhere in the world expect a woman to bear children; there are not very many strong-willed and rebellious women who could fight such pressure (see Ratner, 2000). Childless women have been burned as witches, persecuted as lesbians, and refused the right to adopt if unmarried. Because women are physically the primary progenitor and, by social convention, the primary caretaker of the human species, the female psyche has been conditioned and shaped to accept having children. Women are generally brought up to expect the role of motherhood and not to apply intellectual arguments against it. Once a baby is born, this helpless and needy new person can effortlessly dominate her love; she sees it as an extension of her body, of her self; the possibilities of enabling her baby to have a better life than hers seem endless. However, can mothers alone achieve these goals?

The assignment of long-term, daily child-care responsibilities to mothers rather than to fathers has left men free to acquire economic, political, and social power, which can, and too often has, been used against women (Treblicot, 1984). Several writers have pointed out that the unpaid work of mothers serves capitalism: mothers produce the next generation of workers and service the current generation as unpaid labor (Crittendon, 2001). The fact that mothers and others see women's primary job as childbearing helps to justify low levels of job training, high levels of unemployment, and low pay for women. Thus, women form a pool of cheap labor. In twentieth-century socialist societies, the provision of paid maternity leave, day care, and family allowances has helped to mitigate some of the costs of motherhood to women, in theory to spread the sacrifice more evenly. This has rarely been a goal of capitalist societies, though European countries have gone further than the United States in providing social services that reduce the imbalance in the price of motherhood.

The Cultural Shaping of Biological Events

Attitudes Toward Pregnancy

A woman's emotional state, attitudes, and reactions to her social environment can influence the way she experiences the physiological process involved with motherhood. How women encounter pregnancy, for example, will depend in part on whether the pregnancy was wanted or not. It will also depend on the social support system they have, their perceptions of motherhood, perhaps their relationship with their own parents, and their relationship with the father of the expected child. It will also depend on whether this is a first pregnancy, on the nature of a woman's previous experiences, and on her expectations.

Pregnant women must adjust simultaneously to both physiological changes (in hormones and body shape and weight) and changes in self-perception. These adjustments will affect dramatic changes in other people's reactions to their pregnancy. Most societies have sets of rules and beliefs that dictate how a woman ought to feel and act during pregnancy. Depictions of pregnant women in painting and sculpture are found far back in early antiquity, probably even in the Paleolithic era. Current interpretations suggest that the ancient "Venus" figurines of heavily pregnant women represent the notion of fertility and that pregnancy was a desirable, even a venerated state.

The veneration of pregnant women ceased in societies with patriarchal monotheistic religions as the act of sexual intercourse came to be seen as "the fall of man," a reminder of a sinful event even within marriage, or the consequence of private conduct that should be properly covered up in public; hence, the billowing "maternity dress." In the middle and upper classes of European society, pregnant women were once secluded from public life. Even in the twentieth century, pregnant women who were teachers were obliged to relinquish their jobs in some places. Early in the twentieth century in the United States, obstetricians advised pregnant women to avoid a variety of activities, including bathing, physical exercise, and sexual intercourse. Today, however, healthy pregnant women in the

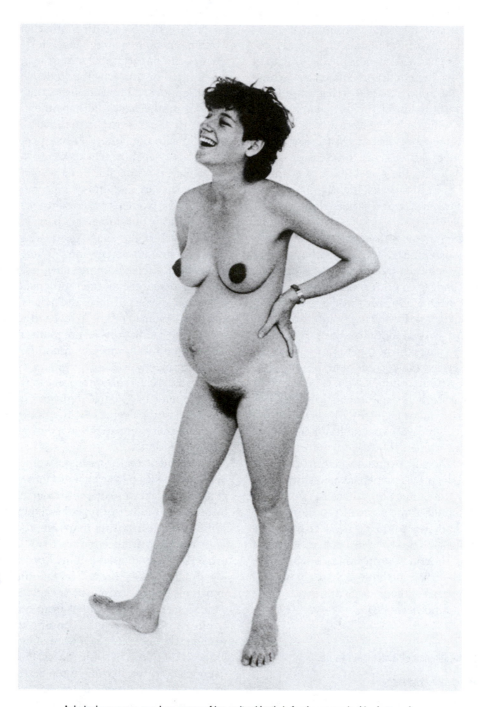

A desired pregnancy may be a source of joy, as it evidently is for the woman in this photograph.

Box 8.2 BECOMING A MOTHER IS A LIFETIME JOB

In the twenty-first century more women are confessing to negative feelings about motherhood.

. . . Motherhood, for me, was a sort of compound fenced off from the rest of the world. I was forever plotting my escape from it, and when I found myself pregnant again when Albertine was six moths old I greeted my old cell with the cheerless acceptance of a convict intercepted at large. . . .

. . . Birth is not merely that which divides women from men: it also divides women from themselves, so that a woman's understanding of what it is to exist is profoundly changed. Another person has existed in her, and after their birth they live within the jurisdiction of her consciousness. When she is with them she is not herself; when she is without them she is not herself; and so it is as difficult to leave your children as it is to stay with them. . . .

. . . It is possible, I sense, to make a specialism out of anything and hence unravel the native confidence of those you address. The more I read, the more my daughter recedes from me and becomes an object whose use I must re-learn, whose conformity to other objects like her is a matter of liminal anxiety. Most of these books begin, like science fiction, with a sort of apocalyptic scenario in which the world we know has vanished, replaced by another in whose principles we must be educated. The vanished world is the mother's own. It is the world of her childhood, and her own mother was its last living inhabitant. In those days, the story goes, mothers were told what to do by *their* mothers.

Source: Cusk, 2002:2, 7, 111–12.

United States and elsewhere are encouraged to engage in all activities until they no longer physically can do so.

Male parents are not immune to the taboos and proscriptions of society. The Arapesh of Papua New Guinea, for example, believe that sperm contribute to the growth of the fetus, so parents are expected to engage in frequent sexual intercourse to enable the father to supply the necessary material for his child's formation during pregnancy (Mead, 1963). Such social beliefs have no obvious relation to the strict biological facts of pregnancy, but they can affect its course through influencing the emotional and physical state of the pregnant woman and her partner.

The speculation that modern science will soon have the capacity to eliminate pregnancy altogether is gaining some force, in spite of religious and moral considerations. It is now possible to fertilize the ovum in a dish. Will it be long before a fetus can be brought to term in an artificial womb? Science fiction (like Marge Piercy's *Woman on the Edge of Time*, 1976) has long considered the possible implications of such a development. Would it help to equalize female–male relations by producing a more balanced parenthood? Much will depend on who controls the technology.

Childbirth: A Cultural or a Natural Event?

In the United States today, due to poverty, 18% of women have little or no prenatal care (Madrick, 2002). In many parts of the world, women lack appropriate health care during pregnancy and delivery. In sub-Saharan Africa, excluding South Africa, only 66% of women receive prenatal care; in Western Asia, where the majority of women are Muslim, the number rises to 82%; in the countries of Europe, the Caribbean, and East Asia, it hovers around 95%. While in developed countries the number of deliveries aided by a skilled attendant is 99%, in southern Asia it drops to 39% (United Nations, 2000). Most women in the United States, however, give birth in hospitals, where the process is monitored and controlled by medical professionals (see Chapter 11). A significant subset of women have increasingly preferred to have their children at home, assisted by a midwife, believing that there is something "unnatural" about hospital births. In general, every society has customs that provide the basis for shaping the birthing event. It is the culture that informs women and other participants about what should be done, who should do it, and how.

Typical birth procedures in the United States are unusual in a number of respects. Hospitalized women generally give birth lying on their backs, for the convenience of the obstetrician (see Chapter 11); but elsewhere in the world, more common birth postures are kneeling, sitting, and squatting. Ample evidence shows that the latter positions facilitate the delivery of the child. Hospitals in the United States rarely allow friends and relatives to attend births, although the presence of the father has become quite common. In most areas of the world, however, a large number of women, midwives, female kin, and friends are present in the room, but no strangers.

The father aids the birth directly or indirectly through prescribed rituals. The U.S. experience has shown signs of changing attitudes toward giving birth; for instance, photographing or filming the process was introduced several decades ago, inviting more people, even strangers, to participate in the event through this visual medium. Childbirth

varies from one culture to the next. In some, as in the United States, it is treated like a sickness and the woman is rushed to the hospital to be attended by professionals. In others, it may be a cause for celebration or considered a defiling of the premises as fluids spill from the woman's body. The act of giving birth is a part of the general attitude toward women in that society; therefore, the event is influenced by gender politics.

Population growth is a public concern in most countries, but it takes many forms. In the United States during the mid-twentieth century, when a decrease in population among the mostly white middle class rang alarm bells, women were exhorted to have more babies to preserve their race and even "civilization" (Gordon, 1976). To encourage women to have babies, men in the clergy, medical sciences, and politics took it upon themselves to glorify motherhood, to emphasize that it was a woman's duty, and to promise a near-painless childbirth aided with ether and other drugs. There were also scientists who advised women, contrary to those who promoted the use of drugs, that pain during childbirth was the result of culturally induced fear.

In Europe after the two world wars, which had caused immense losses in population, French and Russian physicians, attempting to reverse the trend of a low birth rate, introduced a new approach to childbirth. "Prepared childbirth" involved mental concentration so that women could enhance their awareness of the different stages of muscle contraction involved in giving birth, learning to concentrate on controlling them rather than just passively experiencing them as pain. Learning the stages of labor, they could concentrate on different methods of breathing, orchestrated to manage their responses to each stage. A French doctor, Fernand Lamaze, who was sympathetic to such ideas, adopted the approach. His name came to be commonly associated with prepared child-birth in the United States, where it became popular (Karmel, 1965). In the "Lamaze method" of giving birth, the importance of mental preparation replaced anesthesia, but increasingly mechanical monitoring complicated the hospital situation.

The concept of childbirth during which the mother is not drugged was promoted among pregnant U.S. women by holding group sessions in which the experiences of pregnancy and giving birth were shared and discussed and husbands were encouraged to attend and learn to help the woman monitor her breathing. The increased awareness that resulted from the movement has led to greater demands for individual, private control of childbirth and to a gradual drift away from the more ritualized approach used in prepared childbirth classes. The current resistance by many women to the vigorous demands of natural childbirth and the more relaxed attitude toward taking painkillers when needed are manifestations of these new trends. Feminists respect the diversity in childbirthing choices for women but still urge women to be well informed of the process of childbirth and to not let themselves be placed in any particular birthing situation without asking questions of the medical establishment.

Breast-Feeding: Attitudes and Choices

Social and cultural factors and judgments, as well as the physical context of motherhood, also affect breast-feeding practices. The biological aspects of lactation, like the treatment and welfare of babies, are shaped by a combination of physiology and society. Women who are supported by their social environment are more successful at breast-feeding; stress and distractions can interfere with a mother's production of milk. Physiology is on the side of the mother and her child when she breast-

feeds. Mother's milk builds immunity in the newborn baby, which it needs vitally at this stage. Mother's milk also contains almost all the nutrients that larger amounts of prepared milk "formula" can provide; hence, babies who consume their mother's milk do not gain unnecessary weight. If the process proves satisfactory, the sensation of breast-feeding can accord the mother with pleasure, likened to a sense of sexual and emotional fulfillment. Breast-feeding usefully reduces the pressure on overflowing breasts and most significantly can help in pacing the birth of children. At least for a short period of time after giving birth, conception is hindered by lactation. In those societies where cultural factors place taboos on having sexual intercourse with a lactating mother, a mother is aided by not conceiving another child immediately. This natural contraception, though far from perfect, provides her with some respite from continuous pregnancy and ensures enough milk for the child until another one arrives and claims the breast.

Prepared milk formula for babies has become a huge business. When the dangers of feeding a baby unrefrigerated milk, not boiling the water intended to mix with milk powder, not disinfecting the bottles, or adding more than the necessary water are not explained well to mothers—or present problems that cannot be overcome—-infant mortality may rise. In the 1950s and 1960s, when the Swiss company Nestlé pushed its "prepared or fortified" powdered milk in developing areas of south Asia and Africa, where some of these precautions could not be met, there were detrimental effects on babies. For the sake of the child, therefore, when mothers can successfully breast-feed, such nutrients should be used as supplements, not replacements. With the development of safe milk and sanitary bottles early in the twentieth century, women who found this alternative useful in their busy lives, as well as those concerned

Mother and child sculpture from Kongo culture (Zaire, Angola, Congo), nineteenth century. In this wood sculpture, a mother holds an infant so sick he refuses to nurse, pointing instead to where his belly hurts. The back of the mother's head has been carved to allow space for a medicine shelf, to be filled with herbs and other healing substances to help her remedy her child's distress.

about maintaining media-advertised "desirable" body imagery—fearful of sagging breasts after nursing babies—took refuge in bottle-feeding their babies.

Most women in most parts of the world over history have had no choice however; breast-feeding has always been the only way to nourish infants. Mothers carry their infants with them wherever they go, to gather food (as do the dwellers of the Kalahari Desert in South Africa) or on their jobs (as do the domestic workers in South and Central America). For working middle- or upper-class women in economically developed countries, new devices such as "breast pumps" are being introduced into the market so that they can store their milk to be fed to the child in their absence. In many countries, including the United States, there are cultural proscriptions against revealing the breast in public, even for feeding babies. In most professional workplaces, babies and children are rarely welcome.

Substitutes for breast-feeding actually have a long history. In imperial Rome, as in seventeenth-century France and eighteenth-century England, wealthy women and working women had an option other than nursing: the use of "wet nurses" who breast-fed other women's infants. Like the use of bottles, the use of wet nurses was induced by the desire to preserve youthful-looking breasts, to appease a male who was resentful of sharing the women's breasts, or because a woman needed to devote herself to work. Though some women find nursing their babies sensually and emotionally gratifying, others, particularly among the working and educated groups, resent the idea of being tied down to a nursing schedule or feel that breast-feeding is uncomfortable and exhausting. It should be possible for women to make choices concerning breast-feeding, as well as childbirth, not on the basis of stereotypes or cultural strictures in which they have had no say at all but to suit their own personal beliefs, desires, and circumstances.

Support Systems: Fathers, Women's Networks, and Institutionalized and Societal Support

If motherhood is a social institution, as we have thus far suggested, support for the woman who has given birth or has become a mother by adoption or fostering ought to be provided by the state. Yet, like almost all aspects of motherhood, support for mothers is highly politicized and debated. Fathers, even when willing to assist their mates, are restricted by society: laws and rules regulate a father's role and his closeness to the mother and their children. In some cases, he may have access to her only if they are legally married; in others, he may have to work away from his family. In the absence of a father's support, women with significant resources may pay for help, hiring a nurse or a nanny. More often, help comes from other women who are kin or friends. The women who help a mother are often older, like grandmothers (Hrdy, 1999:282–6). If the mother is forced to seek employment to support herself and her child and has no help at home, she depends on the government or community-provided day-care centers. In their absence, a mother may look to other women for informal day-care networks. Otherwise, she may be forced to take her child everywhere she goes, as is the practice among the !Kung of the Kalahari Desert in South Africa, where a mother carries her child with her as she forages for food.

Maternity-leave benefits are also subject to politics and do not hinge on the wealth of a country (see Table 8.1). Among the developed countries, Japan grants 14 weeks of maternity leave at 60% of paid wages; in Sweden, 450 days' paid parental leave is given: 360 days at 75% and 90 days at a flat rate. In the United States, a woman is entitled to 12 weeks of *unpaid* leave for the birth and care

TABLE 8.1 Maternity-Leave Statistics Compared, 2000

Country	Length of Maternity Leave	Wages Paid During Covered Period (%)
Egypt	50 days	100
Ghana	12 weeks	50
Kenya	2 months	100
Senegal	14 weeks	100
South Africa	12 weeks	45
Argentina	90 days	100
Brazil	120 days	100
Cuba	18 weeks	100
Jamaica	12 weeks	100 (for 8 weeks)
Nicaragua	12 weeks	60
China	90 days	100
India	12 weeks	100
Philippines	60 days	100
Turkey	12 weeks	66.7
Vietnam	4–6 months	100
Australia	1 year	0
Canada	17–18 weeks	55 (for 15 weeks)
France	16–26 weeks	100
Hungary	24 weeks	100
Japan	14 weeks	60
Russia Federation	140 days	100
United States	12 weeks	0

Source: United Nations, *The World's Women, 2000: Trends and Statistics.* New York: United Nations, 2000: 140–3.

of the newborn, the same as a woman in Swaziland, Africa.

Fathers

The female of most mammalian species chooses, whenever she can, an able, strong, and well-formed mate to father her offspring, one that would provide for her and her progeny and protect her while she bears and nurses them. Likewise, a woman of the human species does better in her partnership if she chooses an able and resourceful mate who would provide for her and her children while she is pregnant with and breast-feeding them. One of the reasons that many women have traditionally married older and estab-

lished men has been for their support at this stage of their lives.

The support that a father can offer should be not only financial but also emotional, for after giving birth a woman, in a weakened state, has the obligation of feeding her child often and caring for it. His willingness to relieve the mother from the routine of child care, his words of encouragement, his display of sincere love for the child strengthen the bonding between them and the child.

A father's support for his mate and their children has usually been forthcoming if he is sure of paternity. The segregation of women in many traditional societies, as in the rural areas of South Asian countries like Pakistan, and the strict separation of public and private spheres in Middle Eastern countries, like Saudi Arabia, controls women's productive potential and ensures the paternity of husbands. Even in a Western society like the United States, not providing mothers with paid maternity leave stems from the effort to control motherhood. An economic and social system that ensures that most women are paid less than men (see Chapter 12) is one way to ensure that they are made financially dependent on their husbands. A federal law passed in May 2003 that rewards married couples with a greater tax cut is part of such a policy, for in its ramifications it encourages women to get married and be unpaid workers at home. Often-repeated phrases such as "family values" and "keep the family together" are ultimately meant to segregate women in their homes.

Fathers as parents can share the burdens of mothers. Yet, most fathers easily become distracted and frustrated with child care or have to attend to business or work outside the home. Rachel Cusk, a British author, tells of how, after the birth of a daughter, she remained with her baby while her partner continued to work outside their home. She came to think that their life began to resemble a kind of feudal relationship, in which she was wholly dependent on the lord of the manor for the maintenance of herself and their child (Cusk, 2001:5–7). The majority of societies disrupt or prevent a closer bonding that might have taken place between father and child by forcing him to work out of the house. Even when the man wishes to do so, he cannot devote himself fully to his child. Biological necessity, that only a woman can breast-feed, can be sidestepped by a bottle-feeding father, but a stay-at-home father is still rare.

Women's Networks, Community, and Institutionalized Support

Next to a child's father, a mother's help comes from other women, sometimes her women kin, especially those who have passed the childbearing age and have no small children of their own to demand their attention. Widowed or unmarried mothers, aunts, and sisters extend their assistance to a mother in need of help to care for her child. In the United States at the beginning of the twenty-first century, grandmothers are the primary caregivers of approximately 4 million children (Hrdy, 1999:282–6). However, when a second child arrives, an elderly grandmother or aunt may find the task of child care too burdensome, and many either withdraw their help completely or reduce it. The second child makes a forceful impact on a marriage, especially for middle-class American families according to a study by a University of Michigan anthropologist Rebecca L. Upton at the Center for the Ethnography of Everyday Life.

> Women's full-time participation in the labor market drops off dramatically with the second child. While most paid professional women return to the work force full-time after the birth of their first child, more than 50 percent change to part-time or take a leave of absence after the birth of the second. A second child also profoundly affects a couple's relationship to each other, with even the most egalitarian men and women assuming more traditional gender roles. (Upton, 2003; see also Chapter 12)

When help from mates or kin is unavailable or not forthcoming, mothers turn to friends. Mothers may pool their resources and take turns in caring for each other's small children. This practice has been institutionalized in the form of cooperative day-care centers in many towns in the United States. Unlike kin- and friend-based support systems, institutionalized community support in the form of day-care centers is a fairly recent phenomenon. In the former Soviet Union, in socialist countries such as Cuba, and in many European countries, government-supported day-care centers are common, as are privately run day-care centers. In an economically developed country such as the United States, day-care centers are sometimes viewed by ideological conservatives as a threat to the nuclear family, giving the mother the opportunity to leave her young children and earn wages, which supposedly she does for extra income, not economic necessity. This view runs against the actual norm of family conditions in the United States, where woman-headed families are on the rise (see Chapter 7). The United States stands almost alone among the industrialized societies in having a very limited national family policy with regard to such supports as family allowances, mandatory parental leaves, and child-care facilities (Crittendon, 2001). Although a law passed in May 2003 offered an increased child tax credit of $1,000 to families in upper income brackets, about 50 million households—36% of all households in the nation—were to receive only $400 per child; these low-income families include 2.5 million single parents (Fireston, 2003). This highly politicized "tax reform" punishes poor women, especially those with children, who need to work but receive very little relief from the government.

Political ideologies in the United States have simply not kept up with the social realities, have denied the changes in family configurations, and have turned a deaf ear to the plight of mothers. As more women and children are pushed into poverty, the future of motherhood for millions of women in the United States cannot be very bright. It is the obligation of this generation of feminists to insist that lawmakers in Congress acknowledge the realities of changes in U.S. society, especially in the issues surrounding motherhood, and make the overdue adjustments.

Box 8.3 MOMMY TAX

Unpaid female care giving is not only the life blood of families; it is the very heart of the U.S. economy. A spate of new studies reveals that the amount of work involved in unpaid child care is far greater than economists ever imagined. Indeed, it rivals in size the largest industries of the visible economy. By some estimates, even in the most industrialized countries, the total hours spent on unpaid household work—much of it associated with child-rearing—amount to at least half of the hours of paid work in the market. Up to 80 percent of this unpaid labor is contributed by women.

This huge gift of unreimbursed time and labor explains, in a nutshell, why adult women are so much poorer than men even though they work longer hours than men in almost every country in the world.

. . . But mothers' choices are not made in a vacuum. They are made in a world that women never made, according to rules they didn't write. To take just one example, what many mothers really want is a good part-time job, yet there is no rich and vibrant part-time labor market in the United States . . . we have many more choices in breakfast cereal than we do in work arrangements. To take another example, married working mothers . . . pay the highest taxes in the country on their earned income, in addition to the mommy tax. Mothers obviously played no role in writing a tax code that takes most of their earnings away from them. But this heavy taxation powerfully affects their choice of whether to work or not.

Source: From *The Price of Motherhood: Why the Most Important Job in the World Is Still the Least Valued*, by Ann Crittendon. © 2001 by Ann Crittendon. Reprinted by permission of Henry Holt and Company, LLC.

Whether divorced or never married, single mothers, mostly of the less-affluent groups, are overburdened with their workload. The Bush administration's welfare plan (2003) requires poor single mothers to work 40 hours a week in addition to caring for children. As for the tasks of caring for children, such as preparing their food, washing their clothes, helping them with their homework, and taking them to doctors, these remain unpaid work and welfare regulations do not count them as real work.

Childrearing Manuals

Modernity has shaken the roots of traditional families. Since the late nineteenth century, families have been on the move, especially from rural areas to urban centers, in search of work and a better life; and education for children has consistently been a foremost consideration. In these moves, mothers have generally lost the direct support and advice of their mothers and other kin in rearing their children. Finding themselves alone and bewildered, mothers have turned to manuals, which offer advice in caring for children. Ann Hulbert's *Raising America* (2003) is a history of the major handbooks of this kind. According to Hulbert, most of the child-care experts have been men. These theorists, pediatricians, and psychologists have advised women about regulating the behavior of their children, from eating habits to cuddling. Dr. Benjamin Spock is one of the authors discussed. His book, *The Common Sense Book of Baby and Child Care*, first appeared in 1946 and has gone into a seventh edition; translated into 39 languages with 50 million copies sold, it has had the widest influence on mothers (see Acocella, 2003). The writers of manuals reflect the consensus of men of the day toward childrearing. By imposing their views on mothers, they have directed the practice of motherhood. The existence and wide acceptance of such books undoubtedly reveal a need for guidance in child raising, while handbooks by experienced and practicing mothers might be better suited to the practical concerns of women. The feminist mothers of this generation need to offer their counsel to their sisters and daughters.

Choices and Control: The Politics of Motherhood

We have seen in this chapter that women's reproductive rights are constructed by laws, customs, governments, and religions. The politicizing of motherhood and the control over women's bodies and lives seem to be directed at curbing the power of women as the sole bearers of children. (Although it is scientifically possible to clone humans, the ethical objection renders this prospect moot for the time being.) Whether it is to ensure the continuity of individual families or the human species, men are in the forefront of regulating women's bodies. It seems childbearing bodies are too precious to entrust their ownership only to women. The regulations imposed on women's reproductive rights limit men's accessibility to women's bodies but also curb women's rights to exercise free will in terms of choice of mates, of when and how and how often to have children, and of how to raise them. Men, when in doubt of paternity, often withdraw their support for the care of their partners' children. They thus force women to restrict their sexual activities to monogamous relationships.

The biological clocks of women's bodies also regulate when and, to a lesser extent, how often they bear children. Against such cultural and biological restrictions women have an uphill fight to own their bodies and control their lives. Women's destinies in almost every society, with the exception of northern European countries where women's rights to their bodies are legally accepted, seem to be centered on their reproductive capacity. Women's control of their bodies must start with their free and unrestricted access to reasonable and sound birth control, including, if necessary, abortion.

Whether, When, and How Often to Become a Mother

The development of safe and effective contraceptive methods is as recent as the twentieth century. Contraceptives have been made available to women but only after many battles fought and not all universally won (see Chapters 7 and 11). Literacy and education among women are linked to the knowledge of birth control (see Box 8.4).

To regulate the frequency of children and to relieve families from the difficulties of maintaining large numbers of children, couples have taken various types of precaution to control birth. Birth-control techniques range from the so-called rhythm method practiced traditionally among Catholics, which takes a woman's ovulation period into consideration, to infanticide, euphemistically called "overlaying," when infants a "accidentally" smothered by their caretakers. Coroners' reports for London between 1855 and 1860, for example, list 3,900 deaths, mostly of newborns, from

"overlaying" (Hrdy, 1999: 290-1). Aborting a fetus is another form of birth control. Despite the imbalance in responsibility assigned to women and men for having or not having babies, there has been a history of legal obstacles to women's reproductive freedom. In Britain, the first laws banning abortion altogether were passed in 1803; the Catholic Church worldwide banned abortion for its communicants in 1869. In the United States, abortion up until *quickening* (when a fetus is first felt moving), usually the second trimester of pregnancy, was legal in most states until the middle of the nineteenth century. After the Civil War, probably as a result of high numbers of deaths caused by the war, many states adopted pro-natalist policies and outlawed abortion entirely. In 1873, as part of a new restrictive attitude toward sexual expression ("social purity"), the federal government passed the Comstock Law, which banned distribution of pornography, methods of abortion, and all means of preventing conception (Yalom, 2001).

Efforts to open birth-control clinics in Europe and the United States in the late nineteenth and early twentieth centuries were met with strong state and church opposition. The

---

Box 8.4   POPULATION ESTIMATES FALL AS POOR WOMEN ASSERT CONTROL

Gita Sen, professor of economics at the Indian Institute of Management in Bangalore, said . . . "For a very long time we've had a huge problem in terms of 50 to 60 percent of the female population being illiterate." The most recent census, the 2001 census, shows the biggest increases in literacy happening in some of the poor northern states, big jumps in literacy, and that means girls are going to school.

"Those same girls are going to be making fertility decisions in another 10 years or so," she said, and "I don't think they are going to make them in the same way that their mothers may have."

Source: From Barbara Crossette, Population estimates fall as poor women assert control, *New York Times*, March 10, 2002, A3. Copyright © 2002 by The New York Times Co. Reprinted with permission.

depression of the 1930s, when economic conditions discouraged large families, resulted in the loosening of restrictions on birth control in the United States. By 1940, every state except Massachusetts and Connecticut had legalized access to contraceptive information. Family-planning clinics, some publicly funded, were established. In 1965 (*Griswold* v. *Connecticut*), the Supreme Court held that an individual's right to privacy encompasses a woman's right to make decisions on whether to conceive children and, therefore, to have unrestricted access to contraception. Elsewhere in the world, some countries that are predominantly Catholic, like Poland, outlaw abortion and severely limit the use of contraceptives. Other countries, concerned about severe poverty in the midst of a rapidly expanding population, have made it official policy to encourage contraception, as in India or the People's Republic of China, and to restrict by means of serious financial and other disincentives the number of children couples may have.

Limiting the number of children is motivated in a family or in a nation by the acknowledged economic burden of raising children. Little or no attention is paid to the wish or health of women when it is state policy, as in the People's Republic of China. Contraceptive devices have been developed for both women and men, although the majority are for women, upon whom lies the burden of their use. On the other hand, to the extent that there is choice about and responsibility for birth control, these devices emphasize the woman's role. Women, in order to make their own choice about pregnancy, need not only legal backing and access to technical devices but full knowledge and awareness of the options. Social conditions have not fostered an atmosphere conducive to real choices. Rather, women have usually been pressured to become mothers from early childhood. Traditionally, men could divorce women for bar-

renness; women who depended on husbands for economic support and protection had no choice but to try to become mothers. For many teenage girls living in poverty, having a child may seem like a chance for happiness and self-esteem, though many become pregnant from lack of sexual information and knowledge of the difficulties of raising a child alone.

Today, many women in developed and also in some developing countries, like Turkey, have the opportunity to ask themselves whether they want a child. They have become aware of the options available to them and are making choices with regard to reproductive technology. However, questions about the rights of women around the world remain. Should such rights be granted to a pregnant woman's parents if the woman is a minor and unable to support a child? The U.S. Supreme Court said no to this question in 1964, but such issues continue to be debated. Because it is women who undergo the burdens of pregnancy and of giving birth, it seems appropriate to place the sole right to determine conduct over childbearing in their hands. Many, however, including some women, are unwilling to accord this power only to the women involved.

Surrogate motherhood, a form of bearing a child that is on the increase, is when a woman is inseminated with an unrelated man's sperm in order to give birth to a child to be raised by others, for example, if a man and his wife are infertile or if a gay man wants to have a baby. It also is used when a fertilized egg is implanted in the womb of a woman who will carry the embryo to birth for the genetic parents. The issues involved in surrogate mothering that concern both feminists and the courts are the likelihood of exploitation of poor women who receive payment for bearing a child and whether a surrogate mother who contributes her ovum may be permitted to change her mind about giving up her child.

Nevertheless, the practice is increasing, especially in the state of California; and these issues remain to be resolved.

There is, at present, almost no help from public sources for infertile women who cannot pay the high fees demanded for the new birth technologies. Even these technologies, like artificial insemination, may not help or may result in multiple births, oftentimes at high risk to mother and babies. Infertility may also be the result of restricted options, such as parental leave and child care, which make women delay having children until it proves too late to conceive. Furthermore, infertility may be caused by workplace and environmental hazards that need to be controlled (see Chapter 11).

Control over Children

While women in the past were obligated, for the most part, to bear children if they could, the extent to which they had control over their children once they were born varied in different times, places, and classes. Patriarchal societies, such as the traditional Muslim countries, have often viewed children legally as well as by custom as the "possession" of their father and his kin group; and these relatives have determined how children should be raised, taught, married, and employed. Often, this kin group was not formally obligated to consult or even inform the children's mother about decisions that had been made for them. If women lost their husbands through divorce or widowhood, they were often obliged to leave their children as well. Patriarchal patterns have characterized Europe and the United States until the modern era. Not until the 1850s, for example, did laws in Victorian England make it possible for women to claim physical custody of children under 7 years old. In the United States, the issue has been dealt with on a state-by-state, case-by-case basis.

From the early twentieth century until recently, when marriages ended in divorce, women were often given custody of their children on the grounds that the decision was best for the child. However, some states have lately made changes in custody decisions that reflect the changing view of the best interests of the child. A father, instead of declaring his wife unfit as a mother, now has to argue why his custody is better for the child. The women's movement and concurrent rethinking of parental roles have led more fathers to seek physical and legal custody of their children. More common is joint custody of children shared by their parents.

Mothers who dissolve a partnership with a man upon the realization of being a lesbian have not done well in the courts when they seek the custody of their children. Too often, they are viewed as "unfit" mothers by judges. The general tendency to be intolerant of homosexuality in many societies, including the United States, leads judges to put their biases before the welfare of the child. Yet, there is no indication that children of lesbian mothers fare less well than children of heterosexual ones.

Laws designed to protect children ironically have been used as weapons against poor women and women of color. Because of their poverty, lack of education, or lack of familiarity with local practices, these mothers have often been blamed for abuse, neglect, or simply being slovenly in their care of the house and children. Children may be removed from the custody of their mother because of neglect or abuse and placed in foster homes or put up for adoption, permanently cutting all ties with their mother. Poor women are often unable to fight in the courts because they lack funds for adequate legal help.

Questions about women's rights to keep and make decisions about their own children are often related to their financial responsibilities. Traditionally, the father has had the primary responsibility for the economic support of children, but it must fall on the mother if the father fails to provide for his children. If mothers are to be legally responsible for the economic support of their children, how are they to have the means to provide it? This brings us to the issue of work and motherhood.

Working for Wages

In many countries, women with small children under age 5 spend less time on paid work and more time on unpaid work. The responsibility for child care lies mainly with women, who spend more than twice as much time as men do on it. Child care includes all direct physical care, reading to and playing with children, but excludes secondary child care, for example, watching children while engaged in other activities. With the exception of the Republic of Korea, where, on average, both women and men spend less than 1 hour per week on child care, women everywhere spend between 2 and 5 hours per week on child care compared with less than 2 hours for men. Compared to men, women spend considerably more time doing unpaid work and much less time doing paid work, almost universally (United Nations, 2000).

Making real choices, not only about whether and when to become a mother but also about how to mother and how to spend time with one's children, depends on having the right and opportunity to choose whether or not to work for wages. This issue in the United States, like birth control, is much affected by public policy. Public welfare policy has in the past fostered the traditional arrangement in which mothers stay home to care for their children. Now, welfare policy for mothers is to insist that they do work for wages outside the home, even though those wages will be minimal, potentially limiting their choices and ability to bring up their children in dignity.

"Unnatural" Mothers: Mothers Who Give Up Their Children

So far, this chapter has focused on "natural," or "birth," mothers. The idealized picture of the mother is a young woman embracing her infant child. The picture that has been handed down from generation to generation would lead us to believe that mothers are instinctively committed to nurture their children. We do not take into consideration that there are women who, for one reason or another, are unable to care for their children; there are unwanted children who are born to single, very young, very poor mothers, sometimes already with more children than they can handle. When a woman gives up her child because she feels unable to bear the responsibility of raising it, she is readily blamed for not behaving in the normal way, for being "unnatural." Some critics also label a woman who abandons her child as "unnatural" or lacking in maternal instincts. A mother who gives up her child may do it to protect herself from a society which reacts harshly to unwed mothers or to procure a better future for herself because she can then work or earn an education. This would be impossible with a small child. An unmarried woman who is desperately poor and has been a victim of rape may wish to abandon her child in the hope that both she and her baby will be better off—she with one less burden and the baby with a chance of being adopted by those who want it. There are mothers around the world to whom babies are born with such alarming frequency that their milk would not be adequate, and they give up one with the hope of keeping another alive. There are countries, like the People's Republic of China, that discourage more than one child per couple; and because boys are preferred, daughters may often be relinquished (see Chapter 6).

Laws that criminalize abandoning a baby and prosecute the mother do not discriminate about the kind of circumstances that lead to abandonment, calling all such mothers "unnatural." This judgment emanates from the socially constructed view of mothers as women who should love and care for their children unconditionally. An ideology that assumes the existence of "maternal instinct" and "motherly love" blinds us to the possibility that a woman may give up a child exactly for that reason: to give it a better chance in life. A mother who relinquishes her child to be adopted by persons who can provide this opportunity gains her goal.

Orphanages and foundling "hospitals" have existed in many countries. The most complete historical records on infant abandonment exist in Italy; for example, in 1640, 22% of all children baptized in Florence were abandoned babies. In the worst years on record, during the 1840s, 43% of all infants baptized in Florence were abandoned. According to these records, the majority, about 90%, of children abandoned to a foundling home died there (Hrdy, 1999: 304). Babies and children in orphanages in poorer countries, as in Romania at the beginning of the twenty-first century, still die as a result of negligence, malnourishment, lack of funds, and lack of concern for abandoned children. Society judges mothers who relinquish their children as unnatural, but provisions for helping them or their children remain minimal.

Women Other Than Birth Mothers Who Mother

Stepmothers

Any woman who substitutes for the "natural" mother does not fare well in our collective imagination. We learn the story of Cinderella and her stepmother in many languages and versions; the stepmother is not only an ugly woman but also evil. The negative image of the stepmother in myth and fiction, the resentment a child may feel toward the woman who replaces the mother, the absence of an early bonding between the child and the stepmother, and her possible preference for her own children over the stepchild are potential reasons to anticipate the difficult role that awaits the stepmother. However, in almost every country today, second marriages with stepchildren are becoming common, solutions are eventually worked out in most families, and close bonds can be formed.

What of stepfathers? Men, however, are less likely to care for the children of another man. Child homicide is uncommon and tolerated nowhere. Yet, in the United States when the father of offspring under 2 years of age no longer lives in the home and an unrelated man or stepfather lives there instead, this rare event is seventy times more likely to occur. Among the Ache of South American forests, mothers themselves sometimes kill fatherless infants after a conscious evaluation of what the future holds (Hrdy, 1999).

Foster Mothers and Adoptive Mothers

In the United States, abandoned children are often placed in foster care. Foster mothers provide children with homes in exchange for wages; although there are unfortunate incidents in some foster homes, children can be reasonably well cared for and intimacy and love can grow between foster mother and child, which in some cases may lead to adoption. Adoptive mothers are generally married women because most adoptions are governed by the state. When a child is adopted into a married household, the child fares quite well because it is a wanted child and the parents are usually older and financially comfortable. In a second marriage, the wife may adopt her husband's child, especially if she does not have children of her own or if the child has no mother.

Godmothers

Since human children mature over a very long period, they need to be entrusted to the supervision of some adult if the parents are unable to care for them. The designation of a godmother is made in good will by the parents of the child. In the West, the tradition of asking trusted friends and especially influential people to serve as godparents is widespread. The goal is to ensure fictive parents who, if needed, will look after the offspring. Similarly, in some societies, including the Yanomamo of Brazil and Venezuela, sexual liaisons are part of the way a mother sets up networks of well-disposed men to help protect and provision her offspring (Hrdy, 1999:246).

Summary

Being a mother is the most significant, responsible, intimidating, controversial, and politicized role there is for a woman. Images of motherhood permeate most societies in multiple cultural forms, mostly stereotypical. For example, mothers have been depicted in ancient Greek myths as all-powerful and in European paintings as the center of domesticity. U.S. ethnic literature abounds with depictions of the complex relationships of Jewish, African American, and Asian American mothers with their daughters and sons.

The dominant Western media, in particular, has idealized mothers and depicted them as weak and dependent. With the feminist movement, a more positive image of mothers is evident; yet, few women can achieve such representations of perfection, which contribute to anxiety, frustration, and isolation.

The marketing of motherhood also fosters feelings of personal inadequacy in women. Contemporary feminists are beginning to write about the contradictions of motherhood, including its oppressive conditions.

Although women in general bear children, mothering is cultural behavior. Parental roles among humans do not develop by instinct but are primarily learned. Because human children are dependent for so long, the role of parenting is extended. Biology dictates women's capacity for motherhood, but society enlarges the task of "mothering."

U.S. society has high expectations and standards of mothering; yet, mothers and their tasks remain undervalued, and their role is not appreciated as "real work." Assigning parenting to women almost exclusively contributes to women's dependence and men's superior attitude toward women. Until very recently, fathers have been excluded from and oftentimes have not demonstrated an active role in childrearing. Feminists disagree about motherhood. For some, it contributes to women's oppression; for others, it can be a source of pride and empowerment.

Some women become mothers willingly, after consideration; others fall into the role without much thought; and on many women motherhood is foisted. The role of motherhood is everywhere manipulated by society, for example, the choice a woman makes for her mate and the manner she chooses to give birth, to raise her child, and whether or not to breast-feed. Capitalist economies and men, in particular, have benefited from women being assigned the primary responsibility for childrearing. Men are free to acquire more economic, political, and social power.

The attitudes of women and men toward pregnancy, childbirth, and breast-feeding are culturally shaped by their societies and have changed over time and with the women's movement. Prenatal care varies widely across the globe. Class is also a factor in the United States as poor women suffer most from lack of prenatal care. Although the medical establishment has institutionalized childbirth in the United States, women (and men) are demanding a more active role.

Support for mothers is highly politicized. The culture of each society prescribes the definition of motherhood, the fathers' role, and women's support networks. State support for women as mothers, including maternity leave and child-care centers, varies widely globally. In the United States, current public policy that requires welfare mothers to work outside the home does not adequately reflect or support the social realities of contemporary families, especially for low-income single mothers, and may even penalize mothers and children. In contemporary Western societies, manuals written by "experts," who are largely men, have come to dominate childrearing information.

Women's reproductive rights, like the definition and role of motherhood, have been and continue to be constructed by laws, customs, governments, and religions. Safe and effective contraceptive methods have become available only as recently as the latter half of the twentieth century. Although surrogate motherhood is on the increase, feminists and the courts raise concerns about the exploitation of poor women. New technologies are increasing the possibility for infertile women to bear children, but there are health risks and financial costs.

Women's control over the children they have born has varied in different times, places, and classes. Poor women and women of color are more vulnerable to losing custody. Although by necessity, women in many countries must spend time at paid work, their governments, for the most part, have not recognized the unpaid work that women contribute through the care of small children, which benefits each society.

Women have many reasons for giving up their children; sometimes it is for the children's survival and benefit. Women who do so are often viewed harshly by their cultures as "unnatural" mothers, yet their societies provide little support to help women and children in need. Institutions, such as orphanages, have existed to attend to abandoned children but, for the most part, are not ideal.

Women other than birth mothers also mother. Stepmothers have been maligned in mythology and fairytales. In real life, the stepmother–child relationship varies but can include a close bond. Fostering adoption, and being a godmother are other ways in which women who do not give birth can mother.

Discussion Questions

1. What are some of the sources from which a woman in the United States learns how to be a mother? Does race or ethnicity matter?
2. Examine the role and image of mothers for your generation, your mother's, and your grandmothers'. How has it changed in the past 10 years?
3. What changes do you hope for and what changes do you expect in mothering in the twenty-first century?
4. How would you define the role of grandmother and mother-in-law (hers and his)?
5. The "good and nurturing mother" and the "terrible mother" are important mythic figures. Find examples from literature and popular fiction, films, and folk tales to represent the devaluation and simultaneous exaltation of mothers.

Recommended Readings

Colette. *My Mother's House and Sido* (1930), translated by Una Vincenzo and Enid McLeod. New York: Farrar, Straus, and

Giroux, 1953. The distinguished French writer lovingly reminisces about her mother and the beneficent influence that she had. The author depicts the warm, rich atmosphere of the rural home where she grew up—a product, she claims, of her mother's creation.

Crittendon, Ann. *The Price of Motherhood.* New York: Henry Holt, 2001. The author provides a timely study of the costs to women who bear and raise children. The "mommy tax" includes loss of current and future income and exclusion from retirement benefits. She argues that men and society should share the costs of raising children, criticizing mainstream feminism for not campaigning for appropriate wages and security for motherhood.

Cusk, Rachel. *A Life's Work: On Becoming a Mother.* New York: Picador, 2002. In this lively memoir of mothering by a novelist, Cusk reacts against the conservative "family values" of the late twentieth century. The author acknowledges her resentment at her loss of freedom and personhood as well as the pleasures of mothering.

Folbre, Nancy. *The Invisible Heart. Economics and Family Values.* New York: New Press, 2001. The author, an economist, provides a wide-ranging theoretical discussion of women as caregivers set in the context of social values.

Hrdy, Sarah Blaffer. *Mother Nature. A History of Mothers, Infants and Natural Selection.* New York: Pantheon, 1999. An anthropologist looks at primates, including humans, and reconceptualizes such traditional ideas as the "maternal instinct" and the devaluation of postmenopausal women. She revises accepted Darwinian views to include women's agency in human evolution.

Rich, Adrienne. *Of Woman Born: Motherhood as Experience and Institution.* New York: Norton, 1976. Rich examines motherhood as a social institution and the way that it has evolved from antiquity to the present. She shows how relationships between women and men are reflected in the institution of motherhood and how concepts related to this institution change with changes in women's status. Rich, a feminist and poet, draws from her own experience as well as the scholarly literature.

References

Acocella, J. Mother's helpers. *New Yorker,* May 5, 2003.

Angelou, Maya. *I Know Why the Caged Bird Sings.* New York: Knopf, 1969.

Baruch, Elaine Hoffman. *Women and Power: Literary and Psychoanalytic Perspectives.* New York: New York University Press, 1991.

Bienstock, Beverly Gray. The changing image of the American Jewish mother. In *Changing Images of the Family,* edited by Virginia Tufte and Barbara Myerhoff. New Haven: Yale University Press, 1979.

Bittman, Sam, and Sue Rosenberg Zalk. *Expectant Fathers.* New York: Dutton, 1978.

Chesler, Phyllis. *With Child: A Diary of Motherhood.* New York: Crowell, 1979.

Colette. *My Mother's House and Sido* (1930), translated by Una Vincenzo and Enid McLeod. New York: Farrar, Straus and Giroux, 1953.

Collins, Patricia Hill. *Black Feminist Thought: Knowledge, Consciousness, and the Politics of Empowerment,* 2nd ed. New York: Routledge, 2000.

Crittendon, Ann. *The Price of Motherhood.* New York: Henry Holt, 2001.

Crossette, Barbara. Population estimates fall as poor women assert control. *New York Times,* March 10, 2002, A3.

Cusk, Rachel. *A Life's Work: On Becoming a Mother.* New York: Picador, 2002.

de Beauvoir, Simone. *The Second Sex,* translated by H. M. Parshley. New York: Knopf, 1953.

Desai, Anita. *Fasting, Feasting.* Boston: Houghton Mifflin, 1999.

Duncan, Carol. Happy mothers and other new ideas in French art. *Art Bulletin,* 55, 570–83, 1973.

Fireston, David. 2nd study finds gaps in tax cuts. *New York Times*, June 1, 2003, Sec. 1.

Firestone, Shulasmith. *The Dialectic of Sex*. New York: Morrow, 1970.

French, Marilyn. *The Women's Room*. New York: Ballantine Books, 1977.

Friedan, Betty. *The Feminine Mystique*. New York: Dell, 1963.

Gilman, Charlotte Perkins. *Herland* (1915). New York: Pantheon, 1979.

Gordon, Linda. *Woman's Body, Woman's Right: A Social History of Birth Control in America*. New York: Grossman, 1976.

Held, Virginia. *Feminist Morality: Transforming Culture, Society, and Politics*. Chicago: University of Chicago Press, 1993.

Hrdy, Sarah Blaffer. *Mother Nature: A History of Natural Selection, Mothers, and Infants*. New York: Pantheon, 1999.

Hulbert, Ann. *Raising America: Experts, Parents, and a Century of Advice About Children*. New York: Knopf, 2003.

Karmel, Marjorie. *Thank You, Dr. Lamaze*. New York: Dolphin, 1965.

Kingston, Maxine Hong. *The Woman Warrior*. New York: Knopf, 1976.

Madrick, Jeff. Economic scene. *New York Times*, June 13, 2002, C2.

Mead, Margaret. *Sex and Temperament in Three Primitive Societies*. New York: Morrow, 1963.

Meehan, Paula. *The Man Who Was Marked by Winter*. Loughcrew: Gallery Press, 1991.

Miller, Sue. *The Good Mother*. New York: Harper & Row, 1986.

Mukherjee, Bharati. *Desirable Daughters*. New York: Hyperion, 2002.

Piercy, Marge. *Woman on the Edge of Time*. New York: Knopf, 1976.

Ratner, Rochelle, editor. *Bearing Life: Women's Writings on Childlessness*. New York: Feminist Press at the City University of New York, 2000.

Rich, Adrienne. *Of Woman Born: Motherhood as Experience and Institution*. New York: Norton, 1976.

Ruddick, Sara. Maternal thinking. *Feminist Studies*, 6, 342–67, 1980.

Tan, Amy. *The Joy Luck Club*. New York: G. P. Putnam's Sons, 1989.

———. *The Bonesetter's Daughter*. New York: G. P. Putnam's Sons, 2001.

Treblicot, Joyce, editor. *Mothering. Essays in Feminist Theory*. Totowa, NJ: Rowman & Allanheld, 1984.

United Nations. *The World's Women 2000: Trends and Statistics*. New York: United Nations, 2000.

Upton, Rebecca. The American family: from good to bad, from bad to worse? *University of Michigan Magazine*, spring, 11–13, 2003.

Yalom, Marilyn. *A History of the Wife*. New York: Harper Collins, 2001.

Part *III*

Women in Society

The earlier sections of this book explored the various ways women have been defined by others—in society and culture, in the family, and the alternatives they have chosen for themselves. This final section deals with women's relationships to what has often been called the "public sphere." Here, we explore the contributions of women to the fields of religion, education, health, work, and political power.

Women have always participated in the world beyond the family circle, but all too often these contributions and efforts have been undervalued, ignored, or treated as invisible. For many people, the threat of feminism has been the growing power of women in the public domain and the redefinition of women's roles in what has been misleadingly called the "private" domain.

Religion has been a continuing force in many women's lives. Varieties of religion prescribe human behavior and provide models for human aspiration. Women have often been viewed as saints or sinners. Many women through history have chosen a "religious life" as an alternative to secular life and marriage. They have not only been involved as worshippers and followers but have also taken leadership roles, ranging from curers to clergy.

Feminists involved in religions and religious life have reinterpreted religious doctrines and questioned the sexist basis of the language and cultural practices in which religious dogmas are framed. Today, feminists also seek a religious expression for self-affirming beliefs in womanhood.

Education stimulates us to ask questions and search for answers. Too often, those who do not have the advantage of an education do not learn how to question the nature of our environment and experience. In many parts of the world, parents without the necessary resources choose not to educate their daughters but only their sons. Women's education can be a controversial issue. Will education provoke them to challenge the status quo? What is appropriate for women to learn? Access to certain fields often requires specific educational preparation. In the past, women were not permitted to obtain instruction in the male-dominated professions of the ministry, law, and medicine. Today, women are challenging long-held beliefs about their lack of ability for scholarship. In doing gender-conscious research, feminist scholarly questions differ from the traditional approaches of the past, and such research is adding to the knowledge base about both women and men.

Standards for the health of women have very often been based solely on women's reproductive roles. The norms for women's physical and emotional health have usually been defined by men. Women have not been encouraged to be responsible for their own well-being, especially as men have controlled the field of women's health care. When women have rebelled against their traditional roles and asserted themselves, the health-care system has labeled them "sick."

Health and medical care have become major political means for controlling the activities of women. Who should make decisions about women's bodies is a controversial national and international issue. Similarly, contraception and sterilization are significant political issues. The international women's health movement has begun to challenge antiquated notions of women's health care.

Work has usually been devalued when labeled "women's work." Much of the work done by women has been interwoven with the traditional roles of housewife and mother. Within the context of the household, women have rarely, if ever, been paid or given credit for their daily work. With the advent of industrialization and modernization, much of the work formerly done by women in the home was transformed into activities performed outside the home for wages—for example, spinning, sewing, education of the young, and care of the sick. Some of the traditional areas of women's work were taken over by men in factories, schools, and hospitals. When done by men, the status of the work and the pay received for it rose. In the industrialized world, technology continues to change the nature of work, and more women are seeking a place in the paid labor force than ever before—as well as demanding respect for those tasks that they have traditionally performed.

The growing number of women and mothers in the workforce has led to demand for changes in the workplace and the family to accommodate women's needs. Child-care facilities, flexible working hours, and parental leave have been implemented by employers and government in response to the influx of women into the workforce.

Politics and the power to change society are crucial to women's lives. Where there is power, there are means for exerting social control. Those who wield power are not quick to redistribute or relinquish this advantage. In societies where power is accorded to certain groups of people by virtue of race, religion, ethnic origin, or gender, it has been difficult for oppressed groups to gain sufficient power to alter the status quo. This pattern can be seen in women's struggles for their political rights.

The struggle for women's political power has become international. Through international conferencing, women from different countries come together to share their common experiences and work together to improve women's lives. Despite the differences that separate women, the women's movement and feminism are global phenomena.

Should women strive to reform the existing social system, or will nothing less than a radical restructuring be necessary? Different women have different political objectives. Women do not make up a homogeneous group, but they can and do support one another in realizing a variety of shared goals.

chapter 9

Women and Religion

Religious Beliefs

What Is Religion?

Women are often at the center of political conflict about religion, which provides a rationale for both liberal and conservative reformers in their arguments about controlling or liberating women. What we call "religion" is something about which people feel passionately. Wars have been fought, people have been hideously maimed and tortured, and some have even sought martyrdom in the name of "religion." The subject has not lost its force in modern times by any means and remains a major element in world politics.

Religion is among the most elusive of the concepts we use to describe human societies. Some theorists distinguish religion in terms of its reliance upon a supernatural element, but it is possible to be an adherent to some religions without believing in any god. Furthermore, many religions that have a distinctive label, such as "Hinduism" or "Christianity," incorporate many distinct variants that are so different from one another, occasionally even hostile to one another, that they cannot be described as unitary in any sense. To generalize in any way about women and religion would therefore be futile. In many societies, including U.S. society, religious belief permeates, at least for some women and men, virtually all aspects of

life. Planting a garden, eating a meal, having a baby, and burying the dead have both secular and religious aspects. This is so even in societies which have sought rigorously to establish and enforce a separation between religion and secular society; many societies have not sought to separate in this way but, rather, have combined a mutually reinforcing religious and political establishment.

While many have come to see religion as a relic of the past, representative of older traditions and bastion of conservatism, it has long been a force for change and continues to be so in the present. Religious believers often seek reform rather than acceptance. They criticize what they see as injustice, oppression, and evil and try to change the behavior both of individuals and of whole societies. At times they attempt to do this through established religious institutions—the churches, the clergy, and so forth—and at times through new religious movements (in which women sometimes play leading roles) within or outside of established religions.

We can speak of varieties of religion just as we can speak of varieties of society. On the one hand, there are the diffuse religious beliefs and practices of societies that have few or no specialized religious institutions, small-scale societies which have little social hierarchy or specialization. On the other hand, there are the major world religions, diverse in character but each claiming millions of adherents, in state-organized societies, which have specialized ordained clergy and which play roles recognized and protected by state-level political institutions. These often contain sects which, though established, are extremely different from one another, some granting prominent roles to women and others being more patriarchal in character. Finally, there are religious movements, often on the fringe or even outside of the established large-scale religions, such as what are called "fundamentalist" religions and "new" religions.

Many religious traditions appeal to a "higher authority," something above human will or desire, for a formulation of right and wrong. For some women and men, this appeal strengthens the dicta about morality. Sometimes this authority involves sanctions, such as blessings for those who do right and punishments for those who do wrong. However, the motivations of believers do not lie only in sanctions but also in the wish to do and to see done what is right. Some women and men resort to interpretations of texts for guidance into what is "right" and what is "wrong," while others look to the vision of charismatic leaders or even direct religious experience (though this itself is usually much influenced by leaders and customs). Generally, it is not a live-and-let-live world. Believers are not usually satisfied with following the right path only for themselves or even for themselves and their children. They want others to see and follow the right path and to avoid supporting systems that take the wrong path. The vehemence with which they insist on this in part determines whether outsiders label them as "fundamentalists" or "fanatics."

Religion and Social Reform

Usually, we associate doctrines, teachings, and customs concerning right and wrong with reli-gion. Religions not only set standards for good behavior but also tell their adherents how to achieve a state of "goodness," whether this is defined as moral health or conduct which sets things right with the world. Religion is often associated with healing, a matter which we will explore in this chapter. Healing, or achieving a better state, can be directed toward the individual or to the society as a whole. When directed toward the individual, it can involve diagnosis (discovery of what is wrong, whether through divination, confession, or some other means) and repair (through penitence, atonement, or restoration—by sacrifice or making amends). The individual tries to improve by correcting what is wrong and doing what is right.

When the society as a whole is believed to have gone wrong, individual improvement is not enough. Religious institutions and movements attempt to bring about social change as well as individual change. Some of that change may come from within established religions, which may deplore poverty, what is regarded as depravity of various sorts, injustice, or simply failure of compassion. It may attempt to restore an earlier state of affairs in which such evils did not occur or at least were less evident, or it may seek to correct wrongs by changing or establishing institutions. In other words, established religions may criticize society for having gone astray and seek to correct evils by changing society.

In both respects, women can be expected to be active, in part because of the unfavorable position in which they so frequently find themselves. As individuals, they may be deeply unhappy and turn to religion for help. They may also seek change for themselves and others like them, obliging their society to establish justice, compassion, harmony, and whatever else their belief system teaches them is right and proper.

While feminists in modern times have critiqued major world religions for prejudice against women and the many devices used to control women and keep them in a secondary role, it cannot be denied that the majority of the women in the world have found value in their faith and their religious communities and that some have found the means to change society for the better through their religions. Thus, for example, although their churches may have told Christian women in the United States in the nineteenth century that their place was in the home, it was through their churches that many women fought slavery and organized the abolitionist movement.

It is paradoxical, then, that the major religions of the world have been so repressive toward women, usually mandating far stronger constraints on women than on men and excluding them from positions of leadership. Yet, even in these religions, we often find women in the forefront, sometimes venerated as saints and holy women, sometimes as leaders in the spheres allocated to them. Today, feminist theologians analyze the sexism in major world religious traditions and reformulate received doctrines to meet feminist ideals (see Sharma and Young, 1999).

Established Religions

Religions in Small-Scale Societies. Women often play important roles in small-scale societies' religious practices. In these societies, there may be little specialization in social roles beyond those determined by age and gender. Some women and men are regarded as gifted in their ability to attain communion with spiritual entities and are able to use their gifts and training from more experienced practitioners to perform healing ceremonies, for the purpose of enhancing physical as well as spiritual well-being and harmony between humans and nature. In the past, anthropologists and others have sometimes referred to such individuals as "shamans," though recently many have preferred to use culturally specific terminology that reflects the distinctive understandings of the settings in which such healing practices occur.

Women in these, as in more complex, societies need to know the rituals associated with their assigned activities and to perform them in order to have them come out well. In small-scale societies, the roles of women in the performance of rituals and ceremonies may be regarded as critical to essential elements of social survival, such as fertility, protection from environmental disasters, health and safety, and prosperity.

World Religions. World religions are those which number their adherents in the millions. Some of these are more unitary in their beliefs. Confucianism, Buddhism, and Christianity, for example, trace their origins to their namesakes: Confucius, the Buddha (Siddhartha Gautama), and Christ, and Islam to its Prophet, Muhammad. Judaism traces a common ethnic history as well as a common set of scriptures. Taoism has a coherent set of beliefs. Hinduism, like Judaism, is grounded in an ethnic/national history, yet it contains immense diversity of belief. Indeed, each of these, with a history of movement through conversion and migration, has been transformed through time into a multitude of different variants, often with different names and different beliefs and practices.

These world religions are frequently associated with political structures, particularly the state itself or an arm of the state. In the past, for example, Christian states recognized an official religion, a particular variant of Christianity, and designated practitioners served important roles in government; conversely, the ruler had to be legitimized by the Church. Today, there are a number of Islamic nations in which Muslim clerics rule (such as Iran) or have great influence (such as Pakistan). While states have varied in their degree of tolerance of other religions, a close linkage between the state and the religious establishment has been the rule, rather than the exception, in the history of complex societies. However, the separation of church and state no doubt has made possible religious tolerance and democratic governance.

As with secular leadership, women have long been excluded from positions of authority in these world religions. Women in the more male-dominated major religions are almost never permitted to be educated in the texts or the liturgy and often banned from participation in the central rituals and sometimes from places of worship. They tend to be valued primarily as mothers or as symbols of motherhood; otherwise, they are devalued and their sexuality is regarded as dangerous to men. Women's religious rights are secondary to those of men, and when they are denied rights by the secular state, this denial is supported by religious doctrine.

Nevertheless, women are adherents of these faiths. Those who do achieve positions of power and wealth become patronesses of their religious establishments, endowing religious institutions, supporting the construction of religious edifices, and patronizing sacred arts and artifacts. Regardless of the lower status to which they are assigned, millions of women have found spiritual gratification in the major established religions of the world. Further, they have found the rewards of sisterhood through these religions, gathering together in mutual support and for the purpose of nurturing their own religious communities, as well as in support of charity, social services, and social reform.

Origin Myths

Most religions provide a creation myth, which tells of what are thought to be the first humans and how they came to be. The creation myth to which Jews, Christians, and Muslims subscribe, the story of Adam and Eve, is much more, of course, than a tale of the first humans. Like other people's creation myths, it provides a "charter" and a "plan" for relations between people and the supernatural, between women and men, and between humans and nature. We have already discussed some of the implications for women of the Adam and Eve myth in Chapter 1. A myth that tells of the descent of the Iroquois nation from females was recorded by Father Louis Hennepin, a missionary working in New France (Quebec, 1679–80; see Box 9.2).

Females in the Supernatural World

Most forms of religious belief include some conceptualization of a supernatural world that is inhabited by forces with superhuman qualities. These saints, ghosts, and spirits of various sorts are often considered more approachable and more interested in "ordinary" people than the great deities. Although the formal traditions of Judaism, Christianity, and Islam are *monotheistic* (believing in a single divinity), their "folk" or "popular" versions have always included belief in lesser supernatural forces.

Immortal Women: Souls, Saints, and Ghosts. The question of what happens to the soul after death is a critical one. Many people believe that the soul persists, to occupy a place in the supernatural world or to return to life in another body. The latter, called *reincarnation*, as represented in Hinduism and Buddhism, involves belief in a scale of perfection that an individual can ascend or descend, through successive lifetimes, depending on how virtuously each life was lived. Individuals are destined to be reborn again and again, to endure the pain of existence, until they reach the pinnacle of perfection, after which they are released. In Hinduism and in some, but not all, Buddhist traditions, the most virtuous life is one

Box 9.1   PHILLIS WHEATLEY: THOUGHTS ON THE WORKS OF PROVIDENCE

Phillis Wheatley (1753–84) was brought from Senegal to Boston at about the age of 7. After a period of slavery her owners, John and Susanna Wheatley, freed her. She was intensely religious. Her poems were published in England in 1773.

Arise, my soul, on wings enraptur'd, rise
To praise the monarch of the earth and skies . . .

Creation smiles in various beauty gay,
While day to night, and night succeeds to day:
That *Wisdom*, which attends *Jehovah's* ways,
Shines most conspicuous in the solar rays:
Without them, destitute of heat and light,
This world would be the reign of endless night:
In their excess how would our race complain,
Abhorring life! how hate its length'ned chain!
From air adust what num'rous ills would rise?
What dire contagion taint the burning skies?
What pestilential vapours, fraught with death,
Would rise, and overspread the lands beneath?

Hail, smiling morn, that from the orient main
Ascending dost adorn the heav'nly plain!
So rich, so various are thy beauteous dies,
That spread through all the circuit of the skies,
That, full of thee, my soul in rapture soars,
And thy great God, the cause of all adores. . . .

Infinite *Love* where'er we turn our eyes
Appears: this ev'ry creature's wants supplies;
This most is heard in *Nature's* constant voice,
This makes the morn, and this the eve rejoice;
This bids the fost'ring rains and dews descend
To nourish all, to serve one gen'ral end,
The good of man: yet man ungrateful pays
But little homage, and but little praise.
To him, whose works array'd with mercy shine,
What songs should rise, how constant, how divine!

Source: From Shields, John C., editor, *The Collected Works of Phillis Wheatley*, pp. 43–50. The Schomburg Library of Nineteenth-Century Black Women Writers, Henry Louis Gates, Jr., editor. New York: Oxford University Press, 1988.

Box 9.2   THE VARIED CREATION STORIES OF NATIVE AMERICANS

The Cherokee say they came from Corn Mother, or Selu, who cut open her breast so that corn could spring forth, giving life to the people. For the Tewa Pueblo people, the first mothers were known as Blue Corn Woman, the summer mother, and White Corn Maiden, the winter mother. The Iroquois believe that they were born into this world from the mud on the back of the Earth, known as Grandmother Turtle. The essentials of life—corn, beans, and squash—were given to them by the Three Sisters. The Iroquois refer to the Three Sisters when giving thanks for food in everyday prayers. The Apache believe that they are descendants of Child of the Water, who was kept safe by his mother, White-Painted Woman, so that he could slay all the monsters and make the world safe for the Apache people. . . . For the Sioux, White Buffalo Calf Woman gave the people the gift of the Pipe, and thus a gift of Truth.

[According to the Western Apache creation myth] There was a time when White Painted Woman lived all alone. . . .

  Longing for children, she slept with the Sun and not long after gave birth to Slayer of Monsters, the foremost culture hero. Four days later, White Painted Woman became pregnant by water and gave birth to Born-of-the-Water (also known as Child-of-the-Water). As Slayer of Monsters and Child-of-the-Water matured, White Painted Woman instructed them on how to live. Then they left home and, following her advice, rid the earth of most of its evil. White Painted Woman never became old. When she reached an advanced age, she walked toward the east. After a while, she saw herself coming toward herself. When she came together, there was only one, the young one. Then she was like a young girl all over again.

Sources: Cherokee story from Rayna Green, *Women in American Indian Society*, p. 21. © 1992 by Chelsea House Publishers, a subsidiary of Haights Cross Communications. Apache story from Thomas E. Mails, *The People Called Apache*, Englewod Cliffs, NJ: Prentice Hall, 1974:76.

---

devoted to study, meditation, and unconcern about worldly things (like marriage, children, wealth, and comfort, even eating and sleeping). However, women are very unlikely to have the opportunity to pursue a life of study and meditation in Hindu and Buddhist societies. In Hindu mythology, women came to symbolize the eternal struggle that men must wage between materiality and spirit. Kali (the goddess) symbolizes the womb, connected with rebirth and consequent illusion and entanglement in the world (Caldwell, 2000).

Christianity and Islam teach direct individual immortality, with the soul experiencing punishment or reward in accordance with the virtues and vices of a single lifetime. These religions strongly espouse the idea that souls are essentially without sex and that salvation is open to both women and men. Some souls, because of unusual virtue, become saints. They continue to provide blessings for the living who appeal to them. Fiorenza (1979:140) argues that "the lives of the saints provide a variety of role models for Christian women. What is more important is that they teach that women, like men, have to follow their vocation from God even if this means that they have to go frontally against the ingrained cultural mores and images of women."

Many religions believe in the existence of ghosts as opposed to immortal souls. A ghost is someone whose spirit outlasts the physical body for some period. Ghosts are thought to be capable of beneficence, particularly as protectors of their survivors in the family. However, if maltreated or forgotten, they are also believed to be capable of vengeance. Bad luck, sickness, nightmares, and even psychic persecution are often blamed on ghosts. Ghosts differ from saints in that they are interested in their own families and require appeasement and respect, not veneration (Harrell, 1986).

The family is usually regarded as the proper channel for the satisfaction and control of the dead. This is true of ancestors as well as ghosts. In most ancestor-worshiping societies, however, women do not fare very well in receiving the worship of descendants. In such societies, the significant ancestors usually are male and require male descendants for their worship. The male ancestors of wives are not worshiped by husbands and sons. In the ancestor cults of China, only the mothers of sons are included on the family altars of husbands (Jordan, 1999). In many modern cults, the spirits of women are considered weaker than those of men and not entitled to worship as ancestors (Lewis, 1971).

Despite, or perhaps because of, the poor position of women as ancestors, they figure extensively as ghosts. For example, in a study of a Taiwanese village, a high proportion of the ghosts that were thought to regularly disturb the villagers were divined to be the spirits of women demanding a place on a family altar. These spirits were generally women who had died before being received into a husband's family or whose marital histories featured some irregularity that left them stranded between family altars (Jordan, 1999).

Goddesses. Many people believe that the supernatural world consists of elevated regions inhabited by deities of wider sway than spirits, saints, and ghosts. This cosmos is generally perceived to be inhabited by a number of divine persons paired and grouped in relationships not unlike those found on earth. The Hindu Shiva and Devi, for example, are regarded as the primeval twofold personification of the Absolute.

The goddess, like the unfettered woman of male fantasies, is often envisaged as a threatening and terrible being. This is the case with the Inuit goddess Sedna. In Hindu mythology, the goddess is dark Kali (see Chapter 1), whose orgiastic dancing brings death and destruction on the world. However, when she submits to her husband, Shiva, the goddess becomes beneficent and her energy is harnessed for good by the rational principle of maleness. In the countryside, peasants in the nineteenth century prayed to Kali alone as the good mother:

> Though the mother beats the child . . . the child cries mother, mother, and clings still tighter to her garment. True I cannot see thee, yet I am not a lost child. I still cry mother, mother. All the miseries that I have suffered and I am suffering, I know, O mother, to be your mercy alone. (Eliot, 1962:287–8)

Tamed and controlled, a goddess may become a great and well-loved figure, worthy of the worship of men as well as women.

Buddhism has sometimes been called an atheistic religion because in its most sophisticated vision of the cosmos all personality and individual attributes are wholly dissolved into divine unity, *nirvana* (the state of enlightenment or supreme bliss). However, the religion provides a focus for worshipers in figures of *bodhisattvas*, personages whose perfection has freed them from mortal life but who choose to remain in a personalized existence in order to be accessible to the appeals of the struggling faithful. The greatest and most popular of all is Avalokitesvara, the bodhisattva of compassion, who appears as a goddess in one manifestation. Avalokitesvara originated in

India but is worshiped in Tibet as Chenresig, in China as Gaun Yin, in Japan as Kannon, and by other names throughout Asia. Guanyin is the very quintessence of the compassion of the Buddha. Pregnant women turn to her for help, and she cooperates with mediums seeking communication with ancestors or ghosts.

In the great polytheistic religions of later antiquity, goddesses appear with a variety of powers and attributes. They are patronesses of cities (Athena), marriage (Hera), and sex (Aphrodite). They are in charge of agriculture (Demeter) and human fertility (Artemis). Isis was an amalgam of female deities of the Mediterranean world, gathering their attributes, powers, and myths into her own cult. She also controlled powers usually attributed to male divinities. She began as a local Egyptian goddess associated with the cult of Osiris, who was both her brother and husband. By Hellenistic times, when the Greeks ruled Egypt, her cult was one of the most popular in the ancient world, promising immortality to its adherents. Women were active participants in the cult of Isis as priestesses, members of religious societies, and donors. However, male participants far outnumbered females, and the chief priesthoods were held by men (Pomeroy, 1975).

In the sixth century B.C.E., Jews returning to the Holy Land from their exile in Babylon enforced their belief in one male divinity, outlawing the worship of all other gods and goddesses. When European pagans became Christians, they turned their backs on the gods and goddesses of the Greek and Roman worlds, reducing them to hollow idols. Some second-century Christians favored endowing the Holy Ghost with a feminine persona; this impulse was rejected by the dominant faction, and all three persons of the Christian Trinity became male or without gender. In the seventh century, Muslims in their turn rejected the goddesses of their ancient Arabian tribes in favor of the one (male) god.

For most ordinary worshipers, however, monotheistic religions have not entirely excluded the older idea of a female deity. For example, Christians exalted the memory and attributes of Mary, "mother of God (Jesus)," in direct proportion as God himself became increasingly patriarchal (Fiorenza, 1979, 1983). In many respects, Mary seems hardly distinguishable from the great goddesses of the ancient world whom she supplanted. A stranger unacquainted with the formal theology of Catholicism would not hesitate to advance the idea that the great cathedrals and shrines were devoted to the worship of a great goddess (Mâle, 1949).

The Gender of God

Some feminists feel that the social position of women can be enhanced by the worship of a goddess and that belief in a female deity would give religion more usefulness and meaning. This position has been taken by such leading theologians and feminists as Mary Daly (1973), Carol Christ (1979, 1987), and Naomi Goldenberg (1979). They believe that the image of the deity we worship is important to our understanding and appreciation of ourselves. In patriarchal religions, divinity is male; hence, men see an image of themselves in the divine, while women are denied this identification with divinity.

Mythologists have sometimes argued that the rule of a great goddess in the early periods of human civilization was reflected on earth by a matriarchy (see Stone, 1979). In periods for which we have historical documentation, cults and sects that accorded the deity a female nature, in part or in whole, accorded women an active position in religious practices. The six Vestal Virgins who were devoted to the cult of Vesta in ancient Rome

Box 9.3 **INVOCATION TO THE GODDESS**

Queen of the night
Queen of the moon
Queen of the stars
Queen of the horns
Queen of the earth
Bring to us the child of light.

Night sky rider
Silver shining one
Lady of wild things
Silver wheel
North star
Circle
Crescent
Moon-bright
Singer
Changer!
Teach us!

See with our eyes
Hear with our ears
Breathe with our nostrils
Kiss with our lips,
Touch with our hands,
Be here now!

Source: From *Changing of the Gods: Feminism and the End of Traditional Religions* by Naomi Goldenberg. Copyright © 1979 by Naomi Goldenberg. Reprinted by permission of Beacon Press.

were respected and provided with special honors by their social peers, but they were subject to the authority of the *pontifex maximus* (chief priest). Although the few women selected to serve as priestesses for such cults might have enjoyed a higher status than secular women, it has not been possible to establish any necessary correlation between the worship of goddesses and the status of women in ancient societies (Pomeroy, 1984). Nevertheless, the presence of a goddess or quasi-goddess in a religious system has the psychological value of providing women with a role model and an object for supplication. On the other hand, such figures can be employed as models to confine the ambitions of women.

Some gods are thought to incite enthusiastic female worship and appear to prefer female devotees. Dionysus, Krishna, and Jesus have all been particularly venerated by women. Dionysus liberated some of the frustrated and confined women of ancient Greece periodically with ecstatic experiences of dancing and frenzied activity. Krishna, who is often represented as a baby, is associated with a sect of female worshipers who call themselves "mothers of God" (Freeman, 1980). As young men, all three gods are represented as

Box 9.4   THE PRAISES OF ISIS

Isis announces her divine powers and titles in this second-century Greek document found in Asia Minor. This document is a copy of a text from Memphis, Egypt.

Demetrios, the son of Artemidoros, who is also (called) Thraseas, a Magnesian / from (Magnesia on the) Maeander, an offering in fulfillment of a vow to Isis. / He transcribed the following from the stele in Memphis which / stands by the temple of Hephaistos: I am Isis, / the tyrant of every land; and I was educated by / Hermes, and together with Hermes I invented letters, both the hieroglyphic I and the demotic, in order that the same script should not be used/ to write everything. I imposed laws on men, / and the laws which I laid down no one may change. / I am the eldest daughter of Kronos. I am the wife and sister of King Osiris. I am she who discovered (the cultivation of) grain / for men. I am the mother of King Horos. / I am she who rises in the Dog Star. I / am she who is called goddess by women. By me the city of Bubastis / was built. I separated earth from sky. / I designated the paths of the stars. The sun and the moon's / course I laid out. I invented navigation./ I caused the just to be strong. Woman and man I / brought together. For woman I determined that in the tenth month she shall deliver a baby into / the light. I ordained that parents be cherished by their children. / For parents who are cruelly treated / I imposed retribution. / Together with (my) brother Osiris I stopped cannibalism. I revealed initiations to men. / I taught (men) to honor the images of the gods. I / established precincts for the gods. The governments of tyrants / I suppressed. I stopped murders. I / compelled women to be loved by men. I / caused the just to be stronger than gold and silver. / I ordained that the true be considered beautiful. / I invented marriage contracts. Languages / I assigned to Greeks and barbarians. I caused the honorable and the shameful / to be distinguished by Nature. I / caused nothing to be more fearful than an oath. He who unjustly / plotted against others I gave into the hands of his victim. On those who commit unjust acts / I imposed retribution. I ordained that suppliants be pitied. / I honor those who justly defend themselves. / With me the just prevails. Of rivers and winds / and the sea am I mistress. No one becomes famous / without my knowledge. I am the mistress of war. Of the thunderbolt am I mistress. I calm and stir up the sea. / I am in the rays of the sun. I sit beside the / course of the sun. Whatever I decide, this also is accomplished. / For me everything is right. I free those who are in bonds. I / am the mistress of sailing. The navigable I make unnavigable whenever I choose. I established the boundaries of cities. / I am she who is called Thesmophoros. The island from the depths I brought up into the light. I / conquer Fate. Fate heeds me. / Hail Egypt who reared me.

attractive and loving of women, posing in their lives as protectors. They continue to attract the warm affection of women in their apotheosized state.

The position of goddesses in polytheistic societies varies widely, as did the position of women in ancient Egypt, Athens, and Rome.

Similarly, there is such wide variation in the position of women in monotheistic societies that it becomes difficult to generalize about the influence of women's roles on beliefs about the gender of God and vice versa. Not everyone is convinced, then, that a female deity is needed to improve the status and position of women in society or that belief in such a deity would support that goal. While some argue that it is necessary to recognize both "masculine" and "feminine" attributes in the objects of our worship, this is not sufficient to address the social injustice of sexism.

Religion and Social Controls

Religion provides more than the imagery by which we can conceptualize the supernatural world. It provides a basis for a code of ethics to govern human conduct. In highly organized religions, clergy and other specialists interpret and sometimes enforce a code of ethics grounded in religious belief. However, all religious systems have some means for exerting control over human conduct.

Religion and the Family

Laws concerning family matters, particularly marriage, childrearing, and sexual relations, nearly always refer to religious beliefs. In most large-scale societies, such laws have supported patriarchal structures. As an accommodation to multiculturalism, some nations today even bow to the more conservative rights of religious minorities to adhere to "tradition" (usually to the detriment of women's rights), while others override these group rights to protect women (Foblets, 1999, see Howland, 1999, for many international examples of family law and religion).

Life-Cycle Rituals. As we have already seen, the family provides the framework within which women are confined and socialized. Public performance of rituals during the life cycle—for example, at puberty, marriage, and death—enhances the power of the family, the relationships considered proper for its members, and the control of those individuals in accordance with the decorum of the commu-

nity. In traditional Greek society from antiquity to the present, death rituals have been almost entirely the responsibility of women (Danforth, 1982). For men, life-cycle rituals are usually occasions that help to define and enhance their potency and social power as they advance toward full adult membership in the community. The major life-cycle rituals for Jewish males, for example, are the *brith millah*, the circumcision ritual of 8-day-old infant boys, which provides them with a physical identity as Jews, and the *bar mitzvah*, the ritual of first participation in adult study and prayer, which marks the entry of a 13-year-old boy into the community of adults. For infant girls, there is no equivalent of the briss, but for Conservative and Reform Jews, there is a girls' equivalent to the bar mitzvah, the *bat mitzvah*. Unlike the bar mitzvah, the bat mitzvah is not essential to girls' membership in the Jewish community, nor does it mark their "coming of age" in the traditional sense.

In patriarchal, patrilineal societies, the most important life-cycle ritual or rite of passage for women is likely to be the wedding ceremony. This marks the major transition from the family of birth to the husband's family. Since divorce may be difficult or even impossible for women in such societies, they are likely to undergo this ceremony only once. It may last for days, preceded by months of preparation and preliminary rituals. In Western societies, weddings have traditionally spotlighted the bride. Neither menarche nor childbirth (unless it is the birth of a royal son and heir) is accompanied by equivalent attention.

This is not the case in some matrilineal societies. Marriage does not substantially alter women's social position since women remain in their own matrilineage for life. If there is a major life-cycle ritual, it is likely to be associated with menarche, when women become of reproductive age, ready to contribute new members to the matrilineage. A good example is the *chisungu* ceremony of the matrilineal Bemba, a large and complex society in Zambia (Richards, 1956). Periodically, all the girls of a district whose first menstruation has occurred since the last *chisungu* participate in the month-long ceremony. The initiates are honored by the whole community; the women sing and dance before these girls, and parents, fiancés, and prospective in-laws contribute to the expenses of the ceremonial feasting.

During the complex ceremony of initiation, Bemba girls pass through several role changes, beginning with separation and seclusion, physical degradation (such as being prohibited from bathing), and testing for strength and courage. The ritual ends with reentry and renewal. After initiation, Bemba girls are prepared for marriage and reproduction, related to other women in a new and more intimate way, and newly knowledgeable about the role requirements of women.

Female circumcision (removal of the clitoris and/or labia minora) is prevalent in East Africa, particularly in the Muslim nations of Sudan and Egypt and in Christian Ethiopia. It is also found in West Africa. Feminists within these countries as well as elsewhere have condemned this genital mutilation of women as an odious and oppressive custom. Unlike the circumcision of boys, it is not dignified with religious prescription. Instead of being a mark of honor, it is intended to keep women from becoming sexually active before marriage and from enjoying their sexuality when married. African American novelist Alice Walker has explored this issue in her novel *Possessing the Secret of Joy* (1992), including the complicity of older women who perform the cutting.

Feminist critics of Western religious systems have favored the establishment of a meaningful life-cycle ritual for women in connection with menarche. Theologian Penelope Washbourne (1979) believes that such a ritual would help young women deal with ambivalent feelings about menstruation and achieve their new adult identities.

Sexual Controls. At puberty in most cultures, the freedom girls might have enjoyed when they were little is sharply curtailed. Adolescent girls may be told that they are unclean and must learn to control the possible ill effects of their "polluted nature." At the same time, they may be schooled in the hard facts of their vulnerability, to both public censure and physical attack. The leaders of every major literate religion in the world have produced literature against the sexuality of women. Representatives of the major religious hierarchies have continually urged women to contain themselves within the narrow limits of their homes and the narrower limits of female modesty and decorum, threatening them with both earthly and eternal punishments for the sins of their "nature."

The most effective method of controlling the dangers represented by women's sexuality is to ensure that they are kept under the authority of their male kin. At puberty, men are proclaimed mature and ready to undertake public responsibilities. Some societies begin a process of weakening the control of the father over his son at this point, to free the son for service in the greater community. Women, however, are not released from their fathers' power; rather, fathers (or other male kin) are given the right to hand them over to the power of a husband. This right to "give" a daughter in marriage has been, until recently, the sovereign right of a woman's male kin. Even in Christian societies that defended the individual's right of consent to marriage, the economic dependence of daughters usually made them subject to paternal authority.

Religious laws in patriarchal societies often protect men from the "dangers" of pollution inherent in close proximity to women during their menstrual periods. In the Koran, the sacred book of Islam, men are ordered to separate themselves from their wives until the women have taken the ritual bath at the end of the menstrual period (Delaney et al., 1976). The same religious proscription on sexual relations between husband and wife applies to Orthodox Jews. Some feminists argue that such laws reinforce women's own fears about menstruation and undermine their self-esteem by labeling them as periodically "unclean." However, some adherents to these religions feel quite differently about them. These women feel that the ritual bath enhances their self-

regard, the sanctity of their marriages, and even the warmth of their relationships with their husbands.

The codes of most religions urge husbands to use their authority prudently. They warn of the damage that may be caused to a family by the despair of unhappy women. They remind men of the blessings of a home cared for by a contented wife. However, while men are subjected to moral suasion, women are subjected to physical coercion. The Koran instructs husbands on how to ensure the right behavior in their wives: "Say to the believers, that they cast down their eyes and guard their private parts; that is purer for them" (XXIV:30; see Arberry, 1955). Nearly

---

Box 9.5   THE RITUAL BATH: POSITIVE AND NEGATIVE

Rachel's experience [with the Jewish observance of mikveh, the ritual bath taken after menstruation] has been one of relative ease. Still even for Rachel, a New York City professional in her 40's, mikveh has always been a "mixed bag. . . .

Rachel says "I don't resent having to go." She finds something powerful about total immersion in water, a substance connected to the flood of Jewish history and the miracle of the parting sea.

When she emerges from her seventh dunk, she recites personal prayers. Concerning the label, "impure," which defines women during niddah, Rachel says: "I really don't think about it at all. It's not on my radar screen."

When Rachel was younger, in child-bearing mode, she says, "every menstrual cycle became a missed opportunity for life as opposed to seeing myself as impure."

Asked if the observance strengthens her marriage, Rachel closes her eyes to the din of the Upper West Side Starbucks. She thinks.

"Yes, I do," she answers. "There is an element of longing. I liken it to a business trip. When I'm away I miss my husband."

During the days of niddah, before Rachel goes to the mikveh, when physical intimacy with her husband isn't possible, she senses a different dynamic in her marriage. "It makes it easier to talk because you know that's all you are going to do."

[On the negative side], she complains of the long wait at her local mikveh. . . . Often Rachel spends three hours there.

"Even if you have a miraculous experience, even if the spiritual mikveh lady is there, you leave praying your husband hasn't fallen asleep. What kind of date is that?"

Source: ©Elicia Brown. By Permission. Excerpted from Immersed in a dilemma, *The Jewish Week* Nov. 14, 2003, p. 62.

every written religious code is based on double-standard morality. Christianity, whose rhetoric consistently states that what is not allowed to women is not allowed to men either, has never made wide practical application of the rule.

Control over women's sexuality and reproduction is a high priority for what are called "fundamentalist" groups (Brown, 1994). Fundamentalist controls on women are often associated with assertions of nationalist or ethnic identity. Women represent holy motherhood, their virtue reflecting the purity of the group and their subservience, the source of strength and dignity of men.

Protection of Women

Religious laws generally offer some protection to the obedient weakling. While they justify authority and preach obedience, they also restrain human authority in the name of a higher power and teach the limits on an insubordinate will.

In this spirit, Jewish, Christian, and Islamic laws are concerned with the economic responsibilities of men toward their wives and daughters. The rights of women to dowries, inheritance, and other economic protections are spelled out carefully. Arbitrary divorce is discouraged, and polygyny is regulated to ensure the rights of co-wives. Catholic canon law sanctifies the consensual basis of marriage and protects wives from repudiation by husbands. It defines rape as a crime of violence against women and denies men the right to kill their wives. All the "peoples of the Book" are urged to protect and support widows and orphans and to treat moral and observant women with respect and kindness. A major attraction of evangelistic religions is their requirement of men that they assume the responsibilities of marriage and parenthood (Toulis, 1997).

Within that framework, religion acts to establish and enforce the norms of family life.

Sexual relationships between wife and husband resulting in the birth of children are universally viewed as divinely ordained. Deviation from that pattern is sometimes considered immoral and sometimes violently punished. While many religious constraints on women were rationalized as being for their protection, this notion has been challenged by feminist critics and sometimes rethought.

An Algerian Muslim scholar's analysis has concluded that the function of the veil at the time of Muhammad was to protect women, and thus the veil's most appropriate modern equivalent is education and schooling that in our times gives the most protection to a woman. (Helie-Lucas, 1999:24)

Beyond the Family

Outside the religious activities of the family, most societies engage in a wider set of ceremonies, celebrations, and rituals devoted to the deities worshiped in the community. These require the services of a professional and trained clergy who enjoy the accoutrements of public art and architecture, conduct time-consuming and often occult rituals (sometimes in a language unknown to the laity), and make use of an extensive tradition of myth and law to enforce their social authority.

Women as Worshipers. Nearly all religions encourage, indeed command, the active participation of women as worshipers. Even as worshipers, though, women are subjected to a variety of restrictions. Lay participation in the performance of rituals is often restricted to men.

Except in Orthodox Judaism, Jewish women are nowadays counted in the *minyan*, the quorum of ten required for the conduct of certain services. In the past, there were no female altar servers in Roman Catholic churches. Yet, any traveler in a Catholic country must be struck by the idea of the church as "woman's space." It may be dominated by an all-male hierarchy, but every day the women spend hours there in devotion and conversation with one another. From earliest times, Christian moralists complained about women's habit of using the church as a social center. Similarly, the shrines of Sufi saints are centers where Islamic women meet daily for rest and relaxation and to confide in the sympathetic saint (Fernea and Fernea, 1972). Underneath the restrictive and apparently prohibitive structure of the great religions is the elusive, often undocumented world of women.

Syncretistic and Evangelistic Religions. On the fringes of the "established religions" are hosts of syncretistic religions, each of which combines elements from a variety of others. They flourish today, as they have throughout history. For the sake of simplicity, we shall restrict our discussion to a small sample of groups. However, the findings of historians and anthropologists bear ample witness to the presence of similar "popular" religions throughout the world.

Many syncretistic religions have spun off from Catholicism. Santería, practiced throughout the United States and the Caribbean, as well as Candomblé, found in Brazil, have both African and Catholic roots. The black leaders of the ancestor religions of the Caribbean see no contradiction between their beliefs and Catholicism. Indeed, they maintain that the one is not possible without the other (Simpson, 1978). Women play important roles of leadership in Santería and Candomblé, outnumber men four to one in these religions, and are the principal dancers in the Shango and Big Drum sects. Similarly, the women of Haiti dominate the popular religions such as Vodun.

In North America, where the dominant form of Christianity has generally been Protestant, Mambo and other African cults have been syncretized to particular sects,

principally variants of Baptism (Simpson, 1978). In these groups, women often emerge as preachers and leaders. Women are also prominent among the Quakers and other nonhierarchical dissenting sects. Women assume much more important places in both leadership and participation in dissenting and popular religions than in established ones, whether or not they see themselves as opponents to established authority. In the United States, women comprise 75%–90% of the participants in the activities of black churches. In some denominations of the Sanctified Church, women are equal to men. In the Pentecostal Assemblies of the World, women may offer communion and perform marriages. Even in the denominations that prohibit the ordination of women, they exercise a powerful influence through women's departments. Women's economic contribution and roles in education and community work are essential to the survival of these churches, and women's expression of spirituality is likewise central to their theology.

Pentecostalism provides a major source of identity for African Caribbean women (mostly of Jamaican origin) in Britain. Attendance at black Pentecostal churches is double the national rate, and the great majority of church members are women. Through religion, these worshipers in a discriminatory and hostile social environment redefine their world and themselves in ways consistent with their own experience and aspirations. While men dominate their church officially, it is said that "man is the head, but woman is the neck." Women support and guide; without them, there is no church (Toulis, 1997:225). This is just one of the many examples of the way that evangelistic movements serve immigrant minority groups, but it is typical.

Women and Religious Movements. Religion often becomes a vehicle for social change. In some cases, this involves the formation of a new or the joining of an existing religious movement.

Today, unlike in the past, such movements are not necessarily labeled "heretical" and might not risk their members' lives and freedom, but they are often called by pejorative terms, like *cults*, and feared by mainstream religious groups and secular people alike. Religious movements, whether conservative or not, tend to protest and challenge contemporary social conditions, critiquing family and society as well as established religious institutions (Puttick, 1997:3; Palmer, 1994).

Some such movements, known as "new religious movements," offer women the means to escape traditional family and community constraints and provide alternatives to these structures. In the West, new religious movements are often inspired by Eastern religions, while in the East, sometimes (but not always) they are inspired by Western ones. Others, more conservative or even reactionary in character, called "fundamentalist" or some other label by critics, seek to establish or reestablish traditional structures and roles, placing women in subordinate positions and confining them to the roles of homemaker, wife, and mother. Generally, these latter identify themselves with mainstream religions such as Christianity or Islam yet criticize them for their liberalism and acceptance of "modernism"; they often ally themselves with right-wing political groups. In these, women may well be very prominent, even though the beliefs of the group may relegate women to secondary status and bar them from public roles. While both ends of the spectrum are enormously diverse in their beliefs and practices, what is important to recognize is that they are an expression of dissatisfaction with the status quo and an attempt to repair its ills (and the malaise of their adherents) through religion.

Fundamentalism and Women's Human Rights. It is hard to read a newspaper without coming across a reference to "fundamentalists" in some part of the world. Though originally a term certain

U.S. conservative Christian reformers applied to themselves (Hawley, 1994), it has now come to be applied to other religious movements. These consist of groups who challenge (sometimes violently) the authority of governments, oppose specific laws or reforms, or impose ideas derived from their interpretations of established religions on others who do not share their beliefs. Almost invariably, those called "fundamentalists" oppose liberalization of women's rights in all areas, including education, control of their bodies (reproduction), and participation in public life by having jobs and holding political office. Generally, these groups teach the subordination of women to men in the family and in the public arena, whether church or other areas of social life.

The issue of human rights, specifically women's human rights, lies at the center of the debate about fundamentalist religious movements (Howland, 1999). On the one hand, it seems obvious that certain international agreements concerning the rights of all people to a basic education, control over their bodies, freedom to choose a mate or a job or a form of religious expression are violated by a denial of these rights to women. Thus, the Taliban regime of Afghanistan's denial of women's right to education in the name of Islamic law exemplifies a violation of their human rights by an Islamic state. On the other hand, multiculturalism and respect for religious diversity would argue for tolerance of religious practices which differ from one's own and especially from those of the majority. A number of multicultural nations do in fact have judicial procedures and legal accommodation to the religious beliefs and practices of minority groups. In an effort to respect diversity of religious expression, some liberals defend the rights of the minority to practice their own interpretations of religious beliefs which might violate the norms of the majority, including many which appear to discriminate against women, such as in divorce law. In several European nations, such as Belgium, courts permit divorce according to the laws of the home nation of immigrants (Foblets, 1999); in India, accommodation of the Muslim minority has recently included imposition of divorce settlements far less favorable to wives than is the case for the Hindu majority (Hawley, 1999; Awn, 1994).

Women as Religious Leaders

Only rarely do women enjoy the authority of clergy, and when they do, their range of activities is usually restricted. The most highly organized religions welcome women clergy the least. Thus, in Catholicism, the clergy has been restricted to not only men but celibate men since the eleventh century. Eastern Christianity (the Greek and Russian Orthodox churches) allows women to marry priests but not to be ordained. Only very recently have a number of women been ordained in some of the larger, institutionalized Protestant churches.

Women tend to emerge as ministers in sects that do not control their clergy and that depend on genuine spontaneous religious emotion, as opposed to a weighty establishment supported by endowments and state cooperation. Thus, the loosely organized pentecostal or evangelical sects are frequently ministered by women.

Women have customarily been kept from the rabbinate. Since Jewish girls are not required by religious law to study the Scriptures and sacred texts as boys are, it has only been the exceptional Jewish woman who has qualified, in the past, for the specialized learning of the rabbi. However, Judaism, like Protestant Christianity, lacks a single central hierarchy, so it allows for a proliferation of congregations of varying opinions on matters of administration and discipline. In Conservative and Reform Judaism, the predominant forms in the United States, female rabbis are now ordained. Islam, like Judaism, has no formal clergy and no "church" hierarchy. Professional mullahs and ayatollahs in the Shiite branch along with other teachers and prayer leaders serve many of the functions of clergy, such as officiating at marriage and funeral rites and interpreting customary law. Women are not numbered among these revered individuals. The conventions of *purdah* (segregation of women) and veiling severely restrict Muslim women from participating in services and prayers with men, not to mention leading them. These same conventions have in some places given rise to a class of female mullahs whose job is to minister to women, to teach the rudiments of the Koran, and to conduct rituals with women at home.

Healers

In folk traditions around the world, both in the countryside and in the cities, women have served their communities as healers and midwives. These traditional arts are generally thought to have a supernatural or spiritual component as well as a practical one. Both illness and childbirth are widely viewed as spiritually dangerous states. Curers, sometimes termed "shamans," are active in societies where it is believed that illness—or certain types of illness—is caused by supernatural agency. Both curers and midwives are thought to have esoteric knowledge about how to fend off or appease threatening supernatural beings. Traditional curers of this sort need not be exclusively female but often are, and midwifery almost everywhere is a women's profession.

To cure an illness, the healer often enters a trance state, during which she (or he) communicates with the spirit world for assistance in the restoration of health. The curer, the midwife, and the medium (who puts her clients in touch with departed souls) have a nurturing, supportive relationship to clients, unlike the

The Reverend Pauli Murray (1910–85), the first African American woman to be ordained an Episcopal priest, January 8, 1977.

often depersonalized and authoritarian relationships that male physicians and priests tend to have with those who come to them for help. Yet curers, midwives, and mediums can be professionals too, often devoting years of training to such careers (Hoch-Smith and Spring, 1978). As a result, curers can become powerful individuals in their communities who possess greater economic and social independence (Bacigalupo, 1996:89).

Among Native Americans, women healers perform cures, lead hunting ceremonies, and

The Reverend Ellen Barrett, the first declared lesbian to be ordained an Episcopal priest, January 10, 1977.

create artifacts, such as baskets, ornaments, and talismans. They officiate at burials, births, child namings, and menstrual and pregnancy rituals. The healers perform these rites through dancing and chanting, as well as songs they sing and stories they tell. Native American women writers reflect in fiction and poetry the woman healer's connection to the spirit world (Allen, 1988). One such work is the novel *The Woman Who Owned the Shadows* by Paula Gunn Allen (1983), and another is *Ceremony* by Leslie Marmon Silko (1977).

Women play these spiritual roles in vastly different sorts of society, from South Africa to north Florida, from Southeast Asia to Latin America. Some feminist authors have deplored the loss of these roles among the middle-class and wealthy women of the Western world as the healing professions have been gradually taken over by men (Ehrenreich and English, 1979). Herbalists, midwives, and other sorts

of female healer have often been classed with fraudulent mediums by professional clergy and professional male healers, whose reasons for doing so may involve a defense of their professional (and male) monopoly.

Missionaries and Martyrs. The great religions of the world, distinguished by monumental places of worship, professional clergy, written literature, and a large following, reflect the institutionalized worlds of men. However, the great religions started as popular religions, often as sects of rebels against a greater system, as the Christians within the Roman Empire or the Buddhists in India. All have known periods of danger and persecution; all have entered into periods of struggle to win recognition for themselves. During these times, women often played significant roles.

Where the role of a missionary is dangerous and the reward often death, women have

Rabbi Sally Priesand, the first woman to be ordained a rabbi, June 2, 1972.

found favorable conditions for the expression of their zeal and spirit of adventure. Women were welcomed into the original Buddhist fellowships for their missionary contributions but later restricted as the religion became established and more secure (Carmody, 1979).

Women have enjoyed a long and honorable history in Christian missions. The Samaritan woman Jesus sent to spread news of his coming among her people might be called the first of all Christian missionaries (McNamara, 1996). In the conversion of Europe, Christian queens opened the way for priests and monks by marrying pagan kings and converting them; the most famous of these was Clotilda, wife of Clovis, king of the Franks at the beginning of the sixth century C.E. (McNamara, 1966). Modern Christian missionary women tend to fall under the control and supervision of men: Catholic nuns by supervisory priests and Protestant missionaries by husbands, male relatives, or male mission heads.

Religious Rebels. In the early centuries of Christianity, women were active in heretical movements such as Montanism and Gnosticism. As historian Jo Ann McNamara explains, women's participation in these movements arose from social rather than intellectual motives. Women saw in early Christianity a vehicle for liberation, for activity on a broader scale than was offered by the traditional homebound destiny. Some rebelled against versions of Christianity that imposed restrictions on women (McNamara, 1983).

In the major religious rebellions in Europe in the sixteenth century, Protestant churches freed themselves from the authority of the pope and his orthodox establishment. In the process, women again took an active part as defenders and preachers of both new and old religions. However, Catholics and Protestants alike were alarmed by the apparent assumption on the part of women that the new conditions would offer them a broader field of

Box 9.6   "WITHOUT A HUSBAND I SHALL LIVE HAPPILY"

According to folk tales dating to the early seventeenth century, the Nishan Shaman was a young widow who dutifully took care of her mother-in-law and her domestic duties. But she had a far-reaching reputation for her ability to communicate with the dead and bring them back to life. She had a lover who assisted her in her seances. On one ghostly journey, she met her deceased husband who begged her for resurrection. She refused, saying:

Without a husband
I shall live happily.
Without a man
  I shall live proudly.
  Among mother's relatives
I shall live enjoyably.
  Facing the years
  I shall live cheerfully.
Without children
  I shall live on.
Without a family
  I shall live lovingly.
Pursuing my own youth,
I shall live as a guest.

Source: From The Nishan Shaman caught in cultural contradictions by Stephen Durrant, *Signs* 5, 345–46, 1979. Copyright © 1979, by The University of Chicago Press. Reprinted by permission of the University of Chicago Press.

activity. Both acted to put an end to the threat. Catholic women like Angela Merici (1474–1540) and Mary Ward (1585–1645), who championed a more active public role for nuns, were severely disciplined. Protestant women like Anne Askew (1521–46) were executed for thinking that the priesthood of all believers urged by Luther and his contemporaries included women (Dickens, 1964).

The late medieval period in Europe had also been a time of great social upheaval. From the fifteenth century on, women were perceived to behave in a variety of eccentric and unconventional ways. An example from the early fifteenth century (c. 1412–31) was Joan of Arc, who led troops of French soldiers against the invading English armies. The English burned her at the stake as a heretic

and witch; however, the French supported her memory as a martyr, and she was finally canonized by the Catholic Church (see Box 9.7).

Historians have recently been reinterpreting the great witch hunt in Western Europe in light of the work of anthropologists on witchcraft in other cultures. The accused witches in eastern England, southwestern Germany, and Switzerland, for example, seem to have been the same sort of women accused in Africa and elsewhere outside Europe: old women, deprived of the protection of husbands or sons, living on the risky margins of society. These were the women who irritated and angered neighbors with efforts to gain assistance and ill-tempered cursing of the ungenerous.

Another theory, advanced by Margaret Murray (1967) and made popular recently by

Box 9.7   THE TRIAL OF JOAN OF ARC

Joan of Arc, at the instigation of "voices" sent by God, took up arms against the English occupation of France in 1428. Her military victories against the English began the process of ultimate French victory in the Hundred Years' War (1337–1453). She was captured by the English and tried. Her prosecutors dwelt particularly on her insistence on wearing male clothing:

You have said that, by God's command, you have continually worn man's dress . . . that you have also worn your hair short, cut en rond [a "bowl" cut] above your ears, with nothing left that could show you to be a woman; and that on many occasions you received the Body of our Lord dressed in this fashion, although you have been frequently admonished to leave it off, which you have refused to do, saying that you would rather die than leave it off, save by God's command. And you said further that if you were still so dressed and with the king and those of his party, it would be one of the greatest blessings for the kingdom of France; and you have said that not for anything would you take an oath not to wear this dress or carry arms; and concerning all these matters you have said that you did well, and obediently to God's command.

Source: From W. S. Scott, editor and translator. *Trial of Joan of Arc.* London: Folio Society, 1968:156, © The Folio Society, 1956. Reprinted by permission of the Folio Society.

some modern feminists, is that there really was a witch religion to which large numbers of common people, including Joan of Arc, subscribed. Although much of Murray's evidence has not withstood scholarly scrutiny, we do know that under the apparently monolithic facade of the medieval church, there was a world of popular religion. Wise women devoted to healing and prophesying flourished, not unlike the female curers found in Catholic countries in Latin America today. The popular religion of the Middle Ages was full of vestiges of paganism, rituals, incantations, herbalism, and magic, both beneficial and malevolent. The medieval church systematically dealt with that religion in a successful manner. The harmless and beneficial practices of the country people were "Christianized"; for example, incantations to old goddesses were retained, with the names of Christian saints substituted. The demons of hell were reduced to mischief makers of limited intelligence and minimal power.

Another set of theories associates witchcraft with heresy. In this view, the sixteenth-century belief in demon worshipers and witch churches with covens, sabbaths, "black masses," and other paraphernalia of witchcraft developed as a result of the mentality of the Catholic Inquisition and the fear of women that the Protestant Reformation awoke.

There may indeed have been witch cults. One or two such groups have been uncovered. The women may have been religious visionaries or sexual nonconformists, antisocial rebels of one sort or another. These witches may have been women who had seized upon the illusion of religious and moral freedom that the Reformation seemed to offer, only to learn that the leaders of the new churches were no more welcoming than had been those of the old.

Religious Expression

The Religious Experiences of Women

Today's contemporary feminists argue that established world religions reflect and enhance profoundly sexist values prevailing in the societies in which they are found. They have not

The Penitent Magdalene (c. 1560) by Titian. The painting presents a picture of a beautiful woman, representing Mary Magdalene, depicted in the Christian Bible as a fallen woman redeemed by Jesus. Versions of the biblical story include her as a close companion and disciple of Jesus. She has remained a popular image for Roman Catholicism, and Titian painted at least seven versions of this subject.

only denied women a place in leadership but have promulgated ideas that devalue women in general (see Chapters 1 and 2). Why, then, are women in great numbers the world over devoted members of religions?

Women's personal experiences of religion suggest that they see and feel something beyond and apart from the negative messages that male clergy, ritual, and teaching convey. Women often make aspects of religion that are underplayed by the male hierarchy the essence of their own belief. For example, many Christian women have concentrated on Mary, on Christ as healer and nurturer, or on a loving, benevolent, even maternal God (Bynum, 1982). For Phillis Wheatley (see Box 9.1), Christianity was the inspiration for some of her most lyrical poetry.

While the major religions have produced formal codes, the great masses of their adher-ents have developed their own versions of belief and practice. Catholic women are every-where excluded from the clerical hierarchy of Catholicism. In belief and practice, rural Italian Catholic women may well resemble rural Mexican, Irish, or Peruvian Catholic women more closely than they do the urban Roman priest. In some respects, rural Catholic women may have in common certain religious attitudes and interests with rural Islamic and Hindu sisters that neither shares with the men who dominate their systems of codified knowledge. The popular versions of the reli-gions of the world have often provided a scope for women's activities denied them by the male governing elite in the formalized versions of these religions. For the majority of religious women in the past, this standing appears to have been enough. For a few, as we shall see, it was not; and today numbers of

---

Box 9.8   A MOROCCAN STORY

One day two old ladies decided to invoke the Devil and persuade him to part with some of his magic secrets. So they pretended to quarrel, for it is well known that the devil appears whenever there is a dispute. "I am sure that the Devil must be dead," said one old woman. "And I am sure that he is not; what makes you say such a silly thing?" retorted the other, and they went on arguing furiously. The Devil was very flattered to be the subject of their argument and he decided to make himself visible. "Indeed, I am very much alive—here I am!" he said, appearing before the two old ladies. "How can we be sure that you are really the Devil?" asked one shrewdly. "You must prove it to us by doing something extraordinary. Let's see you squeeze yourself into a sugar bowl," added the other. "Easy!" said the Devil and he slipped into the bowl. As soon as he was inside the old ladies put the lid on and held it down firmly. "Let me out and I will do you a good turn," begged the Devil. "How can you do that, Father of Evil?" demanded the old women. "I shall teach you how to dominate men," he replied, and so he did. And that is why witches are feared everywhere to this day, especially by men.

Source: Epton, 1958:44. Reprinted by permission of Cassell.

---

women are demanding an equal place "at the top."

We have seen that while women have made many dramatic and effective accommodations to the restraints placed on them by organized religion, their participation is often viewed by men as marginal. Religion is simply one of the most universal and distinctive of human activities, and women are human in every way, subject to all the multiplicity of impulses, emotions, and inquiries that lead men to faith. In this sense, religion is necessary to many women for reasons of pure individual satisfaction. For Marta Morena Vega (2000), a Santería priestess, religious practice has enabled her to fulfill her mission in life. Some women, particularly in patriarchal monotheistic religions, seek individual fulfillment in a greater union with God by means of a life of prayer and meditation. These women seem to compensate for their exclusion from the religious hierarchy and their ignorance of occult languages and rituals by developing a more personal, idiosyncratic approach to religion (Gross, 1996).

One Yemenite Jewish woman said her mother never suffered from not learning Hebrew: "My mother says what she wants to God." Similarly, the Muslim saint Leila Mimouna, illiterate like most of her sisters, said "Mimouna knows God and God knows Mimouna" (Fernea and Bezirgan, 1977:197). Barred from the study of theology even after Protestantism had made the Scriptures available in the languages of its adherents, women used vehicles such as the novel, poetry, or the popular hymn to make religious statements. Contemporary artists have imaginatively interpreted biblical texts, as in Judith Kates and Gail Twersky Reimer's collection of writings by many distinguished authors inspired by the biblical Book of Ruth (1994).

Women and Possession

The popular religions of the poor, marginal, and alienated make their mystics the visionaries of ecstasy cults and the mediums of "possession" sects. The possessed woman may be regarded as holy or unclean, depending on the circumstances. Possessed women may become healers or be thought of as diseased or infected by a spirit whose purpose is malicious, a spirit that is an enemy of the recognized deities of the group. Women who are thus possessed often have reason to complain of their circumstances in the first place. They are frequently the victims of an exogamous marital situation, vulnerable to hostile charges of witchcraft when misfortune strikes any member of the husband's kin, as well as vulnerable to repudiation, isolation, and lack of support.

Possession has been found, sometimes in mass outbreaks, among women in every area of the world. Possession tends to afflict alienated people who are responding to the strains of oppression. It is an experience that is guaranteed to gain attention for a discontented woman, and it provides a vehicle for revenge against an oppressive husband, co-wife, mother-in-law, or, in the case of nuns, father confessor (Simpson, 1978).

Possession serves a variety of purposes for the possessed. First of all, it frees women from the guilt associated with rebellion and from responsibility for antisocial behavior. Women can say and do things that would never be permitted if they were in control of themselves. Where the religious structure is not too rigid or highly controlled, possession gives women access to real cultic power. Many possessed women are believed to gain sufficient control over spirits to have the ability to work healing magic, divination, or other powerful spells. Such women are particularly useful in curing similarly afflicted women. For many women, possession, like mysticism, has proven to be the first stage of a liberating experience that culminated in a more active life of social service and reform (Hoehler-Fatton, 1996; Simpson, 1978).

The male establishment tends carefully to control possessed behavior. The mechanics of exorcism, for example, often involve much physical abuse of the possessed women (to guard against faking). The saint is never far from accusations of malicious witchcraft or heresy. Like Joan of Arc, saints will be allowed to obey "voices" only up to the point where established authorities are not discomfited. However, the dominating powers are generally willing to allow some latitude to these strong spirits to avert a more general social disruption. Thus, female cults, like some of the more expressive churches organized by black prophets in America, are often on the edge between the socially acceptable role of releasing strong emotions and the socially unacceptable role of revolution.

Women's Religious Groups and Orders

In countries where religion is effectively separated from the state, women enjoy a fairly wide opportunity to participate in religious sects of their own devising. Women who have been excluded from positions of active leadership in more formal religions have been welcomed into spiritualist and Pentecostal sects that emphasize the individual experience of grace above the organized ministry. The testimony of grace is an invaluable experience to many women. Amanda Smith (1837–1915), an African American woman who was a former slave, testified at a camp meeting that the experience of grace freed her from reticence, her fear of whites, and her fear of men and enabled her to begin preaching and speaking of her own experience with confidence (Hardesty et al., 1979).

Women often find spiritual support and some degree of empowerment through single-sex groups within their religious establishments. Many established religions have community-level women's groups—women's auxiliaries, committees, and sisterhoods—that do "good works" for the community and others in need and provide an outlet for the creativity and spirit of their members. Such groups express their religious devotion in part through the care of the place of worship (flowers at the altar, cleaning the sanctuary, maintaining the holy objects). They do this together, taking turns at tasks, making decisions as a group. Often, they play a prominent role in the community as organizers of charities, raising scholarships, taking care of people in need, and beautifying public spaces. Sometimes, they organize beyond the community level to the national and even international levels, such as the Jewish charitable organization Hadassah.

Such women are usually also involved in family life as wives and mothers. Some religions also offer the option of an alternative to family life, a life completely devoted to religion. Women's religious orders have a long history in Christianity and Buddhism.

Women and Religion in the United States

The formal separation between church and state in the United States has not prevented special forms of dialogue between religious organizations and the government. Religious groups committed to major social reforms have spearheaded important political and legal changes; other religious groups, more conservative in orientation, have provided focal points for resistance and reaction. It has been largely through their participation in religious groups, rather than in government itself, that women have had a strong voice in political processes. In particular, feminism, with its call for women's rights and its role in other legislative reforms (most notably abolition of slavery and suffrage), has had a significant impact on the history of religion in America.

Leadership by Women

Protestant Denominations. Women emerged as religious leaders and reformers early in American history, in the notoriously intolerant context of colonial New England. Anne Hutchinson, a Puritan woman of Massachusetts Bay Colony, was banished for her refusal to stop preaching her doctrine of salvation by grace alone. In 1638, she was driven out of Massachusetts with her husband and children and excommunicated from the Puritan community in Boston. She led her followers to Rhode Island, where she helped to establish a new colony and pursued her evangelical ministry. In 1642, she migrated yet again to East Chester, New York, where the following year she and her family were killed by Native Americans. Her friend Mary Dyer, who supported her throughout her trials in Massachusetts, died on the gallows in 1660 for defending the Quakers who had begun to preach in the colony and for refusing to accept banishment (Dunn, 1979).

The Quakers, or Society of Friends, believed in the equality of all people, including the equality of women and men. They opposed settlement on lands claimed by Native Americans and particularly opposed the institution of slavery. Despite the hostility of the colonies to Quakerism, the movement spread. Nearly half the Quaker missionaries were women, mostly traveling without husbands and often with other women. They continued to travel and do missionary work through the seventeenth century. In these early years, while numbers of women's "meetings" (congregations) were established, there was some difference of opinion on how strong they should be or even how legitimate they were. Some women's meetings deferred to men; others were quite assertive of their autonomy and conducted their own affairs. When permanent meetinghouses were built, it became common to construct a building to house both women and men, who sat on separate sides. A partition down the center was open for worship but closed for the conduct of their separate business (Dunn, 1979).

Quaker women's experience in the organization of religious meetings provided training in the public arena that few women of colonial or postcolonial times had an opportunity to gain. The "Friends" became accustomed to public speaking, to creating organizational structures, and to feeling equal to others. Quakers were disproportionately represented among American women abolitionists, feminists, and suffragists (Dunn, 1979). Sarah Grimké (1792–1873), Angelina Grimké Weld (1805–79), and Lucretia Coffin Mott are among the most famous of these women in the nineteenth century.

Although Lucretia Mott grew up as a Quaker, she held her own convictions on social reforms, not limited by the views of more traditional Quakers. For example, she was a radical abolitionist, whereas many Quakers preferred gradual emancipation. Mott's reformist views particularly influenced and shaped the abolitionist and feminist movements in America. The formation of her views dates from the time when she attended the World Anti-Slavery Convention in London in 1840 together with Elizabeth Cady Stanton. At the opening of the convention, the question of seating the American women delegates arose. After a long debate, the effort to seat them failed, and Mott and Stanton were relegated to sit behind a bar and curtain and thus forbidden to voice their opinions (Buhle and Buhle, 1978). When Mott and Stanton returned to America, they brought a firm objective: to continue to work for both the abolition of African American slavery and an end to women's inferior property and family rights. Eight years later, under their leadership, the Women's Rights Convention took place in July 1848 at Seneca Falls, New York (see Chapters 7 and 13). The convention is considered the official beginning of the women's rights movement in the United States (Seneca Falls is now the site of a national museum).

The United Society of Believers in Christ's Second Appearing, better known as the Shakers, was founded and led in colonial America by Ann Lee (1736–84). The Shakers believed that the "Godhead is defined in four persons—Father, Son, Holy Mother Wisdom and Daughter" (Zikmund, 1979:209). They lived a communal life and practiced celibacy. Few practitioners are left.

Christian Science, a late nineteenth-century sectarian religion, also supported women's rights. Its founder, Mary Baker Eddy (1821–1910), believed and preached that God is both masculine and feminine. She frequently referred to God in her writings as Father–Mother God. Christian Science has a very successful and extensive establishment today, including its widely read newspaper the *Christian Science Monitor*, published in Boston, and free reading rooms in towns and cities throughout the world.

Seventh-Day Adventism, an evangelical religion, was guided by Ellen Harmon White (1827–1915) from its beginning in Battle Creek, Michigan, in 1860 (Zikmund, 1979). She emphasized temperance, education, and health, particularly in diet. Her hegemony over Adventism lasted 50 years and was responsible for much of its influence and growth.

Many other U.S. women, black and white, rose to prominence and leadership in evangelical and revivalist movements in the nineteenth and twentieth centuries (Gilkes, 1985). Today, Holiness denominations "have a higher percentage of ordained women than does their mother church, the United Methodist Church" (Hardesty et al., 1979: 240). Like Quakerism, the evangelical and revivalist movements have been a training ground for women activists, providing them with unique opportunities for public speaking and group organizing. Religious activity was practically the only important extrafamilial activity permitted to most women in the nineteenth and much of the twentieth centuries. Reform-oriented women had to work through the church, and sectarian religions offered them precisely this opportunity. The initial entry of women into reformist movements through evangelical religion served them in good stead during later periods when they entered nonsectarian public arenas as well.

Jewish Denominations. American Jewish women contribute to religious life as professionals and through domestic activities; the latter role reaches back beyond the Jews' arrival in the United States through a long history. The heart of Judaism since the *diaspora* (exile from the Holy Land) has been the ritual of hearth and home. Of major importance to Jewish self-definition is *kashruth*, or purity, particularly of diet. It is the responsibility of religious Jewish women to keep kitchens *kosher*, to see that meat and milk are not mixed and that the family consumes no "unclean" foods such as pork or shellfish or improperly butchered meats. Women prepare the festive foods for holidays and most particularly for the celebration each week of the Sabbath. The conduct of Jewish life is completely dependent on women's perpetuation of religious traditions in the home.

In 1988, Conservative Judaism moved women to the focal point by declaring that the home was the center of Jewish religious life. Various Jewish women's groups, particularly charity organizations, provide an arena for major public activities. Prominent among these is Hadassah, founded in 1912 under the leadership of an American woman, Henrietta Szold (1860–1945). In 1893, Hannah Greenbaum Solomon (1858–1942) initiated the National Council of Jewish Women, dedicated to education, social reform, and issues concerning women. These organizations and others like them provide vehicles for women to learn how to organize, how to manage money, and how to raise funds; they raise and distribute millions of dollars in the causes they espouse.

Catholicism. Catholic women, in contrast to Jewish women, have had the option of following a "vocation" in religion by becoming nuns. As nuns, American women have played a number of influential roles in American life, particularly in education and nursing. Today, nuns may be women in street clothes who may or may not wear symbolic head scarves and crosses. They are no longer found only in the shadows of a cloister but also in public places. Since medieval times, nuns have held professional responsibilities in education and attending the sick and elderly, but today they are also found in executive positions, managing self-supporting philanthropic or educational institutions and projects.

The decision to join a convent and become a nun may be prompted by expectations for the future that have nothing to do with religion. For a poor Catholic girl, convent life means moving to another class with privileges that she may not have if she remained in secular life. She might be seeking an orderly and secure life where education is offered, friendship of sisters is promised, and marriage and children are prohibited. Organized religions do offer spiritual security and, above all, ethical and moral codes that are time-tested. Catholic women have choices to make and require the freedom to follow their sincere beliefs.

The dedication of nuns to education, health care, and social welfare is well illustrated in the life of Mother Elizabeth Bayley Seton (1774–1821) and the order of Sisters of Charity that she founded. In 1975, Seton was canonized as the first American-born saint. It was she who founded the first sisterhood in the United States and the first Catholic free school in America, in Emmitsburg, Maryland. She governed her religious community and administered her school through many early hardships. At the time of her death, Seton's Emmitsburg community numbered fifty sisters. Now, six branches claim her as their founder and have remained independent North American groups.

In following Christian beliefs, Native American women often find themselves at conflict: some of their ancestral traditions are at opposite ends of the monotheistic/patriarchal scriptures of Judeo-Christianity. The scholar Paula Gunn Allen, who herself is part Native American, asserts "Traditional tribal lifestyles are more often gynocratic than not, and they are never patriarchal" (Allen, 1988:2). One can begin to judge the basic conflicts that arose when Native Americans were gradually converted to Christianity by missionaries and conquerors. The work of Mary TallMountain (Athabascan) demonstrates the "difficult and uneasy alliance between the pagan awareness that characterized tribal thought and the less earthy, more judgmental view of medieval Christianity" (Allen, 1988:172). TallMountain is a devout Roman Catholic, and her poetry reveals the conflict between her faith and her tribal awareness (TallMountain, 1981).

Feminist Contributions to Religious Change

Religious change comes from many different sources and in many different forms. The spokeswomen for the numerous sectarian branches of religion in the United States mentioned here all sought changes in established practice and belief. Elizabeth Cady Stanton, one of the presidents of the National Woman Suffrage Association and cofounder in 1868 with Susan B. Anthony of the radical magazine *The Revolution*, went further than most of her coworkers and even today's feminists in confronting the sexist language of the Scriptures. Maintaining that the Bible contributed to the low self-image of women, she attempted twice to organize a group to write

commentaries on passages from the Old and New Testaments dealing with women. Eventually, between 1895 and 1898, she succeeded in publishing *The Woman's Bible*, parts I and II, and an appendix (see Stanton, [1895–8] 1972).

This work is the result of Stanton's belief that the language and interpretations of passages dealing with women in the Bible were a major source of women's inferior status because women turned to the Bible so much for comfort and inspiration. She maintained that the language of the Scriptures had to be rendered in such a way that it would not center only on man, celebrate man as the superior creation, or allow man to dominate woman. Certain passages in the Bible, Stanton believed, could be interpreted to conform to women's experiences as humans, as well as men's experiences.

Stanton's attempts were not well received by the majority of suffragists, and the National American Woman Suffrage Association disclaimed any official connection with *The Woman's Bible* in 1895. The organization feared a backlash from society at large on purely religious issues, a reaction that could have halted the political and social changes being sought. The decision was based on the view that it was possible to separate political and secular issues from religious ones. Stanton, on the other hand, saw the traditions of religious belief as an important cause of women's subordination. Nowadays, some biblical historians criticize Stanton for expressing anti-Jewish views in *The Woman's Bible*. They urge caution about belief in unsubstantiated theories concerning the history of the Israelites that result in blaming Judaism for the existence of patriarchy (Bird, 1989; Plaskow, 1979).

In addition to changing the language of devotion, feminists in the United States have developed new versions of traditional rituals. They have taken out the sexist bases of general rituals and added new rituals for women to complement those specifically intended for men. For example, some Jewish women have written a complement to the boy's *brith* to bring their daughters into the covenant (Plaskow, 1979). Aviva Cantor (1979) has composed a woman's *Haggadah*, a version of the Jewish Passover text that traditionally celebrates freedom from slavery and oppression, while others have developed Sabbath prayers for women (Janowitz and Wenig, 1979).

Feminist theologians and philosophers address the deeper issues of belief and practice in all the world religions, including Buddhism (Gross, 1999; Peach, 1999), Confucianism (Woo, 1999), and Islam (Hassan, 1999; Helie-Lucas, 1999), as well as Judaism and Christianity. For some religious feminists, the old traditions are insufficient, even when revised. While looking for spiritual growth and healing, they find the established religions outmoded and meaningless and look to mysticism, paganism, and other sources to create new religions. They believe that "the margin may also be the leading edge, whose experiments create the future" (Puttick, 1997:2). They may, in fact, have had an impact in some areas, most discernibly in the incorporation of respect for the environment into religious doctrines as well as the promotion of alternative medicine and health approaches.

Summary

Religion and society affect each other. As societies become more complex and hierarchical, so do their religious institutions. In societies that deny leadership roles to women, religious institutions do so too. Religious beliefs about what is "good behavior" influence societies.

Despite their devalued status in religion, women have been active participants in religions throughout history. Many women focus on certain aspects of religion (such as the healing Christ or the Virgin Mary) that appeal to their concerns and evolve from their beliefs and practices. "Popular" versions of traditional religions often provide scope for women's activities.

Some ancient religions included goddess worship and gave priestesses status. The origin myths of many of the major religions support the dominant religious and social roles of men. Most religions have conceptions of supernatural beings, and females are featured among them. These beings may be souls, saints, ghosts, and goddesses. The goddess is often envisaged as a threatening being who is tamed and controlled by being linked to a male god. As monotheism entered religious belief, the goddesses of ancient religions were dropped in favor of a single male God. Some feminists believe that worship of a female God would enhance women's social position.

Religious codes govern human conduct and exert social controls. Life-cycle rituals for men enhance their power and status in the community, but the wedding ceremony, the most important ritual for women in patrilineal societies, serves only to shift control over women from father to husband.

Religious leaders in many societies attempt to control female sexuality by urging women to stay within the home and to be modest and decorous. Many religious laws require women and men to be separate during the menstrual period. Religious codes also protect women and promote family life and procreation.

In public worship, women are subject to a number of controls. They are frequently prohibited from lay participation in rituals and sometimes segregated from men. Even so, it is women who spend the most hours of devotion in the church.

The most highly organized religions are the least welcoming to women as clergy. Many women find that they can play far more active roles in the religions that are on the fringes of or in conflict with "established" religion. Often, women emerge as preachers or leaders of these sects.

Women excel at ritual and spiritual services connected with nurturance and healing. That is why so many women are numbered among the healers of societies. Women have also served the various religions as missionaries and martyrs.

Women have also been active as rebels in religious movements, probably because they have often seen rebellion as the only means of winning more liberation for themselves. During the Reformation, women heretics were frequently accused of being witches. Some women have found fulfillment in religions through an idiosyncratic approach. Mysticism and possession by spirits are both highly personal expressions of religion.

Women, especially Quakers, were among the early religious leaders and reformers in U.S. history. In the nineteenth century, women had important parts to play in the founding and organization of the Shakers, Christian Scientists, Seventh-Day Adventists, and a number of evangelical movements. Jewish women have been responsible for maintaining religious traditions in the home and are active in the public arena by means of various Jewish women's groups. American nuns have played influential roles in education and nursing in the United States.

Feminists have contributed to religious change. In the last century, Elizabeth Cady Stanton wrote a commentary on the Bible, *The Woman's Bible*, while feminists today are developing new versions of traditional rituals and adding new rituals for women.

Discussion Questions

1. Nearly everyone receives some religious education—in the home, in school, in church, in the community at large—on both a conscious and an unconscious level. What do you think you learned about rela-

tions between women and men from this background? What were the sources of what you learned (the Bible, ritual, prayer)?

2. Religious movements challenge the status quo, looking to the past as well as the future. Select one, either fundamentalist, evangelist, or new, and examine how the roles assigned to women relate to its vision of the world.

3. Does the gender of God matter to you? Why or why not? What have been the arguments offered on both sides of this issue?

4. Study some of the representations of Isis, Diana, the Virgin Mary, and Avalokitesvara (Guan Yin or Kannon). What do these images have in common? What type of convictions do you think they reflect?

Recommended Readings

Christ, Carol P. *Laughter of Aphrodite: Reflections on a Journey to the Goddess*. New York: Harper & Row, 1987. Reflections on the spiritual and intellectual journey of a feminist theologian through her first encounters with graduate studies on the holocaust to her questioning of male religious language to her exploration of the goddess tradition.

Howland, Courtney W., editor. *Religious Fundamentalisms and the Human Rights of Women*. New York: St. Martin's Press, 1999. A collection of original essays on the conflicts between international fundamentalist movements and international human rights, examining legal, political, cultural, as well as practical issues.

Mernissi, Fatima. *Dreams of Trespass. Tales of a Harem Girlhood. Reading*, MA: Addison-Wesley, 1994. The author, a sociologist, describes her girlhood in a harem in Morocco in the 1940s, where women constantly dreamed of trespassing and staged theatrical performances in which they impersonated famous Arab feminist leaders.

Plaskow, Judith, and Carol P. Christ, editors. *Weaving the Visions: New Patterns in Feminist Spirituality*. New York: Harper & Row, 1989. A sequel to *Womanspirit Rising* (1979), these essays attempt to reconceptualize central religious categories through the experiences and voices of white, black, Chicana, Asian American, and Native American feminists.

Ruether, Rosemary, and Eleanor McLaughlin, editors. *Women of Spirit: Female Leadership in the Jewish and Christian Traditions*. New York: Simon & Schuster, 1979. A collection of original essays on women's religious leadership, with an emphasis on historical developments in Europe and the United States.

Sharma, Arvind, and Katherine K. Young, editors. *Feminism and World Religions*. Albany: SUNY Press, 1999. An edited volume of essays about the roles of women in established religions, their resistence to sexism and misogyny in these religions, and their search for reinterpretations and change both historically and in the present.

References

Allen, Paula Gunn. *The Woman Who Owned the Shadows*. San Francisco: Spinsters, Ink, 1983.

———. *The Sacred Hoop: Recovering the Feminine in American Indian Traditions*. Boston: Beacon Press, 1988.

Arberry, A. J. *The Koran Interpreted*. New York: Macmillan, 1955.

Awn, Peter J. Indian Islam: The Shah Bano affair. In *Fundamentalism and Gender*, edited by John Stratton Hawley. Oxford: Oxford University Press, 1994.

Bacigalupo, Ana Mariella. Mapuche women's empowerment as shaman-healers (machis) in Chile. In *Annual Review of Women in World Religions*. vol. IV, edited by Arvind Sharma and Katherine K. Young. Albany: SUNY Press, 1996.

Bird, Phyllis. Women's religion in ancient Israel. In *Women's Earliest Records: From Ancient Egypt and Western Asia*, edited by Barbara S. Lesko. Atlanta: Scholars Press, 1989.

Brown, Elicia. Immersed in a dilemma. *Jewish Week*, Nov. 14, 2003, 62.

Brown, Karen McCarthy. "Fundamentalism and the control of women." In *Fundamentalism and Gender*, edited by John Stratton Hawley. Oxford: Oxford University Press, 1994.

Buhle, Marijo, and Paul Buhle, editors. *The Concise History of Woman Suffrage: Selections from the Classic Work of Stanton, Anthony, Gage, and Harper*. Urbana: University of Illinois Press, 1978.

Burstein, Stanley M., editor. *The Hellenistic Age: From the Battle of Ipsos to the Death of Kleopatra*, VII. Cambridge: Cambridge University Press, 1985.

Bynum, Caroline Walker. *Jesus as Mother: Studies in the Spirituality of the High Middle Ages*. Los Angeles: University of California Press, 1982.

Cantor, Aviva. Jewish women's haggadah. In *Womanspirit Rising: A Feminist Reader in Religion*, edited by Carol P. Christ and Judith Plaskow. San Francisco: Harper & Row, 1979.

Caldwell, Sarah. *Oh Terrifying Mother: Sexuality, Violence and Worship of the Goddess Kali*. New York: Oxford University Press, 2000.

Carmody, Denise. *Women and World Religions*. Nashville, TN: Abingdon, 1979.

Christ, Carol P. Why women need the goddess: Phenomenological, psychological, and political reflections. In *Womanspirit Rising: A Feminist Reader in Religion*, edited by Carol P. Christ and Judith Plaskow. San Francisco: Harper & Row, 1979.

———. *Laughter of Aphrodite: Reflections on a Journey to the Goddess*. New York: Harper & Row, 1987.

Daly, Mary. *Beyond God the Father: Toward a Philosophy of Women's Liberation*. Boston: Beacon, 1973.

Danforth, Loring M. *The Death Rituals of Rural Greece*. Princeton: Princeton University Press, 1982.

Delaney, Janice, Mary J. Lupton, and Emily Toth, editors. *The Curse: A Cultural History of Menstruation*. New York: New American Library, 1976.

Dickens, Arthur G. *The English Reformation*. New York: Schocken, 1964.

Dunn, Mary Maples. Woman of light. In *Women of America: A History*, edited by Carol Ruth Berkin and Mary Beth Norton. Boston: Houghton Mifflin, 1979.

Durrant, Stephen. The nisan shaman caught in cultural contradictions. *Signs*, 5, 338–47, 1979.

Ehrenreich, Barbara, and Deidre English. *For Her Own Good: 150 Years of the Experts' Advice to Women*. Garden City, NY: Doubleday, 1979.

Eliot, Charles. *Hinduism and Buddhism*, vol. II. London: Routledge & Kegan Paul, 1962.

Epton, Nina. *Saints and Sorcerers: A Moroccan Journey*. London: Cassell, 1958.

Fernea, Elizabeth W., and Basima Q. Bezirgan, editors. *Middle Eastern Muslim Women Speak*. Austin: University of Texas Press, 1977.

Fernea, Robert A., and Elizabeth W. Fernea. Variation in religious observance among Islamic women. In *Scholars, Saints, and Sufis: Muslim Religious Institutions Since 1500*, edited by Nikki R. Keddie. Berkeley: University of California Press, 1972.

Fiorenza, Elisabeth Schussler. Word, spirit, and power: Women in early Christian communities. In *Women of Spirit: Female Leadership in the Jewish and Christian Traditions*, edited by Rosemary Ruether and Eleanor McLaughlin. New York: Simon & Schuster, 1979.

———. *In Memory of Her: A Feminist Theological Reconstruction of Christian Origins*. New York: Crossroad, 1983.

Foblets, Marie Claire S. F. G. Family disputes involving Muslim women in contemporary Europe: Immigrant women caught between Islamic family law and women's rights. In *Religious Fundamentalisms and the Human Rights of Women*, edited by Courtney W. Howland. New York: St. Martin's Press, 1999.

Freeman, James M. The ladies of Lord Krishna. In *Unspoken Worlds: Women's Religious Lives in Non-Western Cultures*, edited by Nancy Falk and Rita Gross. New York: Harper & Row, 1980.

Gilkes, Cheryl Townsend. "Together and in harness": Women's traditions in the sanctified church. *Signs*, 10, 687–99, 1985.

Goldenberg, Naomi. *Changing of the Gods: Feminism and the End of Traditional Religions*. Boston: Beacon, 1979.

Green, Rayna. *Women in American Indian Society*. Philadelphia: Chelsea House, 1992.

Gross, Rita. *Feminism and Religion: An Introduction*. Boston: Beacon, 1996.

———. Strategies for a feminist revalorization of buddhism. In *Feminism and World Religions*, edited by Courtney W. Howland. Albany: SUNY Press, 1999.

Hardesty, Nancy, Lucille Sider Dayton, and Conald Dayton. Women in the holiness movement: Feminism in the evangelical tradition. In *Women of Spirit: Female Leadership in The Jewish and Christian Traditions*, edited by Rosemary Ruether and Eleanor McLaughlin. New York: Simon & Schuster, 1979.

Harrell, Steven. Men, women, and ghosts in Taiwanese folk religion. In *Gender and Religion: On the Complexity of Symbols*, edited by Caroline Walker Bynum, Steven Harrell, and Paula Richman. Boston: Beacon, 1986.

Hassan, Riffat. Feminism in Islam. In *Feminism and World Religions*, edited by Courtney W. Howland. Albany: SUNY Press, 1999.

Hawley, John Stratton, editor. *Fundamentalism and Gender*. Oxford: Oxford University Press, 1994.

———. Fundamentalism. In *Religious Fundamentalisms and the Human Rights of Women*, edited by Courtney W. Howland. New York: St. Martin's Press, 1999.

Helie-Lucas, Marie-Aimee. What is your tribe: Women's struggles and the construction of Muslimness. In *Religious Fundamentalisms and the Human Rights of Women*, edited by Courtney W. Howland. New York: St. Martin's Press, 1999.

Hoch-Smith, Judith, and Anita Spring. *Women in Ritual and Symbolic Roles*. New York: Plenum, 1978.

Hoehler-Fatton, Cynthia. *Women of Fire and Spirit: History, Faith, and Gender in Roho Religion in*

Western Kenya. New York: Oxford University Press, 1996.

Howland, Courtney W., editor. *Religious Fundamentalisms and the Human Rights of Women*. New York: St. Martin's Press, 1999.

Janowitz, Naomi, and Maggie Wenig. Sabbath prayers for women. In *Womanspirit Rising: A Feminist Reader in Religion*, edited by Carol P. Christ and Judith Plaskow. San Francisco: Harper & Row, 1979.

Jordan, David K. *Gods, Ghosts, and Ancestors: Folk Religion in a Taiwanese Village*. Berkeley: University of California Press, 1999.

Kates, Judith, and Gail Twersky Reimer, editors. *Reading Ruth: Contemporary Women Reclaim a Sacred Story*. New York: Ballantine, 1994.

Lewis, I. M. *Ecstatic Religion: An Anthropological Study of Spirit Possession and Shamanism*. Harmondsworth, UK: Penguin, 1971.

Mails, Thomas E. *The People Called Apache*, Englewood Cliffs, NJ: Prentice-Hall, 1974.

Mâle, G. *The Gothic Image: Religious Art in the Thirteenth Century*, translated by Dora Nussey. New York: Harper & Row, 1949.

McNamara, Jo Ann. *A New Song: Celibate Women in the First Three Christian Centuries*. New York: Haworth, 1983.

McNamara, Jo Ann Kay. "Sisters in Arms: Catholic Nuns through Two Millenia." Harvard University Press, Cambridge, Massachusetts. London, England. 1996.

Murray, Margaret Alice. *The Witch Cult in Western Europe*. Oxford: Clarendon, 1967.

Palmer, Susan Jean. *Moon Sisters, Krishna Mothers, Rajneesh Lovers: Women's Roles in New Religions*. Syracuse: Syracuse University Press, 1994.

Peach, Lucinda May. Buddhism and human rights in the Thai sex trade. In *Religious Fundamentalisms and the Human Rights of Women*, edited by Courtney W. Howland. New York: St. Martin's Press, 1999.

Plaskow, Judith. Bringing a daughter into the covenant. In *Womanspirit Rising: A Feminist Reader in Religion*, edited by Carol P. Christ and Judith Plaskow. San Francisco: Harper & Row, 1979.

Pomeroy, Sarah B. *Goddesses, Whores, Wives, and Slaves*. New York: Schocken, 1975.

———. *Women in Hellenistic Egypt: From Alexander to Cleopatra*. New York: Schocken, 1984.

Puttick, Elizabeth. *Women in New Religions: In Search of Community, Sexuality and Spiritual Power*. New York: St. Martin's Press, 1997.

Richards, Audrey I. *Chisungu: A girls' initiation ceremony among the Bemba of Zambia*. London: Faber & Faber, 1956.

Scott, W. S., editor and translator. *Trial of Joan of Arc*. London: Folio Society, 1968.

Sharma, Arvind, and Katherine K. Young, editors. *Feminism and World Religions*. Albany: SUNY Press, 1999.

Shields, John C., editor. *The Collected Works of Phillis Wheatley*. The Schomburg Library of Nineteenth-Century Black Women Writers, edited by Henry Louis Gates, Jr. New York: Oxford University Press, 1988.

Silko, Leslie Marmon. *Ceremony*. New York: Penguin Books, 1977.

Simpson, George E. *Black Religions in the New World*. New York: Columbia University Press, 1978.

Stanton, Elizabeth Cady. *The Woman's Bible* (1895–8), parts I, II, and appendix. New York: Arno, 1972.

Stone, Merlin. When God was a woman. In *Womanspirit Rising: A Feminist Reader in Religion*, edited by Carol P. Christ and Judith Plaskow. San Francisco: Harper & Row, 1979.

TallMountain, Mary. There is no word for goodbye. *Blue Cloud Quarterly*, 9, 1981.

Toulis, Nicole Rodriguez. *Believing Identity: Pentecostalism and the Mediation of Jamaican Ethnicity and Gender in England*. Oxford: Berg, 1997.

Vega, Marta Moreno. *The Altar of My Soul: The Liviing Traditions of Santería*. New York: One World, 2000.

Walker, Alice. *Possessing the Secret of Joy*. New York: Harcourt Brace Jovanovich, 1992.

Washbourne, Penelope. Becoming a woman: Menstruation as spiritual challenge. In *Womanspirit Rising: A Feminist*, edited by Carol P.

Christ and Judith Plaskow. San Francisco: Harper & Row, 1979.

Woo, Terry. Confucianism and feminism. In *Feminism and World Religions*, edited by Courtney W. Howland. Albany: SUNY Press, 1999.

Zikmund, Barbara Brown. The feminist thrust of sectarian Christianity. In *Women of Spirit: Female Leadership in The Jewish and Christian Traditions*, edited by Rosemary Ruether and Eleanor McLaughlin. New York: Simon & Schuster, 1979.

chapter **10**

Women and Education

We do not think of the ordinary person as preoccupied with such difficult and profound questions as: What is truth? What is authority? To whom do I listen? What counts for me as evidence? How do I know what I know? ... [Yet our answers] affect our definitions of ourselves, the way we interact with others, our public and private personae, our sense of control over life events, our views of teaching and learning, and our conceptions of morality.

(BELENKY ET AL., *WOMEN'S WAYS OF KNOWING*, 1986:3)

Epistemology and the Politics of Knowledge

Everything in this book constitutes "knowledge." It is knowledge presented from a feminist perspective and, therefore, *like all knowledge*, reflects a conscious, subjective point of view or interpretation of "reality." How can we claim to "know" anything? This question is called a problem in *epistemology* (coined from ancient Greek words meaning the "study of knowledge"). Knowledge involves what we understand about our world and ourselves: *what* we know and *how* we know it. Studying epistemology demonstrates that there is, and always has been, a "politics of knowledge." This means that what we know always reflects either a conscious interpretation of information or an unconscious interpretation based on unexamined assumptions. This is true for all knowledge, including what we call "science," despite its claims of a higher level of objectivity (Kuhn, 1962; see also Hrdy, 1986). Education involves ideas about who should possess formal knowledge and what that formal knowledge ought to be, based on what is culturally assumed to be the proper social roles for women and men in society (see Chapter 5). When what is taught and how it is taught are based on the assumption that women's place is "naturally" subordinate to that of men and when education

does not specifically question the reason for these fixed gender roles, it is as much engaged in politics as an education that specifically raises such questions.

Women's Ways of Knowing, quoted above, investigates what women say about their education and their learning experiences in the United States. The authors assert that there are distinctive "women's ways of knowing." The claim is not based on some biological or essentialist definition of "women" but on the ways the specific women in this study were introduced from childhood (by their families and schools) to the voices of others in authority. The women accepted these voices as "all-powerful," and the messages given by these authorities left the women feeling "passive, reactive, and dependent" (Belenky et al., 1986:27). The women in the study grew up learning that they had to struggle against the social forces at work to keep them silent; it was a struggle to claim the power of their own minds, based on their personal experiences. It is a struggle that can be identified for women going back in time and continuing into the present.

Epistemologies as Political Systems

Knowledge is a social construct. As people in a particular culture agree upon the meanings they give the world around them, they classify their experiences and encode them in order to think and talk about them. What we "know" is subject to what we believe, and what we believe depends on how we think about or conceptualize our experiences. Knowledge is not an accumulation of facts but an interpretation of those facts. This accounts for worldwide cultural differences about what constitutes knowledge. There is not a single fixed knowledge system that all people share. The scholarship on which this text is based, for example, is grounded in a Western, indeed a largely Anglo-American, feminist belief system. It differs, to some extent, from the ideologies that underpin, say, French or Egyptian or Latin American feminist thinking, no less than any nonfeminist thinking (which generally includes the thinking of most traditional academic disciplines).

One fundamental difference between non-feminist systems of thought and this book is the way women and women's concerns form the center of the search for knowledge. Aware of our location in Western knowledge, the authors of this text attempt to let voices of those outside that framework express themselves or at least to make known how those experiences differ from ours. Feminist methods and interpretations continue to change over time, and the voices of women from all cultures are increasingly brought into interaction. The process enables all feminists to build on feminist thinking and on what has been learned over the past 30 years, both in the United States and elsewhere. These new perspectives now inform the work of many scholars—women and men—in the traditional disciplines, in both their theories and methods.

A hundred years ago, few scholars anywhere questioned the prevailing view that to understand society and how it has changed over time, it was necessary, primarily, to study the lives and actions of men. Scholars—and men as a group—might acknowledge that women had always had important reproductive and family roles but that those roles were relatively fixed and therefore did not require further scholarly scrutiny. Women's productive roles remained invisible because it was assumed that they were not important. By the end of the nineteenth century, this belief system was identified with the ideology of "separate spheres," which explained that, by their "nature," women in general inhabited the private sphere of home and family, while men—both elite and working men—were the active agents in the public sphere. Men, by their "nature," were responsible for ruling and working. To understand the world meant studying men's ideas and men's activities. The new discipline of anthropology, however, did note that women might take part in activities outside the domestic sphere in other, "less developed" cultures, and their roles were seen as emblematic of those "lesser" cultures (Mascia-Lees and Black, 1999).

The Politics of Knowledge and the Rise of Feminist Scholarship

When feminist scholars began to ask questions about what women had been doing in the past, what they learned changed their understanding about women's pasts and men's pasts as well. They learned that what questions a discipline asked and did not ask shaped how men had developed their basic theories about the world. The decision not to ask questions about women and their lives—because they were deemed unimportant—was a political one. Disciplines were built on this value system and their "knowledge" taught to generations of students; as a result, this political decision became accepted as the framework for knowledge. Thinking only within such a framework makes it difficult to see what does not fit. As Thomas Kuhn (1962) pointed out in his study of the development of scientific knowledge, a prevailing framework, which he called a "paradigm," remains uncritically accepted as true until a new paradigm replaces it. A change occurs only when what has been excluded, and therefore not explained, by the prevailing paradigm suddenly becomes visible and can no longer be ignored simply because it does not "fit in." Making women visible was the task undertaken by increasing numbers of feminist scholars in the 1960s and 1970s. They asked what women were doing, setting in motion a revolutionary paradigm shift in what we understand to be knowledge.

Feminists created what became the women's liberation movement, deliberately engaging in consciousness raising. This process brought women together to share their personal experiences and thereby to learn that what each had considered an individual problem—in relation to men, families, and work—was in fact a systemic one shared by other women. Women began to notice that what they had been learning was primarily about the ideas, writings, and activities of men and what they had been taught as a universal perspective was a specifically male one. The spread of feminism around the world has allowed more women in all cultures to see this discrepancy.

In the late 1960s and 1970s, women—in and outside of universities—began to do their own research and to pool their newly acquired information to write new books and create new courses to teach about women's lives, experiences, and accomplishments. Within a few years, thousands of college courses focusing on women and asking woman-centered questions were created. Hundreds of women's studies programs followed. It was a scholarly revolution of intellectual discoveries integrally related to questions of who and what should be taught.

Education as a Contested Arena: *Who* Should Be Educated?

In the early 1970s in the United States—as they always had—men outnumbered women in higher education, a situation found throughout the world. Despite advances, disagreements continue to the present, particularly in the developing world, about who should be educated. One extreme point of view flourished in Afghanistan in the 1990s, where the Taliban regime won political control and prohibited girls and women from attending any kind of school outside their home. Before this regime, a significant number of those who achieved university education in Afghanistan had been women. What was the Taliban's objection to girls and women being educated? Theirs was a fundamentalist religious position: it was not women's "place." Throughout history, elite males of all religions have striven to control access to reading and writing (see Chapter 9).

Nearly two-thirds of the people in the world who are not literate today are female. The United Nations Educational, Scientific, and Cultural Organization (UNESCO) defines literacy as a person's ability, with understanding, "to read and write a short simple statement" about their everyday lives (United Nations, 2000:86). What causes this unequal access to education? One obvious answer is the pattern of social subordination that women experience globally. In every society, daughters and wives are still expected to be responsible for domestic duties, even when they undertake income-producing labor outside the home as well (see Chapter 12). The idea that domestic duties should be the goal of any girl's education has a long history. Even educators who have wanted to offer some schooling to girls have had different goals for them compared to their brothers. Through the centuries, daughters who aspired to the same kind of formal education considered proper for their brothers have had to struggle to achieve it.

Women's Struggles for Formal Education in the Past

In the ancient world (c. 800 B.C.E.–400 C.E.), young Greek males of the small, privileged citizen class (perhaps 10% of the population) were educated in athletics, music, and reading. Despite the small numbers who were allowed to become citizens, ancient Greece is often given pride of place in the history of Western civilization as the birthplace of enlightened ideas. The sisters of elite citizen men were only occasionally taught to read and write however. A few studied and practiced poetry, music, and philosophy. Even more rare were women who learned medicine in classes taught by physicians, a few writing gynecological texts (Pomeroy, 1975, 1977). Formal education was not available to the rest of Greek society, made up of the lower classes or slave men and women. In ancient Rome, propertied citizens similarly educated their sons, but unlike the Greeks they were more inclined to think it desirable that their daughters read Latin and Greek literature, play the lyre, and know how to dance (Snyder, 1989; Pomeroy, 1975).

Late in the ancient world, in Egypt, a truly exceptional woman named Hypatia (c. 370–415), taught by her learned father, became a teacher of mathematics, astronomy, and philosophy at the school at Alexandria. By her lifetime, Alexandria had become a Christian city. As a prominent pagan philosopher, Hypatia was the subject of great hostility from the church authorities and suffered a horrific death. A crowd of angry monks set upon her, cut up her body, and set it on fire (Ronchey, 2001; Dzielska, 1995). Wherever learning existed elsewhere in the world during this period, it remained in the hands of elite men, who used it to maintain their privileged positions.

In the thousand years that followed (c. 400–1400), formal education in medieval western Europe continued within Christian monasteries and convents. In the late eighth and early ninth centuries, a small number of royal tutors taught the daughters and sons of rulers like Emperor Charlemagne. Throughout these years in Europe, men of titled and propertied families were more concerned about swordsmanship and field sports than in learning to read. Formal education was left to the clergy, who used their skills on behalf of their secular rulers, and to cloistered nuns as well as some women of the upper social ranks placed in convent schools by their families to become nuns or as a safe harbor until marriages could be arranged (McNamara, 1996; Lucas, 1983).

Despite these obstacles, there were a few notable learned women in medieval Europe. Their intellectual achievements include Latin plays by Hroswitha (935–1001), a dramatist and nun in Gandersheim, Germany; the mystical writings by the abbess Hildegard (1098–1179) of Bingen, Germany (Thiébaux, 1994); and song poems by women troubadours in southern France in the twelfth and thirteenth centuries (Bogin, 1976). Trotula (c. 11th century), the wife and mother of physicians, taught at a medical school in Salerno, southern Italy, that was exceptional in allowing both women and men to study and teach there. She wrote books on gynecology and obstetrics used for centuries thereafter (Green, 2001). By the thirteenth century, however, European universities came to dominate formal learning; and admission to these institutions was solely for the purpose of training men for careers in theology, law, and medicine.

Elsewhere in the world during the fifth to fifteenth centuries, only women who belonged to aristocratic or royal families could learn to read and write. Only a few examples are known. Several women at the Japanese emperor's court in the Heian period (794–1192), for example, kept diaries and wrote letters to each other. One royal woman, Lady Murasaki Shikibu (c. 978–1030), produced the world's earliest epic novel, the *Tale of Genji*, a story about the love adventures of a prince at court (Jayawardena, 1986). In Islamic Spain, Walladah Bint Mustakfi (c. 1001–80), the daughter of the caliph (ruler) of Cordoba, composed love poetry in the flourishing intellectual climate established by her father. At the Sung court in Confucian China, Li Quing-zhao (c. 1084–1151), the daughter and wife of scholars, wrote poetry as well as essays and was a keen observer of the corrupt court politics around her. In the Middle East generally, Islam as a religion required both women and men to study the Koran, creating a measure of literacy for girls. In the thirteenth to fifteenth centuries, a number of Muslim women from scholarly and noble households were educated to a high degree. They were generally taught in the homes of family members or religious scholars, and a few of them contributed notably to literary and theological writings (Nashat, 1999).

From the fifteenth to eighteenth centuries in Europe, government bureaucracies developed, giving employment to learned men. An urban commercial class, dependent on a high level of literacy, grew in importance. Expectations for formal education increased for secular men as knowledge became a means for governing the state more efficiently and for serving the expanding needs of business enterprise. Although new avenues of scholarly inquiry developed, assumptions about women's inferior "nature" and impaired mental capacities persisted (Boxer and Quataert, 2000). Humanist ideas increased the value of formal education for sons of many aristocratic families. A small number of privately educated "learned ladies" existed in Italy and delivered orations and wrote dialogues, treatises, and poems in the style of the male scholarly humanists of their day. Although highly praised for their achievements, these women were not received as equals in the company of learned men, nor were they given opportunities to enter the learned professions. Learned women ultimately faced an absolute choice: either marry and abandon their studies or withdraw from the social world to a convent in order to continue them (King, 1980).

A small number of educated women did dare to speak out against the dominant view that denigrated women's capacities. Christine de Pizan (c. 1364–1430) accompanied her physician father from Venice to the French court. When she became a young widow with children, she supported herself by writing lyric poetry, courtly romances, and tracts on moral conduct and public matters. In *The Book of the City of Ladies* (1405), she wrote of the achievements of famous women of the past, chiding male writers who had distorted women's abilities when writing about them in their secular and religious texts (Boxer and Quataert, 2000). With the invention of the printed book, literacy flourished among men, who benefited from schools available to them in villages and in growing cities. These schools did not admit females. As before, women of the wealthier classes might be tutored privately. In Catholic countries, convents educated a small number of elite women in religion and some elements of reading, writing, and arithmetic (Lee, 1975).

There were two powerful women rulers in Europe in the sixteenth century, Catherine de Medici (1519–89) in France and Elizabeth I (1533–1603) in England, both well-educated humanist scholars. As the Protestant Reformation took hold in a number of countries, some educated women aristocrats sought to influence court life with discussions of the Scriptures and church reform (Boxer and Quataert, 2000). Protestant reformers of the period promoted reading the Bible as the proper education for both girls and boys but soon placed restrictions on women. While such activities opened up opportunities for women in a growing middle class to become literate, religious reformers emphasized the need for women's moral training, not their intellectual development.

European Colonization and Women's Education

After 1500 and until the second half of the twentieth century, Western countries expanded their possessions overseas in search of far-flung sources of trade and wealth through the use of force. In imposing European power, institutions, and practices on many parts of Asia, Africa, the Middle East, and the Americas, the issue of who should be educated soon became a critical one within these colonial regimes since the primary goal of the colonizers was to create an empire with an orderly and disciplined local labor force. For women, the consequences were mixed. Christian missionary schools for girls often provided colonized women with their first opportunity for formal education, but Western education introduced new concepts of European racial and cultural superiority. As the West increasingly began to view the education of women as a symbol of modernity, indigenous elites who identified with their colonial masters sought to redefine their traditional concepts, including that of womanhood (Edwards and Roces, 2000; Berger and White, 1999). In new Latin American nations in the latter part of the nineteenth century, for example, indigenous women received schooling after enlightened local leaders expanded secular education for women in order to demonstrate the modern nature of their states (Sànchez Korrol, 1999).

Local men of privilege sought to replicate nineteenth-century European codes of conduct. In the multiracial British Caribbean, for example, lower-class black girls and boys attended schools together but studied different subjects, which prepared females to be domestic servants and males to be artisans. At the secondary level, upper-class white males were educated for the professions and senior positions in the colonial administration, while middle-class males, many of whom were of mixed race (then called "colored" or "mulatto") received training for the civil service and commerce. Middle-class and upper-class females were groomed to be able wives for educated husbands. While they received more

years of schooling, the curriculum, with its emphasis on household subjects such as needlework, differed little from that provided to black lower-class girls (Ellis, 1986). The content and nature of education, following Western models, were meant to prepare colonized women to play supportive domestic roles within a patriarchal family system, facilitating the advancement of local male elites in a system differentiated by color, caste, and gender (Jayawardena, 1986).

By the twentieth century, many colonies had government-supported elementary schools for girls and boys, which increased access to literacy; but boys more than girls were consciously encouraged. A few private secondary schools and a very small number of universities aimed at training indigenous men as professionals and political leaders were established as well. Some colonial subjects, including a few women, studied at educational institutions and church-related schools in Europe or the United States. Such opportunities enabled a select group of women in India, for example, to return home as teachers, midwives, doctors, and lawyers (Burton, 1998; Jayawardena, 1986) and a small number of women in colonized eastern and southern Africa to train for vocations deemed suitable for women, such as teaching, nursing, and social welfare (Berger, 1999).

Some colonial governments simply neglected educational services, as in the Portuguese African territories of Angola, Guinea-Bissau, and Mozambique (Lindsay, 1980). In the Belgian Congo, discrimination against women in schooling was a matter of colonial law, resulting in one of the lowest literacy rates for women in the world (Yates, 1982). Where it existed, European-sponsored education mirrored traditional European gender values, which meant that secular schools for colonial peoples emphasized formal education only for boys. Where local women had previously wielded a measure of political and economic power in their pre-colonial societies, there was a measurable decline in their status (see Chapter 13).

Education in the Developing World Today

Though more women than men around the world lack literacy, the situation has slowly begun to change. Women reformers in the developing world have successfully challenged the colonial view of women's education. Feminist literature of the late nineteenth and early twentieth centuries in these societies debated the nature of women's education and shared information about common struggles for change. Though literacy remained possible for relatively few women in the developing countries, those few gained wider access to the ideas being aired around the globe. After 1906, for example, literate Iranian women could obtain a weekly newspaper called *Danish (Knowledge)*. It was published by one of several women's secret societies that had been founded to expand educational opportunities for girls. By 1914, literate Egyptian women had fifteen journals in Arabic from which to choose. In 1919 in China, where revolution had removed the ruling dynasty, there were 400 new nationalist and feminist periodicals and magazines openly questioning Chinese women's subordination, including foot binding and traditional marriage customs (Jayawardena, 1986).

Women actively supported and served as fighting soldiers in independence movements and wars of national liberation that ended Western colonialism in the three decades after World War II (see Chapter 13). In the 30 and more years since achieving nationhood, the women of these new countries have increasingly acquired more schooling. Because developing nations represent a wide range of cultures, religions, political ideologies, and economic resources, their commitment to ex-panding educational opportunities for women has varied and wide discrepancies remain in the literacy statistics between women and men (United Nations, 2000). Whether because of traditional or renewed religious fundamentalism or because of the enormous costs of national reconstruction, social and economic choices are often made at the expense of women's development. Such was the case in Eritrea in the 1990s, when decisions by male leaders to direct fewer resources to women's education began to reverse the earlier gains made by women during the war of independence, 1961–91 (Stefanos, 1997).

Gender inequity has accompanied many efforts on behalf of economic development, a key concern of developing nations since the 1970s. Feminists in both the developing world and the West have been critical of the strategies used by most developing states in education and economic planning. Development planning that imposes traditional Western values and standards upon developing nations tends to perpetuate gender roles that discriminate against women, depriving them of access to resources, ignoring their real but "invisible" contributions to economic growth, and relegating them to the West's notion of the domestic sphere. Where educational opportunities do exist, too often they prescribe a gender-specific curriculum that tracks women mainly into specialized fields in any given society. The greater number of women to suffer from such gender inequity has been the poor, rural, and illiterate (Edwards and Roces, 2000; Rogers, 1980).

As the global community has come to accept access to formal education as a human right for all, feminists have expanded the debate about women's education. They have called for transforming the education system, including incorporation into the curriculum of the values, perspectives, and experiences of women everywhere and their full and equal participation at all levels of education (Martin, 2000). As in earlier centuries, the struggle for ever higher levels of formal education has been led primarily by women who simply refuse to accept the view that they are intellectually inferior.

Affirmative Action in the United States

Patterns of discrimination against women and other disadvantaged groups in society continue to limit access to formal education. Before the U.S. Civil War, the South had been without any system of public education. When public schools were introduced, they were formally segregated by race, with educational facilities for black children seriously underfunded. After 1865 and a brief period of reconstruction, state laws began introducing segregation in public facilities, including schools, and erected barriers to exercising the right to vote. For 50 years after the Civil War, the majority of African Americans continued to live in southern states, where economic debt and local laws maintained a structure of economic, social, and political discrimination. This segregated system was upheld by the U.S. Supreme Court in *Plessy* v. *Ferguson* in 1896 on the southern claim that their public schools were "separate but equal." It took half a century and the U.S. Supreme Court case *Brown* v. *Board of Education* (1954) to overturn that decision. The court condemned these practices as inherently "unequal" based on arguments concerning the adverse psychological effects of segregation.

Many schools and universities in the south attempted to resist the implementation of desegregation. A few courageous African Americans—schoolchildren and university students—acted on their new legal rights, and federal troops had to protect them in the face of local resistance. A growing civil rights movement in the 1950s and 1960s focused on ending segregation and winning back African

American voting rights. The Civil Rights Act of 1964 condemned all forms of discrimination "based on race, color, religion, sex, or national origin." Titles (paragraphs) VI and VII explicitly extended the terms of the act to higher education, as did Title IX of the Education Amendments of 1972. According to the latter, "No person . . . shall, on the basis of sex, be excluded from participation in, be denied the benefit of, or be subjected to discrimination under any educational program or activity receiving Federal financial assistance." The policies adopted by employers and higher-education institutions to conform to the spirit as well as the letter of these laws came to be known as "affirmative action." Ending discrimination meant acting affirmatively to compensate for the long-existing patterns of discrimination that had barred white women and women and men of color from enjoying equal access to studying and teaching at professional schools—law and medical schools in particular and higher education in general.

Affirmative action was actively challenged in the late 1980s and into the 1990s by a growing conservative movement in the United States, which called it "reverse discrimination" against whites, particularly white males (Messer-Davidow, 2002). The 1978 U.S. Supreme Court in *Regents of the University of California* v. *Bakke* sustained affirmative action policies by a single vote. As affirmative action increased the numbers of white women and women and men of color admitted to universities as students and hired as faculty and administrators, resistance to these policies gained support in conservative circles. In November 1996, in California, a statewide referendum, Proposition 209, sanctioned the end to affirmative action policies in public universities. In May 2001, however, in arguing for the desirability of diversity among its student body, the regents of the University of

In September 1957, nine black children attempted to integrate Central High School in Little Rock, Arkansas. The young woman in this photograph shows the courage necessary to face the jeers and threats of local people encouraged by Governor Faubus. President Eisenhower called out the national guard to protect these students.

California system once again asserted the value of diversity as one factor, but not as the sole criterion, for undergraduate admissions. In June 2003, the Supreme Court upheld the admissions policy of the University of Michigan Law School, specifically citing Justice Sandra Day O'Connor's ruling that a student body's diversity justified the use of race in university admissions (see below), even as it struck down the point system used by the University of Michigan for undergraduate admissions.

> **Box 10.1 DIVERSITY AS A "COMPELLING INTEREST" IN HIGHER EDUCATION**
>
> The fourth goal asserted by petitioner is the attainment of a diverse student body. This clearly is a constitutionally permissible goal for an institution of higher education. Academic freedom, though not a specifically enumerated constitutional right, long has been viewed as a special concern of the First Amendment. The freedom of a university to make its own judgments as to education includes the selection of its student body. Thus, in arguing that its university must be accorded the right to select those students who will contribute the most to the "robust exchange of ideas," petitioner invokes a countervailing constitutional interest, that of the First Amendment. In this light, petitioner must be viewed as seeking to achieve a goal that is of paramount importance in the fulfillment of its mission.
>
> *Source: Regents of the University of California* v. *Bakke,* 438 U.S. 265 (1978).

Diversity in Higher Education

When Supreme Court Justice Lewis Powell wrote the deciding opinion in the Bakke case, he justified his action in terms of the legitimacy of the educational goal of achieving a diverse student body (see Box 10.1).

Affirmative action raises the status of diversity on an academic campus in terms of gender, race, and ethnicity as a positive value in its own right. In a nation and world characterized by diversity, if we are to understand what this means in terms of culture, values, points of view, and the complexities of individual views despite labels and identities, we need to see that diversity at work in terms of people's lives, thoughts, and actions. Diversity up close reveals similarities as well as differences. Experiencing diversity and that "robust exchange of ideas" to which Justice Powell refers is an education that we cannot afford to miss. The learning experiences of all are enhanced by the multiple diversities of those who come together in a spirit of inquiry and investigation. The issue of diversity is also basic to the contested arena of educational equity. This is the question of what should be taught.

Education as a Contested Arena: *What* Should Be Taught?

Women's Traditional Knowledge

Through the centuries and across cultures, women have taught themselves and their daughters the knowledge needed to survive. Women's traditional knowledge has played a crucial role in the survival of their families and communities in terms of food and clothing as well as healing, birthing, and mourning rituals. Among most nomadic peoples, women designed, built, and transported the tents that housed their families. Among settled villages, women bartered goods and, in some areas, organized long-distance trade. Women's productive role was constant but varied with societies and regions. In some instances, women were acknowledged as crucial to all aspects of village life, but too often they remained relatively invisible to the men around them, subsumed under their domestic roles.

Formal Knowledge Defined by Men

Often, women themselves have accepted the male devaluation of women's knowledge. As a result, women have accepted men's claims and have sought to gain access to men's formal education on the belief that it would give them educational equality. Only with the second wave of feminism in the twentieth century has it become clear that what privileged men have defined as formal knowledge is only a partial knowledge. Traditionally, men's formal knowledge, the greater part of formal education for so long, has excluded large portions of human experiences and achievements, those for which white women and women and men of color are largely responsible. To include this neglected portion changes the whole. Yet, men's knowledge has been accepted through history as the standard of intellectual excellence, and women worldwide have sought to share it.

The Goals of Women's Education Debated

Over the last four centuries, conservatives and progressives have debated the proper goals of women's education. Abbé Fénelon, an influential cleric at the court of King Louis XIV of France, for example, endorsed the idea that girls should be taught primarily "women's subjects," which he defined as the duties of a good (obedient) wife (Lougee, 1976). Contemporaries who opposed him included three Englishwomen who founded schools for girls that provided the more rigorous academic education taught young men, including logic, Greek, Hebrew, math, and poetry. Bathsua Makin (1600–75), learned in many languages and tutor to one of the daughters of King James I of England, argued in 1673 that an academy for young women would not harm their chances for marriage but would benefit their families and the young women themselves (Boxer and Quataert, 2000; Teague, 1998). In 1694, Mary Astell (1666–1731) protested that it was solely custom and prejudice, not nature that limited women's educational development (Hill, 1986). Hannah Woolley, seventeenth-century commentator on the female sex, spoke her mind in more crude and witty terms (see Box 10.2).

In the late eighteenth century, the popular and widely read French philosopher Jean-Jacques Rousseau set out his views about the ideal education for a young man in *Émile* ([1762] 1974). For Émile's wife, Sophie, he

---

Box 10.2   THE RIGHT EDUCATION OF THE FEMALE SEX

The right Education of the Female Sex, as it is in a manner everywhere neglected, so it ought to be generally lamented. Most in this depraved later Age think a Woman learned and wise enough if she can distinguish her Husbands Bed from another. Certainly Man's Soul cannot boast of a more sublime Original than ours, they had equally their efflux from the same eternal Immensity, and [are] therefore capable of the same improvement by good Education. Vain man is apt to think we were merely intended for the Worlds propagation, and to keep its humane inhabitants sweet and clean; but by their leaves, had we the same Literature, he would find our brains as fruitful as our bodies. Hence I am induced to believe, we are debar'd from the knowledge of humane learning lest our pregnant Wits should rival the towering conceits of our insulting Lords and Masters.

Source: From Hannah Woolley in Joan K. Kinnaird, Mary Astell and the conservative contribution to English feminism. *Journal of British Studies* 19, p. 53, 1979. Reprinted with the permission of the University of Chicago Press.

recommended an education that would make her a charming companion, one submissive to her husband's will and domestic needs (Keohane, 1980). Rousseau's prescription was challenged by Catharine Macaulay (1731–91), author of the eight-volume *History of England* (1763–83), who called for women learning alongside men and sharing the same curriculum and physical exercises (Boos, 1976).

The more passionately written response to Rousseau's views came from Mary Wollstonecraft (see Chapter 2). Supporting herself from the age of 19 as a lady's companion, needleworker, governess, schoolmistress, journalist, and translator, the middle-class Wollstonecraft deplored the useless "accomplishments" society thought appropriate for young women. Her *Vindication of the Rights of Woman* (1792) pointed out that since Sophie's abilities were left uncultivated, she would make a poor mother for Émile's children. Young women must have the same education as men, she argued, to enable them to be rational, competent, and independent. She insisted that women could fulfill their domestic roles best if they learned first to respect themselves as individuals (see Sapiro, 1992).

This debate was not limited to European societies. In China, Confucian ideology maintained a patriarchal system and gave its greatest rewards to males who mastered the learning required to become a scholar-official. A few exceptional scholar-officials advocated some forms of education for women. Lu K'un, in 1590, for example, encouraged women to gain practical expertise, such as medical knowledge. Ch'en Hung-mou (1696–1771) argued that all people were educable in some fashion and that women should not be neglected. Women of the upper and middle ranks around the world were also more likely to lead less restricted lives than the conventional prescriptions of societies required; a few even managed to become scholars, writers, artists, and poets.

The Debate in the United States

In colonial America, formal education for women beyond their "letters" was considered inappropriate, dangerous, and unsettling to the performance of domestic duties. Male literacy rates may have been as high as 80% at the time of the American Revolution, while women's literacy remained as low as 45% (Cott, 1977). After the Revolution, women were expected to be virtuous examples for their brothers, husbands, and sons and exemplary mothers for future heroes and statesmen (Kerber, 1980). Turned down by the New York State legislature to finance a public female seminary to train teachers, Emma Willard (1787–1870) went on to establish a private academy in Troy, New York, in 1821 (Cott, 1977). Willard's message to each graduating class of young women over the next three decades became important in reshaping women's education throughout the nation. She told them that women were capable of studying any academic subject they chose, that they should prepare themselves to be self-supporting in a profession, and—most daring of all—that marriage was not an end in itself. Graduates of her Troy Female Seminary, renamed the Emma Willard School in 1814, formed a widespread network committed to the education of women and to the professionalization of teaching. Similar wide-ranging networks were created by Catharine Beecher (1800–78) in her Hartford Female Seminary and Mary Lyon (1797–1849) at Mount Holyoke (Solomon, 1985).

By the 1870s, when men were discovering new careers in industry, young women began to replace them in what had been a male-dominated teaching profession. Taught by society to value their own efforts as less than men's, they readily agreed to accept far lower wages than men had been paid (Kaufman, 1984). Susan B. Anthony spoke out against this inequity (see Box 10.3).

Box 10.3   EQUAL PAY FOR WOMEN TEACHERS, 1853

In 1853, Susan B. Anthony, a teacher and leader in the nineteenth-century women's rights movement, attended an education convention at Rochester, New York. She listened to long discussions of the low prestige in which the teaching profession was held, compared to the law, medicine, and the ministry. The discussion was conducted entirely by men, "the thousand women crowding that hall could not vote on the question," nor did they venture to speak. After asking to be heard, and waiting for a further half-hour discussion on whether her request would be granted, she spoke:

It seems to me, gentlemen, that none of you quite comprehend the cause of the disrespect of which you complain. Do you not see that so long as society says a woman is incompetent to be a lawyer, minister, or doctor, but has ample ability to be a teacher, that every man of you who chooses this profession tacitly acknowledges that he has no more brains than a woman? And this, too, is the reason that teaching is a less lucrative profession, as here men must compete with the cheap labor of women. Would you exalt your profession, exalt those who labor with you. Would you make it more lucrative, increase the salaries of the women engaged in the noble work of educating our future Presidents, Senators, and Congressmen?

Source: Quoted passage from Gerda Lerner, *The Female Experience: An American Documentary.* New York: Oxford University Press, 1992:235–6.

By the twentieth century, women made up over one-half of the more than 200,000 teachers in U.S. public elementary and secondary schools. When women sought entry into higher education, they were accepted in a few of the new government-supported "land-grant" state universities being established. Only Iowa State University permitted women to enroll from the outset, starting with two women out of thirty-two students in 1869. By 1870, eight state universities were open to women, but they were often enrolled in separate "female departments" (Newcomer, 1959). Separate private colleges for women were also established in this period: Vassar (1861), Smith (1871), Wellesley (1875), Bryn Mawr (1885), and Radcliffe (1894).

The lack of funds available for higher education for blacks in general discouraged the creation of separate colleges for African American women. The exceptions—Bennett College (1873), Miner Teachers College (1873), and Spelman College (1881)—were located in the South and established with the assistance of white Northern philanthropists and missionary associations (Ihle, 1986:III, IV). One African American woman, Anna Julia Cooper (1858–1964), who made the education of girls her special concern, was born in slavery and ended life with a Ph.D. in Latin earned in Paris. She wrote eloquently on the need for the higher education of black women (see Box 10.4).

Modern Culture Wars

The Struggle for Equal Access to Knowledge

The contested areas of who should be educated and what should be taught discussed in the previous two sections continue and have been referred to in the present as the modern "culture wars." Beginning in the late 1800s and until today, the debate over what should be taught women has not changed significantly. It

---

Box 10.4   ANNA JULIA COOPER ON THE HIGHER EDUCATION OF WOMEN

In the very first year of our century, the year 1801, there appeared in Paris a book . . . entitled "Shall Woman Learn the Alphabet?" The book proposes a law prohibiting the alphabet to women, and quotes authorities weighty and various, to prove that the woman who knows the alphabet has already lost part of her womanliness. The author declares that women can use the alphabet only as Moliere predicted they would, in spelling out the verb amo; . . . while Sappho, Aspasia, Madame de Maintenon, and Madame de Stael could read altogether too well for their good; finally if women were once permitted to read Sophocles and work with logarithms, or to nibble at any side of the apple of knowledge, there would be an end forever to their sewing on buttons and embroidering slippers.

. . . Now I claim that it is the prevalence of Higher Education among women, the making it a common everyday affair for women to reason and think and express their thought, the training and stimulus which enable and encourage women to administer to the world the bread it needs as well as the sugar it cries for . . . that has given symmetry and completeness to the world's agencies.

Source: Loewenberg and Bogin, 1976:318–19, 321.

---

has been couched in terms of either a curriculum attuned to women's primarily domestic duties or a curriculum that represented exactly what men were taught (Delamont, 1978; Wein, 1974). Those advocating for the same curriculum argued that only by studying the same curriculum as men could women win full public recognition for their educational achievements. Educators who resisted the same curriculum were influenced by the writing of a retired Harvard medical school professor, Edward Clarke, whose book *Sex in Education* (1873) warned that developing a young woman's intellect could be done only at the expense of her physical health, in particular her reproductive capacities (see Walsh, 1977).

Expansion of Access to Higher Education

The second half of the twentieth century was marked by an extraordinary increase in access to higher education. Beginning with the 1944 G.I. Bill, offering to pay education expenses for returning World War II veterans, millions of students, including a small number of ex-service women, sought admission to institutions of higher learning. As colleges welcomed male veterans and expanded their facilities to meet their needs, women, including college graduates, were urged to seek early marriage and early motherhood.

Re-entry Women

By the 1960s, *re-entry women*—adult women who "dropped out" of colleges earlier in their lives—became the fastest growing component in higher education. A growing women's movement led more adult women to "drop back in" to prepare themselves for employment or career transitions (Chamberlain, 1988). Further incentives came from the U.S. government. New State Commissions on the Status of Women set up by President John F. Kennedy in 1960 began to track patterns of institutional discrimination against women. In answer to Sputnik's launch into space by the Soviet Union in 1957, the world's first

---

Box 10.5 WOMEN'S EDUCATION AT HUNTER COLLEGE

Established in 1870 as New York City's first public normal (teacher training) college for women, by 1914 Hunter had developed into a full liberal arts college named after its first president, Thomas Hunter. In 1964, it became coeducational. Hunter College ranked first in a study of the number of female graduates of undergraduate institutions who obtained doctorates in the period 1920–73 (Tidball and Kistiakowsky, 1976). Now a part of the City University of New York, the student body at Hunter has always been at least 70% female, with a large proportion of adult women. Its diverse student body reflects the many cultural, ethnic, and religious groups that make up New York City. The women's studies program, initiated in 1971, became official by 1976, offering now both a major and a minor (Paludi and Tronto, 1992; Helly, 1983). As a result of efforts initiated by the women's studies faculty, as of 1993 all students are expected to complete at least one course focusing on gender or sexual orientation as part of their general education requirements.

---

artificial satellite, the United States sought to reinvigorate higher education with funds to train scientists and other professionals. Women as well as men benefited from the scholarships offered. A growth of community colleges, offering a 2-year curriculum in vocational and liberal arts, opened up new opportunities for re-entry women. Early research indicated that even attending college for only one semester helped strengthen a mature woman's concept of her abilities (Denmark and Guttentag, 1967). For how women's education fared at Hunter College, where this textbook was initiated, see Box 10.5.

Since the 1970s, women's higher-education enrollment in the United States has continued to increase, encouraged by Title IX in 1972 and affirmative action policies (see above), the demands of the women's movement for equity, and women's own educational aspirations. New financial aid programs brought in women of color, immigrant women, and working-class women, many of them adults, in greater numbers than ever before (Hune, 1998). Table 10.1 reveals women's gains, their predominance at the bachelor's and master's levels and their pursuance of doctoral and professional degrees in recent years.

Transforming the Curriculum

With the rise of the second wave of feminism in the late 1960s, feminist scholars began to interrogate the nature of the traditional curriculum. Among the efforts to transform the male-centered curriculum were programs undertaken to acquaint faculty in all disciplines with the advances in knowledge being achieved by studies that focused on women, gender, race, ethnicity, class, and sexuality (Fiol-Matta and Chamberlain, 1994). As a debate developed with those who saw their traditional core values being challenged (Messer-Davidow, 2002; Boxer, 1999; Aiken et al., 1988), a backlash to the new curriculum took place—the "culture wars" of the 1990s. Those unsympathetic with the goals of gender

TABLE 10.1 Degrees Awarded to U.S. Women as a Percentage of the Total Awarded, 1980–1 and 2000–1

	1980–1	2000–1
B.A.	49.8%	57.3%
M.A.	50.5%	58.5%
Ph.D.	32.4%	43.9%
Professional	26.8%	46.2%

Source: Harvey, 2003.

inclusiveness and multicultural education accused those who were instituting curriculum changes of "watering down" the traditional curriculum in terms of the achievements of "Western civilization." The catch phrase used to denigrate those who favored inclusiveness was to accuse them of "political correctness," a term that implied a politicizing of the curriculum for the first time (Levine, 1997; Graff, 1994). Feminist scholars alarmed that multiculturalism introduced a cultural relativity that might be used to justify patterns of oppression against women in other cultures complicated the debate (Okin, 1999). The debate aired for public consumption some of the intellectual ferment stirred up by challenging the traditional European- and male-centered knowledge base and recognized the importance of the questions of *who* should be taught and *what* should be taught.

Schools as Socializers

Schools have helped socialize girls to be obedient, nice, respectful, and quiet, in contrast to instilling competition and independence of thought in boys. By replicating society's gender roles, they perpetuate the structures of sexism in the classroom. Schools do not consciously set out to discriminate in this way, but investigators have found that insofar as teachers and administrators represent the values to which they in turn have been socialized, they perpetuate these structures in educational settings (see Box 10.6).

Elementary Schools

One of the first tasks feminist scholars undertook in the 1970s was to analyze the content of children's books to see what sorts of aspiration are held out to young girls. Elizabeth Fisher (1974), for example, pointed out that the fantasy world of the much-admired picture books used widely with small children is primarily a male world, including the works of the very popular Maurice Sendak, Dr. Seuss, and Richard Scarry. Women on Words and Images (1974), a task force of the Central New Jersey National Organization for Women (NOW), analyzed 134 elementary school books with 2,760 stories and found that boys outnumbered girls five to two as the central focus.

School textbooks in the 1970s, especially in science and mathematics, reinforced that girls would grow up to be passive and boys active. Even the wording of mathematical problems revealed gender bias. In "new math" texts, which arranged people in sets, groups of men

---

Box 10.6   SEXISM IN THE SCHOOLROOM IN THE 1980s

If a boy calls out in class, he gets teacher attention, especially intellectual attention. If a girl calls out in class, she is told to raise her hand before speaking. Teachers praise boys more than girls, give boys more academic help and are more likely to accept boys' comments during the classroom discussions.

Source: Myra Pollack Sadker and David Miller Sadker, Sexism in the schoolroom in the 80s. In *Women: Images and Realities. A Multicultural Anthology,* edited by Amy Kesselman, Lily D. McNair, and Nancy Schniedwind. Mountain View, CA, London, and Toronto: Mayfield Publishing Company, 1995, p. 66. Reproduced with permission of The McGraw-Hill Companies.

appeared as doctors, firefighters, chefs, astronauts, pilots, letter carriers, painters, and police officers, ignoring the existence of women in several of these occupations (Federbush, 1974). Girls were rarely depicted as capable of independent thinking, even in textbooks written by women, who had been socialized to reflect these dominant values (U'Ren, 1971: 325).

Under pressure from feminist revelations of biases against girls and women in educational texts, by the 1980s changes began to be made but too often solely in terms of using pictures of girls and women, while texts continued with "sexism as their subtext" (Sadker and Sadker, 1994). Only since the mid-1980s have introductory social studies and history texts, for example, acknowledged this discrimination, using more gender-neutral terms, such as *Political Behavior* and *Industrial Life*, in their chapter titles in place of *Political Man* and *Industrial Man* (Smithson, 1990).

Secondary Schools

Girls at the secondary level also continue to be discouraged from intellectual achievement, especially in mathematics and science, in which boys are expected to excel. Gender bias subtly influences the use of educational technology, leaving girls behind by making them less likely to use computers or to enroll in computer-programming courses (Smithson, 1990). Many high school counselors, well socialized in their society's values, still urge girls to avoid the more rigorous courses of study and to set their sights on traditional female occupations. Within this context, Carol Gilligan and her associates explored the complexities of female adolescence, including girls' conflicts between a desire to find an autonomous self and identity and a desire to establish relationships or connections (Gilligan et al., 1990). Though it has been supposed

that the central preoccupation of adolescents is to achieve independence, investigators have found that this notion is not sufficient for young women. Adolescent girls seek both autonomy and connection (Stern, 1990).

The teenage years also present young women with many problems that their secondary schools do not do enough to help them resolve. For example, two studies in the 1990s pointed to the serious and pervasive unsupportive environments in which girls in high schools were expected to learn. The American Association of University Women report *How Schools Shortchange Girls* (1992) cited the unequal treatment girls still experienced in curricula, classroom materials, testing, and teacher attention, problems identified decades ago. A joint Wellesley College Center for Research on Women and NOW Legal Defense and Education Fund study (see Stein et al., 1993) added the shocking revelation that girls are sexually harassed in public daily by male classmates and by teachers. The study showed how the high school curriculum continued to teach young women to accept this abuse and how young men continued unchallenged in their intimidating behavior (Stein et al., 1993). A 2001 report of the National Council for Research on Women, *Balancing the Equation*, has identified strategies that successfully increase female participation in such male-dominated fields as math and science. These include, for example, cooperative and hands-on teaching approaches, integration of computer technology into other fields such as politics and health, and supportive mentors and role models.

Higher Education

Gender bias flourishes in higher education as well. Vocational counseling too often has sent women students into traditional, gender-segregated career paths. One study shows that college women, encouraged by both male and female peers to emphasize their attractiveness over their intellect and to value being in a romantic relationship over academic achievements, may choose to drop out or downgrade their educational plans as a way of winning peer approval. Also, African American college women may spend as much time and energy as their white sisters on romantic relationships but are less convinced that their future financial support will come primarily from such a relationship (Holland and Eisenhart, 1990).

In the 1980s and 1990s, the Association of American Colleges' Project on the Status and Education of Women began to focus on women's experiences in higher education. A series of reports discussed those experiences that trivialize and marginalize women's intellectual pursuits, contributing to a decline in college women's academic and career goals. Roberta Hall and Bernice Sandler have examined the "chilly climate" for women as students, faculty, and administrators (Sandler and Hall, 1986; Hall and Sandler, 1982, 1984). Female students of color report how race and gender bias together compound the unwelcoming climate and lack of support they find in higher education. They identify university policies and practices that render women of color invisible, along with the everyday inequities experienced in the classroom and the curriculum and with faculty, staff, and students to the detriment of their academic achievement (Hune, 1998; Moses 1989).

Schools as Gendered Workplaces

At every level of formal learning, gender plays a distinctive role. In elementary and secondary education, with the feminization of elementary school teaching in the United States in the nineteenth century, a gender hierarchy quickly emerged. As the profession came to be dominated by women and pay was lowered, principals and supervisors remained more highly paid men. In high schools, women have usually taught what men called the "softer" subjects of literature, languages, art, and music, while men became the more highly paid specialists in physics, chemistry, mathematics, and the social sciences. At the college and university level, more women now hold faculty positions but they occupy the lower-paid lower ranks (Table 10.2). Women faculty are still absent from some departments. Women faculty, administrators, and staff also face issues of sexual harassment, as do women students. This gendered world of education, from the earliest years, socializes students into a model of power relationships they continue to face at home and in the work world.

A small group of senior women scientists at the Massachusetts Institute of Technology (MIT) analyzed the usually invisible gendered hierarchy of their workplace. In "A Study on the Status of Women Faculty in Science at MIT" (Committee on Women Faculty, 1999), they reported that the percentage of women faculty in the School of Science remained small (8%) despite the existence of a national pool of qualified women scientists. Junior women faculty in general felt supported within their departments. They did not believe that gender bias would hinder their advancement but identified family–work conflicts as potentially having a more detrimental effect on women's than men's careers. Senior

TABLE 10.2 Women by Faculty Rank in the United States by Percentage, 1981–2 and 1999–2000

Faculty Rank	1981–2	1999–2000
Full professor	10.3%	20.9%
Associate professor	20.8%	35.5%
Assistant professor	33.5%	45.8%
Instructors and lecturers	42.8%	51.3%

Source: Harvey, 2003.

women faculty, on the other hand, reported being marginalized and excluded from important committees and decision-making channels within their departments. Data revealed that senior women faculty received less salary, research space, resources, and other supports from MIT than did their male colleagues. Yet, junior women faculty tended to believe that gender discrimination had been "solved" by the previous generation.

Today, more women in the United States have achieved the educational credentials traditionally associated with men but receive disproportionately fewer rewards and less professional acceptance. Historically, women have argued that equal access to formal education would give them gender equity. Why does gender discrimination in the academy remain subtle, all-encompassing, and persistent into the twenty-first century? Virginia Valian (1998) sought to explain why women do not advance professionally as far and as rapidly as men. In addition to overt discrimination against women, she concludes that in early childhood both women and men acquire the same implicit or unconscious hypotheses about sex differences that affect their expectations about women's and men's roles, including how their professional work should be evaluated. These "gender schemas" contribute to small differences in how women and men are treated, but over time they result in pronounced gender disparities in salary, rank, promotion, and prestige. Women's professional advancement is slowed because women accumulate disadvantages while men accumulate advantages. For women to break through the glass ceiling requires attention to stereotypes and gender biases, both hidden and overt, held by both women and men (see Chapters 5 and 12).

A number of women are breaking through the highest levels of higher education administration to become college and university presidents. Women served as presidents of 688 (21.5%) of the more than 3000 colleges and universities in the United States in 2003, an increase from 15% in 1993 (Harvey, 2003). Some distinguished women presidents include Johnnetta B. Cole, Susan Hockfield, Shirley Ann Jackson, Donna Shalala, Ruth Simmons, and Shirley Tilghman.

Education as Cultural Assimilation

Before settlement by Europeans, what is now the United States was home to Native American societies. As a British colony and then a new nation, it also became a new home to Africans, introduced by force as slaves to work the land for the European settlers. This mixed cultural history was added to in the nineteenth and twentieth centuries by new waves of immigrants from eastern Asia and Mexico, northern and western Europe, central and southern Europe, and more recently from the rest of Asia, the Caribbean, Central and South America, and elsewhere. Many were sought as a labor source to help build the nation. Others immigrated to reunite with family members.

Until the mid-twentieth century, access to education for indigenous people and Americans of African, Asian, or Central/South American descent, if available at all, usually meant coeducational but racially segregated and poorly funded schools. The predominant European American group always called for the cultural assimilation of those who differed from them. Schools, whether those of Quaker missionaries in colonial days or the public ones of the new republic, played a leading role in assimilation (Almeida 1997). Each culturally different group, beginning with Native Americans, many of whom were subsequently confined to reservations, and then African Americans once freed from slavery, were taught the European American social and cultural values of those who controlled the nation. By the early twentieth century, this process became known as "Americanization."

Donna E. Shalala, president of Hunter College 1980–7; chancellor of the University of Wisconsin, Madison 1987–93. After serving under President Clinton as U.S. Secretary for Health and Human Services (1994–2001), she became president of the University of Miami in 2001.

Johnnetta B. Cole, president of Spelman College 1987–97, president of Bennett College since 2002, formerly a faculty member at Hunter College. Both Spelman and Bennett are historically African American women's colleges.

Susan Hockfield, a neuroscientist and a former provost at Yale University, became the 16th president of the Massachusetts Institute for Technology in 2004. She is the first woman to hold this office in what has been a traditionally male-dominated institution.

Ruth Simmons, president of Smith College 1995–2001, president of Brown University since 2001.

Shirley Ann Jackson, president of Rensselaer Polytechnic Institute since 1999 and the first African American to earn a Ph.D. (Massachusetts Institute of Technology) in physics in the United States.

Shirley Tilghman, first woman to become president of Princeton University, 2001–present.

The American Indian Experience

To accelerate the assimilation of Native Americans into the European American culture, the U.S. government adopted an off-reservation boarding school program for children from 1878 to 1928 and reinstated it between 1950 and 1980, despite the generally poor facilities available. The boarding schools had a limited and gendered curriculum. Girls learned household work and boys received technical training. Through the "outing system," girls were placed in white American homes during the summer months to develop their English language skills and to gain greater knowledge of European American culture while providing cheap domestic labor (Almeida, 1997).

Today, many American Indian children live in urban areas and attend mainstream public schools, where the curriculum and pedagogy are often in conflict with tribal cultures. Other Native American children attend schools run by the Bureau of Indian Affairs or tribally controlled schools that are often underfunded (Almeida, 1997). College opportunities now include thirty-three tribally controlled American Indian colleges (the first was founded in 1968) where young women and men can be trained in both indigenous and mainstream subjects (Putman, 2001).

Under these conditions, what has been the cost or benefit to Native American women of a formal education? In many cases, relocation from their tribal lands has contributed to high drop-out rates. Some women also become culturally alienated from their tribes and disengage from tribal gender roles and indigenous knowledge that once empowered women. Other Native American women have returned to their peoples with new training to benefit the community. During the 1960s and 1970s, some American Indian women became political activists, to promote Native American rights and to preserve and advance the participation of women in tribal matters (Almeida, 1997). One of the most distinguished is Wilma Mankiller. In 1957, Mankiller and her family were among those forced by government policy to relocate from Oklahoma to California. After attending the University of Arkansas, she returned to her ancestral lands to become a nationally known expert on rural community development. Appointed in 1985 as principal chief of the Cherokee Nation, the second largest tribe in the United States, she became the first woman in modern history to lead a major Native American tribe. Subsequently, she was elected in 1987 and re-elected in 1991 (Mankiller and Wallis, 1993). She retired from that position in 1995.

The African American Experience

Free African Americans before the end of slavery sought education outside the South; afterward, freed slaves turned to education in great numbers for personal and community advancement. Historically, African Americans have placed a high value on education and have considered educated black women as assets to their communities. Educated black women could affect the status of children, secure gainful employment other than domestic work, and ensure that African American culture be preserved and transmitted to the next generation (Collins, 2001).

Who taught African American girls and boys after the Civil War? Typically, white males were supervisors and upper-level teachers, while white women from the North and a few educated black women taught the lower levels. African American women were frequently assigned to remote schools, sometimes facing hostile situations in which they were in danger of being whipped, raped, and even killed (Ihle, 1986:I). Despite the intimidation and lack of resources, many black women persevered and established schools of their own. Lucy Craft Laney (1854–1933), born in slavery, graduated from the first class of Atlanta University in 1873. In 1886, Laney opened Haines Normal and Industrial Institute in Augusta, Georgia, a state that did not provide public high schools for blacks. Her school was unique in offering liberal arts courses at a time when Southern state educators viewed vocational training as a sufficient education for African Americans (Giddings, 1984). Other African American women and the schools for girls they founded include Janie Porter Barrett (1865–1948), the Janie Porter Barrett School for Girls in Virginia; Mary McLeod Bethune (1875–1955), Bethune-Cookman College in Florida; and Charlotte Hawkins Brown (1883–1961), the Palmer Memorial Institute in North Carolina.

By the end of the nineteenth century, African American women teachers taught black children in all regions of the country, largely in segregated schools woefully lacking in books, equipment, and other supports, although deemed by law to be "separate but equal" (Randolph, 2001; Weiler, 1997). Teaching had become for black women the highest paid and most prestigious position available. Until World War I, domestic service and laundry work remained the only other alternatives (see Chapter 12). As with other female teachers, employment was restricted to unmarried women, and black women teachers earned less than black men and all whites (Ihle, 1986:I).

African American women educators participated in the debate between the value of industrial education for blacks, identified with Booker T. Washington (1856–1915), and the position of Harvard-educated W. E. B. DuBois (1868–1963) that an academic program of liberal arts better prepared African Americans for a rapidly changing economy. Activist Ida B. Wells-Barnett (1862–1931), a co-founder of the National Association for the Advancement of Colored People (NAACP), joined DuBois in condemning industrial education for blacks as simply providing menial labor for the nation's economy while severely restricting them from opportunities for advancement.

Through the first half of the twentieth century, most African American women, like American Indian and immigrant women (see below), were trained in domestic science—sewing, laundering, and cooking—with an emphasis on moral virtues and good work habits. While they could find employment as teachers or domestics, they lived in a dominantly white society that, until late in the twentieth century, took as its family model the middle-class household in which men were expected to be the sole breadwinners. Working outside the home, which was a necessity for poor women, was considered by middle-class white society to be a temporary situation, one that remained secondary to meeting the needs of husbands and children (Collins, 2001; Ihle, 1986: I) (see Chapter 12).

Black women, on the other hand, sought education as a tool of liberation, to empower their communities, uplift those in poverty, and become scholars in their own right (Collins, 2001). Today, aided by the expanded access to education of the last 30 years, African American women have moved into many professional fields. Following in the tradition of a long line of distinguished black women educators, three notable college presidents have blazed new paths. Johnnetta B. Cole became the first African American woman to serve as president of Spelman College (1987–97) and in 2002 was named president of Bennett College, both historically black women's colleges. Shirley Ann Jackson, who in 1973 became the first African American (either sex) to earn a Ph.D. in physics, became president of Rensselaer Polytechnic Institute in 1999. Ruth Simmons has moved from the presidency of Smith College

(1995–2001) to that of Brown University, (2001) and is the first African American to lead an Ivy League institution.

The Immigrant Experience

Prior to the Civil War, immigrant girls and boys—largely German or Irish in origin—were taught reading, writing, and arithmetic alongside native-born children in the North. With industrialization, urbanization, and the arrival of East Asian immigrants to Hawaii and the Pacific Coast states (1840s–1920s) and eastern and southern Europeans to Midwestern and Northeastern cities (1880s–1920s), the U.S. educational system was radically transformed. In need of skilled and unskilled laborers, yet fearful of the racial and cultural differences of immigrants, the nation's policy makers looked to the public school system to help "Americanize" immigrants and prepare them for their "proper" places in an industrial economy. Immigrant girls were taught skills and habits for use in the workplace, which included hygiene and patriotism as well as the English language, Protestant values, and European American culture (Seller, 1981). A similar phenomenon occurred among Mexicans in the Southwest.

Immigrant communities relied on the U.S. educational system to provide new opportunities for their children. At the same time, hoping that their U.S.-born children would retain the language and culture of their parents and grandparents, immigrant communities supported (and many continue to do so) ethnic and religious based school programs held at community sites after public school hours or on weekends (Seller, 1977).

Immigrant women struggled to overcome the gender restrictions and conflicting expectations of the dominant society and their own ethnic communities. Access to formal education, often denied to women in their home countries because of tradition, colo-nialism, and limited family resources, was now available to them through the U.S. system of public education. Work and family responsibilities, however, hindered immigrant women from obtaining a formal education. It was their daughters who were "Americanized" in the schools in the first half of the twentieth century. A few grew up to be writers who recorded their experiences. Mary Antin, a Jewish immigrant and author of *The Promised Land* (1912), considered her schoolbooks "a badge of scholarship" and proudly carried them home every day (Seller, 1981:201). In *Nisei Daughter* (1953), Japanese American Monica Sone compared her modest behavior during afternoon Japanese school, with its formality and politeness, to her public school in Seattle, where she was a "jumping, screaming, roustabout Yankee" in the years prior to World War II (Sone, 1953:231). Not all immigrant girls were joyful about the new worlds opened to them. There were painful memories of how they were ridiculed for their accents, dress, and food habits and of being treated as socially inferior during their school years (Gibson and Ogbu, 1991).

Immigrant girls rarely obtained more than elementary education prior to World War II. While young men left school for factory work, young women left school to take care of younger siblings or to earn a small wage for the household. Immigrant families, like most families worldwide, tended to use their limited resources to support boys, rather than girls, in obtaining more education. As in the past globally, higher education for women was viewed as a detriment rather than an asset since marriage was their ultimate goal. Often, a woman's desire for more education contributed to conflict in immigrant households and could mean a temporary or permanent estrangement with her family (Newby, 1977). Women teachers were among the few role models for immigrant girls until the latter part of the twentieth century. Mothers and other female relatives have also encouraged young immigrant women, past and present, to use the educational system to widen their opportunities (Hune, 1998; Seller, 1981).

Since the 1970s, new immigrants and refugees far more diverse in their national origin, culture, language, and social class than previously have demographically changed classrooms from kindergarten through college and professional school. The new ethnic diversity and the demands of people of color for greater inclusion in the curriculum, including ethnic studies at the college level, have contributed to the development of new curriculum and pedagogy in schools. These innovations, often referred to as "multicultural education," like the scholarly revolution in terms of gender occurring contemporaneously, have aimed at greater inclusion of the knowledge from the various cultures of the nation's diverse population and serve as a more democratic model than that of "Americanization" (Sleeter and Grant, 1988). While multicultural education is controversial and has not replaced cultural assimilation and a male-defined Eurocentric bias in the curriculum, immigrant girls and women today find more opportunities in their schooling to express themselves as both American and ethnic and to fulfill their potential (Danquah, 2000).

Empowering Women Learners

Women's increased presence in higher education is complex. It varies across fields and educational levels. At the undergraduate level, women continue to be overrepresented in the field of education itself and in the health professions, while remaining underrepresented in engineering (Harvey, 2003). While more women are earning graduate and professional degrees, they are often undersupported in terms of teaching and research fellowships.

Why, despite extensive education and academic achievement, do women still face a pattern of limited career choices and less support from schools and society for their goals? Virgina Valian (see above) has given us one answer.

The Importance of Education

Educational experiences *do* encourage achievement in women, but what kind should they be? M. Elizabeth Tidball investigated women who were listed in *Who's Who of American Women* and whose college experience occurred between 1910 and 1960. She found that women's colleges produced more achieving women than did coeducational institutions. She concluded that the greater number of women faculty and administrators in women's colleges, who served as role models, made the difference (Tidball, 1973, 1980).

Using Tidball's measurement, Oates and Williamson (1978) compared different types of institution and found that during the 1930s elite Ivy League colleges for women (called the "Seven Sisters") produced more women achievers than other women's colleges and coeducational institutions. They also found that women graduates of coeducational colleges achieved greater prominence as government officials and as faculty members and administrators in professional schools, producing teachers, librarians, and home economists.

Rice and Hemmings (1988) suggested that Tidball's findings can be explained by the highly selective process at the Seven Sisters, which recruit motivated women largely from families with social and economic advantages. Tidball (1991) reasserted the importance of a supportive institutional environment for women's achievement. She argues that coeducational settings frequently have a climate of lower academic expectations for women, a conclusion that Holland and

Eisenhart (1990) made regarding romantic relationships (see above). Tidball (1991:411) claims that all women would benefit from increased numbers of women as faculty, administrators, and trustees and endorses the view of the "chilly climate" (Hall and Sandler, 1982, 1984; Sandler and Hall, 1986) investigators that more equitable classroom and campus environments would benefit both women and men. The influence of single-sex institutions versus coeducation on women becoming achievers after college continues to be debated.

Professional Advancement and Women's Realities

More attention also needs to be given to how women's achievement is defined. The traditional professions requiring higher education have been the professorate, ministry, law, and medicine. Because these professions are practiced outside the domestic sphere, they have been considered men's activities. Men have guarded the custom and privilege of these professions as their "right," and generally women have been socialized to agree with them. Since the 1980s, more women have broken through these barriers to become professors, ministers, lawyers, and doctors (see Table 10.1).

To judge from the field of education, women have not yet gained equity in the professions. They remain the majority of elementary and secondary schoolteachers and continue to be underrepresented as college professors. Since the 1980s, women have been earning more doctorates, generally a prerequisite for college teaching; but they are not being hired as faculty at the same rate and are more likely to be found at the lower ranks (see Tables 10.1 and 10.2). Women are more likely to hold faculty positions in community colleges and public 4-year teaching institutions than in research universities, considered by the educational establishment to be the most prestigious institutions. At 21.5% of all college presidents in 2003, women are also underrepresented at the highest administrative level (Harvey, 2003). Women's salaries at every level remain below those of men at the same level.

Women's Studies and Critical Feminist Pedagogy

The proliferation of courses and programs in women's studies in the United States has heightened the self-consciousness of women in education and has challenged the assumptions about women trained in traditional disciplines. In 1970, California State University at San Diego became the first institution to develop a program of women's studies courses. Among the "founding mothers" of women's studies in its first decade were scholar-activists who brought their organizing skills and experiences in the movements for civil rights and against poverty and the Vietnam War to the struggle to establish women's studies on U.S. campuses (Buhle, 2000).

Women's studies as an intellectual approach challenges the traditional hierarchical structure of higher education. The first women's studies courses were often collaborative efforts that introduced critical new pedagogies that sought to decenter power in the classroom. They also sought to engage students in the classroom by calling on their life experiences to aid the learning process and to promote participatory democracy (Buhle, 2000).

Women's studies remains a feminist critique of the knowledge taught by traditional disciplines. Scholars have sought to correct the distortions and omissions that underpin disciplinary theories of knowledge about the past and contemporary society. Past research has been revisited, and every field of knowledge has been scrutinized for its assumptions and the language that it uses to describe women because even the vocabularies used in the disciplines have communicated traditional male perspectives. Mary Field Belenky and her colleagues (1986), with whom we began this chapter, and scholars such as Patricia Hill Collins (2000), Sandra Harding (1991), and Elizabeth Kamarck Minnich (1990) are among those who have questioned the assumption that there is a "universal" path of development, learning, and knowledge construction.

Today, women's studies is a prominent feature within higher education. New journals, created in the early years of the second wave of feminism to disseminate scholarship in women's studies, such as *Hypatia, Feminist Studies, Gender and Society, Psychology of Women Quarterly, Sex Roles, Signs,* and *Women's Studies,* have become well established and respected. Many university and trade presses have adopted book series on women and gender because they have found an increasing market for them. Scholarly works on feminist theory in many fields and readers in feminist theory for classroom use abound.

By 2000, there were more than 600 undergraduate women's studies programs at institutions public and private, large and small, single-sex and coeducational. These programs enroll the largest number of students of any interdisciplinary field. Undergraduates can take majors and minors in the field. There are more than 100 programs at the master's-degree level, and a small number of doctoral programs have sprung up and they are growing. Graduate students can usually find a wide choice of women's courses within their traditional disciplines. Many programs provide a forum for larger educational issues, including the problems of re-entry women students; gender discrimination in faculty appointments, promotion, and retention; free expression of sexual preferences among students and faculty; provision of health-care, legal, and child-care services for students; and transformation of the knowledge base to reflect the perspectives not only of gender but also of race, ethnicity, class, and sexual orientation (Fiol-Matta and Chamberlain, 1994).

The institutionalization of women's studies on campuses is not monolithic; it involves healthy debate among feminists. Women students and faculty of color and lesbians, bisexuals, and transsexuals, for example, have expressed concerns when they do not feel fully welcomed in some women's studies programs. Many criticize feminist theories and agendas that seem to universalize white middle-class heterosexual women's lives, excluding the significance, perspectives, and experiences of race, ethnicity, national origin, sexuality, class, and other differences among women. Where feminists exist, they take diverse positions. For example, some engage in writing and teaching feminist theory. Others criticize feminist theory as being an approach, and using a language, that is as elitist as that of male writers, which reinforces traditional hierarchies in higher education and ignores the grounding democratic tendency of women's studies. Some feminists have also sought to reconceptualize women's studies as gender studies (Messer-Davidow, 2002; Scott, 1997; Pesquera and Segura, 1996).

The future of women's studies depends on the presence of women students, faculty, and administrators who consider it essential to the educational experience. Women students were in the forefront of initiatives to establish women's studies; they will have to take the responsibility, along with committed faculty, for ensuring that their institutions continue to respond to their needs. Resistance on the part of conservative-minded male faculty and administrators continues. Part of the price that feminists have had to pay for their success in academe has been intellectual harassment of their teaching and scholarly publications (Clark et al., 1996) and continued marginalization in the profession as a whole (Eisenhart and Finkel, 1998). Women will remain underrepresented at the full professor level and in

---

Box 10.7   WOMEN'S STUDIES AS AN INTELLECTUAL REVOLUTION

[S]econdary and higher education constitute an initiation into Western culture, leading students into the ways of seeing and listening and speaking that over the centuries have created both Western civilization and the need for Women's Studies. To see the absence of women as a significant omission means to change civilization, to reform the disciplines, and thereby to change higher education. Thus if women students—half the university population—experience their perceptions or their questions as disruptive, it may be because, in fact, they are so.

Source: Reprinted by permission of the publisher from *Making Connections: The Relational Worlds of Adolescent Girls at Emma Willard School,* edited by Carol Gilligan, Nona P. Lyons and Trudy J. Hanmer, p. 6, Cambridge, MA: Harvard Unversity Press. Copyright © 1990 by the President and Fellows of Harvard College, Copyright © 1989 by the Emma Willard School.

---

many disciplines so long as they continue to experience gender discrimination in hiring, tenure, promotion, and wages. Women's greater familial responsibilities and historic exclusion in the academic community still deny them a full understanding of specific male-defined cultural norms that limit their professional capacity to participate fully (Aisenberg and Harrington, 1988). As with other occupations where women remain in subordinate positions, only mutual support and advocacy will overcome the organizational barriers found in higher education.

In its focus on women's realities and new theories to explain them, women's studies holds the possibility of restructuring knowledge to make it resonant with women's perceptions of the world and women's consciousness as well as men's and thereby has the potential of bringing forth a true intellectual revolution (see Box 10.7).

Summary

Epistemology is the study of what we know and how we know it. Knowledge is not objective but a social construct and part of a political system that has historically and continues to marginalize women's experiences and taught

women to be passive. The rise of feminist scholarship worldwide has challenged a specifically male perspective of knowledge and sought to make women visible and to validate their perspectives.

Societies worldwide always have debated who should be educated. That women's proper place has traditionally been viewed as within the domestic sphere and men's as in the public sphere explains in part why women comprise two-thirds of illiterate persons worldwide today. In the ancient world, in Europe and elsewhere, and through the medieval period, only a few exceptional women became accomplished in literary and scientific endeavors. Religious requirements provided girls and women with opportunities to learn to read; however, the emphasis was on women's moral training, not their intellectual development. Across cultures and over time, women have struggled for access to formal education.

From the 1500s until the 1960s, European colonialism has had varying consequences for colonized women's education. Western ideologies of race, color, class, and gender roles and models for economic development often have contributed to a decline in indigenous women's status from their precolonial period. Today, women in developing countries have gained more schooling, but this varies greatly given the wide range of cultures, political ideologies, and economic resources among these states.

In the United States, *affirmative action* refers to policies to act affirmatively to end historic and long-standing discrimination experienced by women and people of color. A diverse student body contributes to the "robust exchange of ideas" that enhances the educational experiences of all students.

Societies of all cultures past and present have debated whether girls and women should have the same curriculum as boys and men to achieve equity or be schooled in subjects to prepare them primarily to be traditional wives and mothers. Feminists who sought to provide a rigorous education for women often established their own schools. As more women, including adult "re-entry" women, and students of color have enrolled in U.S. higher education and efforts to diversify the curriculum have succeeded since the 1970s, a backlash has occurred to defend "Western civilization" in the curriculum and to oppose affirmative action.

For the most part, the U.S. educational system at all levels—through textbooks, curricula, and teacher preparation—has socialized women to be quiet and submissive, to accept male authority rather than their own experiences, and to choose traditional women's careers. Schools shortchange girls, and in higher education women experience a "chilly climate," which is even more unwelcoming for women of color. That women and men are evaluated differently, resulting in women accumulating disadvantages and men accumulating advantages, contributes to gendered workplaces. Women faculty are concentrated in the lower ranks and paid less at all ranks than their male counterparts.

The educational system is a tool of assimilation in the United States. American Indians, African Americans, and immigrant groups experience pressures to acculturate to the European American values taught in American schools. Although girls and women of color find new opportunities in schooling, the U.S. educational system continues to treat them as inferior and less capable.

Feminist scholars have also debated what kinds of educational experience benefit women's academic achievements. Since the 1970s, women's studies as a feminist critique of knowledge has been established as a distinct field of study in higher education and has begun to be taught in traditional disciplines as well. There is also healthy debate among feminists about the nature and institutionalization of women's studies in the academy. Its future and substance as an intellectual revolution depends on the presence of women students, faculty, and administrators.

Discussion Questions

1. Why did early feminists believe that education was important for women, and why was this idea resisted? How do the world figures for literacy and school enrollment reflect the position of women in various societies?
2. Investigate the statistics for women at your college. Compare the numbers of women and men enrolled, breaking this down by race and ethnicity if possible. Are women to be found in all majors? Are there women faculty in all disciplines? If not, why not?
3. Do you think there are any special advantages or disadvantages to gender-segregated education? On your campus, what institutional supports and resources, if any, are available to women of color; lesbian, bisexual, and transsexual women; women who are differently abled; and adult re-entry women?
4. Trace the educational history of the women in your family as far back as you can go. What were the educational experiences of specific women (your grandmothers, aunts,

mother, sisters, and so forth)? How do their experiences compare with your own, and how do you account for the differences and similarities?

5. What are the opportunities and obstacles you now face in making a career choice? (If you have yet to decide on a career, select an interesting one to think about.) Have your previous educational experiences readily enabled you to pursue this goal? Are there any social expectations by your family and friends that might cause difficulties in carrying out your goal?

Recommended Readings

Belenky, Mary Field, Blythe McVicker Clinchey, Nancy Rule Goldberger, and Jill Mattuck Tarule. *Women's Ways of Knowing: The Development of Self, Voice, and Mind*. New York: Basic Books, 1986. This work challenges the traditional male model of knowing that renders women "voiceless" and considers how women's ways of knowing are legitimate although different because of their experiences and place in society.

Conway, Jill Ker, and Susan C. Bourque, editors. *The Politics of Women's Education: Perspectives from Asia, Africa, and Latin America*. Ann Arbor: University of Michigan Press, 1993. This excellent collection of interdisciplinary articles on the undereducation of women in Asia, Africa, Latin America, and the Middle East focuses on the determinants, nature, and outcomes of women's education in developing countries.

Howe, Florence, editor. *The Politics of Women's Studies: Testimony from Thirty Founding Mothers*. New York: Feminist Press at the City University of New York, 2000. Thirty feminist scholars and activists who helped shape the study of women in the academy from the late 1960s reveal their personal and professional goals, how they met the challenge of institutional resistance, and the nature of the politics they engaged in to construct a new curriculum in the face of sexist attitudes and hierarchical structures.

Lightfoot, Sara Lawrence. *Balm in Gilead: Journey of a Healer*. Reading, MA: Addison-Wesley, 1988. This biography of an African American woman with educational experiences in the South and North provides a moving personal story behind the analysis offered in this chapter. Born in Mississippi in 1914, she eventually attended Cornell University and went on to become a physician and child psychiatrist.

Woolf, Virginia. *A Room of One's Own* (1929). New York: Harcourt, Brace, 1957. This classic work explores the ways women have been prevented from achieving higher education and what this has meant for their lives, independence, and creativity.

References

Aiken, Susan Hardy, Karen Anderson, Myra Dinnerstein, Judy Lensink, Judy Nolte, and Patricia MacCorquodale, editors. *Changing Our Minds: Feminist Transformations of Knowledge*. Albany: SUNY Press, 1988.

Aisenberg, Nadya, and Mona Harrington. *Women of Academe: Outsiders in the Sacred Grove*. Amherst: University of Massachusetts Press, 1988.

Almeida, Deidre A. The hidden half: A history of Native American women's education. *Harvard Education Review*, 67:4, 757–71, 1997.

American Association of University Women. *AAUW Report: How Schools Shortchange Girls*. Washington, D.C.: American Association of University Women, 1992.

Antin, Mary. *The Promised Land*. Boston: Houghton Mifflin, 1912.

Belenky, Mary Field, Blythe McVicker Clinchey, Nancy Rule Goldberger, and Jill Mattuck Tarule. *Women's Ways of Knowing: The*

Development of Self, Voice, and Mind. New York: Basic Books, 1986.

Berger, Iris. Women in east and southern Africa. In *Women in Sub-Saharan Africa: Restoring Women to History*, edited by Iris Berger and E. Frances White. Bloomington: Indiana University Press, 1999.

Berger, Iris, and E. Frances White, editors. *Women in Sub-Saharan Africa: Restoring Women to History.* Bloomington: Indiana University Press, 1999.

Bogin, Meg. *Women Troubadors.* New York: Norton, 1976.

Boos, Florence S. Catherine Macaulay's *Letters on Education* (1790): An early feminist polemic. *University of Michigan Papers in Women's Studies*, 2, 64–78, 1976.

Boxer, Marilyn. *When Women Asked the Questions: Creating Women's Studies in America.* Baltimore: Johns Hopkins University Press, 1999.

Boxer, Marilyn J., and Jean H. Quataert. Women in the early modern era: Religious upheaval, political centralization, and colonial conquest. In *Connecting Spheres: Women in the Western World, 1500 to the Present*, edited by Marilyn J., Boxer and Jean H. Quataert. New York: Oxford University Press, 2000.

Buhle, Mari Jo. Introduction. In *The Politics of Women's Studies: Testimony from Thirty Founding Mothers*, edited by Florence Howe. New York: Feminist Press at the City University of New York, 2000.

Burton, Antoinette. *At the Heart of the Empire: Indians and the Colonial Encounter in Later Victorian England.* Berkeley: University of California Press, 1998.

Chamberlain, Mariam K., editor. *Women in Academe: Progress and Prospects.* New York: Russell Sage Foundation, 1988.

Clark, Vévé, Shirley Nelson Ganer, Margaret Higonnet, and Ketu H. Katrak, editors. *Antifeminism in the Academy.* New York: Routledge, 1996.

Collins, Alicia C. Black women in the academy. In *Sisters of the Academy*, edited by Reitumetse Obakeng Mabokela and Ann L. Green. Sterling, VA: Stylus, 2001.

Collins, Patricia Hill. *Black Feminist Thought: Knowledge, Consciousness, and the Politics of Empowerment*, 2nd ed. New York: Routledge, 2000.

Committee on Women Faculty. A study on the status of women faculty in science at MIT. *MIT Faculty Newsletter*, 11:4, 1999.

Cott, Nancy F. *The Bonds of Womanhood: "Woman's Sphere" in New England, 1780–1835.* New Haven: Yale University Press, 1977.

Danquah, Meri Nana-Ama, editor. *Becoming American: Personal Essays by First Generation Immigrant Women.* New York: Hyperion, 2000.

Delamont, Sara. The domestic ideology and women's education. In *The Nineteenth-Century Woman*, edited by Sara Delamont and Lorna Duffin. New York: Barnes & Noble, 1978.

Denmark, Florence L., and Marcia Guttentag. Dissonance in the self-concepts and educational concepts of college and non-college-oriented women. *Journal of Counseling Psychology*, 14, 113–15, 1967.

Dzielska, Maria. *Hypatia of Alexandria.* Cambridge, MA: Harvard University Press, 1995.

Edwards, Louise, and Mina Roces, editors. *Women in Asia.* Ann Arbor: University of Michigan Press, 2000.

Eisenhart, Margaret A., and Elizabeth Finkel. *Women's Science: Learning and Succeeding from the Margins.* Chicago: University of Chicago Press, 1998.

Ellis, Pat, editor. *Women of the Caribbean.* London: Zed, 1986.

Federbush, Marsha. The sex problems of school math books. In *And Jill Came Tumbling After: Sexism in American Education*, edited by Judith Stacey, Susan Béreaud, and Joan Daniels. New York: Dell, 1974.

Fiol-Matta, Lisa, and Mariam K. Chamberlain. *Women of Color and the Multicultural Curriculum: Transforming the College Classroom.* New York: Feminist Press at the City University of New York, 1994.

Fisher, Elizabeth. Children's books: The second sex, junior division. In *And Jill Came Tumbling After: Sexism in American Education*, edited by Judith Stacey, Susan

Béreaud, and Joan Daniels. New York: Dell, 1974.

Gibson, Margaret, and John Ogbu, editors. *Minority Status and Schooling: A Comparative Study of Immigrant and Involuntary Minorities.* New York: Garland, 1991.

Giddings, Paula. *When and Where I Enter: The Impact of Black Women on Race and Sex in America.* New York: Bantam, 1984.

Gilligan, Carol, Nona P. Lyons, and Trudy J. Hanmer, editors. *Making Connections: The Relational Worlds of Adolescent Girls at Emma Willard School.* Cambridge, MA: Harvard University Press, 1990.

Graff, Gerald. *Curriculum Reform and the Culture Wars.* New York: Garland, 1994.

Green, Monica H., editor and translator. *The "Trotula": A Medieval Compendium of Women's Medicine.* Philadelphia: University of Pennsylvania Press, 2001.

Hall, Roberta M., and Bernice R. Sandler. *The Classroom Climate: A Chilly One for Women?* Washington, DC: Association of American Colleges, 1982.

———. *Out of the Classroom: A Chilly Campus Climate for Women?* Washington, DC: Association of American Colleges, 1984.

Harding, Sandra. *Whose Science? Whose Knowledge?: Thinking from Women's Lives.* Ithaca: Cornell University Press, 1991.

Harvey, William B. *Twentieth Annual Status Report on Minorities in Higher Education, 2002–2003.* Washington, D.C.: American Council on Education, 2003.

Helly, Dorothy O. Women's studies at Hunter College: Strategies in an institutional environment. *Women's Studies Quarterly,* XI, 41–4, 1983.

Hill, Bridget, editor. *The First English Feminist: Reflections Upon Marriage and Other Writings by Mary Astell.* Aldershot, UK: Gower/Maurice Temple Smith, 1986.

Holland, Dorothy C., and Margaret A. Eisenhart. *Educated in Romance: Women, Achievement, and College Culture.* Chicago: University of Chicago Press, 1990.

Hrdy, Sarah Blaffer. Empathy, polyandry, and the myth of the "Coy" female. In *Feminist Approaches to Science,* edited by Ruth Bleier. New York: Pergamon, 1986.

Hune, Shirley. *Asian Pacific American Women in Higher Education: Claiming Visibility and Voice.* Washington, D.C.: Association of American Colleges and Universities, 1998.

Ihle, Elizabeth L. *History of Black Women's Education in the South, 1865–Present: Instruction Modules for Educators,* 4 vols. Washington, D.C.: U.S. Department of Education, 1986.

Jayawardena, Kumari. *Feminism and Nationalism in the Third World.* London: Zed Books, 1986.

Kaufman, Polly Welts. *Women Teachers on the Frontier.* New Haven: Yale University Press, 1984.

Keohane, Nannerl O. "But for her sex . . .": The domestication of Sophie. *University of Ottawa Quarterly,* 49, 390–400, 1980.

Kerber, Linda. *Women of the Republic: Intellect and Ideology in Revolutionary America.* Chapel Hill: University of North Carolina Press, 1980.

King, Margaret L. Book-lined cells: Women and humanism in the early Italian Renaissance. In *Beyond Their Sex,* edited by Patricia H. Labalme. New York: New York University Press, 1980.

Kinnaird, Joan K. Mary Astell and the conservative contribution to English feminism. *Journal of British Studies,* 19, 53–75, 1979.

Kuhn, Thomas. *The Structure of Scientific Revolutions.* Chicago: University of Chicago Press, 1962.

Lee, Vera. *The Reign of Women in Eighteenth-Century France.* Cambridge, MA: Schenckman, 1975.

Lerner, Gerda. *The Female Experience: An American Documentary.* New York: Oxford University Press, 1992.

Levine, Lawrence. *The Opening of the American Mind: Canons, Culture, and History.* Boston: Beacon, 1997.

Lindsay, Beverly, editor. *Comparative Perspectives of Third World Women: The Impact of Race, Sex, and Class.* New York: Praeger, 1980.

Loewenberg, Bert James, and Ruth Bogin, editors. *Black Women in Nineteenth-Century Life: Their Words, Their Thoughts, Their Feelings.*

University Park: Pennsylvania State University Press, 1976.

Lougee, Carolyn C. *Le Paradis des Femmes: Women, Salons, and Social Stratification in Seventeenth-Century France.* Princeton: Princeton University Press, 1976.

Lucas, Angela M. *Women in the Middle Ages: Religion, Marriage and Letters.* Brighton, UK: Harvester Press, 1983.

Mankiller, Wilma, and Michael Wallis. *Mankiller: A Chief and Her People.* New York: St. Martin's Press, 1993.

Martin, Jane Roland. *Coming of Age in Academe: Rekindling Women's Hopes and Reforming the Academy.* New York: Routledge, 2000.

Mascia-Lees, Frances E., and Nancy Johnson Black. *Gender and Anthropology.* Prospect Heights, IL: Waveland Press, 1999.

McNamara, Jo Ann Kay. *Sisters in Arms: Catholic Nuns Through Two Millennia.* Cambridge, MA: Harvard University Press, 1996.

Messer-Davidow, Ellen. *Disciplining Feminism: From Social Activism to Academic Discourse.* Durham: Duke University Press, 2002.

Minnich, Elizabeth Kamarck. *Transforming Knowledge.* Philadelphia: Temple University Press, 1990.

Moses, Yolanda T. *Black Women in Academe: Issues and Strategies.* Washington, D.C.: Association of American Colleges, 1989.

Nashat, Guity. Women in the Middle East, 8,000 B.C.E.–C.E. 1800. In *Women in the Middle East and North Africa,* edited by Guity Nashat and Judith E. Tucker. Bloomington: Indiana University Press, 1999.

National Council for Research on Women. *Balancing the Equation: Where Are Women and Girls in Science, Engineering and Technology?* New York: National Council for Research on Women, 2001.

Newby, Elizabeth Loza. *A Migrant with Hope.* Nashville: Broadman Press, 1977.

Newcomer, Mabel. *A Century of Higher Education for American Women.* New York: Harper, 1959.

Oates, Mary J., and Susan Williamson. Women's colleges and women achievers. *Signs,* 3, 795–806, 1978.

Okin, Susan Moller. *Is Multiculturalism Bad for Women?* Princeton: Princeton University. Press, 1999.

Paludi, Michele, and Joan Tronto. CUNY–Hunter College feminist education. In *The Courage to Question: Women's Studies and Student Learning,* edited by Caryn McTighe Musil. Washington, D.C.: Association of American Colleges and National Women's Studies Association, 1992.

Pesquera, Beatriz M., and Denise A. Segura. With quill and torch: A Chicana perspective on the American women's movement and feminist theories. In *Chicanas/Chicanos at the Crossroads,* edited by David R. Maciel and Isidro D. Ortiz. Tucson: University of Arizona Press, 1996.

Pomeroy, Sarah B. *Goddesses, Whores, Wives, and Slaves: Women in Classical Antiquity.* New York: Schocken, 1975.

———. Technicai Kai Mousikai: The education of women in the fourth century and in the Hellenistic period. *American Journal of Ancient History,* 2, 51–68, 1977.

Putnam, Betsy Mennell. Can tribal colleges maintain identity while seeking legitimacy? *Tribal College Journal,* 13:1, 18–23, 2001.

Randolph, Adah Ward. Fear of miscegenation: Black women educators in Columbus, Ohio (1898–1909). In *Sisters of the Academy,* edited by Reitumetse Obakeng Mabokela and Ann L. Green. Sterling, VA: Stylus, 2001.

Rice, Joy K., and Annette Hemmings. Women's colleges and women achievers: An update. *Signs,* 13:3, 546–59, 1988.

Rogers, Barbara. *The Domestication of Women: Discriminaton in Developing Countries.* London: Kogan Page, 1980.

Ronchey, Silvia. Hypatia the intellectual. In *Roman Women,* edited by Augusto Fraschetti, translated by Linda Lappin. Chicago: University of Chicago Press, 2001.

Rousseau, Jean-Jacques. *Émile* (1762), translated by Barbara Foxley. New York: Dutton, 1974.

Sadker, Myra Pollack, and David Miller Sadker. *Failing at Fairness : How America's Schools Cheat Girls.* New York: Charles Scribner's Sons, 1994.

————. Sexism in the schoolroom in the '80s. In *Women: Images and Realities. A Multicultural Anthology*, edited by Amy Kesselman, Lily D. McNair, and Nancy Schniedwind. Mountain View, CA: Mayfield, 1995.

Sànchez Korrol, Virgina. Women in nineteenth- and twentieth-century Latin America and the Caribbean. In *Women in Latin America and the Caribbean*, edited by Marysa Navarro and Virginia Sànchez Korrol. Bloomington: Indiana University Press, 1999.

Sandler, Bernice R., and Roberta M. Hall. *The Campus Climate Revisited: Chilly for Women Faculty, Administrators, and Graduate Students*. Washington, D.C.: Association of American Colleges, 1986.

Sapiro, Virginia. *A Vindication of Political Virtue: The Political Theory of Mary Wollstonecraft*. Chicago: University of Chicago Press, 1992.

Scott, Joan Wallach, editor. Women's studies on the edge. *differences*, 9:3, 1997.

Seller, Maxine Schwartz. *To Seek America: A History of Ethnic Life in the United States*. Englewood, NJ: Jerome S. Ozer, 1977.

————, editor. *Immigrant Women*. Philadelphia: Temple University Press, 1981.

Sleeter, Christine, and Carl Grant. *Making Choices for Multicultural Education*. Columbus, OH: Merrill, 1988.

Smithson, Isaiah. Introduction: Investigating gender, power, and pedagogy. In *Gender in the Classroom: Power and Pedagogy*, edited by Susan L. Gabriel and Isaiah Smithson. Urbana: University of Illinois Press, 1990.

Snyder, Jane McIntosh. *The Woman and the Lyre: Women Writers in Classical Greece and Rome*. Carbondale: Southern Illinois University Press, 1989.

Solomon, Barbara Miller. *In the Company of Educated Women: A History of Women and Higher Education in America*. New Haven: Yale University Press, 1985.

Sone, Monica. *Nisei Daughter*. Seattle: University of Washington Press, 1953, 1979.

Stefanos, Asgedet. Women and education in Eritrea: A historical and contemporary analysis. *Harvard Education Review*, 67:4, 658–88, 1997.

Stein, Nan, Nancy L. Marshall, and Linda R. Tropp. *Secrets in Public: Sexual Harassment in Our Schools*. Center for Research on Women, Wellesley College and NOW Legal Defense and Education Fund. Wellesley, MA: Wellesley Centers For Women, 1993.

Stern, Lori. Conceptions of separation and connection in female adolescence. In *Making Connections: The Relational Worlds of Adolescent Girls at Emma Willard School*, edited by Carol Gilligan, Nona P. Lyons, and Trudy J. Hanmer. Cambridge, MA: Harvard University Press, 1990.

Teague, Frances. *Bathsua Makin, Woman of Learning*. London: Associated University Press, 1998.

Thiébaux, Marcelle, editor. *The Writings of Medieval Women: An Anthology*, translated by Marcelle Thiébaux. New York: Garland, 1994.

Tidball, M. Elizabeth. Perspective on academic women and affirmative action. *Educational Record*, 54, 130–5, 1973.

————. Women's colleges and women achievers revisited. *Signs*, 5, 504–17, 1980.

————. Comment on women's colleges and women's career attainments revisited. *Journal of Higher Education*, 62:4, 406–9, 1991.

Tidball, M. Elizabeth, and Vera Kistiakowsky. Baccalaureate origins of American scientists and scholars. *Science*, 193, 646–52, 1976.

United Nations. *The World's Women 2000: Trends and Statistics*. New York: United Nations, 2000.

U'Ren, Marjorie B. The image of women in textbooks. In *Women in Sexist Society: Studies in Power and Powerlessness*, edited by Vivian Gornick and Barbara K. Moran. New York: New American Library, 1971.

Valian, Virginia. *Why So Slow? The Advancement of Women*. Cambridge, MA: MIT Press, 1998.

Walsh, Mary Roth. *"Doctors Wanted: No Women Need Apply": Sexual Barriers in the Medical Profession, 1835–1975*. New Haven: Yale University Press, 1977.

Weiler, Kathleen. Reflections on writing a history of women teachers. *Harvard Educational Review*, 67:4, 635–57, 1997.

Wein, Roberta. Women's colleges and domesticity, 1875–1918. *History of Education Quarterly*, 14, 31–47, 1974.

Women on Words and Images. Look Jane look. See sex stereotypes. In *And Jill Came Tumbling After: Sexism in American Education*, edited by Judith Stacey, Susan Béreaud, and Joan Daniels. New York: Dell, 1974.

Yates, Barbara A. Church, state and education in Belgian Africa: Implications for contemporary third world women. In *Women's Education in the Third World: Comparative Perspectives*, edited by Gail P. Kelly and Carolyn M. Elliott. Albany: SUNY Press, 1982.

Women's Health

Clayquet Indian healers were predominantly women and they sang songs to compel the spirits to relinquish control of the sick person. One such song cautioned:

Do not listen to the other singing.
Do not be ashamed to sing your own song.

(Jaskoski, 1981)

To understand women's health, we must investigate how the women's healing songs were lost and displaced. We must learn how women have begun to reclaim their own songs.

The Women's Health Movement

Health issues have galvanized political consciousness among women globally. In part, this is because these issues relate to the most fundamental of political questions: Who is to control women's own bodies, their physical selves? Additionally, such issues relate to how the health-care system operates to reinforce and sustain power hierarchies within a given class, race, age, and gender structure. In an interview shortly before her death, physician, activist, and advocate for the underserved Helen Rodriguez-Trias said, "What brought me to the women's movement was the women's health movement. The cultural elements of feminism didn't resonate with me, but abortion resonated with me" (Wilcox, 2002). Such an experience is not unique. The "genitalizing" of women's health has served as both a motivating and an organizing force in the contemporary women's movement. Understanding the issues involved in women's health thus helps us understand an important impetus for women to organize and reform society.

The publication in 1971 of the book *Our Bodies, Ourselves* by the Boston Women's Health Collective marked the coming of age of the modern women's movement. This volume analyzed the implications of patriarchal society for the total well-being of women and provided three critical routes to change: *(1)* empowerment through self-knowledge, *(2)* establishment of women's right and obligation to choose what to do with their own bodies, and *(3)* reliance on mutual support among women.

Redefining Health

As a first step to improving women's health, *health* itself needed to be reconceptualized and a new model for understanding it devised. This might seem strange at first since we often tend to think of health as simply the "absence of disease." However, health is not a static state: the parameters that define health reflect a dynamic, shifting adaptation to the environment over the life cycle of an individual and are influenced by the values inherent in a specific culture. Definitions of *health* are culturally variable: what is considered normal and what is considered an illness vary widely across societies.

In 1946 the World Health Organization (WHO) defined health as "a state of complete physical, mental, and social well-being and not merely the absence of disease and infirmity" (United Nations, 2002a). Today, current Western attitudes have expanded the definition to include the physical, emotional, social, intellectual, and spiritual dimensions of

The Broken Column (1944) by Frida Kahlo (1907–54), oil on canvas. The painter was in a trolley accident as a teenager and had to wear a variety of corsets to support her spine the rest of her life. In this painting, the scattered pins and her naked and corseted upper body display both her pain and her courage.

thus has both subjective and objective components, which influence the way it is defined, the nature of the data collected to study health and disease, and the way different groups of people will be treated by the medical establishment.

New Approaches

The women's health movement has been largely responsible for the view that health is not just the absence of disease but an integral part of a woman's total life experience, inextricably linked to her place in society. This ecological, or social embeddedness, model analyzes the impact of social factors such as race/ethnicity, gender, educational attainment, and socioeconomic status on health. This model has shown that each of these factors locates an individual or group in the structure of society, giving differential access to power, privilege, and desirable resources (Williams, 2002).

One example of how this model has been successfully implemented to uncover obstacles to women's health comes from the Black Women's Health Imperative (formerly the National Black Women's Health Project). A group of African American women living in Atlanta recognized the benefits of physical activity. However, unlike women privileged by class, they lived in neighborhoods without parks that were dangerous for them to walk alone (especially after work and in the dark), making physical activity difficult, even if desirable. Knowing this, Byllye Y. Avery, the founder of the Black Women's Health Imperative, devised a strategy to meet their health needs after recognizing the particular obstacles black women faced. She helped the women to organize walking groups that met and walked together safely through their Atlanta neighborhood. Such efforts to overcome obstacles can have unintended outcomes: participants might become empowered as a group and organize to create a safer

neighborhood, perhaps beginning by urging the city government to install more lights or to create accessible recreation resources.

Reforming the Health-Care System

Women in the women's health movement not only developed new approaches for understanding women's particular health needs but also undertook steps on multiple fronts to reform the health-care system and make it more responsive to women's needs. For example, they called for a personal reappraisal by women of their own bodies and health. Now, women are encouraged to ask questions: What is a state of health for women, and how do women obtain and sustain such a condition? What are the appropriate means of dealing with illness or disease? These questions are essential for women's health, both because women's health has been perceived differently from men's and because women's bodies and biological processes are different in some respects from men's.

The women's health movement has also called for changes in the services a society provides for women, based on its recognition that women have been discriminated against not only as recipients but also as providers of health-care services. For example, medication and treatment for medical conditions not specific to women, such as heart disease, had long been investigated and norms established primarily on the basis of research on men. Medication has too often been prescribed for women when there were too few data on appropriate amounts, side effects, and effectiveness of such treatment for women (Sechzer et al., 1994). This situation has only recently begun to change as women have lobbied for changes in medical testing protocols. In addition, U.S. women have pushed to extend to prescription drugs, including oral contraceptives and hormone replacement therapies (HRT), the Food and Drug Administration (FDA) requirement that manufacturers list a product's ingredients and side effects on package inserts.

U.S. women's health activists have made other important gains in health policy. Over the years, they have managed to keep abortion legal despite many threats to this right. Women now demand reproductive choice, more information about their bodies and health, and stronger roles in the decision making regarding health-care policies. In the United States, the creation of the Office of Research on Women's Health (ORWH) in 1990 and of the Women's Health Initiative (WHI) in 1991 has led to slowly increasing gender parity in both research and opportunities for women-led research projects. The recent findings regarding HRT, which we discuss below, were funded through the WHI. This reflects a victory won by U.S. feminist activists in the 1990s: to have more federal funds allocated to research on women's health (Morgen, 2002). Activists have also struggled for improvements in accessibility to affordable health care for women and less tolerance for discrimination based on gender, race, sexuality, class, or age.

The efforts of health-care movements under the conditions that prevail in many poor nations around the world are somewhat different from those found in wealthier nations. For example, in developing countries, a primary focus is delivering basic resources such as food, clean water, and shelter to people as well as provisions to alleviate the suffering of the weak and the poor. Around the world, women health activists have lobbied for widespread inoculations against disease, hygiene for infected wounds, creation of more hospitals, and availability of medicines.

Uncovering the Gender Dynamics of Western Medicine

Another important contribution of the women's health movement has been its investigation of how and why women have

TABLE 11.1 Comparing Life Expectancies by Gender, Country, and Year

	1900	*1950*	*1998*
United States			
Female	48.3	71.1	79.5
Male	46.3	65.6	73.8

	1997	
	Female	*Male*
Japan	83.8	77.2
Canada	81.4	75.8
Russian Federation	73.0	61.0

Source: Health, United States, 2002. Hyattsville, MD: National Center for Health Statistics, 2002.

been underserved in terms of their health. Understanding these reasons was an important first step in finding solutions. Feminists have shown how in the nineteenth century a Western male medical establishment co-opted women's role in healing and documented its consequences for women.

In most societies, at most times, and in most places, women have been the primary caretakers of human bodies from birth to death. It has been women's work to tend to birthing, to care for infants and children, and to teach basic habits of sanitation and nutrition to young people. Women care for the sick and wounded, the ailing and weak, and the infirm elderly; usually, women also tend to the dead. Thus, when the caretaker herself requires assistance, especially in later years, in many industrialized nations there is often no one to help her. Although regular day-to-day caretaking has been, and continues to be, done largely by women, male authorities in many Western societies have taken control of the more prestigious forms of healing, organizing into a professional group that has largely excluded women from its ranks.

By the end of the nineteenth century, the Western health-care system had begun to crystallize into the professionalized form it takes today. Men prevailed as leaders of the professional health-care system and propagated ideals about what a normal woman's health was like. These ideals reflected not only gender bias but class, race, and heterosexist biases as well. As we discuss in the following sections, society increasingly assigned health-care authority to men, who perceived women as "other." For men, who do not menstruate, menstruation seemed unhealthy, abnormal, and dangerous (see Box 11.1). For men, who could not experience pregnancy and childbirth, these conditions were mysterious, frightening, and threatening. If men are the authorities to whom women turn for information about these events, certainly men's subjective interpretations are conveyed to women, who learn to perceive the world through men's "expert" eyes. Today, the female body in Western societies has been increasingly medicalized, constructed as an object of medical knowledge, thereby placing it under the gaze and control of the medical establishment. Such normal functions as menstruation and giving birth, once the domain of female family members and midwives, are now the domain of the medical establishment.

Woman as Deviant. Although Western medicine was not professionalized and put into men's hands until the nineteenth century, the assumption underlying it—that a woman is an aberrant man—has much deeper roots (see Chapter 2). One of the earliest writers on the subject of the health of women was Soranus of Ephesus (98–138 C.E.), in whose work the topics of obstetrics and gynecology are treated as but one aspect of health. Soranus declared that women and men had the same physical and health problems, with the sole exception of the area of reproduction (Dean-Jones, 1994). Galen (c. 130–200 C.E.), a Greek physician whose writings influenced Western medicine for centuries, taught that women were "inside-out men." According to Galen, women had insufficient body heat to force

genitals outward. Thus, using man as his measure, Galen viewed women (as Aristotle had) as "defective" persons. Since women were "inferior," it followed that their diseases were caused, almost entirely, by their inferior genitalia (Dean-Jones, 1994).

In later centuries, as the new "science" and "reason" began to overtake the dominant role of the spiritual/religious leaders in Western societies, many moral and spiritual concerns became the domain of science. Professional physicians displaced lay midwives, who had long aided women in childbirth, and provided information about birth control and abortion. As we have seen, male "experts" now provided guidance and information for women that they had formerly found in other women.

Woman as "the Weaker Sex." As the Industrial Revolution began to change the structure of modern Western society, women were placed in an illogical, dichotomous position. While their bodies continued to be considered pathological, women were considered the moral guardians of society (Martin, 1987; Ehrenreich and English, 1977). Upper- and middle-class women were perceived as physically weak, of delicate health, and vulnerable to a great variety of ailments arising from the fact that they had wombs. The uterus itself was believed to be the source of a vast array of illnesses, both of body and of the mind. Excessive physical and mental challenges were thought to be damaging to women's most exalted function, procreation. Women of the upper classes were believed to have little or no sex drive. If they did exhibit some, this was thought to be symptomatic of severe illness, to be treated surgically. Any form of rebelliousness or deviance from expected gender roles was met with severe medical measures (Barker-Benfield, 1977). Refusal to be satisfied with housework, a tendency to masturbate, an overeagerness to be educated, or a desire for the vote might be deemed cause for

Box 11.1   IF MEN COULD MENSTRUATE

Living in India made me understand that a white minority of the world has spent centuries conning us into thinking a white skin makes people superior, even though the only thing it really does is make them more affected by ultraviolet rays and wrinkles.

Reading Freud made me just as skeptical about penis envy. The power of giving birth makes "womb envy" more logical, and an organ as external and unprotected as the penis makes men very vulnerable indeed.

But listening recently to a woman describe the unexpected arrival of her menstrual period (a red stain had spread on her dress as she argued heatedly on the public stage) still made me cringe with embarrassment. That is, until she explained that, when finally informed in whispers of the obvious event, she had said to the all-male audience, "and you should be proud to have a menstruating woman on your stage. It's probably the first real thing that's happened to this group in years!"

Laughter. Relief. She had turned a negative into a positive. Somehow her story merged with India and Freud to make me finally understand the power of positive thinking. Whatever a "superior" group has will be used to justify its superiority, and whatever an "inferior" has will be used to justify its plight. Black men were given poorly paid jobs because they were said to be "stronger" than white men, while all women were relegated to poorly paid jobs because they were said to be "weaker." As the little boy said when asked if he wanted to be a lawyer like his mother, "Oh, no, that's women's work." Logic has nothing to do with oppression.

So what would happen if suddenly, magically, men could menstruate, and women could not?

Clearly, menstruation would become an enviable, boast-worthy, masculine event:

Men would boast about how long and how much.

Young boys would talk about it as the envied beginning of manhood. Gifts, religious ceremonies, family dinners, and stag parties would mark the day.

To prevent monthly work loss among the powerful, Congress would fund a National Institute of Dysmenorrhea. Doctors would research little about heart attacks, from which men were hormonally protected, but everything about cramps.

Sanitary supplies would be federally funded and free. Of course, some men would still pay for the prestige of such commercial brands as Paul Newman Tampons, Muhammad Ali's Rope-a-Dope pads, John Wayne Maxi Pads, and Joe Namath Jock Shields—"For Those Light Bachelor Days."

Statistical surveys would show that men did better in sports and won more Olympic medals during their periods.

Generals, rightwing politicians, and religious fundamentalists would cite menstruation ("men-struation") as proof that only men could serve God and country in combat, "You have to give blood to take blood," occupy high political office. "Can women be properly fierce without a monthly cycle governed by the planet Mars?", be priests, ministers, God Himself ("He gave his blood for our sins") or rabbis ("Without a monthly purge of impurities, women are unclean").

Male liberals or radicals would insist that women are equal, just different, and that any woman could join their ranks if only she were willing to recognize the primacy of menstruation rights ("Everything else is a single issue") or self-inflict a major wound every month "You *must* give blood for the revolution."

Street guys would invent slang ("He's a three-pad man") and "give fives" on the corner with some exchange like, "Man, you lookin' *good*!"

"Yeah, man, I'm on the rag!"

TV shows would treat the subject openly. (*Happy Days:* Richie and Potsie try to convince Fonzie that he is still "The Fonz," though he has missed two periods in a row. *Hill Street Blues:* The whole precinct hits the same cycle.) So would newspapers. (SUMMER SHARK CASE THREATENS MENSTRUATING MEN. JUDGE CITES MONTHLIES IN PARDONING RAPIST.) And so would movies. (Newman and Redford in *Blood Brothers!*)

Men would convince women that sex was more pleasurable at "that time of the month." Lesbians would be said to fear blood and therefore life itself, though all they needed was a good menstruating man.

Medical schools would limit women's entry ("they might faint at the sight of blood").

Of course, intellectuals would offer the most moral and logical arguments. Without that biological gift for measuring the cycles of the moon and planets, how could a woman master any discipline that demanded a sense of time, space, and mathematics—or the ability to measure anything at all? In philosophy and religion, how could women compensate for being disconnected from the rhythm of the universe? Or for their lack of a symbolic death and resurrection every month?

Menopause would be celebrated as a positive event, the symbol that men had accumulated enough years of cyclical wisdom to need no more.

Liberal males in every field would try to be kind to women. The fact that "these people" have no gift for measuring life, the liberals would explain, should be punishment enough.

And how would women be trained to react? One can imagine right-wing women agreeing to all these arguments with a staunch and smiling masochism. ("The ERA would force housewives to wound themselves every month": Phyllis Schlafly. "Your husband's blood is as sacred as that of Jesus—and so sexy, too!": Marabel Morgan.) Reformers and Queen Bees would adjust their lives to the cycles of the men around them. Feminists would explain endlessly that men, too, needed to be liberated from the false idea of Martian aggressiveness, just as women needed to escape the bonds of "menses-envy." Radical feminists would add that the oppression of the nonmenstrual was the pattern for all other oppressions. ("Vampires were our first freedom fighters!") Cultural feminists would exalt a bloodless female imagery in art and literature. Socialist feminists would insist that, once capitalism and imperialism were overthrown, women would menstruate, too. ("If women aren't yet menstruating in Russia," they would explain, "it's only because true socialism can't exist within capitalist encirclement.")

In short, we would discover, as we should already have guessed, that logic is in the eye of the logician. (For instance, here's an idea for theorists and logicians: If women are supposed to be less rational and more emotional at the beginning of our menstrual cycle when the female hormone is at its lowest level, then why isn't it logical to say that, in those few days, women behave the most like the way men behave all month long? I leave improvisations to you.)

The truth is that, if men could menstruate, the power justifications would go and on.

If we let them.

---

*With thanks to Stan Pottinger for many of the improvisations already here.
Source: From *Outrageous Acts and Every Day Rebellions* by Gloria Steinem. Copyright 1983 by Gloria Steinem © 1984 by East Toledo Productions, Inc. Reprinted by permission of Henry Holt and Company, LLC.

surgical practices ranging from *clitoridectomy*, the removal of the clitoris, to *hysterectomy*, the removal of the uterus (Marieskind, 1977). These actions or their threat kept women of the more privileged classes more or less in line. Women of the lower classes and women of color were less vulnerable to such strictures, for they were not thought to share the weakness of those of privilege.

By the end of the nineteenth century, women health-care specialists, healers, and midwives were prohibited from practicing even among low-income women (Petchesky and Judd, 1998). The assumption of healing roles by the medical establishment had special repercussions for low-income women, who did not have the same access as wealthy women to professional medical practices.

As recently as 1970, less than 8% of all U.S. physicians were female. A class lawsuit filed against every medical school in the country by the Women's Equity Action League (WEAL) forced an examination of medical school admission policies. By 1975, the number of female medical students had tripled. However, over a quarter of a century later, the number of female physicians as full professors in medical schools and as heads of hospital medical units (especially surgery) has remained small, limiting the ability of such women to make institutional changes.

The Medicalization of Life Processes

Medicalization involves organizing a broad (and ever-expanding) range of behaviors and aspects of everyday life into categories of health and illness (Boston Women's Health Collective, 1971). Western society has medicalized menstruation, childbirth, menopause, and sexuality, even though these are normal parts of the life cycle and experience of most women (see Box 11.2). Nevertheless, some women rarely, if ever, menstruate; some women never give birth; some women do not

experience any symptoms, such as hot flashes, with the onset of menopause. Among those who do experience these processes, there are wide variations in the experience.

Menstruation

Menarche (the onset of menstruation) can occur when a girl is only 10 years old or later, even at 18; menstruation may occur every 28 days or be less regular; it may last a whole week or only a couple of days; it may be accompanied by a blood flow that is heavy or light, with strong abdominal cramps or none at all; it may be preceded by a variety of changes in a woman's body or emotions or it may not.

It was once thought essential for women of the privileged classes to take to bed while menstruating, during the latter phases of pregnancy (*confinement*), and for several weeks after childbirth. However, no such strictures applied to women of the working classes. Despite class disparities, menstruation was persistently conceptualized as a form of illness; and pregnancy, childbirth, and menopause also became medicalized events. Brumberg (1997) notes that by the late nineteenth century, physicians began to share with mothers the role of socializing adolescent girls about their bodies, a strategy that enlarged the constituency of the physicians, who thus defined and treated menstruation.

The Tremin Project (now known as the Tremin Research Project), begun in 1934 to examine the statistical implications of menstrual regularity, is a little-known yet important source of information on women's health. Initially established to challenge the commonly held medical myth of the 28-day menstrual cycle, this is one of very few scientific studies to view menstruation as a component of healthy women's life experience (Mansfield and Bracken, 2003). (Despite this and other research, the "normal" 28-day cycle remains a widespread belief, thus causing

Box 11.2   **WISHES FOR SONS**

i wish them cramps
i wish them a strange town
and the last tampon.
i wish them no 7–11.

i wish them one week early
and wearing a white skirt
i wish them one week late.

later i wish them hot flashes
and clots like you
wouldn't believe. let the
flashes come when they
meet someone special.
let the clots come
when they want to.

let them think they have accepted
arrogance in the universe,
then bring them to gynecologists
not unlike themselves.

concern for those many women who do not have such a cycle.)

Birth Control

The ability to control pregnancy has also been a boon to women in many ways. However, as with the other life processes, once it became medicalized it had mixed benefits.

Women in many societies, past and present, have been able to control pregnancy through the use of herbal remedies. In nineteenth-century New York City newspapers, abortifacient medications, abortion providers, and condom manufacturers advertised freely. However, their services gradually became illegal. The Comstock Law (1873) prohibited the sale of birth-control information and materials (such as condoms) through the U.S. mail. Early in the twentieth century, efforts were increasingly made to deny women access to birth control as the eugenics movement sought ways to increase the population among the "better classes," while limiting family size among the vast numbers of recent immigrants to the United States. With growing concern about overpopulation, especially among the "lower" classes and less-favored races, and frequent use of birth control for families of the upwardly mobile middle classes, there came a dramatic reversal of public policy. Eugenic sterilization became public policy, depriving those deemed "unfit" (often non-English-speaking immigrants as well as the mentally disabled) of the capacity to reproduce. Concurrently, access to birth control for the upper classes was not restricted, in an attempt to increase the numbers of children born to the upper classes relative to those born to new immigrants and other members of the "unfit" classes (Luker, 1996).

In the 1960s, hormone pills and intrauterine devices were distributed freely among millions of U.S. women before adequate testing and other precautions were taken. Some of these devices were later found to be damaging to women's health (Rathus et al., 2000; Ruzek, 1978; Seaman, 1977). New methods of contraception have recently become available or are being developed. These include transdermal patches, soft silicon vaginal rings, and various injectables that would protect against pregnancy for 90 days. However, funding levels for research into new methods of contraception remain miniscule relative to other health concerns. The testing of birth-control devices and medications has become increasingly required in Western nations. However, this is not without its consequences: now, women from poor nations are often the experimental subjects in medical trials for products that will be primarily consumed by Western women.

Abortion

Abortion, sometimes a last resort for women for whom birth control has failed, has also been placed in the hands of medical practitioners as part of the process of professionalization discussed above. In the late nineteenth- and early twentieth-century United States, it was through the efforts of the nascent American Medical Association that control of abortion was wrested from midwives and ultimately suppressed as a legal option (Luker, 1984). There is a consensus in the women's health movement that the decision to have or not to have an abortion should be in the hands of the pregnant woman (Ruzek, 1978). Although legalization of abortion allowed many women to make decisions about pregnancy for themselves and vastly improved the conditions of abortion, the abusive treatment of women seeking abortions (and those women and men who aid them) by abortion opponents continues. The current shift in many parts of the world from medicalization to politicization provides an additional area of concern (WHO, 1998).

For example, the right of women to this ultimate control over their own bodies has been one of the first issues to be challenged in the formerly communist countries of Eastern Europe and the former Soviet Union (Funk and Mueller, 1993). In the United States, harassment of abortion clinic staff has even escalated to the point of assassinating physicians and support personnel. Studies of women who encountered antiabortion protesters when entering a clinic show that the protesters made them feel angry, accosted, and guilty. However, the protesters had no effect on most women's decision to follow through with the abortion (Cozzarelli and Major, 1998).

During the 1980s, the administrations of Presidents Ronald Reagan and George H. W. Bush supported the efforts and tactics of antiabortion forces. It was not until President Bill Clinton was elected that Attorney General Janet Reno used federal resources against the most extreme and violent sectors of the antichoice movement. After Clinton's election in 1992, many changes in the abortion movement took place, including the lifting of the *gag rule*, a statute that previously prohibited any health facility from mentioning abortion as an option for pregnant women. In response, violence perpetrated by antichoice activists increased. Abortion clinics across the United States have sustained a great deal of damage and loss of revenue due to the actions of violent antiabortion activists, and many medical residencies in obstetrics/gynecology and surgery no longer provide training in abortion procedures. However, the overall impact on many clinics has been to reinforce their provision of abortion services and increase their political involvement to fight for these rights. The political debate regarding abortion continues, as do the threats to the prochoice movement, due in large part to right-wing politics and a conservative Republican administration (Morgen, 2002). One of the first administrative decisions of the George W. Bush administration in 2001 was to reinstate the gag rule and suspend monies to international organizations that provided information about abortion.

Childbirth

As childbirth fell into the hands of professionalizing male medical specialists, it was experienced even more passively by women in hospital settings. It came to involve medicines, instruments, and procedures that served to remove childbirth from the realm of normal experience. With the application of anesthetics, the placing of the woman in a prone (lithotomy) position, and a variety of other procedures, the birthing mother became literally incapable of giving birth and now had to be "delivered." Until recently, this meant the routine use of forceps. In recent decades, delivery has also frequently meant the routine performance of *caesarean sections* (surgical delivery of the fetus). Although these procedures are convenient and profitable for physicians and hospitals, and extremely useful in medical emergencies, they are disabling for a large number of women (Martin, 1987).

The acceptance of innovations such as anesthetics during childbirth, hospital-based births, and use of fetal screening through amniocentesis and other testing reveals that not all medicalization should be seen as forced upon women. Rather, the use of new technologies reflects a confluence of sociocultural attitudes and the availability of medical proce-

dures. Many women today are grateful that such technologies exist. However, the potential for abuse through such innovations is not always sufficiently evaluated before widespread acceptance occurs, though past experiences have made increasing numbers of women and health activists more wary.

Until the twentieth century, the risks of childbirth were grave for women everywhere; they remain serious for low-income women in the modern industrial world as well as in less industrially developed countries. Mortality rates for Latinas in the United States and their infants, for example, are higher than for other groups. The health risks for pregnant and childbearing adolescents and their infants are also great since teenage mothers are found disproportionately among groups with low income (Elise, 1995).

The immediate causes of maternal death are, in the main, hemorrhage, sepsis (infection), toxemia, obstructed labor, and complications of abortion. Underlying these are causes related to poverty: lack of prenatal care; lack of trained personnel, equipment, blood, or transport at the time of obstetrical emergency; lack of family planning to avoid unwanted pregnancies and too many or too closely spaced births; and preexisting conditions like malaria, anemia, fatigue, and malnutrition that predispose to obstetrical complications (United Nations, 2000).

Of the half-million women who die each year in childbirth, 99% live in poor countries. For each maternal death, women worldwide contract 100 serious illnesses. This results in approximately 62 million serious childbirth-related health problems every year. Other illnesses caused by childbirth that appear only later are uncounted in these estimates (Elise, 1995).

Menopause

Generally speaking, *menopause* refers to what happens in a woman's body as she reaches the end of her childbearing years. The increased life span for women means that more now reach menopause. Problems related to menopause, and their treatment, have therefore become more central as a health issue. Since all of women's other reproductive processes have become medicalized, it is no surprise that menopause, or the cessation of menstruation, has as well. Here again, the medical establishment has sought to manage an event all too often perceived through images created to support a patriarchal view of women. If it is claimed women's principal function in life is to reproduce, then cessation of menstruation, and hence of fertility, means the cessation of women's reason for existence. In a society where women's dependence, immaturity, and association with children are idealized characteristics, the mature woman with adult children can be regarded as socially useless, unattractive, and morbid.

The biological shifts that come with menopause, seen through this patriarchal and medical perspective, are regarded as pathological (though in fact a wide range of different experiences is quite "normal") and in need of medical management, including dosing with hormones and even surgical removal of the uterus, among other measures. While it is true that many women do suffer discomforts that might be relieved medically, there remains the question of whether such measures are needed, whether they are worth the cost in terms of health risk, and whether alternative measures have been adequately considered. The years prior to menopause have now been identified as *perimenopause*, providing yet another opportunity for medical intervention.

Most women cease menstruating between the ages of 45 and 55. During or just prior to that time, there may be a period of some irregularity in the timing and character of the menstrual cycle; many women also experience other physical changes or sensations. These experiences are thought to relate in large part to the reduced production of estrogen, which also results in eventual cessation of the menstrual cycle. The negative experiences of many women in menopause are not an illusion, but there is also documentation that psychological and cultural factors shape these experiences. A number of sensations and bodily conditions associated with menopause have been linked directly to shifts in the body's production of estrogen. Although some women report no special physiological experiences during the menopausal years, others report a wide variety. The most widely reported negative experiences related to estrogen changes is the *hot flash*, a feeling of body heat that spreads from one point in the body to others, often accompanied by flushing, sometimes by intense perspiration. Physicians (and sometimes women themselves) frequently attribute to menopause other conditions— headaches or depression, for example—which may occur at any age and from a number of causes.

Lack of substantial funding (reflecting traditional research priorities) has resulted in continuing gaps in our understanding of the mechanisms of menopause as they affect individual women. Once again, wide dissemination of pharmaceuticals (which now target an enormous number of the so-called aging baby boomer generation) creates a conflict of interest between pharmaceutical profits and women's lives. In July 2001, the WHI suspended a study funded by the National Heart, Lung, and Blood Institute of the National Institutes of Health (NIH) 3 years before the scheduled conclusion because preliminary findings demonstrated that serious health risks outweighed the potential benefits of long-term estrogen plus progestin HRT. This was a groundbreaking event because the claims which had been made for HRT could not be replicated by this study. Thus, once again, women had been prescribed drugs that were inadequately tested and had potentially dangerous effects without the opportunity to make an informed choice (Rexrode and Manson, 2002).

Sexuality

Sexuality has also become a medical concern, one that is often closely tied to existing gender ideals and expectations. This requires continued analysis of the "politics of sexuality" and how it differentially affects men and women (Vance, 1984). Viagra, the medication developed in the last decades of the twentieth century to treat male "sexual dysfunction," is a case in point. During most of the twentieth century, Western concerns with masculinity were intimately tied to ideas of virility and men's ability to perform sexually. This link is evident in the very medical term used to describe a man who has difficulty getting an erection: *impotence*. This word implies not merely a physical difficulty but also a loss of vigor, strength, and power (Tiefer 2002:150). Although early in the twentieth century it was typical to view impotence as a psychological problem, throughout the century it increasingly became understood as a physical problem in need of medical intervention. In the pre-Viagra days, the cure for impotence was usually surgical implantation of a device into the penis. Despite the costs and risks of this procedure, many U.S. men opted for this solution because it offered an explanation and solution to "impotence" that removed responsibility for "sexual failure" from men themselves (Tiefer, 2002). In 1998, the U.S. FDA approved Viagra, an oral medication that treats men's erection problems.

No such drug has been produced for women. Women seeking enhanced sexual pleasure began using Viagra (both with and without a physician's prescription), even though no research had been undertaken to assess its effectiveness and safety for women. This use of a nontested medication is just one example of how commonplace has become the medicalization of not only physical processes but also lifestyle choices as well. It is not unusual today in the United States, for example, for people, both men and women, to search for a "magic bullet," a pill or cream or device, that will make them feel better and perform better. Tiefer (2000) has warned of the dangers inherent in the profitability of lifestyle drugs (such as those to address lifestyle concerns like weight, sexual functioning, memory) as doctors and drug manufacturers become more closely linked. The newly identified condition, female sexual dysfunction (FSD), is another example of how medicine is seen as the place to provide a quick fix. When men and women turn to Viagra, or women to some other drug, for increased sexual performance, they dismiss the cultural and emotional aspects that may affect a person's sexual functioning (Hartley and Tiefer, 2003).

The Impact of Gender, Social, and Cultural Disparities on Women's Health

Health Status and Risks

Women's bodies and men's bodies are more alike than they are different from one another. They are largely subject to the same hazards to their health: illnesses, accidents, and disabilities. However, there are some significant differences, which can be identified by comparing men's and women's health status. Health status is typically depicted according to rates of *morbidity* (illness) and *mortality* (death). Disparities in health in the United States as well as in many other parts of the world have been persistent over time. What explains these disparities? Some hazards are unique to women because they concern the female reproductive organs and female reproductive experiences. Other hazards are shared by women and men but experienced differently because of the different roles assigned to women (such as jobs resulting in different workplace hazards) or because society supports different behaviors that are potentially a threat to health. Behavioral differences that affect health risks, such as substance abuse and driving behavior, also clearly are patterned by gender (Travis, 1988). Thus, in addition to greater understanding of the biological component of health, the role of risk factors, such as poverty or racial/ethnic and gender discrimination, requires examination of risk-taking behaviors such as driving after heavy alcohol consumption.

In the past, men on average had greater access to nutritional foods and lived longer than women. However, in the United States today and in all countries of the world, for every age group, women on average outlive men (United Nations, 2002). The leading cause of death for both women and men is coronary heart disease, but each year more women die of it than men (Gupta, 2003). However, according to indicators such as disability days, hospitalization, and visits to physicians, women display greater rates of illness than men.

Poverty

Poverty is probably the single greatest hazard to women's health; it is often lethal when combined with other serious hazards. Two out of three women around the world presently suffer from poverty, which is perhaps the most debilitating disease known to humanity. Currently, the two poorest groups in the United States are women raising children alone and women over 65 living alone. These women experience at higher rates than others such ailments as chronic anemia, malnutrition, and severe fatigue. Sufferers exhibit increased susceptibility to infections of the respiratory and reproductive tracts. Premature death is a frequent outcome of poverty.

Poverty explains many of the differences in health found among different groups of hu-

mans and is directly related not only to disease incidences but also to avenues for cure. For example, low-income women are likely to be poorly educated and, hence, unlikely to have sufficient knowledge to identify and avoid risks or respond adequately to them (even if they had the means to do so). In the United States, health insurance coverage is often employment-linked and increasingly workers may find themselves without health insurance. Low-income women are unlikely to have the financial resources to pay for medical treatment or the means of obtaining it, even when it is offered free, because of the costs of transportation or time lost from work. Poverty means lack of adequate housing for shelter and adequate clothing and shoes for protection. It means inadequate sanitation due to insufficient or unclean water, food storage, and waste removal. It means exposure to risks of violence as a result of living in unprotected neighborhoods, and it means dependence on others for survival. So "choosing" to avoid a potentially dangerous situation, as many women are warned to do, may not, in fact, be a choice for many poor women.

Women are more likely than men to be poor, and women who head their own households are much more likely to have a low income than male heads of households (Kemp, 1995). Poverty poses special health risks to disabled and elderly women, especially those who live alone. These are vulnerable populations who lack assistance as even economically able nations increasingly cut back on the "safety nets" of social services.

Racial/Ethnic Discrimination

Race/ethnicity also affects the health risks of women. Health statistics show that African Americans are subject to higher rates of morbidity (such illnesses as cardiovascular disease, diabetes, and cancer) and mortality (including infant mortality due to low birth weight) than white Americans (Dressler, 1993). These differentials persist even when a study takes socioeconomic status into account. When African Americans and whites earn the same income, African Americans still have higher rates of illness in many categories. Although researchers have often attributed these health differentials to biological factors, Dressler (1993) demonstrates that race is a social construct, having no biological common denominators. Although genetic factors can increase health risks among members of any group, genetic inheritance alone is inadequate to account for overall differences in morbidity and mortality rates across different groups. Thus, although among Americans of African origin, rates of sickle-cell anemia are indeed higher than those among the general population, this would not be enough to account for overall rates of illness and death among people classified as "African American."

Yet, models that account for differences in wealth or lifestyle are equally inadequate to explain the persistence of racial differentials in health. Instead, Dressler (1993) proposes a "social structural model," in which wealth or class and status are analyzed for their combined effect on life chances. The stress of "race" status affects physical disease (such as cardiovascular problems) as well as mental health (as in depression). This stress, combined with preconceptions and misconceptions within the health-care industry about the health needs and risks of African Americans, conspires to maintain health inequalities even when controlling for heredity and poverty. Dressler's (1993) model helps to explain the health risks faced by African Americans. Although all women face additional health risks because of gender, factors such as poverty and racial status combine to pose even greater health risks for some women.

Box 11.3   TIPS ON SEARCHING HEALTH INFORMATION ON THE WEB I

Searching for current, reliable information in health sites on the Internet is a useful skill but one that requires care. Some suggestions for "health information surfing" by Laura Buchan of the Canadian Women's Health Network are repeated here:

The URL gives you some information right away. The last part of the domain name (.com, .org, .edu) is significant: .com for commercial sites, .org for non-profit organizations and .edu for educational institutions. Educational sites are generally a safe bet, with "org" sites generally a safe bet (if you can identify the organization and who's funding it) and commercial sites as the most problematic, though there are exceptions (such as Alzheimers.com).

Health on the Net (HON) Foundation provides accreditation for websites and can be searched by language. A Geneva-based NGO (non-governmental organization), HON accredited sites provide trustworthy information. Does the site tell who's paying for it? Is there an "About Us" section that provides such information, including their mission? How current is the information? Are addresses provided for visitors that seek further information or support?

Source: Adapted from Networking: Searching for health information on-line by Laura Buchan. Canadian Women's Health Network (accessed 7/15/03, http://www.cwhn.ca/network-reseau/fall98/fall98net.html) and HON Code of Conduct for Medical and Health Web Sites. Health on The Net Foundation (HON is free and depends on the generosity of internet users and private and public donations; accessed 9/7/03, http://www.hon.ch/HONcode/Conduct.html)

Box 11.4   TIPS ON SEARCHING HEALTH INFORMATION ON THE WEB II

The following discussion on Go Ask Alice, a question-and-answer service available through the Internet from Columbia University in New York, covers many of the concerns a young woman may have about health/gynecological health exams:

Should I Tell My Gyn I'm Having Lesbian Sex?

Dear Alice,
Is it necessary to tell my gynecologist that I am bisexual and engaging in lesbian sex when I go for my yearly checkup?

Dear Reader,
Being honest and complete with the information you give to your health care providers is one of the most important things you can do to insure yourself thorough health care. Of course, it's also understandable that you may be reluctant to tell your gynecologist that you're having sex with another woman, or to talk about your bisexuality. Like other women in your situation, perhaps you are worried that:

• talking about this will be awkward
• you will be misunderstood
• your health care provider will ask a lot of embarrassing questions
• your statement will be ignored
• you will be mistreated
• assumptions will be made about you and/or your behavior
• the provider will refuse to treat you

These are all reasonable concerns since, unfortunately, there are still many people out there, including health care providers, who don't understand or accept same-sex relationships. However, there are also lots of providers who are sensitive and open to *all* of their patients' needs and issues and, in fact, some who even specialize in providing services to lesbian, bisexual, gay, and/or transgendered people.

If you already have an established relationship with your gynecologist, you have an idea of how s/he has handled your needs in the past. Has s/he been sensitive when listening to your health concerns? Have you had the time to discuss all of the different aspects of your sexual health? Have the services provided been thorough, gentle, well explained, and followed up? These are some questions to ask yourself. Talking about this issue might be hard at first, but if you don't tell your gyn, it is quite possible, unfortunately, that s/he will assume that you're sexually active with only men (if you discuss being sexually active). This can lead to a lot of

Occupational Health Risks

Women can suffer from different occupational health risks compared to men. Although men are injured at work more often than women, women suffer illnesses related to work conditions that are harder to detect and less often re-

ported (Muller, 1990). Higher rates of illness among people of color are often attributed to factors related to biology or culture, rather than being sought in their work roles. However, African American women work in riskier and lower-paying jobs compared to white women. As a result, they experience more confusion, complicated, vague wording on your part, and possibly unnecessary or inappropriate discussion and suggestions for your health care.

If you have felt comfortable with your gyn up until now, you may want to just go ahead and mention the fact that you are having lesbian sex. Perhaps you consider yourself bisexual, but are currently only involved with women. You might have one partner, or multiple partners. You may have physical relationships with both men and women. Whatever your situation, choose the wording that's most comfortable for you, and that best describes you and your sexual activity. You can say something like, "I have a female partner now," or "I'm bisexual, and sometimes I have sex with women, and sometimes with men," or "I know the last time I saw you I wasn't having sex with anyone. Right now I'm involved with a woman." Your gynecologist will probably ask some questions to get more specific information. Having a productive discussion with her/him can allow you to explore some or all of the following issues:

- how this affects your need, or lack of need, for contraception
- how to effectively protect you and your partner(s) from sexually transmitted infections (STIs), including HIV
- whether you're also having sex with men, and the health care needs associated with this
- your possible interest in having children some day
- whether there's any stress for you associated with your same-sex relationship(s)
- anything in your intimate relationships, whether with women or with men, which is troubling to you: emotional, physical, or sexual abuse, for example

If you do not yet have a gynecologist that you work with, or are unhappy/too nervous about your current one, you can search out a good match for you in a number of ways. Word of mouth is definitely one of the best ways to find out how a particular provider deals with LGBT health care issues. Ask your friends, school-, or work-mates if they can recommend a gynecologist or nurse practitioner they like. While you're at it, ask about primary care providers, dentists, dermatologists, and others . . . you never know when you'll need a good specialist.

You can also contact your local gay and lesbian services center for some names. If you're in the New York area, contact The Lesbian and Gay Community Services Center. You can also try The Gay and Lesbian Medical Association.

If you're a Columbia student, all of the providers in Primary Care and throughout Health Services are open to discussing the needs of LGBT students.

Take care of yourself,

Alice

Source: Accessed 9/23/03, http://www.goaskalice.columbia.edu/1709.html

work-related injuries and illnesses. A large number of African American women work at low-paid health-service jobs, and studies show that workers at these jobs experience a high rate of occupational illness. Many Latinas and Asian immigrant women work in the garment industry in cities like Los Angeles, Miami, and New York, often in sweatshops where workers face health risks from overcrowding, lack of adequate ventilation, danger of fire due to inadequate escape routes and fire-prevention features in the work facility, and other hazards. Work and pregnancy have been more problematic for women of color in the United

States than for white women of the higher socioeconomic classes because more of the former have had to work during their childbearing years, without access to health care.

Violence

Physical Abuse. A fairly large proportion of women who show up in emergency rooms of hospitals for treatment of injuries are victims of intimate partner abuse and sexual violence. Nonfatal violence between intimate partners compromises the health of millions of women worldwide. Studies in 48 countries reveal that 10%–69% of women report having been physically assaulted by an intimate partner during their lifetime. In the United States, this figure is 22%. In the United States, battering is the greatest single cause of injury to women (Browne, 1993). Physicians and nurses are "legally mandated reporters" and, as such, must report suspected cases of sexual and/or physical abuse. However, often, women are treated for broken bones and other bodily wounds and then sent home again. It is likely that in a large number of cases battering is not reported in the medical record. However, after women repeatedly appear for treatment for such injuries, medical practitioners may respond by blaming the victims. Discovering that many battered women who reappear for treatment also use alcohol or other drugs, medical practitioners might begin to regard this behavior as the cause of their problems. If such cases are followed up, it is the victim who is regarded as "sick" and in need of treatment by various therapies that will change her ways so that she will not "cause herself to be beaten."

One study found that although some physicians did provide supportive care, there were still some who did not. Some women still report that their physician examined them roughly, minimized an injury or the abuse in general, accused the patient of lying, or blamed the patient for the abuse. This indicates a continued need to educate less skilled physicians who may be causing physical and emotional harm to abused women (Hamberger et al., 1998). Although in many cases this is difficult for a woman to do, options can include leaving the relationship or going to a shelter.

Nations and cultures vary in the extent of their domestic violence against women, but the phenomenon appears pervasive worldwide, with few minor exceptions in small societies (Heise, 1993). Rape and sexual assault are also pervasive, and while not usually included in the statistics covering domestic violence, the perpetrators of these violent acts are known to the victims in the majority of cases—often friends, relatives, and household members (Heise, 1993). Both nonsexual and sexual assault results in severe health consequences for women, including not only chronic disabilities, both physical and mental, but also death. It has been estimated, for example, that in the United States, "every 15 seconds a woman is beaten, and four battered women die each day" (Smyke, 1991:53). It has also been estimated that at least one out of ten women has been sexually abused as a child (Courtois, 2000).

Rape. Rape has obvious health consequences, both physical and mental, including subjection of the victim to exposure to sexually transmitted diseases, including acquired immune deficiency syndrome (AIDS). A further consequence, resulting from the stigma attached to loss of virginity by unmarried women in some cultures, has often been missed. Rape victims may become unwanted, "unmarriageable" members of the household and, hence, further victimized. They may even be murdered by their own male kin for their loss of "honor" (Heise, 1993). In addition, rape victims are among the highest risk groups for *posttraumatic stress disorder*, a debilitating psychological syndrome that involves detailed reliving of the traumatic event, panic attacks, depression, nightmares, and sleep disorders. Therapeutic measures designed to help patients overcome posttraumatic stress disorder include systematic desensitization training, cognitive–behavioral therapy, group therapy, and self-help therapy (Campbell, 2003; Wallace, 1999; Weaver et al., 1997). At particular risk for such violence are women in war zones and refugee women. Understandably, many women are reluctant to come forward when they are raped because of the way they believe they may be perceived and/or treated by both legal and medical personnel. The concern with a "second rape" during postassault interactions places unnecessary blame on rape survivors and may result in exacerbating the possibility of long-term health problems (Campbell et al., 2003).

Women and Physical Health: Some Specific Concerns

Heart Disease

One in every two U.S. women will develop heart disease (also known as cardiovascular disease) (Laurence and Weinhouse, 1997). Women appear to be diagnosed with heart disease at later stages, to have their illness treated less aggressively by physicians, and to require different medical and surgical treatment from men. Even risk factors such as cholesterol and triglyceride levels appear to pose different risks according to gender. Yet, most cardiac medication has been tested only on men, and awareness of the dangers of heart disease to women is underestimated by both professionals and women themselves. According to the World Heart Federation, women have more severe first strokes at an older age than men, require longer hospitalization, and remain disabled. In addition, the risk factors for stroke differ from those in men. Prevention of heart disease must begin young, and early detection and awareness is needed to more effectively manage women with cardiovascular disease.

Cancer

After heart disease, the most prevalent cause of death in the United States is cancer. A variety of different possible factors causing higher risk for cancer have been investigated. Dietary fat and obesity are factors that can be affected by behavioral change, but so far, it is not clear whether, or to what extent, either fat or calories increases the risk of breast cancer. Alcohol consumption has been implicated, but questions remain about how the age at onset of drinking or amount of drinking is related to risk (Porzelius, 2000). The major types of cancer in U.S. women are breast, lung, colon, uterine, ovarian, and cervical. Four of these six are associated directly with the reproductive organs. The most common type of cancer among women is breast cancer (which only very rarely occurs in men). The incidence of breast cancer varies substantially among different ethnic groups. As with the majority of cancers, the risk of breast cancer increases with age. This may be due to the long-term effect of exposure to environmental and other toxins as well as to other not yet understood factors.

The effects of hormones, specifically estrogens, on breast cancer, have been examined in numerous studies. Recent studies show an association between estrogen replacement therapy and harmful diseases: HRT has been associated with increased risk of stroke, cardiovascular disease, and breast cancer. Due to the increased suggestion of the potential for harm to women, use of HRT has been called into question (Waters et al., 2002; Cummings et al., 1999).

The incidence of breast cancer has gone up dramatically in recent years (Hewitt and Simone, 1999; Kemeny, 1994). If detected early, it can often be treated effectively; but according to a recent study, women who examined their own breasts were unable to reduce their risk of dying from breast cancer

Box 11.5   WIND CHILL FACTOR

When my grandmother had hers removed,
She complained of the cold.
We wandered down the windy beach in the evening.
You don't think of that beforehand.
She crossed her arms over the flat plains
Of her chest as she spoke.
Our walks were always after the sun had gone down.
Post radiation, the bright light of day was forbidden.
Her cool, dark bedroom was forever fringed
with the hats she would take off and toss.
Within the mahogany dresser drawers
I glimpsed the bulky white contraptions
She strapped on each morning
After shooing us out and closing the door.
Even her daughters were left outside.

My aunt had to forfeit only one.
Do you want to see?
she asked, six months after the surgery.
She pulled open her soft, pink nightgown,
revealing herself.
She and I both looked, curiously.
I shrugged, was nonchalant,
But privately thought
that I could have done the job just as well myself
blindfolded with a dull hatchet.
My aunt buttoned up her flannel.
I'm too small to need a prosthesis.
But there are times I look down at myself
and it seems like someone has
made the bed and left off a pillow.

Now it has come down to you,
drifting though the air,
the water, the years,
who knows.
Before surgery, you write on the good one:
NO! DO NOT REMOVE!
And draw arrows to the bad one.

Source: From *Women's Studies Quarterly* 31, nos. 1 & 2 (Spring/Summer 2003):185–6. Copyright © 2001 by Charlotte McCaffrey, by permission of the Feminist Press at the City University of New York, www.feministpress.org.

A former model but still beautiful, "Matuschka" displays her naked torso with pride. This photograph, entitled *Beauty Out of Damage,* first appeared on the cover of the *New York Times Magazine* of August 15, 1993.

by detecting the tumors themselves. There was almost no difference found in the rate of death from breast cancer between those who were taught breast self-examination and those who were not (Thomas et al., 2002). Performing breast self-examinations, however, contributes to awareness of possible changes in a woman's body and can be important for this reason. It is also crucial that women understand the importance of clinical breast exams to reduce breast cancer mortality. Physicians or nurse practitioners may detect breast cancers through manual examination, which should be performed at regular gynecological examinations. Other technologies for detecting breast cancer exist. Probably the most commonly used today is mammography, which uses radiation to take an image to see if there are any abnormal tissue masses. The effectiveness of mammography has recently been called into question by new research, and further developments should be examined closely. Additional methods are used to confirm the diagnosis, and these involve examination by ultrasound and taking a sample of cells (*biopsy*) from the suspicious mass. Cancers of the ovaries, uterus, and cervix cannot be detected by self-examination. Early detection of cervical cancer is possible, however, by use of a Pap smear, which detects abnormalities in sampled cells. This test should be administered at regular gynecological examinations. An abnormal Pap smear is an indication that further examination is warranted, not direct evidence that there is cancer.

In the last several years, there has been an increase in research on breast cancer. This is partly due to increased government research funding that advocates from the National Breast Cancer Coalition and other organizations have fought so hard to win. Women physicians, health-care workers, breast cancer survivors and their families, as well as women in general have been at the forefront in demanding more funds for breast cancer research. Often, their activities include grass roots movements, such as marathons, to raise awareness about breast cancer.

Sexually Transmitted Diseases

Sexually transmitted diseases are quite prevalent in the world today, with major repercussions for women's health. They are a major cause of infertility and can contribute to blindness and brain damage as well as to difficulties in childbearing. Chlamydia infection is the most common bacterial sexually transmitted disease in the United States, with 3 million new cases estimated each year. Worldwide, 89 million new chlamydia infections occurred in 1997. According to the Institute of Medicine (IOC), untreated chlamydia, which is largely asymptomatic in women, can result in pelvic inflammatory disease, which in turn may cause infertility, ectopic pregnancy, and chronic pelvic pain (IOC, 1997). Certain types of human papillomavirus are linked to cervical cancer, which is the second most common cancer among women worldwide (World Health Organization, 1998).

Human immunodeficiency virus (HIV), the precursor of AIDS, is transmitted through genital secretions or through blood. At the end of 2002, an estimated 42 million people worldwide—38.6 million adults and 3.2 million children younger than 15 years—were living with HIV/AIDS. Approximately 70% of these people (29.4 million) live in sub-Saharan Africa; another 17% (7.2 million) live in Asia. Approximately 50% of adults living with HIV/AIDS worldwide are women (UN AIDS, 2001). Numbers continue to rise among ado-

lescents. One particular consequence for women with these diseases is that they can transfer them to their fetuses.

Approximately 40,000 new HIV infections occur each year in the United States, about 70% among men and 30% among women. Of newly infected women, approximately 64% are black, 18% are white, 18% are Latinas, and a small percentage is members of other racial/ethnic groups (Centers for Disease Control and Prevention, 2001). The Centers for Disease Control (2001) also estimates that approximately 75% of women were infected through heterosexual sex and 25% through injection drug use. Poverty is the critical factor accounting for racial group differences; that poverty itself is disproportionately found among African Americans is the product of a history of racial discrimination.

AIDS, like other sexually transmitted diseases, is avoidable for adults who have control over their own bodies. Protected sex (using a latex condom) is the most common effective alternative (although "safe sex" alternatives, using fantasy and masturbation, have also been recommended). Unfortunately, some women engage in casual sexual relations without using condoms. The reasons they give include inconvenience, shame, and refusal by their male partners (Eversly et al., 1990; Hinkle et al., 1992). In sub-Saharan Africa, for example, where problems of HIV transmission are acute, women run high risks of abuse by male partners for insisting on condom use. There, poverty forces large numbers of women into sex work, hence into extreme vulnerability to exposure to AIDS and abuse. Women's lower status may prevent them from having the control to protect themselves from HIV transmission. Many young women in sub-Saharan African countries have cited that their first experience of sexual intercourse was forced (UN AIDS, 1998). Similar data exist in the United States. Issues such as lack of knowledge, inaccessibility, and lack of concern for one's own safety are some of the reasons for the lack of contraception use.

Women who engage in heterosexual intercourse with an HIV carrier are at greater risk of contracting HIV than are men who have sexual intercourse with an HIV-positive woman. Female condoms, sometimes referred to as "vaginal pouches" (because they are inserted in the vagina), can help women exert greater control over HIV transmission. While these are available in some parts of the world, they require practice to use correctly and are expensive. Microbicides appear to provide a new means of female protection, and research into them continues.

Birth Control, Sterilization, and Abortion

Birth-control options for women have been limited, in part owing to the lack of research into effective new technologies. As we have seen, when this research has been done, it has been tested on impoverished women and women of color. Although many women find them to be effective and convenient, contraceptive methods such as Norplant, Depo-Provera, and intrauterine devices can pose health risks and must be provided by a physician.

Sterilization has a long history of use in the United States as a form of birth control. Many women each year choose to control their fertility through sterilization, generally in the form of a *tubal ligation*, a medical procedure which blocks the tubes carrying a woman's egg to her uterus so that it cannot be fertilized. However, sterilization has not always been chosen by the woman undergoing the procedure. It has often been performed on women of color, mentally retarded women, disabled women, and poor women by authorities interested in reducing their ability to procreate. Forced sterilization dates back to the eugenics movement of the early twentieth century, when physicians specifically

sterilized impoverished women who were officially judged to be genetically unfit to reproduce. This practice was modified after World War II, when forced sterilization was legally acceptable only in the case of developmentally disabled women (Reilly, 1987).

Sterilization without informed consent continued well into the twentieth century. During the 1960s, for example, Puerto Rican women in the United States were sterilized without informed consent in large numbers. Even where sterilization was not technically forced, its use was prescribed in the propaganda from the government of Puerto Rico to combat overpopulation; and where other birth-control alternatives were lacking, sterilization became the only family-planning "choice" available. As a result of these policies, for example, in Hartford, Connecticut, in the mid-1980s, 51% of Puerto Rican women of childbearing age had been sterilized (Lopez, 1987). Native American women have also been sterilized in extremely high numbers relative to their population's size, according to a U.S. Senate General Accounting Office Report (Rodriguez-Trias, 1997). The U.S. practice ended in the 1960s, after being overwhelmed by court challenges and the civil rights movement (Morgan, 2000). Today, the denial of abortion reimbursement by Medicaid also contributes to making sterilization the only viable "option" for birth control among impoverished women (Lopez, 1987).

The availability of legal abortion, in light of the realities of the limitations and failures of birth control, is vital to the health of women. When hygienically and correctly induced, abortion is extremely safe. It has been estimated that at least 200,000 women die annually as a result of poorly performed abortions and hundreds of thousands more suffer serious complications, including sepsis, hemorrhage, uterine perforation, and cervical trauma, often leading to permanent physical damage. These unnecessary consequences are largely the result of women still resorting to clandestine and illegal means of terminating unwanted pregnancies. Women still suffer from a shortage of facilities that can provide safe, prompt, and affordable abortions and that can also safeguard their anonymity if they desire it (Coeytaux et al., 1993).

When conservative politicians are in the majority in the U.S. national government and U.S. Supreme Court, the right to safe and legal abortions and women's reproductive rights is at risk. Despite the fact that "13% of global maternal mortality" is attributed to complication from unsafe, illegal abortions, the biggest problem facing women wanting or needing an abortion service is accessibility (World Health Organization, 1998). Eighty-five percent of counties nationwide have no abortion provider. It remains true that women with money can always access abortion but women with less cannot (Morgen, 2002).

Hysterectomy

Hysterectomy, or removal of the uterus, has been the second most frequently performed surgery among the population of the United States for about the past century. Since only half of that population has a uterus, this statistic demonstrates how common this operation has been for women.

Hysterectomies can be performed for a variety of reasons, but it remains unclear why they are so common. In the nineteenth century, the uterus was thought to be the principal source of women's ailments; its removal was the obvious cure. Although modern medical science rejects this idea, hysterectomies continue to be performed on women possessed of a healthy uterus. Physicians have offered to perform this "service" for women who no longer wish to bear children, citing two primary reasons: It is an effective form of sterilization and it is a preventive measure since the uterus *may* be the site of cancer at some future time.

Currently in the United States, hysterectomy is the most common major non-obstetrical procedure performed on women, with over 600,000 performed each year. The percentage of hysterectomies performed that are truly necessary remains under debate. According to the results of a recent study, as many as 70% of hysterectomies performed in the United States may be recommended inappropriately. This presents a problem when there are alternative procedures available, such as localized treatments, surgery to remove fibroids, and heat treatment for endometriosis, especially because hysterectomies may have long-lasting negative physical, emotional, and sexual effects (Sellman, 2000).

Osteoporosis

Osteoporosis, another process associated with estrogen changes, has been more closely examined, although its rate of occurrence is difficult to gauge. Osteoporosis is associated with a decrease in bone density and occurs in all humans after the age of 35, but it is greatly accelerated in some women after menopause, resulting in bone ailments and a highly increased vulnerability to bone fractures. It is estimated that more than 25 million Americans are affected by osteoporosis, and 80% of this group are women (Galsworthy, 1994). Women sustain 1.2 million bone fractures annually as a result (American Medical Women's Association, 1990). It is further estimated that osteoporosis will cause one woman out of three over the age of 65 to develop a vertebral fracture and one out of three over the age of 75 to develop a hip fracture. Mortality rates resulting from hip fractures are quite high, and morbidity is 50%. Osteoporosis is a major cause of physical disability in older women (twice as common as for older men) (Galsworthy, 1994). The risk of osteoporosis, however, is not uniform among women: African Americans and some African groups rarely show symptoms of this disease (Stoppard, 1999; Doress-Worters and Siegal, 1994). Medicalization in this area may occur in the form of bone density screenings and medications prescribed for women who are not at risk of osteoporosis.

Women and Mental Health

In the realm of mental health, the interconnections between perceptions of health, diagnoses of the causes of illness, and women's place in society seem unavoidable. Critical literature in this field is extensive. Phyllis Chesler's classic work *Women and Madness* (1972) brought attention to the way ideas about "madness" in U.S. society were used to oppress and control women. While the interpretation of human behavior as mentally healthy or mentally ill clearly contains a subjective element, it equally clearly reflects social values. For example, until the mid-1970s homosexuality was listed as an illness in the *Diagnostic and Statistical Manual* of the American Psychiatric Association.

Humans are extremely plastic, and most individuals in a society will tend to fit themselves into a pattern of behavior they are taught is "normal." However, behavior that is considered "normal" in one society might be interpreted as "insane" or at least "neurotic" in another. Notions and behaviors associated with female modesty in Western society, if found in, say, a woman in a traditional Middle Eastern rural village, would indicate fairly extreme deviance and vice versa. Just as a Muslim woman parading about in shorts and a halter top in such a village might be thought to be behaving "crazily," so a modern Western Christian woman who was ashamed to show her face in public might be suspected of having a "mental problem." As in the case of physical health, women and men

are more similar than different in most respects in mental health and illness; it is in the area of difference that feminist criticism is most brought to bear. In a very useful review of the literature, Karen Pugliesi (1992) depicts two basic positions regarding gender differences in mental health. One, which she terms the "social causation approach," looks at aspects of women's experience in society that affect women's mental well-being. Thus, the social conditions mentioned earlier, such as greater likelihood of experiencing poverty, sexual abuse, violence, and the double discrimination of gender and race, produce stresses that endanger women's mental as well as physical well-being. Mental health advantages can also be attributed to social conditions that differentially affect women and men. For example, the fact that women are encouraged to express emotions while men are encouraged to repress them might have specific mental health repercussions favoring women (Klonoff and Landrine, 1995). The second position Pugliesi describes, the "social constructionist approach," finds a major source of difference between women and men in methods of conception and diagnosis of mental health and illness. Phyllis Chesler's (1972) work falls squarely in this category. Certain behaviors by women are labeled as the product of mental disorders by sexist psychiatrists and psychologists (Lopez et al., 1993). While both approaches locate the source of difference in women's and men's mental health in sexism, one takes the discovery of gender differences as "real," the product of different experiences in a gender-biased society, and the other treats this discovery as an artifact of biased diagnosis, a misinterpretation of what actually exists. These approaches complement one another in possibilities for dealing with treatment. We shall return to this point later.

Women and men differ with regard to many aspects of behavior that fall into the mental health realm, which clearly reflects social circumstances. Substance abuse is one area in which men and women differ. Research indicates that women are less likely than men to be abusers of alcohol and tobacco, for example, but when their lifestyles more closely resemble those of men, so do their substance abuse patterns. Yet women, especially pregnant women and women with children, who seek treatment for substance abuse are more likely than men to be turned away from programs or to encounter problems with the legal system over child custody. As women entered the workforce, for example, they more frequently used alcohol and tobacco. On the other hand, women make greater use of prescription drugs, again, most likely as a reflection of social patterns. Women are more likely to request psychotropic drugs from physicians, and physicians are more likely to locate women's complaints in the psychological domain. Hence, with greater access to the drugs, women are more likely to use and abuse them.

Depression

One of the most consistent findings in the literature on gender differences in mental health is that women are at about twice the risk for depression as men, and this finding applies not only to the United States but also on a global basis. Depression is characterized by the persistence over a prolonged time (2 weeks according to current diagnostic procedures) of a number of symptoms from a list. Typical symptoms include feeling sad, anxiety, decreased capacity to experience pleasure, diminished ability to think or concentrate, indifferent grooming, change in appetite, sleep disturbance, and many more. Psychiatrists and psychologists recognize a variety of types of depression. The report of the American Psychological Association's National Task Force on Women and Depression (McGrath

et al., 1990) urges a "biopsychosocial" perspective on depression, with regard to both diagnosis of causes and prescription for treatment. The biological component of this perspective includes a consideration of the biological and psychological consequences of reproduction-related events, including menstruation, pregnancy, childbirth, infertility, abortion, and menopause. The psychological component also refers to characteristics of female personality as constructed by society and the ways that women are oriented by this construction toward certain patterns of perception, social interaction, and coping with stress. The social component refers to the stresses produced by the roles to which women are assigned and to the risks to which women are subject, such as rape, sexual and gender discrimination, and poverty. Because women are subjected to particular gender expectations, the source of their depression may be misidentified. A woman herself, for example, might feel she needs to seek help because she feels "depressed," locating the source of the problem in herself but not recognizing that her social situation might be the major contributor to her feeling. Her consultant, psychiatrist, or psychologist might compound this by "blaming the victim," characterizing a perfectly normal reaction to a terrible situation as a symptom of mental illness.

If the risk for depression or diagnosis of depression is higher among women than among men, the risk for members of racial and ethnic minority groups is also high and higher for women of these groups than men. The conditions affecting rates of depression for African Americans, Latinas, Asian Americans, and Native Americans vary according to the situation of the groups and subgroups in question; while discrimination produces stress and depression at a greater rate than for the population of women in general, the ways in which they are experienced and expressed are specific to each group.

A second important dimension for variation in risk of depression for women is age. Adolescence and old age are considered high-risk categories, life stages characterized by both biological changes accompanying changes in reproductive status and social changes resulting in adjustment challenges.

A final dimension of risk for depression is sexual orientation. Alcoholism and drug abuse continue to affect lesbians, gay men, and transgendered persons at two to three times the rate of the general population; programs are needed that address the special risks of these populations. Lesbians also report higher levels of stress than heterosexual women. Adolescents may be particularly vulnerable. Lack of family and social acceptance can place a significant burden on mental health (U.S. Department of Health and Human Services, 2000). Positive factors reducing the likelihood of depression for lesbians include group support from the lesbian community (among those who have come out and have a community to consult) and the sharing of housework and child care in lesbian households. Legislation supporting same-sex unions and adoptions also is beneficial, though still controversial.

Issues in Therapy

Feminist critiques of psychotherapy generally argue that the fundamental error of traditional therapy is one of attribution. This means that the cause of the client's problem is seen to lie in the person. It is thus to the person herself that the cure is directed, rather than to the social forces that contributed to her "disorder." This focus on the individual as the source of the problem ignores the social conditions and processes affecting women that exist outside them and are beyond their direct control.

Feminist Therapy. Feminist alternatives to traditional therapy arose in direct response to this situation. These alternatives demand recognition of two basic points: first, that women must be viewed in their own terms, not as deviations from a male norm or in terms of their fulfilling roles in relation to males, and second, that their experience, like all human experience, must be located in a social context and that social context has been, and continues to be, one of inequality. Different feminist philosophies argue for different applications of these basic principles.

Greater awareness of the effects of social bias and the nature and consequences of gender-related dominance and dependence are essential aspects of feminist analysis of the human psychic condition. Helping women clients through feminist therapy includes assisting them to understand their circumstances at least partly in terms of societal conditions and gender relationships. It also includes helping them to determine some means of coping with the stresses that are posed to them by their life conditions that do not deny their worth as human beings, do not require their acceptance of behavior or roles simply because society has assigned them, and do not require their perpetual subordination simply because they are women. This may mean actively changing their social interactions and even their social conditions.

Addressing Homophobic Bias

As Beverly Greene (1993) points out, feminist therapists, to be effective, must recognize the biases experienced by women as a result of discrimination by such factors as gender, race, class, and sexual orientation. For example, the problems facing a lesbian seeking assistance through therapy must be understood in terms of the negative bias in the larger social environment against homosexuality and the struggles the woman may experience with negative self-image resulting from taught prejudice. If therapeutic practices are based on an assumption of heterosexuality, their impact can be devastating (Glassgold and Iasenza, 1995). Feminist therapists also call for recognition that clients' behaviors may be adaptive responses to an unhealthy society rather than just a form of pathology. The goal of feminist therapy is empowerment, which is attained by making changes at the personal, interpersonal, and psychological levels (Wyche and Rice, 1997).

Drug Therapy

Psychotropic drugs (tranquilizers, sedatives, hypnotics, and stimulants) are prescribed more frequently and for longer durations to women than men. This pattern becomes marked after the age of 45. The most frequent prescribers of these drugs are general practitioners (Travis, 1988). There are considerable risks in the use of these drugs, including undesirable side effects, negative drug interactions, overdose, and dependence.

Gender differences in this phenomenon can be traced to two sources: patients and physicians. Women are more likely to go to a physician for help. This may be because they experience more problems, they more readily admit they have problems, they feel less able to cope with these problems without help, or they have readier access to physicians due to more flexible working hours. It may be a combination of some or all of these factors that explains why women seek physician assistance more frequently than men. Physicians, on the other hand, are more likely to attribute problems reported by women to psychic causes and to deal with these problems by prescribing psychotropic drugs (Calderone, 1990).

Women as Special-Risk/Vulnerable Populations

Life situations may expose particular groups of women to greater levels of ill health and injury as well as more limited access to care. These groups include the following: refugees, elderly, disabled, and incarcerated women.

Refugee Women

Some 80% of the world's 30 million refugees are women and children. Although many refugees are homeless, impoverished, and terrified, women refugees have special vulnerabilities:

> Refugee women are subject to sexual violence and abduction at every step of their escape, from flight to border crossings to life in the camps. . . . Many refugee women who have been raped are shunned by their families and isolated from other members of their community. (Heise, 1993:178)

Women refugees often find themselves settled temporarily in camps with minimal sanitation and health care, little shelter from the elements, little nutritious food or clean water, and rough treatment on the part of camp officials. Finally, when refugee women are resettled, they find themselves in a strange new land, frightened and lonely, not knowing the language and customs, and resorting to health-care workers whose understanding of illness and disease might be very different from their own (Smyke, 1991).

Disabled Women

Disabled women tend to be stigmatized everywhere. Disabilities include impairments ranging from vision and hearing to mobility at various levels. Poverty and isolation from a supportive family unit generally compound disability. It has only been in recent years that many high-income countries have made accommodations to empower the disabled to participate "in the mainstream," by providing means of access in public places; poorer countries lag far behind (Boylan, 1991). Disabled women enter a world of "sexism without the pedestal" (Fine and Asch, 1988). In contrast to disabled men, who are thought of as weak but interested in sex, women who are disabled are thought of as ugly and not interested in sex. Nonetheless, disabled women have claimed the right to sexual lives, to marry, and to bear children and have shown that they, their partners, and their children can thrive as families (Linton, 1997).

Elderly Women

Much of what has been said of disabled women could also be (and has been) said of elderly women, who are often treated as disabled persons, with the entire stigma that goes with assumptions about disability. With improvement in health care, there are more and more women living to advanced ages. However, they are frequently disabled, too, with chronic diseases. Isolation exacerbates their difficulties in coping with disability as women live longer than their male partners and, in urban areas, often live apart from their families (Fried et al., 2001; Gillick, 2001). Membership in an ethnic or racial minority group may exacerbate the problems women experience as aging persons who are female and poor. However, it should be pointed out, they also have coping strategies within their families and communities that counteract larger societal disadvantages (Padgett, 1989). Often, their families need their help, and they offer one another support.

The United Nations Second World Assembly on Ageing took place in Madrid in April 2002 and produced a plan of action, which includes protection of elderly consumers (United Nations, 2002b).

Incarcerated Women

In the United States, in particular, women have been incarcerated in swiftly rising numbers. Their health needs include all the concomitant issues of poverty, violence, and racism that have an impact upon male prisoners; however, institutions must also focus on concerns specific to women, such as reproductive health, including pregnancy and abortion, and mental health needs.

Conclusions

Women's health movements, both in the United States and elsewhere, have made great strides in identifying health as a feminist issue and in challenging patriarchal assumptions about women's bodily processes; but there is still tremendous work to be done. Questions of health cannot be divorced from issues of social stratification, especially poverty, race, and gender. Until such forms of social differentiation are transformed, women around the world will continue to suffer disproportionately in terms of their health and life chances.

Summary

Around the globe, women's political consciousness has been galvanized around health issues. Those in the women's health movement have sought to empower women about their own bodies. They have also undertaken to reform the health-care system and public policy by making them more responsive to women's bodies and women's needs and by ensuring that women's issues are addressed.

Women's health has been perceived differently from men's because women's bodies and biological processes are different in some respects from men's. Feminists, however, have uncovered biases in the gender dynamics of Western medicine. Greek physicians in the ancient world considered women to be physically defective. After the Industrial Revolution, women became increasingly viewed as the "weaker sex." With the professionalization of the Western health-care system in the nineteenth century, men displaced midwives and male "experts" came to predominate in providing guidance and information, previously offered by women kinfolk and other women.

Western society has medicalized the normal parts of the life cycle and experiences of most women, such as menstruation, childbirth, and menopause. Its male experts, along with policy makers, have enormous influence and control over women's access to health information and health care. Control over women's bodies is especially politicized around birth control and abortion.

In the past, women in many societies had knowledge of herbal remedies to control pregnancy. In the early twentieth century, birth-control information and materials became increasingly illegal in the United States. Since the 1960s, new medications and devices have been developed and made available but only after having been tested on women in poor nations. Recent conservative administrations prodded by antichoice organizations have sought to severely limit women's access to abortion.

Childbirth has become the domain of medical specialists, who are predominantly male, with women as passive consumers of their expertise and medical procedures. In developing countries and among the poor everywhere, childbirth remains a risk to the health of the mother and her child.

Male biases are seen in the treatment of menopause and women's sexuality. Menopause is viewed as pathological rather than normal and something to be managed by surgery or hormones. When the medical profession has intervened, for example, with HRT, it has often done so without adequate testing of drugs and treatments, which can place women at risk. The invention and marketing of Viagra to treat male "sexual dysfunction" is another example of the "politics of sexuality" that places men's needs as primary.

Poverty is probably the single greatest hazard to women's health; it is often lethal when combined with other serious hazards. Race and ethnicity also affect women's health risks. The stress of racism contributes to physical disease as well as mental health. African Americans, for example, receive unequal treatment from the U.S. health-care system and its professionals.

Women's work roles, which are often in low-paying and hazardous conditions, contribute to health risks that are harder to detect and less often reported than men's occupational health risks. Physical abuse and rape are forms of violence that women experience and that are very much underreported.

One in every two U.S. women will develop heart disease, yet the health-care system underdiagnoses and undertreats women in this area. Much more attention has been given to breast cancer, largely because of women's efforts to demand more funds for breast cancer awareness and research. Women need to become better informed about sexually transmitted diseases because of the implications for infertility and other health issues. Due to lack of information, condoms, and other devices as well as women's lower status, women, especially those who are poor and those in developing countries, are at great risk for contracting HIV.

Birth-control options for women remain limited, due in part to lack of research into effective new technologies. The availability of legal abortion is vital to women's health. The politicization of abortion and predominance of conservative politicians in the United States jeopardize women's right to safe and legal abortions and other reproductive rights. The frequency of hysterectomies and the risks of osteoporosis are two other physical health issues that require women's attention.

Women also have mental health issues. They experience depression at a much higher rate than men. Feminists question traditional (male-centered) therapy for its gender bias and homophobia. Drug therapy is also prescribed for women more frequently and for longer than for men.

Some groups of women, such as refugees, the disabled, the elderly, and the incarcerated, are especially vulnerable. They are at special risk for violent attacks and neglect and have limited access to good health care.

The women's health movement has made great strides in bringing women's health issues to the public and to women's own agendas. Structural factors will also need to be incorporated to counter gender, racial, ethnic, and class biases toward improving women's health and addressing their issues.

Discussion Questions

1. What would be the consequences for women's health if women had greater control of reproduction? What factors affect their control; how might their control be increased? What concerns might arise in the future?

2. Select a group of women at special risk for health problems as a consequence of disability, age, political status, or other factors. Discuss problems, their causes, how they are addressed in the present health-care system, and how health-care delivery might be improved.

3. Describe health care in a society very different from your own, say, in a less economically developed nation, a traditional indigenous society, a socialist or communist country (or one that has recently been socialist or communist and is now capitalist) or during a time period in the distant past. Who are the health-care practitioners? How does treatment differ from that with which you are familiar?

Recommended Readings

Angier, Natalie. *Woman: An Intimate Geography*. New York: Anchor Books, 2000. A well-researched, passionate, and pithy discussion of female anatomy and physiology by the chief science writer for the *New York Times*.

Gordon, Linda. *The Moral Property of Women: A History of Birth Control Policies in America*. Chicago: University of Illinois Press, 2002. A substantially revised and updated edition of *Women's Body, Women's Right*, an important text in understanding the interstices of health, politics, and the struggle for gender equity.

Morgen, Sandra. *Into Our Own Hands: The Women's Health Movement in the United States, 1969–1990*. New Brunswick, NJ: Rutgers University Press, 2002. A comprehensive account of the U.S. women's health movement by an anthropologist involved in the movement since the 1970s. Firsthand accounts by many participants are especially of interest.

References

American Medical Women's Association. AMWA position statement on osteoporosis. *Journal of the American Medical Women's Association*, 45:3, 75–9, 1990.

Barker-Benfield, G. J. Sexual surgery in late nineteenth-century America. In *Seizing Our Bodies: The Politics of Women's Health*, edited by Claudia Dreifus. New York: Vintage Books, 1977.

Boston Women's Health Collective. *Our Bodies, Ourselves*. New York: Simon and Schuster, 1971.

Boylan, Esther. *Women and Disability. Women and World Development Series*. Atlantic Highlands, NJ: Zed Books, 1991.

Browne, A. Violence against women by male partners: Prevalence, outcomes, and policy implications. *American Psychologist*, 48, 1077–87, 1993.

Brumberg, Joan J. *The Body Project: An Intimate History of American Girls*. New York: Random House, 1997.

Calderone, K. L. The influence of gender on the frequency of pain and sedative medication administered to postoperative patients. *Sex Roles*, 10, 587–99, 1990.

Campbell, Rebecca, Tracy Sefl, and Courtney E. Ahrens. The physical health consequences of rape: Assessing survivors' somatic symptoms in a racially diverse population. *Women's Studies Quarterly*, 31, 90–7, 2003.

Centers for Disease Control and Prevention. *HIV Prevention and Strategic Plan Through 2005*. Atlanta: CDC, 2001.

Chesler, Phyllis. *Women and Madness*. Garden City, NY: Doubleday, 1972.

Clifton, Lucille. Wishes for sons. In *Quilting: Poems 1987–1990*. Rochester, NY: BOA Editions, 1991.

Coeytaux, Francine, Ann Leonard, and Carolyn Bloomer. Abortion. In *The Health of Women: A Global Perspective*, edited by Marge Koblinsky, Judith Timayan, and Jill Gay. Boulder, CO: Westview Press, 1993.

Courtois, C. The aftermath of child sexual abuse: The treatment of complex posttraumatic stress reactions. In *Psychological Perspectives on Human Sexuality*, edited by L. Szuchman, and Frank Muscarella. New York: Wiley, 2000.

Cozzarelli, C., and B. Major. The impact of antiabortion activities on women seeking abortions. In *The New Civil War: The Psychology, Culture, and Politics of Abortion*, edited by L. J. Beckman and S. M. Harvey. Washington, D.C.: American Psychological Association, 1998.

Cummings, S. R., S. Eckert, K. A. Krueger, D. Grady, T. J. Powles, J. A. Cauley, L. Norton, T. Nickelsen, N. H. Bjarnason, M. Morrow, M. E. Lippman, D. Black, J. E. Glusman, A. Costa, and V. C. Jordan. The effect of raloxifene on risk of breast cancer in post-menopausal women. *Journal of the American Medical Association*, 281, 2189–97, 1999.

Dean-Jones, L. *Women's Bodies in Classical Greek Science*. Oxford: Clarendon, 1994.

Doress-Worters, P. B., and D. L. Siegal. *The New Ourselves Growing Older*. New York: Simon and Schuster, 1994.

Dressler, William W. Health in the African American community: Accounting for health inquiries. *Medical Anthropology Quarterly*, 7:4, 325–45, 1993.

Ehrenreich, Barbara, and English, Deirdre. Complaints and Disorders: The Sexual Politics of Sickness. In *Seizing Our Bodies: The Poli-*

tics of Women's Health, edited by Claudia Dreifus. New York: Vintage Books, 1977.

Elise, S. Teenaged mothers: A sense of self. In *African American Single Mothers*, edited by B. J. Dickerson. Thousand Oaks, CA: Sage, 1995.

Eversley, Ravi, D. Beirnes, A. Newstetter, G. Wingood, K. Hembry, L. Gotch, and A. Avins. Ethnic predictors of sexual HIV risk among young adult women attending family planning clinics. *Multicultural Inquiry and Research on AIDS*, 3:3, 4–5, 1990.

Fine, M., and A. Asch, editors. *Women with Disabilities: Essays in Psychology, Culture and Politics*. Philadelphia: Temple University Press, 1988.

Fried, L. P., C. M. Tangen, J. Walston, A. B. Newman, C. Hirsch, J. Gottdiener, T. Seeman, R. Tracy, W. J. Kop, G. Burke, and M. A. McBurnie. Frailty in older adults: Evidence for a phenotype. *Journal of Gerontology*, 56A, M146–56, 2001.

Funk, Nanette, and Magda Mueller. *Gender Politics and Post-Communism: Reflections from Eastern Europe and the Former Soviet Union*. New York: Routledge, 1993.

Galsworthy, Theresa D. Osteoporosis: Statistics, intervention, and prevention. *Annals of the New York Academy of Sciences*, 736, 158–64, 1994.

Gillick, M. Pinning down frailty. *Journal of Gerontology*, 56A:3, M134–5, 2001.

Glassgold, Judith M., and Suzanne Iasenza, editors. *Lesbians and Psychoanalysis: Revolution in Theory and Practice*. New York: Free Press, 1995.

Greene, Beverly. Psychotherapy with African-American women: Integrating feminist and psychodynamic models. *Journal of Training and Practice in Professional Psychology*, 7:1, 49–66, 1993.

Gupta, Sanjay. Those fragile hearts. *Time*, Feb. 10, 2003, 84.

Hamberger, L. K., B. Ambuel, A. Marbella, and J. Donze. Physician interaction with battered women. *Journal of the American Medical Association*, 7, 575–82, 1998.

Hartley, H., and L. Tiefer. Taking a biological turn: The push for a 'female viagra' and the medicalization of women's sexual problems. *Women's Studies Quarterly*, 31, 42–54, 2003.

Heise, Lori. Violence against women: The missing health agenda. In *The Health of Women: A Global Perspective*, edited by Marge Koblinksy, Judith Timyan, and Jill Gay. Boulder, CO: Westview Press, 1993.

Hewitt, M., and J. Simone, editors. *Ensuring Quality Cancer Care*. Washington, D.C.: National Academic Press, 1999.

Hinkle, Yvonne, Ernest Johnson, Douglas Gilbert, Linda Jackson, and Charles Lollis. African-American women who always use condoms: Attitudes, knowledge about AIDS, and sexual behavior. *Journal of American Medical Women's Association*, 47:6, 230–7, 1992.

Institute of Medicine. *The hidden epidemic: Confronting sexually transmitted diseases*, edited by Thomas R. Eng and William T. Butler. Washington, D.C.: National Academy Press, 1997.

Jaskoski, J. Helen. My heart will go out: Healing songs of Native American women. *International Journal of Women's Studies*, 4:2, 118–34, 1981.

Kemeny, Margaret M., and Paula Dranov. *Breast Cancer and Ovarian Cancer: Beating the Odds*. New York: Addison-Wesley, 1994.

Kemp, A. A. Poverty and welfare for women. In *Women: A Feminist Perspective*, 5th ed., edited by J. Freeman. Mountain View, CA: Mayfield, 1995.

Klonoff, E. A., and H. Landrine. The schedule of sexist events: A measure of lifetime and recent sexist discrimination in women's lives. *Psychology of Women Quarterly*, 19, 439–72, 1995.

Laurence, L., and B. Weinhouse. *Outrageous practices: How gender bias threatens women's health*. New Brunswick, NJ: Rutgers University Press, 1997.

Linton, Simi. *Claiming Disability: Knowledge and Identity*. New York: New York University Press, 1997.

Lopez, Iris. Sterilization among Puerto Rican women in New York City: Public policy and social constraints. In *Cities of the United States*, edited by Leith Mullings. New York: Columbia University Press, 1987.

Lopez, S., A. Smith, B. Wolkenstein, and V. Charlin. Gender bias in clinical judgment: An assessment of the analogue method's transparency and social desirability. *Sex Roles*, 28, 35–45, 1993.

Luker, Kristin. *Abortion and the Politics of Motherhood*. Berkeley: University of California Press, 1984.

———. *Dubious Conceptions: The Policies of Teenage Pregnancy*. Cambridge, MA: Harvard University Press, 1996.

Mansfield, P. K., and S. Bracken. The Tremin Program: Sixty-eight years of research on menstruation and women's health. *Women's Studies Quarterly*, 31, 25–41, 2003.

Marieskind, Helen. The women's health movement: Past roots. In *Seizing Our Bodies: The Politics of Women's Health*, edited by Claudia Dreifus. New York: Vintage Books, 1977.

Martin, Emily. *The Woman in the Body*. Boston: Beacon, 1987.

McCaffrey, Charlotte. Wind chill factor. *Women's Studies Quarterly*, 31:1, 2, 185–6, 2003.

McGrath, Ellen, Gwendolyn Keita, Bonnie R. Strickland, and Nancy F. Russo, editors. *Women and Depression: Risk Factors and Treatment Issues. Final Report of the American Psychological Association's Task Force on Women and Depression*. Washington, D.C.: American Psychological Association, 1990.

Morgan, D. Yale Study: U.S. eugenics policies akin to Nazis' sterilizations went on for decades. *Chicago Tribune*, Feb. 15, 2000, 3.

Morgen, S. *Into Our Own Hands: The Women's Health Movement in the United States, 1969–1990*. New Brunswick, NJ: Rutgers University Press, 2002.

Muller, Charlotte. *Health Care and Gender*. New York: Russell Sage Foundation, 1990.

National Center for Health Statistics. *Health, United States*, 2002. Hyattsville, MD: NCHS, 2002.

Padgett, Deborah. Aging minority women: Issues in research and health policy. In *Women in the Later Years: Health, Social and Cultural Perspectives*, edited by Lois Grau and Ida Susser. New York: Harrington Park Press, 1989.

Petchesky, Rosalind P., and Karen Judd. *Negotiating Reproductive Rights: Women's Perspectives Across Countries and Cultures*. New York: Zed Books, 1998.

Porzelius, Linda Krug. Physical health issues for women. In *Issues in the Psychology of Women*, edited by Maryka Biaggio and Michel Hersen. New York: Kluwer Academic/Plenum, 2000.

Pugliesi, Karen. Women and mental health: Two traditions of feminist research. *Women and Health*, 19:2–3, 43–68, 1992.

Rathus, S., J. Nevid, and L. Fichner-Rathus. *Human Sexuality in a World of Diversity*, 4th ed. Boston: Allyn & Bacon, 2000.

Reilly, Philip. Involuntary sterilization in the United States. *Quarterly Review of Biology*, 62, 153–70, 1987.

Rexrode, K. M., and J. E. Manson. Postmenopausal hormone therapy and quality of life. No cause for celebration. *JAMA, 287*, 641–42, 2002.

Rodriguez-Trias, Helen. Interview with Kathy Rolland, Eugene, Oregon, Feb. 8, 1997.

Ruzek, Sheryl Burt. *The Women's Health Movement: Feminist Alternatives to Medical Control*. New York: Praeger, 1978.

Seaman, Barbara. The dangers of oral contraception. In *Seizing Our Bodies: The Politics of Women's Health*, edited by Claudia Dreifus. New York: Vintage Books, 1977.

Sechzer, Jeri A., Vita C. Rabinowitz, Florence L. Denmark, Michael F. McGinn, Bruce M. Weeks, and Carrie L. Wilkens. Sex and gender bias in animal research and in clinical studies of cancer, cardiovascular disease, and depression. *Annals of the New York Academy of Sciences*, 736, 21–48, 1994.

Sellman, Sherrill. *Hysterectomy Hysteria*. NBC News Article, 2000.

Smyke, Patricia. *Women and Health*. London: Zed Books, 1991.

Stoppard, M. *HRT: Hormone Replacement Therapy*. New York: DK Publishing, 1999.

Thomas, D. B., D. L. Gao, R. M. Ray, W. Wang, C. J. Allison, F. L. Chen, P. Porter, Y. W. Hu, G. L. Zhao, L. D. Pan, W. Li, C. Wu, Z. Coraty, I. Evans, M. G. Lin, H. Stalsberg, and S. G. Self. Randomized trial of breast self-examination in Shanghai: Final results. *Journal of the National Cancer Institute*, 94:19, 1445–57, 2002.

Tiefer, Lenore. Sexology and the pharmaceutical industry: The threat of Co-optation. *The Journal of Sex Research*, 37, 273, 2000.

———. In pursuit of the perfect penis: The medicalization of male sexuality. In *Readings in Gender and Culture in America*, edited by Nancy McKee and Linda Stone. Englewood Cliffs, NJ: Prentice Hall, 2002.

Travis, C. B. *Women and Health Psychology: Mental Health Issues*. Hillside, NJ: Erlbaum, 1988.

United Nations. *The World's Women 2000: Trends and Statistics*. New York: United Nations, 2000.

United Nations. Department of Economic and Social Affairs. *International Plan of Action on Aging*. New York: United Nations, 1998.

———. *Population and Vital Statistics Report*, series A, vol. LIV. New York: United Nations, 2002a.

———. *Report of the Second Assembly on Ageing*. Madrid: United Nations, 2002b.

UN AIDS. Force for change: World AIDS campaign with young people. In *World AIDS Campaign Briefing Paper*. Geneva: UN AIDS, 1998.

———. *AIDS Epidemic Update*. New York: United Nations, 2001.

U.S. Department of Health and Human Services. *Healthy People 2010*, 2nd ed. *with Understanding and Improving Health Objectives for Improving Health*, 2 vols. Washington, DC: US Government Printing Office, Nov. 2000.

Wallace, H. *Family Violence: Legal, Medical, and Social Perspectives*. Boston: Allyn & Bacon, 1999.

Waters, David, Edwin L. Alderman, Judith Hsia, Barbara V. Howard, Frederick R. Cobb, William J. Rogers, Pamela Ouyang, Paul Thompson, Jean Claude Tardiff, Vera Bittner, Lyall Higginson, Michael Steffes, David J. Gordon, Michael Proschan, Naji Younes, and Joel Verter. Effects of hormone replacement and antioxidant vitamin supplements on coronary atherosclerosis in postmenopausal women. *Journal of the American Medical Association*, 288:19, 224–32, 2002.

Weaver, T. L., D. G. Kilpatrick, H. S. Resnick, C. L. Best, and B. E. Saunders. An examination of physical assault and childhood victimization histories within a national probability sample of women. In G. Kaufman Kantor and J. L. Jasinski, editors. *Out of Darkness: Contemporary Perspectives on Family Violence.* Thousand Oaks, CA: Sage, 1997.

Wilcox, Joyce. The Face of Women's Health: Helen Rodriguez-Trias. *American Journal of Public Health*, 92:4, 566-569, 2002.

Williams, D. Racial/ethnic variations in women's health: The social embeddedness of health. *American Journal of Public Health*, 92, 588–97, 2002.

World Health Organization. *World Health Organization Constitution. Introduction.* New York: 1946.

———. World health day/safe motherhood, 7 April 1998: Address unsafe abortion. WHD 98.10, http://www.who.int/archives/whday/en/pages1998/whd98_10.html (accessed April 7, 1998).

Wyche, K. F., and J. K. Rice. Feminist therapy: From dialogue to tenets. In *Shaping the Future of Feminist Psychology: Education, Research, and Practice*, edited by J. Worell and N. G. Johnson. Washington, D.C.: American Psychological Association, 1997.

Women and Work

Human societies generally organize the work needed for survival by dividing tasks among their members. Individual work assignments are decided in a variety of ways. Strength and skill are obvious and basic determinants. Status and value also influence work patterns, and some tasks are thought to merit higher rewards than others. All known societies have used gender as a criterion for work assignments; these are largely arbitrary, however, because the content of roles varies from culture to culture and time to time. Yet, a gender division of labor exists.

Gender affects who is assigned which tasks, but class and race/ethnicity further intervene so that women of color and poor women are usually found in the most undervalued work. These class, caste, and racial/ethnic divisions among women are reinforced by *globalization*, an economic, social, political, and cultural process in which industries operate on a worldwide scale to take advantage of cheap labor costs to enhance their profits.

Many societies judge the value of work in terms of economic rewards. "Do you work?" means, for many people, "Do you earn money?" That is why the idea that a housewife does not "work" is so common. Although housekeeping services can be bought and sold, when this labor is performed for "free," it is not considered "work." During the past century, many feminists have challenged the basic assumptions that most people hold about the nature and definition of "work" itself.

Unpaid labor often contributes enormously to the goods and services that keep a society well and functioning. Masking the economic value of women's unpaid labor serves the interests of those who have property and power. If women's unpaid household tasks were included in national income accounts, economic output would increase by 20%–30% (United Nations Development Program, 1993). Failing to acknowledge the value of such work in economic terms distorts an accurate assessment of a country's gross national product and keeps in place a system that undervalues both the producers of this labor, women, and their work.

Many societal theories hold that relationships between people are fundamentally based on economic power. The economic inequality between women and men has contributed to a widely held stereotype of women as dependent. A vicious cycle develops in which women's dependence is cited as the reason for their economic inequality. Hence, social inequalities between women and men are often the result of economic inequalities. This chapter examines some aspects of these ideals in order to understand women's roles in reproduction and production and the impact of economic change on women's roles within and outside the family. It considers various types of work that women do and have done and the obstacles they face as workers. Finally, the chapter examines the roles played by support groups, government, and the women's movement in influencing women's opportunities for paid work.

The Labor of Women

Division of Labor by Gender

Every known society has had some sort of division of labor by gender, but the work done by women and men has varied by geographical region, by historical era, and from society to society. While clerical work is typical for women in developed Western countries and in many developing countries in the Asian/Pacific region, employed women in the Middle East/North Africa are found predominantly in the professional/technical occupations and women in other developing countries are concentrated in production work (Anker, 1998). The Asia/Pacific region has the lowest concentration of occupational sex segregation; the Middle East/North Africa region has the highest level. Table 12.1 indicates the extent to which occupational sex segregation (defined as an occupation in which one

gender accounts for 80% of the workforce) is an enduring feature within societies. In the past three decades, there have been changes in the gender division of labor. Women have entered some occupations previously held by men—architects/engineers, legislative and government officials, managers, and buyers—as Table 12.1 illustrates. However, the other four predominantly male occupations—protective services; production supervisors and foremen; blacksmiths and toolmakers; and bricklayers, carpenters, and construction workers—remain strongly male-identified. Women who have entered traditionally male occupations find that advancement is very difficult, and they typically remain at the lowest levels (see Box 12.1). Men, on the other hand, have always found work in "female" occupations, and they continue to do so. Once employed in a typically female occupation, men also move quickly into higher-level administrative or supervisory positions (Kimmel, 2000).

The division of labor by gender has often been related to the differences in the reproductive roles assigned to women and men. Since women necessarily bear, and until recent times have necessarily nursed, infants, they have always been assigned the additional social role of child care, even though this assignment is not necessitated by either

TABLE 12.1 The Eight Most Typical Occupations for Women and Men Globally and the Percentage of the Dominant Sex in the Occupation

Eight Typical Female Occupations	%	Eight Typical Male Occupations	%
Maids, housekeepers, domestics	85	Protective services	96
Typists	85	Bricklayers, carpenters, construction	95
Nurses	82	Production supervisors, foremen	95
Tailors, dressmakers	64	Blacksmiths, toolmakers	95
Hairdressers, beauticians	60	Managers	86
Cashiers, bookkeepers	52	Legislators, government officials	84
Teachers	50	Sales supervisors, buyers	83
Salespersons, shop assistants	50	Architects, engineers	79

Source: Richard Anker, *Gender and Jobs: Sex Segregation of Occupations in the World*, p. 265. Geneva: ILO, 1998. Copyright © 1998 International Labour Organiztion.

Box 12.1   BREAKING BARRIERS: FIREFIGHTERS

Brenda Berkman, Lieutenant, New York City Fire Department, Ladder Company 12:

The overwhelming impetus for me to become a firefighter was exactly what the whole world witnessed the day of the 9/11 attacks: the opportunity to help somebody in the direst hour of need. After practicing law for five years, I became the named plaintiff in a 1978 lawsuit [won in 1982] challenging the physical abilities exam for firefighters as being discriminatory and not job-related. . . .

About forty of us went into the Fire Academy at the same time. . . . About a dozen of us were allowed to graduate on time; the rest were held over for "re-training," since they kept changing the requirements. . . . But nothing was done to prepare firefighters in the field for the fact that women were on the way. . . . So there were some years of total misery, from minor incidents (guys put feces in women's boots and nasty things in our beds) to major ones (women's firefighting equipment was tampered with; women weren't backed up in firefighting situations). . . . As of 2002, [there were] 25 women—among 1,100 firefighters.

. . . [Women] become firefighters for exactly the same reasons as men. There's the service aspect, plus the hours are good, and there's a halfway decent salary with pension and health benefits. The job is interesting, too. . . . Furthermore, women have changed the job for the better: parental leave, increased professionalism, more emphasis on training, more attention to human relations. . . .

. . . But we're deeply concerned that little girls are seeing only the faces of men as heroes of September 11. That's totally out of touch with reality, because women were there. . . . And we're going to *go on* being there.

Source: From Brenda Berkman, Breaking barriers: Firefighters. Abridged by permission of Pocket Books, an imprint of Simon & Schuster Adult Publishing Group, from *Sisterhood Is Forever,* edited by Robin Morgan, pp. 331–34. Copyright © 2003 by Robin Morgan.

function. Yet, the physical burdens women bear while pregnant and nursing are often assumed to place some limitation on their ability to participate fully in the productive economy (see Chapter 8). An examination of women's roles in a variety of preindustrial and developing societies, however, shows that they do engage in fairly strenuous economic activities even while pregnant and nursing.

The labor involved in reproduction itself is essential for any society. With the exception of those employed to care for the young, most women receive no economic compensation for mothering, even though societies could not exist without the work involved. Using the Department of Labor's figures for the hourly wages paid for certain types of work, Table 12.2 estimates what women in the United States would earn if they were paid for their unpaid labor.

Maintenance of the Domestic Unit

To the extent that women are involved in child care—and this extent varies historically and cross-culturally—the other work they do must be possible to do at the same time. "Housework," such as cooking and cleaning, generally falls into this category. As with reproduction, this work serves an important

TABLE 12.2 What Women in the United States Would Earn if They Were Paid for Their Unpaid Labor

Role	Number of Hours per Week	Hourly Rate ($)	Dollar Amount ($)
Food preparer	18	8.72	157
Cleaner	6	6.36	38
Washer	3	6.36	19
Ironer	3	6.36	19
Chauffeur	10	12.17	122
Social secretary	18	10.00	180
Psychologist	10	150.00	1,500
Child-care worker	51	7.65	390
Health-care worker	1	9.17	9
Repairer	2	15.72	31

Source: Calculations are based on data found in U.S. Department of Labor, Bureau of Labor Statistics, 2002.

function: it "services" the male worker so that he can return, fed and refreshed, to the workplace the next day. However, the housewife is not compensated for this work either.

In most parts of the world for most of human history, virtually all productive labor was domestic, performed without compensation for the benefit of family members. Under these conditions, the labor done by women and men, although often differentiated, was viewed as making equivalent contributions. *Social labor,* labor done for the good of the larger community beyond the family, did have value, earning esteem for the laborer beyond family rewards. As the social labor sector grew with increasing urbanization and capitalism, it became a larger component of the whole economy. With this change, women began to lose ground. That women's domestic work was essential to the total economy but deemed lacking in economic or social value also diminished women's opportunities to participate in valued social labor outside the home (Dalla Costa and James, 1975).

Feminists have challenged such traditional conceptions of the separate "private" and "domestic" spheres of life as misleading and damaging to women. Women combine many

sorts of work with child care, which is often overlooked. Work, such as weaving and making pottery, and running businesses, such as beauty parlors and family grocery stores, can be carried out in or near the home. Alternatively, societies may take responsibility for making child-care facilities available so that both parents can work at other jobs.

Women's Work in the Marketplace

Despite women's assigned responsibilities in the domestic sphere, many have managed to sell some of their labor, and larger numbers are continuing to do so. Because of the devaluation of women, resulting in part from the devaluation of their domestic labor, a woman's labor sold in the marketplace is valued less than the same work done by a man. Women find more restrictions in their job choices than men, men rarely take the jobs largely filled by women, and women's jobs are stereotyped in the workplace just as they are in the home. An activity that is highly regarded in one society, when done by men, may be considered unimportant in another society, when done by women. A more insidious pattern of integrating women into the labor market is illustrated by an early twentieth-century example. This pattern encouraged women's entry into bookkeeping, which had been formerly occupied by men. Compensation was then lowered and office management, the traditional authority associated with the position, was eliminated. A new office position, accountant, was established, with higher prestige and pay, and became a male-identified occupation (Machung, 1988). When work is divided along gender lines, it is not the work itself that determines its value but the gender of the person doing it.

The Contribution of Women to Economic Development

As long as women are expected to be the primary caretakers of their children, they will be forced to choose between child care, wage labor, or a compromise, part-time work. In Western societies, part-time work, as a solution to problems associated with the lack of day care, penalizes the female wage earner. Employers typically pay part-time workers lower hourly wages and provide few, if any, benefits compared to full-time workers in the same job. For those who must work for wages or who choose to do so, the problems of arranging for adequate child care may be severe, especially when fathers continue to maintain that these are the mothers' problems. Even in dual-career households, women, whether employed full-time or part-time, often have a "second shift": they assume the major share of household and child responsibilities after a "work day." This inequality strains marital relations and women's health and life satisfaction (Hochschild with Machung, 2003).

In contemporary developing countries, models of economic growth and change have tended to follow patterns set by Western industrialism. Where women were once heavily involved in small-scale agriculture based on intensive labor and simple technology, there is now a tendency to consolidate land holdings, to use industrial machinery, and to emphasize production for the market rather than for the home. It has consistently been men who have been taught to use the new machinery (such as tractors) and given the means to acquire it. As a result of being excluded from modernized agricultural production, women in developing countries have lost their influence over the deployment of resources, even within the home.

When men lose their "jobs" through the shift from labor-intensive to capital-intensive production, they are viewed as "unemployed." Because what women do outside the home has been considered by societies to be economically negligible, women similarly "unemployed" often are not considered an economic casualty. Feminists question this standard interpretation of economic "development" and women's invisibility in it (Acosta-Belén and Bose, 1990; Boserup, 1970).

The Domestic Mode of Production

Anthropologists use the phrase *domestic mode of production* to describe the organization of economic systems such as hunting–gathering, small-scale, frontier, and peasant economies. In such systems, the economic roles of women and men are integrated into other domestic roles within the household, which serves as the basic unit of both production and consumption. The division of labor is by age and gender, with relatively little specialization within these two categories. Women's contributions in these economies are variable in type and extent.

Food Production

Although women's roles in food production (subsistence) are quite variable, some general patterns can be found. In hunting–gathering societies, women are primarily responsible for the collection and processing of plant foods; in some cases, they do the fishing. Men hunt large game. In horticultural societies that depend on cultivated plants, women tend to be mostly responsible for planting, weeding, and harvesting; men are often assigned the more sporadic tasks of clearing the forest for new gardens and the like. In pastoral societies that depend on herding large animals (sheep, goats, cattle, yak, horses, llamas, alpacas, reindeer), women are often associated with milking, preparing butter and cheese, and care of young herd animals, while men are in charge of protection of the herd from raiders and predators. Yet, in certain societies, herding is women's work and, in others, farming is men's work.

Increased technology curtails to some extent the participation of women in those traditional activities. For example, women in herding societies are rarely directly involved in ranching operations, which are oriented toward markets rather than household consumption. When agricultural production is intensified by the use of plow and oxen, men assume the tasks of cultivation. Although the digging stick is often a woman's tool, the plow rarely is. Women are generally credited with inventing most of the techniques of agriculture and storage (pottery and baskets). Further, it is probable that women were the inventors of spinning (and later of the spinning wheel), weaving, and other techniques of cloth production. However, as with so many of the genuinely creative people in world history, women's names and records have been forgotten while the records of military adventures, the activity of men and their inventions, survive.

Maintenance

Simply producing food by gathering, cultivating, fishing, or herding is not enough to provide for family needs. Researchers who attempt to find a relationship between subsistence activities (food production) and women's status often overlook this point. Food processing, for example, may be a critical task in subsistence. While Mexican peasant men are primarily responsible for growing their food staple, corn, Mexican peasant women spend considerable amounts of time and energy turning corn into food—husking and shelling it, grinding it, forming and cooking tortillas. Food preservation and storage are critical tasks. Fish and meat may be dried or smoked or preserved in oil. Such tasks often are assigned to women.

Women also tend to take on the tasks of making clothing. The Inuit (Eskimo) men who hunt for sea mammals and caribou could not do so unless provided with warm parkas, leggings, and boots made by women. In societies that use plant or animal fibers for clothing, women generally do the spinning, weaving, and sewing. Women also construct tents and houses in many societies. They also have considerable responsibility for the care and health of their families. In many societies, women play important roles as healers of the sick, midwives, and "morticians" (laying out the dead) (see Chapter 9).

Exchange and Marketing

Although economies based on the domestic mode of production are geared toward production for household use, some wares become commodities, exchanged to obtain goods and services not produced in the household. In some societies, like those in West Africa and the Caribbean, women play a significant role as traders, merchants, and brokers. Their participation in the market has tended (though not invariably) to be limited to short-distance trade in necessities, such as food and utensils, rather than long-distance "luxury" items, such as precious metals, gems, and ivory. Where women do engage in mercantile activities, they tend to retain considerable control over their income, enhancing their autonomy and status.

The Capitalist Mode of Production

Urbanization and Class Distinctions

The development of *social stratification*, the division of a society into layers of social classes that commanded vastly different shares of the economic resources of the community, was one of the by-products of the development of civilization. Urbanization and capitalism accelerated that process. Cities provide a wide range of socioeconomic and cultural opportunities and depend on migrants for population growth and maintenance. Younger daughters and sons of the rural population come to the city with the hope of finding employment and social mobility.

Until recently, women migrating into a city rarely found a dazzling array of choices open to them. Previously, they usually entered into the class structure as the appendages of fathers or husbands. If totally on their own, they probably most readily found work as servants or entered the ranks of "unskilled" laborers. Such women were paid little, transient, and obliged by the discrimination of most societies against working women to supplement their meager incomes with prostitution. For women who lack skills, education, and social networks, this situation has not changed dramatically even today.

The idea of selling "labor" introduces a distinctive set of notions about work. It distinguishes members of a family (whose labor is not sold) from those who interact outside the family (where labor is sold). Such distinctions are especially applicable in urban contexts, where people interact with others who are mostly non-kin. Under the capitalist system, workers are separated (alienated) from the means of production, distribution, and exchange, which are privately owned and directed by small numbers of individuals and corporations, who become enormously wealthy by retaining part of the value of the workers' production as profits.

Working for Wages: Its Organizational Prerequisites

In order to "free" labor from the household, which requires work to sustain itself, certain basic arrangements must be made. One kind of arrangement involves a division of labor in the social sphere whereby some workers provide, on a regular basis, goods and services once produced only in the home for family consumption.

Labor directed strictly to household use, for example, the weaving of cloth for clothing, benefits only the family. When the same labor is sold in specialized production, the owner of the resources, tools, and products takes part of the value (after costs) produced by labor and allows the worker to take only a small share back to the family in the form of wages. The profit taken by the owner is accumulated and reinvested in more materials, tools, and products to increase future profits and personal wealth.

To the extent that women are paid lower wages for their work than men (as has invariably been the case), women have "subsidized" the development of industry and capitalist economies as a whole. Currently, women in developing nations not only provide cheap labor in industry but also continue to produce food and clothing in the rural countryside for their families, who work for industry. The African or Latin American male laborer who works for low wages in a mine or a factory depends on his wife to grow food to feed the family. The wife's efforts, however, are rarely appreciated as contributing—as they do—to the gross national product of the nation: they are a free subsidy to the nation's development.

It is doubtful that any country now considered "developed" could have achieved economic development through industrialization had it not been for a similar subsidy by women (Acosta-Belén and Bose, 1990; Mbinlinyi, 1987; Beneria and Sen, 1982).

Women's Work

Slaves and Serfs. In some economic systems, slaves, who were not paid at all for working, were the lowest level of worker. African American slaves prior to the U.S. Civil War were worked to obtain the maximum amount of labor possible, generally by means of coercion. In addition to the work performed for their masters, female slaves cooked and cared for their own families and produced more slaves for their owners. Unlike other women in this era, slave women were defined first as workers (Jones, 1985; White, 1985).

In Europe, after the slave-based economic system of the Roman Empire was overturned in the fifth century and replaced by small-scale economies of free and slave labor, there developed a system of serfdom that bound female and male workers to the soil, which existed for centuries. Serfdom gradually gave way to economic systems based on "free" wage labor. "Free" labor has been the most effective source of work in western European economies since the fourteenth century. The broad base of most contemporary economies is the "working class." With the development of industrial capitalism, the vast majorities of workers outside the home sell their labor for wages and cannot exist without doing so. They are "free" to accept what work they can find but are not free to withhold selling their labor for wages if they are to survive economically.

Prostitution. *Prostitution* is defined as the sale of sexual services. In the United States historically, prostitution has primarily been organized into relationships of economic dependence, very often with third parties as the employers or "bosses," as in the case of procurers, pimps, or madams. Men, but also women (parents, spouses, lovers, employers, brothel owners), play these intermediary roles; and both gain by the dependent relationship involved (Butler, 1985; Rosen, 1982; Hirata, 1979). In developing countries, where foreign governments have established overseas military installations, third parties often include host government officials, such as local police officers, and various military personnel of the foreign government (Enloe, 2000).

Most women do not intend or aspire to become prostitutes; rather, in certain circumstances, prostitution may provide the only means of generating an income. Poor females, both women and children, are the most vulnerable group (Brennan, 2002; Bertone, 2000). It is not uncommon for poor women across the globe to be trapped into international prostitution rings, lured by false promises of good wages for working as "entertainers." Considered deviant by "good women," female prostitutes are vulnerable to crime and diseases such as syphilis and acquired immune deficiency syndrome (AIDS); are brutalized by pimps, madams, and clients; and do not control the remuneration for their services.

Working-Class Women: Skilled Labor. Production was generally a household enterprise until the development of the factory system and workplaces designed to fit the industrial model. Although all the family shared the work, members did not do the same tasks and were not equally recognized for their contributions. In small-scale craft enterprises, it was commonplace for the man to work at the craft, producing goods, while his wife ran the shop, sold the goods, and kept the books. In Europe, where this division of labor was most pronounced, the more elite, urban professions and crafts had organized themselves into guilds by the thirteenth century. However, women were barred as members (except, in some cases, as widows) from the most skilled and lucrative occupations, and the knowledge of crafts was a "mystery" to them, opened for the most part to licensed male apprentices.

In some guilds, women did participate as independent and active working members. Out of several hundred crafts registered in thirteenth-century Paris, six were composed exclusively of women: silk spinners, wool spinners, silk weavers, silk-train makers, milliners of gold-braided caps, and makers of alms purses. In England, fourteenth-century guilds listed women as brewers, bakers, corders, and spinners and as working in wool, linen, and silk. It is likely that these guilds were organized by employers or civil authorities for the purpose of placing women under surveillance, to prevent them from pilfering materials (Shahar, 1983).

Working-Class Women: Domestic Wage Labor. A vast proportion of wage-earning women have worked as domestic laborers: maids, cooks, and nursemaids. They have contributed to the maintenance of a distinctive standard of living for women and men of the middle and upper classes, enabling them to occupy large, sometimes sumptuous, residences and to enjoy elaborate lifestyles.

Domestics had only a little more freedom than slaves. Their personal lives were closely supervised, and their working hours were ill defined and long, with very little time off. The less skilled were treated with little respect; indeed, they were often "invisible" to their employers. They had little or no job security, bargaining power, or opportunity to organize to protest their working conditions or low wages.

Today, in industrially developed nations, many of the former tasks of female domestics are provided by service industries such as hospitals, day-care centers, hotels, and restaurants or by machinery in the home, such as washing machines. However, were it not for the availability of relatively cheap domestic labor, filled largely by immigrant women, many middle-class professional women would be obliged to stay at home to care for their families since few men are willing to do so or to share parenting responsibilities equally. Many women acknowledge their dependence on child-care workers; but not all are conscious that their own ability to pursue careers is built upon a form of exploitation, paying poorer women relatively low wages for this domestic labor. In some areas, domestic workers have begun to form associations to enforce minimum-wage levels.

Working-Class Women: Factory Workers. The proportion of women in the U.S. labor force has increased steadily since 1900 (Table 12.3), beginning with a major influx of European immigrants, many with previous experience in the needle trade and garment factories. Female factory workers were not new to the U.S. economy in 1900. In the 1820s and

TABLE 12.3 Women in the U.S. Labor Force: Selected Years

Year	Women in the Labor Force (Thousands)	Women in the Labor Force as a Percent of the Labor Force
1900	4,999	18.1
1910	8,076	21.2
1920	8,229	20.4
1930	10,396	21.9
1940	13,007	24.6
1950	18,412	28.8
1960	23,272	32.3
1970	31,560	36.7
1980	41,283	44.2
1990	56,554	45.3
2001	57,933	47.9

Source: U.S. Department of Labor, Bureau of Labor Statistics, selected years.

When workplaces moved outside the home with industrialization, women found jobs that were extensions of the work done traditionally at home. This scene demonstrates the conditions that would have been found in nineteenth-century Europe and the United States.

1830s, single women were employed in textile mills throughout New England. They labored 12–13 hours a day, 6 days a week, and were paid half or less the pay of men. Most were young daughters of farmers who worked for a short period before marriage to help support their families and themselves. At the new model factory at Lowell, Massachusetts, they lived in company housing and their lives were closely supervised.

From time to time, the women workers resisted their situation. However, their efforts to improve working conditions through protest, strikes, organizations, and alliances with men's groups met with little success. By mid-twentieth century, poorer immigrant women, initially Irish, rapidly outnumbered native-born female factory workers and took over the struggle to organize and protect factory workers. These struggles produced labor leaders like Mary Harris ("Mother") Jones (1830–1930) and Elizabeth Gurley Flynn (1890–1964).

Immigrant women worked in a wide variety of industries but were predominant in the garment industry—and still are. It was in this industry that their union activities had the greatest impact. A strike of women shirtwaist workers in New York City in 1909 brought tens of thousands of members to the International Ladies' Garment Workers Union (ILGWU). Although beaten by hired thugs, the picketing women managed to win an increase in wages. Another goal, recognition for the union, was not achieved until 1913. While 80% of the garment workers were women, the ILGWU was dominated by men; not surprisingly, it classified the male-dominated crafts of cutting and pressing as highly paid skilled labor and the female-dominated tasks of joining, draping, and trimming as un-skilled, with women being paid accordingly. The union leaders did not press for the safety regulations demanded by the women in 1909, and many women perished in the Triangle Shirtwaist Factory fire in 1911 (Kennedy, 1979).

Beginning in the 1970s, the garment sweat-shop was revitalized in cities like New York, Miami, and Los Angeles, utilizing a new im-migrant force—women from East Asia, Latin America, and the Caribbean. Part of a global workforce in the apparel industry, immigrant women's exploitation and their resistance to it has remained largely unchanged over the decades (Louie, 2001). In 1982, for example, in the largest labor strike in the history of New York City's Chinatown, 20,000 Chinese women garment workers defended their right to a union contract. In addition, so they could both work and mother, the women wrenched financial support from the ILGWU for a day-care center, a demand that the union had ig-nored for 6 years (Bao, 2003).

Working women have had to contend with society's view of the proper role of females. During the Great Depression of the 1930s, employed women were told they were taking jobs from men. This propaganda ignored the fact that most of the jobs women held were low-paid, traditionally female ones, which men had not previously performed. After World War II, they were told that to work away from home was unfeminine and harmful to their families. Women who had worked in heavy industry during both wars to help the nation and support their families were made unwelcome there when the men came home. Women lacked the power to fight for their interests, to resist layoffs, and to hold on to their high wages.

In the 1970s, a few women began to obtain high-paying heavy industrial jobs at twice the wages they could earn as secretaries. Many women have fought for legal reforms to ban gender discrimination in hiring and promo-tion but remain rare in technical, industrial, and "skilled" trades. To increase women's par-ticipation in the skilled trades, the U.S. De-partment of Labor in 1978 established regula-tions that required companies receiving any federal funding to adhere to goals and timeta-bles and to set aside apprenticeships for women. However, there has been a lack of ef-fort to enforce these regulations on the part of the government, notably during the presiden-cies of Ronald Reagan (1981–9) and George H. W. Bush (1989–93). Those few women who have entered the nontraditional trades report job isolation and sexual harassment, despite Department of Labor regulations against such activities, with the effect of fur-ther reducing women's participation in the skilled trades.

With global competition (see globalization below), employers face more demands to keep costs down. One solution has always been to turn to women as their labor can be purchased at a lower rate than that of men. In the Mid-west of the United States, for example, since the 1980s immigrant Mexican, Laotian, and Vietnamese women have worked in various capacities in the meatpacking industry, now no longer a male domain (Broadway, 1994).

The Pink-Collar Worker. Women today predominate in clerical work, sales, and services. Although both women and men work as salespeople, they sell different things. Men generally sell cars and insurance; women sell cosmetics and women's clothing. In the United States, most women who work do so in the service sector, which involves the sale and distribu-tion of goods and services themselves. These exclusively female jobs are called *pink-collar* work.

Office workers are the largest occupational category for women today. Women occupy

This photograph shows women in Lesotho, a country in southern Africa. These women are accomplishing the kind of heavy work, requiring great physical strength, that has traditionally been associated with men.

administrative support positions, while men primarily hold the management positions (Bravo, 2003). In part, the gender segregation of office workers is something of an illusion, a product of labeling the things done by women and men differently. For example, men might be hired as administrative "analysts" and women as administrative "assistants," though they end up doing the same job. By giving the same job two different titles, one for men and one for women, companies can classify the title used for women at a lower wage rate.

Heavy mining labor pays women far more than white-collar or factory jobs, even at the lowest entry levels. These three women express the joy of sisterhood in sharing their hardships together.

Pink-collar workers are paid at rates comparable to those of unskilled blue-collar workers, and the work is generally routine and lacks career advancement. They are expected to be deferential rather than ambitious, and preference may be given to women who are young and sexually attractive. Often, part of the "job" is to look and be "feminine" in dress and manner.

Clerical and secretarial work became available to women late in the nineteenth century, especially with the introduction of the typewriter. Computers and other new technologies have further changed the nature and conditions of office work. The lowest-level clerical jobs, which have served as entry points for women, are disappearing. Also, learning a word-processing program does not establish the kind of skills that can lead to the higher-paying information technology positions, such as operations, programming, or systems analysts, held largely by men (Gutek and Bikson, 1985). Many women have had the challenges of varied work replaced by long hours of repetitive word processing, which is linked to health hazards, including eye fatigue and wrist, neck, and back aches (Stellman and Henifin, 1989). Others find their jobs include greater responsibilities, such as database management and desktop publishing, but they are not viewed as professionals. New technology with electronic surveillance capabilities, for example, the timing of customer-service calls, has enabled employers and supervisors to more closely monitor a woman's work, contributing to a loss of her sense of security and control. In other cases, jobs are being "outsourced" to "cheaper" labor overseas as corporations compete globally, drawing women in other parts of the world into automated office work. Although the new technologies do provide new opportunities for women, they also reinforce gender and economic inequalities worldwide (Bravo, 2003).

U.S. women working full-time and year-round earn about 70% of what men earn (Table 12.4). The differential has improved only slightly in some 30 years, although women are entering the workforce in increased numbers and are working in jobs formerly held only by men. In some countries, the pay differential between women and men is even greater. In the Republic of Korea and Japan, women earn only 47% and 51%, respectively, of what their male colleagues earn (United Nations Development Program, 1993). One argument sometimes made to explain this discrepancy is that the pay differential results from women having less

TABLE 12.4 Median Weekly Earnings of Women and Men, 2001 (All Workers, 16 Years and Over $597)

	Females ($)	Males ($)
Age 16–24	354	392
Age 25 and over	542	722
Married with spouse	548	759
Race		
White	521	694
Black	451	518
Hispanic	385	438
Union affiliation		
Union member	643	765
Non-union member	494	647
Educational attainment		
Less than high school diploma	314	415
High school diploma	441	610
College graduate	784	1082
Occupation		
Managerial/professional	732	1038
Technical sales/ administrative support	473	667
Service occupation	335	438
Precision, production, and repair	332	374
Operators, fabricators, and laborers	368	501
Farming, forestry, fishing	308	366

Source: U.S. Department of Labor, Bureau of Labor Statistics, 2002:21.

experience than men, which ignores the impact of gender discrimination. To test this argument, economists have held constant the variables of age, experience, and duration of the job and have found that women still get paid less than men and are still promoted more slowly (Rotella, 1980).

The Contingent Worker. Contingent workers include part-time, temporary, and free-lance workers. They comprise a "flexible" workforce and are increasingly prevalent. Employers rely on these workers when they perceive a need and release them when there is no future need. Some contingent workers are voluntary, preferring this particular work arrangement, while others are involuntary and are looking for full-time, regular employment.

Included in the category of temporary workers are "leased" employees, who work for one company (the leasing company) but perform all their job duties for a different company, leading to concerns such as who exactly the employer is and what rights the employee has. In many cases, employee leasing, as a cost saving to the employer, is a means of reducing benefits or breaking unions (Axelrod, 1987).

Home workers and independent contractors are another part of the flexible workforce. Most home-based white-collar workers are self-employed (75%) and married women (75%). Home workers list four major reasons to work at home: *(1)* family responsibilities; *(2)* control over work hours and setting; *(3)* elimination of the expense of traveling and of office politics; and *(4)* the need to earn extra money (Christensen, 1988). Women performing home work report stress in trying to balance work at home with household responsibilities.

Contingent work raises disturbing issues concerning the development of a new workforce of women dependent on the capricious demands of employers. Contingent workers

rarely receive the benefits and security associated with full-time employment. Employers feel less need to provide training and occupational advancement. Some of these workers report feeling "out of it" at their workplace and isolated at home. On average, home workers receive lower wages than on-site employees. Yet, for many women, a contingent job with a weak attachment to an employer is the only solution to the problems of inadequate child care, partial retirement, and continuing education.

In the United States, 25% of all female workers worked part time in 2001. In Finland and Denmark, 45% of all women who work are part-timers. Part-time work may become a trap for women who, in seeking full-time employment later on, will be at a disadvantage because of their history of low wages, low skills, and irregularity of work (Bollé, 2001).

The Professions. The professions include the arts, law, medicine, teaching, and management. They often require more training and education than other kinds of work, although critics claim that the structure of the professions is often designed more to preserve class privileges (by requiring, for instance, lengthy training that only the rich can afford) than to enhance the quality of the work performed. Most of the professions set their own standards for qualifications and performance and generally pay more than blue- and pink-collar work.

Work in the professions is also highly segregated by gender. Most fall into one of two categories: those that society deems "female" and those that society deems "male." For example, in the United States, nursing, elementary and secondary teaching, social work, and library work are considered women's professions and women outnumber men in them. Women are underrepresented in most other (men's) professions, especially in medicine, science, engineering, and higher management and as stockbrokers. The issues for women in the two kinds of profession are somewhat different.

Within the "women's professions" there is gender segregation that places men at the highest levels. More men than women, for example, are principals, superintendents, chief officers, and faculty and administrators of professional schools. For the most part, these female professions offer limited career mobility to women; they are the lowest-paying and least prestigious of the professions. Yet, they are enormously important to society. They provide large numbers of women with the opportunity to pursue gratifying careers, although society has not elected to reward them with high pay or status. It is likely that women are poorly paid and even sometimes belittled *because* they are in women's professions.

Although many women have been trained and are active in the arts, few have held top-ranking positions in architecture or design or as producers or directors in theater or film. Women have also experienced systematic discrimination as artists, so it is harder for them than for men to gain recognition and to make a living in the arts. In recent years, thanks in part to the women's movement and in part to antidiscrimination laws, increasing numbers of women have entered and achieved success in professions formerly reserved for men.

Women in "male professions" often encounter serious obstacles. Not only will they be in the minority among their peers but also their subordinates, whether female or male, may have difficulty relating to them and vice versa. The more negative a male subordinate's opinion is of women in general, the less likely he will be to attribute the success of a female manager to her own ability or effort (Garland et al., 1982). The same could be said of women and men as co-workers.

Gender segregation is evident within "male professions" as well: female physicians tend to go into pediatrics; female lawyers, into pro-

bate (dealing with wills and property dispositions to widows and offspring); and female professors, into the humanities and social sciences rather than the physical sciences. Gender segregation between and within the professions is in part the result of gender discrimination in education (see Chapter 10).

For female professionals who pursue both career and family, there are many role conflicts since both jobs and families make demands on a woman's time and energy. The male model of professional development is especially problematic for women who are raising a family. Many professions and employers within the professions, especially male-dominated ones, assume that individuals dedicate most of their time and energies to work. Some professional women now in their thirties and forties are choosing to leave careers that had been closed to their mother's generation and previous generations of women, albeit perhaps only temporarily. Having experienced the fast track to a law partnership or corporate management, for example, they have found the male-defined work conditions enormously dissatisfying. Although this option is open primarily to the wealthy or those with high income–earning spouses, their decision to "opt out" goes beyond the issue of balancing work and family to questioning the place and satisfaction of work itself in life (Belkin, 2003).

Corporate Management at the Highest Levels. Corporate leaders are much admired for their power and influence, and chief executives are certainly well remunerated. Some feminists hope to reform the corporation from within by gaining positions of power. The ability to do so remains questionable. Corporations have traditionally employed men in the management of the business enterprise. Worldwide, women account for more than 40% of the labor force but rarely hold more than 20% of the management jobs.

In the United States, affirmative action suits, affirmative action policies of companies, and the women's movement have called attention to the gender gap in the corporate ladder. More women are reaching middle-management ranks, but few are senior managers, being skipped over while male peers or juniors are chosen for these positions. Not surprisingly, women executives continue to be compensated at a lower rate than male executives. In a 1999 survey of the 500 largest U.S. corporations, women accounted for 11% of all corporate officers and 5% of the most senior corporate officers (Fortune, 1999)—very low percentages indeed. Yet, one study found a positive correlation between high numbers of women in executive positions and high profits within the same industry, suggesting that including women in leadership roles benefits business (Adler, 2001).

Why do women experience difficulty in attaining positions of authority and responsibility in the corporate setting, and why do corporations fail to see women as assets? Historically, employers have argued that women do not have the aptitude or training required for many of the jobs men have traditionally held. They tend to believe the social stereotyping that women would perform those jobs poorly. They also view women as identified with family and home and see non-traditional jobs for women as inappropriate. Therefore, they choose to hire men and pay them higher wages.

In a survey conducted by an executive search firm, executive women reported their greatest obstacle to advancement was not family responsibilities but simply "being a woman" and the multifaceted pattern of gender discrimination due to male attitudes and behavior (Korn/Ferry International, 1990). One early feminist work on women in corporations in the 1970s found that they had to try to "fit in." Many of the women in this study lacked the opportunities to acquire the skills associated with (male-defined) upper-management jobs and were seen as incompetent (Kanter, 1977). Feminine work practices (information sharing, cooperation, and nurturing) continue to be undervalued, and women who engage in such behaviors are more likely to have their responsibilities and authority eroded (Kolb and Meyerson, 1999). Many women who have put in the long hours and attained senior-level management positions have often delayed motherhood, chosen not to marry or to become mothers, and/or had significant amounts of domestic help, including supportive spouses.

Although women leaders have just as much need as men to enhance their personal power, women tend to express a more helpful leadership style and to inhibit the exhibition of power (Claes, 2001; Chusmir and Parker, 1984; Colwill, 1982). In the twenty-first century, some businesses are beginning to value those management styles, often identified with female leadership styles, which stress teamwork, flexibility, and collaboration in problem solving as making them better able to adapt to the current global economic environment characterized by uncertainty and the need to constantly evolve.

Whether women earn high salaries as professionals or low wages as caregivers, salesclerks, or sex workers, discrimination against them is found at all levels and categories of work. Women experience the "glass ceiling" and the "sticky floor": the glass ceiling keeps them from reaching the highest levels of corporate and public responsibility, and the sticky floor keeps the vast majority of the world's women stuck in low-paid jobs (Kimmel, 2000; Albeda and Tilly, 1997).

Globalization and the Transformation of Work

Today, globalizing forces have profoundly altered national economies and the workplace. Globalization entails "the internationalization of the capitalist economy in which states, markets, and civil society are restructured to facilitate the spread of global capital" (Peterson and Runyan, 1999:82). Since the conclusion of World War II, capitalism has integrated the world's countries into a single global economy, a process that accelerated with the end of colonialism and the collapse of communism in Russia and Eastern Europe. To facilitate this restructuring, governments accommodate the interests of multinational corporations to compete in selling their products in the global economy.

In industrialized nations, which tend to have higher labor costs, manufacturing industries have moved some of their operations to low-wage regions of the world. Since the 1970s, the number of manufacturing jobs in the United States and other industrialized countries has declined. Work is being transformed from full-time with decent wages and benefits to short-term or part-time with lower wages and few, if any, benefits (Ehrenreich and Hochschild, 2002; Carnoy, 2001). Men formerly employed in well-paying manufacturing jobs have had to find other jobs, often with lower wages and fewer benefits. Many women have been pulled into the workforce to make up for the loss of the male breadwinner's income. For working-class and poor women with few or no skills who must work, the low wages and lack of benefits earned laboring as maids, waitresses, and salesclerks are not enough to make ends meet (Ehrenreich, 2001; Wichterich, 1998). Middle-class and well-educated women in developed countries, on the other hand, have made significant gains in finding employment in the professions that traditionally discriminated against them.

Globalization also touches the lives of women and men in developing countries. As manufacturing industries have relocated to low-wage countries in search of cheap, docile labor, many women in developing countries have joined the global assembly line in industries as diverse as clothing, food production, and electronics. The governments in the Caribbean and Latin America, Eastern Europe, and many countries of Asia advertise the availability of a large supply of female labor. Work in multinational corporation factories compromises workers' health and life expectancy; women perform repetitious tasks and are exposed to dangerous chemicals. However, the women in these countries face extreme poverty and need even the lowest wages for survival; they have almost no possibility of resisting exploitation.

As economic conditions in developing countries worsened over the past four decades, governments were forced to implement specific policies of international financial institutions like the International Monetary Fund, the World Bank, and the World Trade Organization. These policies benefited the global economy as determined by the advanced industrialized countries. In exchange for loans and aid, developing countries have had to agree to cut government spending on health, education, and welfare; reduce the number of government jobs; sell off government-owned and -operated businesses; and open their economies to foreign investors. These structural adjustment programs have caused enormous hardships (Dickinson and Schaeffer, 2001; Wichterich, 1998). Migration becomes an economic strategy for family survival in developing countries; women often lead the way.

Those women who cannot find work in their own country migrate to developed countries or wealthier developing countries. They find jobs performing traditional women's tasks. The less-educated often work as nannies, maids, and sex workers and send remittances back home to feed, clothe, house, and educate their families there. They make it possible for women in industrialized countries to go out and work with the knowledge that their child will be looked after, their homes cleaned, and their elderly relatives attended. These immigrant workers are poorly paid, have little or no rights in the host country, are often subject to emotional and physical abuse, and for sex workers, run the risks of acquiring the human immunodeficiency virus (HIV) and contracting AIDS and other sexually transmitted diseases. Today, women account for one-half of the world's 120 million migrants (Ehrenreich and Hochschild, 2002). For the small numbers of educated and skilled women from developing countries who seek to continue their professions in the developed countries, their experiences have generally been of downward mobility, that is, starting over again (for example, by taking licensing exams) and getting little or no credit for their skills and years of experience.

Globalization creates winners and losers. The winners include professional women in developed countries who earn decent salaries in order to consume cheap goods made by women in developing countries paid low wages. However, many feminists do not wish to achieve economic advancement for themselves at the expense of women elsewhere. The avoidance of this dilemma will require the development of more enlightened policies on the part of corporations and better foreign economic policies by the United States than are now in effect.

Race, Ethnicity, and Work in the United States

Women from all backgrounds can feel the experience of gender discrimination in the labor force. Women of color—African American, Asian American, Latina, and Native American—are victimized by racial/ethnic discrimination as well. Although women of color have common experiences, it is impor-

tant to recognize that they have different experiences as well.

African American women's career expectations and pursuits are not fully appreciated (Collins, 2000). African American women have been a significant part of the labor force since the days of slavery. When slavery was abolished, many of them turned to employment as domestics, laundresses, and child-care workers and continued to work alongside their men in the fields as needed. Because African American men often found it more difficult to gain employment in cities, African American women became heads of households when necessary. They experienced high labor force participation along with family responsibilities through the periods when fewer white women carried this double burden.

Because of racism, African American women have generally been employed at the lowest rung of the labor market. In recent times, their participation in government-funded training programs, such as the Manpower Development and Training Act (MDTA), the Comprehensive Employment and Training Act (CETA), and the Job Training Partnership Act (JTPA), has not increased their employment rates or conditions. Under the MDTA, African American women were forced into two narrow fields, health and clerical occupations. Those enrolled in the CETA program received lower incomes after training than either white and black males or white women (Wallace, 1980).

Given the obstacle of racism, African American families have always stressed the value of education, especially for daughters (see Chapter 10). Professional and managerial black women are making gains, but job ceilings and sector segmentation persist. The majority of them are employed in the public sector, by small independent firms, or in the black community (Higginbotham, 1994). In 2000, African American women are frequently found

Robert F. Goheen Professor at Princeton University, Toni Morrison, recipient of the Nobel Prize in Literature in 1993, started to work at 13 years of age at a job that was available to a young African American girl: cleaning house after school. When asked if she felt a sense of triumph when she received the Nobel Prize, she answered "I felt a lot of 'we' excitement. It was as if a whole category of 'female writer' and 'black writer' had been redeemed. I felt I represented a whole world of women who either were silenced or who had never received the imprimatur of the established literary world" (Dreifus, 1994).

in the occupations of clergy, social work, teaching, and nursing (Costello et al., 2002).

Latino cultural patterns are built around the values of *machismo* for men and *marianismo* for women (Comas-Diaz, 1987). *Machismo*, with its emphasis on the display of male power and authority, means literally "maleness" or "virility." Under *marianismo*, women are expected to be spiritually superior to men and to adjust selflessly to male *macho* behavior and to a role of childbearing and motherhood. These cultural messages restrict the choices of girls and women and give men more freedom, placing them in a privileged position as the breadwinner and overseer of the family.

Confinement of Latinas to the home is *machismo* ideology; the reality is that Latinas have a long tradition of contributing to the family economy (Kessler-Harris, 2003). Paid employment or participation in the informal economy has been a traditional role for most working-class and peasant women in Latin America. For example, by the 1930s, Puerto Rican women outnumbered Puerto Rican men in the cigar and needlework industries (Ammott and Matthaei, 1991). In the mid-1960s, middle-class Cuban immigrant women in Miami, who had never worked outside of their homes in Cuba, joined the paid labor force and revived the garment industry (Portes and Stepick, 1993). For Latinas,

Box 12.2   LIFE IN THE CANNERIES

Chicana and Mexican immigrant women express the joys, demands, and constraints of combining work in California's food processing industry with family life in the following account.

According to [Vicki] Ruiz [1990], cannery culture is "a curious blend of Mexican extended families and a general women's work culture, nurtured by assembly line segregation and common interests." . . . At work the women talked with each other on the line, exchanged pictures of their children during breaks, and established close friendships that continued outside the plant.

. . . A Chicana who worked in the canneries for twenty-five years explained that work in the canneries gave her a brief escape from the drudgery of housework and childcare . . . "When I'm not working, I stay home and take care of my grandchildren. I love them, but I need time to myself. When I'm working, I'm happy. I see my friends. I have my own money."

Work in the canneries did not free the women from the "double day.". . . they still had the main responsibilities for child-rearing, cooking, laundry, and housecleaning.

Traditional Mexican family roles limited women's activism. As one woman explained, "My husband would tell me, 'You work all day and weekends. Leave the union to others who don't have kids.'" Gender stratification and the union structure also severely restricted women's participation in the union.

Source: From William V. Flores, Mujeres en huelga: Cultural citizenship and gender empowerment in a cannery strike. In *Latino Cultural Citizenship*, edited by William V. Flores and Rina Benmayor, 218–9. Boston: Beacon Press, 1997.

language barriers reinforced by residential patterns and lack of transportation make it difficult to find decent and good-paying jobs (see Box 12.2).

In the United States today, a large number of Latinas are undocumented workers having no U.S. work visa; to avoid apprehension, these women often live in isolated situations. Many Latinas work as domestics and nannies; as migrant farm laborers, traveling all over the country picking fruits and vegetables; and in factory work (sweatshops), doing piecework. These endeavors are generally exploitative, giving women little power to shape their work environment.

Second- and third-generation mainland Puerto Rican women are less traditional, more assertive, than first-generation Puerto Rican women, and education is considered the major reason (Soto and Shaver, 1983;

Rosario, 1982). Nationally, however, only 11% of all Latinas achieved a college degree in 2000. As Puerto Rican women have become more educated and geographically dispersed, they have increased their labor force participation. The result is an emerging split within some Latino communities. Among Puerto Ricans, for example, recent migrants are found in lower-level jobs while mainland-born Puerto Ricans, having attained more education, are relatively upwardly mobile, although not assimilated. Overall, by 2000, many Latinas were found working as dental assistants and social workers (Costello et al., 2002).

Compared to Latinas, Asian American women in general have higher labor force participation, education, and economic status. Their population is complex, comprising about a dozen large ethnic groups and many smaller communities from east, south, and southeast Asia. In 2000, the most frequent occupations for Asian American women were computer processors, data-processing equipment repairers, and physicians (Costello et al., 2002). Employment experiences and choices vary widely, depending on class, ethnicity, national grouping, English language facility, generation in the United States, and citizenship status (Hune and Chan, 1997).

Aggregate data distort employment disparities between and within Asian American ethnic groups. For example, many Asian Indian and Filipina women are professionals, particularly in health care, while many Chinese and Japanese American females hold white-collar jobs. However, Chinese, Indian, Korean, and Vietnamese American women also are unpaid or low-paid workers in small family businesses; a few head their own small businesses, such as restaurants and nail salons. Other Chinese, Vietnamese, Cambodian, and Hmong American women are employed as factory operatives or service workers, and other Filipinas as home caregivers; they are among the working poor (Hune and Chan, 1997).

What role does culture play in Asian American women's work choices? Historically, Asian cultures have privileged males, dissuading women from developing "masculine" traits such as competitiveness, independence, and activism. Females are socialized to be modest, responsible, and self-sacrificing and to assume traditional roles at home (Mau, 1990; Fillmore and Cheong, 1980). Like Latinas, these notions about Asian American women being homebound and submissive are idealized; in reality, Asian American women work outside the home and as an economic necessity to support families and to supplement the low income of spouses. Feminist scholars have argued that structural factors, such as racism, xenophobia, and restrictive immigration laws and professional licenses, as well as cultural factors, contribute to Asian American women's work roles (Hune 1997; Chu, 1988).

Many Asian American women seek advanced degrees. Yet, sociologist Deborah Woo (1989) finds that highly educated Asian American women are not economically rewarded commensurate with their education and that few progress beyond the middle levels of management. Asian American women who have developed both feminine and masculine aspects of their self-concept experience higher self-esteem, work satisfaction, and occupational attainment (Chow, 1987).

Native American women are the most economically disadvantaged group in the United States. Unemployment rates are high (12%), and of those who do work, more than two-thirds hold part-time jobs. For those with college degrees, many have found jobs in the public sector, working as professionals and technicians on reservations. However, cutbacks at all governmental levels have made it difficult for them to secure employment opportunities. Native American women constantly struggle against inadequate education and discrimination in the labor market (Amott and Matthaei, 1991).

Self-Employment

Historically, few women have been self-employed due, in part, to the different socialization of girls and boys. Girls tend not to be taught to take the initiative or to be assertive or independent. When girls do show these qualities, which underlie successful self-employment, they often receive fewer rewards than boys or even negative sanctions.

Financial institutions globally have long maintained discriminatory practices, denying loans and credit that could enable women to start or run a business simply on the basis of gender. As women in the industrialized countries campaign to legislate against such discrimination, it is not easy to end traditional attitudes translated into business practices.

Despite the obstacles, quite a few ambitious women have managed to overcome many of the financial barriers to self-employment. Madame C. J. Walker (born Sarah Breedlove, 1867–1919), for example, was an early African American inventor and entrepreneur, who in 1905 developed and sold hair products for black women. With her wealth, she became an activist against lynching and a philanthropist (Bundles, 2001).

The factors that propel women to become self-employed vary. In developed countries, self-employed women include those who previously worked in major corporations but left to start their own enterprises because of dissatisfaction over gender inequities in pay, power, and promotion (Wirth, 2001). However, the vast majority of self-employed women in the world choose self-employment for other reasons. For many women who must combine work and family responsibilities, self-employment allows them to earn needed income and to take care of their families at the same time. In developing countries, when government structural adjustment programs jeopardized a family's economic survival, households set aside cultural beliefs about women in the workforce and marketplace. For example, women in south Asia, Africa, and the Caribbean have entered the workforce as traders (Seligman, 2001).

Globally, self-employed women have some commonalities: they tend to work out of their homes; they are found in enterprises at the lower end of economic productive activities, particularly those with little barriers to entry (food, child care, and craft production); and they start enterprises that allow them to use their traditional skills and knowledge. In developed countries, more self-employed women are engaged in commerce and services than in developing countries, where self-employed women typically establish businesses involving artisan crafts and agriculture (United Nations, 2000).

In the United States, women own about 32% of small businesses. Self-employed women tend to experience higher autonomy, self-development, and satisfaction from working than women who are employees (Mannheim and Schriffrin, 1984).

Unemployment

Most countries recognize the responsibility to provide jobs to those who cannot find them, even though many governments may fail to avoid high levels of unemployment. The United States is almost alone in denying this obligation. Governmental attempts to encourage or stimulate private sector employment are often unsuccessful, especially for women, the working class, and minorities, who are routinely "last hired and first fired." It has been argued that the right of an individual to employment, provided by the government if not available otherwise, should be recognized as a human right (Sen, 2001; Nickel, 1978–9).

Unemployment rates are almost always higher for women than for men, and young women experience more unemployment and longer periods of unemployment than young men (United Nations, 2000). If women are to be able to lead decent, productive lives, among the first priorities must be the assurance that when they seek employment, jobs will be available. To be able to compete on equal terms with men for an inadequate number of actual jobs will not be enough.

The Politics of Work: Barriers and Strategies

Conflict and Competition Between Women and Men

As daughters, sisters, wives, and mothers, women have special relationships with men. Women in the workplace are not simply competitors with men; women cannot entirely separate their own interests from those of the men to whom they are in some way related.

This is a multifaceted issue. First, men may feel that having their wives work for wages will threaten their own authority within the household. Second, women at home usually perform tasks that enhance men's status and leisure time. Third, men's social status often relies on their being the primary breadwinner in the family. This situation is changing. Many households require more than one wage earner. Almost 60% of men in the United States who are married with children have wives who work. Then why do men whose wives *must* work for wages not support women's advancement in the workplace? Men's concern for having a status superior to that of their wives operates here, too; but the explanation must also incorporate a broader view of the economic system. In industrialized economies, jobs—or at least "good" jobs—are scarce: there are generally more workers available than there are attractive jobs. By reducing the pool from which prospective employers can draw, those who have or could have "good" jobs hope to reduce competition, to better their chances and force up their pay. By supporting both sexist and racist discrimination in employment, white male workers may believe they are improving their own lot, even though such discrimination undermines their daughters, wives, sisters, and mothers, as well as their own positions.

As more women work, conflict between women and men over child care and housekeeping responsibilities divides the genders. Women make up over 47% of the U.S. labor force, yet men and policy makers operate as if the majority of households have only one breadwinner, the man. Among women who require the flexibility of taking time off to meet their domestic responsibilities, many will be relegated to the "female"

occupations—jobs that pay less, are part-time, offer little in the way of training, and fail to lead to career advancement. Until men share equally in caregiving and other household responsibilities, societies must find ways to help women meet their responsibilities both at work and at home. Expanded day-care and after school–care facilities funded by governments are examples of what could be done. One such model is that of the Scandinavian governments, which provide educational opportunities, paid parental leave, health care, extensive day-care services, child or family allowances, government–guaranteed child support, and other social services to enable women to seek and hold employment (Melkas, 2001).

The future cooperation of women and men is encouraged by studies of children whose mothers work outside the home compared to those whose mothers work at home. These studies indicate that daughters and sons of working women have less traditional views of marriage (Stephen and Corder, 1985). They also view both women and their employment more positively than children of "nonworking" mothers (Powell and Steelman, 1982). In another study of young people who have grown up with a working mom, two-thirds of the young men interviewed hoped to share parenting and work (Gerson, 2003). There is evidence that men who have high self-esteem and are comfortable with their own masculinity accept the changing role of women at home and at work (Archer, 1984; Corder and Stephen, 1984).

Sexual and Gender Harassment

Sexual and gender harassment has only recently come under legal scrutiny. This pervasive problem for women workers is very much underreported, though the testimony given by attorney Anita Hill in 1991 against

---

Box 12.3   LEVELS OF SEXUAL HARASSMENT

- Gender harassment: generalized sexist statements and behavior not designed to elicit sexual cooperation but to convey insulting, degrading, and/or sexist attitudes toward women or homosexual people.
- Seductive behavior: unwanted, inappropriate, and offensive physical or verbal sexual advances.
- Sexual bribery: solicitation of sexual activity or other sex-linked behavior by promise of reward.
- Sexual coercion: coercion of sexual activity or other sex-linked behavior by promise of reward.
- Sexual assault: physical assault and/or rape.

Source: From S. R. Zalk, Harrassment on the job: What everyone ought to know. Dental Teamwork 1991; May–June: 10–5, p. 13. Copyright © 1991 American Dental Association. All rights reserved. Reprinted by permission.

Supreme Court nominee Clarence Thomas encouraged more women to come forward about their experiences (Morrison, 1992).

Sexual harassment is an abuse of power. In the workplace, sexual harassment occurs when an employer or supervisor demands sexual favors from an employee under threat of dismissal or other reprisal, often not made explicit, or when an employee is subjected to persistent unwelcome sexual advances or innuendoes (see Box 12.3). It includes not only the harassment of females by males but also the harassment by customers of women whose job requires that they wear sexually provocative clothing, male employees by female supervisors, and homosexual advances (Christensen, 1988). Studies have found that many men view certain sexual behaviors (sexual advances or solicitation of sex in exchange for a reward) as flattering to women. These behaviors are anything but innocent. They contribute to a hostile work environment and may inflict great harm upon a victim. Sexual harassment can interfere with a woman's ability to meet financial obligations, can block her career choices, and can damage her self-esteem

and personal security (Paludi, 1990). Other studies view sexual harassment simply as a means of putting women in their place. Sexual harassment is costly: approximately $7 million is lost annually due to the high turnover of female employees, absenteeism, and productivity declines that result (Kimmel, 2000).

In the past, women who were victimized by sexual harassment were unlikely to complain. They felt that speaking up or confronting a harasser would make no difference. However, as more workplaces establish codes of conduct to regulate such offensive behaviors (see Box 12.4), women are increasingly seeking redress at their workplace and in the courts.

Countries as diverse as Argentina, Canada, Costa Rica, Japan, New Zealand, the Philippines, South Africa, the United States, and the members of the European Union have defined sexual harassment as a legal wrong that merits sanctions and remedies. New Zealand has made sexual harassment a violation of its 1993 Human Rights Act amendment; it is the only country in the world with detailed procedures for handling sexual harassment cases (Aeberhard, 2001).

Box 12.4   U.S. GUIDELINES FOR EMPLOYERS ON SEXUAL HARASSMENT

The U.S. government has adopted guidelines for employers to eliminate sexual harassment in the workplace. Here is an excerpt:

Prevention is the best tool for the elimination of sexual harassment. An employer should take all steps necessary to prevent sexual harassment from occurring, such as affirmatively raising the subject, expressing strong disapproval, developing appropriate sanctions, informing employees of their right to raise and how to raise the issue of harassment under Title VII, and developing methods to sensitize all concerned.

Source: U.S. Equal Employment Opportunity Commission.

Social Support for Working Women

Unions. The labor union is the principal organized support group for working people outside the family. In the past, unions have not always been particularly supportive of women workers. It is noteworthy that many primary fields of women's employment, whether blue-collar, pink-collar, or professional, are not unionized. A large proportion of working women have the additional disadvantage of racial and ethnic discrimination; many unions have tended to exclude or discriminate against racial and ethnic minority groups and immigrants.

The conditions militating against women's participation in trade union activity today are much the same as they were over a century ago. Women are seen as dependents, whose primary role is in the home. The demands of domestic responsibility leave women little time to devote to union activities. Women traditionally lack training and experience in public speaking and self-assertion, important aspects of union activity. As the least skilled and lowest-paid workers, they have had little bargaining leverage with employers. Women have also faced considerable hostility from working men, who often view female colleagues as direct competitors for jobs or union positions and are made uneasy at home by wives who are too "independent" (Kennedy, 1979).

Despite these obstacles, many women have organized themselves or joined with men to fight for unions and collective-bargaining rights. One of the earliest successful women's trade unions was the Collar Laundry Union of Troy, New York, which had some four hundred members at its peak, many of them Irish immigrants, and lasted nearly 6 years in the 1860s (Kennedy, 1979). The Knights of Labor, a national union founded in 1869, offered support to women and African American workers but was soon replaced by the more conservative crafts union, the American Federation of Labor, which was interested mainly in skilled white male workers. Despite union organization among women who worked during World War I in machine shops, foundries, railroad yards and offices, streetcars, and telephone exchanges, union support for women subsequently fell. Fearing that the presence of women in these workplaces would change working conditions at their expense, many men defended traditions that barred women from employment. Women either were relegated to auxiliary groups in unions or remained unorganized (Greenwald, 1980). The highest levels of leadership within labor unions have remained male preserves.

Unionization has proven beneficial to working women, and existing unions are gradually becoming more aware of women's issues. The United Auto Workers, for example, has endorsed equal pay, gender-integrated seniority lists, day care, and the Equal Rights Amendment. Despite unions' growing awareness of the importance of organizing for working women's rights, most women do not join unions. In the United States, only 7 million out of a total of 58 million working women (11%) belong to unions or professional associations. To improve the status of all working women, three thousand women representing fifty-eight trade unions formed the Coalition of Labor Union Women (CLUW) in 1974. During the past decade, a number of significant efforts have been made to organize clerical women workers and to negotiate contracts that would address their interests.

One model for a trade union association sensitive to the productive and reproductive needs of women is the Self-Employed Women's Association (SEWA) in India. Formed in 1972, SEWA is a trade union of women who work as petty vendors and home-based producers. The union establishes savings and credit cooperatives to provide working capital to its members. Its producer cooperatives help women secure a higher price for their goods, enhancing their income. Through SEWA, members have been able to learn about plumbing, carpentry, radio repair, accounting, and management, thereby upgrading their skills. SEWA also provides legal services, which assist members in obtaining the benefits of labor legislation enacted by the Indian government, and welfare services, such as maternal protection schemes, widows' benefits, child care, and training of midwives (United Nations Development Program, 1993).

Professional Organizations. Since women have not been well represented in the professions in the past, they have not been prominent in the leadership of professional organizations. Beginning in 1969, groups of professional women began to take responsibility for raising the consciousness of the members of professional organizations to the problems and rights of women and to the need to include women in leadership positions. One of the authors of this text, Florence Denmark, helped develop a section on the psychology of women for the American Psychological Association and became its president for 1980–81. Many other professional organizations, such as the American Historical Association, the American Philosophical Association, the American Anthropological Association, and the American Political Science Association, have experienced the development of women's caucuses. As a result, women are playing a greater role than in the past in keeping these groups alert to the problems of women professionals and to the need to include gender in the curriculum of these disciplines.

Networks. The family, the union, and the professional association are formal organizations that have a legal standing. Networks are loose connections among individuals who know one another (or of one another) and support one another; they are informal and have no legal standing. They are, for many, the most significant support group in the workplace. Networks are at once powerful and "invisible," operating to influence career opportunities and the workings of the business and professional worlds but not legally liable or open to attack.

Men in power have always relied on networks. The "old boys' network" often begins in school, especially private schools, or at colleges, where young men get to know others who share their interests. These acquaintances are often kept up through a lifetime and broadened and shaped through other associations: clubs, civic groups, and special membership organizations. Networks provide their members with access to important information and resources. Leaders in virtually all fields—business, the arts, politics, and the professions—rely on them for their continued success. For the most part, white men have worked to exclude white women and women and men of color from their networks.

Women who share experiences and interests have developed their own groups and relationships for mutual aid, sometimes on a formal but more often on an informal basis. The women's movement has created a supportive climate for the formation of women's networks by keeping women aware of their need for one another and by encouraging women's mutual support. Women use professional caucuses, newsletters, and regular meetings as more or less formal networking instruments.

Laws Against Sexist Job Discrimination

Although there is no U.S. constitutional amendment that guarantees to its female citizens equality under law, two federal statutes enacted in the 1960s provide the legal basis for women's equality in the workplace. Title VII of the Civil Rights Act of 1964, particularly Section 703(a), prohibits discrimination on the basis of sex in hiring or discharging individuals and in terms of compensation and conditions of work. It also prohibits classifying (on the basis of sex) either applicants or employees, to avoid adversely affecting women's opportunities. The Equal Pay Act of 1963, amended by the Education Amendments of 1972 (Higher Education Act), guarantees to women equal pay for work equal to that of male employees. The 1972 amendments extended coverage of both acts to executive, professional, and other job categories.

Affirmative action requires that employers who have discriminated against women and mi-

norities set goals for reducing or ending such discrimination. For instance, if it can be shown on the basis of population figures or numbers of qualified applicants that a nondiscriminatory hiring policy would have resulted in about a quarter of the workers in a given category being women, an employer may be required to set a goal of 25% women employees in that category. Preference has often been given to groups, such as veterans, to compensate for their previous personal sacrifices in the national interest (though many individual veterans suffered little). Affirmative action is an effort to compensate for past (and present) wrongs done by employers, both public and private, to women and members of minority groups.

White males often charge that affirmative action subjects them to "reverse discrimination." Usually, it is younger white men who feel this way because they have not yet established themselves in jobs or careers. Older white males with seniority may be relatively unaffected by affirmative action, yet they are the ones who have benefited most from past discrimination against women and people of color. Instead of attacking affirmative action as unfair, as many have, fairness would require its burdens to be more equally shared among all white males. It is clear that without evidence of the decrease of discrimination, as can be provided by the meeting of goals for women and minorities in employment, employers can go back to excluding women and minorities, no matter how qualified, from all the better-paying and most desirable kinds of work (Bishop and Weinzweig, 1979).

Many of the gains women achieved during the late 1960s and 1970s were reversed in the next decades, beginning with the Reagan administration, which came into office with the support of various groups bitterly opposed to affirmative action. During the Reagan administration, both the Equal Employment Opportunity Commission and the Civil Rights Commission rejected the concept of comparable worth (see below). In the 1990s and up to the present, a more conservative Supreme Court has adopted a less supportive approach to women's equal rights on affirmative action grounds.

Within the European Union, the European Court of Justice has ruled favorably on affirmative action cases for women. Its rulings in the 1990s allow employers to take into consideration the fact that women competing with men for jobs may have had breaks in their careers in order to meet their family responsibilities. The development of European law with respect to women, work, and equality has led to the advancement of women's rights on issues related to pay, pensions, part-time work, night work, and work in the armed services. The European Court of Justice has ordered member states of the European Union to end discriminatory treatment of women in the workplace. As a result, national laws that discriminate against women in the workplace have been overturned.

Equal Pay–Comparable Worth

Those who have enforced laws against discrimination in the past have applied them only to persons doing the same work. It was illegal for an employer to pay a man more than a woman for doing exactly the same job with the same job specifications. This interpretation may be in the process of changing. Only if it does will a real attack on the inequities faced by women in the labor force be possible, for few women do the same work as men. "Women's work" is generally compensated at rates substantially lower than what men get for work of comparable value. Discrimination against women begins with initial gender segregation of tasks and persists into the sphere of remuneration.

If economic forces alone were at work, there would be a uniform pay scale since capitalists would seek to raise their profit by utilizing cheap labor. This does not happen. Instead, institutional features of the job market reflect a society's gender discrimination, which is found in the traditional customs, prejudices, and belief systems about the way one group of workers should be paid because of gender, ethnicity, age, or race.

The labor market is split into primary and secondary segments. Institutional features of the primary segment are career ladders, on-the-job training and retraining, education requirements, higher rates of pay, good working conditions, and security. These jobs are typically found in industries with large investments, unionization, and advanced technology. Jobs in the secondary segment typically provide poor rates of compensation, little or no training, little or no security, poor working conditions, and unpredictable work rules. Most important, they do not have career ladders to the primary segment (Ammott and Matthaei, 1991; Treiman and Hartmann, 1981). Women are traditionally found in the secondary segment and men are most often employed in the primary segment.

Juanita Kreps, the secretary of labor in the Carter administration (1977–81), has pointed out "that many of the occupational groups in which women are concentrated pay low wages while requiring higher than average educational achievement. . . . These higher levels of education do not pay off for either men or women in these 'female' occupations" (Kreps, 1971:40). Demands have developed for "equal pay for work of comparable value." Comparable worth proceeds beyond equal pay for women and men in the same job as women and men are rarely found in the same job category. Instead, the theory of comparable worth states that wages reflect the skills, training, and conditions of the work, with women and men receiving equal pay for positions assessed as having equivalent value.

To date, the U.S. Supreme Court has been unwilling to rule on comparable worth.

However, if it can be proved that an employer intentionally discriminates in pay rates between women and men performing similar jobs, the courts will rule that violation of Title VII has occurred. In contrast to the United States, the European Union, in both judicial rulings and legislative action, has contributed to growing support and respect for the principle of equal pay for work of equal value. In a case involving pay differentials between mostly (male) pharmacists and mostly (female) speech therapists, the court ruled that the employer (the British National Health Service) was obligated to abide by the principle of equal pay for work of equal value (Heide, 2001).

The Impact of the Women's Movement

The current women's movement has demanded recognition of a woman's right to engage in useful, meaningful, and rewarding work. It has also stood for equal pay and respect for women in the workplace, equal opportunity in job and career advancement, and improvement in opportunity, pay, and recognition for women of color.

Practical arrangements to relieve the burdens of women who work outside the home have been few and far between. The number of day-care centers has increased but not nearly enough to accommodate all working mothers, and they are still too costly. A few work organizations have experimented with *flextime*, instituting a system of flexible work hours so that women and men can carry out home and family responsibilities during the day and work as well. However, such arrangements are unusual. While consciousness and gender images have changed somewhat, practical accommodations have changed little.

One of the most important developments within the U.S. women's movement in recent years is the growing recognition that deeper and more fundamental changes than these are needed in the economy. Women cannot achieve feminist objectives without a substantial breakdown of the class differences that pit the interests of advantaged women against those of disadvantaged women. An equal opportunity to exploit the weak is not the aim of the women's movement. More humane and less hierarchical organizations of work are needed, along with a concern on the part of society with what work is for, what investments shall be made, and what products shall be made. Work that serves human needs and interests while respecting the environment is better for both women and men than work for increased profits. Progress toward these objectives will require fundamental changes in the way the work of both women and men is organized and conducted.

Summary

Every known society has assigned work by gender, and the work done by women has traditionally been valued less than that done by men. Women's reproductive functions have been used as an excuse for the division of labor by gender. Although the labor involved in reproduction and childrearing is essential for any society, often it is not recognized and almost never adequately compensated.

Maintaining the domestic unit is essential to the functioning of society and the economy, but it has been given neither economic nor social value. Women who sell their labor in the marketplace find their jobs devalued; they are restricted in their job choices and paid less than men.

When a society's economy is based on a simple domestic mode of production, economic and domestic roles tend to be integrated for both women and men. As a society modernizes and work becomes capital-intensive rather than labor-intensive, women tend to be phased out of the economy and confined to the domestic sphere. Women "subsidize" capitalist enterprises by servicing workers for free, producing and caring for the next generation of workers, and providing a cheap pool of labor when needed.

As slavery and serfdom gave way to "free" wage labor, a working class evolved. Within this class, women have been barred from most trades of skilled labor by guilds and craft organizations. Most working-class women have been employed as domestic wage labor. In past centuries in the United States, increasing numbers of women, particularly immigrants, have found work in factories. Today's immigrants, pushed by the forces of globalization, find work in the service sector as nannies, maids, and sex workers. Most women today are employed as pink-collar workers in clerical work, sales, and services, jobs considered "female." A growing economic trend is the use of contingent workers, who do not receive the benefits, security, and earnings of full-time workers.

The professions are also segregated by gender. Within the "female professions," men hold most top-level jobs. Women sometimes find it difficult to enter a "male profession," much less to rise within it, but some gains are evident. A few professional women are choosing to "optout" of their careers, questioning the male-defined conditions of the work itself.

Women are largely confined to middle management. Those who have advanced to high levels are under pressure to conform to corporate standards. Women experience the "glass ceiling" of blocked entry up the corporate ladder and the "sticky floor" that keeps the vast majority in low-paying jobs.

Economic competition between companies and countries has intensified as a result of globalization. Multinational corporations move their operations to regions where the labor costs are cheaper. Some women in developing countries migrate to developed countries or wealthier developing countries, where their labor often benefits middle-class and upper-class households, including allowing many professional women to advance their careers.

African American, Latina, Asian American, and Native American women experience racial/ethnic discrimination and gender discrimination in the workplace. Although they share the experience of exploitation, differences in occupations and opportunities exist among the groups and within each racial/ethnic group.

Few women are self-employed, perhaps because women have not been socialized to be assertive and independent. Women have less access than men to the financial resources needed to establish an enterprise. The right of an individual to employment, it has been argued, should be recognized as a human right.

Women find it difficult to compete with men for jobs because their interests are not entirely separate from those of the men to whom they are in some way related. Many men do not support women's attempt to gain economic equality because they believe this would threaten their superior status in the job market and at home.

Women on the job may be subject to sexual or gender harassment. Women who work can find social support in formal organizations, such as unions and professional organizations. Women's informal networks are especially important for mutual aid and information and resource sharing.

More countries are passing laws to lessen job discrimination. The Equal Opportunity Act and Equal Pay Act help U.S. women challenge job discrimination. Affirmative action programs attempt to improve the opportunities of those who have suffered from discrimination. Many women today are calling for laws that will require equal pay for work of comparable value.

The women's movement has raised women's aspirations and brought about some changes in attitude. However, it appears that feminist objectives will not be achieved without structural changes in the economy and society.

Discussion Questions

1. Choose three households you know that vary in a number of ways: income, educational level, race/ethnicity, age of adults and children, or other variables. Interview a woman in each household to find out what she does each week with her time. How can you account for differences and similarities in the activities that the three women do?

2. Select a place of work—a hospital, a business firm, a school—to which you have access. List all the positions and who holds them by gender. Are particular types of work done mainly or exclusively by women? Are women found mainly at some levels and not at others?

3. Many women feel that family obligations pose special problems for them as they pursue careers. In what ways does our society provide "relief" for women who work or study outside the home? To what extent are these services satisfactory or unsatisfactory? What are some alternative means for alleviating this problem?

4. Research the experiences of working women in another country or region of the world. What kinds of work do these women do? What child-care options do they have? How do they balance family and work responsibilities? What are the similarities and differences between women in your society and the one you chose to study?

5. If you have a particular career goal, study the roles of women in that career or profession in the past and at present. What proportion of people in the field is female? If there are obstacles to women's success in this field, might they be overcome?

Recommended Readings

Ammot, Teresa L., and Julia A. Matthaei. *Race, Gender, and Work.* Boston: South End Press, 1991. The authors explore how race, ethnicity, class, and gender shape the working experiences of women in the United States and provide a historical look at the types of work performed by Native American, Chicana, European American, African American, Asian American, and Puerto Rican women.

Ehrenreich, Barbara, and Arlie Russell Hochschild, editors. *Global Woman: Nannies, Maids, and Sex Workers in the New Economy.* New York: Henry Holt, 2002. The book examines the impact and consequences of globalization on women around the world. The lives of women migrants from the Dominican Republic, Taiwan, Vietnam, Mexico, Thailand, Sri Lanka, and the Philippines are analyzed.

Kessler-Harris, Alice. *Out To Work: A History of Wage-Earning Women in the United States,* 20th ed. Oxford: Oxford University Press, 2003. This history of working women from the colonial period to the end of the twentieth century looks at the interrelationships of work, family, and ideas about work and family.

Pearson, Allison. *I Don't Know How She Does It: The Life of Kate Reddy, Working Mother.* New York: Knopf, 2002. In this novel, a woman attempts to balance her successful and challenging career as a hedge-fund investment manager with the demands of her husband and two small children.

Ruddick, Sara, and Pamela Daniels, editors. *Working It Out: 23 Women Writers, Artists, Scientists, and Scholars Talk About Their Lives and Work.* New York: Pantheon, 1977. An extraordinary roster of women in all fields provide personal accounts of the problems they encountered as they carved out their work against the grain of society's expectations.

References

Acosta-Belén, Edna, and Christine Bose. From structural subordination to empowerment: Women and development in third world contexts. *Gender and Society*, 4:3, 299–320, 1990.

Adler, Roy D. Women in the executive suite correlate to high profits. *Harvard Business Review*, Nov. 16, 2001.

Aeberhard, Jane Hodges. Sexual harassment in employment: Recent judicial and arbitral trends. In *Women, Gender, and Work*, edited by Martha Fetherolf Loutfi. Geneva: International Labour Office, 2001.

Albeda, Rany, and Chris Tilly. *Glass Ceilings and Bottomless Pits: Women's Work, Women's Poverty*. Boston: South End Press, 1997.

Ammot, Teresa L., and Julie A. Matthaei. *Race, Gender, and Work*. Boston: South End Press, 1991.

Anker, Richard. *Gender and Jobs: Sex Segregation of Occupations in the World*. Geneva: International Labour Office, 1998.

Archer, C. J. Children's attitudes toward sex role division in adult occupational roles. *Sex Roles*, 10, 1–10, 1984.

Axelrod, J. G. Who's the boss? Employee leasing and the joint employer relationship. *Labor Lawyer*, 3, 853–72, 1987.

Bao, Xiaolan. Politicizing motherhood: Chinese garment workers campaign for daycare centers in New York City, 1977–1982. In *Asian/Pacific Islander American Women: A Historical Anthology*, edited by Shirley Hune and Gail M. Nomura. New York: New York University Press, 2003.

Belkin, Lisa. The opt-out revolution. *New York Times Magazine*, Oct. 26, 2003, 42–7, 58, 85–6.

Beneria, Lourdes, and Gita Sen. Class and gender inequalities and women's role in economic development—Theoretical and practical implications. *Feminist Studies*, 8:1, 157–75, 1982.

Bertone, Andrea Marie. Sexual trafficking in women: International political economy and the politics of sex. *Gender Issues*, 18:1, 4–22, 2000.

Bishop, Sharon, and Marjorie Weinzweig, editors. Preferential treatment. In *Philosophy and Women*. Belmont, CA: Wadsworth, 1979.

Bollé, Patrick. Part-time work: solution or trap? In *Women, Gender, and Work*, edited by Martha Fetherolf Loutfi. Geneva: International Labour Office, 2001.

Boserup, Esther. *Women's Role in Economic Development*. New York: St. Martin's Press, 1970.

Bravo, Ellen. The clerical proletariat. In *Sisterhood Is Forever*, edited by Robin Morgan. New York: Washington Square Press, 2003.

Brennan, Denise. Selling sex for visas: Sex tourism as a stepping-stone to international migration. In *Global Women: Nannies, Maids, and Sex Workers in the New Economy*, edited by Barbara Ehrenreich and Arlie Russell Hochschild. New York: Metropolitan Books, 2002.

Broadway, Michael. Beef stew: Cattle, immigrants, and established residents in a Kansas beefpacking town. In *Newcomers in the Workplace*, edited by Louise Lamphere, Alex Stepick, and Guillermo Grenier. Philadelphia: Temple University Press, 1994.

Bundles, A'Lelia Perry. *On Her Own Ground: The Life and Times of Madame C. J. Walker*. New York: Scribner, 2001.

Butler, Anne M. *Daughters of Joy, Sisters of Misery: Prostitutes in the American West, 1865–90*. Urbana: University of Illinois Press, 1985.

Carnoy, Martin. The family, flexible work and social cohesion at risk. In *Women, Gender, and Work*, edited by Martha Fetherolf Loutfi. Geneva: International Labour Office, 2001.

Chow, Esther N. L. The influence of sex-role identity and occupational attainment on the psychological well-being of Asian-American women. *Psychology of Women Quarterly*, 11, 69–82, 1987.

Christensen, A. S. Sex discrimination and the law. In *Women Working: Theories and Facts in Perspective*, edited by Ann H. Stromberg and Shirley Harkness. Mountain View, CA: Mayfield, 1988.

Chu, Judy. Social and economic profile of Asian Pacific American women: Los Angeles County. In *Reflections on Shuttered Windows*, edited by Gary Y. Okihiro, Shirley Hune, Arthur A. Hansen, and John M. Liu. Pullman: Washington State University Press, 1988.

Chusmir, Leonard H., and Barbara Parker. Dimensions of need for power: Personalized vs. socialized power in female and male managers. *Sex Roles*, 11, 759–69, 1984.

Claes, Marie-Thérèse. Women, men and management styles. In *Women, Gender, and Work*, edited by Martha Fetherolf Loutfi. Geneva: International Labour Office, 2001.

Collins, Patricia Hill. *Black Feminist Thought: Knowledge, Consciousness, and the Politics of Empowerment*, 2nd ed. New York: Routledge, 2000.

Colwill, Nina L. *The New Partnership: Women and Men in Organizations*. Palo Alto, CA: Mayfield, 1982.

Comas-Diaz, Lillian. Feminist therapy with mainland Puerto Rican women. *Psychology of Women Quarterly*, 11, 461–74, 1987.

Corder, Judy, and Cookie W. Stephen. Females' combination of work and family roles: Adolescents' aspirations. *Journal of Marriage and the Family*, 46, 391–402, 1984.

Costello, Cynthia B., Vanessa R. Wight, and Anne J. Stone. *The American Woman 2003–2004*. New York: Palgrave Macmillan, 2002.

Dalla Costa, Mariarosa, and Selma James. *The Power of Women and Subversion of the Community*. Bristol, CT: Falling Wall Press, 1975.

Dickinson, Torry D., and Robert K. Schaeffer. *Fast Forward: Work, Gender, and Protest in a Changing World*. Lanham, MD: Rowman & Littlefield, 2001.

Dreifus, Claudia. Chloe Wofford talks about Toni Morrison. *New York Times Magazine*, Sept. 11, 1994.

Ehrenreich, Barbara, *Nickel and Dimed: On (Not) Getting by in America*. Henry Holt, 2001.

Ehrenreich, Barbara, and Arlie Russell Hochschild, editors. *Global Women: Nannies, Maids and Sex Workers in the New Economy*. New York: Metropolitan Books, 2002.

Enloe, Cynthia. *Maneuvers*. Berkeley: University of California Press, 2000.

Fillmore, Lily Wong, and Jacqueline Leong Cheong. The early socialization of Asian-American female children. In *Conference on the Educational and Occupational Needs of Asian-Pacific-American Women*. Washington, D.C.: U.S. Department of Education, National Institute of Education, 1980.

Flores, William V. Mujeres en huelga: Cultural citizenship and gender empowerment in a cannery strike. In *Latino Cultural Citizenship*, edited by William V. Flores and Rina Benmayor. Boston: Beacon Press, 1997.

The Fortune 500. *Fortune*, 139:8, April 26, 1999.

Garland, Howard, Karen F. Hale, and Michael Burnson. Attributes for the success and failure of female managers: A replication and extension. *Psychology of Women Quarterly*, 7, 155–62, 1982.

Gerson, Kathleen. Work without worry. *New York Times*, May 11, 2003, A15.

Greenwald, Maurine Weiner. *Women, War, and Work: The Impact of World War I on Women Workers in the United States*. Westport, CT: Greenwood Press, 1980.

Gutek, Barbara A., and Tora K. Bikson. Differential experiences of men and women in computerized offices. *Sex Roles*, 13, 123–36, 1985.

Heide, Ingeborg. Supranational action against sex discrimination: Equal pay and equal treatment in the European Union. In *Women, Gender, and Work*, edited by Martha Fetherolf Loutfi. Geneva: International Labour Office, 2001.

Higginbotham, Elizabeth. Black professional women: Job ceilings and employment sectors. In *Women of Color in U.S. Society*, edited by Maxine Baca Zinn and Bonnie Thornton Dill. Philadelphia; Temple University Press, 1994.

Hirata, Lucie Cheng. Free, enslaved, and indentured workers in nineteenth-century Chinese prostitution. *Signs*, 5, 3–29, 1979.

Hochschild, Arlie Russell, with Anne Machung. *The Second Shift*. Penguin, 2003.

Hune, Shirley. *Teaching Asian American Women's History*. Washington, D.C.: American Historical Association, 1997.

Hune, Shirley, and Kenyon S. Chan. Special focus: Asian Pacific American demographic and educational trends. In *Minorities in Higher Education: Fifteenth Annual Status Report*, edited by Deborah J. Carter and Reginald Wilson. Washington, D.C.: American Council on Education, 1997.

Jones, Jacqueline. *Labor of Love, Labor of Sorrow: Black Women, Work, and the Family from Slavery to the Present*. New York: Basic Books, 1985.

Kanter, Rosabeth M. *Men and Women of the Corporation*. New York: Basic Books, 1977.

Kennedy, Susan Estabrook. *If All We Did Was to Weep at Home: A History of White Working Class Women in America*. Bloomington: Indiana University Press, 1979.

Kessler-Harris, Alice. *Out to Work*, 20th ed. Oxford: Oxford University Press, 2003.

Kimmel, Michael S. *The Gendered Society*. New York: Oxford University Press, 2000.

Kolb, Deborah M., and Debra Meyerson. Keeping gender in the plot: A case study of the Body Shop. In *Gender at Work: Organizational Change for Equity*, edited by Aruna Rao, Rieky Stuart, and David Kelleher. West Hartford, CT: Kumarian Press, 1999.

Korn/Ferry International. *Executive Profile 1990: A Survey of Corporate Leaders*. New York: Korn/Ferry International, 1990.

Kreps, Juanita M. *Sex in the Marketplace: American Women at Work*. Baltimore: Johns Hopkins University Press, 1971.

Louie, Miriam Ching Yoon. *Sweatshop Warriors: Immigrant Women Workers Take on the Global Factory*. Cambridge, MA: South End Press, 2001.

Machung, Anne. *The Politics of Office Work*. Philadelphia: Temple University Press, 1988.

Mannheim, B., and M. Schiffrin. The temporary help industry: Response to the dual internal labor market. *Industrial and Labor Relations Review*, 5, 83–101, 1984.

Mau, Rosalind Y. Barriers to higher education for Asian/Pacific American females. *Urban Review*, 22:3, 183–97, 1990.

Mbinlinyi, Marjorie. "Women in development" ideology and marketplace. In *Competition: A Feminist Taboo?* edited by Valerie Miner and Helen E. Longino. New York: Feminist Press of the City University of New York, 1987.

Melkas, Hellinä. Occupational segregation by sex in Nordic countries: An empirical investigation. In *Women, Gender, and Work*, edited by Martha Fetherolf Loutfi. Geneva: International Labour Office, 2001.

Morgan, Robin, editor. *Sisterhood Is Forever*. New York: Washington Square Press, 2003.

Morrison, Toni, editor. *Race-ing Justice, Engendering Power: Essays on Anita Hill, Clarence Thomas, and the Construction of Social Reality*. New York: Pantheon Books, 1992.

Nickel, James W. Is there a human right to employment? *Philosophical Forum*, 10, 149–70, 1978–9.

Paludi, Michele, editor. *Ivory Power*. Albany: SUNY Press, 1990.

Peterson, V. Spike, and Anne Sisson Runyan. *Global Gender Issues*, 2nd ed. Boulder, CO: Westview Press, 1999.

Portes, Alejandro, and Alex Stepick. *City on the Edge: The Transformation of Miami*. Berkeley: University of California Press, 1993.

Powell, B., and L. C. Steelman. Testing an under-tested comparison: Maternal effects on sons' and daughters' attitudes toward women in the labor force. *Journal of Marriage and the Family*, 44, 349–55, 1982.

Rosario, L. M. The self-perception of Puerto Rican women toward their societal roles. In *Work, Family and Health: Latina Women in Transition*, edited by R. E. Zambrana. New York: Hispanic Research Center, 1982.

Rosen, Ruth. *The Lost Sisterhood: Prostitution in America, 1900–1918*. Baltimore: Johns Hopkins Press, 1982.

Rotella, Elyce J. Women's roles in economic life. In *Issues and Feminism: A First Course in Women's Studies*, edited by Sheila Ruth. Boston: Houghton Mifflin, 1980.

Ruiz, Vicki L. A promise unfulfilled: Mexican cannery workers in southern California. In *Unequal Sisters: A Multicultural Reader in U.S. Women's History*, edited by Ellen Carol DuBois and Vicki L. Ruiz. New York: Routledge, 1990.

Seligman, Linda J., editor. *Women Traders in Cross-Cultural Perspective: Mediating Identities, Marketing Wares*. Stanford: Stanford University Press, 2001.

Sen, Amartya. Work and rights. In *Women, Gender, and Work*, edited by Martha Fetherolf Loutfi. Geneva: International Labour Office, 2001.

Shahar, Shulamith. *The Fourth Estate: A History of Women in the Middle Ages*, translated by Chaya Galai. London: Methuen, 1983.

Soto, E. S., and P. Shaver. Sex-role traditionalism and assertiveness in Puerto Rican women living in the United States. *Journal of Community Psychology*, 11, 346–54, 1983.

Stellman, Jeanne Mager, and Mary Sue Henifin. *Office Work Can Be Dangerous to Your Health*, rev. ed. New York: Ballantine-Fawcett, 1989.

Stephen, Cookie W., and Judy Corder. The effects of dual-career families on adolescents: Sex-role attitudes, work and family plans, and choices of important others. *Journal of Marriage and the Family*, 47, 921–9, 1985.

Treiman, Donald J., and Heidi I. Hartmann. *Women, Work and Wages: Equal Pay for Jobs of Equal Value*. Washington, D.C.: National Academy Press, 1981.

United Nations Department of Economic and Social Affairs. *The World's Women 2000: Trends and Statistics*. New York: United Nations, 2000.

United Nations Development Program. *Human Development Report, 1993*. New York: Oxford University Press, 1993.

U.S. Department of Labor, Bureau of Labor Statistics. *Employment and Earnings*. Washington, D.C.: U.S. Department of Labor, selected years.

———. *Highlights of Women's Earnings in 2001*, report 960. Washington, D.C.: U.S. Department of Labor, 2002.

U.S. Equal Employment Opportunity Commission. *Guidelines on Discrimination Because of Sex*. http://www.lectlaw.com/files/emp32.htm (accessed 10/7/04).

Wallace, Phyllis A., editor. *Black Women in the Labor Force*. Cambridge, MA: MIT Press, 1980.

White, Deborah Gray. *Ain't I A Woman: Female Slaves in the Plantation South*. New York: Norton, 1985.

Wichterich, Christa. *The Globalized Woman: Reports from a Future of Inequality*, translated by Patrick Camiller. London: Zed Books, 1998.

Wirth, Linda. Women in management: Closer to breaking through the glass ceiling? In *Women, Gender, and Work*, edited by Martha Fetherolf Loutfi. Geneva: International Labour Office, 2001.

Woo, Deborah. The gap between striving and achieving: The case of Asian American women. In *Making Waves*, edited by Asian Women United of California. Boston: Beacon Press, 1989.

Zalk, Sue Rosenberg. Harassment on the job. *Dental Teamwork*, 10–15, 1991.

Women and Political Power

Women have been underrepresented in formal political participation everywhere in the world. Historically, subordinated groups have been closed out of formal institutions and structures. Some have wondered how much difference it would make if women occupied more positions of political power, especially at the top. Would public affairs be very different, or would women in power act much the same way as men in power?

(KATHLENE, 1992)

Feminism and Politics

Can women achieve political power without following a male model of success and without imitating men in identifying problems and pursuing solutions? Can they reshape political power to address women's concerns? Do women, as a group, actually have particular priorities and a common set of values relating to political power?

On the one hand, women belong to different racial and ethnic groups. They belong to different social and economic classes, traditionally defined by the membership of their fathers or husbands. On the other hand, all women have some aspects of their lives in common, regardless of their membership in other groups. With a few exceptions, women own—or control— little or no capital, and they contribute free labor for basic social maintenance (housework and reproductive work) that is seen as their "private" responsibility. Women of all groups suffer discrimination by virtue of their gender in jobs and social status. Feminist legal theorist Catharine MacKinnon argues that there is only one "unmodified" feminism: women are at the bottom, irrespective of race or class or mode of production (MacKinnon, 1987). Others argue that the category of "women" as such is of little use because of the great diversity among women (Spelman, 1988).

"The Personal Is Political"

Consciousness-raising efforts of the women's movement of the late 1960s and early 1970s made women, and sometimes men, aware of the political components of their personal lives. A power differential pervades the relations between women and men. The artificial distinction between a "public" sphere of politics and a "private" sphere of domestic life obscures the inescapable fact that excluding women from the public sphere deprives them of control over their presumably private existence. The spheres are, in fact, so linked that in order for changes to take place in the private relations between women and men, changes are necessary in the political structure of society.

Public laws, made and enforced largely by men, have determined women's sexual and reproductive rights by defining marriage, when sexual relations are or are not legal, and whether a woman must continue a pregnancy. Because it was assumed to be a "private" matter, domestic violence was until recently largely ignored by "public" law enforcement and the seriousness of rape minimized, except when it was the rape of "our" women by men belonging to a subordinate minority. Also, the rights of women were not understood to be human rights, to be included on the agendas of those working to promote the international recognition of human rights (Tickner, 2001).

Public policy, made largely by men, determines the effective rights and obligations of women to their children and their ability to carry out their wishes with regard to their children's care, education, and safety. Public policy also restricts and shapes women's rights and capacities to select ways to support themselves and determines the conditions under which they work. In other words, nearly everything women have been brought up to regard as personal is a matter of public concern. To the extent that the private sphere has been the domain of women and the public sphere has been the domain of men, politics has been a means for men to control women's lives.

Feminist legal theorists of color have expanded the critique of the concept of separate public and private spheres. Kimberle Crenshaw (1991) argues for an intersectional approach to domination that incorporates racism and sexism. The dualism of "masculinity" and "femininity" (Crenshaw, 1991; see also Harris, 1991; Williams, 1991) does not reflect the complexity of the African American experience. African American women are generally stereotyped as overly assertive, while African American men are seen to lack the power that white men have to control their own lives.

This is not to say that men's private lives are not also politically controlled or that all men have an equal opportunity to participate in the determination of public policy, laws, and enforcement. Many feminists have been particularly sensitive to the exclusion of anyone—male or female—from power on the basis of race, ethnicity, sexual orientation, or class. Yet, while feminists have been conspicuous in the abolitionist, socialist, and civil rights movements, support from men in these movements for feminists' goals has usually been weak.

In the U.S. civil rights and antiwar movements of the 1960s, women's place was in the kitchen and the bedroom, just as it was outside the movement. Women made coffee and sandwiches, provided men with sexual services, and were excluded from central decision making (Evans, 1980; Brown, 1992). It was the realization that all relations between women and men, including sexual relations, were affected by power, as were relations traditionally labeled as "political," that led women to organize to resist their subordination and to the saying of the women's movement of the 1970s that "the personal is political."

Politics and the "Public" Sphere

Feminists trained in political science have begun to examine the historical and theoretical assumptions that characterize scholarship in this field, and their inquiries show how social sciences that are purportedly gender-neutral have in fact been gender-biased in important ways. Paula Baker, for example, in her study of late nineteenth-century rural New York, found two very different political cultures. Men's public activity involved loyalty to a particular political party and voting for its candidates on the basis of their character and willingness to work for their friends rather than their stands on issues and programs. In contrast, women participated in nonpartisan voluntary associations organized around specific concerns. What women did in the public arena was not viewed by men as "politics" (Baker, 1987). It is "politics" as defined by men that has been privileged.

Most political scientists, being largely middle class and male, had until the women's movement of the 1970s viewed women as of little consequence to their concerns. This view lingers in the ideology of political science: "politics" is what takes place in the "public" sphere of life, and women are identified with the "private" sphere. Traits said to characterize a proper citizen in a liberal democracy, for example, include those identified in the culture of the United States as "masculine": individualism, independence, aggressiveness, competitiveness (Freeman, 1976; Reverby and Helly, 1992). In contrast, qualities such as egalitarianism, caring, pacifism, and cooperation are identified as "feminine." The "citizen" with whom most male political scientists identify is a construct in their own image. What women do in public is often seen as philanthropic or of public service rather than as "real politics." On occasion in the past, women's politics in the public arena have even been viewed as "disorderly conduct" (Lebsock, 1990).

Feminists have advocated that women increase their formal political participation, in part to change the male-centered and male-dominated construction of political activity. At the same time, they have argued that political and social life ought to better reflect women's values of caring and concern for others (Tronto, 1993; Harrington, 1999).

American political scientists who have studied women's political behavior have measured their voting performance, their participation in political campaigns and political parties, and their presence in political office. On all counts, women have been less visible than men. Women's lack of visibility in politics in the past has been explained away as a direct consequence of their domestic roles and reproductive function (Lovenduski, 1981). In short, women's place has been assumed to be in the "private" sphere, to which, it has been said, their temperament and "nature" are better suited.

Feminist social scientists have a different viewpoint and have explored the roles women play in formal and grass roots or community-level organizations; their leadership styles, intraparty roles, and power; and how they organize on issues they consider important

(Bookman and Morgen, 1988). In recent years, women have often voted quite differently from men, forcing candidates and political parties to pay attention to the "women's vote." Also, women have been gaining political power around the world.

No country has ever had, as far as we know, a government that was explicitly designed or run according to feminist principles; but feminist utopian writers, in their imagined alternative societies, reveal both the shortcomings of patriarchal society and visions of new, more just and caring social orders (McKenna, 2001). These writers draw from women's experiences of cooperative organizing to achieve their goals in their families and communities. Decisions in feminist utopian societies tend to be made by consensus, and order is kept not by force but by persuasion (Pearson, 1977).

Sultana's Dream, a feminist utopia written by an Indian Muslim woman, Rokeya Sakhawat Hossain (1880–1932), was perhaps the earliest published in English. In this utopia, "Ladyland," men have been relegated to *purdah* (seclusion) within the home and violent crime and wars, eliminated. The women of "Ladyland" attend two universities, and their research has ended the problems of the environment, society, natural disasters, and poverty.

While such imagined societies have no counterpart in actual human history, governments have varied considerably in the extent to which women have been allowed to participate in public power. This chapter will examine some of these variations in political organization and power, and the roles that women have played in them.

Political Power

What Is Power?

Power is the capacity to get something done, whether directly or indirectly. Women may exercise power in the domestic sphere in

Box 13.1   WOMEN DO NOT BELONG IN THE PUBLIC SPHERE

Then . . .

The civil law, as well as nature herself, has always recognized a wide difference in the respective spheres and destinies of man and woman. Man is or should be woman's protector and defender. The natural and proper timidity and delicacy which belongs to the female sex evidently unfits it for many of the occupations of civil life. The constitution of the family organization, which is founded in the divine ordinance, as well as in the nature of things, indicates the domestic sphere as that which properly belongs to the domain and functions of womanhood. The harmony, not to say identity, of interests and views which belong or should belong to the family institution, is repugnant to the idea of a woman adopting a distinct and independent career from that of her husband. . . .

. . . It is true many women are unmarried and not affected by any other duties, complications, and incapacities arising out of the married state, but these are exceptions to the general rule. The paramount destiny and mission of women are to fulfill the noble and benign offices of wife and mother. . . . And the rules of civil society must be adapted to the general constitution of things, and cannot be based upon exceptional cases.

. . . In my opinion, in view of the peculiar characteristics, destiny, and mission of women, it is within the province of the legislature to ordain what offices, positions, and callings shall be filled and discharged by men and shall receive the benefit of those energies and responsibilities, and that decision and firmness which are presumed to predominate in the sterner sex.

. . . and Now

And if a woman wants to run in the constituency in which she was born she is told, "You left long ago. Go run somewhere else." And if she wants to run in her husband's constituency, she is told, "You didn't come here to rule; you came here to marry."

Sources: Bradwell v. Illinois, 1873; Justice Bradley quoted in Goldstein, 1979:49–51 and Miria-R-K-Matembe, member of the Uganda Constituent Assembly at the USAID Gender and Democracy in Africa Workshop, Washington, DC, July 27, 1995. From *African Voices,* Fall 1995, http://www.usaid.gov/regions/afr/abic/avoices/avfal95.htm#workshop accessed 1998.

terms of their influence within their families. Men's power, in contrast, is "more coordinated and structured within an institutionalized framework" (Ridd and Callaway, 1987:3). Political power is usually exercised by means of institutionalized structures, including the military, the government, the economy, and religious, educational, and legal systems. Such structures protect those who wield power and enable them to disperse their power more widely (Ridd and Callaway, 1987; Hartsock, 1983).

The power that individuals or groups possess involves "a social relationship between groups that determines access to, use of, and control over the basic material and ideological resources in society" (Bookman and Morgen, 1988:4). Except in small-scale agricultural societies (Sanday, 1981), men generally have greater access to and control over resources. Power over others fosters relationships of social distance and subordination.

Power is also the capacity to not do something—to not marry, not bear or be

Box 13.2   SULTANA'S DREAM (1905)

I became very curious to know where the men were. I met more than a hundred women while walking there, but not a single man.

"Where are the men?" I asked her.

"In their proper places, where they ought to be."

"Pray let me know what you mean by 'their proper places.'"

"Oh, I see my mistake, you cannot know our customs, as you were never here before. We shut our men indoors."

"Just as we are kept in the *zenana*?"*

"Exactly so."

"How funny." I burst into a laugh. Sister Sara laughed too.

"But, dear Sultana, how unfair it is to shut in the harmless women and let loose the men."

"Why? It is not safe for us to come out of the *zenana*, as we are naturally weak."

"Yes, it is not safe so long as there are men about the streets, nor is it so when a wild animal enters a marketplace."

"Of course not."

"Suppose some lunatics escape from the asylum and begin to do all sorts of mischief to men, horses, and other creatures: in that case what will your countrymen do?"

"They will try to capture them and put them back into their asylum."

"Thank you! And you do not think it wise to keep sane people inside an asylum and let loose the insane?"

"Of course not!" said I, laughing lightly.

"As a matter of fact, in your country this very thing is done! Men, who do or at least are capable of doing no end of mischief, are let loose and the innocent women shut up in the *zenana!* How can you trust those untrained men out of doors?"

"We have no hand or management of our social affairs. In India man is lord and master. He has taken to himself all powers and privileges and shut up women in the *zenana*."

"Why do you allow yourselves to be shut up?"

"Because it cannot be helped as they are stronger than women."

"A lion is stronger than a man, but it does not enable him to dominate the human race. You have neglected the duty you owe yourselves, and you have lost your natural rights by shutting your eyes to your own interests."

"But my dear Sister Sara, if we do everything by ourselves, what will the men do then?"

"They should not do anything, excuse men; they are fit for nothing. Only catch them and put them into the *zenana*."

"But it would be very easy to catch and put them inside the four walls?" said I. "And even if this were done, would all their business—political and commercial—also go with them into the *zenana*?"

Sister Sara made no reply. She only smiled sweetly. Perhaps she thought it was useless to argue with one who was no better than a frog in a well.

---

*The *zenana* is the women's living quarters in a household.

Source: From Rokeya Sakhawat Hossain, *Sultana's Dream and Selections from the Secluded Ones*, edited and translated by Roushan Jahan. New York: The Feminist Press at The City University of New York, 1988.

responsible for a child, not engage in physical labor, and not have sexual intercourse when another demands it. Only those who have sufficient power to protect themselves from the aggression of others can ensure they will not be coerced to the will of others.

Feminists have pointed out that power need not imply dominance. Power—to get things done—can be shared and distributed evenly. This is the notion behind the organizations of most feminist utopias. The sharing of power has been attempted on a small scale in communes and simple societies throughout the world. In a complex industrial society, the sharing of power has been difficult even to imagine. Feminists seek, at the very least, to reduce the extent to which society is organized hierarchically, with vast disparities of power between those who command and those who must obey.

Some individuals conclude that because men have such power over women, women are powerless; but this is not quite true: power is a social relationship. Power can be wielded by the "powerless," despite the fact that they possess fewer resources and must often organize in larger numbers to offset their "powerlessness." As long as the analysis of power and politics is confined to the study of institutions in which fewer female faces are present—courts, bureaucracies, legislatures, and executive levels—women will be perceived as more powerless than they are. A more fruitful approach to a better understanding of women and politics would be to look at arenas where women can be found—neighborhoods, schools, associations, and organizations (Cott, 1990; Bookman and Morgen, 1988; Dalley, 1988; Moser and Peake, 1987).

Power and Authority

There is an important distinction between *power* and *authority*. Those with *authority* are accepted as being justified in having and using power. People who seize power need eventually to find a way of legitimizing it in order to command obedience to decisions without resorting to the continued use or threat of force. *Economic power and authority* are the ability and accepted right to control the production and distribution of resources; *political power and authority* are the ability and accepted right to control or influence decisions about war and peace, legal protection and punishment, and group decision making in general, including the assignment of leadership roles. In complex societies, political power usually includes a great deal of economic power, but political and economic power can and do operate separately. Sometimes they function in a complementary way; at other times, they are at odds.

Although power and authority are often exercised by the same person, they are distinct, and each may be exercised without the other. Women have from time to time have exercised power (the ability to get someone to do something) but often have not held authority, due to cultural beliefs that women do not possess a legitimate right to power (O'Barr, 1984). Women exercising power are often accused of "manipulating" others because they are not acknowledged as rightfully powerful.

History provides many examples of women who held power by virtue of their relationships with powerful men. Royal mistresses in the courts of European kings even had official status. In the United States in the twentieth century, women married to presidents have occasionally exercised notable political power. When Woodrow Wilson collapsed in office in 1919, his wife Edith Axson Wilson played a crucial role in helping him maintain the presidency. Eleanor Roosevelt was able to undertake major humanitarian programs because of her influence with her husband, Franklin Delano Roosevelt, and his associates. When some of her ideas were not endorsed by the president, she pursued them through women's networks (Cook, 1992). Hillary Rodham

The only woman to be both a first lady and a senator in her own right, Hillary Rodham Clinton, elected to the U.S. Senate from New York in 2002, represents a new kind of feminist leadership in the United States today.

Clinton was the first "first lady" to have a visible role in political appointments but was often criticized for wielding illegitimate power. She was later elected senator from New York and could exercise power in her own right.

The exercise of power based on unofficial influence is difficult to establish or assess. Reference to the power of the "women behind the throne" has often been used by those who wish to justify a status quo in which women have little direct power—or authority—of their own.

Types of Government

As societies have become larger and more complex, forms of government have become more specialized and exclusionary. Full participation occurs only in the smallest, simplest societies, such as hunting-and-gathering bands, where political decisions are made by public discussion and consensus. There are no government specialists, and leaders arise in particular situations according to need and skills. An older woman with experience and skill might organize and direct others in food gathering. A good public speaker might assume responsibility for expressing the will of the community.

Similar principles apply in slightly larger and more complex societies but on a more restricted basis. Some persons hold positions of authority as "chief" or "war leader" or "council member." In these societies, women tend to be more segregated as a group. If women do play a role in political processes, they tend to do so as "women," not as ordinary and equal group members. Among the Iroquois in North America, certain women, and not men, were entitled to select male group leaders. Men, on the other hand, were entitled to hold the leadership positions; women were not (Sanday, 1981).

The most complex forms of government are national states, which exclude most members of society from direct participation in making governmental decisions, though to qualify as democratic they must have periodic elections. At the higher levels of a hierarchical structure, few can participate; but on the local level, small communities can conduct much of their business themselves. Here, participatory democracy may be possible even in a large, complex state. It is at the local level that women's voices are most likely to be heard. For example, more women are found in China on public councils in rural communities and in the United States on school boards and town councils and in greater numbers in state legislatures than at the federal level.

Women's Political Power in the Past

Women have occasionally exercised authority and political power in the past, both in dynastic states in Europe and in some preindustrial societies. Such power often derived from their kinship positions as daughters, sisters, wives, and mothers. In the early Middle Ages in Europe, when a ruler's officials were actually royal household servants (and the head of the household governed the domestic affairs of the royal estate, which was the kingdom), it was considered perfectly natural to place the ruler's wife, or queen, at the head of these servants. When Henry II of England went to war (which was a great deal of the time) he left his queen, Eleanor of Aquitaine (c. 1122–1204), in charge of his kingdom. All his officials were ordered to report to her whenever he was away. As regents for their husbands or sons, queens could wield significant political power. Only when Henry II began to suspect that his queen favored their sons over him did he discontinue making her England's ruler in his absence (Kelly, 1957).

Box 13.3 QUEEN NZINGA OF SEVENTEENTH-CENTURY ANGOLA

The instability of the region allowed an extraordinary woman, Nzinga, to step out of the role most women played to gain control over her own state. Her success stands out particularly because she was able to transform herself from a palace slave into a queen of a new state, Matamba. She began life as a slave in the *Ngola a Kiluanje* palace to the south of Songo. As a palace slave and half-sister of the last *ngola a kiluanje*, or king, Nzinga was closely related to the sources of power in the Ngola kingdom. . . . The court slaves chose Nzinga as an able emissary to the Portuguese in the early 1620s . . .

Eventually Nzinga moved to the northwest, where she established herself as queen of Matamba. As a woman, former slave, and immigrant to the region, she could not call on the local matrilineage to establish her power. Instead, she . . . developed a system of military rule. . . . Shifting alliances characterized the region until Nzinga made a final pact with the Portuguese in 1655. Their support enabled her to reign in Matamba until she died in 1663.

Source: From E. Frances White, Women in West and West-Central Africa, in *Restoring Women to History*, Bloomington: Indiana University Press, 1990:58–59.

As the governments of European states and elsewhere became more bureaucratically organized, women were less likely to share in political power. The recognized offices that might have been delegated to the queen gradually shifted to ministers, judges, councilors, and other functionaries, who were never women. Even in the reign of Queen Elizabeth I (1558–1603), who governed by virtue of inherited right, not a single woman was ever appointed to a ministerial post (Neale, 1957).

Similarly, European colonial rule precipitated erosion of women's power where it had existed. Among the Iroquois of North America, for example, both women and men participated in village decision making. Women were entitled to demand publicly that a murdered relative be replaced by a captive from a non-Iroquoian tribe, and male relatives were morally obligated to join a war party to secure captives. Women also appointed men to official positions in the League of the Iroquois and could veto their decisions, although men controlled league deliberations. Women dominated village life and left interethnic affairs to men, exercising separate but equal political power during the height of the Iroquois confederacy (Sanday, 1981).

In the early nineteenth century, after a steady encroachment on their power by the colonizing British and French over a period of 200 years, the Iroquois became unable to sustain themselves economically. English Quakers, who actually sought to preserve the Iroquoian culture, suggested solutions that fundamentally restructured Iroquois gender relationships. Quaker missionaries urged men to cultivate the soil, a sphere hitherto dominated by women. They also insisted on husband–wife nuclear family relationships, which shut out the traditional power of the wife's mother in the family. In imposing their own cultural assumptions, the Quakers helped develop a new pattern of male dominance where it had not existed before (Sanday, 1981).

Another example of the erosion of women's political power under colonial rule is that of the Igbo of southern Nigeria, where precolonial social arrangements included women's councils. By tradition, these councils exercised peacekeeping powers, including the corporal punishment and public humiliation of the offender and the destruction of the offender's property. Local women's councils had no formal links with one another, but Igbo women maintained a network of rapid communication through an overlapping presence in different marketplaces each week (Sanday, 1981). British colonial rule in the late nineteenth century disrupted these cultural patterns, which had afforded women real power. British authorities bypassed women's councils as irrelevant and created new "warrant" chiefs where none had existed, giving the position to local men (Ifeka-Moller, 1977).

Patterns of Male Dominance

Anthropologist Ernestine Friedl has defined *male dominance* as a pattern in which men have better access, if not exclusive rights, to those activities to which society accords the greatest value and by which control and influence are exercised over others (Sanday, 1981). Thus, male dominance means excluding women from political and economic decision making and includes aggression against women.

Male dominance occurs in various kinds of social relationship. It may consist of cultural assumptions about natural male aggressiveness, about being "tough" and "brave." It may involve designating specific places where only males may congregate, like men's clubs and bars, street corners, legislative chambers, courts, or boardrooms. It may involve wife beating and battering (Gordon, 1988). It may result in murder, as in India where "bride burning" occurs when husbands seek to remarry and to acquire another dowry (for a fuller explanation, see Oldenburg, 2002, especially Chapter 7). Another form is "raiding" enemy groups for wives. Rape is a regular occurrence in many societies (sometimes it is institutionalized as gang rape) and constitutes a form of social control of women by men. The ethnic group rape of Muslim women of Bosnia and Croatia in 1992–3 by Serbian men as part of a general policy of "ethnic cleansing" is an extreme example of the extent to which male dominance is rationalized as a condition of warfare. This kind of control reminds us that although women may wield some political and economic power and authority, they do so by the implicit or explicit consent of men, not from an independent power base or because of authority vested in women as such.

Women as Political Leaders

Throughout history, women leaders have emerged. In modern times, powerful female political figures have included Margaret Thatcher (United Kingdom), Indira Gandhi (India), Corazon Aquino (Philippines), Golda Meir (Israel), Benazir Bhutto (Pakistan), Megawati Sukarnoputri (Indonesia), Eva Perón (Argentina), Gro Harlem Brundtland (Norway), Sirimavo Bandaranaike (Sri Lanka), Mary Robinson (Ireland), and Eugenia Charles (Dominica). In the early 1990s, Bangladesh, Poland, Nicaragua, Canada, and Turkey elected women as heads of government with vast political functions. While it is rare to see women at the summit of power, increasingly they are taking their places in national and state as well as local politics.

Generally, there is an inverse relationship between higher political offices and the presence of women in them. Universally, there are many more women in lower-level political offices than in high ones. On the average, women comprise 10% of national legislators and 7% of executive cabinet ministers worldwide. Table 13.1 reveals that the most promising picture comes from the Scandinavian countries, with their mixed economies and

their concern for both social welfare and social justice. Socialist states have made great efforts to recruit women into national legislatures, but in most of the states of the former Soviet bloc, the number of women in political office declined when tradition and capitalism became more influential than communism. In the Middle East, South Asia, and Africa, women are the least likely to be found in high-level political positions.

The few women who hold high cabinet positions are most likely to be housed in traditional women's fields, such as health and welfare, education, culture, the family, and consumer affairs (Randall, 1987). Worldwide, women are largely ignored when it comes to certain ministerial positions—defense, treasury, foreign affairs—despite the fact that highly capable women can be found in these traditionally male-dominated fields. Madeleine Albright, secretary of state in the Clinton administration, and Condoleezza Rice, national security adviser in the first administration of George W. Bush, are notable exceptions.

Recent Political Gains of Women in the United States

In view of the gender socialization women undergo, the effects of the contemporary women's movement on the pattern of female office-holding are striking. Women's increased political participation in the United States in the 1990s was largely a result of women deciding it was time to change the face of the U.S. Congress and the state legislatures. National attention was given to the dominance of white males in Congress and their male bias during the senate hearings to confirm Clarence Thomas as nominee to the U.S. Supreme Court in 1991. Anita Hill, a former assistant to Thomas, had been called on to testify. Angered by the insensitive treatment of both Hill and the issue of sexual harassment by an all-white male senate committee, women entered the political arena with a

TABLE 13.1 Women in National Legislature and Executive Offices in 2000

Country	National Legislature (%)*	Executive Office (%)[†]	Country	National Legislature (%)*	Executive Office (%)[†]
EUROPE			EAST ASIA		
Austria	25	20	China	22	3
Denmark	37	41	Indonesia	8	0
France	9	12	Japan	11	0
Germany	30	8	Philippines	6	10
Greece	9	5	AFRICA		
Hungary	8	5	Algeria	4	0
Norway	37	26	Ghana	9	9
Poland	13	17	Kenya	4	0
Portugal	19	10	Mozambique	30	0
Russian Federation	6	16	Nigeria	3	7
Sweden	43	44	South Africa	28	15
United Kingdom	17	24	Senegal	17	3
MIDDLE EAST			NORTH AMERICA		
Iraq	8	0	Canada	24	—
Israel	13	0	United States	13	26
Jordan	0	2	SOUTH AMERICA		
Syrian Arab Republic	10	8	Argentina	21	8
SOUTH ASIA			Bolivia	10	6
India	9	8	Brazil	6	4
Nepal	8	3	Cuba	28	5
Pakistan	—	7	Dominican Republic	14	10
Sri Lanka	4	13	Venezuela	10	3

0, none or negligible;—not available.

Sources: *Inter-Parliamentary Union (http://www.ipu.org/wmn-e/classif.htm).
[†]*Human Development Report 2000*, by United National Development Programme, copyright © 2000 by the United Nations Development Programme. Used by permission of Oxford University Press, Inc.

new energy. Many more women decided to run for office. Many more made financial contributions. In addition, women feared the further erosion of specific rights, such as their reproductive rights.

In the 1980s, an important political "gender gap" emerged. It was after the 1980 election that analysts began to note significant differences between women and men in political viewpoints, party identification, and voting decisions. U.S. men, to a greater extent than women, aligned their party identification and voting behavior with parties and candidates conservative on social welfare issues and more in favor of expenditures on defense. Women, to a greater extent than men, sup-

ported parties and candidates that expressed concern for social welfare issues and increased spending on education (Kaufmann and Petrocik, 1999). These tendencies have continued: women are more inclined to favor public policies that support the protection of the environment, fewer militaristic resolutions to disputes, and programs for quality health care, racial equality, and family support. Table 13.2 demonstrates the increased representation of women Democrats and Republicans, the two major political parties in the United States, as candidates and winners for Congress in the period 1970–2000. For the first time in U.S. history, of the six women who ran for senate in the 2000 elections, all

TABLE 13.2 Women Candidates for the U.S. Congress, 1970–2000 (Party and Seat Summary for Democratic and Republican Party Nominees)*

	Senate		House of Representatives	
	Candidates	*Winners*	*Candidates*	*Winners*
1970	1 (1R)	0	25 (15D, 10R)	12 (9D, 3R)
1980	5 (2D, 3R)	0	52 (27D, 25R)	19 (10D, 9R)
1990	8 (2D, 6R)	1 (1D)	69[†](39D, 30R)	28[†](35D, 12R)
2000	6 (4D, 2R)	6 (4D, 2R)	122[†](80D, 42R)	59[†](41D, 18R)

*Includes major party nominees for the general elections, not those running in special elections.

[†]Does not include two (1D, 1R) candidates, one incumbent who won her race and one challenger for nonvoting delegate of Washington, D.C.

Source: Center for the American Woman and Politics (CAWP), Eagleton Institute of Politics, Rutgers, State University of New Jersey, 2001.

were winners, raising the total of U.S. women senators to 13 for the 107th Congress (2001–3).

Women have been even more successful in state legislatures, where their presence has increased fivefold over the past two decades. From 301 legislators in 1969, or 4% of the total, women have grown to 1,663, or 22.4% of the legislators from the fifty states. While the increase in the number of women is significant, in 2003 women still held only 14% of the seats in the U.S. Senate and 13.6% of the seats in the U.S. House of Representatives.

It is not enough for women to be elected or appointed to political office for women's concerns to be heard. Women have far less economic power than men and are hardly represented at all in the upper reaches of the corporate world. The more that economic power and corporate influence affect politics—and the extent of this is enormous in the United States—the less will women's voices be effective.

Political Gains of Women in Office Around the Globe

As more U.S. women have gained access to higher office, their sisters around the world have also increased their share of political seats. In India, a 1993 constitutional amendment created the Panchayat Raj Act, which allocates 33% of seats at the village and district levels to women. As a result of this act, close to 6 million women have been elected to village- and district-level office. In South Africa, the post-apartheid African National Congress government adopted a law to require a 30% quota for women candidates. Today, women hold 29.8% of the lower legislative seats in South Africa. The Nordic countries have made tremendous gains in getting women elected to higher office. Women in Sweden and Norway occupy 42.7% and 36.4%, respectively, of parliamentary seats. Women in Denmark, Finland, the Netherlands, and Iceland hold at least one-third of the seats in their national legislatures. Impressive gains in the number of women running for office and winning were registered in France in the March 2001 elections, following introduction of the *Parité* law of 2000. As a result of a constitutional change, all political parties in France are required to field an equal number of women and men candidates in all elections. The results of the new change were evident in the March 2001 local elections, when the proportion of women elected to town councils jumped from 22% to 47.5% (Mpoumou, 2001). Although more and more women are gaining political office in some countries, one notable exception to this trend has been the declining numbers in

Eastern European countries. Before the end of communist rule in Eastern Europe, women accounted for 20%–40% of parliamentary seats; after 1994, women held only 4%–19% of parliamentary seats in countries such as Albania, Bulgaria, Romania, Slovakia, and Azerbaijan (Inter-Parliamentary Union, 2004).

Do Women in Office Make a Difference?

If women in political office make a difference, what kind of difference do they make? What is the link between women's participation in political office and the advancement of public policy supportive of women's needs? Scholars have noted a critical threshold of 30%; that is, when women make up 30% of political institutions, they are able to influence policy outcomes. In the Nordic countries, where women account for at least 30% of the parliamentary seats, public policy has addressed women's needs. In Norway, the government provides opportunities for women to combine their child-care and employment demands. Women- and family-centered public policies include expanding child-care services; offering flexible work hours; improving pension rights for unpaid care work; and increasing child benefits for families that do not use public child-care services. In South Africa, where government quotas reserve 30% of parliamentary and 50% of local government candidacies for women, the impact has made a difference in women's lives. In 1995, the South African parliament passed the Convention on the Elimination of All Forms of Discrimination Against Women without reservations, and it has introduced "the women's budget process," which analyzes the gender impact of the government's budget. The women's budget process affords women the opportunity to pressure the government for funds for women's empowerment and development (Women's Environment and Development Organization, 2001).

Even in countries that have not attained the 30% threshold, women officeholders generally, regardless of political party or label, take more feminist positions on women's issues than their male colleagues. Studies conducted of women parliamentarians in Europe support this view (Randall, 1987). There is also sufficient evidence that in the U.S. congress "in addition to advocating for their districts, female legislators do exhibit a profound commitment to the pursuit of policies for women, children, and families" (Swers, 2002:132). Women officeholders are more open and inclusive than their male counterparts. In place of carrying out business behind closed doors, women favor involving the general public in the political process and providing increased access to constituent groups often left out of policy making (Center for the American Woman and Politics, 1991, 1992a,b; Kathlene, 1992; Dolan, 2001; Women's Environment and Development Organization, 2001). In a study of Colorado's House of Representatives in 1989, Lyn Kathlene also noted that female legislators sponsored more "innovative" legislation rather than simply modified or updated existing laws, as was the tendency of male legislators (Kathlene, 1992). Women legislators also willingly work collectively across party lines to accomplish specific goals. Former New York congresswoman, the late Bella Abzug found greater support among her female colleagues, both Democrats and Republicans, than from the male members of her own party on issues of concern to women (Abzug, 1984).

Obstacles Facing Women in Politics

Scholars identify three theoretical explanations for why more women are not elected to public office. The sociological theory attributes the low level of women officeholders to culture. Patriarchal cultures socialize their citizens to think in terms of a public/private dichotomy that locates women in the domestic sphere. Women are not expected to hold political decision-making positions. The question raised about female, but not male, candidates is, Who is taking care of the family? (see Chapter 7). As a result, social norms and expectations about women's proper roles act as a brake to recruitment into politics and to political advancement. Women's usual work roles of teacher, clerk, and nurse are not the professions that typically recruit or train people for higher political office. If interested in formal politics, women tend to become involved at the organizational and support levels for other candidates (Lee, 1977). Even when women have the education and the occupational experience necessary for holding higher political office, their fellow citizens must be willing to vote for them. Opinion polls indicate that though the public is more willing than in the past to elect women to higher political office, about 25% of Americans are unwilling to vote for a woman for president (Conway, 2001).

A second explanation for the low rates of women in elected office points to their involvement in nonpolitical activities. Household, child-care, and work responsibilities, with which women are still disproportionately saddled, leave them little time to engage in the political process (Conway, 2001).

A third explanation has to do with institutional impediments. Gatekeepers such as party leaders, interest group leaders, and campaign fundraisers often discourage women from running for office (Conway, 2001). Traditionally, male politicians have sought campaign funds from business and community leaders who are interested in backing candidates as a way of establishing future access to them. Women candidates often face difficulties in finding backers, raising funds, and creating large-scale organizations of devoted followers who see possible benefits in their election. The fundraising success of Hillary

Rodham Clinton, in her race for the senate, was an exception.

In part to overcome this obstacle, EMILY (Early Money Is Like Yeast) was founded in 1982 to support prochoice Democratic women candidates through raising money to launch campaigns in the first stages. EMILY's List is a network of donors and has been one of the largest contributors to female candidates. For prochoice Republican women candidates, WISH (Women in the Senate and House) offers financial support. If traditional financial backers do not take women seriously as political candidates, women are showing that they can fund themselves.

Another institutional impediment to the selection of women to run for office concerns the election procedure. Studies document that gatekeepers are more willing to endorse and promote women candidates running in multimember, rather than single-member, electoral districts. Electoral systems that use some form of proportional representation (with more than one candidate representing an electoral district) have had greater success in getting women to run for and win elections. Proportional representation electoral systems exist in the Nordic countries and elsewhere, but not in the United States.

Women as Citizens

Women have been subject to the decisions of male political leaders and to a male model of citizenship. In this section, we examine women's political subordination in terms of their historical absence from combat warfare, the pattern of their subjection to man-made laws, and their participation in voluntary associations.

Women and War

The dominant male model of "citizen" is often based on the image of the warrior-hero

(Hartsock, 1983). Women are often thought to lack physical strength and to be unsuited for combat warfare. Because war and defense are associated with men and not women, it has also been assumed that diplomacy and other relations between states should be controlled by men (Tickner, 2001). When a woman does have some influence over issues of national security, it is often because she follows patterns established by men.

Women are portrayed as the "protected" and men, as the "protectors," even though, in modern war, it is estimated that "civilians now account for about 90 percent of war casualties, the majority of whom are women and children" (Tickner, 2001:6). The supposedly protected are often, in fact, the victims of war: they are killed, maimed, raped, and captured.

Because women have rarely entered combat, they have rarely participated in councils of war or the governmental positions for which wartime experience is thought an important advantage. Relatively few have shared in any "spoils" of war or special (veteran) postwar benefits. Women are routinely used to support war efforts, then pushed aside. During World War I (1914–19) and World War II (1939–45), women in North America and Europe were recruited to work in supporting industries and given much encouragement, relatively high pay, and other social rewards for their patriotic contribution to the war effort. Women in the United States were provided with opportunities to develop new skills by enlisting in the Women's Army Corps, the Women Marines, the Women's Army Air Corps, the Women Accepted for Volunteer Emergency Services (WAVES), and the Coast Guard *Semper Paratus*–Always Ready (SPARs) during World War II, in part to free men for combat. Many volunteers were lesbians. For the most part, the armed services sought to manage homophobia—against both lesbians and gays. However, after working to produce food and build machines

and serving in dangerous occupations such as field nurses, ambulance drivers, and resistance fighters in enemy-occupied territory, when the men came home, pressure was applied to women to return to the household so that men could have "their" jobs back. "Rosie the Riveter" became "Betty Crocker," and lesbians, like gays who chose not to return to a former life in a small town, began to form communities, primarily in large cities (Berube, 1990). Lesbians who remained in the military in peacetime faced increased repression and the likelihood of a dishonorable discharge in spite of years of dedicated service.

Women have served as fighting soldiers, as documented in antiquity and in modern times, and are increasingly being used in most positions throughout the U.S. Armed Forces. However, these instances are still exceptional. The biblical figure Deborah was a general, as was Joan of Arc in France in the fifteenth century. The modern armies of Israel and Vietnam train most of their women in combat duties, although women soldiers have rarely been deployed in actual combat. Women fighters are more commonly found in the informal armies of rebellions, revolutions, and resistance movements, as in the Warsaw Ghetto uprising, the French Resistance of World War II, the Algerian Revolution, the Chinese Revolution, Zimbabwe's war for independence, and revolutions in Nicaragua during the twentieth century. Typically in postrevolutionary societies, women revolutionaries are told to return to their traditional roles of wife and mother. For example, Zimbabwean women who fought violently and valiantly for independence have since received discriminatory treatment in the allocation of plots of land to those who fought in the war (Jacobs, 1984). More hopeful, however, are postrevolutionary efforts by women in Mozambique and Nicaragua, where autonomous organizations have formed contemporary women's movements

Like Dr. Martin Luther King, Jr., Mahatma Gandhi, and the Dalai Lama, Aung San Suu Kyi has become an international symbol of struggle against repression and brutality. The daughter of a Burmese military hero, a wife, and a mother, she became the spokesperson for her country's beleaguered democracy movement. While under house arrest, Aung San Suu Kyi was awarded the Nobel Peace Prize (1991) for courageous leadership of the Burmese people in their battle against authoritarian rule.

with explicitly feminist goals, involving "development, the economy, education, reproductive rights, health, domestic violence and domestic labor" (Disney, 2003:560).

Wars today no longer depend on physical strength, which disqualified most women previously. Some modern armies employ women on a regular basis for combat warfare using high technology, such as piloting jet fighters or operating long-range missile installations. U.S. women have been admitted to the West Point Military Academy, which produces the highest-ranking army officers, and to other service academies (Stiehm, 1981). Women were first employed in a war zone during the Persian Gulf War in 1990–1, although not in direct combat, and they participated in the U.S. invasion and occupation of Iraq in 2003.

Some people feel that if women are to receive equal rights and benefits, they must assume equal responsibilities; if men get drafted, so should women. Others argue that no one should be drafted, nor should anyone go to war—women or men. Many also argue that until women are granted equality, they should not have to bear the burden of military service in addition to their other burdens. The U.S. Supreme Court decided (*Rostker* v. *Goldberg*, 453, U.S. 57, 64, 67, 1981) that it was constitutional for Congress to call for the registration of men and not women, but the issues raised by the question go to the heart of

---

Box 13.4   "WAR IS A MAN'S WORK"

On the question of the admission of women to combat positions in the United States Marines, General Robert H. Barrow has remarked, "War is a man's work. Biological convergence on the battlefield would not only be dissatisfying in terms of what women could do, but it would be an enormous psychological distraction for the male, who wants to think that he's fighting for that woman somewhere behind, not up there in the foxhole with him. It tramples the male ego. When you get right down to it, you have to protect the manliness of war."

Source: Lloyd, 1986:62–3.

---

gender relationships and the issues of autonomy and power.

Women and the Law

Laws are the governing rules of every human society. The "law" is sometimes conceived to be a force above the vagaries of human will and impulse, an almost divine, implacable, impersonal force. In fact, laws have a history, just as people do. They develop from several sources: ancient custom, legislative bodies, judicial decisions, and administrative agencies.

Feminists are asking new questions about the function of law in society. A feminist jurisprudence is evolving that views the law as a social construction of male dominance. Feminist legal theorists note that "ostensibly legal rules rest on the perspectives of 'the reasonable man'." Catharine MacKinnon (1991:186) argues that "the law sees and treats women the way men treat women." Critical race theorists also conclude that the law is inherently racist. Hence, Mari Matsuda (1989) seeks a jurisprudential method that would incorporate a "multiple consciousness" to give voice to those historically rendered silent and invisible in the law because of race, sex, class, sexual orientation, or physical abilities. As historian Linda Kerber (1998:309) puts it, "whether one is male or female, racially

marked in a system that treats Caucasians as 'normal,' married or single, heterosexual or homosexual, continues to have implications for how we experience the equal obligations of citizenship."

In its regulation of the family, the law's concern has traditionally been to create a space in which the male head of household can exercise power and authority (O'Donovan, 1981). By viewing women as belonging to the "private" domestic sphere, the men who make and interpret laws, like the men who theorize about political power, act on assumptions that make women less than full legal citizens and political beings. These assumptions about women's rightful place are intimately linked to the patriarchal political philosophies that underpin democratic societies (Okin, 1979). For example, laws have explicitly commanded husbands and fathers to control their families. Colonial Americans used ducking stools, stocks, and other instruments of humiliation and torture to correct women found guilty of scolding, nagging, or disturbing the peace. When women are thus classified as a group and subjected to gender-based social policies, their social roles are often reinforced by political and legal sanctions.

Though critics argue that it is not required by the Koran, the traditional Islamic religious law of *shari'a*, in effect in some Muslim societies, incorporates male dominance. It is highly biased against women in matters of marriage, divorce, and custody of children (Meriwether and Tucker, 1999). It limits the mobility of women, who must obtain permission to travel from male guardians.

Traditional moral codes have been based on a sexual double standard for women and men that has affected criminal law and a large amount of civil law, especially family law. Moreover, a society's laws, moral code, and popular conceptions of social norms reinforce each other. Lawmakers and those who enforce the law start from an idea of what the "normal" family is. They act on the basis of their notions of what women are like and ought to do and their unexamined assumptions about what women need and want. Anyone who does not conform to their assumptions is either treated as invisible (as battered wives, incest victims, and working female heads of households have tended to be) or sought out and made the object of pressure to conform (as are lesbians and "welfare mothers").

In studying the lives of young working-class and poor African American women, sociologist Joyce Ladner (1972) pointed out that their lives were in large part governed by laws, customs, and restrictions based on a white middle-class male perception of what is "normal" and what is "deviant." For example, until recently, white middle-class male norms associated "working mothers" with deviance, though it was very common for African American mothers to hold jobs (see Chapter 8).

Based on a double standard of sexual morality, laws have treated prostitutes as "deviant," labeling such women "criminals," but have considered male customers of female prostitutes to be "normal" men indulging a natural appetite. Laws have customarily treated adultery as a serious crime when committed by women, while it is often disregarded when committed by men. The prejudice in favor of the "unwritten law" which excuses husbands who murder adulterous wives is still not entirely eradicated from society's practice of law.

Although many more U.S. women are entering the legal profession and media images suggest that women are often judges, attorneys, and police officers, the law still treats women unfairly in many ways. Lawmakers determine governmental budgets and the respective priorities of health services, day-care centers, education, job creation, and expenditures on weapons and defense. The government shapes welfare regulations that determine the legal obligations of mothers and that fail to recognize unpaid caring for children or others as work.

Women as Interpreters and Enforcers of the Law

We have already pointed out the low levels of representation of women in legislative bodies worldwide. In the United States, laws are interpreted by local judges, whose decisions can be overturned by judges at higher levels. At each level, women judges are rare, although their numbers are increasing. In the U.S. Supreme Court, there had never been a woman judge until the appointment of Sandra Day O'Connor in 1981. She was joined by Ruth Bader Ginsburg in 1993. Below the level of the Supreme Court, today in the United States women account for 14.5% of district court judges and 14.9% of circuit court judges (Palmer, 2001). What difference do women judges make in terms of the law? Their impact has been greatest in the areas of sex discrimination law. Evidence indicates that even with the presence of just one woman judge, courts are more likely to rule in favor of women's rights cases (Palmer, 2001).

Women are also underrepresented in police forces everywhere. Thus, a woman who breaks a law is likely to be arrested and taken into custody by male police officers, tried by a

The first woman to sit on the U.S. Supreme Court, Sandra Day O'Connor's appointment in 1981 by President Reagan broke an all-male tradition that dated to the founding of the country. She has written about her experiences in *The Majesty of the Law* (2003).

male judge, and accused and defended by male lawyers for having broken a law made by male legislators (Adler, 1975; Smart, 1978; Martin and Jurik, 1996).

Women's Voluntary Associations

Prior to achieving the vote for women in the United States, women's primary form of political participation was the voluntary association. Women had, in fact, little choice if they wanted to effect change in the political arena. Women's organizations lobbied the government and other institutions, effectively innovating the strategy of pressure-group politics, now a commonly recognized political practice in the United States (Lebsock, 1990; Cott, 1990; Scott, 1991). Women continue to participate in voluntary associations in large numbers.

In the 1790s, women organized societies to assist the poor. In the period before the Civil War, women organized against the evils of alcohol, the most notable organization being the Women's Christian Temperance Union. Women called for the abolition of slavery, educational opportunities for women, better working conditions, and help for "fallen" women. Beginning in the 1860s, women developed the club movement, culminating in such national organizations as the National Council of Jewish Women, 1893; the National Association of Colored Women, 1896; the National Association of Collegiate Women, 1896; and the National Congress of Mothers, 1897, which later became the

Ruth Bader Ginsburg was appointed to the U.S. Supreme Court in 1993 by President Clinton. In 1972, Ginsburg was the first woman to be hired with tenure at Columbia Law School, arguing a total of six cases involving women's rights before the Supreme Court.

Parent–Teacher Association (PTA) (Lebsock, 1990; Cott, 1990; Scott, 1991).

In the twentieth century, led by Emma Goldman (1869–1940) and Elizabeth Gurley Flynn (1890–1964), radical women became pacifists and socialists. They supported Margaret Sanger (1879–1966) in her campaign for legalizing birth control. When the labor movement resisted women's participation, women formed the National Women's Trade Union League (NWTUL) in 1903. The NWTUL supported the women's suffrage campaign. The campaign became a movement with about 2 million members at the time the National American Woman Suffrage Association (NAWSA) was formed in 1890. Women organized to reform the city, alleviate the evils of industrialization, and

prevent the exploitation of children, working women, and immigrants. In this way, they helped lay the foundation for the modern welfare state (Lebsock, 1990).

Bettina Aptheker (1989) has summarized the "lesbian connection" brought to light by new historical studies on women's organizations. Deeply embedded in the reform efforts of abolitionists, educators, club members, labor organizers, founders of settlement houses, suffragists, and civil rights and peace activists were women who shared emotional and political bonds and, most important, who envisioned a different kind of social structure, one that was woman-centered and caring.

Formal histories have also tended to ignore the importance of grass roots activism. Filling this gap, Patricia Hill Collins has written about

---

Box 13.5   SISTERS IN STRUGGLE: AFRICAN AMERICAN WOMEN CIVIL RIGHTS LEADERS

Black women in their homes, churches, social clubs, organizations, and communities throughout the South performed valuable leadership roles during the modern civil rights movement in the United States. Although race, gender, and class constraints generally prohibited their being the recognized articulators, spokespersons, and media favorites, these women did perform a multiplicity of significant leadership roles, such as the initiation and organization of action, the formulation of tactics, and the provision of crucial resources (e.g., money, communication channels, personnel) necessary to sustain the movement. Sisters in struggle, they were empowered through their activism.

. . . In countless ways, Black women who lived and worked in the South in the 1950s and 1960s led the way in the fight against oppression, in spite of and because of their race, gender, and class. The blood, sweat, and tears that they shed generated protest and activism by other disadvantaged groups—women, farm workers, gays and lesbians, the handicapped, welfare rights activists—all of whom have been in profound ways the beneficiaries of the civil rights movement. The roles that they performed, whether at the grass-roots level or behind the scenes, represent profiles in courage and suggest that they were *leaders* in their communities, *leaders* in the day-to-day fight against various forms of oppression, and *leaders* in the modern civil rights movement.

Source: From Bernice McNair Barnett, Invisible southern black women leaders in the civil rights movement: The triple constraints of gender, race, and class, in *Gender and Society* 7:2, 177, 1993, copyright © 1993 by Sage Publications, Inc. Reprinted by permission of Sage Publications, Inc.

---

definitions of power and resistance and of the activist traditions in the African American community. She emphasizes the individual and group actions "that directly challenge the legal and customary rules governing African-American women's subordination . . ." (Collins, 2000:142). Bernice McNair Barnett has explored the contributions of many ordinary African American women in the South to the civil rights movement of the 1950s and 1960s, looking beyond the men (and women) whose names are usually singled out (Barnett, 1993).

Today, networks of global feminist organizations engaged in grass roots activism are able to challenge and influence governments and their policies through the World Wide Web, the Internet, fax machines, and other telecommunications media. Lori Wallach, director of Public Citizen's Global Trade Watch, organized successful protests against the World Trade Organization (WTO) at its meeting in Seattle in 1999. Effectively protesting the potential consequences of globalization (see Chapter 12) on women and the poor, grass roots activism contributed to the collapse of the WTO meeting. Women's grass roots activism in the United States has been critical in promoting educational opportunities for girls in school, has led to the passage of the federal Violence Against Women Act in 1994, and has mobilized women in the area of health care to ensure their continued access to reproductive health care (Palley, 2001).

Women and Peace Movements

Women have expressed their political disagreement with many men about the excessive use of force, the priority given to militarism versus social agendas, and the effects of nuclear weapons on societies. Women have historically worked for peace through voluntary associations.

In the last two centuries, especially in Europe and the United States, women have organized a number of national and international peace societies. In the late nineteenth century, international socialist leaders Clara Zetkin (1857–1933) and Rosa Luxembourg (1870–1919) were committed to breaking down national borders and ending military competition between nations, positions that were not always taken by their male colleagues. An Austrian woman, Bertha von Suttner (1843–1914), wrote a major book about disarmament, *Lay Down Your Arms* (1889), and suggested the creation of the Nobel Peace Prize. She received it herself in 1905 (Boulding, 1977). Other significant women recipients have been Alva Myrdal in 1982 for her work to further disarmament and peace in international organizations (Bok, 1991) and Rigoberta Menchú Tum in 1992 for her opposition to the cultural genocide of the Indian peoples of Guatemala (Burgos-Debray, 1984).

Harriet Hyman Alonso (1993) has noted that U.S. feminist peace organizations from the 1920s to the present have shared four consistent themes: they make connections between militarism and violence against women; use women's unique perspective of "motherhood," that is, its valuing of creation, caring, and sharing, to secure a world of greater social justice; seek to be responsible citizens, domestically and globally; and strive for independence from male control in the establishment of women-centered and women-run organizations. However, not all women have sought peace. Women's peace organizations have often been challenged by women's patriotic organizations, such as the American War Mothers and the Daughters of the American Revolution, who favored military preparedness and joined other organizations in anti-communist and red-baiting activities (Cott, 1990).

World War I (1914–18) galvanized individual women, particularly suffragists, into forming peace organizations. Jane Addams, founder of the first settlement house in the Chicago slums in the 1890s, became a leader in the women's international peace movement during this war. A cofounder of the Women's International League for Peace and Freedom, Addams called for a women's peace conference in 1915 and helped to form the Woman's Peace Party (WPP) (Steinson, 1980; Rupp, 1997). Mary Church Terrell, a founder of the National Association of Colored Women and of the NAACP, became a member of the WPP's executive committee in 1915 (Alonso, 1993).

During the 1960s, Women Strike for Peace and Another Mother for Peace (now defunct) were founded in response to threats to the world's atmosphere from nuclear testing and to protest the U.S. pursuit of the war in Vietnam. One founder of Women Strike for Peace, Bella Abzug, became a congresswoman. Many women who became involved in feminist consciousness raising in the contemporary women's liberation movement were first active in peace efforts. In the 1970s, Women for Racial and Economic Equality linked the concerns of women of color and the poor, including racism, welfare reform, reproductive rights, employment, housing, health care, and others, to peace and the conversion of military expenditures to social ones (Alonso, 1993; Swerdlow, 1982).

The peace movement has been global. In the early twentieth century, peace was a concern of women's suffrage and internationalist socialist movements worldwide, including the Pan Pacific and Southeast Asia Women's Association and, after World War II, the All African Women's Conference and the Federation of Asian Women's Associations (Boulding, 1977). More recently, women's peace organizations have been active in the United Nations Decade for Women (1975–85).

In 1981, women organized the first peace encampment at Greenham Common to protest the placement of U.S. cruise missiles in England (Snitow, 1985); Nordic women sponsored a peace march across Europe; and women of the Pacific Islands campaigned against the nuclear testing in the Pacific that contributes to the high incidence of birth defects and miscarriages among women in the region. In 2000, women from all over the United States met in Washington on Mother's Day to participate in the Million Mom March in opposition to gun violence. Women have marched on Washington, encircled the Pentagon, petitioned Congress, and sought the closure of nuclear power plants. In their peace organizations, as in their formal politics and other voluntary associations, women have experienced difficulties in fund raising, in finding time for the necessary organizing and fundraising, and in meeting opposition to their goals (Alonso, 1993).

Equal Rights

The movement in the United States for the abolition of slavery raised women's consciousness, showing white women that oppression took many forms. Sarah M. Grimké (see Chapter 9), a leader in the abolitionist movement, was an early champion of women's emancipation. She expressed her feminist views as early as 1837:

> All history attests that man has subjugated woman to his will, used her as a means to promote his selfish gratification, to minister to his sensual pleasures, to be instrumental in promoting his comfort; but never has he desired to elevate her to that rank she was created to fill. He has done all he could to debase and enslave her mind; and now he looks tri-

umphantly on the ruin he has wrought, and says, the being he has thus deeply injured is his inferior. . . . But I ask no favors for my sex. . . . All I ask of our brethren is, that they will take their feet off from our necks and permit us to stand upright on that ground which God designed us to occupy. (Hole and Levine, 1971:4–5)

The Declaration of Sentiments drawn up in Seneca Falls, New York, in 1848, at a meeting to further women's rights reflected the sense of unfinished business women felt as part of a young republican nation dedicated to equality and to the pursuit of happiness for all:

> We hold these truths to be self-evident: that all men and women are created equal. . . . The history of mankind is a history of repeated injuries and usurpations on the part of man toward woman. . . . Now, in view of this entire disfranchisement of one-half the people of this country . . . we insist that they have immediate admission to all the rights and privileges which belong to them as citizens of the United States. (Schneir, 1972:77–8, 80)

The rights of women to full political equality remain unfinished business for feminists today.

The Struggle for the Vote

The Thirteenth Amendment brought an end to slavery in the United States in 1865. When women attempted to eliminate the word *male* in the proposed Fourteenth Amendment, which would ensure the "rights, privileges, and immunities of citizens" to freed slaves, they were advised by male abolitionists that it was not yet their turn. After decades of unceasing work in the cause of black emancipation, women found that they could count on little support from their male colleagues when the matter concerned women's rights, in this case the right to vote.

In 1869, Susan B. Anthony (1820–1906) and Elizabeth Cady Stanton (1815–1902) organized the National Woman Suffrage Association, devoted to achieving national suffrage by a state-by-state effort to change the law. In 1875, the Supreme Court ruled unanimously that the St. Louis registrar of voters could not be compelled to register Virginia Minor as a voter just because she was a citizen. This court ruling made it clear that only a constitutional amendment could achieve the vote for women. By 1878, the Stanton amendment was introduced into Congress: it was this proposal that would be ratified more than 40 years later as the Nineteenth Amendment. In 1890, the National American Woman Suffrage Association was formed (Kerber, 1998).

To dramatize the hypocrisy of Woodrow Wilson's words when he led the United States into World War I "to make the world safe for democracy," Alice Paul's (1885–1977) suffrage group organized a silent picket in front of the White House in 1916. After several months, demonstrators were forcibly removed by the police for obstructing the public way, and 218 women from twenty-six states were arrested in 1917. In prison, they went on a hunger strike. The courts ordered their release several months later, on the grounds that both arrests and convictions were illegal. Despite last-minute efforts by antisuffrage groups after the war, proclaiming that enfranchising women would open up a Pandora's box of evils, the Nineteenth Amendment was passed by Congress in 1918 and ratified by three-fourths of the state governments by August 26, 1920. Finally, American women could vote.

By the time women gained the right to vote in the United States, they could already do so in 10 other countries. The first country to grant women's suffrage was New Zealand, in 1893. Women's suffrage was achieved in England after an equally long but far more militant struggle: women aged 30 and above were allowed to vote in 1918 and women under 30 were given the vote in 1928. Women gained the right to vote in Ecuador in 1929, in Turkey in 1930, while in France they had to wait until 1944. After World War II, women in South Korea, Japan, Greece, and Italy were allowed to vote; but it was not until 1971 that most women in Switzerland won this right (only in 1990 did all cantons permit it). In some countries, such as Saudi Arabia, women are still not permitted to vote.

The Modern Women's Liberation Movement

The origins of the modern women's liberation movement in the United States are usually traced to two main strands of feminist activism beginning in the 1960s. The first strand is identified with national organizations and follows a liberal tradition with an emphasis on women's rights. It had its impetus in the National Commission on the Status of Women established by Pres. Kennedy and chaired by Eleanor Roosevelt in 1961. The commission's report focused on the second-class nature of women's status in the United States and led to the creation of fifty state commissions (Freeman, 1976; Hole and Levine, 1971).

Women dissatisfied with their inability to use these commissions to achieve any practical gains founded the National Organization for Women (NOW) in 1966. Conceived originally as a pressure group to force the government to take seriously the sex discrimination guidelines (Title VII of the 1964 Civil Rights Act) administered by the Equal Employment Opportunity Commission (EEOC), NOW filed a gender discrimination complaint against 1,300 corporations receiving federal funds in 1970. It also became a strong political lobby for many other women's rights issues, including the Equal Rights Amendment, child-care centers, and abortion rights (Hole and Levine, 1971; Dietch, 1993).

Box 13.6   CARRIE CHAPMAN CATT REMEMBERS

To get the word "male" in effect out of the constitution cost the women of the country 52 years of pauseless campaign . . . during that time they were forced to conduct 56 campaigns of referenda to male voters; 480 campaigns to get [state] legislatures to submit suffrage amendments to voters; 47 campaigns to get state constitutional conventions to write woman suffrage into state constitutions; 277 campaigns to get state party conventions to include woman suffrage planks; 30 campaigns to get presidential party conventions to adopt woman suffrage planks in party platforms, and 19 campaigns with 19 successive Congresses.

Source: Goldstein, 1979:62.

A second important source of the modern women's movement in the United States was a relatively younger group active in the civil rights, New Left, and anti-Vietnam War organizations of the 1960s. More radical, grass roots, and local in orientation, this group came to focus on women's liberation and structural change. Young white women from the south and the north, young African American women mainly from the south, and other women of color from across the nation developed a feminist consciousness working in the ranks of the Student Non-Violent Coordinating Committee (SNCC). Women helped run the organizations, yet SNCC's top leadership was male. In being relegated to clerical and housekeeping chores, women were made aware of their relative powerlessness in the male-controlled decision-making process (Evans, 1980; Brown, 1992).

Similarly, women who participated in the Students for a Democratic Society (SDS), which had developed in northern states in 1960, found even fewer opportunities than in SNCC to take up much responsibility. The style of the primarily male leadership was intellectually competitive and aggressive. Women were viewed as attached to particular men or as "implementers and listeners" (Evans, 1980:108, 113). Women joining protests against U.S. pursuit of the war in Vietnam experienced similar subordination.

When the male leadership at the National Conference for a New Politics in Chicago in August 1967 ignored a militant resolution demanding 51% of convention votes for women because women numbered 51% of the population in the country, the women went home and organized. A paper addressed "To the Women of the Left" was circulated, calling on women "to organize a movement for women's liberation" (Evans, 1980:200). Gatherings of women became consciousness-raising groups across the nation. *MS.* magazine, founded in at the end of 1971 by Gloria Steinem and others, gave women a growing feminist voice that drew national attention. By the 1970s, these two main strands of events, built upon women's activism in many areas, merged to form a movement of great political significance.

Lesbian feminist organizations also formed to challenge bias not only in the wider society but also among mainstream feminist organizations and to encourage lesbians to contribute to a collective identity that can exert political influence (Taylor and Whittier, 1992). The political strength of women was particularly significant in the 1992 national presidential elections.

Box 13.7   NOW STATEMENT OF PURPOSE, 1966

To take action to bring women into full participation in the mainstream of American society now, exercising all the privileges and responsibilities thereof in truly equal partnership with men.

... We do not accept the traditional assumption that a woman has to choose between marriage and motherhood, on the one hand, and serious participation in industry or the professions on the other.

The Equal Rights Amendment

An important symbol for all parts of the new women's liberation movement was the passage in the U.S. Congress in 1972 of a constitutional amendment guaranteeing equal rights under the law to all regardless of gender. The National Women's Party first proposed the Equal Rights Amendment (ERA) at the seventy-fifth anniversary conference of the Seneca Falls Convention, in 1923. It was introduced into Congress that year and repeatedly for the next 40 years. The Citizen's Advisory Council on the Status of Women recommended passage of the ERA in 1970. Hearings were held by the Senate Judiciary Committee after pressure from NOW. Seriously debated by Congress for the first time in 1971, the ERA was finally adopted on March 22, 1972. However, it still required ratification by thirty-eight states—three-fourths of the state legislatures—before becoming law.

After the first thirty states ratified the ERA, the process began to slow down as opponents painted the ERA as a threat to personal, social, and religious values (Newland, 1979). By 1980, a more conservative political environment throughout the country made it impossible for the amendment to pass state legislative scrutiny and votes. Time ran out for its ratification by the end of June 1982 (Mansbridge, 1986). Efforts to achieve the legal equality the amendment would have hastened have, however, continued, often with greater resolve.

Global Feminism and Human Rights

Beginning in the 1970s, the development of feminist consciousness and women's increased participation in nation building globally led individuals and groups to place pressure on the United Nations (UN) to take up a year of intensive discussion on the position of women worldwide. Delegates reached agreement on a UN-sponsored examination of the status of women. The first UN-sponsored world conference on women took place in 1975 in Mexico City. The themes of the UN women's conference as well as those of the second (held in Copenhagen in 1980) and the third (in Nairobi in 1985) were equality, peace, and development. The Fourth World Conference on Women, in Beijing in 1995, assessed global progress toward improving the lives of women and girls, as well as the factors that hinder such progress. A special session of the UN General Assembly, designated Beijing+5, was held in 2000 to consider how the platform for action resulting from the Beijing Conference had been implemented.

An important outcome of the first UN conference on women was the creation of a major international treaty concerned with women's rights—the Convention on the Elimination of All Forms of Discrimination Against Women (CEDAW)—which entered into force in 1979. To date, 170 countries have ratified CEDAW, though many have attached reservations that weaken it. While most of the world's governments have ratified the CEDAW treaty, the United States and Afghanistan have yet to do so.

These four UN-sponsored world conferences on women enabled women from all over the globe to share experiences and views. The official UN conferences brought together government representatives (some of whom were men) and the members of many nongovernmental groups, which met in unofficial sessions. At the end of these conferences, global blueprints of action were approved by the UN General Assembly, calling upon governments and communities to eliminate all forms of discrimination against women and to work to improve the lives of women worldwide. At the Fourth World Conference on Women, governments agreed to the idea that women's rights are human rights; recognized the right of women to have control over and to decide on matters relating to their sexuality; referred to the family "in its various forms"; and agreed to end female genital mutilation and prenatal sex selection, to eradicate violence against women and girls, to secure girls' education free of discrimination in schools, and to mainstream international feminism.

In addition to the UN-sponsored world conferences on women, other major UN conferences have benefited from the input of feminist thinkers and activists working throughout the 1980s and 1990s. The 1992 UN Earth Summit in Rio de Janeiro successfully incorporated women's issues related to the environment and sustainable development. The 1993 World Conference on Human Rights in Vienna accepted the principle that "women's rights are human rights," and the Vienna Plan of Action called for the eradication of violence against women in both the public and private spheres. The 1994 Conference on Population and Development in Cairo acknowledged that the empowerment and education of women is a means of improving women's health and that such efforts serve as the best methods to reduce population growth rates.

Global feminist organizing has been very effective at highlighting the issue of violence against women, which affects women globally and cuts across lines of class, race, educational attainment, ethnicity, region, religion, and language. Women experience violence in various forms: in the home, in refugee camps, in prisons, during armed conflict and civil war, and in international sex trafficking operations. The most far-reaching international treaty to work toward the eradication of violence against women is the Inter-American Convention on Violence against Women (ICVW), which entered into force in 1995. The convention defines violence against women as "any act or conduct, based on gender, which causes death or physical, sexual or psychological harm or suffering to women." The ICVW requires states to take immediate action "to prevent, investigate and impose penalties for violence against women" as well as to "modify legal or customary practices that sustain violence" (Meyer 1999; O'Hare, 1999).

Violence against women remains an enormous problem, and women are far from actually attaining equal rights. However, internationally, women have made great progress in gaining recognition of these problems and have had an impact on global issues affecting them. Conferences and meetings have served as a consciousness-raising process as women from around the world have gained new insights on the varieties of patriarchal oppression and have developed a healthy respect for the differences among themselves. In the process, women have changed how gender is understood and lived worldwide.

The Political Climate in the New Millennium

More progress toward feminist goals has been made in the past 30 years than in any other period of modern history. Such success has set off a strong reaction within the United States and elsewhere. The failure to ratify the ERA and the efforts of various U.S. presidents and their administrations to dismantle legislative, judicial, and economic gains made over previous decades present new challenges to feminists of every kind. The elimination of the right of abortion for Medicaid recipients and abortion counseling for women globally has threatened women's rights. Making abortions difficult for some women (especially poor women) to obtain makes it easier down the road to eliminate reproductive rights for all women. The government's opposition to reproductive rights in the 1980s, the 1990s, and the new millennium has contributed to dividing women in the United States who are supportive of many feminist concerns but, for religious and political reasons, oppose government funding of abortion. Even President Clinton (1992–2000), viewed as supportive of women's rights, helped to divide women by setting welfare term limits for poor women and undercutting the recognition that all persons should have, by right, enough resources to stay alive.

Feminists from developing countries or from minority communities in the developed world have struggled with the problems of multiple oppression; for them, racism may be as serious an obstacle as sexism. Women experience oppression because of race, class, ethnicity, nationality, sexual orientation, and religion. Such oppressions may require continued solidarity with other members of their groups even as they strive to decrease the gender inequalities within them. As one group expressed it, "We struggle together with black men about sexism" (Combahee River Collective, 1979:366). Women in the formerly colonized world, the global south, may see their oppression as worsened by the corporate globalization now being foisted on them by the women as well as the men of the privileged, developed, global north (Jaggar, 2002).

Preserving the gains women have made against assaults from those who would turn back the clock requires that women set aside their differences and work together. The phrase made popular during the Black Power liberation movement, "If they come for you in the morning, they will come for me in the afternoon," can be a guidepost. Women must continue to struggle together on issues confronting them as women, while simultaneously struggling to work to transcend divisions.

History shows that women can come together to elect representatives and influence governmental decisions supportive of social justice and equality for all and can promote policies and practices that attend to women's issues. Increasingly, women realize that they have to become the change they wish to see, and they often do this by running for office and seeking appointments themselves.

Globally, differences among women are often enormous. For many, economic survival is the salient concern, while membership in men's clubs is not an issue. Cultural divisions often lead non-Western women to want to work for improvements in women's lives that are very different from those for which Western feminists have striven. However, such differences need not undermine the potential for sisterhood among women.

Can women build together significant political forces to oppose further incursions on the gains made and make further progress? Have women developed the networks, the organizations, the ways of offering support to one another to marshal their forces, get their opinions heard, and make their presence felt in political processes? The answer depends on women.

Summary

Until recently, most political scientists viewed women as of little consequence in politics.

The stereotypical view of women was that they are naturally unsuited to act in the "public" sphere and that they adopt the views of their fathers and husbands.

Women have been far less visible than men in formal political activity. Feminist scholars call attention to the crucial role women play in community-level organizations and the ways they have been socialized to follow rather than lead. The women's movement has brought out the relation between women's exclusion from the "public" sphere and the lack of control over their "private" lives, arguing "The personal is political."

Power is distinct from authority. Women have seldom exercised either power or authority.

As societies become more complex, governmental power tends to be exercised by the few on behalf of the many. Women tend to be segregated as a group and excluded from political power, along with subordinated racial, ethnic, and religious groups. Women who do participate in government tend to do so on the local level.

In the past, some women have exercised political power in their own right in dynastic states and in precolonial African societies. As government became more bureaucratic and as colonial powers altered these societies, the power of these women leaders eroded.

Male dominance is associated with the increasing complexity of societies and societal responses to stress and change. It is manifested in the exclusion of women from economic and political decision making and in violence against women.

The women's movement has encouraged increasing numbers of women to seek public office. In the 1980s, a "gender gap" emerged in the United States, with women and men differing in political viewpoints, party affiliation, and voting behavior. Studies show that regardless of party label or level of office, women officeholders take more feminist positions on women's issues than do men. Nonetheless, women still face opposition, some of which they are attempting to overcome through such methods as raising their own funds to support candidates with feminist viewpoints. In various other countries, women have been able to win political office in greater percentages than in the United States.

One attempt to justify women's political subordination to men asserts that it is men who possess the physical strength to wage wars and thereby to make critical governmental decisions. Aggression is still valued more than nurturance, though feminists are trying to change this. Nonetheless, women have been motivated to fight in informal armies of rebellions, revolutions, and resistance movements and to support their government or state in other war-related efforts. For the most part, however, women have been pressed to return to the traditional roles of wives and mothers after they have made their sacrifices and contributions.

Laws tend to have a sexist bias because they are based on male-defined norms. Many laws and moral codes are based on a double standard. Family law often coerces women into traditional roles. Laws designed to "protect" women often have the effect of restricting women's choices and activities. Women who break the law are subjected to laws made by male legislators, enforced by male police officers, and interpreted by male judges.

Marginalized from "politics" as men define it, women have sought to achieve their objectives through a wide range of voluntary associations. Women's involvement in peace movements testifies to their political opposition to many of men's wars. While women may tend to be more "pacific" than men, this does not mean that they cannot be motivated to fight.

Women's chief struggle at the beginning of the twentieth century was to obtain the right to vote.

The modern women's liberation movement developed from two sources: organizations formed to work for women's equality and a younger, more radical group involved in the civil rights, New Left, and anti–Vietnam War movements and concerned with liberation from male oppression.

The ERA took half a century to pass Congress; in June 1982, it failed to win the necessary ratification by three-fourths of the states. Opposition to the ERA centers on fears that it would disrupt traditional social norms. Yet, more women than ever have joined the political process to pursue its goals.

In the 1980s, a global feminism emerged with the aid of the UN conferences on women, human rights, the environment, and sustainable development. These global conferences brought together women worldwide to share experiences and to develop strategies to eliminate global patriarchy and improve the lives of women.

Feminist unity is made more difficult by the fact that women have different ethnic, national, religious, class, and racial backgrounds, as well as different sexual orientations, and thus have different priorities. Some women carry a double burden in having to deal with both sexism and racism. The need for all women to engage in the political process and to focus clearly on necessary goals is paramount if they are to ensure that recent gains will not be lost and that new gains will be won. Women's unity will benefit from understanding the differences among women.

Women have demonstrated their power to mobilize themselves and others to elect legislators and promote policies supportive of women's issues. Future progress in all areas of women's rights and liberation depends to a large part on women themselves.

Discussion Questions

1. Document the life of a woman political leader of your choice. How did she manage to succeed, given the obstacles to women's political leadership?

2. Find out which women hold political offices or leadership positions in your town, county, or congressional district. On the basis of what you have read in this chapter, design a questionnaire to find out what positions these women hold on a variety of feminist issues.

3. Do an oral-history interview with women in your own family on their role in and views on key aspects of the women's movement. Were members of your family suffragists? Did any participate in the social movements of the 1960s? How many have been involved in voluntary organizations? Which ones? Have any participated in electoral politics? If not, why not?

4. What kinds of organization exist in your locality to deal with issues concerning women, violence, and the law (such as a rape crisis center, a battered wife center, or a group concerned with women in prison)?

5. How do women from different racial or ethnic groups or economic classes differ in their perceptions and attitudes on feminist issues? Select one issue as a "problem" and suggest "solutions." How might women from two groups argue from the perspectives of their different backgrounds?

Recommended Readings

Alonso, Harriet Hyman. *Peace as a Woman's Issue: A History of the U.S. Movement for World Peace and Women's Rights*. Syracuse: Syracuse University Press, 1993. As the first comprehensive history of the feminist peace movement in the United States, this book provides an analysis of the role, activities, and inner workings of key women's peace organizations. It traces the development of the women's campaign for peace from its roots in nineteenth-century abolitionist and suffrage movements to its expression during the 1990–1 Persian Gulf War.

Basu, Amrita, editor. *The Challenge of Local Feminisms: Women's Movements in Global Perspectives*. Boulder, CO: Westview Press, 1995. An examination of the globalized women's movements in 13 countries in Africa, Asia, Europe, and North and South America. The authors discuss the history of women's activism, the state of current struggles of women's movements, the relationship between women's movements and the state, and prospects for the future.

Cohen, Cathy, Kathleen B. Jones, and Joan Tnonto, editors. *Women Transforming Politics: An Alternate Reader.* New York: New York University Press, 1997. An anthology of essays by women scholars and activists who explore the broad diversity of women's contributions to political life. The experiences of women of color of all kinds provide new meaning to "politics."

Evans, Sarah. *Personal Politics, The Roots of Women's Liberation in the Civil Rights Movement and the New Left.* New York: Knopf, 1979. A discussion of the emergence of the women's movement in the context of women's activities in the civil rights and antiwar movements in the 1960s. Evans tells of women's changing roles in these movements as they grew larger and more successful and of the contradictions that emerged.

Schroeder, Pat. *24 Years of House Work . . . and the Place Is Still a Mess, My Life in Politics*. Kansas City, MO: Andrews McMeel Publishing, 1998. Former Colorado Congresswoman Pat Schroeder discusses her two decades in Congress. A witty but sobering look at the challenges faced by women in American politics.

References

Abzug, Bella, with Mim Kelber. *Gender Gap*. Boston: Houghton Mifflin, 1984.

Adler, Frieda. *Sisters in Crime: The Rise of the New Female Criminal*. New York: McGraw-Hill, 1975.

Alonso, Harriet Hyman. *Peace as a Women's Issue*. Syracuse: Syracuse University Press, 1993.

Aptheker, Bettina. *Tapestries of Life*. Amherst: University of Massachusetts Press, 1989.

Baker, Paula. The moral framework of public life: Gender and politics in rural New York, 1870–1930. Ph.D. diss., Rutgers University, 1987.

Barnett, Bernice McNair. Invisible southern black women leaders in the civil rights movement: The triple constraints of gender, race, and class. *Gender and Society*, 7:2, 162–82, 1993.

Berube, Allan. Marching to a different drummer: Lesbian and gay GIs in World War II. In *Hidden from History: Reclaiming the Gay and Lesbian Past*, edited by Martin Duberman, Martha Vicinus, and George Chauncey, Jr. New York: Meridian, 1990.

Bok, Sissela. *Alva Myrdal*, Reading, Mass.: Addison Wesley, 1991.

Bookman, Ann, and Sandra Morgen, editors. *Women and the Politics of Empowerment*. Philadelphia: Temple University Press, 1988.

Boulding, Elise. *Women in the Twentieth Century World*. New York: Wiley, 1977.

Brown, Elaine. *A Taste of Power: A Black Woman's Story*. New York: Pantheon, 1992.

Burgos-Debray, Elizabeth, editor. *I, Rigoberta Menchu*. London: Verso, 1984.

Center for the American Woman and Politics. *The Impact of Women in Public Office: An Overview*. New Brunswick, NJ: Eagleton Institute of Politics, Rutgers University, 1991.

———. *The Gender Gap. Fact Sheet*. New Brunswick, NJ: Eagleton Institute of Politics, Rutgers University, 1992a.

————. *Women Candidates for Congress 1970–1992. Fact Sheet.* New Brunswick, NJ: Eagleton Institute of Politics, Rutgers University, 1992b.

Collins, Patricia Hill. *Black Feminist Thought: Knowledge, Consciousness, and the Politics of Empowerment*, 2nd ed. New York: Routledge, 2000.

Combahee River Collective. A black feminist statement. In *Capitalist Patriarchy and the Case of Socialist Feminism*, edited by Zilah R. Eisenstein. New York: Monthly Review Press, 1979.

Conway, M. Margaret. Women and political participation. *PS: Political Science and Politics*, 25:2, 231–3, 2001.

Cook, Blanche Wiesen. *Eleanor Roosevelt*, vol. I. New York: Penguin, 1992.

Cott, Nancy F. Across the great divide: Women in politics before and after 1920. In *Women, Politics and Change*, edited by Louise A. Tilly and Patricia Gurin. New York: Russell Sage Foundation, 1990.

Crenshaw, Kimberle. Demarginalizing the intersection of race and sex: A black feminist critique of antidiscrimination doctrine, feminist theory and antiracist politics. In *Feminist Legal Theory*, edited by Katharine T. Bartlett and Rosanne Kennedy. Boulder, CO: Westview Press, 1991.

Dalley, Gillian. *Ideologies of Caring: Rethinking Community and Collectivism*. London: Macmillan Education, 1988.

Dietch, Cynthia. Gender, race and class politics and the inclusion of women in Title VII of the 1964 Civil Rights Acts. *Gender and Society*, 7:2, 183–203, 1993.

Disney, Jennifer Leigh. Democratization, civil society, and women's organizing in post-revolutionary Mozambique and Nicaragua. *New Political Science*, 25:4, 533–60, 2003.

Dolan, Julie. Political appointees in the United States: Does gender make a difference? *PS: Political Science and Politics*, 25:2, 213–16, 2001.

Evans, Sarah. *Personal Politics: The Roots of Women's Liberation in the Civil Rights Movement and the New Left*. New York: Vintage, 1980.

Freeman, Bonnie Cook. Power, Patriarch, and Political Primitives. In *Beyond Sexism: A New Woman, a New Reality*, edited by Joan I. Roberts. New York: McKay, 1976.

Goldstein, Leslie Friedman. *The Constitutional Rights of Women: Cases in Law and Social Change*. New York: Longman, 1979.

Gordon, Linda. *Heroes of Their Own Lives*. New York: Penguin, 1988.

Harrington, Mona. *Care and Equality: Inventing a New Family Politics*. New York: Knopf, 1999.

Harris, Alice P. Race and essentialism in feminist legal theory. In *Feminist Legal Theory*, edited by Katharine T. Bartlett and Rosanne Kennedy. Boulder, CO: Westview Press, 1991.

Hartsock, Nancy. *Money, Sex and Power*. New York: Longman, 1983.

Hole, Judith, and Ellen Levine. *Rebirth of Feminism*. New York: Quadrangle, 1971.

Hossain, Rokeya Sakhawat. *Sultana's Dream and Selections from the Secluded Ones*, edited and translated by Roushan Jahan. New York: Feminist Press at the City University of New York, 1988.

Ifeka-Moller, Caroline. Female militancy and colonial revolt: The women's war of 1929, Eastern Nigeria. In *Perceiving Women*, edited by Shirley Ardener. New York: Wiley, 1977.

Inter-Parliamentary Union. *Women in National Parliaments*. www.ipu.org/wmn-e/classif.htm. accessed 2004.

Jacobs, Susie. Women and land resettlement in Zimbabwe. *Review of African Political Economy*, 27/28, 33–50, 1984.

Jaggar, Alison M. A feminist critique of the alleged southern debt. *Hypatia: A Journal of Feminist Philosophy*, 17/4, 119–42, 2002.

Kathlene, Lyn. Studying the new voice of women in politics. *Chronicle of Higher Education*, Nov. 18, 1992, B1–2.

Kaufmann, Karen M., and John R Petrocik. The changing politics of American men: Understanding the sources of the gender gap. *American Journal of Political Science*, 43/3, 864–87, 1999.

Kelly, Amy. *Eleanor of Aquitaine and the Four Kings*. New York: Vintage, 1957.

Kerber, Linda K. *No Constitutional Right to be Ladies: Women and the Obligations of Citizenship*. New York: Hill and Wang, 1998.

Ladner, Joyce A. *Tomorrow's Tomorrow. The Black Woman*. Garden City, NY: Doubleday, 1972.

Lebsock, Suzanne. Women and American politics, 1880–1920. In *Women, Politics and Change*, edited by Louise A. Tilly and Patricia Gurin. New York: Russell Sage Foundation, 1990.

Lee, Marcia M. Toward understanding why few women hold public office: Factors affecting the participation of women in local politics. In *A Portrait of Marginality*, edited by Marianne Githens and Jewel Prestage. New York: McKay, 1977.

Lloyd, Genevieve. Selfhood, war and masculinity. In *Feminist Challenges: Social and Political Theory*, edited by Carole Pateman and Elizabeth Gross. Sydney: Allen and Unwin, 1986.

Lovenduski, Joni. Toward the emasculation of political science: The impact of feminism." In *Men's Studies Modified: The Impact of Feminism on the Academic Disciplines*, edited by Dale Spender. New York: Pergamon, 1981.

MacKinnon, Catharine A. *Feminism Unmodified: Discourses on Life and Law*, Cambridge, MA: Harvard University Press, 1987.

———. Feminism, Marxism, method and the state: Toward feminist jurisprudence. In *Feminist Legal Theory*, edited by Katharine T. Bartlett and Rosanne Kennedy. Boulder, CO: Westview Press, 1991.

Mansbridge, Jane J. *Why We Lost the ERA*. Chicago: University of Chicago Press, 1986.

Martin, Susan Ehrlich, and Nancy C. Jurik. *Doing Justice, Doing Gender*. Thousand Oaks, CA: Sage Publications, 1996.

Matsuda, Mari. When the first quail calls: Multiple consciousness as jurisprudential method. *Women's Rights Law Reporter*, 7, 9, 1989.

McKenna, Erin. *The Task of Utopia*. Lanham, MD: Rowman & Littlefield, 2001.

Meriwether, Margaret, and Judith E. Tucker, editors. *A Social History of Women and Gender in the Modern Middle East*. Boulder, CO: Westview Press, 1999.

Meyer, Mary K. Negotiating international norms: The Inter-American Commission of Women and the Convention on Violence Against Women. In *Gender Politics in Global Governance*, edited by Mary K. Meyer and Elisabeth Prügl. Lanham, MD: Rowman & Littlefield, 1999.

Moser, Caroline O. N. and Peake, Linda. *Women, Human Settlements, and Housing*. London: Tavistock Publications, 1987.

Mpoumou, Doris. From liberty, equality, fraternity to liberty, equality, parité. *WEDO News & Views*, 14:2, 13, 2001.

Neale, John E. *Queen Elizabeth I: A Biography* (1934). Garden City, NY: Doubleday, 1957.

Newland, Kathleen. *The Sisterhood of Man*. New York: Norton. 1979.

O'Barr, Jean. African women in politics. In *African Women South of the Sahara*, edited by Margaret Jean Hay and Sharon Stichter. New York: Longman, 1984.

O'Donovan, Katherine. Before and after: The impact of feminism on the academic discipline of law. In *Men's Studies Modified: The Impact of Feminism on the Academic Disciplines*, edited by Dale Spender. New York: Pergamon, 1981.

O'Hare, Ursula A. Realizing human rights for women. *Human Rights Quarterly*, 21:2, 364–402, 1999.

Okin, Susan Moller. *Women in Western Political Thought*. Princeton: Princeton University Press, 1979.

Oldenburg, Veena Talwar. *Dowry Murder: The Imperial Origins of a Cultural Crime*. New York: Oxford University Press, 2002.

Palley, Marian Lief. Women's policy leadership in the United States. *PS: Political Science and Politics*, 25:2, 247–50, 2001.

Palmer, Barbara. "To do justly": The integration of women into the American judiciary. *PS: Political Science and Politics*, 25:2, 235–9, 2001.

Pearson, Carol. Women's fantasies and feminist utopias. *Frontiers*, 2, 50–61, 1977.

Prinderville, Diane-Michelle, and Teresa Braley Gomez. American Indian women leaders, public policy, and the importance of gender and ethnic identity. *Women and Politics*, 20:2, 17–32, 1999.

Randall, Vicky. *Women and Politics*, 2nd ed. Chicago: Chicago University Press, 1987.

Reverby, Susan, and Dorothy O Helly. Converging on history. In *Gendered Domains: Rethinking Public and Private in Women's History*, edited by Dorothy O. Helly and Susan Reverby. Ithaca: Cornell University Press, 1992.

Rosenthal, Cindy Simon. Gender styles in state legislative committees: Raising their voices in resolving conflict. *Women and Politics*, 21:2, 21–45, 2000.

Rostker v. Goldberg, 453 U.S. 57, 64, 67, 1981.

Ridd, Rosemary, and Helen Callaway. *Women and Political Conflict*. New York: New York University Press, 1987.

Rodríguez, Victoria E., editor. *Women's Participation in Mexican Political Life*. Boulder, CO: Westview Press, 1998.

Rupp, Leila J. *Worlds of Women*. Princeton: Princeton University Press, 1997.

Sanday, Peggy Reeves. *Female Power and Male Dominance: On the Origins of Sexual Inequality*. Cambridge: Cambridge University Press, 1981.

Schneir, Miriam, editor. *Feminism: The Essential Historical Writings*. New York: Random House, 1972.

Scott, Anne Firor. *Natural Allies: Women's Associations in American History*. Urbana: University of Illinois Press, 1991.

Sievers, Sharon L. Women in China, Japan, and Korea. In *Restoring Women to History (Teaching Packets for Integrating Women's History into Courses in Africa, Asia, Latin America and the Caribbean and the Middle East)*, rev. ed. Bloomington, IN: Organization of American Historians, 1990.

Smart, Carol. *Women, Crime and Criminology: A Feminist Critique*. London: Routledge & Kegan Paul, 1978.

Snitow, Ann. Holding the line at Greenham Common: Being joyously political in dangerous times. *Mother Jones*, February/March 1985, 30–47.

Spelman, Elizabeth V. *Inessential Woman: Problems of Exclusion in Feminist Thought*. Boston: Beacon Press, 1988.

Springer, Kimberly, editor. *Still Lifting, Still Climbing: African American Women's Contemporary Activism*. New York: New York University Press, 1999.

Steinson, Barbara J. The mother half of humanity: American women in the peace and preparedness movements in World War I. In *Women, War and Revolution*, edited by Carol R. Berkin and Clara M. Lovett. New York: Homes & Meiers, 1980.

Stiehm, Judith H. *Bring Me Men and Women: Mandated Change at the U.S. Air Force Academy*. Berkeley: University of California Press, 1981.

Swerdlow, Amy. Ladies' day at the Capitol: Women strike for peace versus HUAC. *Feminist Studies*, 8:3, 493–520, 1982.

Swers, Michele L. *The Difference Women Make: The Policy Impact of Women in Congress*. Chicago: University of Chicago Press, 2002.

Taylor, Verta, and Nancy E. Whittier. Collective identity in social movement communities: Lesbian feminist mobilization. In *Frontiers in Social Movement Theory*, edited by Aldon D. Morris and Carol McClurg Mueller. New Haven: Yale University Press, 1992.

Thomas, Sue. Why gender matters: The perceptions of women officeholders. *Women and Politics*, 17:1, 27–53, 1997.

Tickner, J. Ann. *Gendering World Politics*. New York: Columbia University Press, 2001.

Tronto, Joan C. *Moral Boundaries: A Political Argument for an Ethic of Care*. New York: Routledge, 1993.

United Nations Development Program. *Human Development Report 2000*. New York: Oxford University Press, 2000.

Women's Environment and Development Organization. (http://www.wedo.org/factsheet1.htm).

White, E. Frances. Women of western and western central Africa. In *Restoring Women to History (Teaching Packets for Integrating Women's History into Courses in Africa, Asia, Latin America and the Caribbean and the Middle East)*, rev. ed. Bloomington, IN: Organization of American Historians, 1990.

Williams, Patricia J. *The Alchemy of Race and Rights*. Cambridge, MA: Harvard University Press, 1991.

EPILOGUE

Despite decades of feminist political activism, gender continues to differentially structure the experiences and opportunities of women and men throughout the world. There is still a very long way to go before gender equality is attained in most countries of the world. Even in the United States, where twentieth century feminist activism produced the largest social movement in the nation's history (Baxandall and Gordon, 2000:1), widespread discrepancies between women and men still exist. Women and children comprise the majority of people living below the poverty level; women's wages lag behind men's for comparable work; women continue to hit a "glass ceiling" that constrains their opportunities for advancement in many careers; women are more likely than men to experience the double burden of working outside the home while simultaneously having responsibility for work in the home; and women are physically battered by boyfriends and husbands at an alarming rate. For women in other parts of the world, the situation is rarely better: being born female is often a liability.

Although women continue to experience oppression worldwide and many feminist attempts to change society have met with defeat, there is reason for optimism. Some extraordinary gains for women have taken place in some areas of the world over the last few decades. Once barred from national political involvement, women now vote in most countries of the world and hold elected and appointed office, acting as heads of state in numbers unimaginable just 50 years ago. Women's literacy rates are up in many places across the globe, and women's labor has become more highly valued in multiple loca-

tions. Women's intellectual and artistic productions are now often recognized as worthy of the same kind of valuation once only granted to men's.

These and other feminist gains have not come easily. They have been the result of women working together to articulate their concerns, often struggling to find commonalities in the face of genuine differences, and fighting the forces of oppression on multiple fronts. They have come about through the tireless efforts of women activists all over the world. In Asia, Africa, the Middle East, North and South America, and Europe, women have organized in multiple ways to confront gender inequalities and to seek better lives for themselves and their families: they have, for example, come together as workers seeking improved working conditions and freedom from sexual harassment in the workplace; as mothers protesting the murder of their family members by dictatorial regimes; as members of international organizations mobilized to fight domestic and state-sanctioned violence; as participants in local and global environmental movements; as advocates for access to education and healthcare; and as activists seeking protection of women's customary land rights and gay and lesbian rights. Women all over the globe have developed a wide range of organizations to institutionalize their struggles. The Feminist League of Central Asia, the Center for Feminist Legal Research in New Delhi, the Feminist Peasant Network in Mexico, the Working Group Toward a Feminist Europe, the Women's League of the African National Congress, and the National Organization for Women in the United States are just a few.

Bonnie Smith describes the range of women's activism this way:

> Women have carried guns, written diatribes, used shaming and bodily gestures of ridicule against those who would oppress or exploit them. Women have acted heroically on their own, banded together informally, formed national and even transnational groups, and disagreed with one another, sometimes venomously, over politics and social goals . . . women's activism is consistently rich, complex, and vast. (Smith, 2000:9)

In some circumstances, women have fought alongside men in movements for freedom from political domination; at other times they have contested male domination and sexism. Oftentimes, they have had to wage battles on two fronts simultaneously. Although women have been politically active all over the world, this does not mean that there is, or has been, a single global women's movement in which one issue, form of protest, or proposed solution has arisen, joining women in a singular cause. Instead, women's political activism has taken multiple forms because people across the globe have adapted their causes to very different and complex local circumstances. In both the United States and China, for example, women have struggled for expanded reproductive choices. In the United States, however, women have fought for the right to limit family size through access to birth control and abortion, while in China, especially in rural areas, women have struggled against a policy of "one child per family."

Such differences present one of the largest challenges to feminism in the twenty-first century: how to conceptualize women's liberation and to join together in common cause given women's diversity. As we have seen, many feminists have challenged the notion that women share an "essential" nature, situation, set of experiences, or status. This challenge has led many feminists to problematize the very category "woman" and to investigate how other factors such as class, race, ethnicity, religion, sexual preference, geographic location, and physical ability intersect with gender to produce widely different experiences and positions for women both within a society and around the world. This has led to the widespread recognition that the experience of oppression is not the same for all women; indeed it is now widely understood that differences within gender are used to privilege and subordinate women differentially: when men deny women rights, the category woman applies to all who are clearly embodied female, but when men offer privileges, the very entitlements that appear to be rooted in female anatomy can be shown to emerge from the grounds of race and class, heterosexual orientation, and physical ability (Conboy, Medina, and Stanbury, 1997:5).

How, then, given women's diversity, can feminists envision political struggle? There is no simple answer. Many feminists today call for the development of feminist alliance politics, one in which women from various backgrounds position themselves strategically, coming together with other women and men on particular issues of shared concern. Of course, one such issue may very well be a shared commitment to gender equality, one that allows women to transcend local self-interest and fight for broadly conceived forms of liberation. However, since the meaning of liberation for women may vary considerably across cultural and social contexts, it is imperative that feminists truly understand different cultural and social experiences. The feminist historian, Estelle Freedman, suggests that we are closer to this goal than we were just a few decades ago. Indeed, she contends that the recognition of difference among women is now an integral part of feminism:

> By the 1990s the cumulative contributions of working-class women, lesbians, women of

color, and activists from the developing world had transformed an initially white, European, middle-class politics into a diverse and mature feminist movement. Taking into account the range of women's experiences, feminists have increasingly recognized the validity of arguments that once seemed contradictory. Instead of debating whether women are similar to or different from men, most feminists now recognize that both statements are true. Instead of asking which is more important, gender or race, most feminists now acknowledge the indivisibility and interaction of these social categories. Along with demanding the right to work, feminist have redefined work to include caring as well as earning. Along with calling for women's independence, feminists have recognized the interdependence of all people, as well as the interconnection of gender equality with broader social justice movements. (Freedman, 2002:6)

Recognizing that women are differently situated in a global world of power relations has strengthened the possibilities for alliances among women. Recognizing that we must all struggle to keep alive not feminism, but feminisms, makes it more likely that women's diverse needs can be met.

Given both feminisms' gain and defeats, and the complexity of bringing diverse women together into common cause, what do feminists see for the future? Do they look ahead with optimism, anticipating a better world for women? Or does a cloud of pessimism shadow their visions? As this book has indicated, feminists hold different views on the major causes of women's oppression and on how best to overcome that oppression. Thus, their predictions about the future vary. But all feminists believe that women and men are of equal worth and many believe that the social movements associated with women's political activism have been so widespread and significant in the last few decades that there is no "turning back," despite widespread resistances (Freedman, 2002). An essential ingredient for ensuring feminist goals is the continuing development of an understanding of the multiple and often conflicting ways in which women have been oppressed and of the complex history of women's social activism and movements, their successes and failures. We offer this book as a step toward such understanding and a hopeful future for women around the world.

References

Baxandall, Rosalyn, and Linda Gordon. *Dear Sisters: Dispatches from the Women's Liberation Movement.* New York: Basic Books, 2000.

Conboy, K., N. Medina, and S. Stanbury. "Introduction." In *Writing on the Body: Female Embodiment and Feminist Theory*, edited by K. Conboy, N. Medina, and S. Stanbury, pp. 1–12. New York: Columbia University Press, 1997.

Freedman, Estelle B. *No Turning Back: The History of Feminism and the Future of Women.* New York: Ballantine, 2002.

Smith, Bonnie G., editor. *Global Feminisms Since 1945: Rewriting Histories.* New York: Routledge, 2000.

ART CREDITS

Page 27 The Hindu Goddess Kali. Nelson Gallery—Atkins Museum, Kansas City Missouri [Nelson Fund]. **Page 35** Judith and Maidservant with the Head of Holofernes, c. 1625, Artemisia Gentileschi. Gift of Mr. Leslie H. Green. Photograph © 1977 The Detroit Institute of Arts. **Page 36** (left) Blackware Jar. Courtesy of Mark Sublette, Medicine Man Gallery; (right) Maria Montoya Martinez. © Horace Bristol/CORBIS. **Page 37** (top) Visitors at Vietnam Veterans Memorial. Bettmann/CORBIS; (bottom) Maya Lin. Photo courtesy of Cheung Ching-Ming. **Page 38** The Dinner Party. © Judy Chicago, 1979. Photo by Michael Alexander. **Page 51** Simone de Beauvoir. © AP/Wide World Photos. **Page 54** Sojourner Truth. Public Domain Images. **Page 61** Harriet Taylor Mill. The London School of Economics, The British Library of Political and Economic Science. **Page 79** (left) Old-fashioned Corset. © Cheri-Rousseau and Glauth/Getty Images; (right) Madonna in Corset. © Frank Micelotta/Getty Images. **Page 80** (left) High Heels. © Image 100/Royalty-Free/CORBIS; (right) Foot Deformities. Courtesy of Foot.com. **Page 84** Exotic Asian Mail-order Brides. Courtesy of Jack West/ExoticAsianWomen.com. **Page 95** Woman with Tattoos. ©Image 100/Royalty-Free/CORBIS. **Page 97** Portrait of a Punk Woman. © Ryan McVay/ Getty Images. **Page 111** Margaret Mead. American Museum of Natural History. **Page 113** Karen Horney. Association for the Advancement of Psychoanalysis of the Karen Horney Psychoanalytic Institute and Center. **Page 140** Working Girl in Colombia. *Save*

the Children. Photo by Andy Mollo. **Page 144** Storekeepers in Egypt. Courtesy of CARE. **Page 145** Woman Spinning and Weaving. MS Cod. gall. 16 folio 20x, Bayerische Staatsbibliothek, Munich. **Page 147** Veiled Woman. © United Nations/DPI. **Page 156** Chief Wilma P. Mankiller. From *The New York Times*, April 6, 1994. **Page 177** Russian Dolls. Photo by Richard Zalk. **Page 179** (top/left) Christabel Pankhurst. © National Library of Australia; (top/right) Sylvia Pankhurst. Photo by Topical Press Agency/ Getty Images; (bottom) Adela Pankhurst. © National Library of Australia. **Page 184** Anne Frank Photo Strip. Photo by Anne Frank-Fonds—Basel/Anne Frank House—Amsterdam/Getty Images. **Page 188** The Delany Sisters. Photo by Marianne Barcellona/Time Life Pictures/Getty Images. **Page 192** The Anonymous 4. Photo courtesy of Susan Hellauer. **Page 201** The Arnolfini Wedding. Jan Van Eyck (c. 1930–1441). Photo: Erich Lessing/ Art Resource, NY. **Page 204** Wedding Night of Humay. From Khwaju Kirmani, *Divan*, Baghdad, 1936. 32 × 19 cm. London, British Library, MS. Add. 18113, f.45V. **Page 224** Lesbian Wedding. Photo courtesy of Susan Lees. **Page 234** Cornelia Pointing to her Children as Her Treasures, ca. 1785. Virginia Museum of Fine Arts, Richmond. The Adolph D. and Wilkins C. Williams Fund. Photo: Katherine Wetzel. © Virginia Museum of Fine Arts. **Page 235** The Mother, ca. 1670. Oil on canvas, 92 × 100 cm. Inv. 820 B. Photo: Joerg P. Anders, Bildarchiv Preussischer Kulturbesitz/ Art Resource, NY. **Page 237** Mother and

Child, Paula Modersohn-Becker. **Page 244** Pregnancy as a Source of Joy. Photo by Jamie Robinson, 1982. **Page 248** Mother and Child, Kongo Culture. Virginia Museum of Fine Arts, Richmond. The Adolph D. and Wilkins C. Williams Fund. Photo: Katherine Wetzel. © Virginia Museum of Fine Arts. **Page 285** Reverend Pauli Murray. Courtesy of Susan Mullally Weil. **Page 286** Reverend Ellen Barrett. Courtesy of Bettye Lane. **Page 287** Rabbi S. Priesand. Courtesy of Terry H. Layman. **Page 290** The Penitent Magdalene by Titian. The J. Paul Getty Museum, Los Angeles. Courtesy of the J. Paul Getty Museum. **Page 312** One of the Little Rock Nine. © Bettmann/CORBIS. **Page 323** (top) Donna E. Shalala. Courtesy of Donna E. Shalala; (bottom) Johnnetta B. Cole. Courtesy of Johnnetta B. Cole/Bennett College. **Page 324** (top) Susan Hockfield. AP Photo/ Josh Reynolds; (bottom) Ruth Simmons.

Courtesy of Ruth Simmons/Harvard News Office. **Page 325** (top) Shirley Ann Jackson. AP Photo/Mark Humphrey; (bottom) Shirley Tilghman. Photo: Denise Applewhite. Courtesy of Princeton University. **Page 342** The Broken Column. Fundacion Dolores Olmedo, Mexico City. © Banco de Mexico Trust. Photo: Schalkwijk/Art Resource, NY. **Page 361** Beauty Out of Damage. Photo: Matuschka, 1993. **Page 386** Fruit Cannery. © Culver Pictures, Inc. **Page 388** Women in Lesotho. United Nations/ Mudden. **Page 389** Coal Miners. Earl Dotter/American Labor. **Page 396** Toni Morrison. NY Times/Toni Morrison/Princeton University. **Page 420** Hillary Rodham Clinton. AP Photo/Mary Altaffer. **Page 429** Aung San Suu Kyi. AP Photo/Richard Vogel. **Page 432** Sandra Day O'Connor. The Supreme Court Collection. **Page 433** Ruth Bader Ginsburg. The Supreme Court Collection.

INDEX

Note: Page numbers in *italics* denote illustrations on that page; "t" refers to material found in tables.